Praise for Jane Fonda

"A candid, compassionate glimpse of a woman who, by dint of artistic temperament or self-preservation, will always remain stubbornly elusive."
— *Washington Post*

"An engrossing decade-in-the-making biography . . . Bosworth, who not only had her subject's blessing but also had access to her closest family members, acquaintances, and associates, has fashioned a vividly told tale (one with a steady undercurrent of sex given Fonda's varied and constant admirers) filled with revealing firsthand quotes and detailed revelations, including those from the actress herself. The author does a bang-up job probing the fragile, frustrating, and defining nature of Fonda's relationship with her father, supporting her premise that everything Jane did was somehow motivated or shaped by that." — *USA Today*

"Bosworth presents a fuller portrait of Fonda than ever before."
— *New York Post*

"True to her subtitle, author Patricia Bosworth centers her insightful book . . . on the woman more than the performances of the two-time Oscar winner. The *Vanity Fair* writer knows a good personal story when she hears one — and how to tell it with spark and meaning. . . . While a friend of her subject, Bosworth doesn't ignore Fonda's many stumbles along the path of self-discovery — or excuse the pain she has caused others with her single-minded and self-centered pursuits. [Fonda's] has been a remarkable journey, unique for an American woman, and a life Bosworth explores with honesty and empathy in a book as striking as its subject."
— *Associated Press*

"As Patricia Bosworth deftly and comprehensively relates in *Jane Fonda: The Private Life of a Public Woman*, Ms. Fonda, now 73, possesses many strengths — chief among them astonishing drive and personal discipline — but many vulnerabilities as well." — *Wall Street Journal*

"Gracefully written and deeply researched, Patricia Bosworth's *Jane Fonda* is not only a first-class biography but a thoughtful, sympathetic, yet objective, study of a central figure in the preoccupying drama of American celebrity life as it has been played out over the past half century."
— **Richard Schickel, author of *Conversations with Scorsese***

"As an heiress to Hollywood royalty, survivor of childhood trauma, sexpot, movie star, fitness guru, activist, trophy wife, and serial self-reinventor, Jane Fonda has embodied every theme in modern American mythology. And I can't think of anyone better equipped to tell her story than Patricia Bosworth. Her superb reporting, combined with an equally sure understanding of what the details add up to, has produced a clear-sighted but sympathetic and compelling portrait of a woman who really is an emblem of our age." — **Amanda Vaill, author of** *Everybody Was so Young*

"Bosworth has succeeded in capturing Fonda's step-by-step transformation from wide-eyed, apolitical ingenue to the poised personality of recent decades." — ***Publishers Weekly*, starred review**

"Far more than a spellbinding biography, *Jane Fonda* sweeps the reader into a cultural history of the '6os, '7os, and '8os, when this icon helped define the causes of the era. The access gained by Bosworth is impressive — lovers, stepmothers, and ex-husbands share their secrets, adding to what will certainly become the definitive portrait of a woman conflicted, torn between ferocious ambition, family, and feminist causes. Bosworth's rendering of Fonda's interior chaos becomes a revealing probe into the female psyche." — **Gail Sheehy, author of** *Passages*

"Jane Fonda was born with beauty and talent. Now she's blessed with a biographer who knows Hollywood and understands the human condition. Nothing about Fonda's life (her obsession with her looks, her lovers — male and female — her husbands, her money, and her elusive father) escapes the keen eye of Patricia Bosworth, who tells the life story of a cinema icon, one of the most intriguing women of our era. You will be enthralled." — **Kitty Kelley, author of** *Oprah: A Biography*

"Patricia Bosworth's brilliant detective work has unearthed so much about Jane Fonda that I didn't know — so much feeling, so much courage, so much hurt. It reveals Fonda as the archetypal woman of her generation: a woman torn between love and work, family, and accomplishment. Bosworth's book is far from another Hollywood biography; it is a human portrait and, at the same time, a major American life. Reading this book, living Jane's life along with her, is an adventure and a pleasure."
— **William Mann, author of** *Kate: The Woman Who Was Hepburn*

"Watching Jane Fonda wrestle with her many passions has been one of the most fascinating stories of the past fifty years. Brilliant, beautiful, achingly vulnerable, self-wounding, Fonda is one of the greatest film stars to ever appear on the screen. Her life deserves to be reevaluated as it is in Patricia Bosworth's *Jane Fonda*." — **Alec Baldwin**

Books by Patricia Bosworth

Anything Your Little Heart Desires

Marlon Brando

Montgomery Clift

Diane Arbus

Jane Fonda

Jane Fonda

The Private Life
of a Public Woman

PATRICIA BOSWORTH

Mariner Books · Houghton Mifflin Harcourt · BOSTON · NEW YORK

First Mariner Books edition 2012
Copyright © 2011 by Patricia Bosworth

For information about permission to reproduce selections from this book,
write to Permissions, Houghton Mifflin Harcourt Publishing Company,
215 Park Avenue South, New York, New York 10003.

www.hmhbooks.com

Library of Congress Cataloging-in-Publication Data
Bosworth, Patricia.
Jane Fonda : the private life of a public woman / Patricia Bosworth.
p. cm.
Includes bibliographical references and index.
ISBN 978-0-547-15257-8   ISBN 978-0-547-57765-4 (pbk.)
1. Fonda, Jane, 1937– 2. Actors — United States — Biography. I. Title.
PN2287.F56B78 2011
791.4302'8092 — dc22
[B]
2011009144

Book design by Brian Moore

Printed in the United States of America

DOC 10 9 8 7 6 5 4 3 2 1

Photo credits appear on page 567.

The author gratefully acknowledges permission to quote from the following works:
My Life So Far by Jane Fonda, copyright © 2005, 2006 by Jane Fonda, published
by Ebury Press. Used by permission of Random House, Inc. *Fonda: My Life* by
Henry Fonda and Howard Teichmann, copyright © 1981 by Howard Teichmann
and Orion Productions, Inc. Used by permission of Dutton Signet, a division of
Penguin Group (USA) Inc. *Don't Tell Dad: A Memoir* by Peter Fonda, copyright ©
1998 by Peter Fonda. Used by permission of Hyperion. All rights reserved. *Jane: An
Intimate Biography of Jane Fonda* by Thomas Kiernan, copyright © 1973 by Thomas
Kiernan. Reprinted by permission of Sanford J. Greenburger Associates. *The Fon-
das: A Hollywood Dynasty* by Peter Collier, copyright © 1991 by Peter Collier, Inc.
Used by permission of G. P. Putnam's Sons, a division of Penguin Group (USA) Inc.
and Georges Borchardt, Inc., on behalf of the author. *Memoirs of the Devil* by Roger
Vadim, Harcourt Brace Jovanovich, 1977. Reprinted by kind permission of the Estate
of Roger Vadim and Editions Stock.

for Tom

Contents

We are so many selves. It's not just the long-ago child within us who needs tenderness and inclusion, but the person we were last year, wanted to be yesterday, tried to become in one job or in one winter, in one love affair or in one house where even now, we can close our eyes and smell the rooms. What brings together these ever-shifting selves of infinite reactions and returnings is this: There is always one true inner voice. Trust it.

— GLORIA STEINEM, *REVOLUTION FROM WITHIN*

Prologue

ONLY JANE FONDA could upstage Oprah Winfrey. It happened on February 10, 2001, during a performance of Eve Ensler's *Vagina Monologues,* which was being acted out by sixty megastars in front of a sold-out crowd at Madison Square Garden. The show was a fundraiser for V-Day, the international organization that works to prevent violence toward women.

I'll never forget it.

All the celebrities, including Oprah, stood in a semicircle reciting their vignettes about women's sexual triumphs and tragedies from index cards — all the celebrities except Jane, who had memorized her piece and when it was her turn stepped out of the circle and gave a spellbinding rendition about what it's like to watch one's grandchild emerge bloody and screaming from his mother's womb. By turns anxious, tender, and emotional, Jane ended the monologue with "*and I was there in the room. I remember.*"

The audience gave a loud cheer. At that point, Jane curtsied to a dark-haired young woman who was seated in the front row. It turned out the young woman was Jane's daughter, Vanessa Vadim. Months before, Jane had assisted the midwife at the birth of Vanessa's son, Malcolm. Jane was paying her homage.

• • •

Afterward there was a noisy party at the cavernous Hammerstein Ball-room. Jane was surrounded by so many admirers that I had to push my way through the crowd to congratulate her.

"I did it! I did it!" she exclaimed to me, eyes sparkling. She hadn't acted in thirteen years and she suffered from "such God-awful stage fright I was petrified I wouldn't be able to get through it," she confided to me, "but I did."

We gripped hands.

Jane and I have known each other since the 1960s. We were kids then, studying with Lee Strasberg at the Actors Studio. I was an actress for ten years on Broadway before switching to journalism, while Jane was refashioning herself as Barbarella.

I wrote my first article about Jane in 1970 for *McCall's* magazine. She had just been nominated for an Academy Award for her searing per-formance as the suicidal marathon dancer in *They Shoot Horses, Don't They?* She went on to win Oscars for both *Klute* and *Coming Home,* movies that defined her political evolution.

For the next three decades I continued to write stories about her: when she was burned in effigy as Hanoi Jane, and a couple of years af-ter, when the Gallup Poll listed her as one of the most admired women in the world along with Mother Teresa.

Jane polarizes, and the public remains fascinated by her. She has an extraordinary ability to reinvent herself in response to the times. Con-sider that she transformed herself from movie star to political activist to exercise guru to tycoon wife and now, in the twenty-first century, she's turning into an exemplary philanthropist. She doesn't generate, she reacts — to people, places, and events; everything about the fast-paced, chaotic reality that is American life turns her on.

But then I realize that above all she is a consummate actress who has an uncanny ability to inhabit various characters at will. She once told me, "The weird thing about acting is that you get paid for discovering you have multiple personalities." Jane can will herself into becoming whatever she wants to become. Which is why I wanted to write this book about her.

In 2000 I began researching. Jane had given the project her blessing, so I interviewed scores of her friends and colleagues. But Jane herself refused to speak to me. She said it was because she was writing her own memoir and didn't want to give anything away. Then in January

2003, she suddenly changed her mind and invited me to come to her ranch in New Mexico for a week. "I'm going over my FBI files and you can help me. I don't feel like doing it alone," she said. I agreed, and I wasn't surprised; Jane constantly changes her mind. That's the way she is — full of contradictions.

I wasn't surprised either to receive the following e-mail from her a couple of days later:

> Sat 18 Jan 2003
> Subject: Gulp
> From: Jane Fonda
> To: Patricia Bosworth
>   Deep breath. Big gulp. Here's why: I have my own special personal stories about my life and I do have a big fear that I will give them away to you, because I do tend to let things just spill. YET, I do trust you and would like to spend time with you so here goes:
>   I do have all my FBI files like I said and you are welcome to go through them provided you share what's interesting (most isn't) with me. This is a good way to avoid having to do it myself in exchange for you're [sic] being there. How's that? If it's just us, it's truly just us. I am not a cook and eat sparingly when left to my own devices. . . . Aside from that, when not writing I am engaged in heavy manual labor such as cutting down trees and clearing trail. You would be welcome to come along but not required to participate.
> XXOO jane

Two months later I arrived at Jane's 2,500-acre ranch outside Santa Fe. After she showed me around her comfortable, spacious home, we sat down in her vaulted living room, in front of a crackling fire, and drank red wine from oversize goblets. She told me how glad she was that I was writing her biography. There had already been nine published biographies of her, all written by men — all of whom, she believed, felt threatened by her. "I'm glad a woman is writing about me," she said.

I began explaining why I wanted to write this book. Jane has fulfilled every female fantasy, achieving love, fame, money, and success on a grand scale. She's a genuine American icon who won't be remembered for her movies but rather for her outsize serial lives.

Jane interrupted. "I've already written five hundred pages of my book. How many have you got?"

"Not that many," I admitted.

With that, she grinned. "What I really want to know is, who's gonna be first?"

She is the daughter of Henry Fonda. His portrayal of Tom Joad in *The Grapes of Wrath* is embedded in the American consciousness. Jane has always willed herself to be the best at everything. She is also heir to a terrible childhood tragedy: her mother, Frances Fonda, slit her throat when Jane was twelve. Her suicide is the crucial event in Jane's life and it haunts her to this day.

After the suicide Henry Fonda, always the perfectionist, became even more remote, escaping into his work and three more marriages; each wife seemed younger than the last.

Jane kept on battling for his love. She triumphed on Broadway and then went on to make forty-one movies, creating characters as disparate as the naive cowgirl in *Cat Ballou* and the giddy newlywed Corie in *Barefoot in the Park* to the tough-talking call girl Bree Daniels in *Klute,* for which she won her first Oscar. In her twenties she began to reinvent herself to attract and please a succession of father substitutes. She shifted seamlessly from playing film director Roger Vadim's Parisian sex kitten, to political activist and exercise guru when she was married to radical Tom Hayden. Finally, she became the trophy wife of maverick billionaire Ted Turner, a man as famous as she is.

My 2003 visit to her ranch coincided with a turning point. Although she still considers herself primarily a social activist, Jane had decided to recycle herself as a movie star after thirteen years away from the screen. At sixty-five, "It won't be easy," she joked. She'd hired a new agent; she had braces on her teeth; and she was trying out color contacts for her eyes. She'd also just had her breast implants removed. "My kids are so relieved. They tell me I look normal again," she said.

She'd already turned down the remake of *The Manchurian Candidate* because she didn't want her Hollywood comeback to be as a villainess. She told me that Cameron Crowe, who wrote *Fast Times at Ridgemont High* and *Jerry Maguire,* was writing a new movie for her. She said she would be playing Leonardo DiCaprio's tap-dancing mother in the film. She did not say she was now often obliged to audition for parts, including another role for which she was in competition with Anne Bancroft. I found it hard to believe these two Oscar-winning actresses had to compete against each other, but in the end the face-off was merciful: neither got the part. Ultimately, the Cameron Crowe project didn't work out either.

How can I accurately describe our conversations in the five days that followed? Jane is a prodigious talker. I taped and took notes, and everything she said ended up, in one way or another, in this book. She talked and talked and talked on a vast range of subjects: The importance of Michael Moore's documentary on the Columbine massacre; Jimmy Carter; the United Nations; her travels to New Delhi, Mumbai, and Jerusalem. Marilyn Monroe. The joys of being a grandmother. Her first husband, Roger Vadim, and his sexual vulnerability; her dreams; her brother, Peter's, courage; her son, Troy, and his dynamite performance in *Soldier's Girl* where he played a GI in love with a transsexual.

She also talked about Sue Sally Jones, her beloved tomboy friend from grade school, with whom she'd recently reunited. Simone Signoret. The glories of a good martini and the ecstasies of pot. She talked about Carol Gilligan's *In a Different Voice,* the book that has meant more to her than any other book. She talked about her daughter, Vanessa's, talent as a filmmaker. She talked about her obsession with trees — big old trees, with thick, twisted roots. She talked about moving full-grown trees from one of Ted's ranches in New Mexico to her ranch, oak, fir, maple, and poplar. "I am too old to plant young trees." She talked about when she had planted trees at her farm outside Paris and the way Henry Fonda had planted trees years ago at their family home called Tigertail.

While I was listening to her, I decided Jane looked exactly the way she did when I first met her at the Actors Studio, over thirty-five years ago. The same long, sad face, an exact replica of her father's. The same clear-eyed gaze and elegant remoteness. She was warmer than I expected, and sometimes quite funny, but she was so tightly wound I wondered if she could ever really relax. She was impeccably groomed. When I commented on the cut of her tight blue jeans, she said. "Oh, I have fifty pairs." I expressed surprise. "Well, Ted has twenty-seven ranches. I used to keep clothes at every ranch so I would never have to pack."

Every so often the phone rang. Once it was Kofi Annan, the secretary-general of the United Nations. Then it was Ted Turner. Jane spoke to him soothingly, as one might to a child. "You're a good man, Ted. Don't rush into anything too quickly." They talked for quite a while. When she hung up she explained what had just transpired. She spoke in staccato sound bites — a habit she had honed over years of interviews. "Ted is trying to break up with his old mistress Frederique. They just aren't getting along. He's met some new girl, Rebecca something. Ted and I are close. Sometimes we even travel together. He'll probably come to the ranch again. He gave me this ranch as a divorce present. I like to see him. I like to see him go. I feel sorry for him. He can't be alone. Sometimes I take him into my lap and rock him like a baby."

"Aside from the womanizing, what broke you up?" I asked.

"Ted needs constant companionship. Keeping up with him was absolutely exhausting. His nervous energy almost crackles in the air. He can't sit still, because if he does, the demons will catch up with him."

Suddenly she confided she was happier than she'd ever been in her life. "I'm free!" And then she added, "I love living alone for once." She was about to move into her new home in Atlanta, four lofts renovated into a single gigantic apartment in Buckhead, one of the city's wealthiest enclaves.

As she spoke, I was conscious that all around us were photographs of Henry Fonda, reminders that he remained the central presence in her life. She did not deny it. "My dad shadows me," she said. "I dream about him. Think about him. Wonder if he'd approve of what I'm doing now."

She will eventually write in her memoir, *My Life So Far,* "All my life I have been my father's daughter. Trapped in a Greek drama like Athena who sprang from the head of her father Zeus. Discipline and drive started in my childhood. I learned love through perfection."

But she is also her mother's child. Obsessed with her looks. Obsessed with money. Obsessed with sex.

At 7:00 P.M. we ate a supper that Jane prepared herself: broiled salmon, vegetables, and salad. Jane ate rapidly. Her plate was clean in less than five minutes. "Ted used to bolt his food. I got in the habit," she explained.

At 9:00 P.M., after watching CNN for a while, she announced cheerily, "I'm going to bed. I get up before six every morning. Want an Ambien? I get 'em cheap in Paris." I told her no thanks. She returned moments later, looking very glamorous in a black satin nightgown, balancing a big stack of DVDs in her arms. "Brought you some movies. They're from the Academy. All Oscar-nominated films. *The Pianist*, which I voted for. I think that'll win, but we also have *Frida* and *Road to Perdition*."

The following morning sun streamed through the windows as I walked into Jane's gleaming modern kitchen; the air was fragrant with bunches of fresh flowers in crystal vases. Espresso was waiting for me, as were whole-wheat bread, cheese, fruit, and a note from Jane — "I'm in my office. Come and get me" — signed with a smiling face. (Her mother signed her notes that way.)

I found Jane hanging up the phone at her desk. "I just spoke to my grandson, Malcolm. He calls me 'Gamma,'" she said with a look of pleasure. With that she rose and guided me into her bedroom to show me her glittering canopied bed, its draped fabric studded with tiny slivers of mirrored glass. "This is called a sorcerer's bed," Jane told me. "It keeps out evil spirits."

We then moved on to a mirrored dressing room, where she pointed out a portrait of herself at age seven with her mother. Jane's expression in the photo is sullen. Her mother's is melancholy. "I hated to have her touch me," she said. "Isn't that awful?"

There were other photographs in the room — of a youthful Henry Fonda standing tanned and exuberant next to his wife, who in this photo is smiling. They are posed on a tennis court holding rackets. "He never loved her. I always knew that," Jane said curtly. Then she changed the subject: "Let's go for the FBI files."

Finally she led me down a long, tiled hall and into a small, sunny room overlooking the Pecos River. Stuffed animals and an assortment of hats and caps hung on a hat tree. Jane turned on a beautiful Tiffany lamp and pointed to a pile of boxes stacked high. "Twenty-two thousand pages," she said.

She asked me to look for references to the trip she took to North

Vietnam in 1972. Like other activists, Jane had gone there to investigate the bombing of dikes in the Red River delta near Hanoi, which Nixon publicly denied. The dikes protected thousands of acres of villages and rice fields, where 15 million Vietnamese peasants lived. Jane filmed her visits to Hanoi's destroyed dike system, villages, and hospitals, as well as her meetings with Vietnamese children and American POWs. She wanted to document the damage and publicize the evidence back in the United States. The only copy of the film mysteriously disappeared after she screened it at a press conference in Paris. She thought the CIA must have taken it.

For the next couple of days I sifted through piles of reports but found no references to the film. The documents were printed on coarse white paper with thick black lines obscuring informers' identities. Jane told me one of her bodyguards at a rally turned out to be an informer. "I discovered reporters who were informers. It was a whole network."

The files revealed the FBI's obsessive, illegal, and ultimately fruitless surveillance of Jane as she opposed the Vietnam War. FBI agents opened her mail, tapped her phone, combed through her past, even planted a false story in the press that she wanted to kill the president. Meanwhile Nixon kept pressuring the Justice Department to charge her with treason. He hoped to ruin her reputation.

In 1975, Jane filed a million-dollar lawsuit against Richard Nixon, Henry Kissinger, and Charles Colson for conspiring to discredit and destroy her life. In 1979, while Jimmy Carter was president, the U.S. government finally admitted all wrongdoing and released the files it had gathered on her. When she won, she refused the government's offered settlement.

Every so often we took a break and drove around the ranch. We careened along bumpy, winding roads, up and down hills, across mountains, finally splashing through the Pecos River, which curls around much of Jane's 2,500 acres. At one point we passed a gleaming man-made lake stocked with fish. Jane loves to fly-fish. "It's like practicing Zen," she said.

Near us rose jagged, prehistoric-looking cliffs of reddish stone; beyond were rolling hills thick with cottonwood and ponderosa pine.

Bears roam there, and deer and wild dogs. She keeps chickens, because she loves fresh eggs.

About four miles from the house are a big red barn and stables for Jane's six horses, one a white stallion she had just bought from Mike Nichols. A golden retriever named Roxie romped in the field. "Larry David gave Ted and me Roxie when he and the entire *Seinfeld* cast came up to Montana for a visit."

We usually ended up at Jane's fitness gym. It's equipped with every kind of exercise machine imaginable as well as a library of her exercise tapes. Over the next few days I tried to keep up with Jane as we bent and stretched. I was no match for her, but she was kind enough not to point this out.

The phone continued to ring periodically. Once it was her stepdaughter, Nathalie Vadim, who runs Jane's foundation's battered women's shelter in Maine. Then came a call from twenty-nine-year-old Mary Lou Williams, the child of Black Panthers whom Jane unofficially adopted in the seventies. The third call was from her daughter, Vanessa, with whom she has always had a volatile relationship. "Sometimes I think she will be angry with me until I die. She won't forgive me for leaving her to speak out against the war." Jane has no problems with Troy, her beloved son from her marriage to Tom Hayden. "But then I took him everywhere with me when he was a baby," she said.

I asked her why she wanted to go back to making movies, and she answered, "Because I need the money." How was this possible? She'd made a fortune with the Workout tapes and her movies. There were also rumors that Turner gave her $100 million in stock as part of their divorce settlement. "I can't tell you the amount, but it was generous," she admitted. "And he gave me this ranch, too." She added, "I need money because I support a lot of people, as well as my foundations."

"You've always supported so many people, including your first two husbands."

She had paid the gambling debts and back taxes of her first husband, Roger Vadim; she paid for her second husband's political campaigns. Jane didn't mention the money loaned or given to friends in need—hospital bills taken care of, tuitions paid. Recently, she took a college classmate who was going blind to see the Guggenheim Museum in Bilbao. She also invited two of Roger Vadim's former wives and Vanessa to go along. "It was fun," she said.

She'd begun speaking to Tom Hayden again, thirteen years after their acrimonious divorce. "I wanted to be friends; we share our son." Just a couple of weeks before, Hayden had visited the ranch with his new wife and adopted child and then suffered a massive heart attack. A helicopter flew him to a hospital in Santa Fe, where he had a triple bypass and made a full recovery.

Once during that week we both had a massage at the ranch. The young masseuse arrived, literally trembling with excitement, anticipating giving Jane Fonda a massage. "You go first," Jane told me brusquely. I found the experience wonderfully soothing and relaxing. Jane had her massage next. Afterward she padded into my bedroom looking displeased. "She wasn't very good."

"I thought she was great."

"I've been having massages all my life," Jane declared. "My mother loved having massages. Anyhow, I know a good masseuse from a mediocre one." I learned when I should stay out of Jane's way. She confided that she sometimes takes Prozac for her mood swings.

Usually, after she had gone to bed, I'd watch one of the eight movies she had given me, including her documentaries *Fuck the Army* and *Introduction to the Enemy*, the latter of which she made with Haskell Wexler and Tom Hayden in North Vietnam.

Sometimes I couldn't sleep, and I'd wander back into the living room trying to collect my thoughts. A stuffed bear's head jutted out over the fireplace. "I shot that bear," Jane had informed me proudly just after I arrived at the ranch. "After I killed him I started to cry." She added with a bawdy, explosive laugh, "I guess it's not politically correct for me to hunt, but I enjoy it. I didn't want to be a stay-at-home wife when I was married to Ted, so I learned to hunt and fish."

Our time was always scheduled right down to the mini-second; Jane never wasted a minute. An hour and a half for taping and talk, a half-hour for lunch; occasionally I would still be asking her questions. Then a break and she would disappear into her office to work on her own book, or she would go outside to confer with her staff. She was overseeing a big ranch, after all, and there was much to attend to. There were gardens to be planted, and she was building a swimming pool on the hill, as well as a playground for her grandchildren.

Every so often a pleasant young woman named Karen would slip into the kitchen, bringing fresh supplies as well as the newspapers and mail. Karen also worked for Ted Turner; she cooked for him on his various ranches — she was always on call. Ted and Jane shared her, "but it works out," she said. Although Karen was in and out a lot, it always felt as though Jane and I were alone at the ranch. The household gleamed. It was run magnificently.

While I was there, there was a dinner party with a doctor and his wife from Boston who talked to Jane about how she was building her foundation, the Georgia Campaign for Adolescent Pregnancy Prevention (G-CAPP), dedicated to empowering teenage girls and preventing early pregnancy. We were joined by Gordon Miller, an old friend of Roger Vadim's who now lived on an adjoining ranch. At one point he whispered to me, "Jane is coming into her own now that she's left Ted. She is finally becoming Jane Fonda."

Before I left, I showed Jane a photograph I had found in an old *Harper's Bazaar*. It's a portrait of the Fonda family circa 1948; they are posing in their garden. Henry Fonda is in the foreground gazing into space. Jane is watching him intently. Peter glowers next to her, and Frances Fonda hovers in the background, an anxious expression on her face. It's as if she's anticipating that something terrible is about to happen. The image is unsettling, almost eerie.

"I have the same picture!" Jane cried out. "I've been studying all our expressions under a magnifying glass — especially my dad's. It was when our family was about to break apart. Dad was in *Mister Roberts;* my mother and he were barely speaking. She was away at hospitals a lot."

"Did your father ever discuss the suicide with you?"

"No, he never talked about it ever and I never brought it up with him."

"Why?"

"I didn't want to upset him."

She wouldn't discuss her mother's suicide. "Are you in denial?" I asked. "Sure, I'm in denial. That's the way I survive," she snapped.

"Let's say I remember what I *want* to remember. What I can bear to remember."

Once, long ago, Jane told a reporter, "My mother was crazy and my father was never a father, so I had to deal with these lacks and I had to deal with all the people inside my head. I have always dreamed — vivid, powerful dreams, often nightmares. My life did not provide me with a narrative, so I had to make one up."

My last night at the ranch, I couldn't sleep. Around dawn, I realized that in working on our books Jane and I had become locked in a kind of mutual endeavor — and mutual anxiety.

Jane says she often shakes and cries when she writes, and so do I. Maybe it's because we have motives we haven't expressed. We are protecting ourselves; we are both very polite. In later years, we will relax and enjoy each other's company.

I believe Jane is confident that whoever she is and whatever she's accomplished with her life (and that's plenty) will transcend what I have to say about her.

But she also knows that what I write will have some impact on that tangible reality called reputation, and I will be judged by what I write about her. I am drawn to Jane Fonda for many reasons. If I judge her at all, it's because I see many of the same rationalizations and delusions in myself as a woman.

I left the ranch early Friday morning to fly back to New York. Jane and I had breakfast together. She was all set to drive me over the mountains to a taxi that would be waiting outside the ranch's gates four miles away to take me to the airport in Albuquerque. Before I left, I asked Karen to take a picture of us, and I have it tacked to my bulletin board as I write: Jane looking very much like a movie star in her tight jeans and jacket, me looking rumpled and a bit giddy.

Then we climbed into the Land Rover but Jane couldn't start the motor. She was furious. She had just bought the car. "I drove it into Santa Fe yesterday. What the hell?" She got on her cell phone and so did Karen. I think somebody even rang the bell in the bell tower. Within seconds, it seemed, three cars appeared out of nowhere, driven by various ranch hands. One of them chauffeured me down to the waiting cab.

On the plane I began to wonder why Jane had never expressed much interest in any of the people I'd been interviewing for my book. They were friends and colleagues from every phase of her life. "I live in the present," she kept saying. "I live in the moment. I don't want to live in the past." Then I remembered what her brother, Peter, had told me: "Jane has one version of her life, but you should get the others because they are equally interesting."

Peter was right. In the next seven years I gathered an incredible array of stories from lovers, friends, and enemies, many stories that have never been told. They are funny, sad, wondrous, strange, marvelous stories befitting a movie star activist who has played every archetypal female onstage and off — and continues to do so.

Part I

Daughter: 1937–1958

My only major influence was my father. I became my father's "son," a tomboy, the one to bait fishing hooks with bloody worms and pretend I didn't mind. I was going to be brave, to be tough and strong, to make him love me.

— JANE FONDA

1

S HE WAS BORN Jayne Seymour Fonda on December 21, 1937, by cesarean section at Doctors Hospital in New York. Her thirty-two-year-old father, the up-and-coming young actor Henry Fonda, paced back and forth outside the delivery room, smoking cigarette after cigarette while the nurses did their best to ignore him. He'd just flown in from Hollywood, where he'd been filming *Jezebel* opposite Bette Davis. Jane was his first child. Originally he had been nervous about becoming a father. He wasn't sure he was ready. But then he realized how much he wanted to create a family. He'd had it written into his contract that if his wife went into labor during filming, he could be with her in New York.

He was a tall, lanky man, with a slow smile and a modest, self-effacing manner. He'd already starred in *The Farmer Takes a Wife* and *The Trail of the Lonesome Pine*, in which he played a magnetic, hot-tempered idealist. *Lonesome Pine*, which he made in 1936 (and the first to be shot in Technicolor on location), was the movie that established him as the archetypal Midwesterner: shy, honest, with a distinctive loping gait and a homespun drawl.

That evening Fonda could have gone downstairs to the hospital dining room and supped on a quite imaginative menu. Doctors Hospital, located on East End Avenue, a block away from the mayor's home, Gracie Mansion, was famous for its superb chef, who served up delicious food and the finest wines to patients and their guests. Socially prominent New Yorkers — including the Rockefellers, the Pells, and the Vanderbilts — preferred Doctors Hospital because it was "more like a hotel" than a hospital.

Jane's mother, Frances Seymour Brokaw Fonda, wanted her baby delivered there for that very reason. Friends could visit and share a cocktail while she showed off her handsome movie star husband. The view over the East River was magnificent, especially in the evenings when the bridges spanning the river glittered with a million lights.

But Fonda didn't care about the view. As soon as his wife was wheeled out of the recovery room, he started clicking away with his Leica. He was an avid photographer. Taking pictures of his baby daughter would become an obsession.

The pictures, which Jane has kept, show her in her crib or being held by a masked nurse. There are none of Jane with her mother, who made it clear that she wished the baby had been a boy. Frances already had a seven-year-old daughter, nicknamed "Pan," by her first husband, the late financier George Brokaw, and she longed for a son. Jane learned of her mother's preference early on, and it made her feel terrible.

That afternoon Fonda took snapshots of the baby until the nurses insisted he stop; his wife needed her rest. So he vaulted off to a pay phone down the hall and sent a telegram to William Wyler, his director for *Jezebel:*

> I admire your pictures and I would like to work for you. I am eighteen minutes old. Blonde hair and blue eyes, weight: eight pounds . . . and I have been called beautiful. My father was an actor. (Signed) Jayne Seymour Fonda.

Over the next several days Fonda continued taking pictures of his baby daughter — *click! click! click!* He was pleased about becoming a father and never tired of gazing at the tiny pink bundle in the crib. Perhaps he saw himself mirrored in her face — the sad, downturned mouth, the beautiful liquid Mediterranean eyes. "There is a strong Fonda look," he told Lillian Ross when she interviewed him for *The New Yorker* in 1958.

Fonda's ancestors from Genoa, Italy, migrated to Holland in the 1400s and then moved to America in 1642. They were among the first Dutch settlers in upstate New York, where they established the town of Fonda. By 1888, most of the Fondas had settled in Nebraska. In 1900, Hank's father, William Brace Fonda, a stern, unimaginative man, married a lovely young brunette named Herberta Jaynes, who was an ardent Christian Scientist. Their son was born in Grand Island, Nebraska, on May 16, 1905. Six months later, the family moved to Omaha, where Bill established a successful printing plant and bought a white clapboard house in the center of town.

One of the few Democrats among mostly Republican neighbors, Fonda Sr. was the son of a man who had joined the Union forces at the age of seventeen and fought in the Civil War. He was not demonstrative and Hank inherited that trait, along with his father's dark good looks. All his life, whenever he passed a mirror he'd say to himself, "That's my father!"

Of his family, Hank declared, "They were wonderful." His two younger sisters, Harriet and Jayne — both good-natured, friendly, loyal souls — adored him. They were talkers, unlike their bashful brother, who barely spoke. As a little boy he'd communicate by standing on his head or walking on his hands. When he really liked something he'd perform a graceful cartwheel, and he could have been an acrobat, but he also had a great comic gift as a pantomimist. One of his earliest creations was a character he named Elmer, a ten-year-old idiot boy who imitated fishes by wiggling his fingers. He also excelled in athletics and was a top-notch Boy Scout. As a teen, he got into one ferocious fight with a tough Irish boy whom Fonda punched out before being carried home on the shoulders of his cheering friends. His sister Harriet talked of nothing else for days. Yet Fonda remained painfully shy, especially with women. He finally went to bed with a prostitute when he was nineteen, but only after he had gotten very drunk.

Hank Fonda originally wanted to be a journalist, but at the University of Minnesota in 1924 he found that he preferred sketching pictures to doing his homework. After two years he dropped out of college and returned to Omaha, where he took a temporary job at the Retail Credit Agency in town. He earned $30 a week and soon was very bored.

Then, on a fluke, he got into acting. Marlon Brando's mother, Dodie, who ran the Omaha Community Playhouse, encouraged Fonda to apprentice there. He ended up working backstage, running lines with actors, painting scenery, and even playing small parts. Soon he was asked to be the lead in a local production of a play called *Merton of the Movies*, a Broadway hit by Marc Connelly and George S. Kaufman. When he told his parents he had accepted the role, his father became angry and said he shouldn't give up his real job for play-acting and the two began to argue. Both were stubborn, but somehow Fonda's mother calmed them down. For the next few weeks Fonda rose early, hurried to the Retail Credit Agency, then rehearsed in the evenings. He and his father didn't speak; he didn't talk to anyone.

But all the Fondas were at the Playhouse to see him triumph as Merton, a Kansas bumpkin who goes to Hollywood. Hank got a standing ovation. Afterward at a little party at home, Fonda Sr. just sat silently behind a newspaper until Hank's sister Jayne offered a slight criticism. With that William Fonda spoke for the first time in hours. "Shut up! He was perfect!" Whenever Hank told that story to Jane and Peter, his eyes would glisten with tears. "It was the best review I would ever get," he said.

"When I walked out on the stage," he said, "the short hairs on the back of my neck seemed to stand up and my skin tingled. I could forget myself and become another character." He had found himself. Suddenly, all he wanted to do was act, escape from himself. "I always thought I was very boring," he said.

In contrast, Frances Seymour, who would become Fonda's second wife (he was briefly married to the actress Margaret Sullavan), seemed to think she was pretty terrific. "She was always 'up,' the most lively one of all, like a butterfly!" said Laura Clark, who met Frances in 1935 when she was twenty-eight and just widowed. Her husband, George Brokaw, had died and left her a million dollars. "[Frances] invited me to the wonderful parties she gave on her Long Island estate and at the club El Morocco," Laura said. "Men just fell over themselves when they saw her."

She was a volatile woman with pale blond hair perfectly coiffed and a lean, elegant figure kept trim by constant dieting. Her moods rose and fell; she wanted to control everybody. She seemed to radiate sexuality. She liked to claim that her family was both rich and well connected, speaking often of her cousin Millicent Rogers, a Standard Oil heiress. Frances's grandfather, Horatio Seymour, was governor of New York before he ran for president in 1868 and lost to Ulysses S. Grant. However, Frances hadn't started out with many advantages. The eldest of seven sisters, she was born in Brockville, Ontario, in 1908. As a little girl, she and her family moved to a farm outside Morrisburg, New York, on the Saint Lawrence River where her mother, Sophie, raised chickens and sold apples and eggs to neighbors to make ends meet. Ford Seymour, her husband, once a successful lawyer, could no longer hold a job, let alone handle money. He had become a raging alcoholic and was later diagnosed as a "paranoid schizophrenic." In time Cousin Millicent helped with money and packages of clothing, but it was Sophie who was the sole financial provider for the family.

"My mother was from old Canadian stock," Frances wrote in an autobiography she started in 1949. "Any guts I had, I inherited from her. She had one hell of a life with my father." Frances would remember her childhood as utterly miserable; she and her sisters were kept locked in the house and saw no one because Ford Seymour hated visitors. "My father used to spank us so long and hard my mother would scream at him to stop." Then, at the age of eight, Frances was sexually abused by a piano tuner, and that left her traumatized and guilty, though she kept it a secret until she told Henry Fonda after they were married. But he had little sympathy for her. He didn't understand the terrible burden of sexual abuse. He didn't know that if a girl is molested, she will often not blame her adult perpetrator; she will blame herself.

Frances's sexuality became one of the few qualities that had value to her, and it led to promiscuity in her adolescence. In her autobiography she would remember her teenage years as filled with "boys, boys, boys," and she would later refer to her one-night stands as "peccadillos." She would go on to have several abortions. She glowed as a young woman, but she was tormented and insecure.

In 1924, Frances moved to Fairhaven, Massachusetts, to live with the Rogers family and finished high school there. The Rogerses continued to help the Seymours financially, and Cousin Millicent, described by gossip columnists as "the Bohemian debutante," became Frances's inspiration. Millicent's world was one of continuous, extravagant celebration: tennis tournaments, regattas, and gala weekends filled with banquets. By twenty-two she had already been married to and divorced from an Austrian count and had danced with the Prince of Wales. She took Frances to lavish parties at the Ritz in New York, as well as to costume balls. She shared her passion for fashion and collecting Gauguin paintings, Persian rugs, and antique jewels with Frances.

Frances always felt shy and intimidated by her cousin's sleek confidence. "I was the poor relative," she used to say. By the time she graduated from high school Frances had become obsessed with accumulating money, which, she had realized, meant security, a place in society, beautiful clothes and jewels — and power.

Vowing to become "the fastest typist and the best secretary anyone could hire," Frances descended on Wall Street, determined to marry a millionaire. She attended the Katharine Gibbs Secretarial School and found a job at Morgan Guaranty Trust Bank, where she learned about investment firsthand. She educated herself about stocks and bonds and interest rates, studying the market and poring over the *Wall Street Journal*. At age twenty-one, at a penthouse lit by candlelight, Frances met the immensely wealthy fifty-two-year-old industrialist and former congressman George Tuttle Brokaw, who'd just divorced writer Clare Boothe (who went on to marry Henry Luce). Determined to seduce him, Frances confided to a mutual friend that she found older men sexually very attractive; besides, George reminded her of her father. After a whirlwind courtship of six months, she purchased a gold wedding band from Tiffany's, tied it up with a little pink ribbon, and showed it to Brokaw during lunch, saying, "Don't you think it's about time?" His mouth fell open. "When do you want to get married?" he asked.

Clearly Frances knew how to make things happen.

The wedding, which took place in January 1931, was a major event of the New York social season, with five hundred guests including the Fishes and the Stuyvesants. After the honeymoon, the couple lived in splendor in the historic Brokaw mansion on Fifth Avenue and 79th Street, which was spacious but gloomy. Soon Frances had a daughter, Frances de Villers, nicknamed "Pan." But her marriage was a disaster. Brokaw was an alcoholic, and when he got drunk he beat Frances savagely.

In the spring of 1935, Frances persuaded Brokaw to go to a sanatorium in Greenwich, Connecticut, to dry out, but it didn't take. Brokaw sneaked liquor into his room and even hid it on the grounds; the nurses and doctors couldn't stop him. He kept on drinking until May, when he staggered into the sanatorium swimming pool and drowned. Frances's suffering was eased by the settlement. She inherited a million dollars, and Pan was the beneficiary of a trust fund worth several million dollars more. Frances could now take care of her mother financially. She asked her to live with her and to help care for her daughter.

The following year Frances traveled to Europe with her brother

Ford and his fiancée. Their first stop was London, where she was introduced to Henry Fonda on the set of the movie *Wings of Morning*, in which he was starring opposite the French actress Annabella. After one look, Frances decided he would be her next husband, though he was rumored to be having an affair with Annabella. That didn't stop Frances, who asked him to have dinner with her at the Savoy Grill that same night. ("That's the last I ever saw of Hank romantically," Annabella said later. "He was hooked.")

According to Jane in her autobiography, *My Life So Far*, "Then Mother carried a 'strange luminosity'; often victims of abuse carry [this kind of] luminosity because of the sexual energy that was forced into their lives far too early." Fonda described Frances as "bright as a beam from a fellow spot." She was charming and alluring — she had breeding and class, and he was impressed by the way she organized everything. The day after their first date, when she discovered he wasn't filming, she arranged for him to go with her on a boat trip up the Thames and they had a chance to talk. After several more dinners she suggested Hank join her and her brother for a long weekend in Paris: "We have a lovely flat there, we could go over and have fun — go to Maxim's, see the town."

Eulalia Chapin, Frances's best friend at the time, recalled how she must have impressed Hank Fonda. "Frances was very gay, very flirtatious, adorably so. Hank used to tease her about it. She was always talking, talking, talking."

Their courtship moved on from Paris to Berlin, where they attended the 1936 Olympics and saw Nazi soldiers — what seemed like thousands of them — goose-stepping and heiling "*Der Führer*." Fonda managed to snap candids of Hitler with his movie camera, fairly close up. The German dictator was shaking his fist and screaming crazily. "That guy is totally mad," Fonda said at the time. He and Frances were both put off by the Nazis, so they hired a car and drove to the romantic city of Budapest, where they spent hours walking along the Danube. Frances was clearly besotted, but Fonda seemed rather complacent about their affair. He wouldn't pop the question. When they returned to Paris, she drafted a telegram to her mother, which read: "Arriving in New York, will announce my engagement to Henry Fonda." When she showed the wire to him, he shrugged and mumbled, "Sure, fine."

Ten days later they were back in Manhattan, attending dinners in their honor in East Side brownstones and penthouses overlooking Fifth Avenue. Fonda preferred taking Frances to the jazz joints of Harlem. He felt uncomfortable with the wealthy conservative Republicans who dominated Frances's social circle. They hated the Democratic president, Franklin Delano Roosevelt, but Fonda had voted for FDR and supported the New Deal. He started to realize that he and Frances were quite different. But for the moment they tried to compromise and pretend they enjoyed everything about each other.

Frances wanted her husband to love Pan as she did and Fonda tried at first. He spent a few afternoons with the four-year-old before the wedding. Pan remembers, "My first memory of Henry Fonda was when we met and he knelt down so he could be on my level. I must have liked him, because I asked him to read to me right away. He did."

Pan was the flower girl at their wedding, which took place in Christ Church on Park Avenue on September 16, 1936. The bride wore a gown of pale blue taffeta and tulle. The groom sported a black morning coat, top hat, and ascot and remarked to his best man, Josh Logan, that he felt as if he were on a movie set. After the reception at the Hotel Pierre, they flew to Omaha to meet the Fonda family. Frances told the story of their courtship repeatedly to his sisters, how she took one look at their brother and decided that she was going to marry him. It became family lore, along with the fact that Frances's father was directly descended from Edward Seymour, First Duke of Somerset, who was brother to Henry VIII's third wife, Jane Seymour. Edward's cousin, Lady Jayne Grey, was beheaded by Queen Mary I during an attempted takeover of the throne in the sixteenth century. Frances insisted that Hank read Shakespeare's play so he could get a better picture of her dramatic ancestry. Fonda was impressed enough to agree that Lady Jayne Seymour should be the name of their firstborn daughter. (Jane was addressed as "Lady Jayne" by both of her parents until the age of eight, when she refused to answer to it anymore, "because it made me feel too different.")

A week after Jane's birth, the Fondas returned to Southern California to the comfortable ten-room house they'd rented temporarily on Chadbourne Drive in Brentwood. They began looking for a house to buy, but they didn't care for the Moorish palaces and Spanish haciendas the real estate agents showed them and ultimately decided to create something special of their own. They found the property they wanted — a nine-acre tract high on a hill above Sunset Boulevard — but it wasn't for sale. They promised each other they'd just keep after the Mountain Park Land Company until the company changed its mind.

Frances bought a Buick ("Frances always drove a Buick," Fonda said) and purchased a house for her mother and father down the block. Her father, Ford Seymour, was by this time a shadowy figure who didn't seem to participate in family life and who disappeared frequently for weeks at a time. Everybody assumed he was off on a bender. It didn't seem to bother Sophie. "Oh, he'll be back when he needs a pair of clean socks," she'd say.

Frances supported her parents and helped her sisters and brothers as well. She never talked about it and used money inherited from Brokaw, which she kept in a separate account. In the evenings, the Fondas preferred to stay at home with close friends like Jimmy Stewart and the *Life* photographer John Swope. Their tight little circle included Josh and Nedda Logan; Tyrone Power and his wife, Annabella; and a film editor at Fox named Watson Webb, who was especially close to Frances. Then there was Eulalia Chapin, Frances's most intimate confidante. The Fondas attended the A-list dinner parties at David O. Selznick's home and Gary Cooper's ranch, as well as at the opulent Holmby Hills mansion of the producer William Goetz, whose wife, Edith, was one of Louis B. Mayer's daughters. Frances was often the center of attention. "She had the most amazing collection of precious stones," Watson Webb remembered. "The women at these dinners — Joan Crawford, Edith Goetz, Rocky Cooper, Ginger Rogers — were all very competitive about their jewelry. But none of them could hold a candle to Frances Fonda. There was one necklace she wore, aquamarine mounted in platinum with diamonds set in platinum ropes — a knockout. Frances said she had a little man at Harry Winston's in New York who helped her choose her jewels: 'He always shows me the best emeralds and rubies.'"

Back home, Jane was kept isolated in the nursery and overseen by a crisp, efficient nanny who insisted Hank wear a mask whenever he visited his tiny daughter. He complained to his wife, who told him he had to wear the mask; she didn't want her child infected with germs.

"So I never got to kiss Jane goodnight when she was a baby, or hold her in my arms. I think we both felt deprived," he told his biographer,

Howard Teichmann. He did, however, pick her up surreptitiously; and when Jane was a little older, she would crawl into his lap and try to hug him. By then he didn't respond. "Dad never said, 'I love you,'" claimed his daughter.

Hank Fonda always had difficulty verbalizing affection. He seemed to believe it a weakness to show any feeling; his father said it was *disgusting* to break down and cry. So Fonda usually appeared remote. But that didn't stop him from photographing Jane obsessively. It was one of his ways of communicating with her. There was always a visceral exchange between father and daughter whenever she stood in front of him and struck a pose. Early family albums are crammed with seemingly idyllic pictures. Fonda would amass a lively photographic record of Jane and Peter in both stills and home movies.

And he was illustrating for her, too, painting the nursery with fanciful drawings of Oz characters. He decorated the ceiling with nursery rhymes. He loved to paint, to spread bright colors on canvas. He seemed to dance with his brushes. He also sculpted a bust of Frances looking very regal, but it dried out and cracked, so after that he devoted himself mostly to sketching. As soon as she could, Jane began copying him, holding a crayon in her pudgy hand.

But Henry Fonda had little time to paint. Over the next five years he would make ten movies; he starred in *You Only Live Once* (directed by Fritz Lang), playing a young ex-con persecuted for a murder he didn't commit. In *Jesse James* as the tobacco-chewing Frank James, brother of the legendary outlaw, you totally believe Fonda's metamorphosis from Kansas City farm boy to tight-lipped man with a gun. He delivers Jesse from a jail surrounded by soldiers, and then accompanies him in a breathtaking escape scene from a bank ambush. *New York Times* film critic Bosley Crowther called it "a beautiful characterization." Fonda was able to project facets of his own distinctive personality into an amazing variety of characters. But it was his Nebraska upbringing that kept him accessible to the heart of America. John Steinbeck always thought Hank expressed the gentle side of his mother and the harsher qualities of his father.

It was the era when the big studios — MGM, Twentieth Century Fox, Warner Bros., Paramount, RKO — churned out more than four hundred films a year and honed the public images of their biggest stars. The pictures made during this period would become legendary, and so would the actors who starred in them: Clark Gable and Vivien Leigh in *Gone with the Wind;* Orson Welles in *Citizen Kane;* Judy Garland in *The Wizard of Oz;* Henry Fonda in *The Grapes of Wrath.*

Fonda never found his "type" as completely as several of his contemporaries did. He was not as sardonic as Humphrey Bogart was as detective Sam Spade in *The Maltese Falcon.* He wasn't as romantic as Clark Gable or Cary Grant (although he was Grant's equal when it came to playing high comedy—he could be hilarious). He wasn't as laid-back as Spencer Tracy or as tough as Jimmy Cagney. He wasn't as macho as John Wayne, or as mannered as Jimmy Stewart. Like Gary Cooper he projected an almost preternaturalness on the screen. He never seemed to be acting. He invested his performances with a kind of intensity that was forever youthful. "[He] keeps his own grace and talent as light as possible," the film critic Manny Farber wrote. "In his best scenes, Fonda brings together . . . a flickering precision and calculated athleticism mixed in with the mulish withdrawing." He could switch effortlessly from a simple rural type to a civilized urban gentleman, or some enormously attractive combination of the two.

Young Mr. Lincoln, which Fonda made in 1939, established him as the archetypal American, complete with false nose, wart on cheek, and stovepipe hat. His is the definitive characterization of the great man as a young jacklegged lawyer from Springfield, Illinois. His homespun, drawling style, alternately dreamy and tough, illuminated the part. This movie marked the beginning of his association with the director John Ford, with whom he would make five pictures and create his most memorable role, the angry farmer Tom Joad, in John Steinbeck's *The Grapes of Wrath.* It was the story of sharecroppers who leave the Oklahoma Dust Bowl during the Depression to become migrant farm workers in Northern California.

Twentieth Century Fox was producing the movie, and Darryl Zanuck, the shrewd, cigar-smoking president in charge of production, wanted Fonda to play Tom Joad, but only if he signed a seven-year contract with the studio. Zanuck had big plans for Fonda.

At first Fonda said no. He'd been jumping around from studio to studio for seven years and he relished his independence. He disliked

Zanuck because, he said, "all he cares about in life are movies and satisfying his cock."

But Zanuck was adamant about that contract, and Fonda really wanted to play Joad, a character he identified with. He had read every book Steinbeck had written, and he appreciated the rural American characters Steinbeck was immortalizing. His agent, Leland Hayward, got him as good a financial deal as possible so he finally signed. Filming began in the summer of 1939.

Shot on location in dusty Okie camps and the sweltering San Joaquin Valley orange groves, and directed by John Ford, with Greg Toland's sweeping, uncompromising camera work and Alfred Newman's magical use of the Red River Valley folk song as a musical theme, *The Grapes of Wrath* is an American masterpiece.

"There is possibly no more touching utopian speech in pictures than Tom Joad's vision of a better world at the conclusion of this movie," Peter Bogdanovich wrote. "But it is Fonda's extraordinarily beautiful incantation of this man and those words that make the moment both transfixing and ultimately transcendent. 'I'll be there,' he tells his mother. 'When the cop beats up a guy, I'll be there.'" His rural twang and his direct simplicity illuminate this memorable role. Fonda recalled how he and Jane Darwell didn't even rehearse the mother-and-son scene, "but Ford made us wait all afternoon until we were very keyed up. Then we shot the scene in one take and John said, 'Print it,' and he walked off without a word to us. Onscreen it really is brilliant."

Fonda was nominated for an Academy Award. He didn't win — but his best friend, Jimmy Stewart, did, for *The Philadelphia Story*.

He had played one of the greatest roles in film history, but under the studio system his next role was as one of Lillian Russell's tuxedoed suitors in a biopic, starring the very blond singer Alice Faye. It was painful for him to act in such second-rate productions, but he had no choice. And in the next year he also had to act in *The Return of Frank James* and *Chad Hanna*, but he gave strong performances in those movies.

Even so, he deeply regretted signing the seven-year contract with Twentieth Century Fox. He felt enslaved and overwhelmed by "such dumb material." He longed to return to the theater, where he could escape into a role and really create a character. But he couldn't share these frustrations with his wife because Frances thought his complaints about his "lousy movies" were pretty silly, since these same "lousy movies" were making him a rich man.

Frances was happy to be organizing her husband's life, along with his financial affairs. While married to George Brokaw, she had served as vice president of Morgan Guaranty Trust and had become even more knowledgeable about investments. She moved their money around; she bought and sold property, always making a profit. She talked to their Wall Street broker every day. She preferred business talk to show business gossip. Often when Henry came home from the studio, the only thing Frances wanted to discuss was this stock or that bond or such-and-such an interest rate. He would ask about Jane instead.

When Jane was two, Hank taught her how to swim. It was the most loving, most sensuous experience she ever had with her father, and she never forgot it. "He would take me into his arms, walk down the steps into the swimming pool, and play with me in the water. I would bury my nose in his shoulder on the way down the steps and smell his skin. He always had a delicious musky smell that I loved . . . the smell of Man. Yes, he was happy with me when I was little — and deep down I knew his was the winning team, the one I'd do anything to join." Her godfather, director Josh Logan, would sometimes watch them splashing around in the water. "Jane seemed deliriously happy," Logan said. "But when Hank pulled her out of the pool and set her down she would cry hysterically after being taken out of his arms."

She longed to spend entire weekends with her father, but she wasn't allowed to. Weekends were his special private time, when he and Jimmy Stewart would climb the hills behind the house and fly their kites. She would watch them from the living room window — those two lanky movie stars with their rumpled hair and engaging grins — standing on a grassy rise together in the wind. They were both men of few words, and they liked nothing better than to fly their kites in utter silence.

Near evening, as dusk fell, they would wander back to the house and play jazz on the Victrola: Benny Goodman, Hoagy Carmichael, Fats Waller, Duke Ellington. Jane would wonder what they were thinking as they sat together on the couch and listened in rapt attention to the music.

· · ·

Hank and Jimmy Stewart had met in 1928 when they joined a little theater called the University Players on Cape Cod. Other actors included Josh Logan, Myron McCormick, and Margaret Sullavan. Hank played character parts — an Italian nobleman, a has-been boxer — and many romantic leading men. Logan summed up what made him special even back then: "Hank would wipe us all off the stage by seeming to do nothing."

After four years with the Players, Fonda and Stewart moved to New York to try their luck on Broadway. Desperately poor, they shared an apartment on West 63rd Street with Logan and McCormick. They called the place "Casa Gangrene" because the shower curtain in the bathroom stank of mildew.

They would haunt the casting offices and read for shows, but nothing happened. Neither could get any work. At one point Fonda persuaded Stewart to play his accordion in Times Square while he passed the hat to the few people who stopped to listen.

But Hank never even thought of giving up. He had been obsessed with acting from the minute he had started out at the Omaha Playhouse at nineteen. "Acting was a game of make believe," he told *Playboy* interviewer Larry Grobel in 1981. "Like a young kid playing cops and robbers, cowboys and Indians." Once he was onstage he found he could be another person. "I wasn't self-conscious at all [when I was] playing a part," he said.

He kept auditioning and auditioning, and in 1934 his luck changed. Leonard Sillman was casting a new musical revue and Fonda went in to try out (he'd always had fantasies of becoming another Fred Astaire). Asked if he could sing, Fonda said no. Dance? Nope. "Well, what can you do?" Sillman asked irritably.

"I do baby imitations," Fonda told him. "Baby imitations from one week to one year." It was an act he'd been perfecting at family gatherings and parties for years. And with that he began pantomiming a man driving a car and diapering a baby at the same time.

Sillman doubled over with laughter. "You're hired!"

Fonda found himself cast opposite another unknown — a goofy girl named Imogene Coca. They costarred in *New Faces of 1934*, and it was a huge Broadway hit. During the run, he had an affair with Coca, whom Fonda described as an "adorable little clown, with so much talent!"

From then on, his life moved very fast. The debonair Leland Hayward, who had become the most powerful theatrical agent in the country, handling such talents as Garbo, Astaire, and Dashiell Hammett, sent him out to Hollywood, where he signed a movie contract with Walter Wanger for $1,000 a week. The following year, Jimmy Stewart signed with MGM; he and Fonda rented a house together in Brentwood. Orson Welles met them at that time and said, "I thought these guys were either having the hottest affair imaginable or were two of the straightest men in the world. After spending a couple of hours with them, I decided they were the straightest human beings I had ever met in my entire life."

Fonda wished his mother were alive to see his success, but she had died of a blood clot just before *New Faces* opened. As soon as he could, he flew home to visit with his ailing father, who was weak from kidney disease. He took with him a print of *The Farmer Takes a Wife*, and they watched it together. Hank's father wanted to retire and run a chicken farm and so Hank promised he would buy one for him, but he didn't get the chance. Bill Fonda died a couple of weeks later at fifty-five.

Fonda missed his parents. "I adored them," he said. He remained close to his two sisters, who had stayed in Omaha and visited him frequently in California. He still had a hard time believing his great good fortune — so much money in the bank; more scripts than he could read in a week; a beautiful, devoted wife, Frances; and Jane, his adorable baby daughter, as well as his stepdaughter, Pan, to whom he dutifully paid attention.

"All this happening to a boy from Nebraska," he'd drawl when he was in a good mood, and he was in one when he and Frances took off for a vacation in Chile and Ecuador in late 1939, just as war was erupting in Europe. Jane was left in the care of her nanny.

The trip was very important for the Fondas. They forgot about their usual preoccupations, investments and acting, and devoted themselves to each other. They tried to avoid talking too much about the news. The Nazis had invaded Poland, and Britain and France had declared war on Germany. Soon after they returned to California, Frances discovered she was pregnant again, and she was so happy that for a short time she stopped fussing over their investments.

2

ON FEBRUARY 23, 1940, Peter Fonda was born at Leroy Hospital in New York. He weighed nine pounds. Back in Hollywood, his father was so tickled that he ran around the set of *The Return of Frank James*, the movie in which he was starring, yelling, "I've got a fullback!" And then he showed the entire cast the lovely photograph that had been taken of Frances and the baby and had run in all the newspapers. She had a jubilant expression on her face because she'd always longed for a son. (She had planned to adopt a boy if the new baby had been another girl.)

Frances soon fell into a depression. It was her third cesarean and she was having a difficult recuperation. She became agitated and anxious and remained in the hospital for weeks. It's probable she was suffering from postpartum depression, though years later she would be diagnosed with bipolar disorder.

Eventually Hank flew east to be with her, and her mood brightened, but he had to return to Hollywood after the weekend and took the baby back with him, feeding and changing him on the long flight to California. Frances remained in New York for seven weeks at the Hotel Pierre, under the care of a team of doctors, before traveling west in a chauffeur-driven car.

Fonda hadn't been home for more than a couple of days when he showed the home movies of "Mummy and the baby" for Jane and her half sister, Pan. Jane recalls staring at the jiggly color images of her mother kissing Peter's tiny fist over and over, and she burst into tears and ran from the room. "I was not happy, I can tell you," she said. She began feeling doubly rejected when her mother returned and focused all her attention on Peter. She wouldn't let Frances touch her for a long time, and if she did, Jane would cry. "You couldn't forgive your mother," her grandmother Seymour wrote in a letter to Jane. "You thought that she had rejected you for Peter."

In one of the many interviews he gave before his death in 2010, Andreas Voutsinas, Jane's coach, recalled, "Jane told me her mother would come into the nursery and start fussing over Peter, hugging and kissing him, and Jane would just stand there watching. Her mother wouldn't even speak to her except to ask, 'Isn't he the cunningest child?' It got to be unbearable. Since her father seemed unable to show her any affection either, Jane felt totally unloved."

She felt especially ignored on her birthdays. She started brooding about that and grew more and more sullen. As the holidays approached, her mother noticed and asked why, and Jane blurted out that she hated her birth date, December 21, because it was so close to Christmas and she would receive fewer gifts. Frances assured her that she would do something about it.

After a week Frances handed her a beautifully wrapped little box tied with a big satin bow. Inside there was a scribbled note that said, in effect, "Darling — I am giving you my birth date, April 14, as a present. From now on we can celebrate our birthdays together," and she signed it "Love, Mummie," with a smiling little face next to it the way she always signed her notes to her children. It was one of the few warm moments Jane and Frances shared, as were the times when Jane crawled into her mother's bed in the mornings and was read to from Grimm's fairy tales and the Oz books.

At five, Jane was pudgy and frowning and constantly in motion. She had a new friend, Brooke Hayward, also five years old, who had just moved in down the block. Brooke was the daughter of Leland Hayward and his ebullient wife, the actress Margaret Sullavan, who had earlier been married to Henry Fonda. Known for her throaty voice and sharp-tongued manner, she'd just been nominated for an Academy Award for the movie *Three Comrades*. Since their divorce a decade before, she and Hank Fonda had not seen each other much, but now Hank took every opportunity to drop by the Haywards' house with the excuse that he was "picking up Lady Jayne out of the sandbox."

"Our families were united in the most abstract but intricately woven pattern," Brooke recalled in a bit of understatement. "We talked about it many times among ourselves, Jane and I, and Peter, but certainly our parents never discussed it with us and I can't remember how or when we discussed it that once upon a time our mother [Maggie] and their father [Hank] had been married and very much in love."

In 1928 Henry Fonda and Margaret Sullavan were in their twenties and working with the University Players in summer stock. "Theirs was a tempestuous relationship from the minute they met," Josh Logan said. "They starred in a production of the *Constant Nymph* and they were so romantic in that show! I remember they had to sing a duet — neither one of them could carry a tune but they sang anyway and everyone melted as soon as they started crooning off key. They were both natural actors and they had such animal attraction to one another it was palpable. They pretended to despise each other off stage, but as soon as they were in front of an audience they seemed to catch fire."

When they weren't acting they were engaging in verbal duels, which everyone listened in on. Hank taught Maggie how to walk on her hands; they'd do it together and then burst into wild laughter. She had an infectious sense of fun that contrasted with his usually dour nature. He once said, "Maggie was the kind of person, who, if she saw a water pistol, would grab it and shoot it off at anybody who came along."

They fought, they drank, they made up; they bought marriage licenses — they threw them away. Once Sullavan smashed a pudding in Fonda's face, then stormed out of their boarding house and ran down the beach and plunged melodramatically into the ocean, fully clothed. Moments later, Fonda went after her. Wiping the pudding from his face, he walked into the waves to save her.

In 1931 they married and moved into an apartment in Greenwich Village. "They were crazy about each other," Josh Logan said, but they couldn't stop fighting.

Living with Sullavan was like living with lightning, Fonda told his sister Harriet. According to him, Maggie was like "cream and sugar on a bed of hot ashes." But, he added, she always made him feel more interesting than he believed he actually was.

Their fights continued. "It's all a blur now," Fonda recalled. "I can't remember whether I stamped out in a rage or Sullavan threw me out."

Fonda moved to a single room in a fifth-rate hotel in the West 30s.

Weeks later, in a theatrical agent's office, he overheard an actor whisper that Margaret Sullavan was having an affair with Jed Harris, who was then the most successful producer and director on Broadway. Harris could be both cruel and charming; when he wanted a woman, no effort was too great.

After absorbing the news, Fonda stumbled out of the office, afraid he might pass out. That same day, he found himself standing outside the apartment he and Sullavan had shared in Greenwich Village. "I'd lean against the fence and I'd stare up at our apartment with the lighted windows on the second floor," he told his biographer. "I knew Jed Harris was inside with her and I'd wait for him to leave. But instead the lights would go out. More nights than I care to remember I'd stand there and cry.... I couldn't believe my wife and that son of a bitch were in bed together. But I knew that they were. And that ... completely destroyed me. Never in my life have I felt so betrayed, so rejected, so alone."

Eventually Fonda found himself walking into a Christian Science reading room. "A man was sitting behind a desk ... [I] simply spilled out all of [my] agony and the story of the conflict that had gone on between [Maggie and myself].... I don't even know who the man was, but he helped me to leave my pain in that little reading room. When I walked out I was Henry Fonda again. An unemployed actor, but a man."

Sullavan broke up with Harris and went on to marry William Wyler. When that marriage didn't last, she and Hank got back together again in 1935. They were filming *The Moon's Our Home,* a screwball comedy, on location in a ski lodge at snowy Lake Tahoe. They had loved each other before and now they were thrown together, working every day and being together night after night, and they found that the emotions they once felt for each other still existed.

When they returned to Los Angeles, their relationship had become serious enough for them to go house hunting together. Fonda suggested they get married again and Maggie agreed. Then they had a terrible fight and broke up. The next time he saw her on the set, she said, "This is a mistake, Hank. This thing between us — it's not going to work." Fonda said, "She was smart enough to realize that we couldn't make it happen again."

As soon as the movie was finished shooting, he was off to Europe to make another film. That's when he met Frances Brokaw and married her. His son, Peter, believes that he married her on the rebound from Maggie.

As soon as the Haywards moved to Brentwood, Fonda started dropping by their house a lot. "He and Maggie would start fooling around and do crazy things like stand on their heads or do cartwheels," a friend recalled. She could still suddenly turn herself upside down in the living room, and she'd do that whenever Hank visited and then they'd break up laughing. Jane never saw her father behave in that giddy, carefree way with her mother.

Frances was on a different wavelength and she knew it. She accepted only one invitation from the Haywards and never reciprocated. She actively disliked Maggie, disliked her tomboy nonchalance — "She wears shorts and goes barefoot" — and she thought that Maggie had bad taste, because once at a dinner party she had declared, "In the sack Hank comes very fast," and then she'd roared with husky laughter.

Frances didn't enjoy gossip. She felt far more comfortable in the company of men; then she could chat easily about America going off the gold standard or Roosevelt's financial policies with banks. "Frances' favorite subjects were sex, babies, clothes, and money," Logan remembered. "And the subject of money bored the bejesus out of Hank. I often wondered what he and Frances had in common."

Aside from their children, the Fondas did care very much about one thing — the house they were starting to build. The project drew them together.

Early in 1941 they bought the land they'd long been coveting on Tigertail Road above Sunset Boulevard — nine acres of hills and dales with breathtaking vistas of the Pacific Ocean and the Santa Monica Mountains. Peter Fonda remembered, "Pan and Jane and I had picnics together at various points on the property while Dad figured out just where the orchards should be planted and where the barn should be built. My parents designed everything right down to the supper bell in the little cupola on the roof of the main house."

Midway through construction, Frances became terribly agitated when some real estate investments and stock sales she'd made with Hank's movie money had to be sold at a considerable loss. Her own stock and bond portfolio increased in value steadily, but it upset Frances that her business acumen had faltered. She lost confidence in herself.

She believed she'd failed her husband. She became concerned with accounting for every penny. She couldn't sleep. She couldn't eat. She began suffering from blinding headaches. Finally she went off to Scripps Metabolic Clinic in La Jolla for a battery of tests.

The doctors at Scripps Metabolic could find nothing wrong with her, and Frances returned from the clinic in early 1941. By then Tigertail was completed. "It was quite something," recalled Daniel Selznick, producer David O. Selznick's son, "a replica of a Pennsylvania farmhouse — two stories, Dutch colonial fieldstone." Jane remembers how her father designed the place so that it actually *looked* old: "It had shingles made to look weather-beaten, and a lot of Early American furnishings — cobblers' benches, braided rugs, lamps made from early butter churns."

There were barns and a stable and a playhouse for the children complete with child-height sinks, rocking horses, and boxes of toys. The children used the playhouse during the day and at night the adults dropped by to visit. Jane remembers watching John Wayne, Ward Bond, and Jimmy Stewart, wearing cowboy hats and sporting six-shooters, sitting around a table with her father riffling cards.

Sometimes Hank would barbecue thick steaks and roast potatoes outside. "Absolutely delicious," Peter Fonda recalled. Nearby was a jungle gym and swings and a merry-go-round. And there were chickens and a rabbit hutch and "nine old oak trees to climb," Peter added. Beyond that there were clay tennis courts and a freeform rock swimming pool designed to resemble the swimming hole Hank Fonda had swum in as a boy back in Omaha.

Fonda cultivated the land himself. He planted grass, and when it dried he put it into haystacks. He developed one of the first big victory gardens at the start of the war; there were always fresh vegetables to eat. "I was one of the first organic farmers in Los Angeles," he would say proudly. He liked the idea that Tigertail seemed to be in the middle of nowhere even though they were within walking distance of Sunset Boulevard. The rolling fields and the big trees and howling coyotes at night gave the impression they were living in the deep countryside.

There were even skunks. A couple of times, Hank would be sprayed and he'd have to sit in a bath of tomato juice to rid himself of the stink.

In the summer of 1941 Fonda bought Pan a horse, which she rode happily around the grounds. He bought Jane and Peter two burros. They also had three dogs and a cat. Jane said, "My best friends were rabbits for a while."

"It was an absolute paradise," Jane said. "A heaven on earth. It had everything a child — or an adult — could want. It was beautiful and comfortable and private. The house was built especially for *us*. We chose the wallpaper for our rooms, the colors, the furniture."

Her bedroom had a lovely canopied bed with embroidered pillows and a window seat overlooking one of the gardens. She has an early memory of sitting on that window seat and watching her father baling hay and watering the orange groves with a five-gallon drum hauled up from below on his station wagon.

He even plowed the fields. Watching him, Jane wanted desperately to be like him — this tall, lanky man in blue jeans — and to have him notice her. Often she'd run outside and trot behind him as he planted the corn. He would studiously ignore her chatter, even as she copied his walk — weight back on his heels. She was soon able to mimic his graceful, loping stride. By the time she was five, she had learned to ride his horse and ride it well.

Years after she became a movie star, a reporter asked, "Did you used to dress up in your mommy's clothes when you were a little girl?" and she replied, "Oh, no, I always wore what my dad wore — jeans, boots, checked work shirt. Because I wanted to be exactly like my father."

Periodically Frances would insist that Jane replace her jeans with a frilly beribboned frock and be dragged off to a birthday party for Christina Crawford (Joan's daughter) or Marlo Thomas or Candice Bergen, all nine years old or younger. Jane hated attending these parties for stars' children. They were lavish affairs with magicians and clowns and jugglers performing for the guests, "and the richest ice cream you ever tasted," recalled Jill Schary Robinson, the daughter of Dore Schary, who later became head of MGM.

Jane never knew what to do with her hands at these parties, or "how to be polite the way the other little girls were." She would watch Bing

Crosby loudly introducing his four sons; or Lana Turner, invariably drunk, fussing over her tiny daughter, Cheryl, who appeared to be absolutely miserable. Confronted by so many noisy strangers, Jane would start wailing and her nanny would have to take her home.

There seemed to be a new nanny every couple of months. Jane remembers one who was very religious. "Every morning she would come into my room before I was out of bed, and smell my fingers to see if I had my hands 'down there.' She made it clear that pleasuring one's self was a mortal sin."

Then there was another nanny, a very pretty one, who had a boyfriend on leave from the army. One afternoon, she brought him into the bathroom when Jane was having her bath. "She made me get out of the tub and then I remember her turning me around. I felt scared. I have no memory beyond that." Jane doesn't know if the soldier molested her, but something bad must have happened around that time because that's when she began to have recurring fantasies in which she either watched or participated in sexually disturbing, even violent, acts. "This was also when I began feeling terrible anxiety whenever I saw public displays of sexuality: people necking in movies or smooching on the beach. This anxiety lasted until my fifties and I do not know why." Jane did not tell her half sister, Pan, or her brother, Peter, about her fantasies. She did not confide in anyone. "We were brought up in an atmosphere where our parents just didn't express what they felt," Jane said. "So we hid everything — our sorrows, our pain, our joys even. We were being turned into little zombies."

By mid-May 1941 Fonda was fighting with Zanuck and Twentieth Century Fox, still trying to break his contract but unable to, still forced to star in second-rate movies. There were some exceptions, like his wonderful performance in *The Male Animal* as a stodgy professor who suddenly starts fighting for his rights.

And there's the Preston Sturges fast-moving screwball comedy *The Lady Eve,* with Barbara Stanwyck playing a sexy card shark, in which Fonda gives a hilarious performance as a sweetly obtuse man terrified of sex. Jane remembers being carried onto the *Lady Eve* set by her father; she was around six. She'd felt a rush of romance and exultation cuddling in his arms. Fonda introduced her to Barbara Stanwyck, all perfumed and glistening with sequins. "How do you do, Lady Jayne," she'd intoned in her throaty voice. Jane had watched her father light Stanwyck's cigarette, cupping his hand over hers.

During the filming Fonda conducted a stormy affair with Stanwyck, although nobody in Hollywood knew about it. Twenty years later, Fonda confided to his fourth wife, Afdera, "Barbara was the best fuck I ever had because she was gay — no inhibitions. She'd do anything in bed to please a man!" He added that he'd been crazy about her, and if he'd had it to do over again, "Barbara Stanwyck could have been Jane Fonda's mother."

He remained outwardly the faithful husband to Frances, but he continued to see Stanwyck secretly for months after the movie wrapped. Stanwyck provided a diversion from his shifting career, dying marriage, and needy children. He had other affairs; women found him irresistible. One of his other lovers said, "He didn't talk much but he could do everything well. He was a magician with his hands. He could carve a turkey, sculpt, whittle a piece of wood into a beautiful little bird. He could paint luminous still lives. Cultivate beautiful gardens, peel an apple better than anybody in the world."

Frances knew nothing about his other women until one of them filed a paternity suit against him and Frances used her own money to buy her silence. Pan told Jane, "I remember vividly the heavy atmosphere and anguish in Mummy's bedroom . . . her talking with Grandmother."

"In private, Fonda was a horny bastard," his fourth wife, Afdera, said. "But in public and on the screen he acted like a saint. What an act!"

An act, he would say, that he mainly displayed in "dud movies" like the lightweight comedy *Rings on Her Fingers* with Gene Tierney, directed by Rouben Mamoulian. Fonda and the rest of the cast were on location on Catalina Island, twenty miles off the California coast, filming that movie on December 7, 1941. The crew was setting up a shot when the assistant director came running down the beach shouting, "The Japs have bombed Pearl Harbor! Everybody get back on the mainland right away!"

In the next days there were air-raid warnings, and Frances Fonda hung black curtains over the windows at Tigertail. She and the children would lie under the big table in the nursery, and she would read them fairy tales by flashlight until the all-clear siren sounded. Jane began having nightmares — violent nightmares — and then she started walking in her sleep, something she would do periodically for the rest of her life. Jane described one incident in her memoir: as a young star, she sleepwalked around Beverly Hills and woke up naked on Sunset Boulevard.

During that first year of the war, Peter remembers his sister sleepwalking and moving furniture around, most of it against her bedroom window. She "didn't want to let the 'Jap' enemies in," he said. Later she would tell her brother she had no memory of sleepwalking but she did remember waking up, and that they would climb onto the roof, where it was damp and cool, and they would gaze up at the sky and stay there until the dawn streaked the horizon crimson and gold.

Her only real comfort came when Peter orchestrated a tapping signal through the wall between their rooms. They bored tiny holes in the wall so they could whisper to each other through the night. "We had (still have) our very secret word that we would whisper into our little holes," Peter wrote. He maintains that he and Jane still say their secret word to each other.

Jane did not tell her brother about the recurring dreams she was having. "They were always in Technicolor — never in black and white," she remembered, and most revolved around her need to be loved and the frustration she consistently experienced. She often dreamed of being "in a large banquet hall faced with mountains of food but unable to reach any of it." She recalled that another dream consisted of pursuing beautiful objects that always seemed to elude her grasp. Her dreams expressed a longing to be loved and approved, and a desperate need to be emotionally nourished by her father and mother — a need she would have her entire life.

3

B Y MID-1942, AMERICAN defense plants were operating twenty-four hours a day, and movie stars like Lana Turner and Hedy Lamarr were selling their kisses for $5,000 apiece, raising millions of dollars in war bond drives. Hollywood was churning out war films. Irene Diamond, one of the most famous story editors at Warners (she discovered the script for *Casablanca*), remembered, "They were practically on an assembly line, everything from Irving Berlin's *This Is the Army* to *Mrs. Miniver* to Alfred Hitchcock's *Saboteur*."

That summer, right after he completed *The Ox-Bow Incident*, Hank Fonda volunteered for active service as a gunner's mate in the navy, only to be chewed out by a grizzled old commander: "What do fuckin' gunner's mates do in this man's fuckin' Navy? They get killed! You're too smart for that." The commander made it clear that it was both impractical and unrealistic for celebrities to behave like ordinary mortals eager to do their patriotic duty. A star's value lay in exploiting his or her stardom, he said, in selling bonds, or making propaganda films.

All of Fonda's friends were enlisting. Clark Gable and Ronald Reagan enlisted in the Army Air Force; Tyrone Power had abandoned his wife and his male lover to enlist in the Marines. And James Stewart had gained weight in order to meet the requirements of the U.S. Army. Hank finally did enlist in the U.S. Navy, over Frances's vehement objections. He was thirty-seven years old, with three children and a wife to take care of—what was his rationale? He answered that he felt intensely patriotic and wanted to serve his country. He would not change his mind.

The day before he left, Fonda drove over to Grauman's Chinese

Theatre on Hollywood Boulevard, where he and his costars from his latest movie, *Tales of Manhattan* — Rita Hayworth, Charles Laughton, Charles Boyer, and Edward G. Robinson — squatted down and pressed their hands and feet in the wet cement. "It was a real publicity gimmick for this picture, so they all had shit-eating grins on their faces," said John Springer, Fonda's press agent.

But the emphasis Hollywood placed on manufacturing stardom and hype upset Fonda. "What about my *work*?" he'd ask Springer. "Doesn't that count for anything?" He once told Springer he was not about to lose his real identity as a boy from Omaha just to gain some "phony-baloney image of a *picture star.*"

"No matter how much publicity Hank got, he always hung on to his privacy — he never gave away much," Springer said. He kept his real feelings hidden. He was a strange bundle of contradictions. Fonda was a great actor but a bad father, a good friend but a terrible husband; serially unfaithful, he had huge needs he could never articulate. He led a double life most of his life, but all this was hidden beneath his gentle, dreamy face. Everybody in Hollywood knew his marriage to Frances Seymour wasn't working. He could not face what was happening to his wife, but because he didn't believe in doctors, he never consulted anybody about her manic behavior. By mid-1942 he had stopped trying to anticipate her wild mood swings.

His mother-in-law, Sophie Seymour, had been accompanying her daughter to psychiatrists ever since she began suffering from increasing depression. By mid-1942 Frances was floundering helplessly. Outwardly she was still the chic, super-organized wife of a movie star, but inwardly she was experiencing a sense of self-hatred. Her feelings of worthlessness became more intense as time wore on. Sophie tried to explain all this to Hank Fonda, who put it out of his mind. "I never dreamed it would be anything permanent," he said years later. "It was just a bore to have a wife who wasn't always well."

The war gave him an excuse to withdraw. He came home after getting his handprints embedded in Sunset Boulevard and packed up to go into the navy. He spent his last evening at Tigertail with Frances and the children, saying his goodbyes to Pan, Peter, and last, Lady Jayne.

When he entered her room, she sat up in bed and sang him her school song in a sweet, strong voice. "I gave her an extra hug and left before [she] could see me crying," he told his biographer, Howard Teichmann.

And then he was off. But when he arrived at the induction center in San Diego, the shore patrol was waiting to bring him back to Hollywood. Darryl Zanuck had pulled strings so that Fonda could star in an early piece of wartime propaganda, *The Immortal Sergeant*, with Maureen O'Hara. Fonda was furious, but there was nothing he could do about it. As soon as he finished the movie, he returned to boot camp in San Diego; six months later he was sent to the Officer Training School in Rhode Island.

He returned home only once, crewcut, tanned, and very happy. Jane remembered that he "handed out Hershey bars to everybody" and that when she showed off her swimming prowess in the pool, he dived in and joined her. Before he left the next day, he checked on the dozens of trees and bushes he'd planted before he enlisted. Jane trotted silently behind him, mimicking his walk.

For the next two years, Fonda served as Quartermaster Third Class on the destroyer *Curtis* and traveled all over the Pacific — to Hawaii, Guam, Saipan, Iwo Jima, and Tokyo. Late in the war he joined Combat Intelligence.

With her husband away, Frances plunged into a myriad of activities to keep "busy, busy, busy" so she "wouldn't miss Hank so much." She rolled bandages for the Red Cross. She served coffee to soldiers at the Hollywood Canteen. But most of her attention was directed at Tigertail.

"It was a full-time job running that place," said a friend. "Frances behaved like a general commanding her troops. She'd bark out orders to the maids, the cook, the gardeners, the handymen." Before morning was over she'd be in her office, on the phone to Wall Street to discuss their investments. She might stop midafternoon to slaughter a chicken or put up fruit preserves. The house frequently smelled faintly of burnt sugar.

Jane marveled at her mother's efficiency; she always made huge lists. Soon Jane would do that, too. Peter added that their mother would work most of the morning and into the afternoon and then she'd take them to the beach or to a museum when they came home from school. Frances was devoted to Peter and Jane, but she had an especially intimate relationship with her older daughter, Pan, a lovely, slender girl of fourteen who bore a striking resemblance to her mother. The two were real confidantes. Pan later told Jane how their mother spoke to her about the problems she was having with Hank. They just didn't communicate. Unlike her husband, Frances was very modern in her attitude toward sex.

Often after a bout of frenzied activity around the house or a long conversation with her older daughter, Frances would retreat to her darkened bedroom and shut the door. Peter was the only one in the house who was allowed to visit her. The room was off-limits to the servants and to Jane — and her father had been noticeably unwelcome on his brief visit home from the navy.

Peter recalled tiptoeing into his mother's bedroom and finding her lying propped on pillows with a chin strap around her face and wrinkle pads on her eyes. She was obsessed with "staying young," he said, and "hated the idea of aging." She was then thirty-eight. "I have already lost my looks!" she cried.

Outside in the hall, Jane would be fuming because she wasn't allowed in. She was jealous of her brother. He could come and go as he pleased because he was the favorite. She longed to be included, so she would keep standing in the hall, straining to hear them through the door. She was usually rewarded with long silences broken by an occasional *click-click* of the adding machine, a *tap-tap* of the typewriter, the *brrring* of the telephone, and then her mother's low, cultivated voice engaged in a conversation Jane could not make out.

Occasionally the door was left ajar. Peter would march out, ignoring Jane, and go directly to his room, and then Jane would dart in, past the huge rumpled bed, its pillows scattered on the carpet, and into the mirrored dressing room beyond, perfumed and cloudy with smoke. She would find Frances at her dressing table inhaling deeply on a cigarette as she studied herself in the glass. If she liked what she saw, her face would twinkle with animation and pleasure.

When she noticed her daughter in the mirror, standing defiantly in back of her, she would stub out her cigarette impatiently, then light another, and murmur, "Lady, if I gain any extra weight I'm going to cut it off with a knife!"

Jane would shudder. She felt guilty because she hadn't lost any of her baby fat. Her pudgy arms and round cheeks seemed magnified —

almost repulsive to her—reflected in the glass next to her mother's gaunt profile.

Frances would sternly remind her daughter that a woman must be slender to be desirable. She was obsessed with her weight and keeping her body supple. Several times a week a masseuse would come to Tigertail to knead and pound her body. Frances shared the masseuse with Mrs. Gary Cooper and Ava Gardner. Frances loved having her throat massaged—and she agreed with the masseuse that it was her best feature. "My long, smooth patrician neck!"

Midway through the war, a handsome young artist bunked down in the playhouse for a while. "Because he has nowhere else to stay," Frances explained to the children.

His name was Joe Wade, and Frances fell madly in love with him. "He was divinely attractive, a real party boy," Frances's friend Laura Clark recalled. "She was crazy about him. All women were. He drank a lot and was very wild. He carried a gun." Once, when he and Frances were together in the master bedroom, Wade inexplicably shot a bullet into the ceiling. Frances was briefly thrilled, and then panicked when she realized that Hank would ask about the hole in the ceiling after he came home from the war.

Jane was vaguely aware that something was going on with Joe Wade. She remembered hearing that her mother "had taken a fledgling musician under her wing and was trying to manage his career." Wade taught Peter how to play the harmonica and he painted his portrait. Then he disappeared.

Jane remembered walking up the driveway of Tigertail months later, and "out of the blue my mother said, 'Never marry a musician.' I remember it vividly not because it was such an odd thing to say to a seven-year-old but because I can't remember Mother ever giving me any other advice about life. I would wonder about those words over the years."

"I think my mother had an affair with him," Peter wrote. "I hope she did." He knew his mother was very lonely. Occasionally she would go out in the evenings by herself. Once she went to a dinner at the home of former silent film star Carmel Myers in Beverly Hills. Myers was married to perpetually tanned Ralph Blum, a leading Hollywood talent agent, and they often gave big parties. Ralph Blum Jr. remembered Frances making a grand entrance at one of these parties, where she was immediately surrounded by friends and admirers. He recalled that she was dressed very simply but elegantly in a gray silk Valentina jersey. She had fresh flowers in her hair and her jewelry was stunning. During dinner, Frances flirted with an attractive naval officer who was seated next to her at the table. Right after the meal they disappeared into the powder room. When they emerged, their clothes were rumpled and Frances's lipstick was smeared. She said a quick good night and left.

At home with the children, Frances would often start to cry. Tears rolled down her cheeks and onto her dinner plate as they were eating supper. Eventually Jane began mailing her father crude drawings of "a woman standing beside a fireplace and crying because her husband was away to the wars." Henry Fonda would scribble back notes, ignoring the content of the drawings. He'd exclaim, "My darling Lady — How can I tell my friends my daughter not only sings but draws such wonderful pictures?"

And to his son, Peter, he wrote, "I am living now on a big ship . . . the walls of the room are covered with [snapshots] of you and Lady and Pan. . . . There you are when you were just a baby, sitting on Mummy's lap with your finger stuck in your mouth and Little Lady is standing behind Mummy playing with her hair."

He was also thinking of his wife. He arranged with Watson Webb to have a huge bunch of red roses sent to her on their wedding anniversary with a loving note. Webb said, "Frances really appreciated the gesture. Since I was the children's godfather, I was often at Tigertail and I photographed the family constantly." He took dozens of pictures of Jane and Peter when they were little, in the gardens, on the way to Easter services, at birthday parties.

By this time Pan, Jane, and Peter were attending Brentwood Town and Country School along with the Haywards — Brooke, Bill, and Bridget — and other celebrity children. Errol Flynn's son, Sean, was a classmate of Jane's, as were Laurence Olivier's son Tarquin; Gary Cooper's beautiful daughter, Maria; and Dore Schary's daughter, Jill.

"We thought the school was terrific," Jill said. "We were allowed a lot of independence, and there were art classes and outdoor poetry readings, and we acted in plays. Warner LeRoy created puppet shows. He was very thin then and quite handsome. All the girls were in love with him."

Jane got caught up in her studies. (Her third-grade teacher reported that "Jane is well-adjusted, dramatic, has self-confidence and assurance. She is well liked by the children, because she is interesting and vital in her responses. Jane has dramatic ability and a talent for making the common place have life and interest.")

She also excelled in art class, where "she painted the school horse, Traveler, over and over," Jill said in a joint interview with Jane over tea. "We were into horses in a big way. We read *Black Beauty, My Friend Flicka.* Our favorite movie was *National Velvet,* with Elizabeth Taylor."

"Actually, I wanted to be the Lone Ranger," Jane said.

At the age of eight she announced she no longer wanted to be called "Lady Jayne" but plain "Jane," and she began wearing jeans and baggy shirts instead of dresses. She roamed all over Tigertail, climbing mountains and scrambling up trees. "I would get to the top of one particular oak and look out over the Pacific Ocean; triumphant, martial music would ring in my head and I would imagine myself leading an army up the hill to conquer the enemy."

She had a need to transform herself. It was the start of countless self-inventions in the vain hope of being recognized, acknowledged, and noticed by her father. Soon she would chop off her braids. Her mother was furious and told her she had lost her femininity. But when a stranger asked her, "Are you a boy or are you a girl?" she was so excited she couldn't sleep. "I had a deep psychological need to be a boy," she said. "You see, I didn't want to be a girl—I wanted to be like my father."

Periodically, she would get into trouble in school. Once, she was caught in class getting a girl to pull down her panties so she could see her "wee-wee," and she was marched off to the principal's office for a good talking-to. "Sex was starting to confuse and disturb me." This occurred after a traumatic experience with the two burros, Pancho and Pedro. "I was seven years old," Jane said. "I was riding Pancho and leading Pedro. It was a hot day. I was wearing shorts. At the top of a hill all of a sudden two hooves clamped themselves over my bare thighs from behind and all hell broke loose. Pedro had decided to hump Pancho with me astride. Eventually I fell on my back and found myself staring up at . . . well, it was two or three feet long and nasty and scabby. Then it dawned on me Pancho was really Panchita. She'd arrived with a boy's name and nobody had checked her out. See what happens when you don't teach kids the facts of life?"

That wasn't all. She had a crush on a boy in school who was coming on to another girl, and during a game he threw a ball at her, saying, "I'm trying to sex you up." Jane didn't know what that phrase meant, so she ran home to Frances, hoping for some explanation. "I found Mother in her bedroom and asked, 'Mom, what does 'sex you up' mean?' . . . She seemed to go into a sort of slow-motion meltdown . . . I know I left her room as uneducated as I went in, and even more curious about the meaning of those words."

Because Frances was unable to answer, Jane consulted Pan. "She didn't seem surprised at all and proceeded to go into scatological detail." Pan was the one who told Jane the facts of life, and Jane would observe her getting ready to go out on dates. In an interview with Howard Teichmann Jane recalled, "I would watch her in the bathroom when she put on her makeup and she had big breasts. She was [in] the flowering of womanhood . . . at the beginning of liking boys and necking and I used to spy on her. . . . It's nice to have an older sister because you can sort of preview the things to come."

But mostly Jane hung out with a small, tough, sturdily built little girl named Sue Sally Jones, the daughter of Grover Jones, a well-known screenwriter. She and Jane rode horseback together and played "cowboys and Indians." After class, they dressed in buckskins, stuck feathers in their hair, vaulted onto their horses, and galloped across the big courtyard and up into the hills behind the school. "We had so much fun! God, we had fun!" Jane said. Often they'd pelt avocados at students who got in their way.

Some afternoons Jane would end up at Sue Sally's house. Her mother, Jane Avery, was a former ballerina, "and so wonderful to both of us," Jane said, "gentle, nurturing, strong, spiritual. I used to sit on her lap and she'd hug me. She encouraged Sue Sally in every nonconformist thing she wanted to do. I couldn't believe such a close, loving relationship could exist between a mother and a daughter."

When they were by themselves, Sue Sally would boss Jane around and address her as "Lady Jayne." Jane wouldn't tolerate anyone else calling her that in school; it was the first time she was really loved openly by another human being, and she loved Sue Sally back.

As time went on the two girls would watch polo matches at the Riviera Country Club and fantasize about playing polo. Even though only men could play polo professionally, Sue Sally was determined she would do that, too — and she did. After she grew up, she disguised herself as a man under the pseudonym A. Jones and played competitive polo in tournaments for two decades until the U.S. Polo Association changed its laws in 1972 and allowed women to play competitively.

Until she moved east when she was eleven, Jane remained caught up in her friendship with Sue Sally. "The qualities Sue Sally had — physical strength — determination — inspired me for the rest of my life." However, "Dad was my only influence," she said. "Everything I did was *for him*: winning the jumping contests, getting good grades in school. It was all for him. Even if he wasn't around, I never stopped thinking about him, missing him." She counted the days until he was shipped back from the Pacific. "He was the power in our home. And he was famous; that's another kind of power. It was a pressure for both Peter and me."

Jane idealized her father. He was the epic figure in her imagination, a larger-than-life character in her dreams as well as on the screen. She mixed up her father with the roles he played. The dreamy-decent Abe Lincoln and Tom Joad in *Grapes of Wrath* were nothing like the private Henry Fonda at home — the difficult husband, the cold, remote father. For an eight-year-old, it was impossible to reconcile the differences between the private and public man. The father Jane idealized was a myth.

All her life, Jane longed to connect with him and blamed herself when she couldn't. She thought it must be her fault when he didn't appear to love her. Every time she watched him on the screen, she wondered who that man was.

One afternoon, Frances Fonda screened *Drums Along the Mohawk* at Tigertail. During the chase scene, in which Indians almost kill Fonda, Jane hid her head in her hands. Another afternoon Peter, then four years old, saw *Chad Hannah*. Henry Fonda played Chad, a young man who joins the circus and at one point gets into a cage with a lion. Peter became so terrified that he ran up to the screen to touch his father, to warn him that he was in danger. When he discovered that the image of his father's face was something that was totally intangible, he screamed and screamed. His mother had to turn off the projector.

Months later, when Hank Fonda was on leave, he drove to Brentwood Town and Country School to pick Peter up. It was going to be a surprise. As he was getting out of the car, little Peter was running out of a class. Father and son stared at each other and then Peter cried out: "Chad!" Henry Fonda laughed and answered, "No, Dad."

4

AND THEN, SUDDENLY, in August 1945, Henry was back with his family again. On the day he returned from the war, Peter watched him run through the gardens at Tigertail. Tanned and lanky, he was truly formidable in his physical perfection. A Bronze Star for bravery twinkled in his lapel. He'd won it for retrieving critical enemy plans that detailed forthcoming submarine attacks. He gave it to Peter to keep. When he reached the house, he hugged everybody, even the servants, and broke into his dazzling smile. Frances was trembling. Peter said his father was magnificent when he was happy.

Henry beamed all through dinner; the cook had prepared a rib roast — hard to come by, because there was still meat rationing. Jane had gathered fresh flowers from the garden. The entire family was there, including the Seymours. Only Pan was absent, away at camp. Afterward everyone sat around the living room while Fonda held forth on the glories and horrors of battle. He said that shortly before he got out of the service he and another officer had met the crew of *Enola Gay* that was about to drop the atomic bomb on Hiroshima. He did not foresee the kind of devastation the bomb would create.

Not long after he returned home, Jane heard him speak on the radio about the terrible effects of the bomb. She would always remember how sad his voice sounded as he expressed dismay and remorse over the bomb's gruesome aftermath.

For a short time there was a great deal of entertaining at Tigertail — barbecues down at the playhouse, jazz playing on the Victrola. Once Nat King Cole came by and sang. Old friends like Dinah Shore,

Tyrone Power, and Ward Bond dropped by. The Haywards came, too; Leland and Maggie joined in with all of those comparing notes about the outcome of the war. Even Frances left her darkened bedroom to join in the conversation. There was much discussion about the founding of the United Nations in San Francisco, and predictions as to how the new president, Harry Truman, was going to lead America. People still couldn't accept the fact that Roosevelt had died in April 1945. He had been president for twelve years.

From 1945 to 1947 Henry would make eight films, most of them mediocre, with the exception of *My Darling Clementine,* directed by John Ford, in which he played Wyatt Earp, marshal of Tombstone. His diffidence, his honesty, and his authority all combined to make it another unforgettable performance. But most of his other movies from that time were second-rate, and as soon as he remembered that he was being forced to work off the rest of his "blasted contract" with "Fuck-it-all Zanuck," he resorted to his old bad-tempered ways, growing edgy and restless. It seemed the only pleasure he had was flying his kites. He longed to return to the theater, where he could really be challenged to create a role. Getting no comfort from Frances, he took his frustration out on his children. He was starting to feel uncomfortable with Pan. At sixteen, she was tall and lovely but, he said, so jumpy it made him nervous to be with her. She reminded him of Frances. He was glad that Peter and Jane were more like him, but he often got angry with his son because the boy laughed too loudly or cried too much. Peter lost his father's Bronze Star and flushed his goldfish down the toilet. Playing with matches, he started a big fire in the open field by the barn, which he and Jane then tried to put out with tennis ball cans filled with water.

Hank got angry with Jane, too, when he discovered that she had a special closet crammed with dirty jeans and battered cowboy hats and insisted on wearing one of the hats even indoors. Hank would tell her to be more ladylike, and she would talk back to him, or imitate his remoteness with her own increasing detachment. She consciously modeled herself after her father, who kept everything inside himself. At nine she noticed that "Dad was most angry when I was most like him. Oh, but I loved him desperately! I was very much under his spell."

She'd tag along whenever he escaped to his workshop to refinish a chair or lacquer a table, or she'd stand and watch him as he whittled away at a piece of wood until it was shaped into something quite marvelous — an animal, a piece of fruit. He would never speak to her. All she wanted was to be with him and be in his world and just have him say something.

She kept struggling to emulate him and get his attention. She excelled in painting at school and was an accomplished rider; blue ribbons lined the walls of her bedroom. Hank attended a couple of her shows, saw her win prizes, bragged to John Ford about his daughter's prowess as a jumper — but he never praised her directly.

So she suffered from his silence; why couldn't he ever praise her or tell her that he was proud of her? She continued having wild dreams. In one she had over and over again, she could see herself as a little girl chasing clouds of beautiful, delicate butterflies, but the butterflies were always flying beyond her reach. She could never catch them because her hands swelled up, gigantic and misshapen, so huge the fingers could not even grasp a butterfly net.

Even more upsetting was her mother's increasingly unpredictable behavior.

When Hank came home he wanted to relax. He'd mix himself a drink and then take off his shirt and throw it over a chair. Frances would fly into a rage; she'd grab the shirt and stuff it into a laundry bag. At first Hank teased his wife about her compulsiveness, but it grew so irritating that he stayed away from her. Grandmother Sophie Seymour visited Tigertail often now, remaining for long weekends so she could monitor her daughter's escalating mood swings, crying jags, and bouts of depression.

Now and then Frances's mood lightened without warning. She would leave her bedroom and go for a swim, and even join guests Hank had invited over for a Sunday afternoon. Once she saved the director Henry Hathaway's son from drowning. She pulled him out of the pool and toweled him down, murmuring comforting words.

"She was very un-Hollywood," Hathaway said years later. "She was real — [not condescending] and one of the few adults around you could really talk to." He had no knowledge of her mental instability; he just thought she seemed very, very lonely.

Frances spoke openly of her ailments to Jane, noting in her journal that her daughter was very sweet and understanding. "She is a good little girl," she wrote. She described her insomnia to Jane, the pains in her stomach, the blinding headaches. In early 1947, without a word to her husband or her mother, Frances arranged to go to Johns Hopkins for a hysterectomy. She took Peter along and forced him to have a painful rectal examination, because she thought he had a tapeworm. The doctors wheeled him into a large room with lights hanging from the ceiling. "This is just like having your temperature taken," said one voice. Suddenly, Peter felt something "being shoved up my ass." He was terrified and managed to get off the table and run for the door, but the nurses and doctors subdued him and pushed a large, flexible wire up his rectum. "All I could do was cry and scream. I was being raped and no one came to help me." Peter has no memory of the rest of the procedure, except "forty-four years of painful, terrifying nightmares of anal abuse." The doctors could find nothing the matter with him.

When Frances returned to Tigertail, she didn't tell Fonda about her hysterectomy or Peter's ordeal. She seemed determined to attract Hank's attention. She would dye her hair red, then black, then platinum blond in an effort to make him notice her. It was clear to Jane that "Dad wasn't attracted to Mother anymore." He paid no attention to her. Frances kept on trying anyway. She would wander around naked in front of him; but he wouldn't speak to her. In a desperate effort, Frances would crawl on her hands and knees to him, begging him to say something, anything.

The children, who couldn't figure out what was happening, withdrew into fantasies. "We had to make up for the bewilderment somehow," Peter said. He and Jane dressed up as cowboys and Indians and acted out their own version of one of their father's films, *Drums Along the Mohawk*. They smoked the butts of cigarettes they picked up out of ashtrays, puffing away very grandly as they had seen their mother do. Frances caught them at it and as a punishment made them each smoke an entire pack of cigarettes. Peter obeyed and became violently ill but Jane didn't, because she just *pretended* to smoke them.

She wasn't very nice to Peter in those days. She detested him. Peter confirmed this. She was very mean to him and very bossy and sometimes physically abusive. She was still jealous of the closeness he had with their mother. But even so, he insisted, they played together, roughhoused together, explored every inch of Tigertail together. He added, "She meant everything to me, and even though she has told me she was always mean to me, I never thought it out of the ordinary or unloving—it was just the way big sisters treated little brothers. . . . She has said some things that were hurtful . . . but I would never have weathered our storm of abandonment without her."

Jane seemed to be the only person in the family who could cope with their father's huge anger. "His face would get purple—his veins would bulge. His major emotion in those days was rage," Jane remembered. "It came from tension, frustration, repression. It was hard on everybody."

"We were all scared of Henry Fonda," Jill Robinson said. "We'd come over to swim, and if he was sitting by the pool we kept very quiet. If Jane was scared she didn't show it. Even after the dog incident—that story went around the school for quite a while." Apparently when Fonda's Dalmatian ate one of his pet chickens, he chained the remnants of the dead chicken to the dog's collar and they were dragged around the property for days before they disintegrated. (This was once a common practice out in the country, thought to be a way to train a dog not to kill chickens.)

During that incident, Jane was positively "Amazonian," Brooke Hayward remembered. "The worse things got at home, the more together Jane became. Nothing seemed to faze her."

Peter had only one good memory of this time: when he and Jane joined their father and Ward Bond, and John Wayne drove them around in his big cream-colored Cadillac convertible—red leather seats, top down, everyone laughing and telling jokes. They were visiting Fonda on location in the California desert, where he was filming *Fort Apache* for the director John Ford.

"Dad was playing the part of Colonel Thursday, this inflexible, strict hardass, who has to deal with a rebellious daughter and sloppy, undisciplined troops. When people say, 'What was it like growing up with Henry Fonda as your father?' I'd say, 'Did you see him in *Fort Apache*? That's what he was like!'" (In the movie he comes across as totally uncompromising. He had such chilling authority it made you forget he'd played Abraham Lincoln and Tom Joad.)

Fort Apache was the last movie on Fonda's Fox contract. When he finished, he let it be known to his new agent, Lew Wasserman at MCA, that he wanted to do theater. (His old agent, Leland Hayward, had sold his agency to MCA and had moved to New York, where he was now a hugely successful Broadway producer of shows like *State of the Union* and John Hersey's *A Bell for Adano*.) Hayward started looking for plays for Fonda, who was anxious to leave California.

It was a scary time. The House Un-American Activities Committee had begun hearings in the spring of 1947 to investigate the charges that Communists were infiltrating Hollywood with anti-American propaganda. The political affiliations of the industry's most famous actors, writers, producers, and directors were under scrutiny. Hollywood became polarized.

Liberals like Hank, Gregory Peck, Katharine Hepburn, Humphrey Bogart, and John Huston signed an open letter to HUAC expressing their outrage at the committee's tactics. Right-wingers like Jimmy Stewart vehemently opposed Fonda's signing the letter and warned him of the consequences to his career that such an action might bring. After many more arguments they decided not to talk politics anymore or their friendship would be destroyed. Fonda was "graylisted" as a result of his patriotic stand.

As it turned out, he did not star in another Hollywood movie for seven years.

That summer Josh Logan phoned from New York to say he was co-authoring a play called *Mister Roberts,* based on a loosely knit series of stories dealing with navy life by an ex-sailor, Thomas Heggen. Most of the stories focused on a quietly heroic naval officer named Doug Roberts, who is stuck on a cargo ship in the midst of the Pacific and has to deal with the boredom and idiocy of war. He ultimately stands up for his crew by defying their crazy, tyrannical captain, and his crew loves him for that and for his inner strength and humanity. It seemed a part tailor-made for Hank Fonda.

He flew east immediately and listened to a rough draft of the play read in Logan's apartment by the actor David Wayne. Fonda agreed at once to star as Mister Roberts. Logan would be directing it on Broadway and Leland Hayward would be producing it. When he returned to Tigertail, he excitedly described Doug Roberts in detail to Frances. He told her playing this character was going to energize his career and his life. He was sure of it.

They were interrupted in their conversation by a family drama. Earlier that day they had given away a litter of baby kittens six-year-old Peter had been caring for. He was so angry that he threatened to run away. The Fondas paid no attention, and that evening they disappeared into their bedroom so Fonda could begin memorizing the lines from *Mister Roberts,* with Frances cueing him. He felt compelled to immerse himself in the character immediately.

Every so often between reciting speeches, he would wander over to the window. At one point he saw Peter's tiny figure moving across a huge field that was part of Tigertail's sweeping landscape. He was carrying his teddy bear and dragging his red wagon after him. Soon he all but disappeared in the high grass. The field was at least two miles long and Fonda knew it would take him quite a while to reach his destination, which he assumed would be the neighbor's garden in the distance, so he went back to memorizing his lines.

Two hours went by. The phone rang. It was the neighbors saying that Peter was hiding in their garden. Fonda ran out of the house and retrieved Peter. He picked his son up in his arms and comforted him about the loss of the kittens. Then they returned home and Fonda went back to memorizing the play.

"If the show is a hit, will we move to New York?" Frances wanted to know.

"Absolutely!" he said.

Late that summer, Fonda returned east and joined Logan and Heggen in Logan's home in Connecticut where they collaborated on rewrites of *Mister Roberts.* The three men talked and drank and laughed together. Heggen dashed off an entirely new second act in one marathon session. Logan would describe the experience as a "high, happy time," and he would never forget Hank's laugh. "It started with a strangled sob and then soared to a screech. You didn't hear it with your ears, but in your bones."

In February 1948 Henry Fonda opened on Broadway as Mister Roberts, wearing the same battered officer's cap he'd worn during his three years of warfare in the South Pacific. He and Frances had climbed up into the attic at Tigertail and gone through bags and trunks until they found it. Being onstage again after eleven years, gazing out at the pink blur of expectant faces, was a transforming experience — almost electrifying. He had never felt such joy, and he was fearless "because I [didn't] have to be me." He knew that every night the show would be different. That's what made him love the theater so much: that sense of immediacy and connection with the audience, that sense of surprise.

The cheering didn't stop when the curtain came down. All of Broadway royalty was present: the Lunts, Helen Hayes, Katharine Cornell, Elia Kazan, Ruth Gordon, Garson Kanin, Tennessee Williams, Thornton Wilder, Arthur Miller. Noel Coward stood on his seat, and scores of others jumped up, yelling, "Bravo!" The applause went on and on in waves until Fonda stepped out in front of the footlights, grinning. "That's all Tom and Josh wrote." And then he added, "If you want us to do it again, we will." The audience roared its approval. The *Daily News* drama critic John McClain reported, "I hung around hoping they would!"

Each review was a love letter to the star. "Henry Fonda is back on Broadway. He skillfully underplays and plumbs the depths of the play's inner significance," the *New York Times* wrote. "Thank you Mr. Fonda and Mr. Heggen for a royal good time."*

Soon orders for tickets were backed up for the next three years, so Fonda told Frances to put Tigertail on the market immediately. "And find a comparable house in Greenwich," he drawled.

"But we have no friends in Greenwich."

"Greenwich is just a train ride away from New York and you have friends in New York, Frances." Period. End of discussion.

---

* Being the author of a smash hit was too much for Thomas Heggen. He began drinking heavily and taking too many sleeping pills. In May 1949 his cleaning lady found him drowned in the bathtub. He was thirty-one.

5

THE FONDAS MOVED to New York in June of 1948. Pan remained in boarding school in Baltimore. As soon as their plane landed, Frances brought Jane and Peter directly to the Alvin Theatre, where *Mister Roberts* was playing. It was late at night; everybody was exhausted and keyed up. Jane remembered standing in the wings next to the stage manager: "Peter and I waited for intermission to release our father to us. As I peered around the curtains I saw — was it a stage or a sliver of heaven? It was so close, yet far away, bathed in light, awash in an electric energy that crackled back and forth between an unseen audience and Dad in his khaki lieutenant's uniform. But he wasn't 'Dad.' He was a funny, talkative Mr. Roberts. Even the gunmetal gray of the set, the decks, and the antiaircraft guns, and turrets of the navy destroyer seemed to glow from within. No wonder he left us to come to this place: Here he was more alive than life, the eye in the center of a hurricane of love and laughter.

"Suddenly there was thunderous applause," Jane wrote in her memoir. "People began running around backstage, and before I knew it, Dad was next to me giving me a big hug and I could feel some of the energy he'd picked up out there coming through his uniform right into me, along with a heady wave of his musk smell. I didn't want to leave, ever."

After that night Jane visited her father backstage as often as she could. She would climb all over the huge metal set and wander the wings as the stagehands prepared for another performance. Sometimes she sat quietly in her father's dressing room while he lay under a sunlamp so his face would have a perpetually ruddy, South Pacific glow.

The entire cast had sunlamp treatments. His dressing room was like another home, with comfortable chairs, a table, and a couch he could nap on. He could paint in his dressing room; he even set up an easel so he could paint between shows. After the final curtain call, friends would come backstage and he would entertain them. Jane would notice that as soon as he had a couple of belts of Jack Daniel's he would relax and smile and talk more easily.

She liked especially to stand in the wings and watch her father transform himself into Mister Roberts. The lights would dim; the stage manager would murmur, "House to half." Then there would be utter blackness and then a blaze of light as Fonda made his entrance to huge applause. He had remarkable ease onstage and such a commanding presence it made her shiver. "Even when he was cracking jokes there was always an air of pervading sadness about him," she said years later in an interview. "If it hadn't been for that sadness he could've been very cold and lifeless." The audience identified with his private anguish. As time went on he became more and more caught up in playing Mister Roberts. "He was a perfectionist—like a martinet," one of his stage managers, Ruth Mitchell, said. "The cast revered him. He set such an example for concentration and discipline."

He was hardest on himself. One night Gary Cooper and his wife, Rocky, saw the show and dropped backstage to tell him how brilliant he was. They found Hank in his dressing room, banging his head against the wall because he thought he'd given a lousy performance. The Coopers assured him he'd been wonderful.

Hank had rented a little apartment for himself in New York. He was doing eight shows a week and he needed to rest, so the only time he visited his family was Monday, his day off, at their new home in Greenwich, Connecticut. It was an enormous rental called "The Count Palenclar House." It had a garden, an elevator, and a walk-in safe in the basement. The children were in a daze. "We felt we'd been kicked out of paradise," Peter said. Weeks before, he and Jane had trudged up the hill to watch the fog roll in from the Pacific at Tigertail; now they were in Greenwich.

"No orange groves, no avocado trees, no fresh vegetables," as Peter wrote in his autobiography. Frances Fonda became more and more depressed. She realized she'd have to go back and forth to California until she sold Tigertail. She wanted to make a profit, though she wished she could hang on to it. Soon there were bewildering silences at the supper table. Peter cried a lot and rode up and down in the elevator and scrawled "I hate the East" on the walls of his bedroom.

Jane adjusted a little better than Peter. She made friends with a tall, skinny, freckle-faced girl named Diana Dunne. They both loved horses, and Diana introduced her new friend to Round Hill Stables and Riding Club nearby, where Jane learned to "take horses over a jump."

She even began fox hunting with Diana. "I was scared when we'd come to a jump, and I was terrified every time we galloped around a sharp corner when the ground was wet for fear the horse would slip and fall on me. I was used to being scared, but I always felt that courage was the manifestation of character. So I pretended not to be. No one ever knew, especially Diana."

Late that fall Frances had an operation on her kidneys, which left a twelve-inch scar on her stomach. When she came home from the hospital, she was preoccupied with the scar and talked about it obsessively to Jane. She had another scar on her belly from the cesareans, but this new scar really upset her because it was so "thick and red and angry." She wrote a friend, "They have cut me in half." She was experiencing so many violent mood swings that her mother flew from California with her husband and moved in to take care of Peter and Jane.

The Haywards had left California, too, and were living nearby in another big house. The friendship between the two families continued. They were a big comfort. Maggie Sullavan was like a surrogate mother to the Fonda children, just as she had been in Brentwood. "We'd stay overnight and put on plays," Peter said. "Maggie and our nannies were the main audience." Leland Hayward was in New York producing not only *Mister Roberts* but also *South Pacific*. He and Maggie were in the middle of getting divorced; he had fallen in love with Slim Hawks, director Howard Hawks's ex-wife.

Peter was attending Brunswick School in Greenwich, where he had to wear a tie, which he hated, and where he was taunted by the other students for his "incredible skinniness." Jane was enrolled in the sixth grade at Greenwich Academy, with Brooke Hayward and her sister, the pale, ethereal Bridget. "Jane and I really acted up in school," Brooke said, "throwing spitballs and being generally naughty." At recess, Jane found she could make a big impact by telling dirty jokes to a group of her giggling classmates. "It gave me a new identity," she said. But her teachers also treated her with deference because she was Henry Fonda's daughter. They made a big fuss over her and she enjoyed the attention.

Frances was away a lot. The children were told she was having an operation. "There was tension around the house," Jane said. "Grandma Seymour came to take care of everything and Mother's oldest sister tried to help, too."

That first Christmas in Greenwich Fonda gave Peter a set of electric trains, which he had first set up in his dressing room at the Alvin to amuse the cast during intermission. Jane remembered her present, "a Mohawk Indian costume made out of buckskin, complete with beaded moccasins and a strip of fake hair that stood up straight when I pinned it on my head, a real Mohawk hairdo. This was about the most perfect thing Dad could have given me. . . . That very afternoon I put on the outfit and Dad made a home movie of me. He even shot a close-up of my serious little face looking slowly from right to left, before slipping silently back into the forest. It was my film-acting debut."

It was also the end of Jane's cowboy and Indian fantasy life. Looking at the footage decades later, Jane recalled, "It was about that time that I started to hate my round chubby face. I thought I looked like a chipmunk with nuts stored in my cheeks."

By spring of 1949 the Fondas had moved to another house in Greenwich called the "Boomer House." It was set on a big green lawn and had two ponds and a thick green wood nearby. Frances spent very little time there. She was commuting back and forth to California, trying to sell Tigertail. Then she had to go to the hospital again. Grandma Seymour continued caring for Jane and Peter. Hank was home only on his one day off, and he paid less and less attention to his family when he was with them.

Throughout the week he would remain in New York, arriving at the theater in the early afternoon, and he would disappear into his dressing room and paint. He was using pastels. His work was beautiful and very precise.

The entire cast knew that Fonda was seeing another woman, because she was in his dressing room a lot. Her name was Susan Blanchard, and she was just twenty-one. Her mother was Dorothy Blanchard; her stepfather was Oscar Hammerstein II. Her half brother, Bill Hammerstein, was one of the stage managers of *Mister Roberts.*

"Susan was absolutely ravishing," Shirley Clurman (Josh Logan's assistant) recalled. She "looked like Alice in Wonderland with long blond hair down her back, scrubbed Madonna face, husky voice. She used to wear jeans and a man's shirt. Hank would literally melt when he saw her. But he felt guilty because she was so young and he was forty-four and still married."

As soon as Frances returned from California, where she had gone to complete the sale of Tigertail, she realized Hank was having an affair; one minute he'd be giddy with happiness, and he'd talk a mile a minute, which he ordinarily never did; and then he'd be "down in the dumps." She confided to her close friend Eulalia Chapin how he impulsively wanted to give one of his paintings to a mysterious "niece" of Oscar Hammerstein's, and when she asked to know the *name* of this niece, he had exploded.

Then he took her to a dress rehearsal of *South Pacific,* and she caught a glimpse of Susan Blanchard. "I noticed a lovely slender blonde girl sitting a few rows ahead of us," Frances wrote in her autobiography. "She turned around and just stared at Hank, and he stuck his tongue out at her the way he always did with pretty girls."

Frances was beside herself, but she had other things to worry about. Pan had gotten pregnant; she was only seventeen. After much discussion, it was decided that she should marry the father of the child, a young man named Bunny Abry. He came from a distinguished Main Line family in Philadelphia and was heir to the Kresge store fortune. A wedding was hastily arranged in late May with Jane as the flower girl, and Hank Fonda walked his stepdaughter down the aisle. After the ceremony, he whispered to Frances to "make sure Pan knows she can get a divorce whenever she wants."

Frances ignored his comment; that summer she joined her daughter on her honeymoon in Europe. It was Pan's idea. She thought her mother needed to get away from all the tension back home. The trio traveled to all sorts of fashionable spots, including the Riviera. Frances enjoyed being on the Côte d'Azur; it distracted her from thinking about the empty, sinking sorrow that awaited her back in Greenwich. She sailed home on the *Queen Elizabeth* on July 29 after writing friend

Watson Webb "that my better half will find me looking 100% better than when I left."

She had almost convinced herself that everything was going to be all right again in the marriage. But after a few weeks at home, in August of 1949, Hank sat her down and announced he wanted a divorce. He confessed he'd been in love with Susan for a year. Eulalia knew, Shirley Clurman knew, Oscar Hammerstein knew, everybody knew but Frances. She shakily tried to wish him luck although she felt he'd betrayed her. What treachery. But she didn't express her feelings to Fonda, only to friends like Watson Webb and Eulalia. She didn't want him to know he'd broken her heart.

The following morning Jane was on her way to school when her mother walked into the hall and told her calmly, "If anyone mentions that your father and I are getting divorced, tell them that you already know."

In a letter to Watson Webb, she wrote: "The shock of Hank wanting to remarry was almost too much for me. . . . Since he has told me he hasn't been happy during our thirteen years of marriage, all I can say is, I wish him great happiness in his new marriage. I am sad for my children. If it wasn't for them, you know where I'd tell him to go. I'd tell him to have his head examined."

In the following days she rushed around to Bergdorf's and Henri Bendel's and bought an entire wardrobe. She returned everything the next afternoon. Then she met with lawyers over a possible divorce settlement. First, they wrangled over taxes and bills. Her paranoia grew when she was warned by Fonda's attorney that he was not going to be very generous. She had no reason to be paranoid, because she had a small fortune in the bank; even so, she was fearful that she might be left destitute. From then on all her thoughts centered on her money, the savings accounts she had, her many investments, and how the monies should be distributed among her children. Hank was omitted from her newly revised will.

He didn't know that. He behaved as he always had, visiting Jane and Peter on Mondays in Greenwich. He would take them fishing; he would take Jane for drives; he would scold her for biting her nails. Once he slapped her for using the word *nigger*.

"He'd always kiss me when he came into the house," Frances wrote, "and then he would try to kiss me before I put him on the train. The gesture was so hypocritical I finally made him stop."

In the next weeks, Pan suffered a miscarriage and lost her baby. Frances was in despair; she knew her daughter's marriage was very shaky, too, and that she could not help her. Soon she fell apart completely. She began imagining that the maids were spying on her. She would suddenly bolt from the house, get in the car, and drive very fast to New York. She would stand outside Hank's rented apartment, debating whether to go in. She'd end up at Eulalia Chapin's apartment on the Upper East Side.

Her friend would try to comfort her, but Frances was inconsolable; she felt she had lost everything — her husband, her looks, her health, the love of her children. She would spend the night on the couch tossing and turning. She kept repeating, "It is all my fault!" Then she would flee to the bathroom and study her face in the mirror, gazing wild-eyed at her reflection. Once Eulalia came upon her caressing her throat and murmuring, "I wonder where the jugular vein is?"

In January of 1950, Frances was sent to Austen Riggs Psychiatric Hospital in Stockbridge, Massachusetts, where she was treated by Dr. Margaret Gibson. Over the next weeks she sang songs and paced the floor. One day she threw her wedding ring out the window. Moments later she screamed that she wanted it back, and attendants combed the grounds but it was never found. Then she attempted suicide for the first time. Her depressions intensified. The doctors diagnosed her as "suffering from emotional deterioration — extreme depression and suicidal threats."

Unexpectedly she rallied. She wrote notes to Peter, signed "Love, Mummie," with a smiling little face drawn next to the signature. She seemed well enough to visit home on a pass and she went. Once there, she experienced yet another devastating breakdown. Grandmother Seymour called Hank Fonda to inform him of his wife's shocking disintegration.

They met with Dr. Gibson, who told them she believed that Frances should leave Riggs and go to a hospital where she could be more closely supervised. "She is definitely suicidal," she said. Fonda didn't want his wife incarcerated in a "loony bin." It wouldn't look good for the star of *Mister Roberts* to have his wife labeled "crazy." He wanted her to remain at Riggs, where she could heal in "a more normal, less structured fashion."

But Dr. Gibson and Sophie Seymour argued that Frances must leave Riggs, and Fonda finally agreed. Shortly after their conversation, heavily sedated and in a straitjacket, Frances was taken to Craig House Sanitarium, a grim cluster of buildings in Beacon, New York. She was put under the care of Dr. Courtney Bennett. Decades later, Dr. Gibson remembered Henry Fonda with distaste. "He was a cold, self-absorbed person, a complete narcissist. I didn't like him," she said.

Jane grew moodier and moodier. She felt sickened by the impending divorce of her parents, the breakup of her family. She could confide in no one, and her grandmother behaved as though everything was fine. "Nothing is the matter!" she assured her grandchildren.

By the spring of 1950, Frances appeared greatly improved. "She has bounced back," her doctors said. She spoke cheerfully of leaving the hospital for good, and Dr. Bennett told her it was a definite possibility. She asked if she could see her children and he agreed.

On the afternoon of April 7, Jane remembered playing jacks with her brother, Peter, on the third floor of Boomer House and then watching from a window as her mother's car approached the drive, gliding up the long, winding road past the willow trees and the two ponds. Gravel crunched as the car rumbled to a stop. She saw her mother step out of the car, accompanied by two white-uniformed nurses, and disappear quickly onto the porch. Jane didn't know what to expect. She had stopped asking questions long ago. Nobody would tell her anything.

She could hear her Grandmother Seymour greeting Frances downstairs. There was a murmured conversation she couldn't make out, and Frances began calling, "Jane! Jane!" Jane refused to answer and went back to playing jacks with Peter. She was angry at her mother for abandoning her. That's what she'd done her entire life. In the last months it had grown much worse. Jane was eleven, too young to understand just how gravely ill and how utterly despairing her mother was. What mattered was that Peter was her favorite; Frances was always kissing and hugging *him*. In a consciousness-raising group in the 1970s she confided, "My mother was a hypochondriac. I don't like to be around illness. I don't like people to complain."

The cries continued to drift up from the huge polished foyer downstairs: "Jane! Jane! Peter?" Their grandmother was now calling for them both to come down. Jane grabbed her brother's arm. "Don't go down. I'm not going to. Let's stay here and play jacks, okay? I'll let you win." At which point skinny nine-year-old Peter jumped up and headed toward the stairs. Jane held on to him for dear life.

"Peter? Jane?" For another five or ten minutes Frances and then one of the maids continued to call and plead. Nobody bothered to investigate the third-floor hallway, where the children were silently struggling.

At one point Jane thought she heard her mother exclaim, "I must talk to her! Jane?" But Jane wouldn't budge. Her memory leaves her standing alone in the hall, not responding to her mother's cries.

Peter recalled the incident differently. He remembered struggling with Jane and then finally breaking free and running down the three flights of stairs, where his mother was waiting in the library, "fragrant with perfume and telling me she'd be home for good in a week. And I see her giving me a small note saying the usual things, with the same little smiling face at the bottom."

Peter had no recollection of his mother lunging away from the nurses and rushing up to the second floor to her bedroom. But apparently she did. The nurses raced after her. They didn't want to leave her alone because she kept threatening suicide. But Frances told them gaily, "At least I can go potty by myself!" and before they could stop her, she had slipped inside her bathroom and locked the door. It was the one lock Grandmother Seymour had not removed.

When Frances emerged a few moments later, she seemed radiant. She was holding a little porcelain box in her hand. "It's a keepsake. I want to take it back to the hospital with me," she explained. The nurses sighed in relief. If they had opened the box, they would have found that it contained a tiny razor Frances used to shave. (Another version of this story, told by the children's godfather, Watson Webb, says that Frances hid the razor behind a photograph of Jane and Peter.)

Twilight enveloped the green lawns around Boomer House. Jane watched from the third-floor window as her mother slipped through the deepening shadows and into her car. The white-uniformed nurses climbed in after her and the car drove off.

Jane remembered angrily biting her nails and feeling desolate. "What did my mother want to tell me?" she wondered. "And why was she so insistent? She'd never wanted to talk to me that much before." Those questions would haunt her for the rest of her life, as would her mother's plaintive cries of "Jane! Jane! Jane?"

A week later, on April 14, 1950, as dawn broke over the gloomy confines of Craig House, a nurse, Anne Grey, carried a breakfast tray to Frances Fonda's bedroom. She was surprised to find the bed made and the pillows plumped; there was a light under the bathroom door and a scrawled note on the carpet that read, "Don't enter the bathroom but call Dr. Bennett."

The nurse hurried out to find the doctor. Upon returning to the room, they opened the door to the bathroom and found Frances Fonda lying in a pool of her own blood. She had slashed her throat from ear to ear with the tiny razor she'd smuggled out of Boomer House.

Bennett stanched the gaping wound with towels, but Frances had severed her jugular vein and lost so much blood that she was dead less than twenty minutes later. She had killed herself on her birthday — the birth date she'd given her daughter, Jane, as a "gift."

She had written six notes: one for her doctor, one for her nurses, one for her mother, and one for each of her children. The contents of the letters to her family have never been divulged. To her doctor, she wrote, "You've done everything possible for me. I'm sorry but this is the best way out." She left no note for her husband, Henry Fonda. Although they had been in the process of getting divorced, no papers had been signed.

Fonda was notified by his mother-in-law by phone just as he was about to give an interview in his New York apartment.

On hearing the news, he told her, "I can't breathe." Then after a short conversation, he "drove like a bat out of hell" to the mortuary in Hartsdale, New York, where his wife's body had been taken. Sophie Seymour met him there. A private funeral service was held immediately (the two of them were the only ones present). Then the body was cremated and buried in the Seymour family plot in Hartsdale.

Before they returned to Greenwich in their separate cars, they decided that the two Fonda children must never learn the real circumstances of their mother's death. Pan would be told — she was old enough, they felt — but the others were too young to understand suicide.

Late that same afternoon, Jane returned home from Greenwich Academy, and as always she placed her stack of schoolbooks neatly on the hall table. Then she glanced up and noticed her grandmother standing at the top of the stairs gazing down at her. "I don't want you to go out," Sophie said. "You must stay here." She was standing in half shadow so Jane couldn't see the expression on her face, but her voice sounded strained. "You must stay here," she repeated, then added, "Your mother is ill."

As far as Jane was concerned, "Mother was *always* ill." They were forever telling her that. Since she had a date with her friend Diana to go riding, she paid no attention and ran out of the house.

An hour later, when she finished riding, she passed Peter, on the way to *his* riding lesson. They didn't speak. Suddenly she felt anxious about getting home.

It was a ten-minute walk back to Boomer House. By now many cars crowded the driveway. Stillness hovered over the property. The thick grove of willows rustled in the breeze. Her head began to pound. She hurried into the big polished foyer and past the library, where the door was open and she could see her aunt and her mother's secretary sitting. They wouldn't meet her eyes — they bowed their heads and stared at the floor.

Jane marched directly into the living room, where her grandmother was seated, very stiffly, on one couch, her father on the other. He pulled Jane onto his lap and said her mother had died of a heart attack. Peter trotted in a few minutes later, looking expectant, and Grandmother Seymour told him, "Your mother has died of a heart attack." Peter began to cry.

Inexplicably, Jane gave a short laugh, then she rose to her feet and murmured, "Excuse me please, I'm going to my room." And she ran upstairs and plopped down on her canopy bed, waiting, hoping, expecting a huge emotion to engulf her — tears, screams, *something*. But she felt anesthetized, numb. How weird, she thought, I'm never going to see my mother again, and I can't cry.

After a while she walked very slowly back down the stairs to the living room. Her grandmother and father were just as she'd left them, sitting opposite each other on the two couches. Peter was still crying. Henry Fonda didn't try to comfort him. Instead, he left without saying a word.

Jane heard the front door open and close, and a moment later her father's car zoomed off into the evening. He was driving back to New York to appear on Broadway as Mister Roberts. When he walked back-stage he saw Billy Hammerstein rehearsing his understudy, Marshall Jameson, who was already in costume. Fonda went to his dressing room, where he was met by Leland Hayward and Josh Logan. They both told him they didn't think he should do the show, but it was up to him. Logan remembered Fonda staring at his reflection in his dressing room mirror. His face was ashen. Then he said very quietly, "I'm going to go on. It's the only way I can get through the evening." And he did, appearing in the 833rd performance of the play. He was sustained by his professionalism.

Eli Wallach, who was in the cast, remembered, "Hank walked out on the stage and it was as if he'd been spun around three or four times and then pushed into the spotlight. He wasn't with it, but he made it through until the end." Wallach added, "It might seem cold-blooded, but there's that saying 'The show must go on,' and we actors abide by it. Hank knew who he was, when he was onstage. Offstage there was guilt and darkness and confusion and pain."

6

FOR THE NEXT few months all newspapers and magazines were kept hidden so Jane and Peter wouldn't be able to read accounts of their mother's violent death. They knew nothing of the mail their father was receiving, abusive letters criticizing him for his involvement with Susan Blanchard, or the tabloid columns attacking him with invective, because he'd left his wife while she was ill. Meanwhile the children felt uprooted, shuttling back and forth from Boomer House to Sophie Seymour's place nearby. Lawyers hovered; custodial arrangements were being discussed. Sophie wanted to raise her grandchildren herself and make the arrangement legal. Henry Fonda objected vehemently.

There was a great deal of unexpressed anger between the two of them. Although she was too well bred to say anything out loud, Sophie blamed Fonda for her daughter's descent into madness. Frances had been a happy, carefree, beautiful woman until she married Hank, Sophie contended: "Hank's cold remoteness drove her batty."

When Frances Fonda's will was read, Hank discovered that he was not left a penny. Pan and Jane and Peter would each receive trusts to be divided from the good-size fund that Frances had managed so carefully over the years. The atmosphere grew increasingly tense.

Pan disappeared. She divorced her young husband and moved to Italy, where she studied painting. She wanted to get as far away from the Fondas as possible. But she would periodically be in touch with Peter. She would tell him that she had the same nightmare over and over again. She would come upon the figure of Frances lying on the chaise longue they had at Tigertail, completely covered with glistening red blood. Peter brooded that no one except himself and his half sister ever seemed to miss their mother.

"No one talked about her. It was as if she hadn't lived." There was no funeral service and nobody seemed to know where she was buried. He began to have fits of crying; he couldn't eat or sleep. Jane, in contrast, appeared detached. She kept to a vigorous schedule of classes, horse shows, and music lessons. She made endless lists. She polished her saddle relentlessly.

Every so often Maggie Sullavan would try to persuade Hank Fonda to talk to Jane and Peter about their mother's death. Protecting them from the truth would create a web of distortions, she said. He had to talk to them; he couldn't keep something as traumatic as suicide a secret. It would damage Peter and Jane's ability to accept and deal with it. But Fonda insisted on silence.

Years later, he would admit to someone, "I had trouble communicating when I was young. I have trouble now. It's like some people stutter." He was often asked why he hadn't told his children about their mother's suicide. "I thought it was better not to tell them. They were too young." But he did add, "The simple fact was, I didn't tell them the truth."

The children were kept out of school for a mourning period. Brooke remembered that a special assembly was called at Greenwich Academy where the principal got up and said, "I don't want anybody in the school to ever bring up the subject of Mrs. Fonda's death. It will not be discussed."

Nevertheless, in late May of 1950, during a pottery class, Jane and Brooke were sneaking looks at the latest *Photoplay* magazine and Brooke came across a story about "Henry Fonda's tragedy." It said that Frances Fonda had killed herself by slitting her throat.

Brooke quickly turned the page, but Jane grabbed the magazine from her, flipped the page back, and read the story. Brooke recalled, "Her face was absolutely expressionless. She never said a word."

Inside, however, a terrible sadness came over her. As soon as she got home that afternoon, she confronted her new governess, Mrs. Wallace, and asked, "Did my mother commit suicide?" Mrs. Wallace gently answered yes and proceeded to tell her as much of the story as she knew.

After she learned the truth, Jane's first reaction was to confront her father. But she pulled back. She did not tell her brother what she'd learned, either. By now she kept quiet about most things. But the psychic cost of holding everything in was huge, and by the summer Jane began having the same nightmare over and over again. It was identical to the nightmare Pan had, coming upon the figure of their mother lying on the chaise longue, covered with blood.

"Jane would wake up in the middle of the night screaming about her mother," Brooke recalled. They were at summer camp together, and the counselor would have to climb into Jane's bunk bed to comfort her. Jane would pretend to be consoled, but she was not. Jane said, "Before my mother's death I was feisty, I was ambitious, I was brave. Suddenly I was nothing to myself. You could have put what was left of me into a thimble." She was already terrified that she might inherit her mother's instability—her madness. And her terror was visceral; the physical sensation was akin to suffocation or drowning in a pool.

In August, when Jane returned from summer camp, she met Susan Blanchard unexpectedly. She'd gone to Doctors Hospital to visit her father; he was laid up with a knee problem. There was Susan sitting by his bed.

"Dad introduced us," Jane said. "She was the most beautiful woman I'd ever seen. She seemed to be in her early twenties and had light brown hair, pulled back tightly into a large chignon that accentuated her pale blue, slanted eyes, not unlike Mother's." She was warm and friendly and engaging and had such great poise. It was as if she had seen the world. She was everything Jane wanted to be. The two immediately bonded, but Peter resisted Susan's charms for a while. "They were the saddest brother and sister I've ever seen," Susan recalls. "They were so love-starved. I gave them a lot of hugging."

Soon Susan was racing Peter up and down Jones Beach while Hank lolled on the sands and watched. She took Jane to the movies. They went to the ballet and theater. They shopped at Bloomingdale's.

"She'd studied dancing with the fabled Katherine Dunham, and dancing was important to her," Jane said. "She was superb, often twirling or cha-cha-ing around rooms with pretend partners, her waist-length hair flying, while singing Broadway show tunes." After watching her, Jane would go into her own room and try to imitate her. "I imitated her a lot. If I could be like her, maybe Dad would love me more," she said.

Bit by bit, Jane began confiding in Susan, who was then twenty-two; Jane was fourteen. She reached out for advice. She asked questions she'd never asked anyone before. She'd found a woman she could trust. "Susan Blanchard became the mother Jane never had," Andreas Voutsinas said. "For the first time in her life, Jane had a woman she could relate to and emulate. And Susan really *cared* about her. She became the most important person in Jane's life at that time."

The day after Christmas, Henry Fonda and Susan were married in the living room of Oscar Hammerstein's townhouse on East 63rd Street. Jane attended; so did Peter. Then the newlyweds went off on a honeymoon to Caneel Bay in the Virgin Islands. After a day of relaxing at the beach, they received word that Peter had shot himself "by mistake." They flew back to be with him.

Apparently he and two of his schoolmates had been driven over to his grandparents' estate in Greenwich by their chauffeur. They had picked up two guns — a shotgun and an antique pistol — and were dropped off at another estate, owned by the Kress family, where they were going to shoot at tin cans. Peter was trying to load the antique pistol. Somehow the pistol went off and a bullet pierced his liver and kidney.

The chauffeur saved his life by driving him to the hospital in Ossining. Jane and Sophie Seymour arrived at the waiting room just as Peter, under massive doses of ether, began hallucinating. Jane said she prayed that if Peter lived she would never be mean to him again.

Miraculously, a Dr. Charles Sweet, an expert with gunshot wounds because he happened to be the resident MD for nearby Sing-Sing prison, performed the operation. He knew exactly what to do. Even so, Peter lost a great deal of blood and his heart stopped three times. But he did survive.

Peter was in intensive care for four weeks. A rumor went around that he'd attempted suicide in response to his mother's violent death, but he has said that was never even a remote possibility. However, to this day he does show off the big scar on his belly.

After his recuperation, he and Jane spent July and August with their father and Susan. Hank was finishing up the national tour of *Mister*

Roberts in Los Angeles. They stayed in a hotel called Ocean House. It was a "grand mansion, built by William Randolph Hearst for Marion Davies," Peter recalled. "We lay on the beach, and we'd swim, and some nights Jane and I would go dancing at the hotel and rock back and forth to the music. Susan never left our side. She took us two incredibly damaged kids and mended us. In a certain way I feel we owe her so much."

That first summer, "Dad and Susan would often take Peter and me with them when they went out to dinner in swank Hollywood restaurants, like the Brown Derby and Chasen's, one of Dad's favorites," Jane said. "We had never been with him in these kinds of social situations before, so while I knew in an abstract sort of way that he was famous, I didn't know how fame manifested itself in his life. I was struck by how, when he entered a restaurant, there would be a shift in energy, as though he were a magnet. Restaurant owners like Mr. Chasen would call him by name, and as we'd be ushered to Dad's special table, I could hear people saying, 'Why, that's . . . ?'"

Jane noticed that her father behaved differently in public. He was warmer and funnier, and Susan acted differently with him, too. "She was goofy with us, but she became reticent with Dad," Jane said, "less ebullient. He reined her in." She was twenty-two, he was forty-five.

By the end of the summer, Jane had started wearing her hair in a chignon like Susan's, and she bought little black dresses and circle pins like Susan's. She was calling her "Mom" and Peter was calling her "Mom 2." When they returned to New York, they begged to stay with Susan in the apartment she and Hank had rented on East 48th Street instead of returning to the gloomy house in Greenwich with their grandparents.

Sophie Seymour objected; she wanted to take total responsibility for raising her grandchildren. But as time went on, Peter and Jane spent most weekends with their father and young stepmother. Susan focused on Peter because all his behavioral problems were a cry for attention—attention he wasn't getting from his father. When they were together, Susan always gave him a lot of love. "I told him jokes. We laughed and laughed." Jane didn't resent the attention Susan lavished on Peter, because she gave Jane an equal amount.

It was Susan who rushed her to the hospital after she broke her back diving in a lake and Hank—true to his upbringing—was denying that she needed a doctor's care. It was Susan who nursed her back to health, and Susan who saved the day when Jane was asked to her first dance by a boy and broke down in sobs because she was in a cast from neck to crotch and thought she wouldn't be able to go. Susan bought the prettiest gown imaginable from a maternity shop, and the voluminous dress hid the cast completely. Jane went off to the dance and "was the belle of the ball," according to Susan.

A year or so later, Sophie Seymour wrote Susan, thanking her for being such a reassuring presence in her grandchildren's lives. "That note meant a lot to me, because I was very much in love with Hank and all I wanted to do was to create a wonderful home for him and his children. They'd been through such a frightful trauma, I wanted to help them forget and start enjoying themselves — start enjoying life!"

Every so often she'd take Peter and Jane along when she went to visit her own family, the Oscar Hammersteins, who lived on East 63rd Street. For a while when she was renovating her new home, she and Jane lived at the Hammersteins'.

It was a lively place filled with artists and writers and musicians, as well as the lost children of friends who had no other place to go — including a very sarcastic, precocious teenager named Stephen Sondheim. At the center of all this activity was the tall, shambling figure of Oscar Hammerstein II — "Ochie" to his friends — at the height of his career as Richard Rodgers's lyricist. Together they had written the landmark musicals *Oklahoma!, Carousel, The King and I,* and *South Pacific.* These magical shows, with their inspired, melodious songs, created a climate of confidence and promise. "They played a dramatic part in molding the myth of modern America," critic John Lahr wrote.

Susan remembered how she and Jane might be gossiping in the living room and suddenly Oscar would emerge and roar, "How *boring,*" and then at dinner repeat some of the silly things the two young women had been telling each other.

"But he was never cruel," Susan said. "He was actually a stabilizing influence and a different kind of parental figure for Jane to see in comparison to her father. And then there was my mother, Dorothy — she was from Australia, a former chorus girl in the Ziegfeld Follies, now an interior decorator. She and my stepfather were very much in love. You could almost feel their love when you were with them. Oscar was the real man of the house and my mother created a perfect setting for him to live and work in. Theirs was an old-fashioned marriage."

Susan had imagined her marriage to Fonda would be just as loving and old-fashioned. "I was in awe of Hank. I really believed I would be dedicating the rest of my life to this great man, this great actor. I did everything for him. I was like a geisha — no questions asked. I was very subservient."

She would spend hours discussing his children with him. Fonda would listen, but he would rarely comment; he didn't enjoy anticipating what might be in store for either Peter or Jane. He refused to deal with problems, let alone solve them.

Susan was afraid to bring up the subject of Frances Fonda's suicide or the impact it might still be having on everyone, especially the children. It was as if Hank had blocked her death out of his consciousness, his memory. Such behavior was very consistent with him. He held back all his emotions, and he had no patience for anyone who showed emotion. When that happened, he resorted to anger.

Susan hadn't experienced Hank's fury until she happened to burst into tears on their honeymoon. They were on the beach at Caneel Bay. "I'd put his very expensive watch on a rock before we went swimming," Susan said. When they emerged from the water, drenched and laughing, she discovered that the watch had been swept away by the tide. She began to sob. He lashed out at her: "Your crying disgusts me! Stop crying!"

Susan crept behind a tree and remained there until she could contain her emotions. "That's when I realized I was terrified of Henry Fonda — terrified of his anger."

Unable to change her husband, Susan concentrated on being the best possible stepmother. In the fall of 1951, she took Peter up to Fay School in Massachusetts. "I had an ally in Mom 2," he said. "She always made the right clothes choices and encouraged me to look 'cool.'" Susan also accompanied Jane when she enrolled at Emma Willard, the exclusive all-girls boarding school in Troy, New York. (The school guaranteed that its students would be prepared to enter the finest women's colleges — Barnard, Vassar, Wellesley, Bryn Mawr — which was what Hank wanted for his daughter.)

Jane and Susan dragged her monogrammed suitcases across the campus, which consisted of a group of ivy-covered Gothic buildings high on a hill across the Hudson River from Albany. On the way, they discovered that the Gothic buildings were linked to a series of tunnels, making it possible to attend classes even in the midst of a blizzard without putting on an overcoat.

By the time she arrived at Emma Willard, Jane had perfected an air of supreme indifference, and she seemed as insufferably calm and poised and well groomed as her classmates. She was sure that none of them had suffered the way she had.

She was still having that bloody nightmare about her mother. When she screamed at night she woke all the students in her dorm. In desperation she tried to reach out to her father in letters. He always wrote back, enclosing the original notes with her grammatical errors corrected in red ink. It made her feel helpless and inadequate. When he paid her an unexpected visit at school, he radiated charm and affection. She thought she couldn't be fooled by him, but he was so seductive that she would let her guard down and blurt out something personal. As soon as she did, he'd clam up again.

Luckily, Susan visited Jane frequently at school that first year, and they would sit in her room and talk. Susan admitted that she had her own problems communicating with Hank. "I loved her deeply for that," Jane would say years later. "I would never have survived without her support."

The two of them had already had conversations about her mother and the suicide. "No one had raised the subject of Mother with me," Jane said, "much less asked how I *felt*. . . . The problem was that I had no words to offer her. I'd become so unused to expressing my feelings, I was emotionally illiterate."

Jane told Susan she had never been able to cry, and that she'd learned about the suicide from a magazine. Susan was quiet for a long time and then she said, "Maybe your mother's death was a blessing in disguise." Jane said, "It seems strange to me now that I could have found those glib and potentially insensitive words comforting, but my thinking about Mother was so utterly confused that 'blessing in disguise' provided me with a handle, a way to explain the event to myself. Maybe Susan knew I needed a handle."

Jane had a hard time being away from home, and she felt distanced from most of the students at Emma Willard. Near the end of her freshman year she created a group called "The Disorders" for students who felt like outsiders. There was one incident that caused a furor, when

Jane poured lighter fluid from her room to another girl's room, set fire to it, and watched it flame dangerously across the floor, "to let the other girl know Jane Fonda didn't like her."

Gradually, Jane loosened up and began to enjoy her school. She became friendly with another girl, Kevin Bellows, who roomed across the hall from her. Kevin remembered how Jane learned to concentrate during the long hours of study hall and tests and exams, and she studied hard — Latin, French, American history, English literature. Jane often said that the only education she ever got was at Emma Willard, and when she married Ted Turner she gave a great deal of money to the school.

In her sophomore year, "she became best friends with Carol Bentley," Kevin went on. "I called them Snow White and Rose Red because Carol had thick, dark hair and dark eyes and was quite developed, and Jane was blond and willowy. They had this intense, gorgeous friendship throughout their years at Emma Willard." Even so, Jane continued suffering from bouts of depression.

In the summer of 1952, while staying with Hank and Susan at their rented house in Lloyd Neck on Long Island, Jane was so despondent she often slept twelve hours a day. Her father scolded her for being moody and lazy, but she told him she couldn't help it.

On nearby estates debutantes were throwing parties and dancing with boys from exclusive prep schools like Andover and Exeter. Jane longed to be included, but she didn't know how to make it happen. Her father had no connection to that social scene. Occasionally, Susan and he would take her along to the cocktail parties and dinners they did attend in the area. "I could always make people believe I was more experienced and sophisticated than I actually was," Jane said. But inside she felt stupid and ill at ease. "I felt dumb, because I didn't know how to behave the way my father and grandmother wanted me to. Like a conventional young girl." Her grandmother was always encouraging her to think about going out with young lawyers and stockbrokers. "I couldn't stand the idea of being with men like that." She dreamed of falling in love with a rebel or an adventurer. To compensate for her difficulty fitting in, she began developing a repertoire of façades. One was brittle and mocking. Another was warm and eager. But neither reflected how she really felt. "I always thought that I was really weird. That I was really fucked up."

One Saturday night the Fondas attended a dance at the local country club. "Typical WASP bastion," Susan said, "right off a big golf course; blue-haired matrons in pearls, drunken stockbrokers, debutantes with little white gloves." Ashton Hawkins (former legal counsel for the Metropolitan Museum of Art) recalled, "I was on vacation from Harvard with several of my buddies from Cambridge. We all made a beeline for Jane Fonda."

"She was a wonderful dancer," Hawkins said. "But every so often I'd feel a little pinprick at the back of my neck. I'd sort of wince — it hurt — but I tried not to think about it because I was having such fun. That little pinprick happened every time we danced. I mentioned it to the other young men who'd danced with Jane and they experienced the same sharp little pinprick, midway through a foxtrot or a waltz. By the end of the evening, we'd found out she had a hatpin hidden in her hand, and whenever the spirit moved her she'd give us a little jab with it. Pretty hostile gesture! I never saw her again after that night. I admire her for her politics and her acting, but the thing I remember about Jane Fonda is that sharp little pinprick at the back of my neck."

7

J ANE'S MOOD BRIGHTENED considerably that fall after she and Peter moved into the brownstone Hank had bought. It was a lovely house on tree-lined East 74th Street, three blocks away from Central Park. Susan enjoyed redecorating it. At the same time she and Hank adopted a baby girl (they had had trouble conceiving). They named the baby Amy, and for a while they cared for the infant together. Jane observed how adept her father was at diapering. Before she and Peter went back to their respective boarding schools, they moved their belongings into their own bedrooms in the brownstone. Then they all had a meal together. It appeared as if they were going to be a real family at last.

The following summer, when Jane was sixteen, she got her period. She was in the shower when blood coursed down her thighs. Susan was in another room, and she ran in, handed Jane a towel, and cried out, "Congratulations, you're a woman now!" Jane was afraid to be a woman, but she didn't admit it.

They happened to be in California again, where Hank was starring in the road company of *Point of No Return*, a play he'd earlier triumphed in on Broadway.

That same summer, Jane discovered Marlon Brando in *The Wild One*, the movie that gave him legendary status as the alienated biker, all mumbling and scratching and revolutionizing acting with his raw psychological approach, his improvisational wildness. She was so mesmerized by his performance that she began creating her own imitation of Brando, complete with shrugs and long pauses, which she would perform for him years later when they costarred in *The Chase,* and he would chuckle richly.

One afternoon Jane and some of her former classmates from Brentwood Town and Country School — Josie Mankiewicz, Jill Robinson, and Brooke Hayward — drove around West Hollywood trying to find Brando's apartment. They fantasized what it would be like to neck with him. "He was our hero," Jill said, "that hulking brute with the poet's face and the prizefighter's body. We loved him because he seemed out of sync and we felt out of sync."

Boys were beginning to discover Jane. Daniel Selznick said he took her out on her first date. "We started off at an ice cream parlor and ended up at some big party in Beverly Hills, and guys of all ages were coming out of the woodwork to crowd around Jane. She radiated this indefinable magic — she positively glowed. The fact that she was Henry Fonda's daughter just added to her glamour. But it was funny," he went on. Not long before that he and his father, David O. Selznick, the Hollywood producer, had accompanied Jane and Brooke Hayward somewhere. "My dad complimented Brooke's beauty and predicted *she* would be a great star. He totally ignored Jane."

Jane was upset by Selznick's remark. The minute she returned to Emma Willard she began studying her reflection in the mirror. She hated her "chipmunk cheeks," her rather voluptuous hips. Some of her friends at school, like Carol Bentley, were secretly binging and purging in their rooms to lose weight. Jane joined them.

"We'd buy gallons of coffee ice cream and bags of brownies and pound cake, and we'd stuff our faces and then vomit everything out in the john," Jane said. "It started out as a lark," she told Leo Janus in *Cosmopolitan* years later. "I loved to eat but I wanted to be wonderfully thin. It didn't take long for me to be a serious bulimic — binging and purging up to twenty times a day."

She soon spent every waking hour thinking of food, dreaming of food, going out to buy food — mainly junk food. It was the start of a dangerous habit. The disease lasted from sophomore year in boarding school through two marriages and two children.

She was adept at keeping her bulimia hidden, because "I didn't want anyone to stop me and I was convinced I was in control of it and could stop anytime I wanted." To take her mind off eating, Jane began to paint in earnest. Like her father, she had already shown a real talent for it. He'd turned the brownstone's attic into a studio, and he spent all day there before going to the theater. He was now starring in *The Caine Mutiny Court-Martial,* which had opened on Broadway in January 1954. He was less attentive to baby Amy; he seemed to be drifting into another world.

Jane would come home for the weekend and watch him sauntering downstairs from his attic studio in the early evening. He'd say hello to her, but he seemed distant and was equally distant with Susan — so much so that Jane "started feeling jittery."

Jane noticed that he was increasingly critical of Susan for no reason. He would drawl, "She looks so young." Was this because he was now forty-eight and she was only twenty-six? He'd tell her to "put on some lipstick." He was pulling into his shell the way he had with Frances. This upset Jane.

Susan was even more upset. For three years she'd devoted every waking hour to Hank Fonda, "trying to make our life perfect." She'd dutifully picked him up backstage every night and sat with him while he ate his supper, usually in silence. She traveled with him obediently whenever he went on the road with a show. She confided to Jane that, though he rarely spoke to her during the day, when he hopped into bed at night he expected her to make love to him.

"I was young then," Susan went on. "I wanted to see people my own age, laugh and dance and have a good time." She finally confided to her mother about what was going on in her marriage. Dorothy Hammerstein was shocked and furious. "Your life is absolutely wretched with that man."

In an attempt to get a reaction, Susan had recently put on a cheap red wig and confronted him in his dressing room after a show, hoping and praying he'd react. "But he didn't even *see* it. It was incredible." She and Jane laughed about that. "What a funny, strange man." Susan thought his bad moods and ongoing depression might be the result of what had happened on the set of the movie version of *Mister Roberts* the previous summer. It had been a real comedown. Warner Bros. had bought the script, but then the studio decided Marlon Brando or William Holden should play Roberts. Fonda was too old for the part — Roberts was supposed to be thirty years old.

When Warner Bros. hired John Ford to direct, however, he insisted on Fonda, saying he wouldn't do the picture otherwise. But during filming, Ford became increasingly drunk and insulting. Fonda realized that the director disliked the script and had begun to trivialize it, making it "hokey" (Ford thought the story of *Mister Roberts* was "homosexual" because of its intense male camaraderie). Fonda protested, but it did no good. At one point the two men almost came to blows. Midway through the picture, Ford was replaced by Mervyn LeRoy.

The experience was upsetting to Fonda. He hated the film, thought it was "shit," and he fell into a depression. Then *Mister Roberts* opened; audiences loved the picture and it reestablished Fonda as a major movie star.

Even so, he was still depressed when his sister Harriet phoned and told him she wanted him to do a benefit of the play *The Country Girl* for the Omaha Playhouse. Dorothy McGuire, another Omaha native and a close friend, would be his costar, and Jane had agreed to play the ingénue.

Though Hank hadn't known about it, Jane had been appearing in plays at Emma Willard, among them Christopher Fry's *Boy with a Cart,* in which she'd played the male lead, and *The Rivals,* in which she'd played Lydia Languish. Jane had quite enjoyed the experience. So when her aunt called, she thought, "Why not?"

"You mean she's agreed?" her father asked.

"Yes."

Fonda had never seen Jane onstage, so he wouldn't allow her to appear in *The Country Girl* with him without an audition. She was still in school, so she auditioned for the director over the phone. She was letter-perfect; she already knew how important professionalism was to him.

This was a momentous decision for her, a turning point. She was about to appear in public with her father for the first time. She was terrified. She could not and would not disappoint him. She had to be good.

Naturally Jane conferred with her stepmother. "It was the first time she'd given me any inclination that she might choose theater as a career," Susan said. "I thought it was a wonderful idea. She and Hank were so much alike. He was extremely disciplined and so was she. He could always do anything he put his mind to and so could she. I knew that if Jane decided to act she would do it and do it well and of course she did."

As soon as Jane graduated from Emma Willard in June of 1955, she flew out to Omaha with her father, Susan, and Peter, who would be working backstage. He, too, had been dabbling in theater at his school, having acted in and directed his own version of *Stalag 17*. He called it *Stalag 17½*. It was a satire of prep school life.

The rehearsals of *The Country Girl* went smoothly even though Jane had no technique. "I didn't really know what I was doing so I looked to Dad." Sometimes she couldn't believe she was onstage with him — standing opposite him, talking to him, looking at him. She felt she was close to him — emotionally, physically, psychologically close to him for the first time. Acting, it turned out, was the one way to communicate with him and to connect with him totally.

She tried to imitate the way he seemed to relax on stage. He was so erect and graceful, his expression serene. She noticed how he used his slender, tapered hands to gesture and to emphasize points in the dialogue. She was secretly pleased because she had inherited his hands. She had preternaturally long fingers and, like him, was double-jointed.

In one scene Jane had to enter crying. It wasn't easy to walk in at the height of an emotional breakdown. Fonda didn't want to watch. He didn't think Jane could handle it; he thought she'd be phony and overly dramatic. But on opening night "she surprised the hell out of me by bursting into tears on cue." He couldn't believe she was acting.

She wasn't. She had arranged to have one of the stage managers belt her in the face just before she went onstage, something her father never knew. The minute she exited, she ran over to him in the wings and asked, "How'd I do, Dad?" She was grinning from ear to ear because she could see he was surprised and very proud of her.

The critics gave *The Country Girl* enthusiastic notices. After three performances the Fondas, including baby Amy, flew to Rome, where Hank was going to star in Leo Tolstoy's *War and Peace* with Audrey Hepburn.

Fonda had rented a huge estate, the Villa Uscida, on the Via Appia just outside Rome. It had a rambling garden and a fruit and vegetable farm as well as a big wine cellar and a rippling swimming pool filled with mineral water that actually bubbled.

Rome was filled with celebrities that summer. Rock Hudson, Ben Gazzara, Jennifer Jones, Montgomery Clift—they were all making films. Ingrid Bergman and Roberto Rossellini were showing off their new twins to swarms of paparazzi.

"It was supposed to be a great vacation for all of us," Susan said. "We planned to test great restaurants and visit the hill towns in Umbria. Hank wanted to photograph the Stadio dei Marmi, the marble statue-lined stadium that had been built by Mussolini. But we didn't do any of these things."

It was all because Hank wanted to play the part of Pierre the way Tolstoy had written him, as a bumbling nearsighted intellectual. He found a pair of spectacles he liked; he got a funny haircut. But the director, King Vidor, wanted Pierre to be the great romantic. So did Dino De Laurentiis, the producer. Every time he visited the set he'd take Hank's glasses off. It became a running battle. When Fonda came home from Cinecittà Studios, he sulked. He wasn't enjoying himself making *War and Peace,* and he took it out on everybody. He refused all invitations.

"It was an absolute nightmare," Susan said. "I had tried to make him see a therapist but he refused. My heart was ready to burst." She was still in love with him when she decided to break up the marriage, but she'd decided that she had to leave him in order to survive.

At the end of August she told him of her decision. When he didn't respond, she ran down to the kitchen, distraught. It was early morning. Peter was eating breakfast, hard rolls and jam, at the long wooden table. She explained she was leaving his father and taking Amy back to New York. She ended by saying, "You've got to understand that I need to be loved; I need to be courted." Peter listened, and when she'd finished he murmured, "Why did it take you so long?" and then he started to cry. He'd invested so much in her emotionally he couldn't bear to think she would no longer be in his life.

He ran off to tell Jane. Her bedroom was at the far end of the villa, and he burst into it without knocking. There were clothes strewn all over the floor. The shutters were open and sun was streaming into the room. Jane had just awakened and was yawning and stretching with an expression of pure delight on her face.

Peter cried out, "Susan's leaving Dad!" He expected an immediate response, but she didn't react. Instead she began to describe how she'd had a terrific sexual experience the night before. She spoke of "how two bodies holding each other grow sweaty with passion." In truth, at seventeen, Jane admitted, "I was pretty wild, but I hadn't lost my virginity yet. I had done everything but. I couldn't go all the way, although sometimes I pretended to people that I had."

Peter groaned, "Oh fuck, Jane! Oh, fuck!" and then he repeated in anguish, "Mom's leaving Dad!" The Fonda family was disintegrating once again and all Jane could think about was making love. With that, his sister told him that she'd known about it for some time. Scrunching back on the pillows, she raised her arms triumphantly. She was in another world.

Peter ran out of the bedroom and down into the cellar, where he uncorked a bottle of wine and drank the entire contents. He passed out drunk and he didn't wake up until late afternoon. By that time Susan and Amy were gone.

If Jane was upset about her stepmother leaving, she wouldn't say. She was perfecting a façade. To make up for what she lacked, she borrowed bits and pieces of other people's personas. "But generally I looked and behaved as conventionally as seersucker, blending perfectly into the . . . Wonder Bread, predigested world of the fifties." Men flocked around her; she was Henry Fonda's daughter, already something of a celebrity, and she really enjoyed the attention.

Peter's last memory of that summer is one warm August evening when he joined Jane and some of her new friends, diplomats' sons and daughters and a few American expatriates, in the ornate living room at the villa. Candles flickered, wine flowed; there were snatches of conversation and laughter in English and Italian — and then suddenly he heard Jane mention quite dramatically something about "Mummie's suicide."

Five years after the fact, Peter learned for the first time that his mother had slit her throat from ear to ear with a very sharp razor. When she saw the stricken look on her brother's face, Jane reached out her hand. His eyes welled up with tears. Then somebody murmured, "Terribly sorry. Thought you knew."

Days later, he made a feeble attempt to question his father about the suicide as they were careening in and out of Rome in a borrowed Fiat.

Fonda was on his day off and he was trying to teach Peter how to drive. "Whenever I asked questions about my mother's death, he'd just say, 'Keep your mind on driving, son.'"

In the fall Jane went off to Vassar. She'd applied there because Carol Bentley would be there, too. She took courses in French and art history, but she had no idea what to major in; she had no expectations about college, or any idea what a degree would accomplish for her. "I didn't like college at all. I just got by," she said. She was rooming with exotic, raven-haired Susan Stein, the younger daughter of Jules Stein, head of Music Corporation of America, the biggest talent agency in Hollywood. Susan played the guitar and was planning a trip to Asia, but Jane never heard her plans because she was so rarely in their rooms. When the weather was good she could be seen sunbathing nude on the roof of one of the dormitories. She often juggled three dates a night. "Jane was hugely popular," the press agent Bobby Zarem said. "She seemed bound and determined to be a party girl. If she had ambition, she kept quiet about it. She told me once that she didn't think she had what it took to be a great actress, so she was just going to have a great time." Zarem once danced the Charleston with her at a New Haven bar while customers gaped.

Most weekends she would sneak off to Yale to spend time with boys. Dick Cavett, a student then, remembered "listening breathlessly for the click of Jane Fonda's high heels on the tile corridor outside a fellow classmate's room in my dorm *after hours.*"

"Jane was beautiful and icy and she was Henry Fonda's daughter and she had the reputation of being extremely promiscuous. It was an unbeatable combination," novelist Michael Thomas, Brooke Hayward's first husband, said. "It was rumored she had broken a taboo and once fucked in the hallowed halls of Skull and Bones."

He added, "Hank Fonda would phone Brooke and me—we were living in New Haven then—and he'd say, 'Is Jane there?' because Jane would have lied and told him she was staying with us, when in truth she was with some guy—God knows where—and I'd say, 'She's not back yet, Hank,' and he'd say, 'Will you please tell her to call me as soon as she comes in?' He tried to watch her like a hawk but it didn't do much good because she was all over the place."

Thomas thought Jane was trying to annoy her father "because he was carrying on a tempestuous affair with a twenty-three-year-old countess named Afdera Franchetti, and he hadn't divorced Susan yet."

For a while Hank had been on the transatlantic phone every day, pleading with Susan to come back to him. Then he began going out with various starlets, and he had a short romance with Anita Eckberg, who "was the most unsexy woman I have ever been with," he would later say to *Playboy*. Then Audrey Hepburn took him to a dinner party and he'd sat across the table from Afdera. "And I bewitched him," Afdera said. She had curly blond hair and slanting green eyes, and she spoke six languages and wore elegant designer clothes. Her eccentric Venetian family lived in a crumbling palazzo on the Grand Canal. "Fonda had never met anyone like me before," Afdera went on. "He couldn't get enough of me. He kept a picture of my eyes in his shaving kit. He wrote me over six hundred letters which he illustrated with lovely drawings. We had a gorgeous romance."

After Fonda finished filming *War and Peace* they took secret trips to Jerusalem and Berlin. They even spent a few days in Afdera's hometown of Venice. "We did the touristy things. We went on a gondola up the canals. We wandered around Piazza San Marco and fed the pigeons. Hank decided he should see Pan, his stepdaughter. She was studying art in Italy and happened to be in Venice." They hadn't spoken since the suicide five years before. She felt very conflicted about Fonda. They attempted a reconciliation but it was unsuccessful, and they never saw each other again.

Afdera knew he had a reputation for being mean, "but he was never mean to me. He spoiled me terribly. He would always send me baskets of tangerines, because he knew they were my favorite fruit, and he gave me a wonderful mink coat. He was almost too perfect. He never got sick. He never got drunk. He would wake up at seven A.M., get up, stand on his head, and do yoga. He was so private he wouldn't let me watch him shave for a year. He was almost too handsome — too generous — too sexy. Oh, he was sexy. Always with a hard-on."

As soon as Jane learned the details of her father's improbable romance, she burst into tears. The thought that Susan would no longer be her stepmother was agonizing. Susan assured her they would always be close, she would be there for her and for Peter, and she was. In the meantime, whenever she could, Jane would take the train from Vassar and visit with Susan. Susan told her she didn't want to be married to Hank anymore, but she was hurt that he had found another woman so quickly. She couldn't get over how generous he was being to Afdera; she'd heard about the mink coat — Afdera was showing it off all over New York.

Eventually Susan would confront her soon-to-be-ex-husband and demand to know why he had been so different with Afdera — so giving and romantic when he had been none of those things with her. He wouldn't answer. "He had the ability to cut someone out of his life even if they had been close, and it didn't seem to affect him," said Ruth Mitchell, the stage manager from *Mister Roberts* in whom Fonda occasionally confided. "Once he said to me, 'Ruthie, I can be a real son of a bitch.' And you know something? He was."

Susan was determined to hurry the divorce proceedings, and she vowed that she would get as much money as she could out of Henry Fonda. There were fights between their lawyers until a financial settlement was reached. Divorce was granted on the grounds of mental cruelty. They agreed to have joint custody of their adopted daughter, Amy. "We both wanted to raise her, and we did," Susan said.

Susan went on to be one of the most sought-after and popular women in New York. She bought a studio and took up painting. In 1962, she married the actor Michael Wager and they had a son. Fonda was annoyed. "Why couldn't she ever get pregnant with me?" he asked Jane.

The summer of 1956 the Fonda family went up to Cape Cod. Hank had two months off from work, so he rented a big clapboard house on the beach in Hyannis Port next to the Kennedy compound. He'd brought Amy along and Peter was there, as well as Hank's sister Harriet, who had come from Omaha to chaperone. Hank wanted everything to be proper, because Afdera was coming to visit.

Jane was apprenticing at the Dennis Playhouse nearby. The first day of the program she was introduced to a tan, good-looking Yale student named James Franciscus. He was the stage manager and everybody called him Goey. "He was blond, blue-eyed, and movie star handsome.... I was smitten," Jane said. "My previous inarticulate philanderings had not prepared me for true romance." They spent all their free time together. Goey was not only handsome, he was smart and literate and funny. They did not make love that summer: "We waited until fall."

Before Afdera arrived, Jane invited her father, brother, and aunt to see her in a play the apprentices were putting on. It was a bit part in a Restoration comedy. Hank recalled, "Jane had no lines, but the moment she made her entrance you could hear the audience react. Something physical happened. They were drawing in their breath. Jane had presence. You either have it or you don't. Jane had it. I knew it that afternoon."

The next day the manager of the Dennis Playhouse phoned to ask if Hank would for the hell of it act in a show with the apprentices. The play *The Male Animal* would be a perfect vehicle for Hank, he said. Jane would play the ingénue.

Hank agreed. "This time she really knocked me over. None of the amateur self-consciousness. She was absolutely delightful, charming, and natural. I watched her from the wings and I thought, 'If that girl ever wants to do this professionally she'll make out all right.'" Of course he did not say anything to Jane, but she sensed what he was thinking. She remembers when she exited one night he was watching her, frozen in admiration.

She felt closer to him than she had ever felt before. And for the first time she seriously considered becoming an actress. For her father, acting was the most important thing in the world, more important to him than his children or his wives. Maybe they would become close if she was an actress.

Acting might be the only way for them to connect — to viscerally communicate. She wondered what his reaction would be if she took the leap. For two days following the performances, she kept wanting to talk to him about it because she was experiencing more genuine affection from him than she had ever experienced.

But there wasn't a chance to talk, because right after *The Male Animal* closed, Afdera appeared on the scene and she became the focus of Fonda's attention. She had flown in from Europe and she was jet-lagged. "I'd left the Riviera and I hadn't wanted to, but Fonda summoned me to meet the *bambini*," she recalled. "I had already been warned that Jane and Peter adored Susan, so I knew right away they probably would not like me."

And indeed they didn't. Peter and Jane thought Afdera had a certain hard-sell charm that they mistrusted instantly. *Phony* was the word that came to both their minds. Jane said, "We figured he intended to marry her, since he never exposed us to girlfriends unless marriage was at hand. We sensed that this was no Susan, no open-hearted stepmother, but we were just enough older that it didn't matter to us as it would have earlier."

They were staggered by their father's uncharacteristic behavior with Afdera. "He acted like a lovesick schoolboy," Afdera recalled. They'd watch him strolling on the beach with her, hand in hand, kissing her openly on the dock at sunset. He took pictures of her constantly. He kept showering her with little presents. He seemed to give in to her every demand.

"He confided he had failed in all his marriages, so he wanted ours to work. He was committed to us completely," Afdera said.

She would lie on the beach and gossip grandly with Jane about clothes and men. "I thought of myself as a woman of the world," she said. Jane kept watching her. She decided she was vain, spoiled, and greedy and yet somehow strangely endearing. Peter couldn't tolerate her. Jane just wanted to figure out why her father seemed so obsessed.

Was it because she seemed at all times to be enveloped in a sweet rich fragrance? What was it? "Arpege, *cara*." When Hank found out that Jane liked the perfume too, he bought them both little bottles. Jane excitedly daubed some on her wrists and throat, but she was disappointed — she was not enveloped in the same rich sweetness as Afdera. On her skin, Arpege gave off a very peculiar odor. Angrily, Jane threw the little bottle away.

During her second year at Vassar, she barely cracked a book. All that mattered to her was her relationship with Goey. "I had been trying to lose my virginity with three different boyfriends. Then with Goey." She doesn't remember the sex, but the weekends spent alone with him in the country at his parents' farm in upstate New York when it snowed. Taking baths together. Learning how to make whiskey sours. Waking up in the same bed. Her father didn't know about Goey. He did know she wasn't doing well in college, but he had no time to deal with that. He was busy finishing *12 Angry Men*, a movie he was not only starring in but producing.

He was still caught up in his consuming affair with Afdera and he was determined to marry her. He phoned her in Rome and sent her gifts and telegrams, and they would meet whenever he was free and go on trips. He also drove up to Simsbury, Connecticut, and Westminster School, to see Peter. Over lunch, Fonda told him that he planned to marry Afdera. His son was extremely upset, but he knew he couldn't change his father's mind. And in the meantime, Afdera said, "He wore me down. I finally agreed to be his wife, but I cried all night long before the wedding. Hank was very dear; he stayed up with me squeezing my hand."

On May 10, 1957, a small ceremony was held in the Fonda brownstone on East 74th Street. Hank's sister Harriet Peacock and her husband, Jack, were in attendance, as were Jane and a glowering Peter, who was astounded his father wanted him to be his best man.

A judge, "an elderly Jewish fellow, officiated," Afdera said. He told them that none of the couples he'd married had ever been divorced before. With that, Peter declared that he'd just punched out one of his teachers who had told him, "Any man who's been married four times is a no-good SOB." Hank Fonda was properly chagrined but managed a chuckle.

After the ceremony was over, Jane and Peter made a couple of cruel jokes about their father's wives getting younger and younger. Jane predicted that by the tenth wife, Hank would have to diaper her. Afdera was very hurt by these remarks and grateful when Peter changed the subject.

He took his father aside and tried to describe the difficulties he was having at Westminster School. The teacher he'd punched out was a drunk as well as a frustrated actor. He was really out to get him, he said. He was also being persecuted by the other students. "What do you want me to do—take you out of school?" Fonda asked with surprising gentleness. He promised his son, "I'll write the school and settle things with the headmaster."

When Peter returned to school he started picking fights with other students and made a point of saying, "Fuck you!" to the teacher he'd punched out. The letter* his father had promised to write never came, and he felt abandoned and filled with anxiety. He began taking huge

---

* Years later, in 1989, when he was going through his archive at Westminster School, Peter discovered that his father *had* written the letter to the headmaster; Peter just hadn't been informed of it.

quantities of phenobarbital. The medication didn't help—and he had no idea of its deadly consequences. He phoned Jane in a panic, saying he needed help; he was terrified he was going crazy.

She drove up to Westminster and found her brother crouching behind a row of bushes on campus. His hair was dyed blond. When she saw the bad shape he was in, she called their Aunt Harriet, who advised her to put Peter on the next train to Omaha so she and her husband could take care of him.

By the time Peter arrived in Nebraska, he felt "completely unhinged." He'd been off pills for five days and he was in withdrawal: sweating, having convulsions and anxiety attacks. He thought he was going crazy, but he felt better within a week.

Living with Harriet and Jack Peacock was wonderful. "[They] both concentrated on making me feel good in every way. It was the best therapy I could have had." They never pushed him to do anything. "I ate . . . as much or as little food as I wanted—with both of them every day, and was allowed to sleep in. . . . Such leniency was mind-boggling, and I loved them for it."

At first he refused to go back to school—any school; he said all he wanted to do was be a parking lot attendant. Harriet was calm and practical; she persuaded him to face reality and to take some aptitude tests to see what he was good at.

He sat through three weeks of tests (including a batch of personal aptitude tests, multiple-choice general knowledge tests, as well as entrance exams from the University of Omaha, University of California, and Stanford), which showed that Peter had a genius IQ.

The Peacocks invited him to stay with them until he completed his education. So he remained in Omaha for the next four years, graduating from high school and attending college there. Being with his aunt and uncle in a loving, relaxed atmosphere saved his life.

In the meantime, Jane had her own demons to cope with at Vassar. "I drank too much, got hooked on Dexedrine, and failed most of my examinations." She sincerely hoped she'd be expelled, but her teachers just made her take makeup tests. "I was always handled with kid gloves because I was Henry Fonda's daughter." She kept sneaking off campus to be with Goey. Finally she was caught and called in to explain her actions to a teacher. She had an elaborate lie all ready to tell, but the teacher wouldn't let her say a word. He said he understood why she was "rebelling." Her father had just gotten married for the fourth time, so she must be emotionally upset. Jane listened with a poker face. "I wasn't upset about that at all — all I'd done was to go off with some boy for the weekend." But Fonda's publicized marital record got her off the hook time and time again. "Everybody felt sorry for me," Jane said.

She finished her final exam in music history by filling her blue book with figures of women screaming.

The summer of 1957, the Fondas rented a villa on Cap Ferrat near the port of Villefranche. They invited Jane and Peter to come along. First stop — Paris and the Hotel Lotti near Les Tuileries Gardens and rue Saint-Honoré. Susan Blanchard was in Paris, too, studying art, and she sought her stepchildren out. The three of them met for lunches and afternoons at museums. "It was great seeing her," Peter said.

The morning after one of those wonderful times, Peter woke up and heard his father yelling at Jane, something about "How could we be so thoughtless — while he was here in Paris with his bride of four months, we're spending time with his ex-wife!" Peter said he flung open the door and shouted back at him that "*we* hadn't divorced Susan, he had, and we could see her whenever we wanted to and to never yell at my sister about that or anything else. Dad was absolutely stunned. He turned around and left the hotel."

Jane continued, "I was always amazed at Peter when he stood up to Dad and he did it time and time again. I marveled at the extent to which he would, in the face of Dad's anger, remain himself, expose himself to challenging Dad. 'See me for who I am. I will not change in order to make you comfortable.' I on the other hand was loath to be anything that would bring on my father's disapproval until, at a later age, I realized that if I wanted his attention disapproval was the best I could hope for."

As soon as they arrived on the Riviera, they settled in at their rented villa, a large white stucco house with many guest rooms and a swimming pool. It stood on a cliff overlooking the Mediterranean, and below was a little beach that one reached by walking down a steep flight of stairs. Aristotle Onassis's yacht was nearby in Monte Carlo; the Agnellis were their neighbors on the hill above their villa and gave dinners all the time. Afdera knew everybody in the international set so there were endless parties, lunches, even a masked ball in Venice and a benefit in Paris. There were also excursions — one to Picasso's studio in Vallauris, where they watched him paint. "It was like watching Yehudi Menuhin play the violin," Afdera said.

Afdera introduced Jane to Count Giovanni Volpi and he was charmed. "So was Teddy Kennedy — he came around the villa a lot, too. Goey was there for a while but I got the feeling Jane was getting bored by him." She did hang out with him for about a week along with his friend José de Vicuña, a sophisticated Spaniard who knew his way around the Riviera. When Goey left, Jane began having an affair with José.

Near the end of the summer, everyone drove over the Pyrenees to Pamplona to see the running of the bulls. "It was absolute madness," Afdera recalled. "Crowds of tourists, very hard to get hotel rooms. We managed accommodations, but we were not together. The next morning we met for coffee, Jane and Jimmy Franciscus [who kept reappearing in Jane's life], Fonda and me; and then we walked down the street — jammed with people. I was clutching Fonda's one arm; Jane, the other."

They hurried along with the crowd and found a spot on a terrace above the street. In the distance they could hear a rumbling noise. "Where is Peter?" Fonda wanted to know. The sound of hooves drumming on the cobblestones grew louder. "I wish I could see Peter," Fonda said again. He sounded worried. And then they saw him. Peter was there, right in the center of it all, running along with the bulls, hundreds of them, and the young men who wanted to be matadors, all of them running as fast as they could. The unlucky ones were gored or trampled; some gave up and clung to the terraces of the buildings to save their lives. There was noise and dust and cheering. The frontrunners, and Peter was among them, ran triumphantly around a corner. The bulls passed them and Peter lived to tell the tale.

8

T HAT VACATION WAS the start of a couple of aimless years for Jane. That fall she dropped out of Vassar and convinced her father that she should study painting in Paris. Afdera arranged for her to live with an impoverished countess on the avenue d'Iéna on the Right Bank. She moved into the apartment with her paint boxes and canvases. "Everything smelled," Jane remembered. "The furniture was covered in plastic and we had to eat our meals in silence in the dining room. I hated it." Jane enrolled at the Académie de la Grande Chaumière and Académie Julian, an art school on the more bohemian Left Bank.

She felt lost. She made no friends. She couldn't speak French, so whenever she tried to paint in class she was sure the other students were judging her severely. "I felt clumsy and stupid," she said. Gradually she began spending less time in school and more time in Left Bank cafés. For a short while she worked at the *Paris Review* magazine office.

One night Jane attended a dinner party at Maxim's with the actor Christian Marquand. In the middle of the meal a darkly handsome man with burning eyes joined them at their table. Jane recognized his long, tanned, melancholy face from newspaper photographs. His name was Roger Vadim, and he was the director who'd turned Brigitte Bardot into an international star and potent sex symbol with his irreverent movie *And God Created Woman*.

Jane noticed the way the energy in Maxim's shifted the minute Vadim made his entrance: "It reminded me of the effect my father had whenever he came into a room. But Vadim made me uncomfortable, too. He was with his mistress, a beautiful blond actress named Annette Stroyberg, who was hugely pregnant." Jane was still very conventional. She couldn't get used to the habit that some Frenchmen had of getting their women with child and not marrying them. Vadim was aware of Jane, too: "When she got up to dance with Christian, who was a good friend of mine, I noticed she wore a very proper dress with no décolletage and her hair was swept up in a chignon," he said. "The contrast between her and the super-sophisticated Parisienne ladies was very refreshing."

Vadim went on to say that he and Christian used to tease each other "by pointing out and exaggerating the faults of our new conquests. . . . As he danced by us with Jane, I slipped a note in his pocket. I had written, 'Have you seen her ankles?'"

Jane had swollen ankles that evening. When he returned to his table, Christian read Vadim's message, then crumpled it into an ashtray. When he turned away to speak to someone, Jane picked up the note and read it, too. She had heard that Vadim was a great seducer and was intrigued, but the note wounded her. They did not meet that night, and she and Marquand soon left the party.

She was miserable in Paris. The only fun she had was when she was with Susan, who was living nearby and every so often invited Jane to go dancing with her at a popular nightclub called L'Elephant Blanc. Jane began seeing a friend of Susan's, an Italian count in his thirties, who had lost much of his fortune and was now working for an American brokerage firm. He seemed to know everyone in Paris and all he wanted to do was have a good time. "He was a friend of Susan's so I trusted him and besides I was very lonely." She wasn't especially attracted to him, but when he asked her to spend the weekend with him at his country estate outside Paris, she agreed.

She also allowed him to photograph her in the nude. Jane said, "I think the kick he got out of it was he had managed to get Henry Fonda's nineteen-year-old daughter to pose nude for him."

The news soon reached Afdera, who wasted no time in telling Hank. When Jane came home for Christmas, her father told her she would not be returning to Paris. "I was relieved. I didn't want to go back. But my life was spinning out of control."

Her father never mentioned the photographs. "Maybe he was too embarrassed." He did ask, "What are you gonna do with yourself?" Jane had no answer.

For the next six months, she camped out in the Fonda brownstone in New York. "I was at a loss as to what to do with my life. I was deeply depressed, sleeping twelve to thirteen hours a day, and even then I'd fall asleep on dates."

She was aware that her father was as unhappy as she was, especially about the play in which he was starring on Broadway called *Two for the Seesaw* by William Gibson. The play was about Jerry Ryan, an uptight Nebraska lawyer adrift in New York. He begins an affair with Gittel Mosca, a kooky bohemian woman from the Bronx played by the high-spirited Anne Bancroft. Though it was a big hit, Fonda felt his part was both weak and underwritten; he also complained that Bancroft was "too emotional." Every night he had to play a love scene with her, and every night she'd burst into sobs, genuine sobs, tears rolling down her cheeks. He complained to his director, Arthur Penn, "Are you telling me I have to kiss this girl even when she has snot running out of her nose?"

He was reluctant to kiss her but he was a consummate professional, so he did, every night, and he always gave an impeccable performance. Jane saw the play numerous times, often from the wings; she thought both her father and Bancroft were magnificent. She was vaguely aware that they had conflicting acting styles. Fonda was the traditionalist and a superb reactor. Bancroft (a new member of the Actors Studio) listened to Fonda but also tapped into a deep, private pool inside herself.

Fonda couldn't abide his costar's free-flowing emotions, so he was in a terrible mood whenever he was home, and Jane tried to steer clear of him. He also knew his marriage just wasn't working, and this upset him, too.

What in God's name *was* the nature of her father's relationship to Afdera? Jane wondered. Afdera was twenty-three, just a few years older than she was. It seemed to be the most complex and unfathomable of all his marriages, and it certainly flouted her naive conception of how a wife should behave — loving and romantic. Afdera was engaged in an eternal contest with her father, one that resulted in both of them holding each other responsible for their mutual unhappiness.

Their dissatisfaction was combined with a dangerous rage. Hank had recently punched a man out—a perfect stranger—because he had purposely gotten stuck in a revolving door with her. Hank claimed they were coming on to one another. Afdera was unlike any woman he'd ever known, as unpredictable as Maggie Sullavan, who once drove him crazy when he loved her.

"Afdera's lifestyle really bugged Dad, too," Jane said. "He wanted everything to be quiet and sedate." But for as long as Jane was living there, the atmosphere in the brownstone remained highly charged. Phones never stopped ringing, and there were nonstop deliveries of wine and caviar and fresh flowers, as Afdera prepared for yet another dinner party. Reinaldo Herrera recalled an evening when he and Peter Ustinov, Richard Burton, and John Barry Ryan, the grandson of the banker Otto Kahn, along with many lovely women in evening gowns and jewels, threw ice cream and chocolate sauce at one another after drinking a great deal of champagne.

Leland Hayward was there and thought Hank would have a fit, "but he laughed his sobbing screeching laugh along with his guests and threw ice cream right back at them."

Jane didn't join in such antics; she gave her own noisy parties at the brownstone for the *Paris Review* crowd. Afdera remembered, "I'd come home to find Jane on her hands and knees cleaning up a mess of dirty glasses and overflowing ashtrays."

Jane had begun to study drawing at the Art Students League and was taking French and Italian lessons and modeling for *Vogue*. Nan Talese—then a fashion assistant at the magazine—remembered that "Jane caused a scandal by showing up in the fitting room to try on clothes and she wasn't wearing any panties." Eventually, photographed by Irving Penn, Jane appeared on the cover of *Vogue*, wearing a gold sheath. She confided to Afdera that she wanted to earn enough money to buy her father some extravagant gift. "I never knew what the gift was. I do know she gave it to him and he thanked her for it but never opened it, and she was devastated."

He was much more interested in her cover photo. Afdera remembered he took it backstage at the Booth Theatre where he was starring in *Two for the Seesaw* and sort of "flung it at his costar, Anne Bancroft, declaring, 'See how beautiful my daughter is!'"

By then, Afdera says, she and Jane were "getting along pretty well. We were always civil to each other. Jane was sleeping with a lot of different men — so many furtive phone calls, so many cabs drawing up at the curb late at night. I never breathed a word to Fonda. Jane and I used to discuss various kinds of contraceptives — the coil versus the diaphragm, the rhythm system. I thought she knew much more than I did, that she was playing the innocent just to make conversation."

Sometime early in 1958, Afdera introduced Jane to one of her former lovers, twenty-eight-year-old Alexander "Sandy" Whitelaw, a crewcut Harvard graduate who liked to play tennis and ski. He had spent much of his early life in Europe and was fluent in four languages. His Scottish father was a career soldier. Now Sandy was working as a production assistant to David O. Selznick.

On one of their first dates Sandy took Jane to a lavish reception in Selznick's suite at the St. Regis, where he was showing off his collection of "new faces" — Christopher Plummer among them — to friends and business associates.

Plummer remembered Jane as "young, fresh-faced, boyishly sexy. I kept ogling her." Selznick was going around the room, bragging that he was about to sign her to an exclusive contract, just as he had Ingrid Bergman twenty years earlier.

But Jane would have none of it. She had not forgotten Selznick's put-down of her when she was a teenager, when they'd been riding in his limousine with Brooke Hayward and Selznick had predicted, "Brooke will be the movie star, not Jane."

She repeated the remark to Sandy after they left the reception. He laughed and took her in his arms. "And you're going to prove him wrong." They began an affair that continued off and on for a couple of years. She liked his lazy, laconic ways; nothing seemed to faze him. Besides, she enjoyed the perverse sensation of sleeping with a man who had slept with one of her stepmothers. She wondered what her father would say.

Of course, she said nothing to him, but she confided to Susan Blanchard, just back from Paris, that she wasn't in love with Sandy Whitelaw — she wasn't in love with anyone. She was twenty years old and the only sustaining relationship she'd had so far was with Goey. She'd cared for him, but he wasn't enough for her. Along with Sandy she'd been seeing a young French soldier on leave from the Algerian War. "We'd go up to the Cloisters in the afternoons and sit on the grassy hill overlooking the Hudson and neck," Jane said. Many of her girlfriends such as Brooke Hayward and Carol Bentley were already married, but she did not want to get married yet.

She continued to brood about becoming an actress. "That's what I really wanted to do more than anything else," she told *New Yorker* writer Lillian Ross, "so I kept figuring out reasons why I shouldn't act. Acting was selfish. It was egotistical. It gave no enjoyment. I wasn't pretty enough."

"The subtext was 'I'm scared shitless cuz I'll have to compete with my father,'" Michael Thomas said, "because that's what she was gonna have to do, and Henry Fonda was one of the greatest actors in movies and on the stage and how could she ever top him?"

Henry had recently completed *Stage Struck* (the remake of Katharine Hepburn's *Morning Glory,* for which Hepburn had won her first Oscar). Susan Strasberg was playing the Hepburn role. She was an exquisite young woman with a bewitching smile who had triumphed on stage as Anne Frank and who had already made two other movies, *The Cobweb* and *Picnic.* She was then on Broadway in *Time Remembered,* playing opposite Richard Burton, with whom she was having a tumultuous romance.

Jane was impressed with what Susan had accomplished. She felt intimidated. They were exactly the same age, twenty, and she felt as if she had done nothing. Near the end of filming, Jane asked her father if she could visit the *Stage Struck* set. He arranged it for one late afternoon, and she arrived in time to see him playing a love scene with Susan, who was so tiny she had to stand on an apple box to kiss him.

Jane knew how much her father hated playing love scenes. She could tell he wanted to get it over with as quickly as possible, and he did. The scene was the last scene to be shot that day, and as soon as it was finished, the director, Sidney Lumet, raced out of the studio and hopped into a fur-lined convertible driven by his wife, Gloria Vanderbilt, and they sped off into the evening. Fonda disappeared with Afdera, and Jane was left alone on the set.

Susan politely invited her into her dressing room for coffee. The two had met at parties in New York, but they weren't close friends. Even so, Jane pummeled her with questions about what it felt like to kiss Henry Fonda. Susan giggled that it was intimidating because he "reminds me of my father." Her father was Lee Strasberg, the most famous acting teacher in America, who happened to be as cold and detached as Fonda, and just as impenetrable.

Susan said that being an actress made it a little easier to deal with her father's black moods. Then she asked Jane when she was going to act. Jane shook her head. Susan teased, "Oh, come on!" She sensed that Jane was dying to act but, for some reason, couldn't admit it. So she suggested, "You should study with my pop. He could help you." But Jane cried out, "Oh, no!" with such intensity that Susan stopped pushing her. "I didn't know Jane that well then, but when I did get to know her better, I realized she always contradicts herself, saying the opposite of what she is thinking and feeling and wanting to do."

Part II

Actress: 1958-1963

I never wanted Jane to play young mothers or act "reassuring" on the screen. I wanted her to be as bravura as Bette Davis and as defensive as she was in real life. I wanted her to be sexy and glamorous and dangerous and ballsy and comic and ambitious and driven and revealing her pain — the elements she had inside herself that she was trying to push out.

— ANDREAS VOUTSINAS (JANE'S ACTING COACH)

9

J ANE WOULD EVENTUALLY give Lee Strasberg credit for changing her life. "The summer of 1958 was the big turning point," she said. That July she and Peter flew out to California to join Afdera and their father while he was filming *The Tin Star*. The Fondas happened to be renting Tyrone Power's spacious beach house in Malibu, six doors down from the Strasbergs' rented home. Both had splendid views of the booming Pacific Ocean and a coastline that stretched from Santa Monica to Palos Verdes.

For the first week Jane resisted seeing Strasberg. Instead she spent hours with her friend Jill Robinson driving around Malibu. Sometimes they would drive south to the seaside town of Venice, known for its canals and beaches. "We'd walk along the boardwalk and buy ice cream," Jill said. "We'd listen to these shaggy-haired beatniks reciting poetry or watch sailors being tattooed."

In the evenings Jane would come home and help her father as he barbecued steaks for everybody on the beach. He was trying to relax after his difficult run in *Two for the Seesaw*.

As soon as he had a couple of drinks he'd start complaining about the changes in Hollywood. The big studios — Twentieth Century Fox, MGM, Warner Bros. — were breaking up their chains of theaters — no more stables of stars. Instead, the talent agencies were starting to "package" movies and TV shows. As a matter of fact, that summer Fonda was about to sign a contract to star in a TV Western series called *The Deputy*, not because he wanted to but because he needed the money. "Afdera is bleeding me dry," he told Jane with irritation.

And then he'd turn his anger on her — "What in Christ's name are you doing with yourself? You are frittering your life away." She would have no answer, so she would go to her room and write her Spanish lover, José, "I am terribly depressed, don't really see any point in going on. . . . I'm empty, like a vegetable."

"What a pair they were," Afdera said. "I used to study them together. Fonda was such a hidden man, but when you got to know him he had nothing to hide. Jane was much darker — she was hidden, too, but she had a lot she wanted to cover up. When the two of them were in a room, even when they weren't speaking to each other because they were often so angry at each other — there was this unresolved mess between them because they were actually so alike." There was so much tension between them that in the mornings Jane often fled the house just after the sun came up, before he left for the studio, so they wouldn't have to speak.

One morning Jane wandered across the dunes and saw Susan Strasberg curled up on a blanket. Susan looked terrible; she'd lost a great deal of weight and had huge circles under her eyes. She confessed that she was "in mourning for Richard Burton." They'd broken up a month before and she was devastated. She said she had been wearing his T-shirt for days, and she wouldn't take it off. "I will never love anyone the way I loved Richard!" she exclaimed, her eyes welling up with tears, and then she sobbed that for once her father had been wonderful. "For weeks I was hysterical. I couldn't eat, couldn't sleep; Pop held me in his arms and told me, 'Some people never feel or have a great passion to love. Be grateful that you can feel so much.'" The thought made her sob even louder. Jane couldn't imagine her father saying that to her, nor could she imagine feeling so intensely about anyone, although she longed to.

Just then they were joined by thirty-year-old Marty Fried, a swarthy, darkly handsome boxer-turned-actor who was part of the Strasbergs' extended family in New York. He got free acting lessons with Strasberg in exchange for driving him and his friends around in his cab. The friends included Marilyn Monroe; he often drove her to Saks Fifth Avenue or Lord and Taylor and sometimes to her hairdresser. Marty had tried to teach Monroe how to drive, "but she couldn't concentrate, so I gave up," he said.

That morning Marty knelt down and gently wiped the tears from Susan's face with a Kleenex. He made her blow her nose, and after a few moments she stopped crying; he put his arms around her and she snuggled against him and they sat quietly on the sand, watching the waves curl and pound against the shore.

Jane sat down near them. She kept lighting cigarettes; she was chain-smoking and feeling self-conscious because Marty was staring at her.

"Why aren't you acting?" he demanded in his rough, hoarse voice. "You're gorgeous, you're sexy, and you have a lot of energy."

Jane replied she'd been asked the same exact question the night before at a party, when the director Mervyn LeRoy had come over to her wondering why she hadn't appeared in any more plays since she'd acted with her father on Cape Cod. She explained she didn't think she could ever be the kind of actress people expected her to be because she was Henry Fonda's daughter. With that, LeRoy declared he'd hire her then and there to play Jimmy Stewart's daughter in *The FBI Story.* This was a movie he was about to start directing the following week at Warner Bros. "So what about it?" he asked. He was serious.

Jane had panicked and run over to her father, who was also at the party. She whispered the offer to him and he snapped, "If you're going to be an actress, you don't want your first part to be as Jimmy Stewart's daughter!"

"So what shall I do?" she asked Marty and Susan that morning. How should she respond? LeRoy wanted her to come down to Warner Bros. to talk. "The bottom line is," Marty challenged, "you gotta ask yourself, Do you really want to act?"*

Jane refused to answer, although of course she wanted to act. The two times she'd been onstage with her father were the high points of her life, but she didn't want to admit it. She knew if she decided to act, she had to prove to herself that she had talent. But what if she didn't and what if she failed? That possibility was the most frightening thought of all.

So she kept going back and forth about whether or not she should do the movie until Marty was exasperated and Susan ordered her to "please see my pop. Maybe he'll let you study with him." Jane gave in and Susan spoke to her parents that same afternoon, and the follow-

---

* In *My Life So Far,* Jane wrote that in the next week her father felt he had to bring her to Warner Bros. to talk to Jimmy Stewart, who was his best friend. Jane told them both very politely that she had decided not to do the film. "But in light of my subsequent relationship with the Federal Bureau of Investigation, wouldn't it have been ironic if my first role had been in *The FBI Story*?"

ing day Jane found herself face-to-face with Paula, Strasberg's overweight, gossipy little wife, who handled her husband's crowded schedule. Paula spent much of her energy plotting and scheming to make
Strasberg more famous. The minute she heard the name Fonda she
perked up, but she tried to contain her excitement. "Okay, you can see
Lee, but there's no guarantee you'll get into his classes in New York.
There is a long waiting list and nobody is ever pushed to the head of
the line." Then she paused dramatically. "We did make one exception,
though — with Marilyn Monroe."

Jane knew that Paula coached Marilyn Monroe on her movies.
She'd been with her on *Bus Stop* and *The Prince and the Showgirl* and
was now coaching her on *Some Like It Hot*.

"Lee teaches Marilyn privately three times a week," Marty had explained. "He's helping her release her unconscious."

What a combination, Jane thought. A coach for movies and a private teacher as well. Maybe she could have that arrangement, too.
When she mentioned this to Marty, he chuckled. "Why don't you just
start with Lee's classes and see how it goes?"

So, heart pounding, Jane set off across the dunes to meet the most
famous and controversial acting teacher in America.

Lee Strasberg was at his zenith when Jane met him. Artists from all
over the world were crowding in to hear him speak. In his private
classes, he was attracting the brightest untried talents, Dustin Hoffman, Faye Dunaway, and Al Pacino among them. A founder of the re-
nowned 1930s Group Theatre along with Harold Clurman and Cheryl
Crawford, Strasberg was a master teacher. His "Method" techniques
for acting, adapted from Stanislavski, gave the actor a truth, honesty,
and sense of inner life that radiated from the actor's personal core.
Since 1951, Strasberg had been artistic director of the Actors Studio,
and that small private place, founded by legendary director Elia Kazan,
quickly became *the* place in America for the most promising and unconventional performers to practice their craft. The original members
of the Studio included Eli Wallach, Julie Harris, Montgomery Clift,
Marlon Brando, Jerome Robbins, and Patricia Neal.

Admirers said Strasberg had a "jeweler's eye" and praised his ability to dissect a performance down to the slightest nuance. He could
illuminate every element that enriched a character. But detractors

criticized his emotional coldness and his weakness for stars. He was alternately called guru, shrink, god, and devil. Some actors literally trembled in his presence. "He was fucking scary," said Shelley Winters, "but I loved him. He taught me how to use myself."

Marty advised Jane not to be intimidated by everything she'd heard about him. "Lee is going to like you," he promised. "He's going to be kind."

Still, Jane felt distinctly uneasy the afternoon of her meeting. When she arrived at his beach house, Strasberg opened the door himself, his face a solemn and inscrutable mask. There were no polite "how do you do" greetings; instead, they simply moved into the living room, and he sat down in a chair opposite her and stared at her. For what seemed like an interminably long time, he continued to scrutinize her, every so often snorting nervously. (He suffered from a bad postnasal drip, and his conversation was frequently punctuated with snufflings.) Strasberg was fifty-eight, a short man with thick gray hair long on his neck, dressed in a heavy black shirt and trousers, although the California sun blazed outside the windows.

"So, darling?" he finally growled. "You wanna act?" "Yes!" she said. At least she thought so. She told him she had also toyed with the idea of becoming a painter, a veterinarian, even a wife and mother. She quickly corrected herself. She always returned to the idea of becoming an actress, she admitted. She said she could not stop thinking about it.

Strasberg listened. The intelligence and depth in his hazel eyes, even hidden behind heavy-rimmed glasses, were extraordinary. In repose, he appeared distant and remote, armored against all attempts to invade his emotional privacy — rather like Henry Fonda. Not surprisingly, Jane felt strangely at ease with the master teacher.

For a while they discussed the work she might do in his class, and as they talked, it occurred to her that their conversation might itself be a test of her as an actress and as a person. She found herself speaking very clearly and distinctly. She was opening up because "he was treating me like an adult. He spoke to me as if he were interested in me and not because I was Henry Fonda's daughter. I could sense he knew I wanted to act but was afraid to."

He asked her only a few questions. "Have you ever been on the stage? Why are you interested in the theater? Who is your favorite actress?" At the time Jane's favorite actress was Geraldine Page, who would soon electrify Broadway with her flamboyant portrayal of a fading movie star in Tennessee Williams's *Sweet Bird of Youth*. Jane had read somewhere that Page revered Strasberg. "Lee nurtured talent," she maintained in the *Tulane Drama Review*. "He opened up a whole world for me in acting." That's what Jane wanted, too.

The meeting was short. After twenty minutes Strasberg rose and showed Jane to the door, but not before he brusquely agreed to let her study with him in New York that fall. "It'll be thirty-five dollars a month," he said.

Her heart pounded. Next to membership in the Actors Studio, enrollment in Lee Strasberg's private classes was the most coveted position a young performer could aspire to in 1958. She didn't dare ask him how she could become a member of the Actors Studio, too, though that was another of her dreams. Susan had described to her what James Dean had done for his final audition at the Studio. He had written a scene for a couple in love and set it in Central Park, and he rehearsed in the park in all kinds of weather for four months before he and his partner, Chris White, performed the audition; they were now members of the Studio. Jane vowed she would become a member, too.

As she raced back to the Fondas' beach house, she wondered what Lee Strasberg really thought of her. Years later he told a journalist that he felt he had to work with Jane Fonda because "she had such panic in her eyes."

Her father had just returned from filming. She approached him tremulously and said, "Dad, I think I'd like to study with Lee."

Though he privately had no use for Strasberg or the "Method," Fonda shrugged okay. He told Afdera, "Maybe this Lee fellow can help Jane."

After her meeting with Strasberg, Jane started spending more time with Marty. They took drives up into the hills above Malibu and necked. "I suppose we were friends," he said. "But I wasn't fooled. Jane hung around me because I hung around the Strasbergs and I could take her to the Sunday open house. So I did."

By now Paula's open houses were legendary and bicoastal. When she was in New York, she held them every weekend, and when she came to L.A. with Lee, she gave them there. All the New York actors — mostly

Studio members who were making movies or television shows in Hollywood — crowded in for bagels, cream cheese, hot coffee, and bloody marys.

Lee Grant came with her husband, Joey Feury; Rod Steiger with his wife, Claire Bloom; Carroll Baker, Jack Garfein, Sydney Pollack, and Mark Rydell came, too, along with Clifford Odets, who was writing a screenplay about Beethoven for Marlon Brando.

"Everybody came for Lee's blessing," Shelley Winters said. "We would tell him our problems, we would ask for his help with a script or a love affair." He would listen to everyone, nodding and shrugging. He would invariably kiss all of the sexy young girls or he would let them kiss him.

"He was alternately a teacher and surrogate father, or even a psychiatrist," his daughter said. Jane would watch in amazement as every actress there, young and old, competed to sit at his feet. The unknowns dreamed that he would turn them into stars, and stars like Jennifer Jones dreamed he would turn them into actresses.

Paula served everyone, huffing and puffing. As the hours passed by in an alcoholic haze, she grew shiny with sweat. She was heavier than Jane had realized. She guessed that was why she wore only black and was swathed in pastel chiffon scarves. Finally, as the afternoon wound down, Paula would collapse on the sofa and cool herself with a hand-held battery-operated fan.

At the very end of every brunch, Strasberg made ice cream sodas for his favorites. He made the biggest and most elaborate one, with coffee ice cream topped with whipped cream and a cherry, for Marilyn Monroe. She would ooh and aah and wiggle her butt a little, accepting the soda from the master teacher. Jane could see that Strasberg was in seventh heaven. Monroe's husband, Arthur Miller, was standing on the sidelines, a pipe stuck in his mouth. He hated the Strasbergs and he hated Marilyn's dependence on them. He thought they were using her and they were. "Marilyn was Lee's ticket to fame and fortune," said Marty. Estelle Parsons added, "Lee did love movie stars."

Jane was fascinated by the way he behaved with Monroe, showing her more tenderness and love than he showed anyone else. Monroe sat at his feet, too, and his stone face would crack into a smile when she whispered something to him. "Yes, darling, yes. Of course, darling," he would murmur, stroking her hair and whispering back. "Nobody could interrupt him when he was in conversation with Marilyn," Marty said. If Paula asked him to answer the phone he'd growl, "No. Can't you see I'm busy with Marilyn?" If Susan or his son, Johnny, had a problem, too bad. "I'm busy with Marilyn," he would say through clenched teeth.

Not long after Jane's first Sunday brunch, Susan took Jane to visit Marilyn on the set of *Some Like It Hot*. Jane was curious to see how Paula coaxed a performance out of her since she was perpetually anxious and usually on medication. "Paula gives Marilyn confidence," Marty said. "She and Lee have taught her that she should do scenes over and over again until she feels that she's got them right."

The sound stage at the Samuel Goldwyn Studio in Hollywood was huge, high-ceilinged, and quite dark. Jane remembered seeing dozens of crew members running around, moving ladders, adjusting cranes and lights, clustering around big cameras. She found the entire place quite magical. Orson Welles once described films as "ribbons of dreams." Part of her sensed that she was destined to be in some of those dreams. She was Henry Fonda's daughter. But another part of her wondered if it would really happen.

That afternoon the atmosphere was tense because Marilyn couldn't remember her lines. They were written on cue cards and taped on props all over the set. Paula and she kept conferring, and then they would shoot the scene again. After fifteen takes the director, Billy Wilder, was angry and exasperated, but he tried to remain calm as he asked the actors to do it once more.

There was total silence on the darkened sound stage. Jane and Susan held their breath as they watched Marilyn undulating down the train's sleeping car aisle and flirting with Tony Curtis and Jack Lemmon, who were in drag. Finally the little scene worked and a voice yelled, "Cut!" and then "Print!" Everybody relaxed, and the cast and crew scattered to take a break.

Within minutes Marilyn Monroe stepped out of the darkness, "bringing the light with her, shimmering in her hair and on her skin," Jane wrote. "She walked with Paula toward where Susan and I were standing while someone draped a pink chenille bathrobe over her shoulders to cover her revealing nightgown. Her body seemed to precede her, and it was hard to keep my eyes from camping out there.

But when I looked up at her face, I saw a scared, wide-eyed child. I was dizzy. It was hard to believe she was right there in front of me, all golden iridescence, saying hello in that breathy little-girl voice." When they were introduced she murmured, "I'm Marilyn," as if Jane didn't know. They'd seen each other at the brunch, but that afternoon on the set she looked at Jane as if she were seeing her for the first time. Her voice sounded half-playful, half-sensuous. She seemed nice, but preoccupied. "There was a vulnerability that radiated from her and allowed me to love her right then and there and feel glad that she had someone wide and soft, like Paula, to mama her." Jane never forgot her impression of Marilyn Monroe shimmering in the light.

10

B Y MID-SEPTEMBER THE Fondas and the Strasbergs had returned to New York. For a time Jane lived in the 74th Street brownstone, and then Susan Stein, her former roommate at Vassar, suggested Jane share the elegant duplex she was renting on East 76th Street and Third Avenue. Jane moved in and began supporting herself again by posing for fashion magazines. At least it paid some bills.

She disliked modeling and found the long hours and the waiting tedious, but it was a way to get noticed. She hated her face; she didn't think she was photogenic although in fact she was. She obsessed over her body, wanting it to be perfect, to be shaped and toned and graceful. She spent hours at ballet class and she was still bulimic, binging and purging because she imagined she was fat no matter what the scale said. "I was never thin enough," Jane has repeated in her memoir and to reporters.

She kept on taking Dexedrine, which made her hyper. Her weight dropped from 120 to 110 pounds. Soon she was being prominently featured in *Life, Harper's Bazaar,* and *Vogue.* Occasionally she would hang around a newsstand to see how people reacted to her face on various magazine covers, like *Ladies' Home Journal,* then she would go on to acting class. Lee Strasberg's private classes — always separate from the Actors Studio classes — were held on the top floor of the Capitol Theatre building on Broadway and West 50th Street in a grimy little theater called the Dramatic Workshop, which Strasberg rented from his friend Saul Colon.

In those days there was such enormous cachet about being a Lee Strasberg student that crowds of young actors lined the halls outside of the Dramatic Workshop and tried to crash the classes. So many tried to crash, in fact, that Colon had to enlist the help of bouncers. Colon himself also stood guard, and he checked Jane in that first day when she arrived, accompanied by Susan and Marty.

"She behaved like a frightened deer," Colon recalled to Tom Kiernan. "Very tall. Long legs. Hair swept up in a bun on the top of her head. Beautifully dressed in a pale pink Chanel suit. She looked like a society girl, a debutante." It was almost as if she were costumed for another life. She didn't know how to dress as an actress, maybe because she wasn't an actress yet. "She spoke in rapid bursts and she was smoking one cigarette after another and inhaling very deeply," Colon went on. "I could feel her intensity underneath her snooty manners; she definitely had something."

Strasberg did not greet her when she came into the theater. He was sitting in the front row, dressed all in black. Behind him all fifty seats were taken. There were some standing-room visitors. Jane recognized Marilyn Monroe, looking sleepy and huddled in a mink coat on the aisle. Mike Nichols was there, too. So were Ellen Burstyn and a former Miss America, Lee Meriwether.

Jane also noticed a round-faced man with a haughty expression on his face. He wore a beret and was waving a cigarette holder. His name was Andreas Voutsinas, and he was a Greek-born actor and director. "Very close to Lee and Elia Kazan," Marty whispered.

Those first weeks in class Jane didn't know what to expect, but she listened carefully to everything that Strasberg had to say. He kept repeating that tension was the occupational disease of the actor. He emphasized the actor's individuality and the exploration of that individuality. He did not place a high value on versatility; instead he stressed penetrating the talent. The artist's courage lies in his or her ability to plunge into these recesses and confront his or her most secret self.

Over the next months Jane attempted to perform exercises to release her tension. She sat in a chair for twenty minutes, breathing deeply and trying to relax the muscles in her neck and back. She sang songs in a monotone to release inhibitions. Then she acted in her first scene with

Jim Antonio, who remembered how she questioned everything and refused to improvise. She did other scenes where she cried.

"[Lee] made comments based on each actor's individual issues —and one of mine was the need always to be perfect . . . wanting constantly to improve my talent by being very emotional (something that has always come easily for me). So Lee would have me do scenes where I'd play rather dull, slow-speaking, slow-moving characters. Doing nothing was what I needed to learn." She did other scenes where she was required to be emotional, and she chewed up the scenery.

She was impatient to have Strasberg acknowledge her, to pass judgment, say it outright: You have a gift. Maybe she was talented. But she had recurring dreams about failing: she was rowing in the ocean in a boat and was late for an audition; she was terrified because she hadn't memorized her lines.

She had her first success in class when she performed a sense-memory exercise meant to develop concentration. She drank an imaginary glass of orange juice. For a week before, she practiced drinking it over and over again, even performing it for her father, who thought it was "ridiculous."

In class "I closed my eyes and before long felt myself alone in a world of sensation," she wrote. "The nerves in my fingertips felt the cold. I opened my eyes and lifted the glass slowly, testing its weight until I could feel it in my hand, and as I brought the glass to my mouth, the taste buds on my tongue woke up in anticipation of the sweet, acidy wetness. For the first time I was experiencing something unique to actors: I knew I was on a stage before an audience, pretending—yet at the same time, I was all alone and totally in the moment." When she finished, Strasberg complimented her in a low voice, saying, "I see a lot of people go through here, but you have real talent." It was the most important moment of Jane's life up to then to be praised by him, to know she could do something well. "Suddenly I knew what I wanted to do," Jane said. "I wanted to act. To live and breathe acting."

From then on, she was like a woman possessed. She did more scenes and more exercises than anyone else in class. She drove herself night and day—and she never missed a ballet class, either.

"But she still felt very unsure of herself," said Marty Fried. "She sensed resentment from the other students. She was still 'Henry Fonda's daughter.' She took to running out of class without speaking to anyone. They thought she was being stuck-up. She was just very insecure."

Sometimes she'd be so keyed up that she'd want to tell her father what was happening to her. She recalled bumping into him on the street and sharing a cab back to the East Side. "I was panting with excitement," she told reporter Al Aronowitz in an interview for the *Saturday Evening Post.* "I told Dad what I had accomplished that day in class and he listened to me and then he smiled and a curtain came down. I just didn't get to him."

When Aronowitz questioned him for the same article, Fonda's eyes welled with tears. "I don't know what she means 'a curtain came down.' It may be that I am trying to hide my own emotions and to her it is 'a curtain coming down.'" It was interesting that Fonda often hid behind his movie star mask when he spoke to reporters, especially when he was talking about Jane. In the *Post* article he appeared unusually re-laxed, charming, and warm.

He went on to say, "Now I'll relate a story that occurred before Jane became an actress. She was with a young beau of hers who was start-ing in the theater and we were talking about having to feel an emotion on stage. I explained the process I go through, likening it to a seaplane going off. There is a section on the underside of a seaplane called a step. When the plane starts its takeoff, it's very slow in the water but as it picks up speed and gets up on that step and starts to skim across the water before it lifts off, I used to feel that if I could get myself go-ing, I could get on that step and nothing could stop me. That all I had to do was hold back, hold the controls down because then I was soaring. Anyway, a year later I found myself in a cab with Jane going across town. 'You remember the story you told me about soaring? Now I know what you mean. It happened to me today in class.' Well I can get emotional right now remembering Jane tell it. And the curtain prob-ably came down for me to hide that emotion. Because for my daughter to be telling me about it, she knew what it was like. Well, I wasn't going to let her see me like this."

Aronowitz asked, "Why not? Don't you understand she wants to get to you?"

"Well gosh," Fonda replied. "She does get to me."

"I know," Aronowitz said, "but she wants to know that she is getting to you. She is a demonstrative person."

"Well," Fonda said, "I'm not."

Jane found an agent, a rosy-cheeked, cherubic-looking man named Ray Powers, who was working at Famous Artists. He agreed to send her out on auditions, but he advised her to stop dressing like a debutante — "Wear bohemian clothes." She exchanged her Chanel suits for black leotards and turtleneck sweaters and put on less makeup.

By early 1959 her godfather, Josh Logan, called her in for a possible movie role in a film he wanted to do based on *Parrish,* a best-selling novel set in tobacco country. He had always thought she had the potential to be a big star. Jane screen-tested opposite Warren Beatty, age twenty, a handsome former football player from Virginia, who had just appeared on Broadway in *A Loss of Roses.*

It was the first time either of them had done a screen test and they have completely different memories of their filmed kiss. Jane barely remembers it. Beatty's version: "We were thrown together like lions in a cage and told to kiss. Oh my God! We kissed until we had practically eaten each other's heads off. We thought this was all very effective."

Whatever really happened, *Parrish* didn't work out for either of them, but Logan liked Jane's poise and fresh-faced naturalism on camera, so he promptly signed her to a seven-year personal contract that called for her to star in a picture a year for $10,000. He also signed Beatty. They were the only actors Logan ever placed on personal contracts.

Not long after that Elia Kazan began casting *Splendor in the Grass* and decided Beatty should play the male lead. He interviewed Jane for the heroine. She recalled, "Kazan called me down to the edge of the stage, introduced himself, reached up to shake my hand, and said, 'Do you consider yourself ambitious?' I responded immediately with a resounding 'No!' The moment the word left my lips I knew I'd made a mistake. I could read it on Kazan's face. If I wasn't ambitious, I must not have any fire inside, I must be a dilettante. *But good girls aren't supposed to be ambitious.* I went through the motions of the audition but I knew I'd already lost out. Natalie Wood got the role."

She didn't tell Beatty what had happened at the audition because she couldn't admit to him that she had lied to Kazan. "Yes, I was ambitious, but I couldn't admit I was ambitious. What was the matter with me?" When she was with Beatty they spent most of their time discussing their careers, and when they weren't discussing their careers they were discussing sex. "Warren liked to describe his lovers to me. I found that fascinating." Most people assumed she and Beatty were sleeping together because they were seen so much in public acting very affectionate, but Jane denied it: "We were just friends." Throughout 1959, her old boyfriend Sandy Whitelaw remained an occasional lover, and she had brief relationships with two other actors, but they didn't last.

One of her former lovers told Thomas Kiernan, "Jane was so insecure and hungry for love that she tried to swallow you whole. Very intense when she was in love, but very demanding too. She took much more than she was able to give. Oh, she was generous with her time and money and all that, but it was as if she used these as substitutes for real emotion. There was something deep inside her that she kept to herself and would give to no one."

Jane didn't have much time for romance anyway. She was caught up in her career. Josh Logan had — true to his word — found another film project for her that he wanted to direct, a slight comedy called *Tall Story* (originally a play by Howard Lindsay and Russel Crouse), about a basketball star caught in a bribery scandal and his ditzy cheerleader girlfriend. She would be costarring opposite lanky Tony Perkins. Jane immediately went into a panic when she realized this would be her debut on the screen and she'd never really acted professionally before.

She had fantasized, dreamed about what it would be like — being in the movies, being a star. But now that she was actually being given the opportunity, said her agent Ray Powers, "she had doubts she could pull it off." He had doubts, too, because she had no real experience as an actress.

In the summer of 1959, before filming started on *Tall Story*, he arranged to have her play the lead opposite Harold Lang in a summer stock production of *The Moon Is Blue* out in Fort Lee, New Jersey. "It was like a trial by fire," Powers said. "Jane didn't know the first thing about rehearsals or being in a show which was up in a week. She didn't know anything about 'result acting' in front of a live audience. The

Method stuff Lee had been teaching her didn't help. She was so scared she got a terrible case of boils. Her actual performance in *The Moon Is Blue* was only okay. Critics called her 'sweet and promising' but she knew she wasn't very good. And she was so tense she couldn't relax and play her quality. The thing was a disaster."

What impressed Powers was how Jane reacted. "She didn't complain. She told me she'd learned something and she was determined to get better."

"Jane willed herself to change," Marty said. "She is the most determined human being I've ever met. She became even more organized and businesslike in her approach to her career."

When Logan called her over for a meeting in his apartment at the River House to discuss the script, she went at once. She had already memorized her lines. Tony Perkins was there; so was a photographer — "Josh had decided he wanted to promote Tony and me in the movie right away," Jane said. "Within minutes the photographer asked us to pose necking on a couch for a publicity still. Tony and I hadn't even shaken hands but we did as we were told and simulated necking for the camera. Afterwards we had a good laugh about it."

The night before Jane left for Hollywood, her father surprised her by inviting her over to the brownstone for a talk. He had been discussing her future in the movies with Logan. "He was worried I might not be up to it and he didn't want me to be hurt," Jane said. "Josh told him he thought I had real star quality, and he'd show him my screen test if he needed convincing."

Hank seemed relieved. For a while they sat in the living room and talked. He was in an unusually good mood because a hypnotist had just helped him quit smoking. He told his daughter he had been hypnotized into falling asleep, and when he woke up, he had no more desire for a cigarette. He urged Jane to try it, but she said she couldn't. She was too anxious and on edge about going out to Hollywood, and she chain-smoked throughout their conversation.

Fonda laughed and said she must relax and calm down. "Trust Josh. Follow his wishes as a director. He's a professional; he'll do right by you." But he added, "Don't allow yourself to be pushed."

Jane wondered what he meant, but much later she realized, "When you're in front of a camera, you automatically feel as though you have to do things because the film is turning. It was a lesson Dad learned during his first film, *The Farmer Takes a Wife,* and Victor Fleming told him he was mugging. That's all it took — he pulled it down to reality. You don't project anything for the camera. You just do it as you would in your own home, he would say."

Her father's instructions to "do nothing" in front of the camera had lulled her into believing she could act in a movie with relative ease. But Jane hadn't anticipated how difficult the filming of *Tall Story* would be. She was totally unprepared for the enormity of the experience, the armies of people — wardrobe women, makeup technicians, dialogue coaches, electric cameramen, gofers, assistants. Everybody seemed to be coming at her at once.

The morning after she arrived in Hollywood she went directly to the Warners publicity department to go over her bio (and scratch out the references to her mother's untimely death). She asked the PR flacks to go easy on the Henry Fonda daughter connection, but that was going to be impossible. When she arrived at the office, a photographer from *Life* was waiting to snap pictures of her, with a reporter ready to jot down everything she might say.

At lunchtime they followed her to Warners Green Room (the studio's four-star VIP dining room). As she was trying to eat her salad, James Garner came by to tell her that his first job was as a jury member in *The Caine Mutiny Court-Martial.* "I got to watch your dad onstage every night — what a lesson in acting," Garner said. "He taught me all I know."

After lunch the *Life* team accompanied her in a limousine as she was driven over to Revue Studios (the TV division of Universal Studios) to watch Hank shoot some of the first sequences of his Western, *The Deputy.* She was crouching near the cameras to observe him when one of the crew waved her forward to get closer. She shook her head — "I don't want to get too close to Dad when he's acting, otherwise I'll get too emotional." Inside she was furious she'd admitted anything so personal — there was a photographer snapping pictures of her while she watched the person she loved most in the world working, trying to absorb what he was doing, hoping maybe some of it would rub off on her.

He made everything seem so easy. He was using all of himself—his sexuality, his tenderness, his honesty. The realization came to her in a rush.

After a few minutes she slipped away to the ladies' room so she could swallow her tears. She couldn't understand why she had become so upset. Was it because she wanted so much to be as good as he was as an actor? She looked at herself in the mirror and her father's face stared back at her. That unsettled her, too, but she managed to control herself and marched out onto the set. At a break, she and Fonda posed together for a couple of shots and she forced a laugh—the laugh that she had down pat, her father's gulping, coughing laugh.

In the next days she didn't laugh much. The real problems with *Tall Story* accelerated as soon as she was taken to makeup, and the makeup artists lacquered her hair, slathered her face with pancake, and painted her lips into a "different shape because they said my mouth was all over my face." She saw the results of the makeup tests and she wanted to disappear. When she looked in the mirror, what stared back was unrecognizable. "I hated the way I looked," Jane said. "My face was so round and my makeup so unreal. And I definitely didn't have good hair." She felt completely alienated from herself, pretending to be somebody she wasn't.

Apparently Jack Warner had seen the makeup tests, too, and he and Josh Logan decided to suggest that after filming Jane might consider having her jaw broken and reset, and her back teeth pulled to create a more chiseled look—specifically, one that emulated the sunken cheekbones that were the hallmark of Suzy Parker, the supermodel of that time. Logan added, "You'll never be a dramatic actress with that nose—too cute for drama." A last suggestion from Warner: she should wear falsies.

If these comments weren't enough to destroy her sense of self, the actual filming of *Tall Story* was: "I was excited, but I was absolutely terrified, too. I didn't know what the hell I was doing. I'd memorized my lines, but I was totally thrown by the lights, the cameras, the crew milling around." She didn't lose her self-consciousness in front of the cameras until Tony Perkins advised her to do "nothing, absolutely nothing." The gawky twenty-five-year-old actor would eventually become legendary as the sly, crazy murderer Norman M. Bates in Hitchcock's horror film *Psycho*. Jane reached out to him time and time again. She was blinded by the lights; she didn't know how to deal with the glare. "Tony told me, 'Forget about the lights, just forget about the lights.' And I did. And he taught me fascinating things, like the audience's eyes always move to the right side of the screen so you always try to get to the right side of the set." She credits Perkins with helping her learn how to play to the camera when she acted, not to the other actors.

He was a sad, gentle, refined young man, perpetually anxious himself. "I had a huge crush on him," Jane admitted years later. She stopped trying to seduce him after she discovered that he was gay and she met Tony's lover, the dancer Timmy Everett. The three of them became friends, and while she was making the movie she and Tony also spent time together. Perkins remembered, "Jane hated Hollywood." They talked a lot about Hollywood, and then they had their costume tests. Nothing could have been more boring — they'd be waiting around to begin filming and Jane would show up with a pack of cards. "Let's play Gin Rummy and not quit until the picture is over." And they did. A photographer snapped them sitting up in the trees in the back lot, playing marathon games of Gin Rummy.

In the evenings, Perkins would take her to parties and she'd drift in and sit down wearily. She seemed exhausted, and her masseuse followed her around with a little massage table. Whenever Perkins picked her up to take her somewhere, the masseuse was either about to start massaging her or about to leave. Jane explained that she had very little energy and "problems with her circulation." But the truth was, it was her bulimia. It was soaring out of control. She would binge and purge sometimes twenty times a day. She began sleepwalking again, too, as she had when she was a little girl. She would dream she was in bed waiting for a love scene to be shot and would gradually realize she had made a terrible mistake. She was in the wrong bed, in the wrong room, and everyone was waiting for her to start the scene somewhere else but she didn't know where. It was summertime, and so hot she often slept in the nude. One dawn, Jane woke up on the sidewalk cold and naked, searching in vain for where she was and who she was supposed to be.

But she still tried to focus on her character. Whatever free time she had was spent researching her role. She visited college campuses around L.A., mastering cheerleader routines — all in a futile effort to convince herself that she could make the movie more believable. "The dialogue in the script was positively laughable," she said.

Three weeks into filming she knew *Tall Story* was going to be a bomb, and so did other members of the cast like the red-haired, always-cheerful Anne Jackson, who played a professor's wife, and Marc Connelly, who played Jane's chemistry don. They both knocked the picture before it was finished. An air of defeatism pervaded the set even though Josh Logan kept assuring everybody it was all going to be fine. (Later he would admit, "It was not one of my prouder moments as a screen director. I should have known better than to get involved in *Tall Story* and I did it more out of a sense of obligation to Warner Bros.")

The biggest failing had been the casting of Perkins as the college basketball star. After watching the rushes and seeing his gangly bumbling on the courts, Logan decided he would use the movie simply as a vehicle to launch Jane, his great discovery, to the world. He had been studying her in the rushes carefully, and he saw that she was a sheer delight as the cheerleader and was hardworking and a good sport; she had mastered all of the cheerleader routines and performed them with grace and humor.

Logan was trying to do a movie that would establish what he believed was Jane's star potential and would stand as homage to her father and their friendship. It was touching, Perkins thought. Josh would crouch over the camera having her do take after take in the style he had developed when directing Marilyn Monroe in *Bus Stop*. He coaxed a performance out of her. But Jane remembered this differently. "Josh gave me no comfort — we'd shoot a scene and he'd refer to how wonderful it had been to work with Marilyn Monroe — or he'd suddenly bring up my father. 'Your father wouldn't do something like that,' he'd say."

By the time she arrived at the huge cocktail party Warners had organized for her to be introduced to the Hollywood press, she was exhausted from her nightmares, her bulimia, and working with Logan. She felt like screaming. When she saw her father and Afdera, she ran into her stepmother's arms, sobbing hysterically. They gave her a sedative and that relaxed her, but she told them both that she was completely undone by making movies; Afdera said, "She didn't think she deserved the attention, she wasn't glamorous, she wasn't a movie star.

Everyone kept telling her she looked exactly like her father, which she did, but she maintained she couldn't see it. 'I'm a girl; how could I look like my dad?'" But inside she realized how much they resembled each other. She decided to take the comparison as a compliment. Eventually she calmed down enough to talk to reporters and to pose for publicity shots.

The following day she had the obligatory first interview with Louella Parsons, the most powerful gossip columnist in America. Before they started talking, Jane presented her with a bright blue balloon. "I just happened to find it outside of your apartment," she said. "Parsons was charmed by this kind of bullshit," Afdera said. (Actually, a press agent had given it to Jane beforehand.)

Meanwhile, Sandy Whitelaw had been phoning her almost every day since filming began, but she kept putting him off. He didn't know where he stood with her. Were they still lovers? Was there someone else? They had been sleeping together for over a year and he thought it had been good. He knew she had other lovers; so did he, but he couldn't stop thinking about her. "She was so neurotic and so self-involved, I didn't really like her," he admitted later. "But I was sort of in love with her if that makes any sense. She was so ambitious; I wanted to see where that ambition would take her. And she had so much anger in her, I wanted to see how that would play out, too." Sandy added, "I finally did something I am not especially proud of, but I got so bugged she wouldn't answer my calls that one night I broke into her apartment. I thought she was out. Actually, she was in her bedroom and scared I was a burglar so she didn't say a word. I wanted to read her journal because I thought it might give me some clues as to how she felt about me, so I stole it and tiptoed out of the apartment. When I got home, I read it. It was very disappointing. There were only notations in it like 'I went to see Louella Parsons today' or 'I was interviewed by Hedda Hopper.' Nothing else. It was a career journal."

Sandy finally reached Jane by phone and confessed what he had done. She was furious at him. She said, "There were other notations in the journal like 'I don't love Sandy, I know I'm not going to marry him,' and that got him pissed." For a while they stopped seeing each other.

The filming of *Tall Story* ended after thirty-five days, and by then Jane was no longer sleepwalking or having nightmares. She felt more relaxed because she seemed to have mastered some of the basics of acting on camera. When Henry Fonda visited the set, he was impressed by the casual skill with which she and Perkins enacted a love scene. "Jane has made more progress in one year than I have in thirty," he enthused to *Life*. The magazine eventually put father and daughter on a cover together.

A month after she returned to New York, Logan offered her a Broadway play called *There Was a Little Girl* by Daniel Taradash; he thought it would be a great way to capitalize on *Tall Story*—she would open on Broadway in a show about the same time their movie would be released. *There Was a Little Girl* was controversial. The story revolved around a teenage girl who is raped by a hoodlum and then accused of inviting the attack. Hank disliked the premise and advised his daughter to turn it down, but Jane wouldn't listen. The role was a highly charged, emotional one, and she would never be off the stage. She saw it as a way to stretch herself beyond what she had been asked to do in *Tall Story*.

Then Logan started playing money games with her. "He said he would only pay her one hundred twenty-five dollars a week," her agent, Ray Powers, said. "This was ridiculous. She was never offstage. She was the star of the show." Jane turned down the part and Logan started reading other actresses, including Jean Seberg. But he kept coming back to Jane, and she finally agreed to do the play at the original salary. Still, she resented it and resented what Logan had put her through.

The main reason she accepted the role was that she'd become involved with Timmy Everett, and he was urging her to do it. "Timmy had become like her manager," said Ray Powers.

At twenty-two, Everett, slight, curly-haired, hyperenergetic, was called "a triple threat" by directors like Elia Kazan and Bob Fosse because he could sing, dance, and act. He had just won a Tony Award for his sensitive portrayal of a closeted gay cadet in William Inge's *The Dark at the Top of the Stairs*. Before that, he'd danced in shows like *The Music Man*, *Damn Yankees*, and *Reuben, Reuben*.

Everett swung both ways. Tony Perkins recalled how "Jane was attracted to Timmy's edgy theatricality; he was a troubled guy—aggressive, antagonistic, and soulful. And at this point in his life, he was bisexual." Her friend Brooke Hayward added, "Jane went from extra loose sexual behavior at Vassar to her 'gay' period with Timmy. She was always experimenting—possibly in reaction to Hank's rigidity."

She and Timmy began doing scenes in Strasberg's classes, and they often rehearsed at the duplex she was sharing with Susan Stein. "One night Jane asked me if I'd like to stay for a drink," Everett recalled. "Then [she] turned on some music. We talked a while, the lights were low, then all of a sudden we were looking at each other in this strange way. I just got consumed by this wave of tenderness and desire, and so did she. We ran upstairs to the bedroom, tore our clothes off, and stayed in bed for three days."

It was the start of an ardent love affair. "Those two were crazy about each other," Marty Fried said. "They grooved on each other. It was fun to be with them."

Jane had come into her inheritance the year before when she was twenty-one (the trust fund her mother left her was quite large), so she was living off of it, and she began showering Timmy with expensive presents—cashmere sweaters, a Brooks Brothers overcoat. She was always generous to people she cared about, and he was very appreciative.

They used to drive into the country up the Hudson on weekends in Everett's rattletrap car. A couple of times they spent the night in his parents' apartment near the East River. The Everetts were simple, untutored people from the South. Timmy's sisters, Tanya and Sheree, were both in show business, too; his father, Thomas, was a traveling salesman; and his mother, Sally, a bombastic, pushy, wannabe actress, was like Mama Rose in *Gypsy*. The three Everett kids had taken dance lessons from the time they were little. Mrs. Everett recognized Timmy's special talents and fantasized that he would be a great star. She was ecstatic when she realized who Jane Fonda was. Tanya (a dancer who appeared in *Fiddler on the Roof*), said, "Jane liked to visit our family when she and Timmy were going together. She was very sweet to us and kind. And she absolutely adored Timmy. They were very, very happy together."

When Jane signed to do *There Was a Little Girl*, Everett began working with her on her characterization. "Jane was desperate for reinforcement as an actress," Ray Powers said. "She needed psychological support and Timmy gave that to her. Timmy saw himself not only as her mentor and lover but as a teacher, too."

Rehearsals began in early November. Patton Campbell, who designed the costumes for *There Was a Little Girl*, remembered, "Timmy

Everett showed up with Jane every day and went home with her most every night. But this Greek director, Andreas Voutsinas, was hanging around, too. Very grand. Very emotional. He and Timmy avoided each other. Sometimes Timmy had to leave early to teach a dance class and Andreas would mysteriously appear. He would move into Jane's dressing room and play records for her to get her into the 'mood' for the scene. Then Josh would come in and say, 'Stop this hogwash! Just go out and do it like we rehearsed it!'"

Occasionally Logan would taunt her. "I don't think you can do it. You are going to fall behind your old man." "I got so mad," Jane said, "even though I knew he was trying to make me do my best."

Unbeknownst to Jane, Hank Fonda would sneak backstage every so often and stand in the wings watching her during run-throughs. Once, while she was playing a romantic scene, he clutched Logan's shoulder, whispering, "Oh, youth, youth, youth. God! That's the exciting time. Oh, to have it all to do over again!"

Jane opened the show. When the curtain rose she was sitting center stage with a spotlight on her. At the first preview she was about to say her first line when a voice from the audience declared loudly, "Why, she's the spitting image of her father!" Jane told Marty later, "I thought, 'Oh, shit!'"

Although the comment drew laughter from some in the audience, Jane never lost her cool. She remained totally in character — she was a girl who'd been sexually abused and she behaved as if something had been murdered inside her. Her voice sounded flat; she slouched; there was a look of detachment in her eyes.

On New Year's Day 1960, a week before the play's out-of-town try-out in Boston, Margaret Sullavan was found dead of an overdose in a New Haven hotel room. She had been attempting to make a comeback on the stage but then she discovered she was going deaf.

When he heard the news, Logan stopped the run-through; by then Henry Fonda had come into the theater and the two men hugged. Their connection to Sullavan went back to their days at University Players. Logan told the cast to take a break so Jane could go out for a drink with her father. For the next hour she sat with him in a bar as he stared into space, never saying a word. She supposed he was thinking about being married to Maggie and how much he'd been in love with her.

A couple of days afterward, a reporter ran into Fonda at a public function and asked him what it was like to have been married to so many women, two of whom had committed suicide. Onlookers expected Fonda to explode in anger, but instead he paused and said evenly, "Well, I loved them all, in a way I still do. I could've not saved any one of them. And they could not have been saved. Everyone has to save themselves."

For some reason Jane remembered that when she was in her teens Brooke had discovered her mother's scrapbooks, filled with photographs, press clippings, reviews, telegrams from everybody who mattered to her. It surprised Brooke since Maggie had always said that as soon as she began raising a family she no longer had any interest in a career. She told her children that she didn't think any star could support both a career and family life. It just wasn't possible. And she repeatedly told them how much she enjoyed being a mother.

Did Brooke believe her? What had gone wrong? There were no clues and there was no clear moral to the story either.

Two nights after, *There Was a Little Girl* opened at Boston's Colonial Theatre. Logan fired Jane's leading man and replaced him with Dean Jones, who had very little time to learn his lines. Then Louis Jean Heydt, who played Jane's father, died of a heart attack just before he was to have made his entrance in the second act. And two nights after that Logan had a nervous breakdown and disappeared. When the show was in Philadelphia he returned and behaved as if nothing had happened.

The Boston and Philadelphia reviews were not good — although Jane was singled out for praise. In Boston she'd received a standing ovation. Timmy Everett, who was at the opening, recalled, "I've never seen anyone so happy. She was really good in the part. The play had its weaknesses, so did the part for that matter, but she brought more to it than was there. And the beauty of it was that it was instinctual; you could just see it coming out of her once the curtain went up."

Returning to New York, she gave a triumphant performance on opening night on Broadway, February 29. When the curtain rose, her father was standing at the back of the house watching the first scene of the play. He was in another show, *Silent Night, Lonely Night*, down the block, but because Jane's opening was at 6:30 and he didn't have to be at his theater until 8:30, he was able to see most of her first act. This made her feel good.

Afterward, he came backstage and escorted her to Logan's apartment at the River House for a party, then took her to Sardi's for a late dinner. Once again, they were sharing something special; he was supporting her in her work in theater. Theater was what he loved more than anything. She was beginning to love it, too.

When they entered the restaurant, "the crowd had already thinned out because it was after midnight," Henry Fonda remembered, so she received only a smattering of applause.

Father and daughter sat down at a table up front. Soon waiters brought over stacks of the *New York Times* and passed them around. "Jane took one and I took one," Fonda said. "Jane was across the table from me, and I'll never forget the review because it was devastating, and that's what I wanted to save her from.

"Anyway, she read the notice and she looked up at me, because now everybody in the place was reading it and pretending she wasn't there." Her personal notices were glowing, however. Brooks Atkinson allowed that "as the wretched heroine, Jane Fonda gives an alert, many-sided performance."

John McClain in the *Daily News* heralded her performance as "a personal triumph" and described her as "a splendid young woman with exceptional style and assurance." He added, "With the budding talent that she displayed last evening she might become the Sarah Bernhardt of 1990, but she better find herself a more genuine play than this one between now and then."

As for Jane, she had decided, "I'd created a real character in that play. I'd created something for the first time in my life. Now I knew what I wanted to do. I wanted to be the best stage actress in the world."

She began working even harder in Strasberg's classes, and she took dance classes every day, often with Timmy, at June Taylor's, where he taught, and they also performed jazz routines together in front of a floor-to-ceiling mirror.

"Timmy made me get in touch with my body," Jane said. "When he held me in his arms, he danced into my body." She loved to watch him strut and twirl and jive. He taught her how to do the soft shoe, and he performed some of the swooping high kicks he had learned from Bob Fosse in *Damn Yankees.*

In the spring, Jane won both the Theatre World Award and the Drama Critics Award as one of the most promising newcomers of the 1959–60 season. *Life* ran a cover story about her and her father, and she was profiled in *Time. Look* published a piece entitled "The Inevitable Discovery of Jane Fonda." The caption under the photograph of her frolicking in the surf likened her to Brigitte Bardot.

In April, *Tall Story* opened, and the reviews were terrible. "Nothing could save this picture," the *Times* critic Bosley Crowther wrote, "not even a second generation Fonda with a smile like her father's and legs like a chorus girl." But she saw her name on a movie marquee while also starring on Broadway in *There Was a Little Girl.* She walked around Times Square taking it all in, momentarily pleased because it meant "I existed on some level. But it was there and I was here. It all seemed so cockeyed, being famous."

As usual, her father was dancing around the subject of her newfound celebrity. He never talked to her about it, but in the *Life* magazine cover story they were both part of, there are pictures of him watching Jane adoringly on the set of *Tall Story,* smiling and laughing delightedly.

At home he appeared gloomy and on edge, especially when Jane brought Timmy Everett over to the brownstone for dinner. "Timmy made Fonda jumpy," Afdera said. "I'd heard he was gay, but Jane seemed devoted to him. Sometimes I'd catch her running her hand up and down his thigh at the dinner table. Hank never noticed."

But he was obviously very aware of Everett. This was illustrated by an ugly incident that occurred right after *There Was a Little Girl* closed. The producers gave a party for Josh Logan at Sardi's. Jane invited Marty and Timmy. There were a great many toasts, and then she stood up and gave a tremulous little speech about what Logan had done for her career. In the middle of it she burst into tears but managed to carry on. After she finished, everyone laughed and applauded.

Marty was standing next to Timmy and suddenly Henry Fonda hove into view. "He grabbed Timmy by the back of the neck," Marty recalled, "and he hissed, 'What have you done to make her behave that way?' That's all he said, and then he loped off. I guess Jane had never shown that much emotion in public before, or something. But Henry Fonda seemed enraged. Timmy was trembling all over."

Late that spring, Jane and Timmy started psychoanalysis with different doctors. "We were having some problems with our relationship," Timmy said. "Jane was still haunted by the fact that she couldn't feel anything about her mother's suicide. She told me she'd laughed when she heard the news that she'd died." And she still felt guilty that she hadn't run downstairs when her mother began calling her name. What had her mother wanted to tell her? Could she have kept her from killing herself? There were too many unanswered questions. She wanted to find some answers.

Lee Strasberg talked about tapping into one's past experiences to help evoke particular emotions. This was a key element of the Method, which stressed using an actor's real-life experiences. "Turning trauma into drama" was a catch phrase. Strasberg liked to point out that Freud had begun his studies of the subconscious and dreams at the same time that Stanislavski was codifying his system for actors, linking an actor's physical behavior with his or her inner life and spirit. Jane hoped it would be possible to visualize her mother again and re-create some of the times she'd spent with her.

But analysis with a Freudian was an uphill battle. "It just does not work for me," she told Susan Strasberg. She simply could not remember anything.

Peter's memories were not as deeply buried. He didn't feel as guilty about their mother as Jane did, because he had run down to see her in answer to her call. But he was bitter about having been kept in the dark for so long. He said, "Every time I'd come up with a new bit of family life, which I should have known about and didn't, I'd have to deal with it right then and there without any help or explanation." One of his biggest fears (and one of Jane's, too) was that craziness might be inherited, and that "because my mother was bat-shit, I was going to be bat-shit, too."

He had decided to become an actor. He had left Omaha after four years and was living at the 74th Street brownstone. Sometimes he'd cue his father when he was memorizing his lines: "He'd pay me two bucks an hour. What a trip. Dad was so precise, so thoughtful when he worked. It was awesome to see how he created a role."

Peter had signed with the agent Stark Hesseltine of MCA. In the evenings, he hung out with Johnny Strasberg, Lee's son, and mingled freely with the celebrities at the nonstop parties the Strasbergs threw in their cavernous Central Park West apartment. Once he saw his sister, slender and ponytailed, sitting in a chair with her eyes half-closed while the Canadian actress Madeleine Sherwood, who was becoming a close friend, knelt beside her on the rug and massaged her bare feet. Their behavior seemed so intimate and private Peter didn't want to intrude. Mostly he poked around the vast Strasberg library. He estimated there must have been ten thousand books.

He'd been taking private classes with Strasberg, but he really wanted to be at the Actors Studio. "So I asked Lee at one point could I audition, and Lee said the main thing taught at the Studio is getting in touch with one's inner self. He told me my inner self was about to burst through my skin. I had to walk away from it, he said, I had to learn not to act. He suggested I see a psychiatrist, that in order to deal with the turmoil that was boiling under my skin, I had to deal with the root of the turmoil. I asked him how much would he charge for treatment? He loved that comment. 'Well, you do pretend to be a psychiatrist, Lee,' Paula said."

11

THAT SAME SPRING, Jane found herself thrown together more and more with Andreas Voutsinas. They ran into each other regularly at the Strasbergs' Sunday suppers, and they sat next to each other in Lee's class. His first impression of her: "Vassar girl, strong handshake, clear gaze. I thought, 'This is a girl who has no problems.' How wrong I was."

Jane had not forgotten the way he worked with her during rehearsals of *There Was a Little Girl*. Their connection had been very brief, but he seemed to be tuned in to her, and he was able to call attention to what needed to be done in a scene; it was a mysterious process but she felt he really did help center her. In class he commented on her work but kept his distance. She'd laugh when he tried to describe something in his fractured English, but she noticed that his eyes were beautiful and fringed with thick, dark lashes. He was slender; he sported a mustache. She'd heard he was very poor, but he dressed elegantly in expensive clothes. He often draped a black coat over his shoulders like a cape, which gave him an imperious air. Susan Strasberg said, "Andreas looked like Mephistopheles, an impression I'm sure he wanted to give."

At the moment, he was sharing a cramped apartment in Hell's Kitchen with several other actors. He supported himself by working part-time in the Garment District, in the office of a friend of his family. Nobody could figure out how he survived.

He'd been born in Khartoum, Sudan, in 1931, the only child of Greek parents. His father, Angelo, owned a spaghetti factory in Khartoum, but after it failed during World War II he moved the family back to Athens. From then on, Andreas's mother, Anastasia, was the main support of the family. Andreas always dreamed of being in the theater, of being an artist. "I wanted to perform! I wanted to show off! I loved costumes. And I knew I could design them. I loved to dance."

In his teens, he'd escaped to Paris, where he alternately performed in drag in a Left Bank café and trained, briefly, as a designer in couturier Jacques Fath's atelier. After returning to Athens, he had married and fathered a son, Marios. His wife, Diana, whom he eventually divorced, remained in Greece with the boy. In his early twenties, Andreas moved to London and won admission to the Old Vic Theatre School. After graduating in 1957, he headed to Stratford, Ontario, where he says he acted with James Mason in *Oedipus Rex*.

In 1958 he arrived in New York, where a fellow Greek, Elia Kazan, took him in hand and gave him a showy little part in the Broadway hit *J.B.,* for which Andreas received excellent reviews. Kazan also urged him to audition for the Actors Studio. When he was accepted, it was Kazan who introduced Andreas to Lee Strasberg. "Andreas immediately insinuated himself into Lee's inner circle," said Marty Fried. "He'd hang out with Lee and Marilyn and show up at the Strasberg apartment and ass-kiss all the other celebrities there. He was very aggressive." He also began directing and acting in Studio projects. He was especially impressive in scenes from *My Fair Lady,* playing the part of Pickering and singing with Anne Bancroft and Kevin McCarthy.

He soon began coaching actors and, said actress Linda Marsh, "he quickly gained a reputation as a magician when it came to molding raw talent." He taught Sandra Church how to do a striptease dance as part of her audition for the title role in *Gypsy;* when she won the part she gave Andreas an expensive suede jacket as a thank-you present. After that triumph he started coaching actors who wanted to audition for the Actors Studio. He had a talent for choosing material that showed off an actor's "quality." Indeed, what interested Jane about Andreas was that whenever he directed an actor in an audition for the Studio, the actor was invariably accepted. Thousands of performers auditioned for membership in that exclusive workshop where Method acting was defined, nurtured, and experimented with by the likes of Robert De Niro, Ellen Burstyn, and Kim Stanley; only a handful were accepted as members every year.

After a year of taking classes with Strasberg, Jane had not yet dared to audition for the Actors Studio, but she longed to become a member. She decided that if Andreas coached her, she would be accepted. Timmy warned her against it. "Stay away from Andreas," he told her. "He's a user." Andreas had already attached himself to the warm, earthy, exuberant Anne Bancroft, then giving a remarkable performance as Annie Sullivan in *The Miracle Worker*. Andreas had dinner with Bancroft most nights; he shopped for her; he answered her phone. Bancroft was newly famous and uncomfortable with celebrity, and Andreas ran interference for her. But he could be controlling. He disapproved of her romantic involvement with the comic Lenny Bruce — "He's treacherous" — and advised Bancroft to stop seeing the novelist Norman Mailer because "Norman was not worthy of her!"

After hearing these stories, Jane told Timmy, "Keep Andreas away from me. I don't want to be controlled like Anne Bancroft."

"I never controlled Annie," Andreas said. "We collaborated and we shared together. Jane couldn't figure out the emotional dynamic between us. Jane wanted to be controlled. She longed to be as great as Annie and she imagined I could help her. Annie was a stupendous star and a powerful woman. We were very, very close."

Sometimes Jane and Timmy would go to Downey's, a theatrical hangout on Eighth Avenue. She often saw Andreas and Anne squeezed together in a booth, laughing their heads off. They seemed so connected. She envied their intimacy.

Intimacy was not a feeling that she often experienced. Maybe she'd had it with Goey, but now she thought, at this time in her life, intimacy would be found in her intense work relationships. She had been thinking about having a coach ever since she saw how Marilyn Monroe responded to Paula Strasberg and how Paula fulfilled every need. Paula was her nursemaid. Lee was Monroe's surrogate father. Jane was greedy and wanted to have both. Timmy was too sensitive, too loving. She needed somebody to really take over her life.

Weeks went by, and Jane remained wary but intrigued by Andreas. He would flirt with her, come on to her, show her how to do her eye makeup, which he often used himself. He would tell her things she wanted to hear about herself; that she had the makings of a great star but she had to learn how to plumb the depths of her emotions, that she was "definitely not just Daddy's girl." Jeanne Fuchs, a dancer and one of Andreas's closest friends, added, "He was a homosexual preoccupied by women. He understood women's role-playing. He was — if you'll excuse the expression — a macho fag."

Andreas had kept his distance from Jane early on "because I was really caught up in my friendship with Annie. And then Annie met Mel Brooks, so I started spending more time with Jane. Annie was upset but not that upset. I disapproved of Mel and told her so, and she just laughed. And then to humor me we had this all-night discussion. I gave my reasons why I would be a better person for her to spend her life with. Then Mel, who was also present, made a terrific case for himself. Annie sat between us in a rocking chair, rocking back and forth and smiling that wonderful crooked smile of hers. At the end she just said, 'Look, Andreas. I'm in love with Mel. Okay? But you'll always be my friend.' We remained friends till she died."*

During the summer of 1960 Andreas spent more time with Jane, regaling her with extravagant stories of his days in Paris; his summer spent on a Greek island with Jean Cocteau and his young lover, the swashbuckling Jean Marais (the star of Cocteau's fantasy *Beauty and the Beast*). Marais played the Beast and "he fell in love with me," Andreas told her, and then he rambled on about his nights spent as a drag queen in New York, performing in a sequined jock strap.

"Jane knew I was gay," he went on, "and she knew I'd been married and had a son." He noticed when she listened to him that she seemed to relax and become another self, softer and more beautiful. He knew Lee was working with her, encouraging her to reveal her true self — to be authentic — but her façade remained impenetrable. "I thought it would be a challenge to help her break it down; I wasn't sure she was that talented."

Andreas asked her to play the lead in a comedy he was going to direct at the Westport Playhouse "with kids from our class." With some

---

* "Mel Brooks and I became friends, too," Andreas added. "He wrote a great part for me in his movie *The Producers*, which he was about to make with Zero Mostel." In *The Producers*, Andreas, clad entirely in black, is the companion of the flamboyantly gay director, Roger De Bris (played by Christopher Hewitt), who is recruited to direct the Broadway show *Springtime for Hitler*. "I asked Mel, 'How should I play this part?' and Mel said, 'You look like Rasputin and you act like Marilyn Monroe.'"

trepidation, Jane agreed. "I was surprised," Andreas said. "I thought I'd really have to work to convince her."

The play, entitled *No Concern of Mine* by Jeremy Kingston, which had had a three-month run in London, was about a group of aimless young people. "We had fun doing it," Geoffrey Horne, a cast member, said. "It started off as tremendously funny, but it deteriorated into a mediocre melodrama. Rehearsals got intense — a lot of clashing egos. Andreas would try to resolve things by throwing tantrums and screaming a lot. That was his style. He was vicious to the gay actors in the cast. I heard that a couple of them beat him up, they got so mad at him. Jane was upset by the way Andreas treated people — he'd pit one person against another. He'd say terrible things. But Jane never called him on it. At least not then."

She was working with her usual fanatical zeal, taking ballet classes every morning before rehearsal no matter how late she'd been up the night before; scribbling notes in the margins of her script; huddling with Andreas as often as she could while he pontificated about her character and motivation.

Horne recalled, "Andreas was directing Jane in a very deep way — a very personal way — bringing out sensitive areas in herself she hadn't known existed. It made her uncomfortable. He would ramble a lot, like Lee did. He could be sort of hypnotic — a lot of what he said was gobbledygook. But he had this ability to help you create specific behavior for a character. He wove his spell on Jane, and he tested her, too. Sometimes during a break he'd shout, 'Jane!' very imperiously. And she'd, like, jump to attention, and I knew he was getting to her."

Timmy often dropped by rehearsals, and at lunch break Jane would run into his arms and then they'd go back to her dressing room and lie naked together on a cot. They seemed very much in love. But no sooner had Timmy departed to star in a musical out of town than Warren Beatty began showing up backstage, and Jane would disappear with him for a while, and Warren would slip away and Jane would wander around flashing people. "You know — open up her robe and show some skin, then flip it closed," Geoffrey Horne said. "She was a tease." She seemed to need constant sexual approval.

Tom Hatcher, a cast member, said he'd drop by her dressing room and find her scrutinizing her reflection in the mirror. "She'd be wearing bikini panties, nothing else. Her figure was extraordinary—perfectly shaped breasts, flat, flat tummy, incredibly long legs. 'I love looking at my body,' she told me very seriously. 'But I hate my face.'" Like most bulimics, she was a perfectionist and she was working strenuously to make her body perfect; she even had a bar put up in her dressing room so she could do pliés.

Just before dress rehearsal, the stage manager reported to Andreas that he'd heard Jane vomiting in the john. What should he do? Was she sick? Should they call a doctor? Andreas said no.

Earlier that week he'd put his hand on her knee during rehearsal. "She was wearing shorts and her knee was wet. It reminded me of when I worked in a hospital in Athens after the war. Some of the vets I worked with were malnourished and they had water seeping out of their bodies. That's when I realized she had an eating disorder."

At the time he never discussed it with her. Bulimia was a taboo subject in those days, a shameful subject. Afdera, who came to see the show, knew that Jane was bulimic. "Because I was bulimic, too. You had to be, to get into those designer dresses. But we didn't talk about it. It may have been damaging to her health but she wasn't suffering yet. She was very thin—one hundred ten pounds—and she was five feet seven inches. But she looked fantastic."

No Concern of Mine ran only a week—it was summer stock—but the Westport Playhouse heavily promoted it and Jane got star billing. All the local newspapers reported on it. The *Danbury Times* described her portrayal of a drama student as "graceful and completely captivating."

In the fall of 1960, Jane bought a little apartment on West 55th Street, off Fifth Avenue. Andreas said, "I remember how surprised I was when she showed me the place. There was nothing in it, just a mattress on the floor." One of the first things they did together was to go up and down Third Avenue scouring antique shops. Soon the apartment was overflowing with Regency antique furniture, a four-poster bed canopied in gold satin, rococo mirrors, and leopard- and tiger-skin rugs. It was extravagant and overdone, very much in Andreas's taste.

Jane was proud of her new home. She wanted her father to see it but he disapproved of her attachment to Andreas, and he was busy campaigning for John F. Kennedy's run for the presidency. He made several speeches for him, written by John Steinbeck.

"It was a very exciting time for everybody," Afdera said. "Once or twice Jack and Jackie dropped by the house for a drink or we'd go to the Carlyle and have dinner with them. Jack was keyed up and curious about everything and he really listened to you. Jackie usually wore pastels. I am sure she was bulimic because she was so skinny. She had the most amazing mouth, with what seemed like rows of little sharp teeth!"

Afdera added, "I tried to get Jane to work for the Kennedy campaign but she was apolitical in those days; all she could think about was her career." Once she dropped by for tea when Lil Groueff, whose husband, Stefan, ran *Paris Match*, brought Jackie over to the house. But Jane was not that interested, and very soon she traipsed off saying she had to go to her ballet class.

She had decided to do another play on Broadway, *Invitation to a March*, written and directed by playwright Arthur Laurents, celebrated for *West Side Story* and *Gypsy*. He was also a well-known screenwriter who wrote *Rope* and later *The Way We Were*. In *Invitation* Jane played a privileged young college girl whose life is so boring she can barely stay awake. "She's a real Sleeping Beauty," she told Marty. "She's in a trance. She can't get out of her trance by herself; she has to wait for the prince to kiss her awake. That girl was me before I became an actress." Jane often seemed to be attempting to talk herself into existence, to describe a self that she hoped she could inhabit and become.

Initially she'd also been excited about doing the play because Andreas had been hired as Arthur Laurents's assistant. But the two men had a terrible fight, and Andreas was fired after a newspaper item implied that Andreas was really directing the play. After that, he was barred from rehearsals. Jane felt lost. There were other problems as well. The rambunctious blond star of the show, Shelley Winters, wouldn't stop complaining. At the first rehearsal Arthur Laurents read the play to the entire cast and Winters protested, "If a playwright does that he blocks an actor's creativity. He's trying to give us results on the first day." Although Jane said nothing, she disagreed; she'd enjoyed Laurents's reading hugely and had gotten a lot out of it.

But Winters didn't stop there. She was angry because although she had top billing, she thought her part wasn't large enough. She demanded more scenes, but Laurents didn't think more scenes were needed, and he also thought hers were dramatic and funny enough.

Winters continued her tirades throughout rehearsal and on the road in Cleveland, where she campaigned for Kennedy between matinee and evening performances, then mid-run she quit and was replaced by Celeste Holm.

By then Jane had allied herself with Madeleine Sherwood, the intense, petite Canadian actress who was playing her mother in the show. Soon they were holding hands backstage and were constantly trying out new little bits of business during run-throughs where they improvised on their relationship. Once during a performance Madeleine kissed Jane full on the mouth. Arthur Laurents objected, saying, "A mother doesn't kiss a daughter on the mouth." Madeleine recalled, "It was a gentle, loving kiss. We didn't slobber." Hatcher believed "it was Andreas's idea. He was coaching Jane after rehearsals. He wanted to make trouble." Later Jane defended herself. "I knew what I wanted to do with the role, but people in the production had other ideas and we lost the humanity of the girl."

Just before the show opened in Boston, she received word that Bridget Hayward, Brooke's younger sister, had killed herself just ten months after her mother, Margaret Sullavan, took her own life. The mother-daughter tragedy brought back Jane's own terrible memories of her mother slitting her throat, red blood all over, the screaming nightmares in her head. After Jane heard the news, she wasn't sure she could go on in the play. Arthur Laurents found her sobbing hysterically in her dressing room. "Are you afraid you might kill yourself, too?" he asked.

"Yeah — yeah, I am," she admitted. Years later she denied that she would ever commit suicide, "because life is too damn interesting and I think I am too important."

All the Fondas were affected by Bridget's death. They had watched her cycle throughout her childhood in and out of institutions for nervous disorders before she was finally diagnosed as an epileptic. She was beautiful and frail, and bore a striking resemblance to her mother. Peter had been in love with her at one time, but nothing ever came of their romance because in the early 1960s she was sent to Switzerland to be treated for one of her many illnesses.

When he heard the news, Peter was in New York and he hurried home. "My father said, 'Sit down and have a drink.' He hardly ever talked to me, so I couldn't understand why he wanted me to have a drink, but I sat down and he kept saying, 'Poor Leland, poor Leland.'" Bridget was dead from an overdose of pills and "I was falling thirteen floors to the ground and Dad is saying, 'Poor Leland'!"

Bridget's suicide had brought back all of Jane's own fears of going crazy like her mother. Months before, she'd run into Bridget on a train. She hadn't seen her in years. As fate would have it, Bridget was being treated at Riggs in Stockbridge, by the same doctor who'd treated Frances Fonda — Dr. Margaret Gibson.

Jane started asking Bridget questions about Riggs. Jane told Brooke later, "And [Bridget] said to me, 'The hardest part of all is coming out and having to deal with other people's problems; it's all I can do, it absorbs all of my energy to keep myself together — and when I'm out in the world, it's slightly more than I can bear.' Talking to her was like talking to someone through gauze, through heavy filters. There was the same attempt to reveal only the minimum that has to be revealed at a particular time: don't open those floodgates; don't let very much out; be calm as you can; don't rock the boat.

"And then we went back to her apartment, which absolutely shocked me because it was so conventional. I had enormous sadness . . . because it was as if somehow she'd sold out. . . . Somewhere along the way, Bridget was trying to fit into a mold that had nothing to do with her. Her spirit had nowhere else to go."

Jane felt so depressed about Bridget's suicide that she began pouring out her heart to her friends. During the weeks when *Invitation to a March* played out of town, she would go back to her hotel room after the show with Madeleine and Andreas and reminisce about her Hollywood childhood and her friendship with the Haywards. She talked throughout the night in an effort to understand what had happened to all of them. What had gone wrong? Jane described Bridget to Madeleine and Andreas as having "a certain kind of brilliance. A crazy brilliance, erratic, unique. I don't think society offers solutions for people like that, especially women. They are never provided with a constructive way of harnessing that kind of energy and brilliance. It turns inward and destroys them."

Then Madeleine countered with bizarre stories about her childhood in Canada: how from the age of seven on, her father, a dentist, had sexually molested her; his other act of sadism consisted of yanking out all of her lower teeth, "without anesthetic — it was agonizingly painful — see?" Madeleine would cry, and then she'd pull open her mouth and expose her naked pink gums.

"Madeleine told the story of her sexual molestation over and over again," Andreas said. "She held nothing back. After a breakdown in her early twenties, she escaped from a mental institution in Canada and came to New York, determined to be an actress. 'I knew if I could act I would survive,' she said."

She soon made an impact on Broadway in plays like *The Crucible* and *Cat on a Hot Tin Roof,* in which she played the vicious mother of the "no-necked monsters," a part she re-created on film, but she had mood swings. Periodically she would try to commit suicide and Andreas would pull her head out of the oven. "She kept on unraveling her anger and her pain," he said. "It was good for Jane to be around a woman like that, who wasn't afraid to declare herself a self. Madeleine's life force was stronger than her attraction to death. She helped Jane get through that very rough period after Bridget killed herself. She could talk and talk and talk to Madeleine, and Madeleine understood. We all became very close friends."

Madeleine said, "For Jane and me, acting was an escape ladder. We could exorcize our demons and not feel guilty about doing so."

During the out-of-town tryouts, in spite of all the anxiety and tears and panic, Jane triumphed. When she opened on Broadway at the Music Box in *Invitation to a March* in October 1960, her reviews were superlative. Walter Kerr called her "delectable." *Newsday* rhapsodized, "Here is the loveliest and most gifted of young actresses." Kenneth Tynan wrote in *The New Yorker,* "Jane Fonda quivers like a tuning fork. Her neurotic outbursts are as shocking as the wanton destruction of a priceless harpsichord."

Throughout the run of the show she remained in conflict with Arthur Laurents. She wanted to play the part differently, bringing other colors to it. "I was acting for others," she told Lillian Ross in a long *New Yorker* profile, which appeared while the show was running. "I was doing what they thought an audience wanted me to do. I wanted the humor to come out from the conflict in the girl, her struggle with herself and with her mother. Instead I had to do a funny poster of a girl."

The show ran for three months. As usual, Jane spent her free time taking ballet classes or working with Andreas on various projects. Sometimes Timmy would drop by the 55th Street apartment when Andreas wasn't there so they could talk. Jane was always glad to see him. "She was still the same frantic, neurotic girl I loved," he told Thomas Kiernan, "but there was something different about her now. Andreas was helping her get in touch with her power. He had a real hold over her."

Even so, she would often voice her ambivalence about Andreas. She admitted being afraid of his rages; he was excitable and critical and she couldn't fight back. "Don't let him get control of me," she'd plead to Timmy. But then in the next breath she'd turn around and praise Andreas to the skies. He seemed to know exactly what was best for her, whether it was a script or a new dress from Bergdorf's.

"I needed someone else to create my life. I felt more comfortable when I was with him; he could take charge," Jane said. "And as long as the creation was there, I could go off and, even if it were in my head, be me. Take that away — have me be on my own — it was no good. I didn't know who I was. I literally didn't know who or what I was."

Timmy, who was desperate at the thought of losing Jane, started drinking heavily. Over New Year's he insisted that he and Jane meet at her apartment to discuss the state of their relationship. He sounded so manic that Jane phoned Peter and asked him to come over so she wouldn't be alone with him. Peter thought Timmy was "a flake," so he agreed to come over. He arrived late in the evening. Jane gave him her bedroom while she and Timmy stayed in the living room on a foldout couch. A couple of hours later, Peter was awakened by a loud argument. The voices grew louder and more hysterical, and then he heard a scream and he rushed into the kitchen and found that Timmy had stabbed his hand with a butcher knife; there was blood all over.

Peter wanted to call Bellevue Hospital but Jane said absolutely not. She bound Timmy's hand with a dishcloth and took him in a cab to Roosevelt Hospital, where his hand was treated and he was released.

That was it for Jane. "She was finished with Timmy," Marty said. "No matter how much they had shared, she didn't want to have anything more to do with him. Jane was very cold when it came to kicking someone out of her life. Once she was finished, she was finished."*

Andreas said he waited until Jane had totally broken things off with Timmy. Then he moved in with her and took over. "I became nursemaid, lover, brother, father, and mentor," he said dramatically. "We were everything to each other. It's like a dream now. Part of me thought we would be together forever."

Jane's version of their time together is different: "Three years of depression and passivity on my part." She has never been able to talk about this part of her life easily because to her "it was so sad and so false. . . . Not that there weren't happy times, but pain engraves a deeper memory."

She had never lived with a man full-time before, so she had a lot of adjusting to do. She was self-conscious, especially when she realized he was watching her, studying her assiduously as she walked naked from the canopied bed into the bathroom. "I couldn't help myself," he said. "She was so beautiful nude — perfectly proportioned, smooth, tawny skin. I began thinking: that body is part of what will make her a great star — her body, plus her sexuality."

In the morning she was always in a terrible mood, grumpy and depressed. "Years afterwards, when she was with Vadim, she told me, 'He's so cross in the mornings so I wake up and make some coffee and then he's fine.' And I said, 'I used to do that for you, don't you remember?' And she shook her head no."

They were busy all day long; Andreas fielded her phone calls, organized her schedule — ballet, auditions. He would cut and style her hair, he would do her makeup, and he would help her choose her clothes. Sometimes they would read scripts together out loud. Or they would

---

* Timmy went on to shine as a dancer in the movie *The Music Man* with Robert Preston, and he was also in the Broadway show *Marathon* with Julie Harris. "Timmy was a unique dancer, a great dancer," said his last girlfriend, Barbara Flood. "He danced with his heart and his soul." He also acted in a number of TV shows, including *Naked City*. But he never got over Jane, and he began to drink and take pills. He died of a heart attack in 1977.

riffle through magazines, tearing out photographs of women whose looks and styles they admired: Katharine Hepburn, Bette Davis, Ingrid Bergman. "I wanted Jane to learn how to present herself to the world," Andreas said.

Whenever they were scheduled to show up at a premiere or a benefit, Jane would panic. She would get a splitting headache or she would vomit. During this period she was terrified of appearing in public. She would try on all sorts of outfits—a strapless gown, a black cocktail sheath. Should she wear her hair up or down? She and Andreas would argue about her appearance for hours. Finally he would convince her to wear a brocade suit and accessorize it with her mother's jewels. She would study her reflection in the mirror and calm down.

To relax they would dance around the apartment to music. "Jane was a wonderful dancer," said Andreas. "I was pretty good myself, but she would hate it if I got an erection while we were dancing, but I couldn't help it. Oh, yes, we had sex. I don't think Jane enjoyed sex or maybe she just didn't enjoy sex with me. Of course she knew I was gay, but we didn't talk about it. But we did sleep together every night with our arms around each other."

Madeleine said, "Jane was unhappy because she and Andreas couldn't make love. They tried, but it usually didn't work. And sometimes he would go off to the docks, and she knew that. Jane had other lovers, but nobody knew who they were. She never discussed her love life with anyone."

"Up to a point we led separate lives," Andreas said. "She would go out on dates; I didn't know who the other men were." He added, "But I always knew when she was going to be with her father because she'd dress a certain way—very polished and put-together. The clean hanky in her purse, white gloves sort of thing. I was trying to get her to break the umbilical cord. But that was impossible. Jane was totally hung up on her father."

Whenever she'd come back from seeing her father, she and Andreas would have a fight "because I knew he was trying to break us up by innuendo." But mostly they fought about her bulimia. "I wanted her to stop; it was so dangerous for her."

Jane would read cookbooks from cover to cover. "Bulimics do that to torture themselves," Andreas said. Sometimes when they were together she'd prepare a huge meal and ask Andreas to share it with her.

He'd say no and she'd start to cry; she didn't want to eat it all by herself. She'd cry and cry and then she'd start binging.

He witnessed her gorging only once, "and that was enough. I watched Jane consume three roast chickens, a couple of Sara Lee cheesecakes, a loaf of cheap white bread. She literally stuffed her face with food, gagging, then eating; then she rammed her knuckles down her throat and scraped the skin off. Her doctor warned her that ultimately she'd go deaf if she kept on binging and purging, that it would wreak havoc on her body, her stomach lining, her stomach muscles, that she might not be able to get pregnant."

Andreas started reading up on bulimia so he could understand the addiction. He discovered that while a world of change and conflict rages around her, the bulimic takes refuge in the bulimia. It's easier to cope with food, calories, dress sizes. It's a dangerous form of coping because it becomes increasingly addictive. "And then there's this other thing I learned," Andreas said, "that often the bulimic is trying to model her life after her father! Not her mother. Bulimia is a rejection of the female body, an actual cultural rejection of the female body. I read it in a bulletin from the University of Cincinnati. In effect, bulimia is a denial of womanhood!"

Watching Jane, Andreas came to understand that bulimia is a powerful addiction — as powerful as drugs or booze and an even more difficult habit to break. "So I rarely left her side. Whenever we ate in a restaurant, she'd always excuse herself at the end of the meal. I'd follow her into the john, march right into the ladies' room, and say very grandly to the attendant, 'Miss Fonda has forgotten her lipstick so I must give it to her!' So Jane wouldn't be able to vomit her lunch."

He believes the bulimia wasn't quite as intense as long as they lived together. "Of course she compensated by keeping frenetically active — that's what bulimics do. She'd take ballet and jazz classes four hours a day, then we'd go to a movie and then go to Lee's class."

Early in the spring of 1960, Jane decided she wanted to do a private moment in Lee's class about her bulimia. The private moment is a Strasberg specialty; it's his most controversial and misunderstood exercise. Detractors believe it's self-indulgent and self-exhibitionist, but it has many admirers, such as Ellen Burstyn, Anne Bancroft, and Al Pacino. It's an exercise that helps the actor achieve deeper levels of concentration onstage. Most beginning actors are self-conscious and

inhibited by an audience. They can overcome their inhibitions by en-
acting a moment of real privacy in front of people. The end result can
be liberating.

"For Jane it was an unbelievably gutsy thing to do, but that's what
Jane is about," Andreas said. "I will never forget it."

The classroom was packed the afternoon she performed her private
moment. Marty said, "Everyone was waiting for Jane Fonda to fall on
her ass. At first she seemed really tense. She was actually trembling.
She could hardly move. Then she got caught up in what she was doing
and she relaxed and opened up. Her concentration was phenomenal.
You couldn't stop watching her. It was like she was carrying her own
spotlight."

Nobody knew what she was doing, but you could have heard a pin
drop when she covered a rickety ballroom chair with newspapers (in
the private moment exercise the actor must create the surroundings
in which he or she feels securely alone). Later some of the students
guessed the chair was a toilet and the whole exercise had something
to do with her eating disorder. (One student, Hildy Brooks, recalled
"hearing her vomit in the john in the hall. We knew what that meant.
We were all trying to keep our weight down, and we had various ways
of doing it.")

With her back to the audience, Jane proceeded to move around the
stage, around and around. She did not utter a sound. She'd occasionally stop abruptly and stretch her arms beseechingly to the ceiling, then
continue to pace like an animal — around and around the toilet-chair.

Her private moment took no more than five or six minutes at the
most, but the minutes seemed like hours. Marty remembered thinking, "She's gonna heave into that chair." But instead she stopped and
whirled around to face the class, her cheeks deathly white and glistening with sweat. She did not say a word, but her expression registered
disgust, helplessness, and panic, something all bulimics must feel.

Staring beseechingly at Strasberg, she crumpled to the stage in a
heap and waited for his reaction.

"Very good, darling," Strasberg said finally. He seemed nonplussed.

"But Lee — didn't you want me to — ?"

Strasberg raised a finger to his lips and repeated, as he always did,
his definition of the private moment. "The private moment is of use
only to the actor, not to the observer. The actor is dealing with some-

thing so private we almost feel we shouldn't be watching. And you achieved that. However, you have big problems with tension. When your tensions are relieved, you will get a real sense of yourself."

When they left class, Jane was drooping on Andreas's shoulder. She was exhausted. "I took her home and she went straight to bed and slept for fourteen hours."

The private moment didn't stop the bulimia. She continued to binge and purge for the next thirteen years. But she'd proved something to herself that day: that she could at least express her frustration about it, openly, in front of an audience.

12

THE FIRST MONTH they were together, she and Andreas concentrated on her final audition for the Actors Studio. At that point the Studio was the most influential workshop in America. Although Elia Kazan's involvement was minimal now, even Lee Strasberg acknowledged that the reputation of the Studio had been made not by him, but by Kazan — one of the founders — and his distinctive casting of Studio members in his movies: James Dean and Jo Van Fleet in *East of Eden*, Marlon Brando and Eva Marie Saint in *On the Waterfront*, Eli Wallach and Carroll Baker in *Baby Doll*. By 1961, Kazan was still a controversial figure: bold but self-doubting; beloved, yet reviled for "naming names" before the House Un-American Activities Committee. He remained a force to be reckoned with in both theater and film. He had returned to the Studio because he and his wife, Molly, were organizing a playwright and directors unit there. Whenever he attended a session at the Studio, a ripple of excitement filled the air.

Hundreds of actors auditioned for the Studio every year. The standard procedure for admission, which was open to any and all aspirants over eighteen years of age, was to prepare a five-minute scene with a partner. Contemporary material was preferred, something that would show the actor's quality, and that would be easy and simple.

Jane had passed her preliminary audition. She was one of twelve actors out of a thousand who were now about to take their finals. She was determined to get in.

Andreas had chosen a scene from *Butterfield 8*. "I played the lover, the Eddie Fisher part. Jane played the high-class call girl, a blond version of Liz Taylor, who won the Oscar for her performance as Gloria Wandress," Andreas said.

Henry Fonda couldn't fathom why his daughter would be playing a "bad girl" instead of a part "more suitable to her character." Why not Tracy Lord, the epitome of class and breeding in *The Philadelphia Story*? Jane explained that she identified with Gloria's guilt and desperation — not her lifestyle, but her off-the-wall emotions.

"Good and bad are not so much opposites as different kinds of intensity," Andreas had told her. "Women are much more interesting when there is something not quite right about them, when something is off-kilter."

During rehearsals of *Butterfield 8*, Andreas behaved like a dictator; at breaks he would experiment endlessly with makeup and hairstyles. As the date of the audition drew near, he became overwrought because he was also auditioning with someone else that same night. He'd agreed to act with Linda Marsh, a serenely beautiful young actress with long, dark hair and huge, black, melancholy eyes. She would later play Ophelia opposite Richard Burton's Hamlet.

Jane didn't especially like the idea that Andreas was auditioning with someone else while working with her on her audition, but there was nothing she could do. She adjusted to it and he assured her that she was his top priority.

The night of the Actors Studio audition, in January of 1961, Andreas dressed her carefully in a beautiful white satin slip that showed off the curves of her body. Jane borrowed a mink coat from one of her stepmothers to drape over her shoulders. The coat was a key detail in the scene. Gloria had stolen the coat, which belonged to the wife of one of her customers, and she was not going to give it back.

Before they left the apartment, Andreas lit yet another cigarette for Jane and noticed that her fingernails were chewed to the quick. He insisted that she glue false ones on (they kept popping off during the scene but no one paid attention). They were late — it was freezing outside and they had a very hard time finding a cab — so when they reached the Studio they were panting.

Small groups of actors milled about the Studio waiting room. A few huddled in corners, mouthing lines or trying to prepare. One actor kept running around and around the block "to work off excess energy." He was pouring sweat.

Jane's name was called almost immediately, and she and Andreas hurried up the steep steps to the dark cave that was the Studio's theater. The stage was pitch black, save for one harsh spotlight. They knew they were going to be judged by Lee Strasberg, producer Cheryl Crawford, and the legendary director Elia Kazan. The experience was even more nerve-racking because the actors were timed by a stopwatch. They had five minutes to prove their talents. All Jane could think about as she walked across the stage was that Marilyn Monroe had acted in *Anna Christie* in this very same space and she'd been described as "iridescent." Jane hoped she was going to be iridescent, too.

She watched as Andreas set up the props: two chairs, a little table complete with a checkered tablecloth, a wine bottle, and two goblets. The scene took place in a restaurant and ended in an argument, with Gloria attempting to slit her wrists. Andreas had staged it in such a way that Jane would be facing the audience and he would be feeding her the lines from the side, so she would be the focus of attention. But in the middle of the scene, Jane unexpectedly turned away from the audience and smashed a goblet. Then she took a shard of glass between her fingertips and raised it to her throat as if she were about to slash it. She had never done this in rehearsal. Andreas recalled thinking, "What in God's name is she doing?" He darted center stage, grabbed her wrist, and carefully took the glass shard from her — otherwise she could have been badly cut — and placed it on the table. Then he hugged her tightly (this hadn't happened in rehearsal either), and they began rocking back and forth, breathing loudly, the dialogue forgotten. It was visceral, frightening, and hugely theatrical, and both actors, but especially Jane, revealed a spectrum of emotions.

When the judges called, "Time's up!" she gave a little moan; her body was quivering. Then she peered into the darkness, expectant, waiting. She believed she had passed. The reaction from the judges was palpable. In fact, Kazan leaped into the spotlight to congratulate her. "I always thought Jane Fonda was an interesting theater personality," he said, but "seeing her that night made me realize she had something special."

With that, Jane ran out of the theater, and Linda Marsh joined Andreas on the stage to set up her props. "It was the hardest thing I have ever had to do — audition with someone else after what had happened with Jane." But within minutes he and Linda were going through their paces with a scene from *The Dud Avocado.*

Linda recalled that Andreas was selfless. "I think that's why so many actors he worked with got into the Studio. He always put himself in the background, just feeding me the dialogue. I passed my audition that night, too." She adds that she never heard anything about the drama behind Jane's audition. "Studio work was always very private. It was like the Vatican — a secret. We worked on everything in secret."

Meanwhile, Andreas raced off to join Jane at her apartment. A little party was already in progress. Madeleine Sherwood had arrived with Gene Wilder and his wife, Mary; Susan Strasberg came with Marty Fried, who'd operated the lights at the Studio auditions. He kidded about the false nails popping off in the scene. "You really used that," he joked, then he added he thought Jane had been terrific, very intense, very real. Another guest, Jeanne Fuchs, said, "We all drank champagne and toasted Jane. She was elated."

But Andreas was ashen; soon he pulled Jeanne into the kitchen to describe what had happened during the audition, that Jane had started to slit her throat. It hadn't been part of the scene and she wasn't acting, but where had that violent gesture come from? He didn't know what she was doing or thinking or feeling, but it had been mysterious and terrifying. Now he and Jeanne both watched Jane laughing and drinking in the living room with her guests. Her head was thrown back, her thick hair tumbling about her face. Her expression was animated. She was giving a different kind of performance, the gracious, brittle, elegant hostess.

The following morning Andreas asked her if she remembered anything about the audition and she shook her head. He didn't pursue the subject. Then she referred almost casually to her mother's suicide. She remarked that she had discovered her body after going to the sanatorium on her mom's forty-second birthday, carrying a big bunch of flowers. When she walked into the room, "there was mother, lying in a pool of blood."

It was the first time that Jane had ever mentioned her mother's suicide to Andreas. As soon as he could, he phoned her grandmother Sophie Seymour, and she filled him in on the terrible tragedy: how Frances Fonda had slit her throat from ear to ear with a razor at the sanatorium in Beacon, not long after she had learned her husband, Henry, was in love with another woman. "Of course Jane hadn't found her mother; that was a lie," Andreas said. "But obviously she'd wanted to find her mother, to save her mother, maybe even exorcise her mother in that audition."

Bit by bit, Jane opened up to Andreas as she had with Timmy Everett, telling him how numb she'd felt after learning of her mother's death, how she'd laughed. And now how afraid she was she might go mad, like her mother. "She thought the madness might be inherited. After all, her Grandfather Seymour was, to say the least, very unstable.

"Yes, I think Jane considered killing herself," Andreas said. "We slept in the same bed and she would talk in her sleep. She had many nightmares, and in the nightmares her voice sounded almost subhuman, like another person. It was a hoarse, monster voice."

As soon as Jane was accepted as a lifetime member of the Actors Studio, she began attending sessions as often as she could in the battered former Greek Revival church building on West 44th Street in the heart of the Theater District right off Times Square.

The Eisenhower era of repression had just ended and the glittery Kennedy epoch, with its sense of promise and excitement, had begun. American life was changing, but Jane wasn't thinking about that. She was focused on herself and her career.

It was the last of the "golden years" on Broadway. There were distinctive productions up and down the Great White Way, including James Agee's *All the Way Home;* there were prizewinning musicals like *How to Succeed in Business* and *Camelot.* Once *Camelot*'s star, Richard Burton, staggered into the Studio, bleary-eyed and hung-over. Standing downstairs, he recited poetry to anyone who would listen.

Burton was just a tiny part of the heady, creative mix that made the Studio so charged and volatile for Jane. So many varied talents and temperaments crammed together in that brick-walled theater on the second floor, everybody quivering with ambition and the huge desire to become somebody: an artist, a star, a legend.

Where else could you hear Anne Bancroft warbling a song from *My Fair Lady,* Edward Albee presenting *The Zoo Story,* or Tennessee Williams experimenting with *The Night of the Iguana?* Al Pacino could be working on *The Iceman Cometh* and *Hamlet.* While Jane was attending sessions some remarkable work was done: Patricia Neal playing Juliet with Shelley Winters as the nurse; Gene Saks and Gene Wilder regaling everybody with Noel Coward's comedies. Geraldine Page's acting was so bravura as Electra, her performance convinced Kazan to cast her in *Sweet Bird of Youth*.

Strasberg would arrive promptly at 11:00 A.M. every Tuesday and Friday. The theater would be packed, and all talk would cease as he sat down in a camp chair with a painted "Lee" sign on it. He would have his mug of tea, his white metal alarm clock nearby, a pencil, and file cards with the names of the scenes noted on them. Next to him would be a mike and a tape recorder, taking down his voice for posterity.

He would orchestrate every session with witty polemics, a touch of therapy, and some wry philosophy. He could be verbal, outgoing, and witty. He would cajole actors to contact their innermost feelings and express themselves without fear. "Are you a human being?" he would demand. "Then just get up and act like a human being. Don't complicate things."

He was best when dealing with such singular talents as Anne Bancroft, Geraldine Page, Kim Stanley, and Al Pacino. He had the ability to pinpoint exactly what they should be doing with their particular gifts, and his stern manner made them all want to do their best to please him.

So Jane rarely missed the Tuesday and Friday sessions. She and Andreas would hurry to the same seats — front row, stage left — of the crowded Studio theater. Jane was perpetually running out of cigarettes. Someone would hand her a Pall Mall and she'd whisper, "Thank you vurry, vurry much." She had a beautiful, very grown-up speaking voice, supple and mellifluous, with impeccable diction. Sometimes she'd arrange her lustrous honey-blond hair in a French twist, and sometimes she'd let it hang to her shoulders like Alice in Wonderland. Her ballet dancer's posture was amazing — ramrod straight like a soldier's.

Her long, sad face was an exact replica of her father's: the chiseled profile; the clear, steady gaze; the aloofness. She had even picked up one of her father's characteristic gestures, his way of pushing his lips up with a long, attenuated finger; Jane did it when thinking of something.

"If she'd been Jane Doe, nobody would have given her a second thought," actress Collin Wilcox said. "But because of who she was, people sucked up to her, but they still hoped that she'd fail." But she didn't fail, and everyone soon became aware of her steely discipline and her will to succeed. She auditioned for all the plays on Broadway that she was right for, and she made five movies while attending the Studio, including *Walk on the Wild Side,* in which she played a ferocious barefoot hooker.

Lee Strasberg believed she would become the Studio's next celebrity actress, his latest admired creation. So, bit by bit, she became part of his extended family like Marilyn. She and Andreas would attend the open house every Sunday; they would sit at the big table in the kitchen along with Kim Novak and Isaac Stern, listening to Lee talk about the genius of Orson Welles and how great Laurette Taylor was and how Gary Cooper, John Wayne, and Spencer Tracy — and yes, Henry Fonda — who try not to act, but react as themselves, were natural exponents of the Method.

Jane would also attend Lee's luncheons at Sardi's, along with members of his inner circle, which included Marilyn, Madeleine, Shelley Winters, and Marty.

Jane was at the lunch the day that Marilyn contributed $10,000 for Lee and Paula to travel to Russia for a Stanislavski festival. Word came that Paula's visa had come through, but to make the plane she had to leave right from Sardi's, so the group quickly stripped themselves to outfit her. In Jane's fur-lined boots, Shelley's oversize coat with the skunk wrap, and Marilyn's hat, Paula clambered into a cab to take the Soviet Union by storm; Lee followed on another flight.

13

AFTER SHE BECAME a member of the Actors Studio, Jane was still uncertain as to what to do next—a play or a movie? There was one obstacle: her contract with Josh Logan. He literally owned her, and he'd been capitalizing on her as a commodity, loaning her out to various producers and pocketing her acting fees; he paid her $10,000 a year plus expenses.

During the run of *Invitation* she went to him as a friend and asked to be released from her contract. He said no, and he told her he'd just received an offer from Ray Stark to buy her contract from him for $250,000. She asked him again if he would release her. Again he said no, so she decided to take legal action to buy him out. Andreas was encouraging her.

Logan didn't take the negotiations seriously. He'd known Jane since she was a baby; her father was his best friend. He went on loaning her out to other producers; there were a lot of them who wanted to hitch onto her rising star.

In March 1961 he loaned her out for two movies, both of them riddled with script and cast problems. The first was based on Nelson Algren's steamy melodramatic novel *Walk on the Wild Side*. Jane was cast as Kitty Twist, a fast-talking prostitute who ends up in a whorehouse run by a lesbian madam, played by Barbara Stanwyck. Jane was eager to do the part because she thought it would help change her virginal image.

She brought Andreas on location to New Orleans as her coach; the entire cast and crew disliked him and his arrogance, but Jane seemed totally in his thrall and did everything he told her to do while she was filming the movie, including soaking her already tight dress in water so it clung to her hips and bottom; at his suggestion she also wore no panties. Jane's costar, the suave English actor Laurence Harvey, called her an "exhibitionist" and said Andreas Voutsinas was a "creep." Egged on by Andreas, Jane began making outrageous statements such as "Hollywood is run by morons." Gossip columnist Sidney Skolsky visited the set and watched her filming a fight scene with another actress. Jane went all out, bloodying the actress's nose, and the actress ran off crying. That was exactly what Andreas wanted, a different image for Jane that would attract a lot of publicity.

In the evenings, they attended the rushes. The camera always seemed to be moving, the soundtrack crowded with voices and natural sounds. As her image rolled across the screen, Jane thought that she was working much too hard, throwing herself into the part with a kind of desperate voraciousness. She sounded shrill and forced and her eye makeup made her resemble an Abyssinian cat. But she kept her thoughts to herself. Andreas had designed the makeup and occasionally wore it too.

The second fiasco Logan loaned Jane out to was *The Chapman Report*, George Cukor's version of Irving Wallace's racy bestseller exploring the lives of four typical American women who volunteer for a sex survey. Andreas stressed to her that in order to be a big star, she must play roles that exuded sexuality. So they decided she should audition for the role of the nymphomaniac, and she showed up at the audition decked out in a low-cut dress reminiscent of what she'd worn as Kitty Twist. "Cukor laughed at me," Jane said. "He explained he'd already cast Claire Bloom as the nympho. He wanted me to play the frigid widow. But I think if I'd have gone in my frigid widow makeup and costume he wouldn't have hired me." Jane accepted the role, because she wanted very much to work with Cukor, who'd shaped the careers of Greta Garbo, Audrey Hepburn, and Judy Garland.

During filming, Cukor was unfailingly gracious. He told Jane that he believed movies were primarily an actor's medium, not a director's. His function was more of a critic, he said, "pointing out excesses and encouraging the actor's best instincts to emerge." He wouldn't allow Andreas on the set, and he shot take after take of Jane, especially the close-ups. He kept repeating, "Do nothing with your face, nothing."

One Sunday Cukor invited her to lunch at his house. He lived in the

Hollywood Hills above Sunset Strip, surrounded by beautiful gardens, and as she was getting out of the taxi she wondered if her father had ever seen them. After being given a tour of the place, she was served a light lunch in a dimly lit, beautifully furnished living room with a Rouault painting glowing on one wall. Over coffee Cukor told her, "I've let you do certain things now onscreen that if you did them three years from now, I'd knock your teeth in." She realized he was teaching her discipline as an actress and showing her how to play in front of a camera and get the most out of a character.

Cukor commented to reporter Al Aronowitz, "She overacts. I think the only thing she has to watch is that she has such an abundance of talent she must learn how to hold it in."

Soon after filming ended, in May of 1961, the French director Roger Vadim arrived in Los Angeles to promote his new movie, *Liaisons Dangereuses,* and asked to meet with Jane about a project. Jane's agent, Dick Clayton, told her to "dress sexy" to impress the man who had discovered Bardot. Instead Jane appeared at the Beverly Wilshire Hotel coffee shop wearing a man's shirt, jeans, and no makeup.

She was terrified about being alone with Vadim. "I thought he might rape me. I was really put off by his reputation as the great seducer." However, he was gentle and polite and spoke so quietly and seemed so protective of her that she thought, "Oh, boy, is he putting on a clever act." Vadim had sad hound-dog eyes, and he seemed to be fighting depression; he reminded her a bit of her father. The project he told her about sounded so vague it went right out of her mind; they ended up talking about movies and books. Still, after the meeting, she told Clayton that under no circumstances would she ever work with Vadim.

Between films, she was posing for photographers: Richard Avedon, Irving Penn, Tom Palumbo, Jerry Schatzberg, Philippe Halsman. She posed for fashion layouts, movie publicity stills, fan magazines, *Life,* and *Look.* She posed in bathing suits, evening gowns, chic little suits and great hats, lingerie, and bathrobes. Andreas always did her makeup and hair. Often she wore wigs. Her face ran the gamut from Hollywood sexpot to all-American girl — radiant, toothy, vacuous. In some portraits she appears almost mythic, and one is reminded of the old 1930s photographs of movie stars who were objects of physical perfection, glazed and glistening and totally inanimate.

In candid pictures taken by friends, such as Geoffrey Horne, Dennis Hopper, and Jeff Bridges, one catches a different side of Jane — sad, wistful, vulnerable, her eyes watchful and anxious.

She had begun keeping a scrapbook of her photographs and clippings. She enjoyed being famous, and she enjoyed the attention she was getting from photographers and reporters, who clamored for interviews, and from near-strangers who stopped her at her local health food shop on West 57th Street, where she was buying figs, to ask for autographs. "I like fame," she told Collin Wilcox. "I like being famous. My father always hated it."

She had been appearing on TV shows such as *What's My Line* and *Person to Person,* where she popped bubblegum off camera and her senses seemed to be whirring as she explained to Edward R. Murrow what it was like to decorate her own apartment.

Encouraged by Andreas, Jane was sounding off to the press about her "phony life at Tigertail" when she was growing up, and she ridiculed her father's marriage record: "Any man who is 57 years old and has gone through four wives must be very unhappy." She suggested he go to a shrink, and she carped about her brother's politics, too — he had just registered as a Republican.

Peter shot back to a reporter immediately, "My sister's going to self-destruct." As for Hank Fonda, he told the *Saturday Evening Post*, "I'm between planes somewhere, and someone recognizes me, and he has a clipping that says 'Jane Fonda thinks her parents have led a phony life,' or that 'she thinks her father should have been psychoanalyzed 35 years ago.' It's all right for her to think it, if that's what she thinks. But it's not all right for her to say so in interviews. After all I'm her father. It's *disrespectful.* And we didn't lead a phony life. That's the thing I tried most to avoid. I felt we were having a wonderful, normal life growing up with Peter and Jane."

As usual, the Fondas were unable to communicate with each other directly, so they used the media to express their personal feelings. As the years went on, their quotes and stories multiplied as they insulted each other, baited each other, and sometimes tried to seduce each other through the press, depending on what was happening between them. The public ate it up.

Like most movie stars, Hank Fonda suffered from self-absorption, but it made him pull back and try to be private, whereas Jane's egotism expressed itself in a different way. She wanted to be the center of attention. She wanted to be *visible;* it would be a driving force in her life.

Sometimes at night, when Andreas was out, Jane would phone actor Tom Hatcher and say, "I've just taken a Valium; talk to me while I fall asleep." So they would have a long conversation. "I liked Jane," said Hatcher, "but she was so driven, she reminded me of Streisand. She had an absolute craving for fame. I once asked her, 'What about celebrities like Garbo and Salinger who hide?' Jane said, 'That's no fun.' She wanted to be famous much more than she wanted to be a great actress. She dreamed about becoming one of the most famous people in the world. She talked about fame all the time."

In 1961, Jane was instinctively starting to focus on her celebrity, just as the definition of celebrity was changing. That year in his book *The Image,* historian Daniel Boorstin defined "the celebrity" as someone who is "famous for being well-known."

In point of fact, when Jane was growing up in the 1930s, the word *celebrity* was rarely used in print. Most people one read about were described as "famous" or "successful." If they were both, as in Henry Fonda's case, it was because of their achievements.

The same rules applied to other public figures from earlier in the twentieth century, like the inventor Thomas Edison, or the tycoon Andrew Carnegie. In the 1920s and 1930s, publisher William Randolph Hearst began to capitalize on personalities with a vengeance in his tabloids, using photographs to highlight the exploits of Charles Lindbergh, Babe Ruth, and John Dillinger.

Throughout the forties and fifties, Jane watched her father representing his best self in the "goldfish bowl" environment that was Hollywood. He was promoted and protected by his loyal press agent, John Springer, a decent, self-effacing man who worked closely with gossip columnists like Hedda Hopper and Walter Winchell to build up the image of Fonda as the quintessential "American."

By the 1960s, magazines like *Life* and *Look,* radio, and TV were conspiring to build up Jane's image. It was a time of great cultural flux, especially with the rise of the mass media and public fascination with "human entertainment." John and Jackie Kennedy were the newest celebrities. Everything they did in and out of the White House was watched and written about. Then there was Brando, a new sort of culture hero, striving in his ambitions but self-destructive, longing for a kind of transcendence; and the same was true for Marilyn Monroe, who was watched avidly as a kind of show biz victim—the dumb blond bimbo, the sweet lost girl who'd been married to baseball player Joe DiMaggio, another great celebrity, and then to playwright Arthur Miller, a cultural icon.

Marilyn Monroe was not the first star to become a sex symbol or a legend, but she was one of the stars Jane Fonda revered. Jane still had a long way to go before she became a legend herself, an icon emblematic of our culture as she transformed herself into different personas. Her shifting images would become projections of precise social moments. Women's roles were changing drastically, and Jane's life would reflect this.

When the photographer Peter Basch came to her with the idea of being photographed in various well-known movie roles as seen by various movie directors such as Howard Hawks and Roger Vadim, Jane jumped at the chance; it was a great publicity gimmick. She and Andreas worked for weeks on the layout. "It was a huge production—all sorts of costumes, wigs, makeup, locations," Andreas said. The photographs were subsequently published in *Cavalier* magazine.

Basch remembered how "remarkable Jane was. She was seductive, funny, teasing, almost spoofing the pinup. She kept checking her reflection in the mirror. The mirror seemed to confirm the excitement and allure Andreas and I were seeing in her, but she was hypercritical of the way she looked. I got the feeling she was trying on all these disguises, hoping she might find some identity that would fit her. . . . But as far as I was concerned, she was, at the time, a gorgeous empty vessel."

In one shot Jane was photographed half-naked as the betraying woman in *Liaisons Dangereuses*. "You could actually see the curve of her beautiful little ass, complete with pink birthmark," Andreas said. When Henry Fonda heard about the feature, he tried to get it pulled by his press agents, but Jane insisted it be published.

Richard Avedon photographed her bare-breasted for *Vogue*, as he had Baby Jane Holzer, a New York socialite. It was a stunning black-and-white close-up of Jane, wet-lipped and tousle-haired. "She did it to bug her father, but she was in a panic about it," Andreas said, "and

I was in a panic for her." This time her father put pressure on *Vogue* editor Diana Vreeland and the portrait was killed. Avedon gave Jane sheets of tiny contact prints as souvenirs. She burned all the prints except for two, one of which she gave to Lee Strasberg. Andreas kept the other one.

Reporters like Hedda Hopper, who interviewed her in 1961, were "marveling at Jane Fonda's transformation. She's no longer the scrubbed, shy little ingénue of *Tall Story*—she is poised, alert, with great warmth. Her piercing eyes have a refreshing honesty."

But James Bacon, in his column for the Associated Press, said that "Fonda's eyes are very troubled eyes, more troubled than when I interviewed her two years ago."

Frequently, she would come home exhausted from posing for photographers and fret about her "fat ankles." So Andreas taught her ankle exercises, and he periodically bound her ankles in athletic bandages soaked in brine. When the bandages dried, Jane would cry out in pain, but eventually, according to Shelley Winters, it worked. The ankles thinned. But she always felt self-conscious about them. To this day, she invariably wears boots, slacks, long skirts. Even during the minidress craze, Jane would always wear thigh-high boots. "It's ridiculous when you think about it," Andreas said, "because she actually had long, slender, gorgeous legs, and her ankles weren't that fat."

Obsessed as she was with her appearance, Jane was equally obsessed with money. At age twenty-four she knew vaguely that she had quite a lot—lawyers always doled out a generous allowance. "I didn't know how rich Jane was until I moved in with her," Andreas said. "At some point she got hysterical because she didn't think she had any more money in the bank. I went over her accounts and discovered she had all sorts of different accounts. Her mother had left a modest fortune to be divided equally between the three children, so Jane was quite a rich young woman and this freed her from the kinds of pressures most actresses have. She never had to worry about anything. She eventually did learn about her accounts and investments and she kept track of everything." Jane was extremely generous to her friends, especially friends in need, and to people who worked for her. But she never stopped worrying about having enough money.

She may have inherited that feeling from her father, who was always fretting that he didn't have enough in the bank. Work energized him and kept him young—but one of the main reasons he never stopped working was that he was terrified he might not have enough to pay for the house in L.A., the brownstone in New York, and the artwork he kept buying. He often complained to Jane that although he'd been in dozens of plays and movies over the past decade, and they had made him rich, they had left him dissatisfied. None of his projects had been challenging, except for *12 Angry Men,* which he also produced; but he had lost his entire investment in it.

Meanwhile, negotiations to buy out her contract with Josh Logan were still going on. He was asking for $250,000 to release her. He'd already pocketed $180,000 for her services in *Walk on the Wild Side* and *The Chapman Report.* She had received a paltry $20,000 for both, which made her furious. She felt he was exploiting her. Then she discovered that MGM wanted her on loan-out for *A Period of Adjustment,* based on a Tennessee Williams comedy. Without Logan's knowledge, Jane and her agent, Dick Clayton, went directly to MGM to persuade them to advance her the money to buy out the Logan contract. MGM met her stiff fee of $250,000 because they really wanted her to star in *A Period of Adjustment.* Then Jane paid Logan $100,000 for his contract with her. She was exultant; she had taken charge of a business situation for herself for the first time in her life.

When Logan discovered that she'd gone to MGM for the money without telling him, he was shaken, and he was shaken too by her cold, brittle manner when she handed him the check. He was the first person to have faith in her talent and the first person to promote her in the business in a major way. He thought she should have thanked him. He wondered if she appreciated what he'd done.

But Jane would have none of it. She even told a *New York Times* reporter, "All that baloney about being my godfather—that was just publicity. He's a friend of the family but not enough of a friend to pay me what I'm worth. I feel fortunate I have been able to buy out my contract. I paid for my freedom. That's the important thing." She never saw him again and that upset Logan very much. In his memoir, *Josh: My Up and Down, In and Out Life,* he made no mention of Jane, of *Tall Story,* or of *There Was a Little Girl.*

Henry Fonda had just returned from filming *The Longest Day* in

Normandy. He was depressed because Afdera had gone off to Rome, telling him their marriage was over. Then he read Jane's comments about Logan in the newspapers and he felt even worse. He phoned her in L.A. to say how displeased he was, but she said she didn't care. She'd never been taught how to behave in difficult situations. But then, who was her model? She'd watched her father treat her mother with cold indifference while she was slowly going mad, and she'd seen how he'd behaved with her beloved stepmother Susan. Jane would never have much self-awareness when it came to hurting people, so she didn't give Josh Logan another thought. She told Andreas she believed she was finally in control of her career and her income at the age of twenty-four. It made her feel strong.

Elated, she returned to New York on October 6, 1961, for her brother's Broadway debut in *Blood, Sweat, and Stanley Poole,* and his wedding three days later to Susan Brewer, a Sarah Lawrence graduate he'd met the year before. Susan was the stepdaughter of Noah Dietrich, a longtime associate of Howard Hughes. At twenty-two, Peter flew kites, wore cowboy boots with his tuxedo, and drove a silver sports car. He and Jane posed with their father for photographers at the wedding reception. They were all smiling, but Henry Fonda was in a bleak mood.

The reception at the Pierre Hotel, complete with guests from the *Social Register,* was being held in the same room where he and Frances Fonda had celebrated their wedding twenty-five years earlier. The setting was painfully familiar. Running into his radiant ex-wife Susan Blanchard, to whom Peter and Jane remained close, didn't help.

Afdera had wanted to come to Peter's wedding and Hank had said, "Sure, if you come back to me." He did not want their marriage to end. She told him the problem was that she was too selfish and too spoiled, but what had actually precipitated the breakup was her affair with another man. He had tried hard to make their life together work. It was embarrassing to think he'd had four wives.

One evening not long after the wedding reception, he dropped by Jane's apartment to talk. Jane had sent Andreas to see a movie so they could be alone. Father and daughter chatted tensely about this and that; their conversation was punctuated by silences. Fonda didn't comment on the extravagant décor or the photographs of Andreas displayed around the living room. He had already made it clear to friends that he disapproved of Andreas; he called him a "Svengali" and a user, but, as usual, he did not share his thoughts with Jane.

They became animated when they talked about Peter's success on Broadway — his play had been panned but he'd gotten wonderful reviews: "appealing and uncommonly assured," the *New York Times* said. Jane felt relieved that Peter might start sharing the burden of being compared to their father. They also talked about Tigertail, which had just burned down during one of the worst forest fires in California history. Four hundred homes in Bel Air and Brentwood were destroyed. Sophie Seymour's place was razed, the entire contents of the house incinerated, including the three letters Frances Fonda wrote to her children the morning she killed herself, which Peter and Jane and Pan had never read. Jane told her father that she had visited the site while she was finishing up retakes for *The Chapman Report*. She did not tell him she didn't know whether it made her feel better or worse to be there. Neither one of them could ever mention Frances Fonda and her suicide.

Suddenly, Henry Fonda blurted out how proud he was of Jane's achievements; he'd heard from Barbara Stanwyck that she was giving a quirky performance in *Walk on the Wild Side,* and George Cukor had enjoyed working with her in *The Chapman Report.* Jane knew how hard it was for her father to say this to her, because he so rarely spoke personally, but she remained silent. She sensed that he wanted to tell her about his troubles with Afdera, too, but she did not prompt him. There were more long pauses. After about an hour, she glanced at her watch and told him he'd better leave before Andreas got back.

Fonda left immediately. They did not embrace, but when Jane glanced out the window, she saw her father slumped at the curb, unable to move or even hail a cab. When Andreas came back from the movies, Jane ran sobbing into his arms.

That same evening, Fonda returned to the 74th Street brownstone to deal with Afdera, who had just arrived from Rome. He begged her to stay with him, but she refused and repeated that she had to have her freedom; she was too young to live this kind of life — no life, really. All Fonda did was work; they rarely saw each other.

He persuaded her to take one more trip with him to Sweden, because Ingmar Bergman wanted to speak to Fonda — he was his favorite

American actor and he thought perhaps they could do a movie together. "We went to Bergman's house on his island," Afdera said. "He
had two mistresses there, and a flock of noisy children. There was only
one toilet, so I refused to stay. I took the boat to Stockholm and bought
antiques, and Fonda spent the weekend talking movies with Bergman.
He had a great time."

Back in New York, they continued to fight and bicker and decided
to separate. Fonda bought Afdera a Park Avenue co-op and she moved
out, taking Jane's canopied bed with her. Fonda demanded the bed
back. The day Afdera was to leave for Mexico to get a divorce, Fonda
phoned her at 4:00 A.M. "You can still reconsider," he drawled. She
started to cry but said no.

Afdera said, "In Juarez, the courtroom judge asked, 'What grounds,
Mrs. Fonda?' and I told him there were none. He said, 'There have to
be grounds,' and I got annoyed and said, 'Oh — Fonda liked to do it in
the morning and I liked to do it at night!' The decree was granted — 'ir-
reconcilable differences.'"

Fonda had never been so depressed or depleted in his life. He began
going to singles bars on the East Side with male friends. He drank a
great deal and started dating models. He even reached out briefly to
his ex-wife Susan, who had rented a house on Fire Island with their
adopted daughter, Amy, and a friend, Penelope Coker. Coker recalled
that Fonda joined them for a weekend. He spent all his time with Amy
on the beach. After three days, he left on the ferry as quietly and unob-
trusively as he'd come.

Then Garson Kanin offered him a play called *A Gift of Time,* which
he had written about a man dying of cancer. In his final agony he per-
suades his wife to bring him a razor, and she stands over him as he cuts
his veins. Fonda decided to do the play.

The play opened on Broadway at the Barrymore Theatre on February 22, 1962. The audience was stunned by his portrayal. Paul Newman
called it "the greatest God-damnedest performance I had ever seen."
Kanin, who also directed, recalled that "during rehearsals Fonda had
a helluva a time with the suicide scene. I brought in Thornton Wilder
who talked about how the Romans had done it in Julius Caesar's day.
It was very clinical but Hank seemed to need that. He was not going
to get personal." Marian Seldes, who acted with him, said that "Henry

Fonda conveyed all his emotions through his characterization — pain, guilt, anger, resignation. I don't know how he did it — it was a mystery but it was harrowing."

Jane saw the play by herself. Afterward, she went backstage to visit with her father. Marian Seldes happened to be in the hall when she arrived. They said hello and then Marian watched "this beautiful, slender sad-looking girl disappear into Fonda's dressing room and shut the door."

She wondered what they talked about. She sensed that Jane identified with her father's stoic detachment and his commitment to his work. "I never knew whether he knew I knew the true story," Jane said of her mother's death. "I didn't tell him. I never wanted him to be upset. I knew he felt guilty because he'd asked for the divorce."

For several months after seeing the play, Jane lost track of her father. When he was not acting, Fonda haunted the art galleries on Madison Avenue by himself and occasionally hung out at singles bars with Sydney Chaplin.

Late that March he flew to Los Angeles, where he attended a dinner at La Scala with a Beverly Hills press agent to discuss an award that he was about to receive. Shirlee Adams was at the dinner, too. She was an airline stewardess who also did modeling in Dallas. "She was tall and slender, terrific-looking, not much older than Jane," Hank Fonda said. "She had a face with great bone structure and eyes I could drown in." At the end of the dinner, they said good night to the press agent and went for a nightcap at a place on Sunset Strip. They talked for a long time. Hank discovered that Shirlee came from the Midwest, too — Aurora, Illinois, a half-hour from Chicago. She was very religious, a faithful churchgoer. According to Fonda's biographer, she didn't believe in smoking, coffee, liquor, movies, or dancing. "By the end of the night," Hank said, "I was smitten."

They became inseparable. Fonda made it a policy, whenever he flew coast to coast, to fly on Shirlee Adams's flights. If she was working in coach, he rode coach. If she was working in first class, he got a seat up front. "Of course I made it clear at the very beginning, there would be no more marriages for me," Fonda said.

As always, her father kept his own life secret. Jane would not find out about Shirlee for some time.

14

B Y THE LATE SPRING of 1962 Andreas was behaving "like an octopus with Jane," Collin Wilcox said. "Tentacles into every facet of her life." He was increasingly demanding, and he'd fly into a rage if she resisted a suggestion. He often put her down in public, and he kept trying, he said, to "break the umbilical cord." He once barred her father from visiting her while she had the flu. Fonda had made her some hot beef broth and brought it to her apartment himself. "That son-of-a-bitch answered my knock, snatched the package out of my hand, and said, 'Oh, thank you very much,' and closed the door in my face," he told Howard Teichmann. Jane overheard the exchange as she lay in bed burning up with a fever, but she did nothing.

She was still deferring to Andreas, still enduring his tantrums. She laughed at him indulgently when he became too extreme. "Oh, yes, and I was supporting him, too," she said years later. "He had absolutely no money of his own." He had long ago stopped working odd jobs in the Garment District.

She gave frequent parties for his gay friends like Peter DeRhome, who made porn films. Sometimes Marty Fried and Susan Strasberg would join them, "and in front of everybody Jane would take Andreas's face in her hands and kiss him tenderly on the mouth; she was hungry for love and she needed a straight companion who cared for her as intensely as Andreas," Marty said. Andreas would never be enough for her; she was outgrowing him. She was also tired of having him dissect her night and day. He scrutinized her as obsessively as she scrutinized herself. She believed he was putting her personality in chains.

When they returned to Los Angeles that April to begin filming *A*

Period of Adjustment, she rebelled a bit by going off by herself and learning how to drive.

In those days the studios, in this case MGM, would not allow an unmarried female star to live openly with a man, so Jane had rented a spacious apartment for herself in Bel Air while Andreas was shunted off to a hotel room in West Hollywood (which Jane paid for). But because they were separated by a couple of miles, she had more free time for herself and used it to her advantage by taking driving lessons and getting her license. Soon she began tooling all over Beverly Hills — zooming along Sunset Boulevard, driving out to Malibu to visit friends, stopping off somewhere for a coffee or to gossip with high school friends like Maria Cooper or Jill Robinson. "Oh, God, it was glorious!" Jane recalled years later.

When she finally told Andreas what she'd been up to, he felt wounded. "I realized that driving was one less thing I could do for her, but I was concentrating on Jane the actress. I was busy helping her become Jane the movie star. That's what she was when I was with her and that's what she was committed to becoming. I was thinking about her career twenty-four hours a day."

He was trying to turn her into a movie star, but at a time when economic and aesthetic concerns were changing the film industry. The studio system was collapsing because of the inroads of television. Fewer and fewer movies were being made. An actress, even if she was really talented and special, might get only one picture a year — unless she was Natalie Wood or Doris Day or Julie Andrews.

The last great glossy blond movie star, Grace Kelly, had disappeared in 1957 after she married Prince Rainier of Monaco. Even Audrey Hepburn was choosing to do fewer films because she wanted to concentrate on having a family.

There was a larger problem to overcome, as Andreas and Jane both knew whenever they were considering scripts: Where were the great parts for women?

"Whores, jilted mistresses, drunks, sex-starved spinsters, emotional cripples, ball breakers. That's what little girls of the sixties and seventies are made of," the film critic Molly Haskell wrote in *From Reverence to Rape.*

The clichéd roles in movies for women in the 1960s were not for women, they were for girls — "ingénue[s], mail-order cover girl[s]: regularly featured . . . whose real credentials were proved by the inability to convey any emotion beyond shock or embarrassment or inarticulateness that was meant to prove her 'sincerity,'" Haskell continued.

Jane could not fit into that cliché. That's why she decided to play the role of Isabel, the befuddled newlywed in the Tennessee Williams comedy *Period of Adjustment.* George Roy Hill was directing; her costars were Tony Franciosa, Jim Hutton, and Lois Nettleton. The project would offer her a challenge, and she was excited about it.

The entire movie takes place in twenty-four hours, and it's about what happens when a couple realizes their honeymoon is over and compromises must be made in order for the marriage to work.

Jane immersed herself in the role, layering her performance with emotional and sensory exercises she'd mastered at the Actors Studio. You can watch the intensity of her feelings play across her face in the hysterical scene of the phone call to her father, where she touches on farce and pity as she tries to convince him she's having the time of her life on her honeymoon.

Throughout the movie Jane-as-Isabel keeps bursting into tears because she doesn't know how to be sexy so she "acts sexy." Andreas kept telling her, "Think Marilyn Monroe," and he worked hard to help create Isabel's "look" — curly blond wig, false eyelashes she could bat, and frilly dresses he designed to show off her legs and cleavage. He was trying to mold Jane into Hollywood's newest blond bombshell.

(The *New York Times* would later comment, "Jane Fonda as Isabel is appropriately jittery and shallow and sexy and half out of it. Could it be that Fonda is mimicking Marilyn Monroe?")

In fact, she and Andreas were seeing a lot of Marilyn, who was in Hollywood, too, working on *Something's Got to Give* with Dean Martin at Twentieth Century Fox. Marilyn was spending most of her free time with the Strasbergs, and Jane and Andreas had supper with them a couple of times. They commented on how groggy she was. "She had these brutal Nembutal hangovers," Susan explained. Marilyn had just spent the weekend with President Kennedy at Bing Crosby's house in Palm Springs. She never planned to sleep with JFK on a permanent basis, Susan went on. It was okay to sleep with that charismatic president for one night or two — she sort of liked the secrecy and drama of it—but she didn't like being at his beck and call. She made that very clear.

The interlude in Hollywood had been a pleasurable one for Jane. She had treasured her time spent with Marilyn; she'd enjoyed working with director George Roy Hill in *Period of Adjustment.* He had not allowed Andreas on the set, which liberated Jane and gave her free rein during the entire shoot, so she'd been able to create a zany character. She started to enjoy making movies. "Somehow [it] gets to you. It's ego-battering . . . and it's much tougher work for an actor, because with all the various things involved it's harder to create a performance. When I did *Adjustment,* I finally began to feel like an experienced film actress, and I decided movies were for me."

The next movie she did, however, was strictly for money, to help pay back the $250,000 advance from MGM, which she was still funneling to Logan. The movie was *In the Cool of the Day,* costarring Peter Finch and Angela Lansbury. Jane thought the script was trashy, a soap opera. She was to play a dying young widow who goes on a last vacation and has a brief romance with an older married man. The story was set in Greece, amid spectacular scenery, and she looked forward to the prospect of being with Andreas and meeting his family.

When it turned out he couldn't accompany her, because he had never served in the Greek military and would have been drafted the moment he landed in Athens, he opted not to go. Jane then tried to get out of the picture, but the producer, John Houseman, wouldn't let her.

On an impulse she asked Andreas to marry her before she left, but he refused. "I didn't want to be supported by her," he said. "I didn't want to live off her. I really didn't." She asked him to marry her again while she was packing and again he said no. Jane thought they should get married, but privately she had her doubts; she was as ambivalent about him as she'd always been, as she was about most things in her life.

She couldn't figure out what was going on inside her until decades later when she was completing her memoir and discovered that she could not write about the years with Andreas. "It wasn't until I read Carol Gilligan's *In a Different Voice* that I realized that back then I had very successfully separated my body from my psyche. I literally did not know what I was thinking or feeling or what I was experiencing. I had taken myself out of a relationship with myself."

She could not articulate how she felt because at that point in her life she didn't know. She knew she felt different at different times. She knew at some level that she wanted intimacy, security, stimulation, and, above all, reassurance. And, on occasion, a few thrills. But her father's dry Midwestern drawl was constantly sounding in her head, scolding, admonishing her over and over again that Andreas was a user. Didn't he understand that she couldn't bear to be alone? Andreas was the one person in the world who had been trying to save her from destroying herself with her bulimia.

The two of them had a tearful farewell at the airport before she handed him a scribbled note and ran to the plane. He kept the note folded carefully, inside a plastic envelope, for years. In it Jane had written, "If it hadn't been for you, they wouldn't be saying all those good things about me at the Actors Studio, about my acting, and I wouldn't be happy and healthy. Perhaps I wouldn't even be alive. How can I say this to you so you won't get too cocky? Just remember how important you are to me, and how much I love you. Lady Jane Seymour loves you."

They wrote and phoned each other constantly while she was in Greece. During the two weeks she filmed in Athens, she stayed with Andreas's grandmother. The Greek newspapers were filled with stories about her upcoming marriage to Andreas. "Everybody in the Voutsinas family thought they were going to be married," said Marios, Andreas's son. He was nine years old when he met Jane and he never forgot it. "She burst into tears when she saw me and she told me that I looked exactly like my father and that when I grew up, I was going to be as talented as he was."

Six weeks later, when she and Andreas were reunited in London, she couldn't stop talking about how wonderful and loving his family was. She had to appear in the movie's two last scenes, so Andreas came to the set at the Elstree Studios with script and pencil. He remained there through rehearsals and filming. Before each take Jane would emit an earsplitting primal scream, and then she would do the scene. After it was over she would gaze at Andreas for approval over the heads of the director, Robert Stevens, and a very perplexed Peter Finch, with whom she was acting the scenes. "Jane merely screamed to release her tensions and her anger at the script," Andreas said. "The dialogue was unplayable." Peter Finch agreed. He told Jane the only reason he did the movie was to work with her and have a free trip to Athens.

After the two-day shoot, reporters and photographers tagged along with Jane and Andreas as they strolled back to the Savoy, where they were staying. As photographers snapped their picture for the tabloids, reporters moved in to ask questions. "Andreas Voutsinas is as skinny as Miss Fonda, but a couple of inches shorter," the London *Daily Mail* noted. "He has a roundish face and slanting oriental eyes and what looks like a faint moustache. He says he was born in Khartoum and studied design in Paris and London."

Midway through the interview Jane announced, "I've been in love with Andreas for a year." When he ordered her to do something she laughed indulgently. A reporter asked her to comment on her behavior and she answered, "I guess I'm the slave type."

As soon as the feature was reprinted in the Paris edition of the *International Herald Tribune*, it elicited an immediate response from Henry Fonda, which appeared in Leonard Lyons's gossip column in the *New York Post*: "Andreas Voutsinas is a user and a parasite. I've already said he was a Svengali!" He added, "I don't want to see my daughter getting hurt."

Jane made no comment; she appeared more committed to Andreas than ever. In fact, she'd signed to do a Broadway comedy in the next weeks called *The Fun Couple*. Her only stipulation was that Andreas direct. She told friends she was eager to have his talent recognized. She was sick and tired of hearing him constantly put down — especially by her father.

As soon as *In the Cool of the Day* wrapped, they flew to Paris for the weekend. "It should have been so romantic — we were going to be by ourselves in the most beautiful city in the world," Andreas said. They spent most of the first afternoon wandering around the Left Bank, stopping to have a coffee in one of the outdoor cafés, and then they went to a movie. When they emerged from the theater a few hours later, it was dusk. Arm in arm, they strolled up the Champs-Élysées trying to figure out where they should have dinner. They passed a newsstand. Every headline was screaming: MARILYN MONROE EST MORTE.

MARILYN IS DEAD. A SUICIDE. AN OVERDOSE OF PILLS. She was thirty-six years old.

"We couldn't believe it," Andreas recalled. "We'd seen her in April. Oh, she was ill — too many pills — but she was talking about doing *Rain* on TV, you know, the Sadie Thompson role. She seemed very enthusiastic about it. She was going to control every aspect of the production, she said. And Lee was going to direct."

That night they talked about their brief times with Marilyn until it was very late. "So vivid for both of us." The evenings at the Strasbergs where she'd served Chinese takeout at the big table in the kitchen and then afterward washed dishes with Paula. The way she'd appear at the Studio, scrubbed of makeup — no lipstick even — but her skin was luminous; she seemed to glow with an unearthly light. And then there were the scenes she struggled with in Lee's private classes; she was always so scared she trembled. When she played Blanche she brought props from her apartment to make the set look "real." The last scene she did in class was when she recited the Molly Bloom soliloquy from James Joyce's *Ulysses*.

Jane wondered why everyone in her life that mattered to her seemed to commit suicide. Marilyn had inspired her. She had nerve. As soon as she returned to New York she phoned Susan to ask, "Why did she do it?" but Susan couldn't immediately say. Rumor and speculation surrounded Marilyn Monroe's death, including the possibility of suicide, but no consensus has ever been reached on the true events of her death.

Jane had to focus her concentration elsewhere. The Pentagon had just named her Miss Army Recruiting of 1962. She gave an enthusiastic speech in Washington, D.C., to a huge group of young soldiers extolling the virtues of army life and the importance of a strong American army. Also, she was about to go into rehearsal for *The Fun Couple*, so she began to make lists and returned to her ballet classes. She would be wearing a bikini in the play and she wanted her body to look perfect.

The Fun Couple was a satire about newlyweds who don't want to grow up and take on responsibilities because they think they'll be boring. It was a slight premise, supposedly written by "an anonymous dentist with five children," the press release said. In truth it was written by a well-known lawyer named Jay Julien, who was also producing *The Fun Couple*. He had earlier produced the Broadway hit *A Hatful of Rain* with Shelley Winters.

"I did *Fun Couple* as a lark," he said. "It turned out to be the worst mistake of my life." Midway into rehearsals, the situation became so chaotic that Julien confessed that he, not some nameless dentist, was the author. Another writer, Bill Marchand, was brought in to beef up the dialogue and rewrite entire sections of the show. "We had a new second act in Philly and another one in Wilmington."

Meanwhile, D. A. Pennebaker was filming a documentary called *Jane*. Julien thought the film would help promote the show, but Pennebaker had read the script and knew *The Fun Couple* was going to be a disaster, which was why he wanted to record the proceedings. The documentary became not only the story of a monumental Broadway flop, but also a bizarre visual record of Jane's relationship with Andreas. It shows moment by moment her slavish devotion to him even as he screams insults at her. "You wanna see how Andreas really treated me when we were together?" Jane comments caustically today. "Just see this movie!"

During rehearsals, one of Pennebaker's associates, Hope Ryden, taped Jane from morning till night and a camera crew accompanied her everywhere from her apartment to the theater, from costume fittings to meetings with publicists.

"Jane was totally comfortable being filmed," Pennebaker recalled. "She reveled in it and she had no self-consciousness. She chewed gum, swigged from a bottle of brandy, mugged and clowned in front of everybody, and talked nonstop about what it was like growing up in her father's shadow and how much she had to live up to and how she was mourning the death of Marilyn Monroe." Pennebaker thought his documentary captured Jane's raw talent, her fierce ambition.

The camera also captured Andreas, alternately preening, fawning, or going into tirades as he struggled to direct the Broadway flop. When in doubt he'd yell, "Stop it! Let's do it again!" "Do it again!" or "I'm getting angry again!" whenever Jane and others in the cast failed to do something he wanted to make sense out of the inane dialogue.

Throughout, Jane was both submissive and deferential, and she always looked beguiling. At breaks they'd slip into her dressing room and Andreas would present her with a solid gold slave bracelet. "One bangle for every time you do something right for me, darling," he'd say grandly, and they'd kiss each other lovingly. But the affection didn't seem genuine.

Andreas was making all the decisions, but he had never directed a Broadway play before, so he didn't know what he was doing. The script made absolutely no sense, so during the Baltimore tryout Jane tried to write a new second act herself, and she and costar Brad Dillman (who played her husband) even improvised a couple of scenes that took place on their wedding night. She opened the show wearing a bikini and showing off her amazing body to the audience. When everything else failed, Andreas had her dancing and cavorting nonsensically about the stage.

In Philadelphia, Lee Strasberg came to see the show with Susan, and afterward he met with Jane and Andreas, telling them bluntly, "Darlings, this is not a play."

The rest of the cast became hysterical, but they pretended everything was wonderful. "You got a terrific laugh," Dyan Cannon assured Jane at one point backstage. They hugged each other "like we were two drowning rats," Cannon added.

The Fun Couple opened on Broadway on October 24 — the week of the Cuban missile crisis. The reviews were horrific. Walter Kerr rated *The Fun Couple* as one of "the five worst plays" he'd ever seen. The *New York Post* called it "an epic bore." After three performances the show mercifully closed.

Andreas returned to the Actors Studio and threw himself into other projects. For a while Jane stood defiantly by him and did not voice her real feelings, except to Collin Wilcox: "Jane told me Andreas had really let her down bigtime in *The Fun Couple*. I don't think she ever forgave him for that. He embarrassed her and made her a laughingstock. She felt he'd opened her up to ridicule, and of course the documentary recorded it for posterity, chapter and verse."

By mid-October 1962, three of her films had opened — *Walk on the Wild Side, The Chapman Report,* and Tennessee Williams's *A Period of Adjustment.* All three were panned by critics, but Jane emerged as a distinct character in each. She was sexy, she was kittenish, and she made a wonderful impression onscreen.

Then the film critic Stanley Kauffmann wrote a long essay in the highbrow *New Republic,* beginning with "A new talent is rising." "In *Period of Adjustment*," he wrote, "as the nervous Southern bride, [Jane Fonda's] comic touch is as sure as her serious one. Besides the gift of timing, she has what lies below all comedy — confidence in one's perception of what's humorous." He thought she was "vicious, foxy, and tough" in *Walk on the Wild Side,* and he singled out her performance in *The Chapman Report* where she played "a frigid young middle-class widow. The girl's pathological fear of sex, exacerbated by her hunger for love, is expressed in neurotic outbursts that cut to the emotional quick with a truth too good for the material. Miss Fonda is not conventionally pretty," he concluded. "She has the kind of blunt, startling features that can be charged with passion or the cartoon of passion as she chooses. Her tall, slim figure has thoroughbred gawky grace. Her voice is attractive and versatile. Her ear for inflection is secure. What lies ahead for this gifted, appealing young actress? With good parts in good plays and films, she could develop into a first-rate artist."

Jane tore the review out and sent copies to her agent and scores of producers. For a while, she thought the reviews might even be a vindication for Andreas. She told friends she was glad now that she'd trusted him to shape her career. She had not been mistaken. She also sent the reviews to the *Harvard Lampoon,* which had just named her "the worst actress of 1962 for her performance as the frigid woman in *The Chapman Report.*"

She was deluged with film scripts, but before she decided on her next movie, she agreed to appear in Eugene O'Neill's five-hour play *Strange Interlude,* with Geraldine Page, Ben Gazzara, Franchot Tone, and Betty Field. It was to be the much-touted first Actors Studio Theatre production, with José Quintero directing. The play, later described as a "thunderous psychodrama" by *Times* critic Frank Rich, had won O'Neill his third Pulitzer when it was first performed in 1928, but many in the Studio cast now found the drama dated. The rehearsal process was arduous. Rip Torn kicked Andreas out of the theater because he was bullying Jane. Geoffrey Horne remembered, "Andreas was being very difficult. He was terrified he was losing his grip on Jane because she was starting to be a little more independent."

Strange Interlude opened in March 1963 and had a limited run; a number of critics lambasted the show, saying that the production

Jane, age 23, photographed by her friend Peter Basch. She had just begun to study with Lee Strasberg and was auditioning for the Actors Studio in New York. (1960)

Henry Fonda at the height of his beauty and fame as a movie star, around the time he made *The Grapes of Wrath*. (1940)

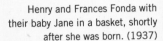

Henry and Frances Fonda with their baby Jane in a basket, shortly after she was born. (1937)

Jane eating some wedding cake at her half sister Pan's wedding, where Jane was the flower girl. (1948)

Peter and Jane with their mother, Frances, outside in the sun at Tigertail. (1943)

The Fondas, photographed for *Harper's Bazaar* in Greenwich in the spring of 1948. Left to right: Peter, Frances, Jane studying her father, and Pan half-hidden behind Henry in the foreground. He is triumphing on Broadway in *Mister Roberts* and about to break up his marriage.

Jane in her first apartment in New York.

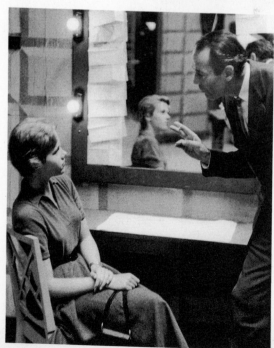

Jane and her father backstage before their first performance of *The Country Girl* at the Omaha Community Theatre. (1955)

Another version of the Fonda family in 1955, on their way to Rome, where Henry was filming *War and Peace*. With Henry, left to right: Peter, Susan Blanchard (Fonda's third wife) and their adopted baby, Amy; Jane looks on.

Jane at a Hollywood cocktail party given for her while she was filming her first movie, *Tall Story*, with Tony Perkins. (1959)

Jane with her director, Josh Logan, during rehearsal in 1960 for her first Broadway show, *There Was a Little Girl*. Logan would sometimes taunt her, saying, "I don't think you can do it. You're going to fall behind your old man."

Peter Basch, Susan Strasberg, Jane, and her coach/lover Andreas Voutsinas attending an Actors Studio benefit in January 1961, just after Jane had passed her final audition and been accepted as a member of the Studio.

Members of the new Actors Studio Theatre in January 1963, about to start rehearsals of their production of Eugene O'Neill's *Strange Interlude*. Jane is in the back row; her idol Geraldine Page is in the front row on the left.

Lee Strasberg, the celebrated artistic director of the Actors Studio and a huge influence on Jane. "He challenged me," she said. "He taught me to depend on my instincts and imagination. He forced me to dig."

Jane on location in New Orleans, on the set of *Walk on the Wild Side*. On the right, Andreas is coaching her intently. She played a feisty prostitute with verve and gusto. (1962)

Jane between takes filming *Sunday in New York*, where she demonstrated her comic gifts and felt at ease in front of the camera for the first time.

Henry, Jane, and Peter posing together on a New York street in 1963. They were each acting in different movies at the same time. In this picture they appear to be getting along. In reality they weren't speaking to one another.

French director Roger Vadim and Jane in their Paris apartment, not long after they fell in love. (1964)

Jane cavorting with Robert Redford in Neil Simon's *Barefoot in the Park*, Jane's most successful movie to date. (1966)

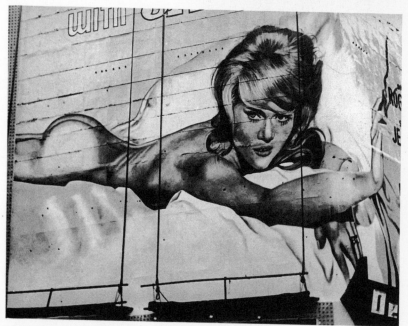

The infamous nude billboard of Jane in Times Square, which was promoting Vadim's *Circle of Love*. More than anything it helped establish Jane Fonda as a sex symbol.

Vadim and Jane in 1966 while filming *La Curée*. When Vadim saw the rushes, he realized he had succeeded in releasing Jane's quirky, powerful spirit—stubborn, flirtatious, spoiled, moody, luxuriating in the celebrity that made her imperious and graceful at the same time.

Roger Vadim on the set in Rome, altering one of the many costumes that Jane wore in *Barbarella*. Vadim imagined Jane would be playing a kind of sexual *Alice in Wonderland* of the future. *Barbarella* was based on the French comic strip that combined science fiction with soft-core porn. (1967)

"lacked distinction" and was "star infested"; others maintained it was "a brilliant revival." Jane, who played Geraldine Page's daughter, was disappointed with her personal notices, which were uniformly bland.

That same spring, the *Saturday Evening Post* published the article entitled "Lady Jane" by Al Aronowitz. It was her first major profile, and Jane had initially been very excited about it, even more so than she had been about the *New Yorker* profile earlier that year by Lillian Ross, who had also interviewed her father in a separate profile. The Ross pieces are precise and informational, and Jane and Hank come across as committed, serious artists.

The *Post* article highlights father and daughter. It was the first time they had talked so much about each other in a piece. They played many games with the reporter, who was completely snowed by Fonda (who was uncharacteristically emotional) and bewitched by Jane. Aronowitz spent weeks taping her rambling, disjointed thoughts on everything from Lee Strasberg to her lonely childhood. At one point she exclaims, "If I had a child who became a bigger star than I was, I'd hate it. I couldn't staaand it!" She is most articulate when she's talking about why she's going to be successful. "I have a persona and I have a presence," she declared. "It's like a commodity."

In this piece, Hank waxes sentimental about his daughter and tearfully describes that when Jane cut off her braids he was very upset. He also predicts, "She's going to be a bigger star than I am. It's kind of scary because she is so loaded. There is no limit to what this girl can do and it's scary because I'm her father."

Jane became more and more displeased as she read and reread the *Saturday Evening Post* story. She didn't see herself as Aronowitz had portrayed her, a kooky, sexy, driven, self-involved young woman. As for her father's fulsome comments about her, she felt resentful because "Dad never told *me* any of those things about myself." In that same interview with Al Aronowitz, she admitted that it was becoming harder for her to do a scene at the Studio, "mainly because I know there are people there who have far more talent than I do." She would watch an actress like Madeleine Sherwood inhabit a role and think she could never do what Madeleine did. But "on film," she told Aronowitz, "I have something else. I have star quality."

As soon as *Strange Interlude* closed, Jane went straight into shooting

Sunday in New York, which costarred Rod Taylor and Cliff Robertson. "It was a role I could do in my sleep," she said, "the archetypal single girl, the naughty, wide-eyed innocent."

For a while Andreas accompanied her to the set, and he carped and criticized until the director, Peter Tewksbury, banished him to an empty dressing room, where he sat sulking. Jane didn't protest. She was having too good a time. Now that she felt she really knew what she was doing in front of a camera, she was relaxed and charming and funny.

She delighted the cast and crew with her antics. "She was a real good sport," said her press agent at the time, John Springer, who remembered when she had to reshoot a one-minute scene ten times. "It took about four hours and was very complicated, because Jane had to run down a circular staircase, answer the phone, and button her jacket at the same time. On the eleventh take, she fell flat on her face, and the director howled, 'Print it!' and everybody laughed, except Andreas. He was starting to lose control of Jane and couldn't deal with that; he was getting panicked."

When they went back to her apartment at night, there was a lot of friction between them. Both Jane's analyst and Andreas's analyst (whom she was paying for) were advising them to be less dependent on one another. "For the past two years we'd been brother and sister, lovers, friends," said Andreas. "We lived and worked together twenty-four hours a day. It was getting to be too intense. Of course, Jane always had a separate life from me and I had a separate life from her, but I was insanely jealous and much too possessive."

He went on, "Every man wanted her — Sandy, Warren, Max Schell, Johnny Frankenheimer. They were all after her and I hated them all. I'd be insane with jealousy every time she'd disappear. I had no right to be that way but I was always suspecting her of being with someone else. Maybe because we were not lovers in the sense that we didn't have sex that often."

Jane, meanwhile, was continuing to enjoy herself making *Sunday in New York*, and her instinct was right. The movie would establish her as a full-fledged movie star in the eyes of the American public. When the film came out, she was praised for her witty performance, and critics paid her the compliment of agreeing that it was time she moved on to more challenging stuff. Jane knew she was in danger of being typecast if she played too many more ingénues. She'd had supper alone with Jean Seberg and listened to her talk about her triumph in Jean-Luc Godard's *Breathless,* a takeoff of a cheap American gangster movie that had been the surprise hit at Cannes that spring.

Seberg told Jane that working with Godard in Paris had been "insane but exciting." He never gave her a full script, just a few grease-spotted pages each day. He never looked her in the eye; he was messy; he stole things from people. He was a misogynist, Seberg said, but he was dedicated to creating a new kind of cinema. The movie was shot with a hand-held camera. Seberg said she loved her role of Patricia, boyish, amoral, assured, "the young American bitch" who betrays her lover without any sense of responsibility or guilt. She added that her lover was played by Jean-Paul Belmondo, a former boxer with a beat-up face. "He was unbelievably sexy."

Only a couple of years before, Seberg had been a tousle-haired twenty-one-year-old Midwesterner, chosen from thousands of applicants to play Joan of Arc for Otto Preminger. *St. Joan* was filmed in London in 1957. She followed that with the starring role in *Bonjour Tristesse,* which Preminger was also directing. Jane had heard about the film from Geoffrey Horne, who had played opposite Seberg. It was Seberg's performance as the disillusioned Parisian teenager living only for pleasure that had brought her to the attention of Godard. He was especially taken with the last image in the film, of her sitting in front of a mirror, expressionless, putting cold cream on her face. Godard was impressed by her cool, detached beauty.

Jane had been impressed, too. She'd seen the movie with Andreas, and she'd wished Godard had chosen her for *Breathless.* She and Seberg were often up for the same roles. In fact, Seberg had been asked to play the part in *There Was a Little Girl* before Jane.

Not long after the dinner with Seberg, while she was in Hollywood finishing *Sunday in New York,* the French director René Clément came to her with an idea. Clément was a distinguished figure in France, the director of such films as *Forbidden Games,* an unforgettable film about war and its effects on children, and *Purple Noon,* a cult favorite. Now he wanted Jane to star in a movie he was developing called *Joy House,* which he described to her as a thriller. The movie would costar Alain

Delon, the hottest leading man in Europe, and be shot in Paris and the Riviera. MGM was financing it. Although Clément was an established filmmaker, the studio was hoping to capitalize on America's fascination with the young French New Wave directors such as Godard and François Truffaut who were using innovative techniques like improvised dialogue.

She accepted Clément's offer almost immediately. It would be a new experience for Jane. "I could separate myself from my father's long shadow," she said, "separate him with an ocean." It would also be a way of breaking with Andreas — she knew MGM wouldn't allow her to bring him with her as her coach.

As soon as she returned to New York, she told Andreas of her decision, just days after she'd signed the contract. Her manner was abrupt. "I want you to move out," she said. She had to live by herself. "When I asked her why," Andreas recalled, "she answered, 'Because I can't keep looking in the mirror and keep hearing you tell me the truth about myself twenty-four hours a day. I need space.'

"But in the same breath, she was saying she still wanted me to be her coach. We might still go to Paris together. Jane lies to people when she doesn't want to hurt them, when she feels sorry for them, but she always knows she's lying. She couldn't let me go totally yet. She had to hold on to me for a while like a life preserver. I knew too much about her. I knew she wouldn't let me go until she found somebody else, and even then she might not want to let me go. I was willing to be there for her always. She said wonderful things about me, how I saved her life, had taken care of her and shaped her, blah, blah, blah. I didn't argue. I didn't put up a fight. I just walked out of the apartment, but I felt as if I'd been hit in the pit of my stomach."

He ran into the actor Gerry O'Loughlin on West 56th Street. "Gerry looked like death warmed over. I told him, 'Jane kicked me out,' and he said, 'Sandy Dennis just left me for Gerry Mulligan.' We looked at each other and laughed, but we were both crying inside. He asked me, 'What are you going to do?' I said, 'I have no idea. I don't even have a place to live,' and he said, 'Take my apartment on West 56th Street. I can never go back there. Too many memories. Sandy and I lived there for over ten years. Take it.' And with that he gave me the keys and walked off. He never saw the place again; it was a rent-controlled cold-water flat."

A few days later an item appeared in the *New York Daily Mirror* column, Sheilah Graham's "Hollywood Today." It was headlined JANE & ANDREAS KI$$ GBYE.

> Jane Fonda and her longtime fiancé Andreas Voutsinas have called the thing off. Their incomes are incompatible. Jane earns $250,000 a year. Andreas works when he can. This type of mismatch rarely works out.

The night before Jane left New York, she attended a party at Franchot Tone's brownstone on the East Side. The place was overrun with Broadway actors, among them the blond, stylish actress Betsy von Furstenberg and her husband, Guy Vincent, an ebullient restaurateur. Vincent loved to read palms, and midway through the evening he insisted on reading Jane's. "You will marry three times, have many children, and become one of the most successful and controversial women in the entire world." He was right on all counts.

Part III

Movie Star / Sex Symbol: 1963-1970

Jane could be . . . sweet, sensuous, and full of laughter.
Her mystery lay in her contrasting moods: she was both
aggressive and vulnerable, intolerant and desperately anxious
to understand other people, open and reserved, charming
and hard as nails — sometimes all at the same time.

— ROGER VADIM, *MEMOIRS OF THE DEVIL*

15

ON THE PLANE to Paris Jane thought about *Joy House* and went into a panic. So far there was no screenplay and, from what René Clément had told her, the story was a confusing collage. The plot revolved around the sleek, dark-haired Alain Delon, who played a small-time swindler and Casanova who finds himself on the hit list of an American gangster. When his enemies attempt to kill him, he hides out in Monte Carlo and gets a job as a chauffeur for a rich married woman. Jane was to play the married woman's niece, Melinda. In the story, she and her aunt fall in love with Delon. Both entice him into their beds.

As soon as she reached her Left Bank hotel, the Relais Bisson, she unpacked her bags and arranged for an impromptu drink with Clément and his producer, Jacques Bar. Both men assured Jane that *Joy House* was going to be a suspense thriller à la Alfred Hitchcock and she had nothing to worry about. They admitted they hadn't cast the rich woman yet, but they were hoping Jeanne Moreau would do the part. (The American actress Lola Albright would ultimately be cast.) The starting date for filming had been changed to the end of September because Delon hadn't yet completed filming on his current picture. She should be relieved because it gave them more time to work on the script.

None of this made Jane feel any better, especially because the conversation was conducted in rapid French. While she thought she understood most of it, she could not answer as completely as she wanted. She felt frustrated. She was determined to speak French fluently as soon as she could. That very evening she arranged for a coach.

Then she phoned Andreas in New York, but he wasn't in his apartment. For close to four months she'd tried to be independent of him,
but she remained in touch, writing him twelve-page letters and phoning him at least once a week. "I was a habit she couldn't break yet,"
Andreas said. The habit would continue until 1970. Right now she
needed somebody in Paris to provide emotional support. That someone turned out to be the Oscar-winning actress Simone Signoret, who
had already sent Jane flowers and invited her to dinner the following
evening.

Signoret lived with her husband, singer and actor Yves Montand, in
an apartment on the Île de la Cité, the little triangle of an island in the
Seine, and Jane began going there regularly. The Montands ran a kind
of salon filled with French and American intellectuals, painters, and
artists, among others the Broadway playwright Herb Gardner, the ex-
istentialist Jean-Paul Sartre and his companion, Simone de Beauvoir,
along with the young Costa-Gavras, who would soon direct the political thriller *Z* with Montand; he was to be Clément's assistant director
on *Joy House.*

Jane had met Signoret in 1959, when she came to New York to be
with Montand while he was performing his hugely successful one-man
cabaret show on Broadway. Jane had gone to see the show with her father and Afdera, and afterward they had dinner with the Montands at
the Algonquin. "I remember watching Simone stare adoringly across
the table at my father," Jane wrote in *My Life So Far,* "and now, in Paris,
she talked to me about the films he'd made — *Blockade, The Grapes of
Wrath, Young Mr. Lincoln,* and *12 Angry Men.* She said it was the values
those films represented, the quality of the characters he played, that
moved her so much, and I began to appreciate him in new ways." "People need heroes they can aspire to," Jane later said. Signoret confided
she had other special heroes, Gandhi and Martin Luther King. She
added that it was mysterious how good people are often very strong.

Signoret would play a special role in Jane's life. She was outspoken
and involved in serious political issues, such as the war in Algeria and
the Vietnam conflict, but she was also a devoted wife and mother. She
gave Jane an idea of what a woman might become: independent, self-
reliant, yet warm, and giving.

Over the years, their friendship would move through a thicket of philosophizing, confession, and gossip. They dined frequently together in Paris and Los Angeles. Jane revered Signoret, and Signoret adored Jane.

In a letter to Andreas she told him she was still being given the runaround about a complete script. Signoret advised her to be tough with Clément, and her French agent, Olga Horstig, warned her to be on guard whenever anyone tried to pull the wool over her eyes. Jane felt frustrated — her French wasn't yet fluent and she often couldn't understand what people were saying to her.

In another letter to Andreas her mood was lightened as she excitedly described the publicity she had been doing nonstop. There were photo ops, press conferences, television appearances, magazine interviews — all part of MGM's efforts to turn her into an overnight celebrity in France, which would help promote *Joy House* all over Europe.

By the end of her second week in Paris she was followed everywhere by photographers and reporters, who quoted her fractured French and silly wisecracks. She was featured in *Elle* and *Paris Match* and all the newspapers, and she was included in a ten-page spread in *Life* in which she modeled the latest creations of French designers such as Balenciaga, Chanel, and Dior. She loved the attention. She did not tell Andreas she was binging and purging so she could squeeze into the couture clothes.

Within a month *Cahiers du Cinéma* had put her on the cover. Inside, the critics raved about her "wall-to-wall teeth and rippling blonde hair." She was "a cyclone of femininity and a panther of desire." This beautiful daughter of Henry Fonda had really captured the French imagination. "It was a magical time to be an American in France," Jane said. "During the Eisenhower presidency, the French had thought of us as gauche, too loud, too styleless: 'ugly Americans.' Now, with Kennedy and Jackie in the White House, everything seemed to have changed. The Kennedys brought us international esteem, and the Americans in Paris benefited from their popularity."

Jane could not understand why the media constantly compared her to Brigitte Bardot; a pop singer had even composed a song about her called "La BB Américaine." "There is only one Bardot," she told reporters, "and I'm not like her at all and she is not like me either!"

Which was true; Jane was sexy, but she had a slender, angular, small-breasted frame whereas Bardot's body was voluptuous, unthreatening, and safe. One imagined she might be innocent and childlike in bed, whereas Jane's manner as a seductress was a bit mocking.

"It was like, Careful, she might sting you," said one of her lovers at the time. "Another thing — she was so hungry for love, you were afraid she might devour you. Monroe and Bardot didn't give off those vibes."

Filming on *Joy House* started on the Côte d'Azur in October, but the production remained disorganized. Clément could not decide whether his thriller should be played for laughs or menace. There was virtually no script; the plot was absurd, and Jane improvised the dialogue in most of her scenes with Delon.*

Her experience at the Actors Studio helped. She moved confidently through the film, creating a vibrant physical life for it whether she was scrambling an omelet for Delon or running gracefully across a highway helping him escape his tormentors. After hours she and Delon flirted. Photographers snapped them celebrating his birthday aboard a yacht. They made a beautiful couple, and she broke up his affair with longtime girlfriend Romy Schneider. "I always fall in love with my leading men," Jane said.

But she ultimately found him boring.

She was quite lonely but she kept up a brave front. She still couldn't speak French very well and she had few friends in Paris, but she wouldn't tell anyone her troubles. Her agent, Dick Clayton, visited her on the set and saw her holding hands with "the little makeup girl." He'd heard rumors that she preferred being with women, "but I put it out of my mind; I thought Jane was very conventional — too conventional to be a lesbian."

She was filming in Paris when John F. Kennedy was assassinated on November 22, 1963. She remembered walking into her hotel lobby and seeing the American actor Keir Dullea on the phone by the reception desk. His face was ashen. "Kennedy's been shot, they think he's dead,"

---

* When it opened the following year in the United States, the film was panned viciously, but Europeans loved it and loved Jane in it. She is funny and seductive. She makes you feel happy whenever she walks into a frame.

Keir told her. "I sat in the lobby, stunned," Jane recalled, "waiting to hear more news." Moments later a reporter from *Cahiers du Cinéma*, who had scheduled an interview with her previously, ran in from the street. He assumed she wanted to cancel.

"No, I need to talk," Jane said, and she and the reporter went upstairs to her room and tried to do the interview. Both wound up in tears. Then Simone Signoret phoned. "She was crying and said that I shouldn't be alone on this night, that she wanted me to come over to their place." So Jane joined Signoret, Montand, and others, and they sat up all night talking and mourning the president.

Jane knew her father must be upset about Kennedy, for whom he had campaigned. She had cut off all connections with him since her move to Paris; she felt she had to do that, or she could never create a separate identity for herself. Yet she was increasingly preoccupied with thoughts about him and was angry that he couldn't reach out to her after the terrible tragedy of the assassination. Months later she learned from a friend that, after watching the news on television that day, Hank Fonda had closeted himself in a spare room and begun to paint. He painted till dawn.

In the days preceding Kennedy's funeral in Washington Jane continued to film *Joy House*. When work was done, she would walk restlessly around Paris — through the Tuileries, up the Boulevard Saint-Michel, past cafés and music halls. The city did not shut down until very late — so much activity, laughter, music, the restaurants and cafés filled with people and cigarette smoke.

Often Jane would end up at novelist James Jones's beautiful apartment on the Île de la Cité, a hangout for American expatriates such as the Irwin Shaws and the Bill Styrons, who were all obsessing about the assassination. Eileen Finletter, a friend of Norman Mailer's, remembered seeing Jane come into the apartment, "very skinny, very blond, in some great designer suit, and she knelt down at Jimmy Jones's feet and gazed up at him with tears in her eyes. She looked like a little lost soul." "Why doesn't my father ever tell me he loves me?" she asked. Jones was too drunk to answer.

Soon Jane's tears evaporated into anger. Some days later on the set, a photographer brought her a publicity still of her father dressed as the clown Emmett Kelly. It was from a terrible movie he'd done in 1959 called *The Man Who Understood Women.* Jane took the picture to her dressing room, tore it into bits, and stomped on it.

On December 21 Olga Horstig threw an impromptu dinner for Jane to celebrate her birthday; the only other guest was her special client and friend, the director Roger Vadim. "I thought the two of you might get along," Horstig said.

She knew he had a project for Jane: *Circle of Love,* a racy revamped version of Schnitzler's *La Ronde,* a sexual comedy of errors set in old Vienna. Vadim wanted to take advantage of her celebrity on two continents to get the movie made, even though she'd stated very clearly that she would never work for him.

On that chilly December evening, they sat close together on the one sofa in Horstig's cramped Right Bank apartment. The shabbiness of the surroundings belied the fact that Horstig handled some of the most celebrated actors in French cinema — Jean Gabin, Simone Signoret, Gérard Philipe. Their photographs hung on the walls near the kitchen, along with portraits of Brigitte Bardot and Danièle Delorme, her other special clients.

While the agent cooked — "I think I served *boeuf bourguignon*" — Vadim drew Jane out in his gentle, hesitant way. "He was irresistible," Horstig said. "He had the magnetism and high-voltage charm of a star himself." She could tell that Jane was captivated by him and by his description of his latest movie, *Château en Suède,* with Monica Vitti, from a Françoise Sagan novel. "We spent three weeks in the Arctic," he said. "The air was so brisk we never slept."

As the evening moved on, much good red wine was drunk and eventually Vadim began singing ribald French marching songs. He kept mispronouncing English. "Oh, Jane, I see no ob-stee-cles in taking you home." She thought, "Oh, God, is he handsome, even though his teeth are too big and his face is too long; his green slanting eyes are filled with so much mystery and promise!" Suddenly she confided that the publicity she'd been getting for breaking up Alain Delon's affair with Romy Schneider was exaggerated. Vadim thought to himself how different she seemed from the edgy, combative young girl he'd met in Beverly Hills two years earlier.

At midnight Olga brought out a cake with candles, and she and

Vadim sang "Happy Birthday." Jane was entranced and let loose a whooping, gulping laugh rather like her father's, a laugh she very rarely released unless she felt at ease with people. Then she glanced at her watch and jumped to her feet, saying she had to get back to her hotel for a little sleep. She was due on the set at 6:00 A.M.

Twenty minutes after her departure the phone rang in Horstig's flat. It was Jane, exclaiming that the evening had been the most fun she'd had since she'd arrived in Paris. "You've seduced her!" Olga told Vadim, who had lingered for a last brandy. He shrugged; he wasn't so sure. However, two days later when his producers, the Hakim brothers, offered Jane a starring role in *Circle of Love,* she accepted immediately.

They did not see each other again until New Year's Eve, when Eddie Barclay, the famous record producer, gave a costume ball. Hundreds of artists, including Jacques Brel and Charles Aznavour, gathered in the huge reception rooms and gardens of Pavillon Armenonville in the Bois de Boulogne.

Jane appeared dressed as a jaunty Charlie Chaplin, complete with mustache, baggy pants, and bowler hat. Vadim had disguised himself as an officer in the Red Army, and he recalled that they played a strange game all evening. "She would avoid me, run into me, and avoid me again."

Around 5:00 A.M. they circled each other for the umpteenth time, as music drifted in plaintively from the garden. There were only about twenty guests left in the huge reception room. "You've forgotten the New Year's Eve kiss," Vadim murmured in his gentle, hesitant way, and he took her in his arms and kissed her deeply on the mouth. Jane gasped and ran off.

A few days later Vadim dropped by the Epinay studios to have a drink with a friend, Jean André, a set designer who'd worked on all of his films and was overseeing the sets for *Joy House.* The two men began smoking and chatting over whiskeys in the small studio bar. It was storming outside.

Suddenly the door opened and Jane flew in, soaking wet from the rain. She'd been shooting a scene in the studio nearby and had thrown a raincoat over her costume to rush across the courtyard as soon as she learned Vadim was in the bar.

"Her chest was heaving; she looked very beautiful, eyes shining, embarrassed to find herself standing in front of me," Vadim wrote. "She had rushed from the set, fearing that I would leave before the end of the day's shooting. That instant I knew I was in love." He promised he would wait for her.

Within two hours they were back at her hotel, embracing passionately. "I had half undressed her and we were about to make love on the sofa when Jane suddenly broke away and ran to the bathroom. She came out a minute later completely naked, and got into bed. I undressed and joined her. But something happened and I couldn't make love to her."

He kept trying but an hour later he had to admit he'd been reduced to total impotence.

"I still don't understand Jane's patience with me during it all. . . . She never refused to let me sleep with her. And I still marvel at my own incredible stubbornness. . . . One evening, in the middle of the night, the curse was broken. We stayed in bed two nights and a day. I had to make up for lost time."

By then Jane was terrified she was falling in love with Vadim. He'd created such a sweet, intense physical intimacy between them that she wanted it to continue, but if it did, she would make herself vulnerable to another human being. "His lovemaking was imaginative, erotic, and tender," Jane wrote. "Though I couldn't understand all that he said (or maybe *because* I couldn't understand), his murmurings sounded to me like messages from some new planet. But what I found as irresistible about him as the sex was his attachment to his little daughter. *He must be a good man to love his daughter that way.*"

"I was Jane's senior by only ten years, but I had long since analyzed and come to grips with my emotions and ideas. . . . Jane, on the other hand, at twenty-four, had not yet come out of her cocoon. She was searching for new roads leading to the discovery of her identity. That I was totally different from whatever she had known so far frightened her somewhat, but fascinated her even more. I was the door that opened onto the adventure of life."

When they weren't making love, he would wander around her hotel suite nude under a voluminous silk caftan — his favorite outfit. He smoked, drank wine, and confided that he was always restless and that he had psychic powers that tormented him — he could literally "see" into the future and predict all manner of wonderful and terrible things.

His moods rose and fell; Jane found his reticence admirable, alien, and sexy. He was amazingly unforthcoming; his detachment reminded her of her father. So did the deep depressions he experienced. To combat them, he tested fate, he told her. He drove racing cars recklessly at dangerously high speeds; he skied down the steepest, slipperiest snowy mountaintops.

At the height of their passion he exclaimed dramatically, "We are going to be living in a beautiful dream but someday we are going to wake up. In the meantime let's savor every moment together — nature — family — colors — smells — the sound of the sea!"

In those first months, Jane was happier than she'd ever been in her life. "I thought my heart would burst. What Vadim gave me when I was young was huge. *Huge.* He reawakened me sexually." She could finally be herself with him. It wasn't an "act." She could communicate with her body (as she suspected her father did with his secret lovers); sex was a way of communicating without words.

"Vadim had an incredible understanding of women. He was able to help me understand myself more than anyone I'd ever met up until that point. He started by telling me to trust myself and listen to myself. And I tried even though I had no idea who I was then!"

"There's no doubt that part of my attraction to him and his life was because it was so different from the repressed style in which I had been raised. Then there was a certain remote dignity about his person that belied his reputation. But what a reputation he had! In the first years of our relationship, walking down the Champs-Élysées, people would react to him as to a major movie star. I was also intrigued by his worldliness: He'd been through war, had risked his life, knew so many interesting people, and was so different from any man I'd known."

At the time, she made little of the fact that they spent so many hours at one of his clubs, where Vadim would go into a side room and bet on miniature electric car races, or that they were driven everywhere by a chauffeur. She didn't pay attention later when he explained to her that he'd had his license revoked for a year for having been in an accident while he was drunk. Catherine Deneuve, his mistress at the time, was in the car with him. She had been pregnant with his child and could have been killed.

Jane did notice that he lied and that he could not handle money; although he worked constantly as a director and screenwriter, he had virtually no money unless he had won at gambling. But at the moment nothing mattered except that she had found a man she truly loved.

Andreas had written her as soon as he discovered that Vadim had moved in with her. "R.V.!" he wrote contemptuously. "I cannot bring myself to spell his entire name." She ignored the letter.

Her former mentor scolded her for cheapening herself: Did she really want to transform herself into another Bardot, when she had the potential of becoming a bigger and better actress than Bette Davis and Katharine Hepburn combined?

And didn't she remember the time they attended a screening of Vadim's disastrous remake of *Les Liaisons Dangereuses* and how they had howled with laughter when Vadim himself appeared on the screen to defend his sexually manipulative heroine and declare in heavily accented English, "Certaine women arre explodeeing lak overripe frut!"

"Jane never thought Vadim would exploit her the way he exploited Bardot," Dick Clayton said, "even though Vadim's relationships were always master strokes of publicity. He was a Svengali three times over before Jane met him. But he was also one of the most charming men I've ever met. And the funniest."

Vadim once asked the journalist Helen Lawrenson, "Do you think I look like Abraham Lincoln?" And she answered, "Nope. All I see is a guy with big ears and a hangdog face." Vadim reported proudly, "Janefonda"—he often referred to her as "Janefonda"—"thinks I look like Abraham Lincoln!"

Roger Vladimir Plemiannikov was born in Paris on January 26, 1928, the son of a French mother and Russian father. His father, Igor, was a diplomat who claimed to be a direct descendant of the great warrior Genghis Khan.

Roger Vadim spent his early childhood living in various embassies in Turkey and Egypt. He described himself to a journalist as "an independent little boy who could speak fluent Turkish, French, Russian and English—I was a fantastic liar," he said.

His young world was idyllic. "My parents loved each other and loved me. Although we had no money, we lived like millionaires." All that changed when his father died unexpectedly of a heart attack when Vadim was nine. It happened during breakfast. "Papa fell into his bowl of coffee." Suddenly his mother, Antoinette, had to take odd jobs, weaving or working in a factory to put food on the table. They were almost always broke.

In 1940 they moved to Paris, shortly after the Germans invaded the city. War was erupting all over Europe. The Plemiannikovs escaped to the south of France, where they survived for three months on nothing but the fresh peaches they could steal from orchards.

"I grew up fast," Vadim said to Aljean Harmetz in an interview in the *New York Times*. He saw men he looked up to "shaking with fear at the bombardments." He saw "priests inform on Jews and Resistance fighters to save their own skin." He saw "the power of money, political hypocrisy, sadism, stupidity." He saw heroism expressed in people he thought weren't capable of courage.

Midway through the war, the Plemiannikovs relocated to a farmhouse high in the Alps. Vadim was fourteen. By day he slept; at night, on skis, he led Jews and downed American pilots through the snowy woods to the Swiss border and freedom.

"The only time I felt like a hero was when I skied through the forest alone at night," he has said, "because I was afraid of ghosts. Crossing the border — even when the Germans shot at me — was easier than going alone through the woods where the ghosts were."

One refugee who escaped from a Spanish prison and hid in their farmhouse turned out to be a handsome young architect who was also a British secret agent. His name was Gerald Hanning, and Vadim's mother fell in love with him; they married and had a child.

There were a few other happy memories. One was in 1944. "I was 16 years old and still a virgin." Vadim had moved back to Paris and enrolled in drama school. One afternoon he and a twenty-one-year-old girl student went to find food on a Normandy farm. "Lying in the hay in the best tradition of popular songs, I graduated from adolescence to manhood. But just at the climax of my initiation something completely unexpected happened. The walls began to move. The ground trembled. The loose planks of the ceiling started to creak menacingly. 'Christ,' I said to myself, 'I didn't know it could be like this!' I had unwittingly chosen to lose my cherry at one of the great moments of history: zero hour, 6 June 1944 — the first wave of the Allied landings in Normandy."

Back in Paris, he continued with drama classes and started writing plays and novels and songs. He read Sartre and Camus; he learned about existentialism, and he also learned about America from the pulp fiction of Dashiell Hammett and James M. Cain. Soon he was discovering Hemingway, Fitzgerald, John Steinbeck, and John Dos Passos. For a while, Vadim says he had a girlfriend who was Hemingway's mistress, "and we would all have dinner together and she would insult him and he would just laugh and tug at his beard." He got a job as a reporter for *Paris Match* magazine — it was, along with *Life*, one of the most powerful magazines in the world before the advent of television. In the evenings he would hang out at places like Brasserie Lipp, drinking and arguing with a group of fellow photojournalists including Sean Flynn, Errol Flynn's son. Vadim said, "We were kindred spirits, shrewd disenchanted kids like myself who'd been hardened by living under the Nazi occupation. We covered everything — arts, sports, revolutions, national disasters. We interviewed kings and movie stars. We were adventurers, ready for anything, capable of anything. . . . But the price of adventure was high. Within ten years, half of my friends were killed in car crashes or plane accidents in Indochina, Africa, Suez, and Cuba."

In order to avoid cynicism and bitterness, he said he eventually developed a kind of philosophy: "I was going to take the best from life. Its pleasures. The sea, nature, sports, Ferraris, friends and pals, art, nights of intoxication, the beauty of women, insolence and nose-thumbing at society."

In 1950 he met Brigitte Bardot, a voluptuous fifteen-year-old schoolgirl who loved animals and dreamed of becoming a ballet dancer. She had just appeared on the cover of *Elle* magazine and had been in a few movies. But "dancing was her life," Vadim said. "She often enjoyed acting, but never took it seriously. Dancing was her life, the cinema a game which she played well."

Brigitte "took to lovemaking with extraordinary intensity," he said. "Sometimes she held up a mirror so she could see me making love to her, as though touching wasn't enough. Before I went off on trips, she asked me to take photos of her, dressed and naked. She wanted me to carry her with me — her face, her body, her sex. She wanted life to be inscribed in a heavenly circle. She would be the sun, radiating life and warmth, with satellites circling in accordance with the dictates of our heart."

Once when he went off somewhere without her, she thought she had lost him and tried to commit suicide. Luckily she was discovered before it was too late. In December 1952 Vadim and Bardot married over the objections of Bardot's father, who wanted his daughter to have a husband who was an engineer, not an artist. Their wedding was celebrated on Bardot's eighteenth birthday. *Paris Match* covered the event, because Bardot was already the media's darling, having just appeared in a film wearing a bikini, which revealed her magnificent body as she rose seductively out of the waves.

After their marriage, Vadim kept his job at *Paris Match* and began working behind the scenes in movies and writing screenplays, all in an effort to create a project for Bardot as the supreme fantasy for the married man. He took photographs of her half-nude and passed them around to talent scouts and producers. He got her cast in nine movies in the next three years.

Vadim says the idea for *And God Created Woman* came to him after he read the news account of the trial of a young married woman who'd been the mistress of her husband's two brothers and had ended up murdering one of them.

"What struck me was not the murder," Vadim said, "but the young criminal's personality, her attitude toward the jury, and the way she replied to the lawyers and the judge. In a flash of inspiration, I had found the subject of my film for Brigitte."

Vadim scribbled notes for *And God Created Woman* while on assignment for *Paris Match* in Rome. He envisioned it as a star vehicle for Bardot and imagined a character like her — a sensuous free spirit, rather petulant, messy, confused — who escapes life in an orphanage only to fall in love with her husband's brother (to be played by Jean-Louis Trintignant).

"I wanted to show a normal young girl whose only difference was she behaved the way a boy might—without any sense of guilt on a moral or sexual level," Vadim said.

He wrote part of the screenplay in a café in Rome while Bardot flirted with a guitar player and later began dancing to his music (she ended up having an affair with him).

One scene in *And God Created Woman,* in which Bardot dances barefoot on a table like a wild Carmen, was inspired by that afternoon in the café. And that particular scene is often cited as a sexual breakthrough in what was considered permissible to show onscreen. Like Jeanne Moreau in *Les Amants,* Bardot would herald a new era in film. She would represent the independent woman who rejects convention to go after what she wants sexually. "There was nothing really so shocking in what Brigitte did on or off the screen," Vadim said. "What was provocative was her natural sensuality."

During filming of *And God,* mostly on the sun-dappled beaches of Saint-Tropez, it was rumored that Bardot and her costar, Jean-Louis Trintignant, were making actual love on camera. Vadim did nothing to quell those rumors.

Soon Bardot confessed that she was having a wild affair with Trintignant. Vadim accepted it. "It was true, I'd been expecting it ever since she slept with the guitar player. Passion is Brigitte's drug, she is ruled by it," he told reporters. "She has to give in to her impulses. I understood. She should neither be idealized nor patronized. We still care for each other. She comes to me with all her troubles. We are like brother and sister." They remained close after they divorced, through Bardot's weight gains, her emotional breakdowns, her many men. They only fought over who would have "custody" of their cocker spaniel, Clown. Vadim ultimately gave the dog to Brigitte, but he missed their pet dreadfully and visited it whenever he could.

And God Created Woman opened in Paris in November 1956. After seeing it, François Truffaut predicted it would open up new horizons for French cinema, which had been "ossified," and Jean-Luc Godard added, "It is pointless to compliment Vadim for being ahead of his time because that is what happened. Everything else [in film] is behind—Vadim is up to date." Even so, most traditional critics trashed the film as "dirty" and immoral, and for a while the public stayed away.

In the United States, the film created a sensation. Committees were formed to protest its lack of morality and to keep the film from being shown in theaters. Speak-outs were organized in churches and synagogues, mostly directed at the scene where Bardot is sunbathing nude. The violent reaction wasn't limited to the United States — it was widespread in Europe, Africa, and Japan. But the publicity about the movie and the curiosity it engendered were huge. By March, the public started streaming into the theaters to see the picture. Suddenly the movie became a big hit all over the world.

Vadim wrote, "The uproar was based on a misunderstanding. People pretended to be shocked by Brigitte's nudity and unabashed sensuality when, in fact, they were attacking a film that spoke without hypocrisy of a woman's right to enjoy sex, a right up to that point reserved for men."

Vadim's next project sounded like big box office. It would be a musical called *Paris by Night,* and Bardot's costar would be none other than Frank Sinatra. Vadim flew to Miami to speak to the singer at the Eden Roc Hotel. He was surrounded by bodyguards. He thought he was in a Mario Puzo novel, but they got along. There was one hitch: Bardot wanted the movie done entirely in Paris, while Sinatra insisted that the movie be filmed entirely in Hollywood. The picture was never made.

Even so, Vadim never stopped being Bardot's mentor. He went on fashioning movies for her even after they divorced and he fell in love with the "golden radiant" Danish teenage model Annette Stroyberg. In fact, Bardot lived with the couple until Annette gave birth to Vadim's first daughter, Nathalie, in 1957.

Then Annette and Vadim got married and Vadim tried to turn her into a star, first in a hastily directed movie about vampires and then in a mediocre remake of *Les Liaisons Dangereuses,* which he set in a modern-day ski resort in Megève. *Liaisons* was held up for two years because of financial and censorship problems. When it was released it solidified Vadim's reputation as a "shameless free-living Pygmalion." Annette was sweet and lazy and not especially talented. All she wanted was to have fun.

Not long after the film was released in 1959, Annette ran away with singer Sacha Distel, who'd earlier been Bardot's lover. An exchange of angry letters between Vadim and Distel was leaked to the press — reportedly by Vadim himself. As a result he became even more notorious. And by then he had a new mistress, the exquisite seventeen-year-old Catherine Deneuve, whom he vowed he would turn into as big a movie star as Bardot. Their relationship was punctuated by breakups and passionate reconciliations. Deneuve gave Vadim his first son, Christian, and then she starred in a movie he directed called *Vice and Virtue*. They fought constantly. She was mercurial, capable of scathing humor, but also downright dictatorial. The more successful she was as an actress, the more difficult she became. "You could be disarmed by her," said Vadim. "No other woman was so beautiful. But then you realized you always had to agree with her — even if you didn't."

Originally Vadim had planned to marry Deneuve after his divorce from Annette was final, but when Annette discovered his plans, she informed him, "If you marry Catherine I will never let you see Nathalie again."

Vadim gave in to her blackmail because he was terrified of losing his daughter. Deneuve knew how much he cared for Nathalie, but she never forgave him for not marrying her. Eventually she ran off with the singer Johnny Hallyday, but she would periodically return to Vadim. She once confided she had been happier with Vadim than with any other man in her life. They were still living rather uneasily together when Jane Fonda entered the picture.

In fact, Vadim was paying rent not only on the apartment he shared with Deneuve on avenue Ingres, but on the one across the hall as well, where Annette Stroyberg lived with their daughter, Nathalie.

To complicate matters further, Vadim's mother, Antoinette Ardiose (nicknamed "Propi"), also lived in the building. Propi — stylish, controlling, emotional — was the most important woman in Vadim's life, according to Olga Horstig. Olga warned Jane, "Vadim has a love-hate thing with Propi — *très, très compliqué*."

Propi was a mystic, a believer in tarot; Vadim inherited her eerie ability to predict the future. He could tell the fortune of anybody accurately with cards. And like his mother, he could purportedly move a table without touching it.

Propi worried about her son's well-being. His risk taking was terrifying to her — his auto racing, his water-skiing. He would explain he had to exhaust himself to keep his "demons" — his intense depressions — at bay. He dreamed often and vividly, and he had no sense of time. He was terribly forgetful and often wouldn't remember lunch dates with loved ones, where he was shooting a movie, or even what the day was.

Not long after he moved in with Jane at her hotel, she ran off to Geneva and didn't say why. He realized "she was afraid of me and attracted, too — so she just decided 'I'll leave, I'll never see him again, and my problems will be over.'" Friends tried to comfort him at a café on the Left Bank. Everybody got very drunk and Vadim "blanked out."

Around 5:00 A.M. he staggered back to the apartment he and Catherine Deneuve still shared. They had not seen each other in weeks. She was furious at him because he had left her for Jane Fonda. Even so, he went directly into their bedroom, undressed, and slid under the covers next to her. Deneuve awoke with a start and sat bolt upright on the pillows, crying, "Will you please explain to me what you're doing?"

It was then Vadim realized he was not back at the hotel. "Pardon," he mumbled. "Went to wrong address," and with that he passed out.

The next morning, very hung-over and wrapped in a blanket, he came out into the living room and found Deneuve standing by the window. "She looked at me in silence — the way an animal might."

"What were you trying to tell me last night?" Vadim asked.

"I was trying to tell you to get dressed and get out," Deneuve said.

"When I went off to sleep, what did you do?"

"I thought of ringing the police. But that wouldn't have worked because it's your apartment. Then I thought of suffocating you with a pillow, but I said it wasn't worth going to prison for someone like you. And I was too tired to drag you out by your heels. So I went back to sleep." After a moment she added, "But aren't you ashamed of yourself, Vadim?"

"Yes, I am ashamed," he admitted.

When Jane came back from Geneva, she confessed she'd gone there to be with an old lover, to test herself, to see if she really loved Vadim. "I also wanted to be away from you so that I could see how I really felt about you."

"And what do you feel?" Vadim asked.

"I love you," she answered.

Later he asked, "Did you sleep with him in Geneva?"

"Yes," she answered. "I already told you I wanted to see what I really felt."

Vadim was shocked and then strangely reassured. "I had never before met a woman who didn't lie."

As soon as *Joy House* finished shooting, MGM stopped paying for Jane's hotel. So she rented a luxurious apartment in a sixteenth-century house on the rue Vieille-du-Temple in the Marais and Vadim moved in with her. The house was on a narrow street near Place Saint-Michel on the Left Bank, in the heart of the student quarter. "There was a huge fireplace, a ceiling with old, craggy beams, and a small staircase leading to a loggia, which took up almost all the upper space."

Although they saw friends, went nightclubbing, and entertained, they spent a great deal of time alone at first. But they had difficulty living together, because Jane preferred going to bed early, whereas Vadim liked staying up all night, arguing and talking with friends for hours in bars on the Left Bank. Sometimes he'd buy champagne for prostitutes and listen to their stories before sauntering off to Les Halles for a café au lait. He loved watching the dawn break over Paris. He would return home just as Jane was waking up; he'd fall into bed and sleep until noon, and then he would start writing or painting until dinnertime.

Jane tried to accept his way of life, which she found messy and nonchalant. "Vadim had created a view of life for himself, a view shared by all his friends, which held that any show of thrift, jealousy or desire for organization or structure was a sign that you were bourgeois. God forbid!" she said. "He could live with dirty dishes stacked high in the sink for weeks."

"Jane always thought that to be happy you must build walls to protect yourself from unhappiness," Vadim recalled. "She cannot relax. Always there is something to do — the work, the appointment, the telephone call."

So he would make love to her slowly and languorously in the early mornings, and sometimes into the late afternoons, and then they would go to lunch at a brasserie, and then they might stroll around Paris, dropping in at a bookstore or a gallery. Jane always wanted to go shopping. She was beginning to collect, a habit she'd inherited from Frances. She spent hours buying religious triptychs, antique dolls, precious stones. She showered Vadim with expensive presents — cashmere pullovers, Italian loafers, long, flowing silk scarves.

She wished he wouldn't drink so much, especially with his best friend Christian Marquand, a tall, handsome actor who was very close to Marlon Brando. Christian dropped by the apartment frequently, often bringing drugs, sometimes hard drugs, because he liked to experiment, and he often brought Brando with him, too; occasionally the three men stayed out all night together.

Vadim loved Christian. He named his son after him (Brando named his son after him, too). Vadim and Christian seemed to have many secrets; they would whisper and laugh, and they often teased each other about their sexuality. They would make pointedly gay innuendos designed to shock; they would send each other suggestive postcards that Jane would be sure to see.

She wished Christian wasn't around so much. But as time went on, she realized that men often prefer the company of other men. They are more comfortable with their pals — *copains* — than they are with their women, because with each other they can act like naughty little boys. She stopped worrying about his deep friendship with Christian — it was part of who Vadim was.

"One of the things I liked best about Vadim was he never grew up entirely," Jane said. "He always inhabited a children's world. He was a magnificent father, infinitely patient and generous with his time." He would concoct stories to tell Nathalie that could go on for weeks. His paintings were childlike, too, primitive, colorful, and sensual. He once painted a three-paneled portrait of Bardot, Deneuve, and Jane, but Jane's face was the dominant one. "Jane was the love of my father's life," Nathalie said.

He could be so touching; he was a kind man. "His gentleness kills me," Jane used to say. He loved listening to his children and playing with them. Preparing one of his special fish stews for his sister and his mother was a joy for him. There were many happy family dinners at the apartment on rue Séguier.

More than anything he was a truly great friend.

Years later another intimate friend, Gordon Miller, told the following story: "I was badly hurt in a motorcycle crash. Nobody thought I would pull through. I had to have a brain operation and I was in a coma for about three months.

"Vadim came to the hospital and sat with me every single day. Finally, when I woke up there was Vadim next to my bed. 'Oh, Gordon,' he murmured in his thick French accent, 'I knew you would pull through. I am so 'appy for you but you look terrible! So feelthy! Tomorrow I am going to wash your hair.'

"The next morning he was back. He had a bowl of warm, soapy water and he slowly, tenderly began to wash my hair. God, it felt so good! And then he toweled my head with supreme gentleness and he said, 'Welcome back to life, *mon ami* — welcome back!'"

As soon as Vadim became involved in preproduction for *Circle of Love,* Jane returned to her ballet class and resumed French lessons, this time with Monique Caron, a tiny, fragile blond Russian who had been married four times and whose mother had committed suicide by hanging herself.

"I didn't tell Jane that," she said. "And I didn't tell her that I'd once been Vadim's lover, either. Right after the end of the war we took acting classes together and had a lovely little affair. We always remained friends."

Monique had met Jane at a party at Christian Marquand's. "Vadim picked me up in his arms and deposited me on Jane's lap. 'Monique will teach you how to speak beautiful French,' he said. And I think I did."

In the next weeks the two women read plays by Molière and Racine out loud, as well as *Madame Bovary* and *Remembrance of Things Past.* "We ate our meals together, shopped, took walks, and went to the movies. We never spoke English," Monique said.

"Jane was the hardest worker I've ever seen, the most determined person I've ever met. She willed herself to speak beautiful French, and she finally did speak beautiful French. She never wanted a free moment — a little unnerving. She had to keep frantically busy. Perhaps she wouldn't have to confront whatever she was afraid of confronting inside herself. A personal persistent emptiness? The emptiness that comes from being a suicide survivor? I related to that, being one myself."

Jane insisted on talking to her in French everywhere, so they might converse while she was trying on clothes or having a massage; Monique once sat with her while she bathed. "Jane had the most beautiful body I've ever seen. Magnificent, flawless, unblemished skin, perfectly proportioned breasts and buttocks, slender arms and legs. She knew her body was beautiful, and she would soap it almost reverently and I would watch and feel uncomfortable. She told me she had gone to bed with so many men she had lost count."

She'd sleep with somebody just in order to connect. She talked on and on about various men, one of whom was not of her "class," and she remembered he had a different kind of smell which appealed to her. It was getting complicated with Vadim because she was afraid she was falling in love with him. She was terrified of intimacy, of being vulnerable: "I'm scared Vadim will roll over me like a bulldozer."

By the time *Circle of Love* was ready to shoot, Jane's French was practically fluent. Vadim gave Monique all the credit. He loved the way Jane sounded. "Her voice was deeper," Monique recalled, "more nuanced when she spoke in French, and the lack of confidence that came from trying to communicate in a foreign language made her even more vulnerable and appealing."

As soon as filming began, the atmosphere on the set grew charged. Jane and Vadim would arrive breathless from their apartment, and it was obvious to everyone they had just gotten out of bed. They would murmur words of endearment to one another while he shrugged off his jacket and she stuck a cigarette in his mouth and lit it. Cast and crew were very aware that an intense romance was being carried on between director and star.

Whenever they rehearsed a scene, Vadim kept trying to break Jane's habit of analyzing every line of dialogue, every gesture; she couldn't be spontaneous. "Andreas had aided her a great deal . . . but by dissecting every feeling and analyzing endlessly she was putting her own personality in chains. All my efforts were directed toward one end: to give her confidence in her looks and in her innermost self." So Vadim would tenderly give her a suggestion but then let her follow through with it, and Jane found that sexually exciting. "I always tried to exceed his expectations and when I did it made me happy." Occasionally he would demonstrate how he wanted an embrace to be done; he would show Jane's costar, Maurice Ronet, by taking Jane into his arms and kissing her passionately; she would often appear to swoon. By the end of the day she had lost her self-consciousness and was romping around on the pillows like a perverse little imp.

Midway through filming, Thomas Quinn Curtis of the *International Herald Tribune* visited the set. "They were about to do another take," he said. "Suddenly Jane grabbed a hand mirror from the makeup girl and stared hard at her reflection in the glass. Her face was flushed and very beautiful. She reminded me of a Narcissus trying to see the image Vadim was fashioning for her and falling in love with and I thought he's like Josef von Sternberg directing Dietrich when they were making *Blue Angel*."

In the last week Jane would do her first seminude scene (which would cause a scandal in the United States). She felt self-conscious, but at this point she would do anything for Vadim. When reporters interviewed her about her feelings, she insisted, "I'm not totally naked. I'm wearing a bra and panties."

Everyone who watched the rushes noticed that she was softer and prettier and more sensual than she'd ever been before onscreen. Vadim realized that, too — he was excited by what he saw, and he began imagining all sorts of movies they could collaborate on.

He wanted to illuminate her paradoxes and what he felt was her mystery, the mystery of her contrasting needs. Vadim's best idea was to create a movie that would explore her need to role-play, because he saw her role-playing as a creative act. At the moment Jane was playing at being his mistress, playing at being the stepmother to his two children; she was struggling through the layers of herself to find an identity. He thought this was very poignant, especially since she already did have an identity, an identity she was trying to shake: her identity as Henry Fonda's daughter.

Several journalist friends were already urging Vadim to write a movie starring not just Jane, but all the important women in his life. That never happened, but near the end of filming *Circle of Love,* something funny occurred that could have been the start of a sex farce.

While showing Serge Marquand how to fall out of a window during a fight scene, Vadim lost his balance and dropped to the floor of the studio, breaking his shoulder. He began moaning with pain.

Annette Stroyberg had just stopped by the set to say hello. She ran to kneel beside him. Jane — who'd been in her dressing room — heard his cry and ran to comfort him. The two women did their best to soothe him. He was now writhing in agony.

It just so happened that Catherine Deneuve was rehearsing on another sound stage nearby. She heard about the accident and rushed to be with Vadim as well.

When the ambulance arrived, Jane, Catherine, and Annette all climbed in with Vadim. At this point, Brigitte Bardot drove into the movie studio's court. The guard ordered her to make way for the ambulance. Then he told her, "Roger Vadim has been badly hurt."

Alarmed, Bardot jumped out of her car and vaulted into the back of the ambulance, crowding in with Jane, Catherine, and Annette.

Vadim saw the faces of these four beautiful women he knew and loved, leaning over him so concerned. Despite the intense pain in his shoulder, he wrote that he was "able to savor that moment."

"He's completely green," he heard Bardot murmur worriedly.

"That's completely normal for a Martian," Deneuve joked. With that, "They all looked at me for an instant — Brigitte, Annette, Catherine and Jane — and burst out laughing."

After *Circle of Love* was completed in January 1964, Vadim stopped courting the press, and he and Jane continued their affair in private. They would disappear for weeks to go skiing in the Alps, or they would visit friends in Brittany, and they went to Saint-Tropez out of season. Jane became more and more caught up in his turbulent life and with the people he cared about. "Never a dull moment."

Once they were awakened at 3:00 A.M. by a phone call from Annette Stroyberg, who informed them weakly that she was so depressed she'd taken an overdose of sleeping pills. A half-hour later, they reached the apartment on avenue Ingres, which Vadim was still renting for Annette. The door was ajar. They ran in and found her on the bed, groggy but conscious. Jane pulled her into the bathroom and forced her to vomit while Vadim brewed a pot of strong coffee.

Soon the story came out. Annette had fallen madly in love with the Egyptian actor Omar Sharif. After spending a weekend with him at the Hotel Georges V, she decided they should be together for the rest of their lives. But Omar had no intention of spending the rest of his

life with Annette. "After their first night together, he had made it perfectly clear to Annette that the adventure ended there." Annette was
devastated.

Jane took over. She sat Annette down on the bed, plied her with
coffee, and started giving her advice. "She spoke in a nice way and succeeded in reasoning with her. She told [Annette] that a woman should
never put herself in the position of depending on a man, either materi-
ally or emotionally."

Annette kissed Jane gratefully and said she'd learned her lesson and
she would never be so foolish again. She was going to think of her
career and she was not going to be a man's plaything, she declared.
Vadim wrote later, "I had never heard Annette talking like this. I
was overwhelmed with admiration for the miracle that Jane had just
wrought."

Two weeks later, Annette fell in love with a man who owned sugar
factories in Casablanca and went off to live with him in Morocco. He
would be her second husband. Before she left, she confessed to Vadim,
"Our daughter Nathalie prefers living with you. I want you to have
custody." Nathalie added, "It was true. My mother knew I'd be happier
with my father. It was the best thing she could have done for me.

"From then on, Jane raised me," she went on. "I was four when we
met. She was ravishingly beautiful. I remember the moment I first saw
her I stuck out my tongue at her and she laughed and held out her
arms. She had never had a mother either. She knew what it was like to
feel lost and abandoned. I absolutely adored her."

They needed more room, so Vadim found a larger apartment for them
in an ancient building called Hotel des Ambassadeurs, where many
artists lived, including Roland Petit of the Ballet de Paris and Charlie
Chaplin. The apartment was in the Marais district. Jane paid the rent;
she was beginning to realize Vadim was not very good about money.

Nathalie remembered that the apartment included a room with
vaults called "the map room, because the walls and ceilings were decorated with images from the sixteenth century. I was studying geog-
raphy at the time and I disagreed with the way some of the images
looked, so I proceeded to do watercolors over them until Jane stopped
me."

There were more parties and dinners with friends at the new apartment, but there were some evenings when Vadim would agree to let Jane prepare a meal for him, and then as she was cooking he would go out, assuring her that he would be back soon. But he didn't come back, and he wouldn't even telephone. She would wait and wait, sitting by herself at the table, finally eating the entire dinner, including the ice cream and cake, then she would go to the bathroom and vomit up everything. She would slink into the bed, angry and tearful, and she would cry herself to sleep. Vadim never knew about the bulimia, or her anger and tears.

The newness of them being together still permitted passion and romance, Jane said. "During the years with Vadim, it never crossed my mind to ask him to help with household chores. I saw it as women's work, even though it meant doing double duty since I often left home for the studios before dawn and returned after dark, while he stayed home and wrote — or went fishing . . . I felt that being the perfect, unselfish housewife would make it impossible for him to leave me — just as my mother had thought about Dad." She also began wrestling with Vadim's finances. He had virtually no money and was deeply in debt to the government. He hadn't paid taxes in years. He owned nothing except his boat and a car — both were in his mother's name.

She had inherited a large trust fund from her mother. "At the time, it was a nice sum, something I could fall back on if I stewarded it carefully," she wrote in her memoir. "Vadim could not comprehend why I hesitated to give him large portions of it so he could hire a friend to come with us to some vacation spot and work with him on a script. At first I was horrified and said so. But over time I began to feel that I was being petty and stingy. So I gave in. Only years later did I realize that Vadim was a compulsive gambler, that the locations for his films or vacations were often chosen for their proximity to a racetrack or casino. I had no idea that gambling was an addictive disease, as difficult to overcome as alcoholism, anorexia, and bulimia. Much of my mother's inheritance was simply gambled away."

Jane set about paying off all his creditors. "It took me five years."

The tax problems hung on even longer. It was a nightmare. She couldn't stand seeing Vadim hounded. She paid off everything, "by sheer force of will," Monique said.

"I loved Vadim," Jane said. "I loved him very much at that time."

16

I N MID-FEBRUARY 1964 Jane flew to New York to do a series of promotions for *Sunday in New York,* which had just opened around the country. It was a trite will-she-or-won't-she sex comedy panned for its coyness; however, she was praised for her stylish charm. (*Time Magazine* said, "Jane Fonda was delectable.") The public loved it. She was interviewed a great deal, but she didn't mention Vadim to anyone while she was there. She even saw Andreas very briefly. Of course, he knew about her affair and was angry and disappointed. "She was all caught up in it," he said. "It was pretty tense between us — we didn't spend more than a half-hour together." He noticed she was dressing like a French woman, in couture clothes; she looked sensational. She was even moving and talking differently. She mentioned she was raising Vadim's daughter, and she seemed very pleased about that. She had started to reinvent herself again.

That summer had started off joyfully. In July, Vadim took Jane, Nathalie, and Christian to a little hotel at Claouey on the Bay of Arcachon, thirty-four miles south of Bordeaux. "Our windows looked out over an oyster bed and beyond that a pine forest," Nathalie said. "From the top of the dunes we had a view of one of the most beautiful and longest stretches of sandy white beach in Europe. The beach was almost always totally deserted."

It was very quiet, very private. Jane wasn't used to such modest surroundings, so the first few days she complained. But then she adjusted to no room service and no phone (except downstairs at the desk) and the communal shower on the second floor.

She grew to love the serenity of the place. She and Vadim and the children took long walks on the beach, collecting shells. They would sunbathe and swim. She would read and Vadim would paint and write.

"That July was the happiest memory of my childhood," Nathalie said. "Jane was always there for us, playing with us, reading to us, telling us stories."

Then there were their car trips. "My father would be driving very fast and Jane would be singing songs like 'Home on the Range.' Christian and I would join her at the top of our voices, howling with laughter, because our American accents were so awful." Soon they would be clinging to Jane's shoulders, and then all three of them would be tapping against the car window with their bare feet, tapping the rhythm of the song against each other's toes. Nathalie called them "footfingers."

After the drives Jane would carry Christian on her back as they trudged down the beach to the hotel, "just as the sun was setting, streaking the sky with scarlet and gold clouds. We would all sing 'By the Light of the Silvery Moon.' We were still terribly out of tune."

Jane remembered "Christian, Nathalie, and me taking our baths together in a tub much too small to accommodate us all. I didn't feel totally sure of myself as a stepmother, but I liked being with the children and having a family. Susan was never far from my heart at those times."

They spent the rest of the summer at Saint-Tropez, staying at the Hotel Tahiti on the beach. Most of the international film set had their headquarters there, and Vadim's ex-wives and some of his old mistresses had rooms there, too.

Jane wasn't quite sure what to think of Vadim's *copains*, his "pals"; they were so direct about everything, especially when it came to love and sex. "If someone coveted someone else's mate, more often than not the someone else would graciously step aside with Gallic civility," Thomas Kiernan wrote.

No one was more civilized than Vadim, or more pragmatic. He had already spelled out his philosophy to Jane months before: "Jealousy is bourgeois." He would go on and on about how the sexual revolution of the 1960s was showing the world what he and his *copains* had always known: that middle-class morality needed to be thrown away and replaced by sexual freedom and open marriage. "If I have sex with someone else, it's not betrayal," he assured her, "because I love you."

Jane kept silent. She was afraid if she disagreed with him or rebelled she might lose him, and that thought terrified her. "[Vadim] helped me rediscover my sexuality (and that of other women in the process), gave me an if-he-loves-me-I-must-be-okay kind of confidence, and helped me move out from under my father's shadow. I had a persona now. I was with a 'real man.' If someone had asked me to describe who I was then, I would have had a difficult time of it. But as film critic Philip Lopate once wrote: 'Where identity is not fixed, performance becomes a floating anchor.' And could I perform! Making the unreal seem real, the sad seem happy, hoping that somewhere along the way it would all work out, that I would discover who I was."

None of their friends suspected how conflicted she was. When her stepmother Susan and her new husband, Michael Wager, came to visit, they thought Jane was blissfully happy.

Meanwhile in Saint-Tropez reporters were clamoring to find out more about the future plans of the couple they jokingly referred to as "Liaison Dangereus." They would ask about their marriage plans, and Jane would tell them, "Why spoil an almost perfect relationship?"

The French novelist Romain Gary, who was then married to Jean Seberg, told Vadim that Jane reminded him of "a mythical creature."

One morning in Saint-Tropez, Gary, unable to sleep, had leaned out his hotel window just as the sun was coming up, and he saw Jane running down the beach, blond hair streaming down her back. "I saw her on the beach at dawn. She was a glorious, naked pagan goddess, followed by a nymph and two fauns. It was an image of the beginning of the world. It was youth, boldness and freedom."

In August 1964, a series of incidents occurring along the North Vietnamese coast in the Gulf of Tonkin were played up in the headlines. An American destroyer, the U.S.S. *Maddox,* was purportedly on the receiving end of a pair of assaults from North Vietnamese patrol boats. After a second purported attack, President Johnson ordered retaliatory air strikes. The reports of the North Vietnamese attacks on American ships were played up in the press, and a congressional resolution was very quickly passed, pledging full support of U.S. forces in South Vietnam and authorizing the president to take whatever action was necessary to protect U.S. forces and stave off aggression. The measure known as the Gulf of Tonkin Resolution opened the way for a major escalation of the war. Only Senator Wayne Morris of Oregon and Alaska's Ernest Gruening opposed the resolution as unconstitutional. (It wasn't until many years later that Americans learned that the Gulf of Tonkin attacks need never have happened.)

Jane remembered vividly a morning in Saint-Tropez: "Vadim and I were having a leisurely breakfast on the balcony of our room at the Tahiti Hôtel when he opened the newspaper. . . . 'Look at this. Your Congress must be out of their minds!' French headlines blasted the news of the Resolution. It gave President Johnson the power, for the first time ever, to bomb North Vietnam."

That summer there were endless discussions in Saint-Tropez about America's "insidious" involvement in Southeast Asia. Most of Vadim's left-wing intellectual friends in Paris, like Yves Montand and Simone Signoret, were contemptuous of Johnson's trickery. They believed that Johnson, along with Secretary of State Dean Rusk and Secretary of Defense Robert McNamara, had misled the Senate into thinking that "retaliation was in the best interest of the nation." Jane listened and absorbed but was not able to understand much yet.

Until she moved to France Jane had never been exposed to people who took such fiercely intellectual approaches to subjects. The unrest in Southeast Asia seemed totally remote to her. She knew vaguely that after World War II, four semi-independent states had emerged from the French empire of Indochina: Laos, Cambodia, pro-French Vietnam with its capital in Saigon, and the Communist Democratic Republic of Vietnam with its capital in Hanoi under the leadership of Ho Chi Minh, who wanted to make North Vietnam an independent country; he and his followers were committed to fight to the death for freedom. The United States was following a policy staked out by the French and was gradually drawn into the Indochina conflict. Americans began to train the South Vietnamese, an interminable process. Internal political rivalries in Saigon increased, reinforcing arguments that the government of South Vietnam was corrupt, and complicating the task of successive administrations in Washington.

Jane continued listening all that summer to arguments about America's involvement in Vietnam. "I wanted to defend my country as a great power acting from the highest political and moral motives," she said, "but suddenly the U.S. was participating in a war halfway around the world, and to what purpose?" She didn't know yet, but she kept listening.

17

JANE AND VADIM STILL didn't have a permanent home. After their summer at the beach Jane realized they would be moving back to Paris into a rented apartment with furniture borrowed from two ex-wives. She wanted them to have their own place, preferably in the country. She wanted to breathe fresh air and bask in the sun; she wanted to plant a garden and walk with her dogs. They were both animal lovers but Vadim didn't have custody of Clown, the black cocker spaniel he and Bardot had raised since it was a puppy. Jane had no pets but she longed for some.

After consulting real estate agents, she eventually settled on a ramshackle stone farmhouse on four acres of land at Saint-Ouen-Marchefroy near Houdan, a tiny hamlet thirty-seven miles outside Paris. She would spend the next three years renovating it with her usual energy and impatience, and Vadim contributed all the money he had from gambling wins and writing. They started collecting a lively menagerie — four ducks, two rabbits, four kittens, and five dogs.

Every morning she would drive from Paris to supervise the workmen. "The house was built around 1830 and what really sold me was the color of the stone walls — a kind of beige honey color like an Andrew Wyeth drawing." She was having the entire house gutted but she kept the walls up. "I wanted to modernize it," she said. The land was flat and there were no trees, so she had a bulldozer come in and move the earth around and give it a more rolling effect, and soon she would order dozens of full-grown trees from nurseries all over France to surround the garden. She would watch the lines of maples, birches, cherry trees, cedar, advancing up the road to the house. The trees were so tall they had to be transported at night and the telephone lines had to be taken down to let them pass. She had them planted with guy wires holding them in place until they had established roots. It was a trick she had learned from her father, who had planted huge pines and fruit trees at Tigertail back in the 1940s.

"Jane had a thing about trees," her stepdaughter, Nathalie, said. "She kept ordering more and more trees, and it was exorbitantly expensive."

There were times when Vadim wondered why she hadn't chosen a farm with trees on the property in the first place. "Because then I wouldn't have had the woods exactly as I wanted them," she answered. Jane was still a movie star's child concocting fairy-tale settings for herself, rather like the Tigertail paradise that Henry Fonda had created for his family when she and Peter were growing up.

The house consumed her.

"She worked with unbelievable efficiency," Nathalie recalled. "I think my father was intimidated by that efficiency. He didn't care about houses or possessions. His friends were what mattered to him — his friends and the beach and his Ferrari and a good bottle of wine, a pot of fresh fish stew. But since Jane wanted the house, he indulged her and gave her what little money he had. He always encouraged her. She did not rest until she finished it. She never missed her daily ballet class, either."

She now had four in help to cook and clean and shop, but she would not allow Vadim to live on the farm full-time, only on weekends. She explained that she needed breathing space. She was trying to be independent. From time to time Vadim would ask her to marry him, but she wasn't sure. She worried about his gambling and drinking, and his first two marriages had been failures.

"Still, Vadim was helping to transform her," Monique Caron said. "Jane had become very chic in her Dior dresses or boxy Cardin skirts and jackets, which she wore when she wasn't in blue jeans. Inside herself she seemed much more serene, much more confident."

People often said Vadim was using Jane, but the opposite was also true: Jane was using Vadim to find a part of herself.

She had gutted the farmhouse and was opening it up into a series of rooms decorated with expensive rugs and artwork. A wall of glass separated the master bedroom from the bath. Both rooms could be seen from the living room. She liked the effect. She seemed content to be a homemaker, experimenting with recipes, working in the garden, and taking care of Nathalie.

David Lean sent her the script for *Dr. Zhivago*. He wanted her to play Lara, the heroine in the epic movie, opposite Omar Sharif. It was the biggest offer she'd ever had; the picture would have an all-star cast that included Alec Guinness, Tom Courtenay, Rod Steiger, and Geraldine Chaplin. The drawback for Jane was that it was to be filmed primarily in Spain for nine months. She didn't want to be away from Vadim for that long. She was afraid of what the separation might do to their life together. So she turned it down. But weeks later she changed her mind and informed her agent she wanted to do it. By then Julie Christie had been signed to play Lara.

Jane wrote despairingly to Andreas, telling him how disappointed she was. He wrote back testily that she should think more about shaping her career and less about holding on to Vadim. "I was her secret sounding board," he said. "We'd write letters. Sometimes I'd read scripts for her. I always told her the truth."

Jane went back to renovating the farm outside Paris. But work stopped in November when she decided to do the low-budget *Cat Ballou*. She hadn't shown the screenplay to Andreas but to Vadim, who encouraged her to do it, "because it's a terrific spoof of a Western." It had every conceivable cliché. In brief, Jane would be playing Cat, an innocent schoolmarm-turned-gunslinger who hires a motley gang of outlaws to avenge her father's murder. Lee Marvin, who was famous for his portraits of sadistic cold-blooded killers, would be playing Kid Shelleen, a whiskey-soaked cowpoke who sobers up long enough to shoot his killer brother (whom Marvin also hilariously portrayed). He wears a fake silver nose, because his real one had been "bit off" in a fight. He would later win an Oscar for his performance. Vadim had ulterior motives about persuading Jane to do *Cat Ballou*. *Circle of Love* was about to come out in the United States; it would be good publicity if he and Jane were there. He could rustle up some business, too; he had another movie for Jane he wanted to peddle.

So she flew out to Colorado in late autumn, just as the leaves were turning orange, and began working. Vadim joined her a couple of weeks later, after getting two speeding tickets for driving too fast out of Denver. He would sit on the set wearing his horn-rimmed glasses and reading *MAD* magazine. Whenever there was a break, Jane would run over to him and they'd talk in rapid French together.

As soon as the filming of *Cat Ballou* ended, Jane and Vadim left for France so she could continue the renovations on the farm. On the way they stopped off in London for the British premiere of *Circle of Love*. In between the opening and various interviews Jane slipped away to see the movie in a theater with an audience. She had developed a habit of always seeing her movies with an audience, usually several times. At this theater in London, studying herself on the screen took on new meaning. She could watch herself in close-up and scrutinize her thick honey-colored hair, or the way she gestured so gracefully with her preternaturally long fingers, and she could somehow separate herself from herself and just drink in Janefonda (as Vadim liked to call her). It was as if she were split in two.

"It was one of the most extraordinary experiences of my life," she would later say to the *New York Post*. "I had seen this movie twice, but I wanted to see it in London and I came in the middle. I saw the last half and then it began again and suddenly — it was no longer that kind of situation where you're only seeing yourself. I was totally relaxed — sitting there watching myself on the screen with people all around me who were watching me on the screen and unaware that I was in the audience. You know how sometimes you say to yourself, 'I wish I could be someone else and see how I appear to other people.' Because you never see how you appear to other people. Certainly not in a mirror.

"Well, I was suddenly seeing myself as someone else. I thought to myself, My God, that's *me*. That's what people see. The me on the screen seemed so much realer than the me in the audience. I was watching the real Jane Fonda. I was panicked and absolutely fascinated."

She told Vadim what she'd seen and experienced in the theater. "Who am I?" She laughed. "What is the real me?" But he didn't answer. Although *Circle of Love* was receiving good reviews in London, he'd heard it was not being received well elsewhere. Reporters had come into their hotel suite; they were being interviewed about their future plans. They described a movie they wanted to make. They were going to call it *Love*. Jane told the reporters she thought it would look marvelous on a marquee. Jane Fonda in *Love*. "You're going to see Jane Fonda in love. Fun, huh?"

In March 1965 they prepared for the American premiere of *Circle of Love*. By now the movie had opened all over Europe and was playing in Berlin, Paris, and Rome to moderately good reviews, although most critics compared it unfavorably to the classic Max Ophüls original. Jane had received some nice notices. *Samedi et Dimanche* commented, "Jane Fonda may be the next woman Roger Vadim molds into a child woman of universal appeal."

Weeks later they flew to New York and arrived at the premiere at the DeMille Theatre on March 24, eager to hear the response from American audiences. It was their first collaboration, and Jane and Vadim were both very proud of it.

They were unprepared for what happened next. Unbeknownst to them, Walter Reade, the owner of the DeMille, had hung an eighty-foot billboard atop Times Square, illuminated with klieg lights. As the audience filed in, they could look up at the billboard, which featured a gigantic image of Jane lying on her stomach, "bare-assed on a bed and gazing seductively across Broadway at another billboard promoting the movie *The Bible*."

Jane was appalled at what Reade had done. "The image was crude, cartoonish, and on top of that the critics were emphasizing the sexual aspects of the story, and nudity, which is misleading and dishonest. I was never nude in the movie." What shocked Vadim most was that the poster was so ugly. "Once again I am the victim of a preconceived idea, that my films are supposed to shock and scandalize people!"

"The media went apeshit if you'll excuse the expression," Fonda's press agent, John Springer, remembered. "Earl Wilson told me he'd received hundreds of letters protesting; the gossip columnist Dorothy Kilgallen accused Jane of indulging in a cheap stunt."

Jane immediately hired the prestigious firm of Paul, Weiss, Rifkind and filed a $3 million lawsuit against Walter Reade. Soon he had a large square of canvas draped over the image of Jane's bare bottom, but that only increased media attention. "It's even more ridiculous with that Band-Aid," she exclaimed angrily.

Eventually Reade removed the offending image and the dispute was settled. *Circle of Love* received mostly bad reviews and did not do well at the box office. But nobody forgot that billboard. "It remained fresh in the public's mind," Dick Clayton said. "More than anything else it helped establish Jane Fonda as a sex symbol."

While they were in New York settling the lawsuit, they stayed at the brownstone. Hank Fonda was away filming; at age sixty he was as busy as ever, giving a tour de force performance as the American president during a fictional nuclear crisis in the movie *Fail-Safe*. He juxtaposed this with lightweight projects such as *Sex and the Single Girl* and Westerns like *The Rounders* and a cameo in *Battle of the Bulge*.

As a matter of fact, he and Jane had bumped into each other earlier that month in the terminal of Charles de Gaulle Airport as he was on his way to the location in Belgium. She was about to fly to New York. They managed to say a few brusque words to each other. They had not spoken for a little over a year.

Jane was out in the city seeing friends or giving interviews, so she didn't spend much time in the brownstone. When he was there, Vadim found the place dark and uninviting. There were piles of art books on tables, and some of Fonda's paintings propped against the wall, as well as a bust of Fonda on a stand.

Sometimes they would have a drink before they went out, and Vadim would find himself fingering the torn fabric on the arm of the sofa he was lounging on. He noticed that there were layers of fabric, one on top of the other. He mentioned this to Jane and she laughed. "Every one of my father's wives has redecorated this house. The layers of fabric represent each marriage!"

They had planned to return to the farm briefly, but as soon as the suit was settled Jane started flying back and forth from New York to Los Angeles on the redeye; she was campaigning hard to get the lead opposite Marlon Brando in *The Chase*. She wanted to counteract the mediocre reception she had received in both *Joy House* and *The Circle of Love*, not to mention the scandalous publicity. But Sam Spiegel, who was producing *The Chase*, liked the controversy. When he screened a rough cut of *Cat Ballou* for himself with his director, Arthur Penn, they decided Jane should definitely be cast. The timing was perfect.

Two months later, in June 1965, *Cat Ballou* opened to ecstatic reviews. *Time Magazine* said: "Jane Fonda does every preposterous thing demanded of her with a giddy sincerity that is both beguiling and hilarious." Her agent, Dick Clayton, was able to get her $300,000 for *The Chase*. She needed every penny. Her expenses were huge; Vadim still had back taxes to pay, not to mention gambling debts. What made her happiest about the movie project was that she'd be working with so many Actors Studio members: the director Arthur Penn, Robert Duvall, Janice Rule, and, of course, Brando. "I just had to work with Marlon," she said.

She knew him from Paris, because he was close to both Marquand and Vadim and he came to their apartment regularly. In California she had a chance to talk to him about the *Chase* script and they started working on it together. She found him otherworldly; he had his head in the clouds. There was a mystery at the center of this man. But he always got to the truth in the script, to the core of the character.

Once he murmured in his oddly light, gentle voice, "You know, Jane, acting is just slipping and sliding. Everybody acts all the time, not just actors." And then with a whisper and a twinkle in his eyes he said, "You gotta keep yourself upset in order to act."

He was asking a lot of questions about the script, which was turgid and overwrought, although no one was willing to admit that yet, because it had been written by the esteemed playwright Lillian Hellman. Jane predicted that the movie would fail. It exploited the hysterical vision that Texans had conspired to kill John F. Kennedy. Jane would be playing a girl of easy virtue who is married to rich guy James Fox, but she is in love with a liberal maverick, Robert Redford, who is about to be lynched for a murder he didn't commit.

It soon became clear that the problems in the *Chase* script could not or would not be fixed. Spiegel did some rewriting himself, which destroyed the story's original spine, and then he decided that most of the action could be filmed on the back lots of Columbia and Universal instead of on location, eliminating any possibility of conveying the atmosphere of a small Southern town. Brando grew depressed; he started to create delays, he gained weight, and he began to mumble his lines. The soundman started complaining.

Jane had a great deal of free time during the shoot, so she spent much of it introducing Vadim to the Hollywood she knew, in the beach house she had rented in Malibu. She invited Brooke Hayward, who was now married to Dennis Hopper, and Roddy McDowall joined them. The former child actor was full of gossip about Elizabeth Taylor and Richard Burton. Then producer David O. Selznick dropped by and he and Vadim played chess. In the middle of the game Vadim started crying, and Jane ran over to hug him and asked, "What's the matter?" And he answered, "I am crying because I am playing chess with the producer of *Gone with the Wind*."

Selznick was part of the "old Hollywood," which, Jane realized, was fast disappearing. The studio system had disintegrated, and in its place were the "Young Turks," directors like John Frankenheimer, who was working with Burt Lancaster on films like *The Train;* and then there were mavericks like John Cassavetes, whose underground hit *Shadows* was the first of a string of rough improvised films. Cassavetes was called the first modern American independent.

There were other young talents, too, like Woody Allen, Buck Henry, Warren Beatty, Peter Bogdanovich, Francis Ford Coppola, Arthur Penn, and Robert Benton, all working on a variety of projects. At the top of the heap at the moment was the charismatic Bert Schneider (whose father, Abe Schneider, was chairman of Columbia Pictures). Along with Bob Rafelson and Steve Blauner he formed a tiny company called BBS and created a TV show called *The Monkees*, a takeoff on the Beatles and their movie *A Hard Day's Night.*

The three men made a fortune on *The Monkees.* Then writer-director Henry Jaglom, rich, gifted, and smart, moved from New York and joined the group in L.A., and they all began to work on projects together. "BBS quickly became a hangout for a ragtag band of filmmakers," Peter Biskind wrote. "There was no hipper place in Hollywood to be." Schneider even had Orson Welles adapting a novel, but he apparently never finished it, although he ran up a bill of $35,000 at the Beverly Hills Hotel and then ran off with Schneider's typewriter.

All these driven, talented people would end up at one time or another at Jane's Malibu house. As a couple, the Vadims were like a magnet, Collin Wilcox said. "The French film world thrown together with the young Hollywood movers and shakers was very sexy. Everybody wanted to make movies. We were hearing about Norman Mailer's underground films, and then there was Warhol; he was starting to attract attention and he showed up in Malibu, too."

Jane and Vadim liked to entertain Warhol and his crowd; they were fascinated by that eccentric group of underground stars, who often camped out at their Malibu house. Vadim thought Warhol, with his avid pursuit of celebrity, perpetual voyeurism, his wild parties with tape recorder and camera always rolling, was setting the tone of the times. Jane loaned money to the foulmouthed Viva, Warhol's biggest underground star, when she wanted to elope with her French boyfriend. They smoked pot together and talked frequently on the phone.

The record business had moved to L.A. and was booming. Rock bands were proliferating in Laurel Canyon. The Byrds lived on Sunset, the Mamas and the Papas on Wildwood Drive. Peter Fonda lived nearby, and he was composing songs and singing them to anyone who'd listen. He hung out with the Byrds and the Beatles and smoked dope with them. Bob Dylan was about to burst forth with songs like "Hey, Mr. Tambourine Man." Supposedly you couldn't really get the lyrics unless you were high.

By 1965 "an amorphous subculture based on the yet to be articulated gospel of peace, love and psychedelics, was just starting to form," Thomas Kiernan wrote. Jane and Vadim were caught up in it.

Meanwhile, their big beach house kept filling up with friends from Paris: journalists, young photographers, and French film directors like Agnès Varda, who would direct *Vagabond,* about a homeless woman truly marginalized. Jane hoped to work with her. There was constant movie talk: gossip about Brando and Anouk Aimée, who might star together in the film of Simone de Beauvoir's *The Mandarins.* And then there was the news that Robert Altman wasn't going to direct the movie he'd developed for Julie Christie about a free spirit called Petulia; he was being replaced by Beatles' director Richard Lester.

Nathalie was enrolled in a summer school right across the Pacific Coast Highway. After classes, Vadim would pick her up and play with her on the beach. When Jane wasn't shooting, she sometimes joined them.

But most of the time she remained at the house entertaining the hordes of children who came by to swim in the pool. Collin Wilcox would bring her four adopted kids, along with Glyn Vincent and his sister Gay-Gay, whose mother was Betsy von Furstenberg. Glyn, now a writer, remembered "how sweet Jane was to us. We came there a lot; there were always some adults swimming naked in the pool, but that didn't bother us. Afterwards, Jane would give us towels, and feed us sandwiches, and we'd go inside and watch TV."

Later she would sunbathe nude on one of the decks. She wasn't at all self-conscious when friends like Brando, Dennis Hopper, Christian Marquand, and Brooke Hayward would wander by. Hopper often took photographs. Nathalie said, "Jane loved having a tan, and sometimes while she was lying there Vadim would kneel down and caress her beautiful body with oil." They never spoke. Jane would grow drowsy; the sun was warm, there was a soft breeze, the waves pounded in the distance; the surroundings turned very sexy. Once a female guest was so overwhelmed by the sensual atmosphere that she knelt down and kissed Jane full on the mouth.

There were continuing rumors that Jane was gay or bisexual. "Look," she said once, "can't we leave something to the imagination?" She added, "Frankly, I've probably done everything. But I will never write about my sex life unless I write about it in a novel. That might be a lot of fun."

Her brother, Peter, was dropping by the beach house, too. He was invariably stoned. He often had his twelve-string guitar with him and he'd play it for her. He'd been practicing for months, for hours and hours until his fingers bled, but he'd mastered all the chords. Sometimes he'd sing a song he'd composed, "Here Comes My Past, Passed." He was "tight" with the Beatles and the Byrds — and "tight" with the Hells Angels, too; he was twenty-five. His hair was shoulder-length; he wore tinted shades and often a crash helmet on his head and usually a rumpled tuxedo or faded blue jeans along with cowboy boots. He survived, he told his sister, "on raw eggs, bananas, and Bosco powder mixed in a blender."

In early 1965 his best friend Stormy McDonald, heir to the $30 million Zenith fortune, had shot himself to death and Peter contemplated suicide himself again. "Oh, yeah, I often thought of killing myself over the years. . . . Like my mother. I thought I might go crazy like my mother." Stormy and he had been like brothers. They'd known each other since their college days in Omaha. "He'd trusted me with his innermost thoughts and I did the same. We told each other everything. He knew about my mother. He helped me with my manic depressions. He was concerned about my past interfering with my present and so was I. We had all sorts of plans to collaborate on movies and books."

Peter later told Rex Reed in *Esquire,* "Not a day goes by that I don't think about my best friend putting a bullet to his head. Hardly a day goes by that I don't think about my mother cutting her throat. There's hardly a day I don't realize this girl whom I was in love with [Bridget] and who was almost like my sister took pills and did herself in. And all the other people who tried to do themselves in. I have no sympathy anymore. Compassion, but no sympathy."

He was at a loss as to what to do next. His movie career had been going nowhere; he was not a conventional leading man. He'd had four flops in a row (including *Tammy and the Doctor,* which he called *Tammy and the Schmuck Face*). He'd fought continually with Warren Beatty on the set of his last movie, *Lilith,* so now nobody wanted to take a chance on him, until American International and Roger Corman cast him in a cheapie movie called *The Wild Angels* about a teenage motorcycle gang. It was a brutal picture featuring outlaw bikers, booze, sex, vandalism, and dope. It had been directed, documentary-style, by Corman. Nancy Sinatra, Bruce Dern, and Michael J. Pollard were in it. Peter played the lead, "a guy called Heavenly Blue."

He would sit with Jane on the beach, describing the movie, for which he'd been paid $10,000. He'd done all his own stunts. The last scene in the movie was an orgy in a church. She just listened to her brother, marveling at him. Somehow he seemed to be getting it together. Somehow he was finding himself. She could not do that in the frenetic, debauched world she lived in. Or maybe she just wasn't willing to "get through the shit," as Peter would say.

She didn't tell him anything about Vadim's gambling and the drinking. "I was in deep denial at that point." Instead she told him about the huge Fourth of July party she was going to give to introduce him to her friends in the film community. Could he arrange the music? Peter promptly asked the Byrds, then the biggest singing group in the country, to perform.

"It was a memorable party," Jill Robinson recalled. "Andy Warhol in one corner drinking with Lauren Bacall; in another corner, Henry Fonda complaining that the music was too loud. George Cukor, holding forth about movies with Sam Spiegel and Marlon Brando. Peter Fonda, Jack Nicholson, Dennis Hopper, all very stoned. Pot smoke thick in the air. Sidney Poitier wandered around in a daze and so did Gene Kelly. They ended up watching Natalie Wood trying to teach Nathalie Vadim how to tap dance."

The Byrds' throbbing music was hypnotic. Everybody was high, floating. The dark felt warm; there were few lights, just guttering candles. Jane had a dance floor set on the beach under a tent, and at midnight there were fireworks — plumes of purple and red and silver stars exploding in the sky and then raining down into the waves.

Jill got very drunk. She remembered "feeling something primitive was rising out of that party — something both destructive and creative. It was the era of LSD, and Dylan and the Beatles and the Stones. It had something to do with the removal of all control — that was what was happening in the sixties; everything about the 'old' America — its repressions, its Puritanism, was disappearing, and in its place there was violence and rebellion and chaos — irrationality — ecstasy."

After a while she staggered away from the house and onto the beach, where she passed out. A group of young men — Jill thought they might have been surfers — picked her up and dragged her back to a nearby hotel and gang-raped her.

"It was like I had dreamed it — wet mouths on my face, big male hands — sandy hands — pawing at me." Hours later she managed to find her way back to Jane's beach house. "I ached all over; my clothes were torn. I felt hysterical but I had to get my car, which was parked in the drive. I had to get back to my kids."

The party was still going on. Jane was passing through the hall when her friend appeared in front of her, disheveled, incoherent, sobbing. As soon as they saw each other, they slipped into the master bedroom, where Jane held Jill in her arms until she stopped crying and calmed down. Then she washed her face, listened to her story, and gave her a tranquilizer. Jill wouldn't let her call the police "because they might not understand."

After about an hour Jane convinced Jill that she should drive home. She made her promise to phone her as soon as she reached her destination.

"For a second I resented Jane's command of my situation. But she was so terrific to me, so kind, so understanding. I'll never forget what she did," Jill said later. The rape was a major incident in Jill Robinson's life; she wrote about it in her semi-autobiographical novel, *Bedtime Story.*

Jane admitted, "I didn't believe Jill's story. Back then I was clueless about any kind of sexual assault against women. I felt no outrage, not even shock. I thought she'd made it up! Now, of course, I'm sure it happened, but back then at least I faked sympathy," Jane said. "As soon as Jill left I felt relieved. I didn't want anyone else to hear her crazy story. I didn't want Vadim's party ruined."

That summer, Henry Fonda phoned the beach house and quietly asked if he could drop by. Jane drawled, "Of course, Dad." They had made brief contact at her party but had not really had an extended conversation for over a year. Her father was curious about this controversial French director named Vadim, his exact opposite, a bon vivant who spoke several languages and loved having a good time above all else. Was he the right man for his daughter? When Fonda arrived at the beach house, he found his prospective son-in-law sitting on the dock fishing. "Fishing was Dad's passion, so it put him at ease and they started to talk right away."

"I wasn't perhaps the ideal son-in-law, but compared to his daughter's ex-fiancés, he found me reassuring. He had never accepted Jane's affair with Andreas Voutsinas. Thanks to the memory left behind by Voutsinas, I enjoyed special status from the very beginning. I was the man who had eliminated the perverse Voutsinas from Jane's life. It wasn't true, but I didn't try to change his mind. I accepted the medal for saving Jane without deserving it."

He had listened for hours to Jane's complaints about her father and he tried to sympathize. "One thing is certain: the father and his children had the greatest difficulty communicating with each other. Jane and Peter turned the misunderstanding into drama. But drama for an actor is like war for a soldier; it's part of daily life. As for me, I was going to help defuse a bomb which, in any case, would never have exploded. For years, I did what I could to 'de-dramatize' relations between Jane and her father."

So when Jane came out on the dock to join them and they tried to talk to each other, "my heart went out to both of them."

• • •

That summer, Vadim was most concerned with writing the best possible screenplay for *La Curée,* an adaptation of an Émile Zola classic novel about a spoiled, pampered young wife of a corrupt tycoon who falls in love with her stepson. For a while he called it *L'Amour.*

Vadim had vowed that *La Curée* would be his masterpiece for Jane. It would showcase her talent. "Vadim wanted it to be a character study of this young woman," Monique Caron said. "But he also hoped the movie would prove to the world he was a serious filmmaker."

So he spent most of that summer writing, until his mother, Propi, came to visit for several weeks. In the evenings Jane would come back from filming and would go into the kitchen and stand next to Vadim as he prepared the meal, broiling fish, tossing salad, explaining what he was doing to Jane while she listened, absorbed. He was continuing to teach her about everything, not just cooking but also history, politics, and art. She felt uneducated and she was thirsty for knowledge. She was still very much in love with him.

After dinner Jane and Propi would laugh and whisper together before dinner. "My mother liked Jane very much," Vadim wrote. "They talked about the role of women in modern society, and bemoaned my laxness in the choice of subjects for films."

With Propi, Jane discussed very earnestly whether or not she and Vadim should get married. She was asking everybody. There was something in her that wanted marriage. Propi thought that Jane was an exceptional woman, and she predicted that "she will be more famous than Brigitte or Catherine and soon being an actress will not be enough for her — she will want more."

Vadim believed that "a happy love life, success in her profession and perhaps a baby would be the fulfillment of her quest. My mother saw further than I."

A few people — her agent, Dick Clayton, included — thought that Jane had decided to marry because her father disapproved of her living openly with a man out of wedlock. "She kept repeating, 'Should I get married?' and most of us told her yes," Dick said.

She would not admit that she was worried about Vadim's heavy drinking as well as his gambling. She said years later, "Boy, if he hadn't been such a drinker, I think we could have always been a team — I mean it." As for the mountains of debts, she had decided she would just keep working to pay them off. "The main thing was, I didn't want Vadim to feel any pressure."

Jane tried to ignore the pressures by keeping busy. In the evenings after filming there were often noisy parties and fundraisers for the Congress of Racial Equality (CORE) at Arthur Penn's. He had rented Sammy Davis's lavish digs on Summit Avenue. There were quite a few intense gatherings in that house. Civil rights was starting to dominate Hollywood consciousness in the 1960s. Some of the biggest stars in the business were getting involved. Brando, Harry Belafonte, Burt Lancaster, and Paul Newman were at Penn's home one night when Jane was there. In 1963 they had all participated in the famous March on Washington where Martin Luther King gave his "I have a dream" speech.

At the meeting Jane noticed that Brando was the most outspoken. She had read about his appearances at student rallies and in churches in the South. He talked on radio and appeared on television, especially after the ugly occurrence in Birmingham when the public safety commissioner, Bull Connor, had authorized the use of cattle prods and water hoses against the demonstrators. They didn't resist or fight because they were practicing nonviolence.

Although he seemed contemptuous of his role as a "movie star," Brando was using his celebrity as a political tool. The public listened to him because he was famous. The comedian Dick Gregory, a radical political activist himself, told Jane that Brando's presence in Mississippi during the sit-ins and the voter registration demonstrations had been very powerful. "Brando had this soothing way about him. You didn't think about him as black or white, just human."

Another night Brando phoned Jane and invited her to a meeting of SNCC (Student Nonviolent Coordinating Committee). "It was at Arthur's, too," she said. "Rita Hayworth was there, I remember, and Burt and Paul. And these SNCC fieldworkers — they were just kids — they were part of a network for the sit-in movement that had started in Greensboro, North Carolina. They had been sitting in at lunch counters, in bus stations, in racially segregated public bathrooms. They spoke about the reasons for SNCC's commitment to nonviolent protest. They spoke about the courage of the Southern blacks who had worked with them during voter registration, some of them beaten or killed. They were so calm and centered as people. People living beyond themselves."

At the fundraiser she saw Vanessa Redgrave for the first time, tall and stately with long, reddish-blond hair. During the question-and-answer period she raised her hand and then stood up to speak. "Unlike all the others, she stood up to speak, turning to look at everyone, owning her space. I will never forget my feelings of awe: Here was a woman who controlled her own destiny."

From then on, whenever she could, Jane would go down to the SNCC office in L.A. to stuff envelopes and lick stamps. "But I wouldn't have become involved if I hadn't been approached by Marlon." He would ultimately tell Jane that acting was child's play, irrelevant when one compared it to the brutishness of racism. He fought to boycott the studios unless black actors were given more opportunities. Jane took note of that, wondering if art and social consciousness could be combined.

"But I was politically ignorant," she said. "I barely knew that President Johnson had signed the Civil Rights Act in 1964." She was not aware of the unrest and rage that had erupted in the ghettos after the riots in Harlem the summer of 1964; she didn't have any idea about the volatility of Compton, one of the black ghettos close to Watts, which was a stone's throw from the opulence of Beverly Hills, until Shirley Sutherland (Donald's wife) pointed it out to her.

On the morning of August 11, 1965, she left early for the studio while Vadim was still asleep. When he woke up, he didn't turn on the TV, so he didn't know about the explosions in Watts, a direct reaction to the brutality and other racial injustices perpetrated in black neighborhoods by the Los Angeles police.

Their black cook, Martha, phoned and asked Vadim to pick her up in Watts, where she lived, because her car had broken down. He agreed good-naturedly. A half-hour later he found himself tooling down the Pacific Coast Highway "in our roomy old Ford convertible. On this particular day I was going to have a chance to show off my virtuosity as a driver," he wrote. "The experience I'd obtained racing Ferraris was not entirely wasted."

Arriving in Santa Monica, he noticed a mushroom of smoke in the distance that seemed to be rising from the center of Los Angeles. He began weaving his way through a maze of police cars and ambulances toward the fire. Heavy machine guns were positioned on the roads; tanks were rumbling down the streets. He wondered what on earth was going on. There was a crackle of gunfire, the sound of explosions punctuated by the wailing of sirens.

He found Martha sitting disgustedly on the curb outside the rubble that had once been her home. He asked her why she hadn't told him what was going on, and she responded, "I forgot to send you a free ticket. Didn't they ask you for it when you came in?"

"I managed to gatecrash," Vadim responded. Martha asked him if he would mind taking her children back to Malibu, as the schools were closed. "I agreed to take the children," Vadim wrote, "and within a matter of seconds my car was invaded by a horde of kids ranging from eighteen months to fourteen years old."

Vadim gunned the motor and they were off, charging through clouds of smoke and zigzagging around tanks and police cars. Bullets whizzed through the air. "The children told me later," Vadim said, "but I was concentrating too hard on what I was doing to bother with details like that."

As soon as they reached Malibu, those twelve little black kids poured out of the car shrieking delightedly. Most of them had never seen an ocean, let alone a beach, before.

Within half an hour a member of Malibu's John Birch Society had phoned the local sheriff to report that "blacks were converging on the beach colony." Squad cars surrounded the house, and police burst in with revolvers pointed at Vadim. After some fast talking he convinced the patrolmen that he should keep the children there until Watts returned to normal but was allowed to do so only on the condition that the kids stayed in the house. Martha subsequently confessed that the children were not all hers. "Just two." She grinned. The rest belonged to neighbors and friends. "I hope you don't mind, Mister Vadim." He assured her he didn't mind at all.

For the next five days, Watts was under siege. There was a bloodbath of rioting, looting, and arson: twenty thousand National Guardsmen finally restored order, but thirty people died and hundreds were injured, and two thousand were arrested. The streets of Watts resembled a war zone.

Jane was very upset about what had happened—unnerved. Even so, *The Chase* continued shooting. Then Vadim had to fly to Paris to do preproduction work on *La Curée.* He was gone a week and Jane fell into a deep depression. She phoned him saying she'd decided they should get married right away. He flew back immediately.

They eloped on August 14. The ceremony was to be private—no press—only Peter Fonda and his wife, Susan; Brooke Hayward and Dennis Hopper; Dick Clayton; Christian Marquand and his wife, Tina; Jane's costar in *The Chase,* James Fox; and Oriana Fallaci, an Italian journalist and close friend of Vadim's, who promised she wouldn't write anything. Propi came, too, armed with cameras; she planned to record the entire wedding.

Everyone packed into a chartered plane that flew them to Las Vegas. "We could see Watts still burning below us," Brooke Hayward remembered.

The ceremony took place in Jane's lavish six-room suite at the Dunes Hotel. While Peter Fonda strummed his guitar, an orchestra of female violinists in skintight blue sequined dresses played "Here Comes the Bride."

Justice of the Peace James Brennan, who'd married Cary Grant and Dyan Cannon six days earlier at the Dunes, officiated. He was so tall—six foot six inches—that he could barely squeeze through the door.

Vadim had forgotten to buy a ring, so he borrowed Tina Marquand's, which was so big that Jane had to hold her finger aloft throughout the ceremony. "It looked as if she was thinking 'fuck you,'" Vadim said. In truth, Jane confessed, she was "feeling like a zombie and wondering, 'I don't know why I'm doing this!'"

Just as Brennan intoned, "I now pronounce you man and wife," Propi slipped into the suite, flushed with embarrassment. She'd been so caught up in photographing Las Vegas that she'd lost all track of time. Now there would be no snapshots of the wedding, certainly no visual record of Jane bursting into tears and locking herself in the bathroom, where she cried and cried.

There was a phone above the toilet. Jane impulsively grabbed it and called Andreas in New York. "I'm married," she sobbed. "Now what do I do?"

"I haven't the faintest idea," her former lover/mentor snapped, and hung up on her.

She hadn't invited her father to the wedding, but when reporters asked him about it Fonda said he was glad. "Vadim is a very civilized man." Five months later he followed his daughter's marriage with his own. He married his fifth wife, Shirlee Adams, in December 1965 between performances of the play *Generation*. The simple ceremony was held in a judge's chambers in Mineola, Long Island, with Elizabeth Ashley and George Peppard as the witnesses, along with close friends John and Jane Springer. Bride and groom were beaming; he couldn't have been happier. "After stepping up to bat five times, I finally hit a home run," he told his biographer.

Word of mouth on *The Chase* was not good; Brando had seen some of it in the editing room and he called Jane. She wasn't surprised, but by then she was concentrating on her next movie, *Any Wednesday*, a lightweight Broadway comedy by Muriel Resnick, which had been adapted by Julius Epstein (who'd cowritten *Casablanca*). He was producing the movie, too, and he'd cast Jason Robards as the millionaire businessman who every Wednesday has a romantic dalliance with his mistress (played by Jane). She wore a wig in the movie and French couture clothes, but she didn't have much interest in the project, although she was nominated for a Golden Globe for her performance. The only reason she accepted the role was so she could pay for the swimming pool that she was planning to put in at the farm and the barn for the pony from *Cat Ballou* that Nathalie was riding.

Vadim remained in Paris in preproduction for *La Curée*. Jane missed him terribly. Epstein recalled, "He would phone her every day at the studio. It was always around 2. We'd be coming back from lunch. Jane would stay on the phone sometimes up to an hour. She'd jabber away in French and I'd be tapping my foot, wanting her to start filming."

Nobody knew how anxious she was about the marriage. Whenever they were separated she was sure that Vadim was up to no good, which was often the case. Part of her concern was that he kept sleeping with other women, although he insisted that it didn't mean he had stopped loving her.

He did not believe in fidelity, he had explained soon after they met. He'd always wanted them to have an "arrangement" like his friends the Vaillands. Roger Vailland was a novelist and a hero of the French Resistance who believed there could never be true love in a relationship without freeing oneself from a sense of ownership and, above all, jealousy on a sexual level.

He and his wife, Elisabeth, had an open marriage. One night when they were spending the weekend at the farm, they talked about it.

Jane listened wide-eyed when the Vaillands first described their "arrangement." Elisabeth not only accepted Roger's extramarital affairs; she also introduced him to various young women — contessas or prostitutes she thought he would enjoy.

"And if your wife made love with another man, would you be jealous?" Jane asked Vailland.

"That's completely forbidden," Vailland said.

"Why?"

"Because she would stop loving me."

"Is that true?" Jane asked Elisabeth.

"Yes!" Elisabeth answered. "I would lose respect for him if he allowed me to come in the arms of another man."

"That's not fair," Jane said. "I don't call that freedom!"

"Perhaps. But Roger and I have found our freedom and we're happy."

Late that night the Vaillands left the farm to drive back to Paris. After they were gone, Vadim and Jane went to bed and made love, and then she asked him, "Do you agree with Roger's theory?"

"No," he lied.

"Why not?"

"Because you're not Elisabeth." And then they embraced and curled up in each other's arms, and they argued about love and its complications until dawn.

Eventually Vadim suggested that they, too, have *"un arrangement."* They had been together for three years; he now confessed he'd never been faithful to her. There had always been other women, but these nameless women weren't important, he insisted. They had nothing to do with the genuine love he had for her. He urged her to try to enjoy "sex for its own sake" so he could tell her about his conquests, and then they could share their experiences. But he assured her he would never embarrass her in public; he would never have a mistress.

Jane was shocked. She believed that nonpossessiveness — sexual freedom — tore the heart out of intimacy in a relationship. She felt diminished by Vadim's suggestion of *un arrangement,* and she felt frustrated and angry, too, because she knew she needed to be controlled by a male authority figure.

Living with Vadim had made her love him more. The attachment had deepened. They had shared so much — the farm, his children, their work together, traveling. They were thinking about having a baby. And then suddenly he blithely asked her to be his *accomplice dans le lit.*

But she kept silent, rationalizing that she had to put up with the arrangement in exchange for the emotional security Vadim gave her. "He validated me. I couldn't conceive of leaving him." So she didn't object when he brought home a beautiful redhead and she welcomed her into their bed. The redhead was a high-class call girl from Madame Claude's, the most elegant brothel in Paris. "I took my cues from him and threw myself into the threesome with the skill and enthusiasm of the actress that I am."

The threesomes continued throughout most of their marriage. Occasionally Jane herself did the soliciting. But she maintained she never got much pleasure from them. She told a friend she felt compelled to supply the women for Vadim so she would have some sort of control. "And the women do invariably fall in love with me," she would add slyly.

What a tangled web their marriage was. Jane seemed to be devoting so much energy to maintaining a double standard for herself. She was often turned on by Vadim's decadence and sensuality but she couldn't admit it. She would complain to friends and act the victim. She was trying to have it both ways, and people who try to have it both ways often come to an unhappy end.

Sandy Whitelaw was working at United Artists in Paris, and he was often at the Vadims'. Their open marriage was the talk of show business, he said. There was much gossip and titillation. Who was in their bed and who wasn't? The crème de la crème from the worlds of politics and the arts. Friends from Hollywood were always eager to participate. "But you had to be invited," said a London producer who was, but refuses to give his name.

It wasn't long before Jane began insisting that Vadim had showed her a different way to live — a European way of life in which there can be no secrets. When Susan Blanchard and her husband, the actor Michael Wager, came to visit the farm, Jane extolled her new sexual philosophy and invited them into the bedroom. Wager said, "We just laughed and said no." However, in Malibu, "for the hell of it," Brooke Hayward and Dennis Hopper joined the Vadims in bed, but just once. "It was not exactly my idea of heaven," Brooke recalled.

Jane would subsequently begin to have her own little affairs and then describe them to Vadim as agreed, "but in ironic tones." "Later, Jane would react, would acknowledge her desires in arms other than mine. There were pangs of jealousy, but no apprehensions, since she, too, told me everything. It still had not dawned on me that by finally accepting her sexual freedom, she also was about to distance herself from me, to escape."

By now, their life was getting pretty complicated. One morning, Nathalie walked in on them and found a strange woman beside her father on the pillows. Jane was in the bathroom. "I was disgusted," Nathalie said. "I turned around and left. I guess I was around nine. After I grew up, I told Vadim he'd been full of shit to behave that way with Jane. I didn't know what Jane thought; I never asked her."

As usual, Jane left a lot unsaid, especially with Nathalie — but she was concerned about her stepdaughter, who was an innocent, impressionable witness to everything that went on at the farm. Without saying anything, she began investigating Swiss boarding schools. After a while she dropped the idea because Vadim didn't want to be separated from his daughter and Jane had so much else to do — overseeing and supporting her huge entourage.

There was an Italian family of three. The mother had been the maid for Deneuve and Annette and had been fired by both. Jane not only hired her back, but hired her husband as well. His job was to keep the farm in shape. When Jane discovered that their twenty-three-year-old son was a Cordon Bleu chef, she hired him as well and then translated all her favorite Italian recipes into French.

There was also Vadim's pretty secretary and *her* lover, and a contingent of Vadim's friends — photographers, writers, actors — who hung around the farm, often spending the night.

Jane had very little free time, but when she did, she would work in her garden. The sunflowers she planted in the courtyard were remarkable. "Like Jack's giant beanstalk," Vadim said, "they never stopped growing, and their magnificent corollas soon reached beyond the roof of the farmhouse."

"What have you done to them?" he wanted to know.

"I know the magic formula that makes everything grow," she replied. She was like her father in that regard. Hank Fonda had a green thumb. His gardens in Bel Air were visual masterpieces of flowers, shrubs, fruit trees, and vegetables, and everything was always flourishing.

She told herself she was almost content. She had the farm and her gardens and her animals, and especially her favorite greyhounds, Mao and Lilliput, to play with. How she loved her menagerie! — the ducks and geese and chickens, the mewling kittens, and twelve barking dogs. She reveled in nature, loved to feel the warm sun on her bare skin. She always sunbathed nude and she swam nude, too, one of the reasons she wanted to build a pool at the farm. But so far she had not earned enough money to do so.

Jane's fantastical life continued during the filming of *La Curée* in January 1966. The film, Vadim's most imaginative, sardonic, cinematic sexual fantasy in luscious Technicolor, seemed a fitting coda to what had preceded it.

Everything about the movie was sumptuous, exaggerated, at times almost nonsensical, beginning with the vicious guard dogs at the start of the picture, which for no reason leap after the young photographer snapping pictures of an older man. He turns out to be the photographer's father and Jane's husband.

Much of *La Curée* was shot in a magnificently appointed townhouse in Parc Monceau, a residential section in Paris for the super-rich. Vadim had a lavish budget for sets and costumes, and he'd hired the great cinematographer Claude Renoir to create the movie's stylish, soft-focus look. There were canopied beds in high-ceilinged rooms filled with priceless antiques, as well as a sleek gym where Jane (as Renee) worked out.

Jane threw herself into the role of Renee, the beautiful child-bride of a corrupt middle-aged tycoon (Michel Piccoli) who falls in love with her stepson (Peter McEnery). During much of the film, in which she is being sexually awakened, she is giddy with passion. It is basically an erotic coming-of-age story, though for anyone who knows the back-story of Jane's private life with Vadim it's a bit too close for comfort, such as the scene when Renee turns on her husband angrily and says, "You like whores."

Vadim collaborated with Jane on every sequence. Whenever she tried to hide behind coy mannerisms or a phony high-pitched voice, he would caution her to "be yourself." He created specific things for her to do during the film, physical, nonverbal stuff as well as improvisations to help her shed her self-consciousness.

In one scene, he has her exercising in the gym; in another, when she is seated at the breakfast table with her husband, he has her belting out part of a song from *Singin' in the Rain*. He also concocted a variety of games for the young lovers to play as they wander, bored and alone, in the great mansion.

The biggest seduction scene in *La Curée* begins in the spirit of children at play — nutty children — with Jane teasing her lover-to-be to the point of exasperation. The two dress up in Genghis Khan costumes, smear cold cream on each other's faces, and chase each other all over the villa. They set the bedclothes on fire — they put the flames out with a bottle of champagne; they smash gilt-framed mirrors and shoot at each other with fake rifles until they fall into each other's arms and make love.

Vadim demanded perfection, and he shot and reshot the scenes. And sometimes he and Jane would quarrel; they often worked till very late.

At the end of the day they returned home as a couple. "If we argued on the set, we made up in bed," Vadim insisted. "No matter how many disagreements we had, our physical life was formidable."

Jane continued to solicit for them on occasion. A female friend recalled, "Jane asked me to join them one evening for some fun and games. I said 'no way' and Jane was so apologetic. 'Oh, I am so sorry. I am so sorry! Forgive me!' she exclaimed, sounding like a schoolgirl. 'Forget it,' I told her. And I hope she did."

In the last days of filming the set was closed for the nude scenes. Vadim had convinced Jane that nudity was essential in creating the character of Renee, and Jane did everything Vadim told her to do, including skinny-dipping in a huge goldfish pond. As soon as she took off her robe and began to rehearse, a photographer, who was hiding on the catwalk, started taking pictures of her naked, which he later sneaked to *Playboy*. In the movie she is seen only from the back.

Jane didn't know about the photographer, but she confided to a friend that she felt "acutely uncomfortable," the way that she had felt when she posed bare-breasted for Avedon. But she said nothing; she just smiled her dazzling smile. "*Ça va*, Teeth," Vadim kidded. His nicknames for her were Teeth and Kiki.

Nathalie said, "Jane put Vadim on a pedestal then. She seemed subsumed by him. I think it excited her to see he was glorifying every aspect of her, even her yielding qualities, and he brought such exuberance to the process. He was absolutely fascinated by female sensuality and he wanted to immortalize Jane. He wanted to create an erotic image of her that would stand the test of time."

Monique Caron watched the rushes and thought "Jane peeked out from behind her mask in *La Curée*. She was always about control and concealment, but she revealed a bit of herself in spite of herself in that movie — her eagerness to please, and her veiled contempt for men, as well as her longing to be loved by men — it's all there and it's gorgeous."

Jane studied the rushes, too, and she seemed pleased. Vadim had succeeded in releasing her quirky/powerful spirit. *La Curée* is a wonderful cinematic documentation of what "Janefonda" was like at the age of twenty-eight: edgy, stubborn, innocent, flirtatious, spoiled, and moody, luxuriating in the wealth and celebrity that sometimes made her so imperious and graceful at the same time.

Jane was exhausted and hoped to relax after *La Curée*. But she was offered a big part in the steamy melodrama *Hurry Sundown* by the controversial German émigré director Otto Preminger. She admired his movies, the film noir *Laura* and the mystery *Anatomy of a Murder*. Preminger convinced her that *Hurry Sundown* could be an important picture about the horrors of bigotry. So she flew to Baton Rouge, Louisiana, and spent the next two months playing a spoiled, self-indulgent woman married to Michael Caine, a scheming plantation owner. (In the most talked-about moment in the movie, Jane, whose character is frustrated by her husband's impotence, puts a saxophone between her legs and blows on it with "a slow and highly suggestive determination." "It is possibly the worst scene I have ever seen in a movie," *Time Magazine*'s Richard Schickel wrote.)

They filmed in the heart of Ku Klux Klan country. The motel they stayed at had never been integrated before, so on their first night in Baton Rouge a cross burned on the motel lawn. Diahann Carroll was concerned because, as a black woman from New York, "she'd forgotten how to behave down here in Klan country." Rumors spread in Baton Rouge that Preminger was making a "nigger gets the best of white folk" movie, because the plot did revolve around blacks trying to keep whites off land the blacks rightfully owned.

Then when the black actor Robert Hooks swam in the motel swimming pool, there were reverberations all the way to New Orleans. "Locals peered from around corners," Jane recalled, "as though they expected the pool to turn black." Tires were slashed on Preminger's car. Cast members began receiving threatening phone calls.

Much of the action of the movie took place in a crumbling mansion, which resembled the plantation house in *Gone with the Wind*. At one point, the location shifted to St. Francisville, a small, one-street town where everybody sat on their front porches fanning themselves in the sweltering heat. Vadim had flown over from Paris to visit with Jane. They were strolling down the sidewalk together as Claude Azoulay, a *Paris Match* photographer, followed them. A small black boy ran over to Jane and gave her a flower, and she bent down to kiss him.

People on the street stopped and stared. "The atmosphere in the street, which only a moment ago had seemed happy and full of life, suddenly became ominous and uncomfortable, full of unspoken threats." Azoulay told Jane in French, "They don't seem to like you kissing blacks." Jane burst out laughing. "Don't be silly," she said. "He's only a child."

The following day, the picture appeared on the front page of the local paper and, Jane said, "all hell broke loose." There were more threatening phone calls, and later that morning the town sheriff confronted Preminger in front of his cameras as he was about to begin shooting a scene.

The director didn't know who he was, so he began bellowing at him in a fury to get out of the way. The sheriff was not impressed. He informed him that the entire production must leave town by midnight that night. After that, he could not guarantee their safety. Preminger realized he meant business. Everyone packed up as quickly as they could and left in various station wagons. When they did, two sedans loaded with armed men pulled off the curb. "As we drove out of town, two of our window screens were holed with bullets," Vadim said, "which could have easily killed the drivers or passengers."

Jane's kiss cost Paramount the equivalent of an entire day's shooting — $60,000.

After *Hurry Sundown* wrapped, the Vadims flew back to Paris and threw a party at the farm for Warren Beatty. Sandy Whitelaw was there, and he recalled, "Jane had gone all out for the dinner and was working up to the last minute with the chef to make everything really delicious. Warren arrived with Brigitte Bardot. They were having an affair."

After a long cocktail hour, dinner was served along with many bottles of red wine. Everybody got very drunk, Sandy said. At the end of the meal, Warren complimented Jane on the food. "It tastes wonderful," he said, and then his eyes twinkled. "But I know something that tastes even better and that I'd like to eat even more," and he gazed lustfully at Bardot.

Vadim added tipsily that "Brigitte is indeed a morsel," and then he murmured, "Jane is not quite in that class."

Sandy turned to Jane, who was trembling with fury and embarrassment, and he tried to smooth things over by saying, "Hey, this will turn out all right."

With that, she snapped, "Oh, shut up! I always thought you were a creep, and now I know it!"

The evening ended in an uncomfortable silence. Jane would subsequently confide in Madeleine Sherwood, sobbing, "Vadim calls me a watered-down version of Brigitte Bardot." Madeleine remembered, "I felt so sorry for her. Jane Fonda was the most insecure person I've ever met in spite of her success. How could she put up with such cruelty? She really loved Vadim, even though he was forcing her to be something she was not. She wasn't a sex symbol. She was essentially a modest person. It seemed as if Jane was locked into subservience by self-hatred and need, and by her unquestioning acceptance of Vadim's right to use and abuse her psychologically."

There was increasing trouble in the marriage, but they kept on trying to make it work. The next time Sandy saw them together, they appeared loving and relaxed, even though by then the August *Playboy* had appeared on the stands showing a nude Jane on the set of *La Cu-rée*. Until the magazine was published, she had no idea she had been photographed during that scene. She subsequently sued the magazine for $9.9 million, claiming that her nudity in the film was her fictional character's, not her own, and that the photographs as published invaded her privacy. The suit dragged on for over a year and she lost, but the film reaped an enormous amount of publicity. Vadim seemed upset; the arty film they'd worked so hard on was all but forgotten and overshadowed by the film's controversial nudity. Jane was told that Vadim had arranged for the photographer to be there, but he vehemently denied it. She suspected differently.

18

JANE HAD TO FLY to L.A. the first week in September to start filming *Barefoot in the Park* with Robert Redford. Vadim was adamant that they go to Saint-Tropez for a few days. He went there religiously every summer. He had to be with his *copains*. Jane was stressed but she agreed. Then she phoned Peter and said he had to come to Saint-Tropez. "She implied she needed me to be there. She always called me when she was bugged. She was like Dad. She could never come out and say what was bugging her directly."

He happened to be in Venice where *The Wild Angels* had opened August 3 at the film festival. It was the invited American entry and it created a sensation. Suddenly Peter was a huge star, and the movie was doing big business; it would eventually gross over $10 million. He was pleased; a crappy little biker movie had taken off and he was about to become famous, maybe more famous than his sister. Peter soon found himself lionized all over Europe as the great American biker. A poster of him astride a motorcycle outsold the biker posters of Brando and Steve McQueen.

When Peter arrived in Saint-Tropez, it was jammed with tourists and topless sunbathers. The weather was flawless — clear blue skies and warm sun. He joined Vadim and Jane at the Tahiti Hotel on the beach. He'd always wanted to get to know Vadim, whom he thought of as "a nicer version of my father." But he never found out anything about his brother-in-law or the marriage on that visit, and Jane never told him what was bugging her. What she did was cling to him, asking all sorts of questions about his experiences with LSD.

In the last year he had taken eighteen trips. He had been "exorcizing his demons," blasting through his despair and his obsession with the past. "Thanks to LSD I am having no further trouble with my past. I've licked it," he told his sister. And because of this "ego death," as he put it, he no longer cared what anyone thought about him — not his father or his sister or "the business." Jane envied him — especially the fact that he no longer suffered nightmares about their mother's suicide. With LSD, he told her, he had felt a kind of spiritual death and rebirth.

He was full of talk about what was going on in America and he had to share it. What was happening was astonishing. The country was seething and changing. Hippies and druggies, music, dress, language, sex — everything was changing with intoxicating speed. Costumes instead of clothes; food was becoming organic. He talked about how people should live their private lives in ways that go along with their politics and their principles.

Jane listened, but she seemed sad and tired to Peter. She and Vadim were not communicating; they weren't even spending much time together. So she and her brother eventually took off on their own, zipping around the bay on Vadim's speedboat, the *Rive,* and always ending up at some grand villa on the Côte d'Azur for dinner. Guests included the Italian Prince Dado Ruspóli and his wife, Nancy; J. Paul Getty and Talitha; Françoise Dorléac; and Christian Marquand. They were "some of the most decadent types I'd ever met, lovely, charming, sensual and outrageous."

They spent their last night together in a restaurant owned by one of Vadim's buddies, and everybody started behaving like giddy kids — drinking wine, smoking, smashing crockery. Peter recalled, "After a fabulous meal and much plate smashing, Vadim, Jane and I were headed back to the Plage Tahiti in the Ferrari [with Vadim at the wheel]. As it was a two-passenger car, Jane sat on my lap. We began singing Everly Brothers songs, something we often did when we were together."

Peter thought Vadim became jealous. Suddenly he "turned the wheel hard to the right, causing the sleek car to swerve. The beautiful handmade aluminum body caromed off a stacked rock wall on the left side of the road, ruining the left rear end. Vadim followed this with a hard turn to the left, smashing the other side of the rear. Jane and I stopped singing. She doesn't remember the incident but I shall never forget it."

The following day, Peter, Jane, and Vadim drove to Nice and then took a flight to Venice, where *La Curée* was being shown at the film festival. They sat with François Truffaut and Jean-Luc Godard. "Jane had dubbed two versions, in French and in English. She had a real triumph," Vadim wrote, adding, "She established her dramatic potential in that movie more than any other." (It opened in January 1967 and was a smash all over Europe; it is now considered a minor classic in France.) It was not as successful in the United States. However, the *L.A. Times* said, "Fonda creates a comprehensive portrait of a woman in love — her joys, her sorrows, her hopes, her fears."

At the Venice premiere, photographers swarmed around her. "She was a photographer's dream," her friend Peter Basch said. He had photographed all the great Hollywood beauties — Taylor, Monroe, Bardot, Lollobrigida — and he believed she could hold her own with any of them. Like everything else she did, Jane informed herself about photography. She asked questions about lights and angles; she used the still photograph to further her career. She knew how to project — she improvised and the camera loved her. The studio system was over and with it, the phony glamour industry. Now stars could be more authentic and genuine. They could also show more skin.

While she was filming *Barefoot in the Park,* she posed for some of the last traditional movie stills, mugging and cavorting with her costar, Robert Redford. They both enjoyed the shoot. *Barefoot in the Park* was based on Neil Simon's zany, bubbling Broadway comedy about Corie, a free-spirited bride who tries to shake up her stuffed-shirt new husband, and it was being directed in lively fashion by Gene Saks. He thought Jane and Bob had real chemistry onscreen.

Some of the early scenes in the movie, including the long honeymoon sequence at the Plaza Hotel, show Jane being humorously seductive as she tries to get her husband to stay in bed.

She liked working with Redford. They became friends and would have long talks between setups when they were filming on location in New York. He confided he was uncomfortable with his increasing fame. He wanted to be able to throw a football in Central Park without

being gawked at. He had already bought huge tracts of land in Timp-
haven, Utah, and was about to build a house there with his wife, Lola.
He intended it to be a hideaway between pictures.

For a while after the *Barefoot* shoot ended, Jane stopped working
and for part of 1967 she stayed at the farm. Vadim wrote a screenplay
and painted; Jane was busy overseeing the renovations; she entertained
film critic Pauline Kael, who remembered the big pack of dogs barking outside in the garden during dinner. Simone Signoret took Jane to
a peace march in Paris where the speakers were Simone de Beauvoir
and Jean-Paul Sartre. For the first time Jane started thinking about the
Vietnam War and realized America was in turmoil. Then on May 18,
1967, she and Vadim were remarried in a civil ceremony in the Saint-
Ouen town hall; they had discovered that their Las Vegas marriage was
invalid in France and they had to comply with French law.

The same month *Barefoot in the Park* opened, two of Jane's other pictures opened as well: *La Curée,* which was moderately well received,
and *Hurry Sundown,* which was savaged by the critics. Words used to
describe the picture included *ludicrous, offensive,* and *tasteless.* Luckily, *Barefoot* saved the day for her. It was her most popular picture so
far; the reviews were enthusiastic. *Time Magazine* noted, "Jane Fonda's
performance is the best of her career. A clever caricature of a sex kitten
who can purr or scratch with equal intensity."

The *New York Times* commented, "Jane Fonda has managed to
maintain two different public images simultaneously in France and
the United States. Over here, she appears in movies like *Barefoot in the
Park* and *Any Wednesday.* She sounds and dresses like the pretty roommate of the girl you dated in college, and everyone still thinks of her
as Henry Fonda's daughter. In Europe, she stars in movies like *Circle of
Love* and *La Curée,* and she sounds like the girl you eavesdropped on
in a Paris café; she undresses like Brigitte Bardot and everyone knows
her as the latest wife of Roger Vadim."

Jane longed to be in a meaningful project. She told Madeleine Sherwood she was tired of playing kooky airheads like Corie. She'd starred
in fifteen films in ten years, and none of them had been especially
memorable. "She was offered everything," Andreas said; he was still

reading scripts for her. "But she turned down *Bonnie and Clyde* and *Rosemary's Baby* when Vadim wanted her to do *Barbarella*."

Initially she had rejected the idea, which had come to her in the form of a letter from producer Dino De Laurentiis. He had asked her to star in the film version of the French comic strip *Barbarella,* which combined science fiction with soft-core porn. Sophia Loren and Bardot had already said no.

Vadim fished the letter out of the wastebasket. He read it and exclaimed, *"C'est formidable, ça!"* He was a huge comic book fan, especially of *MAD*, which he felt perfectly captured life's absurdities.

Within minutes he was conjuring up an image of Jane as Barbarella, the space-age adventuress in the year 40,000, splashed in hot colors. Barbarella's mission is to save the universe, so she flies from galaxy to galaxy in a pink spaceship reminiscent of *2001*. Along the way she's interrupted by a series of bizarre sexual adventures and almost gets killed. But in the end she discovers a new way of making love — intercourse. Her traveling companion is a beautiful, blond, blind angel who has lost his will to fly but gets it back after some delicious sex with Barbarella.

Vadim would take advantage of Jane's dual personas, he said — the dichotomy that had been written up in the *New York Times*. "We will combine these two personas in Barbarella," he went on excitedly. "You will be playing a kind of sexual 'Alice in Wonderland' of the future. There has never been anything like it on the screen. We can create something totally original — a human being in the midst of a cartoon." He believed he could really make a statement about female sensuality.

Jane disliked the idea of *Barbarella* as well as the character. She felt it was misogynistic. But she remained silent and went along with everything Vadim wanted to do.

Indeed, as the months went on, they collaborated as never before on *Barbarella,* including the opening credits (the best thing in the picture), where Jane performs a languorous striptease out of her space suit and floats deliciously naked across the screen for several seconds. That sequence is quite marvelous.

The effect was achieved by having Jane lie on a huge piece of Plexiglas with a picture of the spaceship beneath her. It was filmed from above, creating the illusion that she is in zero gravity. If you look closely, you can see the reflection in the glass as she removes her gloves.

In August 1967 shooting started on *Barbarella* at Cinecittà in Rome, and at the film center nearby, artisans were busy working on the futuristic spacecraft and sets. Dino De Laurentiis was producing. Terry Southern, riding the crest of his success with *Dr. Strangelove* and at his wacky zenith, was writing the screenplay along with seven other writers who were contributing scenes. John Phillip Law played the blind guardian angel who looks after Barbarella; Anita Pallenberg, a lesbian villainess; Marcel Marceau, "the Professor"; and Claude Dauphin, "President of the Earth."

Vadim had originally hoped that Henry Fonda would agree to play the part of the president. When asked, Fonda responded with "Will I have to take my clothes off?" Assured he would not have to, he hastily maintained that he had other commitments. He would tell friends, "Jane has survived more bad movies than I have."

Then there was Andreas Voutsinas, who arrived in Rome from New York, with his goatee beautifully trimmed and a mischievous glint in his eye. He'd been writing Jane, telling her of his acute money problems, and she had felt sorry for him and asked Vadim to give him some kind of a job. Vadim reluctantly agreed.

"So I became dialogue coach for *Barbarella* at a thousand dollars a week, but I did virtually nothing," Andreas admitted. "I collected a nice little bundle, and when the movie finished, I bought myself a sports car, which I later sold and with the proceeds bought myself the Paris apartment I'm still living in to this day."

He said he felt "eternally grateful" to Vadim and told him he had "saved my life." Vadim warned him not to try to coach Jane for any of her scenes. Andreas assured him he would not. But he said he made himself "useful." His "usefulness" included being "a sounding board" whenever Jane complained she didn't want to participate in some of the "orgies" Vadim was trying to organize. Andreas would tell her, "If you don't like them, baby, then don't go along with them."

He soon began urging her to walk out on the marriage. Jane said she couldn't do that; she loved Vadim. Furthermore, she was furious at Andreas for trying to undermine them as a couple, especially after they had given him a job. Vadim knew Andreas was trying to make trouble, but he was so busy with the film that he ignored him.

Jane did as well. She'd get up at the crack of dawn and be driven to Rome for a ballet class. By now her body was as close to perfection as was humanly possible. She'd been taking ballet classes for over ten years and never missed a day. The scant *Barbarella* costumes would reveal every lithe curve, every portion of her anatomy. She was also scheduled to pose for various magazine covers, including *Life*. She told Andreas she had to look perfect and was taking vitamins and having daily massages in addition to binging and purging. It was all part of her unhealthy routine to keep supremely fit — and it seemed to work.

After her ballet class, Jane would arrive at Cinecittà and struggle into her Paco Rabanne costumes. Nathalie would watch as her stepmother was trussed up in too-tight metal ribbed corsets and crammed into tight transparent breastplates. "It was a physical ordeal, but she never complained."

"The actual shooting was hell," Andreas said. "The sets were futuristic, extremely complicated. The special effects kept breaking down. There was one scene that was absolutely nightmarish, where two thousand killer wrens were being blown by a huge fan into a cage where Jane was crouching. The wrens were supposed to peck off her clothes but they did *nada*. Vadim got desperate. He poured birdseed into Jane's costume — guns were fired off — but still the birds did nothing. After three days Jane went into a panic and was rushed to the hospital in Rome, where she was treated for extreme nausea and high blood pressure." The scene was ultimately completed with two thousand trained lovebirds.

There were other difficult scenes — when Jane was chopped at by piranha-toothed dolls, and when she was strapped to a "pleasure-making machine" rigged with smoke bombs and flares that forced her to have constant orgasms. "It ended hilariously," Andreas said. "Jane, as Barbarella, blew a fuse."

After filming, Jane and Vadim would return to the crumbling old villa they'd rented on Villa Appia Antica outside Rome. They were sharing it with fourteen other guests, including Andreas, Peter Fonda, and John Phillip Law, who'd hated his hotel so much that he'd just moved there. Other guests were continually showing up, from Brigitte Bardot to the Rolling Stones.

To cope with her teeming, shifting household, Jane had a domestic staff of three: a cook, butler, and maid. "But the place was totally impractical," Andreas recalled. "Never enough hot water, elevator kept breaking down, birds molted and nested in the rafters."

One noisy Sunday lunch a baby owl dropped into novelist Gore Vidal's lap. "Can I have the recipe?" he joked.

Vadim never appeared for meals until after the first course; he was invariably in his study poring over rewrites with Terry Southern.

Jane presided at table, but "it was never very relaxed," said Andreas, "because Nathalie, age ten, and Christian, age four, would be sitting near their stepmother, amusing themselves by bombarding guests with bread pellets, their shrieks punctuated by shouts of 'Bam! Bam!' as they launched their missiles. I remember one guest whispered, 'I want to kill those children!'"

Other guests might be surprised when Jane's eccentric group of tailless cats and stray dogs appeared at table, often begging for scraps of food. Jane indulged them; she adored her animals. Often at dessert (which she never ate) she would rise and call out to her menagerie to join her in the garden. There a paparazzo, one of several who were lounging nearby, would snap pictures of "Barbarella" and her zoo.

Buck Henry was in Rome writing the screenplay for *Catch-22* for Mike Nichols. He'd drop by the villa in the evenings, "because I'd heard there were orgies, and maybe there were but I never was invited. There was a lot of pot and acid around, too, a lot of drugging." What he remembered best was Jane. "I'd just stand there feasting my eyes on her. She was absolutely ravishing. A great beauty. Those long, long legs, that mane of long gold hair. A true movie star, a celebrity with a capital C."

But she could also be unsettling. "We'd be talking," said Henry, "but I swear she wasn't really listening. She just appeared to be listening. I could never really reach her. I don't think anybody could. But maybe with all that was going on, it was her way of protecting herself."

Her way of protecting herself was to "pop a Dexedrine and plow on. The tensions and insecurities that haunted me during the making of that film almost did me in. There I was, a young woman who hated her body and suffered from terrible bulimia, playing a scantily clad — sometimes naked — sexual heroine. . . . Vadim's drinking had gotten much worse. He was a binge drinker: He would go for weeks and weeks without a drop (unfortunate, because it allowed him to feel he had the disease under control), but then things would seem to disintegrate. Partway through the shooting of *Barbarella* he started drinking at lunch, and we'd never know what to expect after that. He wasn't falling down, but his words would slur and his decisions about how to shoot scenes often seemed ill-considered. When I watch certain scenes from the movie now, I remember all too well how vulnerable I felt at the time. And more and more angry!

"I was also growing more remote," Jane said, "feeling as if I were out on a limb (or a steel pole) by myself, that no one else seemed to care about what I cared about — like showing up to work sober and on time. . . . But I still lacked the confidence to try to take charge when Vadim seemed particularly out of control."

One night in mid-October Joan Baez appeared at the villa. She scrambled eggs for everybody at 4:00 A.M. and described her participation in the march on the Pentagon which had occurred earlier that month. It had been organized by antiwar activist Jerry Rubin at the request of David Dellinger, a longtime pacifist. It was Rubin's idea to "lay siege to the Pentagon inside of the Capital and focus the demonstration at the heart of the American war machine. Six hundred thousand demonstrators came to Washington, among them novelist Norman Mailer and pediatrician Dr. Spock," she went on. The protest began in the traditional way with speeches in front of the Lincoln Memorial. Then the demonstrators moved on across Arlington Memorial Bridge and into Virginia. When they reached the Pentagon itself, twenty-five radicals pushed past a handful of military police guarding a side entrance. They were immediately arrested.

Outside some of the protestors were sticking flowers in the gun barrels of the young troops (some 2,500) while other protestors taunted them. A third group alternated between the two tactics. It was a perfect fragment of the dichotomy that was defining the nation and dividing it as well as binding everyone together in perpetual debate: "flower children versus hard-core practitioners of new radical politics and everyone else in between."

By the time the demonstration had ended at midnight, soldiers and federal marshals had brutally evacuated the plaza in front of the building. The women had been hurt the most, housewives and grandmothers protesting the war. No one moved or got up to leave in spite of the violence. Noam Chomsky thought the demonstration symbolized the transition between resistance and dissent. Over six hundred people were arrested and one hundred injured.

Jane listened to Baez talk and felt homesick. Suddenly she wanted to be informed about what was going on in America. She started to read about "Stop the Draft Week" and the protests from the clergy. She read about Yale chaplain William Sloane Coffin who one morning at services spoke of history's most revered heroes: Socrates, St. Peter, Milton, and Gandhi, who were not disrespectful of the law but who broke it "as a last resort." And then he opened the door of his chapel and the congregation watched as 280 young men burned their draft cards on the altar. Outcries against the war were becoming increasingly intense.

News had just been released from North Vietnam claiming that the United States was dropping antipersonnel bombs on civilians. Children's hands and feet were being blown off. The American government denied this. It was the start of accusations that the Johnson administration was deliberately lying to the public.

The arduous filming of *Barbarella* continued through much of November. "It was really rough on Jane," a crew member recalled, "but she was a wonderful sport; she never complained." The movie was costing De Laurentiis $9 million, the equivalent of $57 million today. Jane often had to pretend to be sick so that the film's insurance could cover the cost of a day or two of shutdown while Vadim and Terry Southern tried to figure out script problems and technical challenges, which were awesome. She endured everything for Vadim's sake — the delays, the script changes, the breakdowns on the expensive, complicated sets.

Jane never dreamed the film would be a cult classic, or that she would be described by film scholars as the first actress to play a character who could evoke the pleasure and pain of an orgasm onscreen. Whenever reporters came on the set, she'd rave about what a wonderful director Vadim was, how relaxed she felt with him, and how she trusted him. "Nobody else could have made this movie except Vadim."

When the film ended its shoot in Rome and moved on to Paris, Jane presented Vadim with a brand-new Ferrari for his birthday, and then rented a DC-4 for the day to fly her many pets (including her silver wolfhounds) and all sorts of new furniture back to the farm. "Some of the furniture was taken from the *Barbarella* set," Andreas said, "weird stuff like a bed in the form of a reclining woman and a table in the shape of a female nude."

They had just one day at the farm before they had to fly to Brittany to complete another project that had been put on hold for *Barbarella*. That film was *Spirits of the Dead*, based on three short stories by Edgar Allan Poe. Louis Malle and Federico Fellini were directing two episodes, Vadim a third.

Vadim's sequence was entitled "Metzengenstein." It was set in the Middle Ages and photographed beautifully. "But nobody took it seriously," said Andreas, who had a bit part. "It got terrible reviews. It was mostly an excuse for Jane to parade around in some gorgeous form-fitting costumes." She played a jaded sensualist who develops a passion for her horse, which is supposedly the reincarnation of her dead cousin and lover (played by her brother, Peter). There were strong overtones of incest.

Peter didn't have much to do in the movie — just a few lines — so between takes he would scribble notes for a project he hoped to do with Dennis Hopper, to be called *Easy Rider*. After filming in a gloomy castle, everybody would go back to the fishing village where they were staying and gorge on food and wine.

On their day off, Vadim and Jane took a long walk over the Brittany cliffs. It was cold and foggy, with the sea foaming beneath, under leaden skies. They stopped at a café, and over hot mulled wine, Jane found herself describing the last time she'd seen her mother. Vadim had never heard a full account, although he sensed that the mystery surrounding Frances Fonda's violent death continued to define Jane's life. She told him how she had hidden from her mother on the third floor of their huge, echoing house as her mother cried out, "Jane! Jane! Jane?" in the foyer below.

Peter had been with her, she said; he wanted to run down and see their mother but Jane tried to stop him. They struggled silently in the third-floor hallway, and then he broke free and ran downstairs.

"Jane! Jane! Jane?" Her mother's melodious, cultivated voice kept ringing in her ears. If only she had run downstairs, too — if only she had embraced her mother, listened to what she had to say, maybe her mother wouldn't have slit her throat.

But what exactly did Frances Fonda want to tell her? She would never know. They had never talked about anything consequential, unless you counted her talk of Peter. Peter was her favorite.

The idea of Peter as the favorite was as upsetting a memory as the recurring dream image of Frances Fonda lying bloody and inert on her chaise. Her mother's death was "like a wound on the brain."

She had recounted painful anecdotes from her childhood to Vadim before, but this was the first time she had told him the complete story of her mother's last visit home. It was a story that haunted her, because she could never stop wondering what would have happened if she had gone downstairs and just hugged her mother. Would she have been able to prevent her from killing herself?

Would it have helped make sense of it all if she'd gone to the sanatorium in Beacon as Peter had? Jane wondered. A couple of years before he had walked through its gloomy, badly lit halls and spoken to some of the nurses who had taken care of their mother. He had touched the wooden organ Frances had supposedly played a few days before she slit her throat. As Jane talked and talked that afternoon on the cliffs, she remained dry-eyed, and Vadim could not comfort her.

Years later she told a journalist for the *Los Angeles Times,* "It may never go away, that memory [of my mother], and it may not be necessary that it go away. Some people go under and remain damaged; I'm not pretending I'm not damaged . . . if I wasn't acting I'd probably be institutionalized. But I'm extremely strong which isn't necessarily good. I have tremendous will. I am not going to be destroyed. I'm going to survive. People have this superhuman image of me and that's not true at all. I am stubborn but I am open, too, and that's a contradiction."

Near dusk, they left the café and drove very fast to the hotel in the fishing village. Peter was already in his room, playing the guitar; he invited them in for some buttery hash-filled fruitcakes. By then Terry Southern had arrived from Rome for meetings with Vadim about the rough cut of *Barbarella,* which he'd just seen and pronounced "silly and wonderful." He joined them for some hash and everyone got pretty mellow that night.

In the following weeks, curled up in a limo on the way to Cinecittà,

Peter told Southern the story of *Easy Rider,* "about two hippie drug dealers who go on a motorcycle odyssey across the country, and they have a love/hate thing about America and parents and authority in general . . . and ultimately they're murdered by right-wingers who are threatened by their eccentricities. . . . But I need a screenwriter!" Peter finished.

Southern exclaimed that he'd do it in a second — he thought it was "the most commercial damn idea" he'd ever heard. Jane was listening and she disagreed; she didn't think it was a good idea. But then, "you're both ripped." She giggled.

Jane was "ripped" too — she'd been smoking right along with them; she loved smoking pot. Once she'd been photographed greedily sucking on a joint in Saint-Tropez. "Let's face it, I have an addictive personality," she told a reporter. "I take laughing gas in the dentist's office, for God's sake. I love getting high."

She would often carry a supply of joints in a tiny silver snuffbox. She had been quoted in *Women's Wear Daily* as saying, "Marijuana is not a bad thing. . . . It makes you much more vulnerable."

Besides, most of her friends in Hollywood were getting stoned. The drug culture was in full flower. Most everybody she knew was on either tranquilizers, hashish, or mescaline. Julia Phillips, who would produce *Steelyard Blues* for Jane five years later, said, "In the sixties and seventies everyone was doing blow."

19

AFTER *BARBARELLA* FINISHED shooting in Paris, they also wrapped *Spirits of the Dead*, then took a ski vacation in Megève in the French Alps. "A week after my thirtieth birthday — December 28, 1967, to be exact — I conceived [Vanessa]," Jane said. "I knew the moment it happened and told him so — there was a different resonance to our lovemaking."

Vadim was extremely happy. Jane thought it would bring them closer.

Inside she was terrified of becoming a mother. "I had to grow up! I had to accept the fact I was getting older!" But she didn't confide her fears to Vadim. She commuted periodically to Paris to see her doctors and to view a rough cut of *Barbarella*, which she confided to Elisabeth Vailland was going to be a huge fiasco. It was crude and leering and not very funny, she said — she was positive she would never get another movie offer.

A month or more into her pregnancy, she began to bleed and was told she couldn't leave her bed for a month in order to prevent a miscarriage. Then she came down with the mumps, and the gynecologist recommended an abortion because of the risk mumps posed to the fetus. She and Vadim discussed the situation at length and decided they wanted the baby.

While she was in bed, she began watching coverage of the Vietnam War on French television news. "I saw images on French television showing damage caused by American bombers that, en route back to their aircraft carriers, unloaded bombs they hadn't already dropped, sometimes hitting schools, hospitals, and churches. I was stunned," she wrote later in her memoir.

Bertrand Russell had convened his international war crimes tribunal in Stockholm in November 1967. That winter Jane read the testimony by journalists and Vietnamese peasants, in which they gave shocking eyewitness accounts of torture and mass starvation.

According to the report, 500,000 citizens had been killed by American bombs in Southeast Asia. In fact, the U.S. Air Force had dropped 4 million pounds of bombs, more than had been unloaded in the South Pacific during World War II. There was indiscriminate use of chemicals, napalm, and antipersonnel bombs. "It was horrifying to me," Jane said.

In early April 1968 Susan Blanchard came to Paris to check up on Jane's pregnancy. By that time Jane felt much better; she and Susan started going out, and at a party they were introduced to some of the American resisters, Vietnam vets, among them a young nineteen-year-old named Dick Perrin. It was the first time Jane had spoken with American soldiers who were actively opposing the war. She was struck by how young they were and how committed they seemed to be. Perrin and his buddies had just created an organization called RITA (Resisters Inside the Army). Its purpose was to spread anti–Vietnam War messages to the troops. Its members said they were neither unpatriotic nor anti-American. They were just against American aggression in Southeast Asia.

RITA had a couple of hideouts; one was at the artist Alexander Calder's old farmhouse outside of Tours, southwest of Paris. Perrin would go there periodically to drop off or pick up soldiers who had gone AWOL. He never knew that the old white-haired man sitting in the kitchen was Calder.

Jane and Susan took Perrin to dinner in Paris with George Orwell's widow, Sonia, and Leonard Bernstein's wife, Felicia, a willowy, fashionable woman with a highly developed social conscience. "We ate at a fancy restaurant called Le Calvados just off the Champs-Élysées," Perrin recalled. That evening he talked to Jane and the others about the Vietnam War and the work he was doing in Paris. After that dinner Jane helped Perrin and other soldiers get dental care, and she gave them a box of Vadim's unused clothing to distribute.

She also asked Perrin and a couple of the other resisters to a screening of *Barbarella*. After the screening, Perrin gave Jane a copy of Jonathan Schell's *The Village of Ben Suc*, the brutal account of how a Vietnamese village had been destroyed by U.S. armed forces, its survivors shunted off to concentration camps. Perrin told her, "Read this and you'll understand." And indeed she did. She was deeply affected when she read Schell's matter-of-fact account of the smugness of high-level U.S. military officers who seemed to revel in the massive destructiveness of Ben Suc. In response to a question from Schell about civilian casualties, one sergeant said, "What does it matter? They're all Vietnamese."

Jane wrote in her memoir that she felt "betrayed as an American, and the depth of my sense of betrayal was in direct proportion to my previous depth of certainty about the ultimate rightness of any U.S. mission." She began telling everybody she knew about the book, and she was shaken by the "we've known this for years, what are you so bothered about" reaction she received from most people, including Vadim.

She wanted to *do* something; she wanted to act on what she was learning and feeling. But what? She fantasized about going home and joining in the antiwar protests, but then she thought of Vadim and the farm they were renovating and the baby they were about to have. She spoke to Simone Signoret, who didn't push or proselytize but just told her, "You will know what to do when the right time comes. Right now, you go and get ready for that baby."

Jane continued to monitor the news. The Vietcong's Tet Offensive, the largest military offensive on both sides, was shattering the public's illusions about America's omnipotence. In January, Communist guerrillas had launched a broad offensive that spread from the cities of the Mekong Delta to Saigon and north to the highlands. President Johnson received word that the American embassy in Saigon was under attack. The assault was especially startling because there was such a huge proportion of Americans — 414,000 U.S. troops — allotted to support and defend in ground operations. The offensive was burned into American memory by the extensive TV coverage, and people realized now that the war could never be won.

In March, Senator Eugene McCarthy, running on an antiwar platform against a sitting president, did unexpectedly well in the Democratic primary in New Hampshire. On March 16, Robert Kennedy announced his candidacy for the U.S. presidency, and on March 31, President Lyndon Johnson went on TV to announce the cessation of bombing in North Vietnam and Southeast Asia, concluding his speech by saying he would not run for reelection.

On April 5 Martin Luther King was assassinated, and the outrage felt by the public resulted in riots all over the country. Sixty-five thousand troops were needed to put down disturbances in 130 American cities. The worst fires were in Washington, D.C., the most dangerous since the War of 1812. Fires and looting spread to within two blocks of the White House, and riot troops took up positions on the president's lawn. There were more antiwar demonstrations and campus revolts around the country. The most theatrical were at the University of California–Berkeley and at Columbia University, where thousands of students rioted, occupying buildings and decorating the lobby of Hamilton Hall with posters of Lenin, Che Guevara, and Malcolm X.

Hearing such news, Jane wondered if she should bring a son — she was sure she would have a son — into such a violently erupting world. Could she be a proper mother in a climate that was so unsettling? Would she make the same mistakes her parents had made and ignore her child? And finally — did she really want to be a mother? And what about her complicated relationship with Vadim?

He knew nothing about her boiling confusion and rage. She could never speak of it to him, but sometimes when they were together she would shiver, and he would ask, "Are you okay?"

Being pregnant was initially a very confusing and emotional experience. She would confess to Vadim that the idea of having a baby made her think of her mother.

Jane "equated anything purely feminine with weakness. Between her mother, destroyed and propelled beyond the brink of madness . . . and the sex-object ideal generally prevalent in America, she could not help having a devastating image of her female identity."

She became even more obsessed with how she looked. "I felt as if I was losing control of my body. I was overweight — it was a shock. I knew I was going to have to deal with the aftermath." She started asking herself, "What am I going to do with this body? Is it going to come back and be thin again? Will I change? Will I be different?"

Gradually, as the weeks went by and her belly swelled and she could feel her baby kick inside her, she suddenly felt better — stronger. Her depression disappeared and she was glad she was pregnant. She thought she might even love Vadim again. She grew briefly happy.

In late spring a student named Daniel Cohn-Bendit, age twenty-four, a French-German binational who had opted for German citizenship instead of French because he wanted no part of the Algerian War, was threatened with expulsion from France. At the time he was attending the suburban Paris West University Nanterre, a hotbed of youthful Marxist activity. He and his friends took to the streets to protest the threatened expulsion. Cohn-Bendit and the other students were already dubbed *les enragés* because of their extreme leftist views. From Nanterre, they carried their protest into the heart of Paris, fighting in the streets with right-wing students and a radical far-right group called Occident. On May 3 there was so much rioting that the rector of the Sorbonne called the police. As they entered the university, the students struck. The Sorbonne retaliated by closing down. The Events of May, as they were called, had begun.

The student riots that started in Paris quickly spread to the rest of the country, growing into a violent national strike supported by all of France's trade unions. Many people were convinced that a genuine revolution was in the making as thousands of students and police fought in the streets of Paris. Millions of workers took over their factories and held their managers hostage, bringing the country to a halt. No garbage was collected; it was impossible to buy a newspaper or find cigarettes; discussion groups replaced all other forms of activity. Trains stopped running, airports shut down, mail wasn't delivered. There was chaos.

Vadim was asked by his fellow directors to temporarily take over the presidency of the French Technicians Union. He didn't want to, but Jane persuaded him, and it was a tumultuous couple of weeks until someone else was voted in.

Six months pregnant, Jane attended the union meetings as well. At one of them, she ran into Jean-Luc Godard, one of the most radical film directors, who was planning to make a series of three-minute films that recorded students and workers discussing the political situation. He was also planning a film about Trotsky, starring John Lennon (it was never made).

Jane remembered sitting at an outdoor café after a meeting and watching the police clear groups of student protesters out of the École des Beaux-Arts. The kids were linking arms and holding hands; their faces were serious, excited, sullen. "Ten thousand students battled police for fourteen hours on May 6, turning Paris into a city under siege . . . streets were being torn up, cars overturned and burned, trees cut down for barricades." The bridges were guarded by riot police; there were endless crowds and traffic jams.

Even the Cannes Film Festival was disrupted; Jane and Vadim accompanied François Truffaut and Roman Polanski to the festival, but the demonstrations were so overpowering that the filmmakers collectively decided to cancel everything.

The June elections proved to be a political failure for the left-wing protesters. However, it was a watershed moment in France, the beginning of a nationwide shift to a more liberal social ideal.

That July the Vadims rented a villa in Saint-Tropez, which they shared with another couple. The husband was an opium addict and had brought along not only his wife but his young girlfriend.

"This added to the alienation I was feeling," Jane wrote in her memoir. "It probably wouldn't have affected me as much a year or two earlier. I would have shrugged it off as part of the dark side of life with Vadim. But now it caused me to retreat into my own world, encapsulated in the cocoon of my pregnancy."

Other close friends surrounded them. Christian Marquand had a house nearby, and so did Bardot; she would wander in and out, spilling out of her bikini, as ripely sensual as ever. She had become involved with animal rights and had taken to collecting stray cats; she must have had fifteen or twenty of them, all smelling and mewing and padding after her. She kept predicting that Jane was going to have a daughter, not a son, and that she would be born on Bardot's birthday. Catherine Deneuve was often there, too, advising Jane to have the baby in the same hospital where she had given birth to her son by Vadim.

Jane wished these women would go away. She started dreaming that when her baby came out of her womb she resembled a miniature Bardot. She hated that idea.

By August, Saint-Tropez was crowded with its usual assortment of royalty; journalists hung around, trying to keep up with the latest celebrity gossip. Jane was eight months pregnant. Photographers snapped pictures of her moving slowly up the beach in her voluminous caftan, big dark glasses covering her face.

She spent hours floating in the Mediterranean on an inflatable raft reading *The Autobiography of Malcolm X*, the journal of "the doped-up, numbers-running, woman-beating, street-hustling, pimping Malcolm Little," transformed into a "proud, clean, literate, Muslim Malcolm X."

"It rocked me to my core," Jane wrote in her autobiography. It was all about "the possibility of profound human transformation."

Every so often, she would attend lunch with a jet-setting group at one of the open-air cafés. But she hated the inane chatter; she never knew what to say; the lunches dragged on and on. At one of them Vadim tipsily stuck his hand inside her caftan and fondled her breast. The incident was written up in the papers the next day.

On an impulse she invited Andreas to Saint-Tropez. She had written him dolefully, saying that Vadim was teasing her about wanting to change the world. "He doesn't take anything seriously," she said.

"I knew Jane needed someone to confide in," Andreas said, "so I went even though I knew Vadim loathed me. I sensed the marriage was in trouble."

It turned out that Vadim needed someone to confide in, too. He was desperate because Jane was having so many mood shifts — elated and happy one minute, morose the next. "He thought maybe I could explain Jane to him," Andreas said. "Which of course I couldn't, except I knew her nastiness had nothing to do with Vadim. It was something internal and agonizing for her. The nastiness had much more to do with her depressions, her self-hatred."

The two men had several lunches by themselves. At one of them, Vadim drank a great deal of wine and confided that Jane had lashed out at him, crying, "How can you love me when I am nothing?"

By then he was so drunk he could hardly get up from the table. "I accompanied him back to his boat, the *Rive* — that's where Jane was.

She wasn't feeling well." She was still upset about Robert Kennedy's assassination, which had happened in June.

Vadim started weaving around. He lost his balance and almost fell off the dock and into the water, but Andreas pulled him back by his shirttails. "I saved his ass."

When they reached the boat, they staggered into the cabin. Jane was fast asleep. Andreas whispered to Vadim that they should both crawl into bed with her, and they did, giggling like schoolboys.

"Then Jane woke up and saw us lying drunkenly on either side of her on the pillows, and she began screaming her head off. She was furious."

She was so furious she did not make Andreas the godfather of her about-to-be-born baby. When she and Vadim left Saint-Tropez and returned to Paris in mid-August, they chose Sargent Shriver, then the American ambassador to France, to be Vanessa's godfather. On August 26, they all watched television coverage of the Democratic convention in Chicago at the embassy together — watched the noisy battles between police and protesters. One of the most articulate and passionate demonstrators was a long-haired, pockmarked man named Tom Hayden, who got himself arrested before the convention was over. Jane barely registered his name.

At the end of the summer, Jane attended Lamaze classes in Paris, but she could not believe that the breathing exercises would alleviate labor pains, so she quit.

Then came September 28. "I woke up at our farm at 5:00 and thought I was dying," she wrote. "The pain was beyond anything I had imagined. . . . Vadim raced to the clinic with me writhing in agony and scared to death. We ran out of gas about a half mile before reaching the clinic and Vadim had to carry me the rest of the way."

Susan Blanchard was waiting in the lobby. She stayed with Jane in the delivery room and comforted her during her very difficult labor. It took fourteen hours before she gave birth to a healthy baby girl whom she named Vanessa.* Everything was fine. The doctor assured them

---

* Most of the time, she said she named her daughter after Vanessa Redgrave, but for years she kept contradicting herself, sometimes denying she had named her child after Redgrave. It always depended on Redgrave's shifting politics.

the baby was normal. Vadim was so relieved he had tears in his eyes.

The baby was born September 28, Brigitte Bardot's birthday, just as she had predicted. "Brigitte sent me a cabbage," Jane said, "with a card that read 'In France babies are delivered in cabbages, not by the stork.'"

Vadim immediately phoned Henry Fonda back in the United States to tell him he was a grandfather. Soon reporters confronted him in a parking lot on Long Island to get his reaction. "If you guys had learned this news before I did I would have killed myself." He grinned. He seemed filled with joy. "Jane had a baby," he kept repeating, almost as if he didn't believe it.

She remained in the hospital for several days, experiencing highs and lows. One minute she felt exultant that she'd become a mother; she'd borne a child! The next minute she was exhausted, depressed, and angry. She wanted to hold the baby, she wanted to nurse the baby, but an orderly took Vanessa away.

Then Jane contracted an infection. When she recovered, and was able to get up, she wanted to lose weight immediately. She began doing ballet pliés in the bathroom and started hemorrhaging, "which meant I had to stay in the hospital for a week, seeing Vanessa only when they'd bring her to me to feed. *Stuck in a hospital. Sick, like my mother!* I was miserable. I did breast-feed a little, but the nurses were giving Vanessa supplements (without telling me), so it wasn't altogether successful — which made me feel I was already failing as a mother."

After a week Vadim took her home. Photographers were outside the hospital and began snapping pictures of her holding her little girl. "I am looking down at the baby in my arms" with "uncertainty on my face."

A cheerful English nanny named Dot was at the farm waiting to take care of Vanessa, "so I felt even more of a failure," Jane said. "I cried for an entire month. She took over the responsibilities of caring for Vanessa, just as nannies had cared for me and my brother."

She had fallen into a deep depression. "Nobody knew much about PPD back then, so instead of seeing my depression as a not-so-unusual phenomenon . . . I just felt that I had failed — that nothing was turning out the way it was supposed to, not the birth, not the nursing, not my feelings for my child or (it seemed) hers for me." Whenever Jane held Vanessa, the baby glared at her.

It was Vadim who tried to teach her how to change diapers and figure out the correct temperature for the supplementary bottle. He had a way with children; he even knew their special language. "I know the difference between whether a baby cries out of anger, or hunger, or just has a stomachache," he'd brag.

Once *Time* reporter Jay Cocks dropped by just as Vadim was heating up some baby formula for Vanessa. He laughed when Cocks did a double take. "I do much more giving than Jane," he explained to the journalist. "In a way, in our relationship she is the man and I am the woman."

Even so, Jane read every conceivable book on childcare, child psychology, and child rearing. And when Vanessa was weaned at four months, she put her on a formula recommended by the health food guru Adelle Davis: goat's milk, cranberry juice concentrate, a little brewer's yeast, and desiccated baby veal liver. Eventually she told her pediatrician what she had been feeding Vanessa and asked why the baby kept throwing up. The doctor just looked at her in disbelief.

20

I N NOVEMBER 1968, *Newsweek* published a story about sex and nudity in the movies with Jane featured half-naked on the cover. The title: "Anything Goes: The Permissive Society." With her seemingly playful, unflappable attitude toward sex, her ironic take on everything, she did seem to personify some of the aspects of the 1960s generation.

The month before, *Barbarella* had opened with a great burst of publicity all over the world. Jane appeared on the cover of *Life* space-suited, booted, and carrying a phallic-shaped gun; she was promoted as "the most fantasized woman in the world." At that moment the fusion of Jane Fonda's image and legend would begin to take hold, although it wouldn't solidify into iconography for another thirty years.

"*Barbarella* was released just as opposition to the war in Vietnam was peaking, and it was right on the cusp of Jane coming out as an antiwar activist," Jerry Lembcke wrote in *Hanoi Jane: War, Sex, and Fantasies of Betrayal*.

In 1968, the public was alternately outraged and titillated by *Barbarella*'s frontal nudity and winking double entendres, and they flocked to the theaters to see it. The critics were divided, most of them calling *Barbarella* "glossy trash." The *L.A. Times* film critic, Charles Champion, carped, "You could title this film *2001 A Spacey Idiocy*," and Rex Reed added, "As seen through the eyes of Helen Gurley Brown and *Vogue* . . ."

But *The New Yorker*'s Pauline Kael insisted, "Jane Fonda having sex on wilted feathers is more charming and bouncy than ever, the American girl triumphing by her innocence over a lewd comic strip of the future — she has the skittishness of a teenage voluptuary and when she takes off her clothes she is playful and deliciously aware of the naughtiness of what she does . . . that innocent's sense of naughtiness — of being a tarnished lady keeps her from being just another naked actress."

The feminist film critic Molly Haskell predicted, "*Barbarella* will be a watershed movie; Vadim is a Svengali — like von Sternberg was to Dietrich. He was ahead of his time portraying female sexuality."

By 2009 film scholar Linda Williams had "charted" the advent of a new carnality in American films through the career of an American icon, Jane Fonda. Williams maintained that Fonda was the first movie star of the late sixties and early seventies to play characters (in *Barbarella, Klute,* and *Coming Home*) whose orgasms, real or fake, were important to the story line of the film.

Suffice it to say, Jane aka Barbarella would give rise to a wide range of interpretation in the next decade. However, back in 1968 Jane had no idea she would ever be a sexual icon. She told friends that the level of exploitation in the film was embarrassing and she hated watching herself in it. "I am not for real. It's like my voice is coming out of my ear. I am totally bizarre. My alienation comes at me through the screen." At the time, however, she publicized *Barbarella* relentlessly with Vadim, appearing on *The Tonight Show* with Johnny Carson, being interviewed around the clock, and defending the movie as "funny and free and nice."

Nevertheless she wanted to blot out the image of herself as *Barbarella* and take on more serious work. Over Christmas she and Vadim flew back to the farm. He was scheduled to direct *Myra Breckinridge;* she had stacks of scripts to read. She told *Life* reporter Tommy Thompson, "I am insatiably ambitious. I know I haven't fulfilled my potential yet . . . I am determined to."

She had been offered the part of Gloria, the suicidal, embittered dance contestant in the movie *They Shoot Horses, Don't They?*, based on Horace McCoy's 1935 novel, in which the dance marathon craze served as a metaphor for the Great Depression. The book had been a cult favorite for years; twenty producers had optioned it, including Charlie Chaplin. Vadim had even adapted it for Bardot. Then in 1963, producer Martin Baum bought it for his new film company, Polimar, and commissioned James Poe to write a script.

Poe believed Jane was the one actress who should play Gloria, not an especially sympathetic character and a dark spirit. The other produc-

ers, Martin Baum and Irwin Winkler, argued that she was too identified with the cartoonish *Barbarella,* but Poe had seen in Jane's eyes the
same "hunted animal" quality that had so impressed Lee Strasberg. He
overcame the producers' resistance and Jane loved the part so much
she agreed to do it. Money was another reason she had to go back to
work immediately. Vadim still owed back taxes; their farm might be
taken away.

So she hired the prestigious New York firm Weissberger & Frosch to
manage their legal and business affairs. Richard Rosenthal, a younger
lawyer in the firm, was assigned to handle them. He'd already had a
great deal of experience dealing with stars, one of his other responsibilities being the care and handling of Elizabeth Taylor and Richard
Burton.

The Vadims met with Rosenthal in December 1968. "They had a
mind-boggling assortment of complicated legal, financial, and other
problems requiring sophisticated attention in both France and the
U.S.," he recalled. "They were confused and uncertain on a number of
points, especially their true legal residence. What was it? They needed
to know for tax purposes. They had virtually no cash between them at
the moment, and outstanding debts of more than four hundred thousand dollars."

Jane would be earning $400,000 in salary for *They Shoot Horses,
Don't They?* She told Rosenthal she'd planned to borrow $200,000 of
it to keep going. She and Vadim were thrilled when the Weissberger &
Frosch office agreed to take them on.

"The Vadims required immediate attention but were in no position
to pay us anything up front," Rosenthal said. "We told them we would
work on a contingency basis and receive a percentage of all income
on account of their professional services on all projects that came into
existence while we represented them. And," he added, "if there were
no projects or income, that would be our tough luck." He recalled,
"How absolutely gorgeous Jane was. Svelte and beautiful in over-the-
knee buccaneer boots that highlighted eye-catching inches of shapely
flesh-colored nylon beneath the hem of her miniskirt. She and Vadim
seemed relaxed and amiable; they gave absolutely no indication at the
time of any marital difficulties."

A week later, in January of 1969, Jane wrote Rosenthal from Los Angeles saying how much she and Vadim had enjoyed getting together,

and they were looking forward to what they felt would be "an exciting collaboration." Rosenthal was young, bright, and ambitious, and he would go on to become one of Jane's closest advisers for the next dozen years.

The Vadims were renting another house in Malibu. It had a terrace overlooking the beach, a guesthouse in the garden, and a huge master bedroom with a superb view of the ocean. The house was filled with light. "A house made for happiness," Vadim said. Jane agreed. She told Thomas Kiernan she was glad to be back. "When you come home, that aggressive American friendliness comes as such a shock after the coldness of the French. . . . Life over there is so entrenched. I adore it here. And all the things that are happening."

Most of all, she was overjoyed at being reconciled with her father. Hank Fonda doted on his first grandchild. He and Shirlee visited frequently. They spent more time with the baby than Jane did because soon she was busy training for the movie. She swam every day in the chilly Pacific Ocean; she jogged for miles up and down the beach to strengthen her body. She dieted strenuously.

She had decided to cut off her long, thick blond hair; it had been part of her identity all the years with Vadim. When she came home with her short, cropped bob, dyed honey blond, her husband quickly realized it was a symbolic gesture. "I had the vision of Jane leading her own life on one side, and of myself leading a separate life on the other," Vadim said. "I knew that the disintegration of our love had started."

But he said nothing, and for a while it seemed as if everything was the same. Guests came and went from the rented beach house; the large, noisy entourage of servants, pets, and friends packed in from Paris. In the midst of entertaining, Jane concentrated on *They Shoot Horses, Don't They?* She organized meetings with James Poe, who by now had written many drafts of the screenplay and was set to direct the movie. He was a gentle, mild-mannered man, one of the top screenwriters in Hollywood. He'd won an Oscar for writing *Around the World in Eighty Days,* and he'd adapted *Cat on a Hot Tin Roof* and *Advise and Consent,* among other movies. *They Shoot Horses, Don't They?* was his first venture as director.

At their meetings, Jane noticed that Poe had a hard time delegating authority and dealing with problems that had already arisen in the production, which was being delayed because the budget had moved way past the $3 million point. Also, Martin Baum, now president of ABC Pictures and the coproducer of the film, grew unhappy with Poe's inability to cope with production details. Baum wasn't satisfied with his latest version of the script, either, so he fired Poe.

Jane agreed with the decision. Vadim was shocked: "Poe had been her biggest fan." When Vadim asked her why she hadn't tried to protect him, she answered brusquely, "He was too inexperienced; Marty and I didn't like his approach."

"This incident revealed to me a new side of my wife's character," Vadim wrote, "her ability to forget compassion when it was a question of better results."

He didn't know that Jane ordered her longtime agency, Ashley-Famous, to propose him as director of the film. Another director, Larry Peerce, celebrated for his film *One Potato, Two Potato,* got the job instead. Jane was furious, fired her agents, and changed to Hugh French.

According to Rosenthal, "Actually Larry Peerce never did get to direct *Horses,* because his agents at CMA couldn't clear him of a preemption right held by Paramount. Peerce then fired CMA and went to Ashley-Famous. Sydney Pollack, who did direct the picture, finally started shooting *Horses* in March 1969, but he wound up firing his agents at William Morris during the negotiations and ended up hiring none other than Peerce's ex, CMA."

Sydney Pollack, a tall, shambling man with a confident, easy manner, had all sorts of ideas. Before Jane knew it he'd pulled her into every aspect of the production — costumes, music, and especially the script — and they began meeting regularly at the Malibu house. "I remember sitting with Sydney at our house," Jane said, "and his asking me what I thought the script problems were and would I read the original book carefully and then talk with him about what was missing in the adaptation. Wonderful Sydney had no idea what this meant to me . . . it was a germinal moment. I began to study the book in ways I hadn't before — identifying moments that seemed essential not just to my character but to the movie as a whole, making sure everything I did contributed to the central theme."

Pollack also had great ideas for casting. He was an actor as well and had been assistant to the master acting teacher Sandy Meisner in New

York. Jane liked Pollack's choice of Red Buttons to play the middle-aged sailor who dies on the dance floor during the marathon, and of Gig Young, who would play the hard-bitten, devious emcee, Rocky.

"Gig came to our audition meeting unshaven and very hung-over," Pollack said. "In private life, he was an alcoholic and a very tormented guy—he would later shoot his own wife and himself. He was perfect for the part. Jane saw that, too." (Young would win an Oscar for his portrayal.)

Jane had been reading books on the Depression and on the grueling dance marathons, which were nothing more than endurance contests. Thousands of Americans crowded into auditoriums in cities like Spokane and Oakland to watch couples—broke, in debt, homeless—dancing nonstop for hundreds of hours. If you were really good, you could win $5,000 for seventy days' work. In the meantime there were other prizes each night for best costume or talent. At the start there were five hundred dancers moving around the floor, and at the end only two couples were still standing. The marathons were outlawed as cruel and inhumane after an incident on the Santa Monica Pier in 1936, when a young man killed his partner in a fury after she collapsed.

Jane had also spoken to her father about the Depression: "It was so much about rootlessness and the dispossessed," he said. Twenty-five years before, he had become "the face of America" with his portrayal of Tom Joad. Jane fantasized that the alienated, masochistic Gloria could be as emblematic. If *Horses* was done right, it could have as much impact as *The Grapes of Wrath*, and she could make as indelible an impression on the screen as her father had. She felt competitive with him, and why not? "It's okay for a daughter to feel competitive with her dad, isn't it?" she asked early on in her career. "I do."

She didn't want Andreas to coach her, and she rejected Vadim's help. She wanted to create Gloria by herself. But when she began thinking about the character, she discovered "something very black inside me that I hadn't known existed." Was it because she was getting inside the head of a suicidal woman? Someone who had given up on life as her mother had?

Jane wondered if she could follow her father's example; he seemed to have relived Frances's suicide when he starred in *A Gift of Time* on Broadway. Jane would never forget her father's arresting portrayal of suicide, but they had never discussed it. Nor would she ever discuss with him the reasons why she was playing the suicidal Gloria.

It had everything and nothing to do with ambition. Somehow Jane had to prove to herself through her imagination that she could experience something as excruciating as Gloria's choice of death over life and come through with a deeper understanding of what her mother had gone through. The movie started shooting in March 1969. It was filmed in an exact replica of the old Aragon Ballroom on Ocean Park in Santa Monica, its bleachers filled with gawkers, a mirrored chandelier whirling, a trio blaring "Brother, Can You Spare a Dime?" Pollack had the set designer build dressing rooms and an office off the ballroom so the camera could move around a 360-degree angle and shoot everything. "We shot it in sequence, in continuity — the story followed the chronology of the script — and by the time the movie ended, the entire cast was absolutely exhausted."

Jane would arrive on the set at 6:30 A.M. and do warm-up exercises. Soon she had all the actors bending and stretching. Before the day's shoot, Pollack made Bruce Dern, Bonnie Bedelia, Susannah York, Red Buttons, and others in the cast run around the room like athletes until they had the look he wanted, "a mixture of fatigue and frenzy."

Everybody in the cast developed an identification with their roles. It became an ensemble piece. They were all becoming downtrodden misfits who had entered the marathon in the hope of winning the big prize money. Jane as Gloria is the most beaten-down and cynical. She's just been released from a mental hospital, where she was recovering from a suicide attempt after being jilted. She has come to Hollywood to pursue her dream of becoming a movie star. The marathon for her is a nightmare. She sees it as corrupt and venal, but essential to her survival even if it requires seducing the male chauvinist pig, Rocky. By the end of the marathon, exhausted and despairing, she convinces her partner to help her commit suicide: "They shoot horses, don't they?"

"Jane worked like a demon," the Broadway dancer-singer Allyn Ann McLerie said. "I've never seen anybody go through so much agony to produce a performance. She seemed possessed by the character. After a while she totally withdrew from the rest of us. No one could reach her between takes."

At one point Jane and Red Buttons danced for fourteen hours straight to see what it felt like, to see how their bodies would react — could they actually fall asleep and still legitimately dance? They could and did.

Every so often Vadim would visit the set, bringing Vanessa. Jane would make a big fuss, hugging and kissing the baby but barely paying attention to her husband. Some of the other actors noticed this. "There didn't seem to be much affection between them," someone said.

As soon as Vadim left, Jane paced around the set — clutching a copy of McCoy's novel. She was moving like Gloria, speaking Gloria in imperious, bitter, weary tones. "I would spend days and nights living at the studio instead of going home to Malibu, partly because I wanted to enhance my identification with Gloria's hopelessness and partly because I just didn't want to go home to Vadim."

Instead, during her free time, she took to driving aimlessly up and down the Pacific Coast Highway before parking at some windswept point. "I was having a mini-breakdown, I think. Naturally I drew on my real-life anguish for all it was worth to feed my role as Gloria."

One evening she went to a screening of a rough cut of *Easy Rider* that Peter had arranged for the entire family. Hank Fonda didn't say much. Vadim pronounced it *"formidable"* and *"très important."* Jane was especially impressed by the performance of an unknown actor named Jack Nicholson, but she was so tired from working that she fell asleep in the middle of the movie. She missed the scene where Peter as Captain America says, "I've always thought of suicide — I've popped pills, driven a car a hundred miles an hour into a ridge," and then later, while high on acid, wanders into a cemetery in New Orleans, gazes up at a statue of the Madonna, and sobs, "You are such a fool mother, I hate you," and then he continues to cry, "Why did you do it, why did you do it?"

Most nights Jane couldn't go home. Instead she moved into Mae West's old dressing room on the Warners lot at the Burbank studio. She'd papered the walls with grim photographs from police magazines — images of gunshot wounds, people decapitated from car accidents. Vadim visited her dressing room at night before she went to sleep. She told him her character was obsessed with death; Gloria had tried to shoot herself once and still had a scar on her temple. Vadim would listen. They spoke in French and that soothed her. They were coming apart and yet she could not have gotten through this agonizing period of creativity without his support. "He was wonderful," she said.

Vadim wrote, "I began to feel I was living a nightmare. The sensation was so fleeting that although I felt a stab of pain whenever we parted I was always able to convince myself that it was only an illusion. The erosion of love is sordid, shabby and absurd." Much of the time he remained in Malibu, periodically phoning Nathalie, who was unhappily in school in Switzerland.

Most evenings Pollack would screen the rushes for the entire cast. "It was obvious that the movie was going to be special," he said. "What Jane was doing was remarkable. She was putting everything into Gloria, pouring out all her frustrations, her own disappointments, and all her aspirations into her work. She wanted to achieve something meaningful, and this was a chance to make an indelible mark as a character fully done, fully executed, and she held nothing back. There was no vanity, nothing hidden, and she went all the way."

Pollack got into the habit of filming her scenes her way, and then if they didn't work, "we would reshoot them after we talked. She was her biggest critic."

They discussed one scene at length. "It's the one where Rocky comes on to her. We talked about how it should be played. I mean it's a scene where she could go down on him, she could unzip his fly, she could really be sexy. But it wasn't about sex. 'Don't touch me' was all she said." Pollack didn't give himself credit for shaping Jane's unique performance, but he did remember how her emotional caginess became central to the drama.

Months later, the film critic Manny Farber would note, "Jane Fonda's stubborn life-loathing is very inside, grudging, thoughtful, always faced toward the situation — nothing escapes [her] suspicious cool observance. It is heroic acting."

Filming lasted until May. Pollack shot the climax of the marathon over and over. At the melodramatic peak, Red Buttons dies in Jane's arms, but she continues to dance and hold him up, screaming, "Walk, you son of a bitch! Walk!" She ends up carrying his corpse on her back, defying the circumstances, defying the Depression. It is a wrenching finish.

When it was over, Jane was weeping with relief and exhaustion. "It was like having a dead baby inside me and I went around wondering why I couldn't give birth. By the last days of shooting, I had delivered Gloria," she said. "The symptoms of her character were gone. I was rid of her. Now a lot of speed freaks have told me they liked me so much they thought I was on speed."

Gloria's bleak spirit was so despairing and negative it took weeks to get the character out of her system. "I felt as if I were physically pulling her out of me."

She didn't feel totally free from Gloria's darkness until she had gone to Vadim's barber and told him to cut off her marcelled bob. He cut it very short and she dyed it dark brown. Someone told her she now looked "like Henry Fonda, only prettier" — which pleased her no end. "I've always had a deep-rooted need to be a boy — now I am one!"

Now Jane had to deal with the way the film was emerging. For a while, Martin Baum didn't want Gloria to die at the end. "Can't she be saved?" he asked Pollack. "We'll make ten million more if she lives." Pollack refused to change the ending, because the book is a minor classic.

However, when Jane saw the edited version, she was disappointed. One whole hour had been cut, scenes about who she was and where she came from — her entire motivation. She hated the addition of the flash-forwards and the dreamy slow-motion sequence of the galloping horses at the start of the picture — "Too artsy." However, when it was shown to preview audiences, they liked it. The movie did become a critical success, and, Pollack added, "It changed my career, and it changed Jane's, irrevocably."

She returned to her life with Vadim at the beach. There were more luncheons and dinners, and posing for photographers while she wheeled the baby in a carriage. She was interviewed by reporters from all over the world. They questioned her endlessly about being a sex symbol and about Barbarella and why she had chosen to do such a grim film as *They Shoot Horses, Don't They?* Jane talked on and on and on.

During one marathon interview with a German journalist, Jane's attention seemed to wander and the reporter pounced. "What are you thinking of right this minute?" he demanded.

"I'm thinking of getting a divorce," she answered. And then she laughed shortly when she realized what she'd said. But before he could probe further, she launched swiftly into another topic.

The truth was that Vadim's frivolous approach to life, which she had once found so charming and joyful, now exasperated her. He would run out of the house to join actor Larry Hagman's evening marches up the beach, everybody in costume and stoned. She wanted to stay inside and talk about how antiwar activism was peaking as Nixon bombed Cambodia relentlessly. Playing Gloria had made her aware of her dissatisfaction with Vadim. She was tired of his drinking and his gambling and the threesomes. She was suddenly aware of how much he had objectified her — how much he had exploited her. Not that she hadn't gone along with it. She had. But she wanted her life to have more significance. She was tired of playing the passive, perfect wife and mistress. In her dreams she imagined going off on a long journey by herself and having incredible adventures. But she didn't believe that she could survive alone.

As for Vadim, he was "less in love with Jane. Her perpetual need for activity and her need to take everything seriously began to tire me. . . . I could not say that Jane was *another* Jane because part of her personality had taken the upper hand and was submerging the rest. She was evolving. She was moving unsteadily toward the future, but it was precisely the submerged part of Jane that I loved. Living with the new Jane interested me less."

Their closest neighbors in Malibu happened to be Donald and Shirley Sutherland. Jane often wandered over to their beach house in the mornings to find someone to talk to. The Sutherlands drank a great deal and didn't seem particularly happy.

Donald was a sad-faced, skinny actor from New Brunswick, Canada, soon to become famous as Hawkeye Pierce in Robert Altman's *M*A*S*H*. Shirley was the daughter of a left-wing politician who headed Canada's New Democratic Party. She was an intense, outspoken woman, harshly critical of the Vietnam War. "Shirley was Malibu's biggest radical," said the producer Julia Phillips. "She raised money for the Indians. She raised money for the Black Panthers." Jane soaked up what she was doing like a sponge.

She had heard about the Panthers from Marlon Brando, who had been supporting them since 1966, when Huey Newton and Bobby

Seale founded the party in Oakland, California, mainly in response to white police who were acting like a hostile army in the ghetto with their guns and clubs. The Panthers started using guns and clubs, too, to combat police persecution and provocation. They called themselves a "party," but they were more like an outlaw gang, Brando told Jane. They were young and tough and a little menacing, and they weren't above using violence and intimidation to get what they wanted for poor blacks. How else can you get justice for the oppressed? Brando wanted to know.

Shirley invited Jane to a benefit for the Black Panthers' Montessori school at Jean Seberg's in Coldwater Canyon. Among the other guests were Paul Newman and a hugely pregnant Vanessa Redgrave, who got into an altercation with Hakim Jamal because he maintained that he was a cousin of Malcolm X. Actually he was married to a cousin of Malcolm X, but Jamal didn't recognize Vanessa and she was miffed, Julia Phillips said.

Jane was taken with Jamal, a handsome, charismatic man with burning eyes who was having an open affair with Seberg. She listened attentively to his speech about the Panther school and about the importance of the Panthers as a political party, and she wrote out a $1,000 check for the school.

In the meantime, Jane and Vadim attempted to conduct their life together as they always had, with quick trips to Paris and New York. In Manhattan they stayed at the Chelsea, the funky hotel on West 23rd Street, and often stopped in at Max's Kansas City, a restaurant-nightclub on Park Avenue South. It was a boisterous and smoke-filled place on Union Square, and it catered to the likes of Patti Smith, Robert Mapplethorpe, Shirley MacLaine, and the Rolling Stones. Max's most famous customer was Andy Warhol, who haunted the place with his entourage: Candy Darling, Viva, and members of his flagship band, the Velvet Underground. They recorded a live album at Max's.

Jane and Vadim usually ended up in the "Celebrities Only" back room at Max's, along with Halston, Liza Minnelli, Tennessee Williams, and Philip Glass. You could buy any drug you wanted: coke, hash, mescaline, opium, pot, LSD. Very few people ate the bad steak and limp salad at Max's. Max's was not about fine cuisine — it was a magnet for artists, actors, musicians, poets, and so-called celebrity fuckers.

Everybody wanted to see the wild, impromptu acts, which were often performed on tabletops by comics and singers on speed.

Jane was attracted to an Andy Warhol protégé, a star of some of his underground films, named Eric Emerson. He looked like a blond angel but he was — according to a Max's regular — "totally amoral. Eric could fuck somebody in the phone booth, then go back to sniffing meth or kidding around at the bar."

On speed he became an astonishing dancer. He could leap as high as Baryshnikov, flying through the air in the back room while customers gasped and applauded. He seemed to hang from the ceiling, suspended for several seconds before he dropped lightly to the floor and began twirling like a dervish.

Emerson reminded Jane of Timmy Everett. They both had muscular little asses and they both enjoyed grooving on their bodies. Emerson got off on moving his pelvis around to the beat of the music. One night somebody dared Emerson to ask Jane Fonda to dance. He marched over to her ringside table and asked her. She accepted, with a little half smile on her face. Everybody watched them dance together. Jane looked so sexy in her miniskirt and thigh-high Barbarella leather boots, hair in a shag. "She had this dissatisfied expression on her beautiful face," a waitress remembered. "She could turn real mean if you crossed her, but she seemed almost happy dancing with Eric. They danced together a long, long time."

Finally Jane went back to Vadim, who had been sitting watching her, smoking cigarette after cigarette. "Eric has suggested kidnapping me," she told him.

"Eric came and went in our life like a charming and perverted elf," Vadim wrote in his memoirs. They accompanied him to parties in an abandoned townhouse in the West Village, where couples danced in the dark and kept switching partners; they were periodically illuminated by blinding strobe lights. After a couple of hours the Vadims and Eric would go back to their suite at the Chelsea Hotel. "Yeah," Jane says, "Eric was my lover."

Back in Los Angeles, Jane and Vadim reconnected with Roman Polanski and his wife, Sharon Tate, at their spacious rented house on Cielo Drive in Benedict Canyon. There were many parties at Polanski's, all-night affairs that turned raucous and druggy, with the Stones' throbbing, sardonic song "Sympathy for the Devil" blasting from the stereo.

One night Vadim watched Jane disappear into a bathroom with Jay Sebring, a sleek, beautifully groomed man who had a hairdressing empire in Los Angeles — salons, products. He had been Sharon Tate's lover and remained her close friend since her marriage to Polanski.

Sebring and Jane didn't reappear for at least a half-hour. For some reason the Polanski housekeeper got upset at the locked bathroom and began banging on the door. "What's going on in there?" she screamed.

"That woman had taken it upon herself to look after the morals of the Polanskis," Vadim wrote dryly. "She had her work cut out for her."

Finally Jane opened the door and marched out, followed by Sebring. Her clothes were in disarray. Their little flirtation had been interrupted, Vadim noted, but Jane seemed indifferent. "I hate it when something is half finished" was all she would say, and she drifted past Vadim and into the living room.

"Jane was particularly beautiful that evening," Vadim thought. "Very self-assured. The butterfly had emerged from its chrysalis . . . and was spreading its wings."

She hadn't kept her little adventure a secret, but it became clear to Vadim that she had no intention of sharing it with him. "I was no longer her accomplice," and he felt "a great chill."

A day or so later, a friend, Jill Robinson, joined Vadim at the beach house and they lay in the sun drinking white wine. Suddenly Vadim confided, "La Fonda can be so cruel. She has used me and I have given her everything. There is nothing left."

Jane overheard the remark and ordered, "Vadim! Stick out your tongue!" And he did, like an obedient lapdog, and she in turn stuck out hers. "There!" she cried. "Yours is longer." Jill recalled how Jane often stuck out her tongue at her father to divert his anger or attract his attention.

Through late spring and into early summer, Jane remained in Malibu. Her father dropped by frequently; he was happy because he thought she had achieved such a fulfilled life. "She doesn't talk to me the way she used to," he said. "She's got this marriage with Vadim and the baby. God knows, I never thought she'd be so maternal. She looks great, she's extremely intelligent, outgoing. Not like me. Look at the life she's created in Malibu — people coming and going from her house all the time. She handles it so beautifully and makes everybody feel so comfortable. I can't do that." He was oblivious to the tensions and conflicts between her husband and her.

In mid-June, Jane and Vadim flew to Maui to visit Peter. It was in Maui that Vadim learned that he would not be directing *Myra Breckinridge* as he'd hoped. The job had gone to an English director named Michael Sarne who had just directed a successful movie called *Joanna*. Vadim was very upset, and he flew back to California almost immediately to rustle up more work, while Jane stayed on with her brother.

Peter's movie *Easy Rider,* which he had conceived, produced, coauthored, and starred in, had opened at the Cannes Film Festival in May 1969, where it won the prize as Best First Work. It was first a critical success and then a huge box office hit. Made for $400,000, it grossed $20 million, proving that the counterculture could be very profitable. Young audiences could identify with the two doomed bikers who, after a big cocaine sale, zoom around the Southwest on their motorcycles before being shot by some trailer-trash yokel. It became one of the most legendary cult films of the 1960s. Not since James Dean's *Rebel Without a Cause* and Brando's *The Wild One* had a movie captured the imagination and the admiration of an entire generation. Peter became a counterculture celebrity as well as a very rich man. He told Jane he felt vindicated because he had proved he could not only express his ideas and get stoned, he could make a lot of money at the same time.

After he talked about the impact of *Easy Rider,* Jane described what had happened to her while she was filming *They Shoot Horses, Don't They?* Playing Gloria had opened her up, forced her to see her life with Vadim differently. "I realized I'd become very cynical. I wanted to change that."

She added she thought she could change her life because she felt she was genuinely changing, too, changing inside — "my attitudes, my awareness." She was always the most excited when she was in the throes of becoming something else. When she first decided to become an actress, she had fantasized about what it would be like — imagining the attention and the celebrity. Then when she actually became an actress, she discovered it was hard, grueling work and that just being an actress wasn't quite enough for her. Even being a movie star had started to bore her. She was losing interest, and she began rejecting that persona as she focused on reinventing herself as a political activist. At the moment she was in the fantasy stage of activism, dreaming about marching and speaking out.

In the next days she and Peter swam nude in Maui's shallow freshwater pools, and they sunbathed and shared joints with the shaggy-haired hippies they met as they explored unmarked dirt roads. It was a lazy, carefree life familiar to Peter but not to hard-driving Jane. She sounded surprised: "I feel free! I feel relaxed!" In the evenings, he taught her how to play twelve-string guitar, and they sang songs on the beach and communicated in their secret language, the language they'd concocted back at Tigertail.

"I knew that things were not very smooth between Jane and Vadim, and that their marriage was just about over," Peter said. "She was not a happy girl, and I felt very protective of her."

Before she left Maui, Jane hugged her brother and told him, "I feel powerful. I feel all my potential is coming together."

By late June she had returned to France, joining Vadim and Vanessa, and she plunged into all manner of activities. She mastered speed reading. She visited a hypnotist so she could break her habit of heavy smoking. She started more renovations on the farm; she wanted to complete the work on the indoor swimming pool in the barn.

She kept in touch with her father; Henry Fonda was the busiest character actor in the movies. He had done four films in 1968, including *Once Upon a Time in the West,* a spaghetti Western for Sergio Leone in which he played a malevolent hired killer who coldly guns down a nine-year-old boy at the start of the picture. He went totally against his "image."

Jane wrote him a fan letter praising his performance.

And then on August 9 came the Manson murders. The very pregnant Sharon Tate, Jay Sebring, the coffee heiress Abby Folger, and the film-maker Wojciech Frykowski were brutally slaughtered by Charles Manson and his tribe of homicidal maniacs inside the Polanski house on Cielo Drive. Joan Didion wrote, "Nobody was surprised." There was a feeling all over Hollywood that "it could have been me." That phrase haunted the hills.

A couple of friends in Los Angeles would eventually reconstruct the horrific event for Jane. Apparently, in the weeks before the murders, things had been very tense in the drug underworld. Dope burns — the selling of diluted drugs at high prices — were common. According to Thomas Kiernan, Frykowski was heading a drug-pusher operation from Polanski's house; he was double-dealing with drugs and was reviled by most of his scrappy hippie clientele, who may or may not have included the Mansons.

It was rumored that Frykowski and Sebring were in the midst of a ten-day mescaline binge and just before Manson arrived, a messenger from Sebring's hair salon had brought a large batch of cocaine and mescaline to the house. Sebring supposedly freaked out because it wasn't enough. Manson himself was a trafficker in all sorts of hard-to-get hallucinatory drugs. In fact, he may have sold these drugs to his victims preceding the murders.

When the intruders broke in, Sharon and her guests were so zonked out on drugs they were unable to move. Police surmised they knew who the killers were, so perhaps at first they didn't take their threats seriously. Sharon was stabbed sixteen times. The word *Pig* was smeared in blood over the louvered doors.

And it seemed as if "everybody who was anybody had been about to visit the Polanski home the night of the murders. It was as if people wanted to be a part of the slaughter, like animals for some dark purpose of their own," Buck Henry said. "Manson was the essence of the 1960s. If Hollywood was the forbidden planet, he was the monster of the id. It was, 'I'm famous. I'm a celebrity. I don't deserve it. Someone is gonna kill me and my family.'"

After the Manson murders, "Toilets flushed all over Beverly Hills," Peter Biskind wrote. "The entire sewer system in L.A. was a river of drugs."

Jane was devastated by Sharon Tate's violent death. "I loved Sharon," she told people. "She was a simple, decent girl. She wanted that baby. She loved Roman." To her, the murders symbolized the worst aspects of this turbulent decade: sex — drugs — hippies — evil gurus — Hollywood excess. She wanted to get away from it.

The rest of the summer was bittersweet. In September Vadim took Jane and Vanessa to Saint-Tropez. The weather was glorious, he remembered: cool breezes, a blue, blue sky. He steered his boat, the *Rive*, along deserted creeks. The water was transparent. Jane lay naked in the sun; Vanessa was happy and gurgling in her little dinghy.

On September 28 they celebrated Vanessa's first birthday with a cake and one candle. Jane snapped pictures and then burst out laughing when her tiny daughter, smeared with chocolate icing, began to eat the candle.

But she was disturbed. Tightly wound as always, and knowing that something was very wrong, "I was trying to be a mother but not really knowing how," she wrote in her autobiography. "I was parenting the way I'd been parented, taking care of all the externals, but not countenancing the personhood of my baby."

Sometimes she would just get up in the middle of dinner and disappear into the bathroom. "I would simply leave the table, go upstairs, purge whatever I had eaten, and come back down again, all chipper and lively. Since the act of purging is somewhat orgasmic, the chipper part was easy. The difficulty would set in within twenty or thirty minutes, when a precipitous drop in blood pressure would flood me with fatigue and necessitate a physical and emotional withdrawal."

"There is one especially powerful memory," she wrote in her autobiography. "It is late at night; I can't get Vanessa to sleep; I am despondent, again deep into the bulimia. I am lying on my back on the floor, with Vanessa lying on my chest. She lifts her head and looks straight into my eyes for what seems like an eternity. I feel she is looking into my soul, that she *knows* me, that she is my conscience. I get scared and have to look away. I don't want to be known."

She was unable to cope with motherhood. She had to find a way out, a plan for escape. But what?

In October she decided to go to India. She told Vadim that she needed to go by herself "in order to figure out what is going on inside me," but she was really fleeing Vadim and their baby. Her first stop was New Delhi. The reality of the teeming city was depressing. She'd expected poverty, but not so much disease and death. The smells and horrific conditions were revolting up close and shot through with vivid colors of women's saris: saffron, purple, magenta, azure, blue.

It was the first time she had ever traveled so far away from home on her own, and she found herself confronting a series of clichés: talking to a Buddhist priest who turned out to be a heroin addict, smoking dope with some hippies. In New Delhi she met some Peace Corps volunteers digging wells. She toyed with the idea of joining them, but could she bring Vanessa? she wondered crazily. She began to suffer such ambivalence about being away from Vadim and her daughter that when she reached Bombay she considered finding an ashram and seeking advice from a guru. Instead, she remained in her hotel room and went over what she felt was wrong about her marriage. But she was putting up a smoke screen for herself as she often did; what was really upsetting her were the harsh facts that she no longer wanted to live with Vadim and she didn't want to be a mother.

Jane wrote Vadim only one letter, datelined from Nepal. She told him she loved him terribly and never wanted to be separated from him and Vanessa again. But Vadim didn't believe her. "If she really loved me, she would have asked me to get on the next plane to join her."

When they met in Paris, he found her "thinner and still unhappy." She had obviously not resolved her discontent; in fact, she seemed even more unsettled. They flew directly to London for two weeks of conferences with the Irish novelist Edna O'Brien for a screenplay that didn't work out.

Jane didn't have time to think about what she had experienced in India until, later that fall, she and Vadim flew to Los Angeles for a screening of *They Shoot Horses, Don't They?* They landed in the dead of night and then woke up in their enormous suite at the Beverly Wilshire Hotel. Jane rolled out of bed and looked out the window.

"I just stood there in a daze," she said later. "I was experiencing culture shock. I called out to Vadim, 'Something's happened. It's like a plague,' all those big houses spread out over Beverly Hills — the immaculate gardens; the silent streets where the rich drive their big cars. India was urine smells and noise and color and misery and disease and masses of teeming people. Beverly Hills was empty — antiseptic. I kept wondering, 'Where is everybody?'"

She continued to talk and talk and talk to Vadim in French. She showed him an article she'd read in *Ramparts,* a left-wing muckraking magazine that she had picked up in the airport.

She told him it was a piece by Peter Collier about a group of militant Native Americans who were occupying an abandoned prison on

Alcatraz Island in San Francisco Bay. They were doing this to remind the public of all the land that had been stolen from them in the past. "Peter had written all sorts of stuff in it about the injustices done to the Indian — the genocide — how our government couldn't care less." She announced that, instead of returning to Paris after *Horses* opened, she wanted to remain in the United States to see what she could do about publicizing the Native American cause.

Vadim didn't answer. As he listened to her talk, he thought, "It was not a home, a husband or a child that she wanted, but a cause she could throw herself into . . . fortunately for her, there are more than enough causes to choose from." He reluctantly agreed to Jane's change of plan.

In mid-December *They Shoot Horses, Don't They?* opened for a week to qualify for the Oscars. Critics all praised Jane's performance as Gloria. Joe Morgenstern of *Newsweek* called the performance "bold, admirable . . . a wounded soul swathed in scar tissue."

The *New Yorker* critic Pauline Kael found "Jane's sharp-tongued Gloria — who expects the worst of everybody and makes them act it out — impressive. Fonda goes all the way with it as actresses rarely do once they become stars, giving in totally to this isolated morbid girl who can't trust anybody. Jane Fonda makes one understand self-destructive courage. She has the true star's gift of drawing one to her emotionally even when the character she plays is repellent. Jane Fonda stands a good chance of personifying American tensions and dominating our movies in the 1970s as Bette Davis did in the 1930s."

The New York Film Critics Circle voted Jane the best actress of the year for her performance in *They Shoot Horses, Don't They?* She was thrilled, and even more so when her father complimented her on her work after seeing the movie at a screening.

A week later Peter and Jane joined their father — this time in L.A. in his Bel Air living room. They were participating in a *Time Magazine* cover story, which was promoting "the Flying Fondas" as the "most potent family act the entertainment industry had ever seen."

Hank Fonda was in a bathrobe and was coming down with a cold, *Time* reporter Mary Cronin says. "He talked about death quite a lot. As I interviewed him it was as if he was trying to wrap up his life and he wasn't especially pleased with what he saw. He was worried about his eyes being puffy and that he was no longer as good looking. Digging around in his psyche made him extremely unhappy. He gave off strong vibes of being jealous of his kids and of the fact that they were eclipsing him."

Jane said, "Dad was in a foul mood. Peter was his usual exasperating self." He inevitably got bored during the interview and wandered out into the garden to light up a joint; even so, throughout the next few hours she tried to be the voice of reason. "We're closer now than we ever have been," she kept repeating cheerily.

When Peter came back, he lambasted the establishment press and *Time* in particular for distorting the truth. Henry Fonda listened in stony silence until Peter seemed to be attacking the correspondents personally, and then he exploded and delivered a furious lecture on manners to his defiant son. Jane said later, "I felt as if I was three years old all over again."

A few days earlier, when she was back in New York staying with the Rosenthals as she often did, she'd had what she thought was an important conversation with Richard and his wife, Teddy. They'd sat up late listening while Jane explained what she felt she must do in the future. She told them she wanted to do something different, something that might not have anything to do with acting. She wanted to find some way that she could be part of all that was going on in the roiling political climate of America. "Somehow I want to make a difference," she added dramatically. She wanted to create a new life, a new persona, but she didn't have a clue as to how she was going to accomplish this.

At that point Jane was very much a political naif. If she wanted to emulate anyone it was Brando, the pivotal figure in Hollywood's changing attitude toward activism. He personalized his causes, sitting in with the Indians, giving the Black Panthers plane tickets so they could attend Martin Luther King's funeral. He was not that involved in protesting the Vietnam War although it was splitting the film community and the nation apart. John Wayne had recently made *The Green Berets* to show the world why it was necessary for the United States to be there. He didn't talk politics publicly like Robert Vaughn (formerly the Man from U.N.C.L.E.), who opposed the war and in 1968 formed a group called Dissenting Democrats, which he took all over the country, challenging President Johnson's war policies with inexhaustible determination and helping Al Lowenstein with his campaign to dump Johnson from the Democratic ticket.

Jane was aware of Vaughn and aware, too, that Warren Beatty and his sister, Shirley MacLaine, were advising the likes of Senator George McGovern. They both believed that McGovern could win the 1972 Democratic presidential nomination. And more than any other politician McGovern saw Beatty and MacLaine as tangible assets and a way to attract media attention and money. It didn't occur to Jane to work with Beatty and Shirley, who tended to do most of their activism behind the scenes. Jane wanted to be visible. She began corresponding with Vanessa Redgrave, who was speaking out for the Palestinians in Trafalgar Square, and she sought the company of other radicals such as the charismatic, mysterious Bert Schneider, who would soon produce the Academy Award–winning documentary by Peter Davis about Vietnam called *Hearts and Minds*. He and formerly blacklisted screenwriter Dalton Trumbo, who had served time in prison for defying the House Un-American Activities Committee, were big supporters of the Black Panthers.

The Panthers were the most romanticized figures of the New Left. "The main white movement heavies chose the Black Panther Party as their leading black heroes and allies," Todd Gitlin wrote. "Alongside the posters of Che Guevara and Malcolm X, there appeared on movement walls the poster of Huey Newton in a black beret seated in a fan shaped wicker throne, spear upright in his left hand, rifle in his right."

Jane enjoyed seeing the Panthers at Dalton Trumbo's parties, a wild mix of dropouts, visionaries, hustlers, lawyers, activists, therapists, and movie stars. Jane met black novelist James Baldwin at a Trumbo party, and she had long conversations with Angela Davis, who was a radical feminist and an associate of the Black Panther Party.

21

I N JANUARY 1970 Jane made her first public foray into activist politics. She flew to San Francisco to support the Indian takeover at Alcatraz, a former federal prison no longer used by the government. The American Indian movement wanted to turn it into an Indian cultural center and bring national media attention to the realities of Indian life — the high rate of unemployment, the low incomes, the high number of deaths from malnutrition and teen suicide.

She had already phoned Brando. He was the only major star who had ever appeared regularly at rallies for Native Americans. Their plight consumed him. He had attended the Washington State fish-in in 1964 with Dick Gregory. Standing on the steps of the state capitol, he had spoken to several thousand people about land rights. He advised Jane to use her fame to attract attention to their cause. "Fame is a useful political tool. For too many years I neglected the forum that was available to me. Now I use every means at my disposal to get across what I want to say."

Jane asked Peter Collier, an editor for *Ramparts,* to accompany her. "She arrived in San Francisco on a foggy morning . . . fresh-faced and confident, taller than I had expected, her hair cut in a boyish shag. As we stood on the wharf waiting for a boat to take us to Alcatraz, Jane stared out at the old maximum-security prison floating ominously in the bay. She said she felt she had been away from America too long; she was glad to be back home where it was 'happening.' I joked that perhaps she had waited too long: the sixties, after all, were over. A look of apprehension crossed her face and she said, 'Oh, I hope not!'"

For weeks the government had been ignoring the Indian occupation at Alcatraz. It was only when Jane appeared on the scene that the public started paying more attention to what was happening. And of course the media did, too.

It was practically a carnival atmosphere at the Embarcadero. There was singing and dancing; wealthy yachters delivered food and blankets and medicine to the Indians while the Coast Guard stood idly by.

Crowds of fans appeared out of nowhere, swarming around Jane and asking for her autograph. Reporters thrust microphones into her face, asking her what she thought. She wondered then, "Here I was a movie star and I was supposed to be an expert. And I didn't know what I thought yet. I had just arrived there."

Ferried out to Alcatraz on one of the local yachts, defying the Coast Guard blockade, Jane spent all afternoon talking with the Indians.

By the time Collier left her, she was squatting in a corner of the deserted prison yard, smoking pot with some of the leaders of the Sioux, the most militant of the tribes, who seemed bewildered at this beautiful movie star in their midst.

Jane had a lengthy conversation with twenty-two-year-old LaNada Means, a young woman whose brother, Russell Means, was one of the leaders of the American Indian movement. They were bitter about white racism and wanted to reestablish traditional Indian methods of government.

Jane also spoke at length with one of the protesters, Sid Mills, a young Yaqui who'd served in Vietnam and was now fighting for his tribe's fishing rights in the state of Washington. It was then that the Sioux leaders suggested she go to a number of reservations around the country to view all their problems close up. She promised them she would.

She came away from Alcatraz filled with rage at white America's treatment of the Native Americans. It was shameful — all the more so because the federal government sanctioned it — and yet the Indian cause and all the oppression surrounding it were ignored in the larger scheme of radical events. Jane determined to do something about it.

The encounters with the Indians and the meetings she had had with the Panthers at Dalton Trumbo's had jolted her out of her indecision. She had been searching for a cause to attach herself to. She decided she would work for both the Indians and the Panthers. She would raise money for both, speak out for both.

Not long after that, Jane told Vadim what he'd been expecting to hear for months — that she wanted a separation. She still loved him very much, she said, but she needed to control her own life; she wanted her freedom.

Until they worked out a legal separation, they decided they would stay together under the same roof for the sake of their daughter, who was then one and a half years old.

Jane went to her father and asked if she could come home. "Dad agreed immediately." She and Vadim moved into the Fonda guesthouse, where they lived for a while along with Vanessa and the nanny, Dot. Jane sent Vadim's secretary and cook and maid back to France. It was partially a question of money, partially because she wanted to simplify things.

It was pleasant in Bel Air. The place was serene and immaculate, Shirlee and the servants were unobtrusive, and Fonda was either painting or working in his gardens. "Dad's way of relating to me [was] complicated. When I was married Dad treated me as a grown-up. Now that I was single again with no man to validate me, I became the little girl for whom he felt responsible and whom he seemed unable to take seriously."

If Fonda objected to his daughter's politics or her lifestyle, he didn't say, nor did he comment on her way of dressing. Jane had started looking like a hippie protester — long, flowing skirts, much Indian jewelry. She went braless under her T-shirts.

However, he became uncomfortable when she invited Angela Davis over and insisted he meet with her. They attempted to have a conversation, but it went nowhere. Davis was imperious and opinionated, holding forth about the injustices against the Black Panthers. She wanted them to know about the FBI's targeting of the Panthers by their Counter Intelligence Program; she said she would be writing about it.

When friends asked her what Vadim felt about her newfound activism, Jane insisted, "Well, he approves of what I'm doing although he doesn't agree with it all." But she added, "He knows he can't stop me."

Vadim was resigned to his wife's choices, although he had little interest in the causes she was fighting for. He was hurt that she had left him, but he was consoled by one thought. "Jane was not seeking a new love affair," he said. "She wasn't leaving me for another man. She was leaving me for herself. She had found her way." Vadim soon left the Fondas' guesthouse and rented a small cottage on the beach. Jane would visit him there on the weekends, bringing Vanessa.

She had started going to places alone. On one of her solitary outings she attended a dinner party Mike Nichols was giving for Michelangelo Antonioni, who had just finished directing the apocalyptic *Zabriskie Point.*

Everybody was talking about the ending of the movie, the best thing in it. A huge modern house explodes in the desert, spewing clothes and food and books amid an orange cloud of flame and smoke, to the pulsing tunes of Pink Floyd.

Jane wandered into the kitchen to get a drink and was introduced to the political activist Fred Gardner, age twenty-seven, dark, brooding, argumentative, said to have been Lillian Hellman's most brilliant student when she taught playwriting at Harvard. Gardner, a committed Marxist, had been hired to do rewrites on the *Zabriskie Point* screenplay, along with Sam Shepard and Clara Peploe. "I'd been inventing what I hoped was 'more authentic dialogue in terms of American radicalism,'" he said.

Gardner was famous in New Left circles for being the driving force behind the GI coffeehouses. For the past three years he had been setting up a national network of coffeehouses outside military bases where soldiers, sailors, and air force pilots could listen to rock music and vent their opposition to the war. An increasing number of soldiers were very supportive of the antiwar campaign. They were a vital part of the GI movement against the Vietnam War.

Jane had never heard of the GI coffeehouses, let alone the GI movement, so Gardner explained how "the GI movement" was a term used by the radical left to refer to that aspect of the antiwar movement aimed at the military. More and more soldiers, as well as Vietnam vets, were banding together with civilian antiwar activists to protest what was going on in Vietnam, he said. Equally important, he added, was protecting GI rights from unconstitutional excesses of military law. (Often after GIs spoke out against the war they were punished.)

After listening to him Jane exclaimed that she would do all she could to publicize the GI movement. Could he please send her everything he'd written on the subject? He brusquely agreed and walked off.

When he returned home to San Francisco, he sent Jane material on the GI movement, expecting never to hear from her again. A week later, she appeared on his doorstep, "burning with questions." He immediately passed her over to his wife, an ardent feminist and activist, while he went over and sulked in a corner. "Jane happened in our lives just as we were trying to patch up our marriage. It wasn't working. At the same time, I was in the process of extricating myself from further participation in the movement, because I was exhausted by the exploitation and backbiting."

By 1970, the male-run movement of the New Left was coming apart out of frustration and factionalism. Initially Gardner had been very involved in the New Left. He and many of his friends had thought of themselves as instruments of change.

At the same time, the women's liberation movement was erupting all over America, taking over much of the rage and energy and commitment the men had had for the revolution. Women around the country were fighting for their equality and independence; the bedroom had become a main area of struggle.

Gardner said he imagined his wife was trying to interest Jane in the feminist cause, but he could tell she was not really listening, because she kept looking at him and trying to draw him into the conversation. When she was unable to, she left.

She started pursuing him. She was fascinated because he seemed totally indifferent to her. However, in the following weeks, his already rocky marriage finally broke up, and they started spending time together.

Gardner had just become president of the newly formed United States Servicemen's Fund (USSF), a money-raising project put together by left-wingers who hoped to expand the GI movement. The first thing he did was to take Jane to some USSF meetings in Los Angeles, where she was introduced to lawyers involved with military law. But mostly he gave Jane a crash course on the GI movement and the issues involved, such as draft resistance, servicemen's rights, the organizing of veterans. The solidarity between vets and soldiers currently serving in the military was growing in terms of protesting the war.

Jane tried to absorb everything Gardner told her. He warned her that the New Left, which she so ardently wanted to be a part of, was dying. "We wanted to change the world," he said. "We had started off with the idea that anything is possible. We wanted to end the war and support civil rights." But nothing had worked out the way he and his friends hoped or dreamed. A lot of it had to do with channeling energy into action.

Now the New Left was a mess. He ended up by telling her that if she became an activist she shouldn't expect rewards. Activism has nothing to do with publicity or heroics or being visible. Being an activist has to do with asking questions, a lot of questions, and being patient and sticking to the cause you're committed to. It's arduous and slow and painful to try to change anything within the democratic system.

Jane kept thanking Gardner for introducing her to radical politics; she'd thank him over and over again in public. He would always minimize his importance in her political evolution. "She gives me more credit than I deserve," he'd always say. Especially since she usually did not follow his advice. She would not stay in the background in order to learn. She had to remain visible and vocal, because she thought if she did she would be accepted and gain credibility with other activists — even though she often didn't know what she was talking about. "Maybe she gives me credit for ideas that I could be proven wrong about and then she could blame me," Gardner added dryly.

They soon became lovers. "But only for a short time," Jane maintained. He reportedly confided to friends that Jane begged him to live with her but he refused. She added, "I was in love with him but I didn't understand him." What she didn't understand was why he was relatively immune to her charms. Most men were dying to go to bed with her because she was so seductive. Gardner played it cool.

In the winter of 1970, they traveled together to coffeehouses in Monterey, near Fort Ord, and in Tacoma, Washington, near Fort Lewis, where she began having long discussions with the soldiers about what had turned them against the war in Vietnam. They would sit on the floor with Jane. "The atmosphere was friendly but somber . . . they had more important things on their minds. . . . Those who had seen combat in Vietnam were the quietest. . . . When I was getting ready to leave, a young man, twenty years old at the most and looking more like fifteen, came up to me wanting to say something. . . . 'I . . . k-killed a young . . . b,' he whispered, and began to cry silently. Up to that moment I had thought only about what we were doing to the Vietnamese. Now, from his suffering, I glimpsed that the war had become an American tragedy as well. *What were we doing to our young men?*"

Through Gardner, Jane met Donald Duncan, a former Green Beret who was now crusading against the war; the press agent Steve Jaffe; and Mark Lane, the burly lawyer who had gained celebrity with his book *Rush to Judgment,* a critical assessment of the Warren Report's findings on the Kennedy assassination.

Some people described Lane as a "political opportunist and an egomaniac," but Jane saw him as fearless. He juggled as many causes as she did: the GI movement, the American Indian movement, the Panthers. He was extremely well informed on all the issues and very theatrical.

Along with Gardner, Lane would take it upon himself to acclimate Jane to the fractious world of the New Left, which was about to splinter over ideology and tactics. Steve Jaffe played a special role; he would strategize with Jane for hours about how best to approach the media. He spent most of his time setting up press conferences and fending off hostile reporters.

As soon as it became known that Jane had offered herself up to the antiwar movement (mostly, but not all, student-driven), there was a mad dash to vie for her allegiance. Organizations like National Mobilization Committee to End the War wanted money. Others, like the National Liberation Front, wanted her to endorse their cause, which was to support North Vietnam. Then there were eccentric offshoots of the movement, such as the Yippies, led by Abbie Hoffman. He practiced street theater and concocted wild stunts to promote peace. Because she was so famous, everybody felt that Jane Fonda, aka Barbarella, could put the movement, and all its warring factions, back in the news.

Everybody wanted to feed off her celebrity—have their picture taken with her, get her autograph, and eat a meal with her. Gardner told her "to be careful. The movement was filled with political fakers. But Jane had a very bad shit detector and she surrounded herself with mediocrities. It eventually got very ugly."

On the morning of March 8, 1970, Jane and Mark Lane marched with Gardner on Fort Lawton, joining 150 protestors from the United Indian People's Council. Some of them scaled the fences surrounding Fort Lawton, draping blankets over the barbed wire and climbing down to set up tepees on the ground. Others brought drums and began singing songs. It was all part of an effort to occupy the fort, led by Bernie Whitebear, a young Native American who'd been inspired by the uprising at Alcatraz.

Some of the Indians rushed the gates; they were met by military police. Jane was part of the group pushing and shoving at the main gate. Her star power was such that the military stopped to ogle her. A few soldiers even took Polaroids while she chatted them up. They took so long talking to her that dozens of Native Americans were able to swarm into the compound unnoticed. Outside the gate fifty more protesters tried to get in while the media recorded the event. There were dozens of photographers and reporters from around the world. The attempted occupation of the fort got international attention, thanks mainly to Jane, who was photographed and roughed up in the melee. Lane tried to protect her and shouted curses. Ten Native Americans were arrested. Trucks were overturned. Tear gas was used to subdue the crowd. Jane and Lane were questioned by the military and then released. Lane took advantage of the crowd of reporters covering the incident to claim that the police were beating up the Native Americans who were still in jail.

One question a reporter from an alternative newspaper kept asking: "Why is Jane Fonda here?" No answers were given, and Jane, Gardner, and Lane then drove to nearby Fort Lewis to protest the beatings to another crowd of reporters and television cameras. This time Jane was arrested and taken into custody for trespassing.

This was her first exposure to violent protest, and she was both energized and angered by it. At a press conference in Seattle the next day, she spoke fiercely about how she and Lane had filed a lawsuit against the army for being barred from Fort Lawton. The suit demanded that they be permitted free access to all bases and all military installations.

Without meaning to, Jane upstaged the Indians by her star presence and caused a good deal of resentment among their leaders, who couldn't get a word in edgewise. "Jane Fonda forgot the crusade she was on," Kahn-Tineta Horn, a Mohawk activist, said. "She started talking about Vietnam. What makes it worse is she's a leftist."

A young reporter on the scene commented, "There was Jane

Fonda—aka Barbarella—in dirty jeans and no makeup, trembling with anger about the injustice of it all. When she spoke in this arch, cultivated, finishing-school accent, 'Vurry, vurry bad situation,' she blew my mind!"

Jane still had no idea what she was doing as an activist. *What was her role? Where could she fit in? With the Panthers, and the Indians, and the GIs?* "She had good instincts and a conscience," Gardner said. "But at the moment she had no political antennae." She was, however, constantly trying to figure out how she could *make things better,* and then she found an answer when she and Gardner flew to New York for two hectic days to sit in at USSF meetings. The office was being run by a political activist named Howard Levy, a young doctor who had been court-martialed and sent to Leavenworth for two years for refusing to train Green Berets in the healing arts. Levy had just been released on parole the summer before and he immediately joined the USSF, and the GI movement got much of its inspiration from Levy when Gardner set up the first coffeehouses in 1967.

"When Jane came to New York," Levy told writer Thomas Kiernan, "she kept saying 'I don't just want to be known as Jane Fonda the actress. I want to be something more than that.' So we said, 'Now, wait a minute, Jane, you are an actress. I'm a doctor, and one of the things I'm trying to do is organize the medical profession, you know, get doctors to give money and support to the movement.... You're an actress. Organizing is what the movement is all about. So go back to Hollywood and start organizing the film industry.' She agreed, and that's what she started doing. She hated going around asking people for money, but she gritted her teeth and did it. . . . Of course, she was very close to Freddie Gardner by then. He was a pretty demanding guy, so I suppose a lot of her drive came about as a result of her trying to please him. But she really went at it." It was the start of her developing her fundraising skills. She had a genius for it.

Jane was also in New York to meet with Elisabeth Vailland, her French left-wing friend, who was arriving from Paris to accompany her on her cross-country trip.

Vadim had insisted she not travel alone. "You are too famous, too beautiful, and too vulnerable. You must have a companion." Elisabeth, whose husband, Roger Vailland, had just recently died, was eager to join her.

When they embraced at Kennedy Airport, Elisabeth would later write, she saw a change in her young friend. "Jane was charged up with what she was doing with the Indians and the GI movement. She felt she now had a real purpose in her life. She spoke intensely about her 'political conscience.' She felt as if she just had been born."

They drove into New York in a limousine with Jane continuing to talk a mile a minute. Elisabeth wanted to see the hippie life in Greenwich Village, so they went on an impromptu tour, stopping to have coffee and poking into a number of antique shops on Bleecker Street.

Later in the day Elisabeth met Gardner, who had accompanied Jane to New York along with LaNada Means, the Indian activist Jane had met at Alcatraz. Jane had paid for her ticket so she could appear on *The Dick Cavett Show* with her on March 13.

Cavett moderated a lively program (he was known as the "thinking man's talk show host"); he had the ability to remain calm and mediate among a wild assortment of guests from Norman Mailer to Gore Vidal and William Buckley. He could also be gently teasing, as he was when Jane appeared that night in a black fringed leather outfit smiling her dazzling smile and laughing angrily because he surprised her by asking, "Do you remember when we met?" "On your show," she answered demurely. In truth she had dated a friend of his, Ed Blier, and Cavett remembered hearing her high heels click across the floor as she sneaked into the Yale dorm to see Blier late at night. Cavett didn't say that, but just the suggestion of Yale caused Jane to bow her head and deny they had ever met. "But we did meet in the Yale dining room. . . ." He went on in that fashion but she refused to fall into the trap of admitting anything personal on camera, so he eventually let the subject drop and started asking her questions about her interest in the American Indians. This was followed by a passionate but slightly incoherent speech about what she felt were the grave injustices perpetrated against the Indians on their reservations, what had happened to her at the Fort Lawton demonstration, and how the press had distorted the issues. Then LaNada Means was brought out, and she attempted to talk about her life as a Native American. The show ended with a surprise appearance by Henry Fonda, Peter Fonda, and Amy Fonda. Jane seemed overjoyed to see her father and threw her arms around him.

Afterward she went back to the hotel and watched a rerun of Cavett with Gardner and Lane. She was mortified by the mistakes she felt she'd made. Jane was often in despair about what she said in public. She spoke too generally; she wasn't specific and often made big errors in the beginning. She would begin to work with both men boning up on the issues and on facts. She really wanted to learn.

It was soon agreed among the various leaders that Jane Fonda was creating problems for the Native Americans. She didn't mean to — her intentions were the best — but the kind of publicity she was getting them was not helpful. The Native Americans did not want to be identified with a big Hollywood star who seemed out to get personal publicity for herself.

Jane was confused and upset by the Native Americans' hostility. Finally an Indian leader who liked her personally told her quietly that she could certainly continue to demonstrate with them but she could not be their spokesperson — she simply did not know enough about the long history of white oppression to be an effective representative.

At the same time, she was making a huge effort to convince her father that he must share her outrage about Vietnam. She wanted him to understand how much news was being suppressed. The public was being kept in the dark about President Nixon's secret plan to end the war, she said. It was actually a plan to escalate it. The president's goal: to reduce American casualties while increasing Vietnamese deaths on the cynical assumption that most Americans didn't care about "nonwhite" body counts.

Mark Lane accompanied her to the meetings she had with her father at his Bel Air mansion. He remembered Fonda's reaction to Jane's revelations: "The guy almost exploded. He refused to believe what his daughter was telling him. 'We do not do these things!' he cried. 'Americans are not capable of doing such terrible things.'"

Jane didn't stop. She took Donald Duncan, the former Green Beret sergeant who was speaking out against the military around the country, to meet her father. (Back in 1966 Duncan had sounded off about what was really going on in Vietnam in the pages of *Ramparts*. A former officer in Special Services, he was the first soldier to talk about civilian atrocities, as well as the indiscriminate bombing of villages, and of faked body counts.) He recounted to Henry Fonda everything he'd seen, along with specific horrors like the beatings of civilians and the raping of women. He then showed Fonda newsreel footage of soldiers setting fire to villages.

"You could tell Henry Fonda was very upset," Lane said. "'What can I do?' he finally asked us. 'Except campaign for peace candidates, which I'm already doing.'"

On the morning of March 26, 1970, Jane and Elisabeth Vailland packed up a rented Mercury station wagon, filling it with bottled water, flashlights, books, and a few clothes. They were about to take off and visit various army bases and Indian reservations around the United States. The station wagon was parked in the driveway of Fonda's Bel Air estate. Hank filmed their departure with his movie camera.

He had not tried to convince his daughter to stay at home, although he privately wondered how the separation would affect eighteen-month-old Vanessa. At the moment she was toddling naked on the grass, watching curiously as her mother and Elisabeth finished packing. Vadim scooped her up in his arms. Jane glanced over at her husband and child and could barely control her tears.

Days before, beside himself about the trip, Vadim had phoned Andreas and asked him to persuade Jane not to go. He'd already pointed out to her that she was behaving just like her mother had behaved toward her when she was a little girl — didn't she realize that? She was virtually abandoning Vanessa in favor of a cause just as Frances had abandoned her years before in favor of Peter.

It's hard to know whether she was in denial or psychologically numbed, or just so self-involved that what she was doing didn't register. As Andreas reminded Vadim, "When Jane wants to do something, you can't change her mind. She has to go on this journey."

Decades later, in 2003, Jane sat with Vanessa Redgrave in her dressing room after seeing her in *Long Day's Journey into Night*. The women talked till 2:00 A.M. about their activism and how it had affected their children. Redgrave, who was a Trotskyite and a fierce supporter of the Palestinians, admitted she often felt guilty about leaving her family when she went off to protest, but she felt compelled to. Did she regret it? Jane wondered. "Yes and no," Redgrave said. "If we were two men talking about our politics and our activism, we would have an entirely different attitude. Women are not supposed to make personal choices at the expense of everything else."

"Have your daughters forgiven you?" Jane asked. And Redgrave said, "I'd like to think so, but I can't be sure. We've talked about it a lot." And Jane confided that she still felt guilty about going off so much to protest the war and said that her daughter had never forgiven her. "She'll be angry about it until I die."

It took a long time for Jane to finish packing. Everybody stood around waiting. Hank Fonda turned off his movie camera, and Vadim cradled baby Vanessa in his arms. There were embraces and kisses, and then the station wagon took off, Jane at the wheel.

In the background, Christian Marquand was convulsed with laughter. After the car disappeared down the drive, Vadim demanded, "What's so funny, *mon vieux*?"

"Because the wife goes off to war and the husband stays behind with the children. It is crazy! It is *fou*!"

Vadim dreaded telling Nathalie about Jane. He had been putting it off because he knew how upset she would be. She had just returned from boarding school in Switzerland because she had been so homesick. A week after Jane left, he called his daughter into his bedroom and announced, *"Jane est partie."*

"My world started crashing," Nathalie said. "She had been my mother for six years. I couldn't believe she wouldn't say goodbye to me. My father was suffering terribly, but he was trying not to show it. He was so hurt. I was furious at Jane for being so thoughtless, so unfeeling." Nathalie didn't speak to Jane for a long time. "I think for close to ten years, we did not have an extended conversation. But finally — I guess it was when I began working in the movie business as an assistant director — I finally had a real talk with her.

"In the next couple of years, she sold the farm at Ouen, and my father never had a chance to salvage any of his own possessions — his chess set, his paintings, his childhood souvenirs, his collection of science fiction and comic books. It was a huge emotional loss. Jane didn't seem to think anything of it. She got rid of all the dogs and cats, the geese, the chickens. She did reimburse my father for the money he had spent on the farm, but money meant nothing to Vadim. It wasn't the money he cared about, it was his personal stuff.

"I told her what I thought. She was having a massage. I told her how cruel she had been to my father and me, and to Vanessa: 'You abandoned us and you never said goodbye.'

"Jane sat bolt upright on the massage table. 'My God!' she said. 'I wasn't aware! I didn't know. I am so sorry.' And she really meant it. She really was sorry. She hadn't been aware.

"'I will make up for it,' she cried. 'I promise you!' And she did. We became close again. She paid for my college tuition when I wanted to get a master's degree at Brown, and she helped me with the battered women's shelter I'd started to run. It's part of her foundation.

"I suppose I've forgiven her now; I don't know whether my father did. Sometimes I wonder if Vanessa has. She really hangs on to her anger. But you know what? No matter what she does, people usually do forgive Jane Fonda."

Part IV

Political Activist: 1970–1988

Jane Fonda is important because she is a celebrity
and unimportant because she is a celebrity.
She is a revolutionary who happens to be an
actress who happens to be a revolutionary.

— TIM FINDLEY, "HANOI JANE FONDA"

22

A S SOON AS SHE slammed the door and gunned the motor of the station wagon, Jane forgot about Vanessa. Oh, yes, she loved her very much, but she had the ability to blot out one reality (in this case abandoning her daughter) and replace it with another one.

Jane drove very fast out of Los Angeles and onto the Pacific Coast Highway. She chain-smoked, her face half-hidden by big dark glasses. Every so often she'd consult a map. Her destination was the Paiute Indian reservation forty miles outside of Reno.

For a while she didn't speak to Elisabeth Vailland, who sat next to her gazing out at the scenery: Hearst Castle at San Simeon, the redwoods rising tall and stately above Big Sur. When they approached the Golden Gate Bridge spanning San Francisco Bay, Elisabeth gasped, *"C'est formidable."* She had never been in the United States before and she was impressed. Every so often she'd scribble notes on a pad. The notes would be part of a memoir she later wrote about their "political journey." It was published in France as *Le Voyage dans L'Amérique de gauche,* but in fact it sheds little light on what actually happened on the trip.

In the memoir Elisabeth writes impersonally about their friendship, but there were always rumors that she and Jane were lovers. In her memoir and in interviews Jane has denied the rumors, saying, "People thought she was my hairdresser, too." But she was intrigued by Elisabeth, with her frizzy black hair and inquisitive nut-brown face. As a young girl she'd been a partisan in Italy during World War II. While married to Roger Vailland, she became part of one of the most vociferous left-wing intellectual groups in Paris.

In his autobiography Vadim described the meeting of the two women in the Vailland garden outside Paris on a cloudy afternoon. They had shaken hands, and then Jane smiled her dazzling American smile, all big white teeth and glistening lips, and began addressing Elisabeth in impeccable French.

Elisabeth seemed mesmerized. After observing Jane for several moments, she started caressing her face and murmuring, "I like your third eye." Vadim thought she meant she admired Jane's power to juggle roles.

They became friends. Elisabeth would see a rough cut of *Barbarella* and the French version of *The Game Is Over,* in which Jane goes mad. She would hang out in the kitchen of the farm when Vadim was teaching Jane how to make mayonnaise; she would be with Jane in the garden as she played with Nathalie and Christian and then frolicked with her dogs. There were so many facets to this woman, Elisabeth would think.

Now on their cross-country trip Jane kept melting into the persona of Madame Vadim as they discussed the curious bond they shared, since they'd both procured many women for their husbands and joined them in bed as well.

"Did you enjoy being with [other] women?" Elisabeth would ask.

Jane would maintain that she thought she did "because I liked having an up-close view of the varied ways women express passion." And besides, she'd said once, most of the women did fall in love with her so Vadim was jealous, and then there was something about those rituals of domination and submission — performing them made her feel more real. But then she'd contradict herself and add, "But to go through with it I'd always have to drink enough to be in an altered state. I always felt scared and competitive — not the best frame of mind to be in when you're having sex."

Vadim preferred young girls. Two or three young girls together helped him get aroused. Jane remembered trying to solicit some nubile young Andy Warhol groupie outside Max's Kansas City late one night. She invited her to come back to the Chelsea Hotel with them. The girl, who had been unlocking her bicycle, was contemptuous — though she recognized Jane and Vadim, she said, "No way!" and pedaled off into the darkness.

• • •

On their trip across the United States, Jane and Elisabeth kept returning to the subject of sex, but this aspect of their lives was just an aside — they were supposed to be exchanging information about Indian water rights. That's what they were talking about as they parked the station wagon at the Paiute reservation in Nevada. It was the morning after they left Los Angeles.

Moments after they arrived, they joined twenty Indians standing on the shore and pouring symbolic vials of water into Pyramid Lake. There'd been a long dispute with the U.S. government about a diversion of water from the Truckee River to a non-Indian irrigation project.

A few of the Indians confided to Jane that they suspected their tribal councils were responsible for permitting the white man's exploitation of the reservation. Jane was still trying to help the Indians although she no longer attempted to be a spokesperson for them. She found most of the Indians apathetic. They were angry, with both their leaders and the white man, but they were divided among themselves and not as militant or dynamic as the Indians she'd met at Alcatraz.

Next she and Elisabeth drove to the Shoshone Reservation at Fort Hall, Utah, where they were joined by LaNada Means, the earnest young activist Jane had met when they were rallying support for the Indian occupation at Alcatraz. LaNada took the two women to meet her father, who spoke sadly about the endless disputes his tribe had had with the U.S. government and the many defeats and betrayals. He had a great many documents from these disputes stuffed into a battered cigar box, and he pulled some of them out to show Jane, a despairing look on his deeply lined face. Jane promised she would do what she could to publicize the Shoshone tribe's troubles.

The meetings at the reservations had not accomplished much. In the next weeks Jane would visit more Indian reservations in the Southwest where she would be shown more of America's illegal exploitation of land grants. But first she had to fly back to L.A. for the Academy Awards.

She'd been nominated for *They Shoot Horses, Don't They?* and had been the odds-on favorite to win Best Actress until her arrest in Seattle. That coupled with her inflammatory public statements about Nixon were jeopardizing her chances. "She may just ruin an otherwise spectacular career," her agent, Dick Clayton, said.

On April 7, Jane arrived at the Dorothy Chandler Pavilion dressed like a movie star in her mink coat and Chanel gown. She swept past the bleachers packed with screaming fans, and as she did she raised her fist and gave the Panther salute. "Power to the people!" There was some applause and lots of boos.

Hours later she lost the Oscar to Maggie Smith, who won for *The Prime of Miss Jean Brodie*. Jane told Vadim that she'd expected to lose but that it didn't matter to her now, "because my life outside of movies was starting to interest me more than being an actor."

Late that night, she attended Elizabeth Taylor's "Oscar losers party" at the Beverly Hills Hotel. She solicited some hefty checks for the Panthers, then went on to a Panther rally to deliver the money. Jane was staying with Vanessa at the beach. The house was filled with hangers-on from Paris.

After the awards ceremony, she had planned to devote her short stay in L.A. to Vanessa. But she found herself on the phone raising money for the Panthers and the GI movement, and that took hours and then she fell asleep on the couch. After two days, on April 9, she left for Denver to participate in a thirty-six-hour "Fast for Peace." It was one of many events planned by Mobe (National Mobilization Committee to End the War in Vietnam). Over a thousand people joined famed baby doctor Benjamin Spock, comedian Dick Gregory, assorted Panthers, and Jane.

At night she and Dick Gregory and Dr. Spock camped out on a small cement island near the United Nations Association in downtown Denver. It was cold and rainy so they huddled in sleeping bags. Cars moved slowly past them, honking their horns loudly in greeting.

The next stop was the Home Front Coffee House outside Fort Carson in Colorado Springs, where Jane had promised to join in an antiwar demonstration. She had already seen plenty of signs of dissent on army bases — heavy peace rings worn as brass knuckles, young officers' jeeps bristling with antiwar stickers.

Many of the antiwar GIs that she'd met told her that hating their personal experience within the military was the first step toward deploring what the unjust war represented. The next step was rejecting U.S. foreign policy. The numbers of deserters and AWOLs had reached a new high, and reenlistment was at an all-time low.

Jane and Elisabeth arrived at Fort Carson on April 11. TV camera-men and reporters had trailed them in another car. Jane Fonda was the biggest thing that had happened to the antiwar movement since Yippie Abbie Hoffman began addressing the politically disaffected through street theater. Thirty GIs were waiting outside the coffeehouse with a lawyer and the base commander. They explained that a few days be-fore, a hundred soldiers had lined up in front of Fort Carson's medical dispensary and flashed peace signs that read "We're Sick of the War." They'd all been thrown into the stockade.

She and Elisabeth were taken into the stockade where they saw pris-oners who seemed catatonic; one appeared schizophrenic. There were rumors that soldiers who were also Black Panthers were being mis-treated. When the commander realized what they were seeing, Jane and Elisabeth were hustled out of the stockade before they were able to determine which prisoners were the protesters.

They returned to Fort Carson the following day but were denied permission to pass out antiwar leaflets. A couple of young officers rec-ognized Jane, and one of them offered to sneak in Jane and Elisabeth in their car. "They wanted me to see an on-base coffeehouse that the brass had created complete with girlie shows to keep the men from coming to the GI movement coffeehouses."

Once inside the coffeehouse, Jane and Elisabeth quickly began handing out the books they'd brought — copies of Jonathan Schell's *The Village of Ben Suc* and an abridged version of *Against the Crime of Silence,* an account of Bertrand Russell's International War Crimes Tribunal. Jane began telling the group of surprised soldiers about the Home Front Coffee House and about what was going on in the stock-ade. By then she'd been recognized by everybody in the place, and GIs crowded around her asking questions. She wasn't able to say much before MPs rushed in and took her into custody.

She was quickly released by one of the generals of the fort be-cause he didn't want any trouble and Jane was going to make a lot of noise.

After that she was arrested a lot for "trespassing" on army bases. Once she was tear-gassed; another time at Fort Meade she and Elisa-beth and Mark Lane were roughed up and pushed and shoved by MPs even as Lane documented the insults with his tape recorder. Invariably they would be taken to an office and fingerprinted. They would sing protest songs and raise their fists as army photographers took mug shots, and then they would be escorted off base where press and TV cameras were waiting to hear Jane's standard speech attacking the military establishment's violation of the rights of servicemen.

Being arrested left her elated. She remembered how Vadim had sarcastically referred to her as "Jane d'Arc." "She really believed she was submitting herself to the radical fires that would burn away her past," Elisabeth Vailland noted.

Jane spent hours listening to GI complaints about how little voice they had in the military and virtually no representation. They could be arrested simply for flashing the "V" peace sign.

Eventually she, Mark Lane, and his companion, the lawyer Carol Mugar, helped to establish a GI office in Washington, D.C., which would act as an important clearinghouse for GI allegations of mistreatment by the military. Over the next months Jane would raise $50,000 for it.

On April 30, as Jane drove into Santa Fe, she and Elisabeth heard Nixon on the radio announcing the bombing of Cambodia. His voice blared out again from a television set as they registered at a local motel. Several reporters appeared in the lobby. "They wanted to know my reaction," Jane said.

She said she felt it was a terrible betrayal by Nixon, who had promised to end the war and was now escalating it. She eventually went on local TV to condemn the president, calling him a warmonger.

On May 4, she was scheduled to speak at the student union at the University of New Mexico at Albuquerque. She hadn't spoken at any big rallies. Whenever she appeared at GI coffeehouses or college campuses, it was for informal conversations. But a student leader urged her to join in an antiwar demonstration about to be held in the university auditorium. He added that a lot of kids there were apathetic about Vietnam; maybe she could shake them a little.

She was nervous and phoned David Duncan in L.A. for reassurance.

She wrote a scholarly speech, but she wasn't prepared for an auditorium jam-packed with seven hundred students, some literally hanging from the balconies. They cheered when she told them in a clear voice that she was not there as an actress but as a participant in a political action. In front of her on the podium was a single word, *Vietnam*, and behind her on a huge blackboard someone had printed the word STRIKE!

"Suddenly I feel the flood gates are opening," Jane cried. "You have to express what you feel. What I feel is rage, rage at being lied to — rage because I am a woman. . . ."

She talked about American planes secretly bombing Cambodia for years; the media just hadn't reported it. She said many GIs did not support this war, indeed many opposed it; they needed support, she said. Students could work for peace in Vietnam by supporting GI rights. "Let the violence stay with those who are really violent — the police and the Administration. . . . Write letters to the President and your Congressman."

When she finished there was an uncomfortable silence. Then a wild-haired, drunken poet named Gregory Corso staggered onto the stage and demanded to know "why in the fuck" Jane Fonda hadn't mentioned the four students who'd just been shot at Kent State University in Ohio by the National Guard?

The Guard had been attempting to calm a milling antiwar demonstration on campus; a thousand angry students taunted young guardsmen wearing gas masks and wielding rifles. The Guard withdrew to a hill with students running after them yelling. That's when the Guard fired, killing four students and seriously wounding eleven others.

"I hadn't heard the news," Jane wrote in her autobiography. "I was shocked by the news and felt like a fool." She immediately joined a march on the home of university president Ferrel Heady. A hundred kids* massed together to demand that the university shut down as a sign of protest against the killings. Before the meeting ended, plans were announced to strike the university, and there was a request that the National Guard not be called in.

Jane flew back to L.A. to help organize more demonstrations around the country. By the time she returned to Albuquerque to support the strike, scuffles had broken out between conservative and radical stu-

---

* In memory of the killings at Kent State, the kids called their group They Shoot Students Don't They?, paraphrasing the title of Jane's most recent movie, which had just played in Albuquerque earlier that month.

dents, the National Guard had been called in, and the university had been shut down.

Similar events of violence were occurring on other campuses all over the country. Student strikes had already closed down more than a hundred universities, and college students were rampaging at Stanford, Princeton, Yale, and the University of Kansas. The favorite target: ROTC buildings.

Nixon had taken to calling the young protesters "bums." Faculty and students from all over the United States joined in condemning the Cambodian invasion, as did leading intellectuals like Norman Mailer, poet Robert Lowell, and countless others. A great plea was rising to end the U.S. military operations in Vietnam.

On May 9, Jane opened a massive rally in Washington, D.C., where one hundred thousand protestors crowded onto the National Mall to demand an immediate withdrawal of troops — not just from Cambodia but from Laos and Vietnam.

Marijuana smoke hung thick in the air. Moments before the speeches started, a black man roped himself to a huge cross at the front of the stage and a group of kids doused themselves with animal blood, symbolic gestures meant to signal that Nixon was crucifying the American people with this war.

Jane ran across the giant stage that had been set up on the Mall. She wore faded jeans, a T-shirt, and no bra. "You can see her nipples," someone shouted. She raised her fist and shouted, "Greetings, fellow bums!" The crowd laughed and roared back in recognition of Nixon's slight and she was off, telling them what the GI movement was all about and how important it was that so many soldiers were speaking out against the war even though they risked being court-martialed. She pointed to some GIs on the edge of the crowd. "Those men may very well have seen combat in Vietnam. They know better than any of us what war is like. Don't assume they are against us for opposing the war." There was loud applause and one of the men threw Jane a peace sign. She disappeared into a sea of performers backstage that included Shirley MacLaine and Dick Gregory, only to surface hours later at another huge demonstration in New York's Central Park before hitting the road again.

As she and Elisabeth Vailland zigzagged across the United States,

Jane became aware she was being followed. She never went over the speed limit but she was stopped over and over again by the highway patrol. She was asked for her license, asked where she was going. She saw it as a form of harassment. "There was a tightening in my stomach. I never knew what would happen next . . . but I also felt a deepening resolve not to turn back."

By now the FBI was really after her. She would stop at coffeehouses like Oleo Strut in Killeen, Texas, which had originally been an indoctrination center on GI rights but by 1970 had been transformed into a cell of political revolutionaries. The staff was totally conflicted about what was the correct approach to radicalize GIs. Jane met with moderates who wanted to concentrate on soldiers' legal rights; there was also another faction, the so-called Trotskyites, who encouraged the antiwar GIs to carry out acts of terrorism and sabotage.

As soon as Jane left places like Oleo Strut, FBI agents would immediately move in and question anyone who'd spoken to her. Teams of informants reported on her every word, and if she gave a speech, they would examine it for violations of the 1917 Espionage Act, which criminalizes incitement, "insubordination . . . disloyalty . . . mutiny . . ." But no one could ever say Jane Fonda was attempting to undermine the U.S. government. Maintained a chaplain's assistant who had been interrogated, mostly "Jane Fonda just listened."

It's not easy to re-create America's apocalyptic state in 1970, the year in which Jane Fonda transformed herself into a revolutionary. The country was still reeling from the assassinations of John F. Kennedy and Martin Luther King Jr., as well as Nixon's betrayal. He'd been re-elected because he'd promised to end the Vietnam War; instead he'd accelerated the bombing. There were protests everywhere: sit-ins, strikes, picketing, and mass marches. Fires blazed in the streets of Chicago and San Francisco, and thousands of students marched on college campuses from California to Maine, pouring blood on draft cards or burning them, as the Berrigan brothers did, with napalm.

As the demonstrations and confrontations multiplied and the civilian antiwar movement, still largely white middle-class, began to make an impact, Nixon lashed out, labeling them "elite intellectuals — out of touch with reality."

He couldn't dismiss the GI movement, made up of sons of the working class — hard hats, the rural poor, blacks, and Latinos — quite so easily, and he went to great lengths to spy, infiltrate, and discredit them as being "alleged soldiers and veterans."

By mid-May Jane and Elisabeth had crisscrossed the United States several times, bumping along back roads and mountain towns, hitting cities as far north as Seattle before veering back down to more GI coffeehouses.

There was no set itinerary; "we would stop when we chose to," Jane said.

Once they passed through a vast trailer camp, where there were hundreds of near-destitute families — hippies existing on pot and red wine. Jane imagined she could make a movie about these families someday, about this trailer camp.

Invariably the two women would end up at some cheap motel near a highway, "and then we'd crash," Jane said. They'd be sick-tired and have to stand in a hot shower for a long time to wash off the grime and ease the ache in their bones.

With supper they would drink whiskey and talk. Now she was struggling with the contradictions of her own privileged life. She had been an activist for less than a year, so how could she possibly understand the problems of welfare mothers when she had a nanny taking care of Vanessa?

Mentioning Vanessa would make her cry. Leaving her child and going off on her own had been reckless — irresponsible — but part of her believed she had to give up something big in order to become a new self. She told Elisabeth she felt as if she'd been reborn when she became a political activist, but she was still very frightened — she was terrified of being judged. Elisabeth would assure her that someday she would be able to reconcile everything and that she should stop feeling guilty, because "the personal is political," to use a New Left motto. She was a small part of that huge revolution of angry women struggling to be independent. She should hold on to her nerves.

Then there was her father. Henry Fonda still loomed large in her life and in her dreams. She'd call him in the dead of night from pay phones on the highway in a never-ending quest for his approval.

She was proud of her work with the GIs, but she couldn't tell him that — she hoped he'd notice her effort on his own and say, in effect, "Bravo, Lady Jane!" He didn't.

In fact, he appeared to be in a bad mood whenever her name was brought up. Once at a party actor John Forsythe congratulated him for having a daughter with the courage to speak out against Nixon. Fonda huffed, "She's keeping me from getting work!"

"How so?" Forsythe asked, and Fonda answered, "Because people think I agree with her!" On top of that he was worried sick that she was being exploited, and he had reason to be. Jane's press agent, Steve Jaffe, had recently gotten a call at 6:00 A.M. from some Black Panthers stranded in Louisiana. "They said, 'Tell Jane to send another Visa card.' I said, 'Another card?' And the Panther said, 'Yeah, we lost the card Jane gave us after we charged a car to it — and then we lost the car!'" It was true: Jane had given them her Visa card and they'd rented a car, then lost both the card and the car.

Henry Fonda had read quotes from speeches she had made, talking of revolution and wanting to change America. He often thought she sounded like a fanatic. In a speech she made on November 22, 1969, during a fundraising tour for Vietnam Veterans Against the War and the Black Panther Party, she made inane comments such as "The Vietcong are driven by the same spirit that drove Washington and Jefferson," and "Black Panther leader Huey Newton is the only man I've ever met that I would trust as leader of this country." At such times Jane wasn't thinking.

Press agent Bobby Zarem thought Steve Jaffe was partly to blame. He didn't prepare her; he let her speak to anyone and everyone in the media.

Years later, Jane wrote in her memoir, "In those first years back home there was hardly a mistake I *didn't* make when it came to public utterances. . . . Instead of reflection, what I did was talk . . . on and on and on in a frantic voice tinged with Ivy League. . . . There I was, up on my soapbox, pronouncing myself a revolutionary woman, while *Barbarella* had just played in a theater around the corner."

But Nicholas von Hoffman, columnist for the *Washington Post* who traveled with Jane to the University of Maryland that spring, thought when she spoke about the opposition to the war *within* the military, she sounded "like a pilgrim — like a Candide. She said a lot of things people wanted to say but were afraid to say; she said a lot of things people didn't know yet about the government."

23

B Y MID-1970 JANE was nearly broke, having spent thousands of dollars of her own money financing her trips and her many causes, especially the Black Panthers. Money was the main reason she decided to do the movie *Klute* and play the part of Bree Daniels, a tough-talking call girl.

Jane liked Alan J. Pakula, a gentle, tall man of forty-two who was going to direct. Pakula had directed only one other film, *The Sterile Cuckoo* with Liza Minnelli, but he'd produced movies like *To Kill a Mockingbird.* Jane appreciated his taste and sensibility. He'd described *Klute* as a psychological thriller set in the world of pimps and brothels. Jane thought it had political connotations because it dramatized how men can exploit women in this society; Jane related to that, remembering her years as a sex object. *Klute* explores in part the mutual dependency of Bree Daniels and a small-town detective, John Klute (played by Donald Sutherland). He is hired to protect her from a sadistic killer; by the middle of the movie they are caught up in an edgy romance.

As soon as she arrived in New York in June, Jane moved into her old room in the Fonda brownstone and threw herself into researching the role of Bree. She started off by creating Bree's look with the help and guidance of costume designer Ann Roth. Roth brought her down to St. Mark's Place to Paul McGregor, who shaped her hair into a shag cut that became her trademark and part of the *Klute* fashion aesthetic. Along with a big fringy bag and a brass buckled belt, Roth also chose a vivid array of taut over-the-knee leather boots, miniskirts, and stretchy sweaters. Jane went braless, another detail that would define Bree and create a particular kind of early seventies cool.

(After the movie was released, thousands of young women — nurses, teachers, secretaries — were taking off their girdles and bullet bras and copying Bree Daniels's slouchily sexy look.) Clothes could make a feminist statement too.

Midway into her costume research, Jane scheduled a speech for a Panther rally in Philadelphia and asked Roth to design an outfit for her. "What do you have in mind?" Roth asked. "Oh, something sheer," Jane answered dreamily. Roth marveled at her quick-change artistry. However, she thinks that sometimes "there are too many Janes."

Once she'd decided on Bree's look, Jane began exploring her worlds. "I was searching for a way to play a call girl differently," Jane said. "I knew she should be tough and angry, but not totally hard." So for the next week she spent time with the madam of a high-class whorehouse and listened to her describe her clients — senators, lawyers, corporate executives. "The more important they are, the kinkier they are."

Sometimes clients could turn dangerous. Pakula arranged for Jane to go to the New York City morgue where police showed her photos of women: call girls who'd been beaten by boyfriends, husbands, johns. Violence against women was something else to think about.

She visited the sleazy walkup of a prostitute who was a cokehead; she got friendly with a couple of streetwalkers; she even accompanied a high-class call girl on a "date" and got upset when she wasn't propositioned by the john she was introduced to. She complained to Pakula, "Even the pimps know I'm not call girl material. Maybe Faye Dunaway should play Bree." He said she was being ridiculous.

Jane would later say that Bree was a composite of the call girls she'd slept with in Paris when Vadim was orchestrating their ménage à trois arrangements. Afterward in the mornings Vadim would disappear and she would make coffee for these girls. They'd sit in the kitchen and talk about their lives. Some of them worked at Madame Claude's, an elegant brothel on the Left Bank.

Those girls had to be whatever their clients wanted them to be, so Madame Claude taught them manners and how to dress, and she'd make some of them get nose jobs or boob lifts. A few of the girls turned out to be dream creatures — soignée and trilingual, they would go with a john to the Élysée presidential palace; a few of them ended up marrying rich, powerful men. In some of them Jane saw "glimmers of talent and hope."

"Most of them refused to be controlled by men," Jane said. "Their main defense was their expertise as sexual actresses — somehow they could figure out the fantasies of the johns and encourage them to act out their fantasies."

Pakula had hired a twenty-three-year-old call girl as a technical adviser. She was on the set every day. "She'd tell us things like how call girls brush their teeth constantly and how they enjoy eating bagels," said Roy Scheider, who played Bree's pimp.

The night before they shot the scene in a hotel room with Bree and a john, Pakula had the call girl coach Jane. "The first thing you do is get your money," she said, "because you get more before. You're not going to get as much afterward. The second thing you do is make the man think he is different."

This discussion resulted in one of the most memorable sequences in the movie, where Jane poses seductively on the couch, looking expectant. They embrace, she chews on his collar, he whispers something in her ear; she laughs throatily, "Oh, that's exciting, but it's going to cost you more." Then comes the famous line "Oh, my angel," as she fakes an orgasm and then glances at her watch. This provided a humorous moment.

But *Klute* was not a happy set. B.J. Bjorkman, the script supervisor, said, "Jane's politics put everybody off." Roy Scheider remembered "Black Panthers hanging around. Jane was raising money for them, but she was also sounding off against the war." One morning the crew hung an American flag over the set in response to her negative remarks about the Nixon administration.

Jane saw the flag and ran into her dressing room. She felt like crying. But she didn't want anyone to know that the crew's reaction to her politics had gotten to her, so she managed to control herself as she was being made up — and since Bree's attitude was "fuck it," that's the attitude she had when she walked out on the set.

At first Pakula worried that Jane had become so politicized her mind would not be on the film. "But I soon discovered she has this extraordinary capacity for concentration. She'd be in conversation with Donald Sutherland or she'd be on the phone hustling people for money for one cause or another and I'd wonder if she knew her lines or devoted any thought to the next scene. I'd say, 'We're ready, Jane,' and she'd say,

'Just give me three minutes.' Then she'd stop what she was doing, stand still, and concentrate. When she'd walk into the scene she was totally involved in the film and nothing else existed for her. When the scene was right, she'd go back to Sutherland or the phone calls."

Roy Scheider recalled, "Jane would sometimes get bugged at the way Alan worked. He liked to improvise — try scenes all sorts of ways and talk about the reason endlessly. We'd often sit for a couple of hours going over and over a scene. Alan had a hard time making up his mind. Once I remember Jane snapped, 'Alan, for Christ's sake, let's do the scene as written, okay?'"

Everybody got caught up in discussions of how a scene could be played and even what objects should be emphasized, like the ever-ringing telephones and the whirring tape recorder that keeps playing Jane's seductive voice over and over. "Alan was paranoid about what was going on in the country with the wiretapping, the FBI surveillance stuff," said composer Michael Small, who wrote the background music for *Klute*. "We even discussed how my score could reflect the paranoia." His eerie quavering music helps to set up a suspenseful, mysterious tone.

But the dark, foreboding cinematography of Gordon Willis is what makes *Klute* so distinctive. "Nobody uses darkness like Gordo," a crew member said. In a documentary on the DVD of *Klute*, Pakula confides that Willis would instinctively realize what he was trying to accomplish with a shot and proceed to achieve the visual effect without any words from Pakula.

It's especially true in one of the most visually striking scenes in the movie — the scene where Bree visits her richest client, an old dress manufacturer who pays her handsomely to tell him a story and then take off her clothes. The sequence takes place in his loft. You see Bree gliding down a shadowy aisle lit by fluorescent lights. She is in a glittery backless gown and feather boa, and she looks magnificent as she undulates over to the old man, finally delivering herself to him in a stunning close-up, "surely the most indelible close-up of Fonda's career," Willis said.

He went on to say that he kept her in the dark as she told her story and then slowly stripped down for her client. Only the old guy sees her beautiful body, although we get a glimpse of her bare back as she slowly pulls the zipper on the dress. "The camera moved further and further away and it got more sensual," Willis said. "It's one of the better scenes I've ever had the pleasure of shooting."

"It also answered some of Jane's concerns," Willis went on. As he was laying out the shot, Jane came to him for a brief discussion of how much would be seen as she stripped. "Now it's funny to me, but she said in so many words, 'Gordo, if we see too much I'll never be able to appear on another army base.' Politics. I didn't agree with Jane's politics or what she was doing but it didn't get in the way of the work. She's a strong, opinionated woman when she's thinking and it shows on her face. She is a powerful presence on the screen. *Klute* ran on her energy."

This is true, but Jane does give Pakula credit for helping her trust her instincts. Throughout the movie Jane used herself. "It was like a melding of souls between the character [of Bree] and me."

She had decided from the start that Bree Daniels was a great actress, as successful call girls often are, and Pakula had agreed with her. This is the psychological study of a woman who can always be counted on to put on a great show; whether she's figuring out her clients' sexual hang-ups or auditioning for a play, she is giving a superb performance, and with Klute she plays various roles: as flirt, ball breaker, or scared little girl.

The improvised sessions with her analyst are especially riveting. In an earlier version of the script the psychiatrist had been a man, but Jane thought Bree would open up better with a woman, so the part was recast with Vivian Nathan, an Actors Studio member and a truly brilliant, sensitive performer. Jane asked that their scenes be filmed last, when she had fully internalized Bree.

She and Nathan and Pakula discussed the subjects they might cover — control issues, trust, and intimacy.

"Jane found sources in herself that she had never known existed," Nathan said. "I posed the questions and Jane talked and talked." It was a moment where life and art intersected. Jane's self-awareness about her sexuality merged with the character.

She would talk about how she was afraid of intimacy and how, when she was in bed with Klute, she'd fight having a real orgasm because she didn't want to lose control.

She said, "I just wish I could let things happen and enjoy it for what it is . . . while it lasts . . . relax about it, but all the time I keep feeling the need to destroy it, to break it off and go back to the comfort of being numb again. I kept hoping it's going to end because I had more control when I was with tricks . . . at least I knew what I was doing when I set things up. . . . [Then she starts talking about the good sex she's had with Klute.] It's so strange . . . the sensation that is flowing from me naturally to somebody else without being prettied up. I mean he's seen me horrible, he's seen me mean, he's seen me more whorey and it doesn't matter; he seems to accept me, and I guess having sex with somebody and feeling those sorts of feelings is very new to me."

Decades afterward Jane confided she really hadn't anticipated the levels in the performance that flowed out of her — it went beyond all the preparation and research. "It was so *deep,* even my voice changed; it wasn't high and girlish, it had lowered — it came from my gut."

She gave Donald Sutherland (her lover of that moment) much of the credit "because our affair was so passionate and I guess I incorporated the feelings I had for Donald, all the intense feelings I was experiencing with Donald. . . ."

As for Sutherland, he told *Playboy,* "It was a time when we were both experimenting — emotionally, politically, personally — it was like being in one big bowl of soup together, it was terrific. You couldn't ask for a more generous, exciting, funny, sensuous woman than Jane. I loved her with all my heart. Jane provided me with the basis of what I guess will be with me for the rest of my life — Jane helped me come out of an intellectual and emotional closet."

On breaks Jane would tell Nathan she was sure her politics were nurturing her acting. Politics had made her more aware, more open.

"Don't you think I'm different than when I was at the Actors Studio?" she would ask. "A year ago I couldn't make phone calls to raise money for the Panthers and then play a scene, for God's sake. I hated making phone calls — I'd break out into a sweat when I had to make a call. Vadim did all the phoning for me — but now — last weekend Vadim was here visiting Vanessa and he watched me making calls — I must have made forty — and he told me he could not believe it — I had changed that much." And then she added, "Don't you see it in my face?"

What Nathan saw was the face of Henry Fonda. "It gave me a start," she said. "Jane and I were sitting opposite each other in every scene, and I kept seeing that implacable Henry Fonda expression reflected back at me." Nathan said she couldn't help remembering one of Henry Fonda's greatest performances, in *Fort Apache* playing the tight-ass colonel. "So little humanity. I'm not saying Jane was her father in drag, but there are elements of his sternness and incomprehension in Jane's portrayal of Bree. Not just in that performance, but in her as a woman."

Director Pakula was so impressed with Jane's hard-edged sensitivity as Bree that in the rushes he expanded her role. The character of the detective Klute remains an enigma to the end — maybe that's essential to the film's meaning because Bree's question — "What's your hang-up, Klute?" — is never answered. If Donald Sutherland was upset about Jane getting so much attention he didn't show it, and he gives a beautiful, self-effacing performance. "He was madly in love with Jane," Nathan said.

Jane's affair with the sad-eyed, gentle Sutherland was intense. However, they weren't living together. Sutherland had a room at the Chelsea Hotel and Jane would visit him there.

By now Vanessa had arrived with her nanny, Dot, from L.A., and after filming, Jane would go home and concentrate on her. She celebrated Vanessa's third birthday with a party attended by Black Panthers; Ann Roth brought the cookies and cake.

Jane had been living in the Fonda brownstone to save money. Halfway through filming in August, the FBI paid a visit. Agents dropped by to question her and to question Henry Fonda as to the whereabouts of "America's number one fugitive," Angela Davis, who had recently disappeared. Earlier that month, Davis had been implicated in the shootout in a Marin County courthouse in which a judge was shot dead, a lawyer wounded, and George Jackson's younger brother Jonathan killed. Davis had purportedly not only masterminded the shootout, she had paid for Jackson's gun. (Eventually, she would be tried for her alleged involvement in the shootings and found not guilty.)

Jane had no information to give the FBI, nor did her father (or Vadim, who'd been questioned in L.A.). Both men had met Davis with Jane months before and at the time Henry Fonda had worried about his daughter's very public involvement with black revolutionaries. He had already received a death threat letter aimed at Jane with a demand of $50,000. He brought it to the FBI office that was directing the campaign against her. Early that year J. Edgar Hoover had pronounced the Black Panther Party the single greatest threat to internal security of the United States. His Counter Intelligence Program had begun to investigate dissidents like Jane who were Panther supporters, "disrupting and neutralizing their lives."

In June of 1970 Hoover sent a memo to the Subversive Activities chief in L.A. authorizing him to mail a phony letter to gossip columnist Army Archerd of *Daily Variety*. In this letter he wanted to maintain that at a fundraising affair Jane and a Panther had led a refrain of "We will kill Richard Nixon and any other mother fucker who stands in our way. . . ." Archerd said he never received the letter.

"This is just one of the few documented instances of a clear-cut frame-up of a private citizen by a high government official," the muckraking reporter Jack Anderson said years later in an interview. "Nixon was desperate to destroy all his critics—remember the enemies list? He and Hoover considered Jane very dangerous, not just because she'd allied herself so firmly to the Panthers but because as a public figure she was so idealistic and plainspoken. She was like Dr. Spock, who was also being intensely surveilled—he was a trusted, beloved authority figure . . . people like Jane and Spock were much scarier to Nixon than terrorists."

After the FBI agents left the brownstone, Jane and her father stepped out onto the den terrace to get some air. "It was very emotional," Fonda told his biographer, Howard Teichmann. "I didn't want to believe that Jane had been duped by those characters [the Panthers]." But he did believe she was being used. He said, "Jane, if I ever discover you're a Communist or a Communist sympathizer, I, your father, will turn you in." Tears trickled down Jane's cheeks. "No, Dad, no."

Fonda added that under the circumstances it would be uncomfortable for both of them to live in the brownstone; he was sorry but she would have to leave. In the next days Mark Lane helped her carry her clothes to the penthouse she rented a few blocks away in the East 60s.

"She was very upset about moving. Her father always got to her," Lane said. He knew Henry Fonda disliked him, but he ignored that and continued to stick to Jane like glue—advising her, cajoling her, boosting her spirits when they needed to be boosted. He also arranged for her to come to Kennedy Airport on August 22 when he introduced her to his client Huey Newton, the handsome, charismatic cofounder of the Black Panther Party, now free on $50,000 bail from the Alameda County jail after a reversal of his conviction for the killing of a policeman in Oakland. Newton was a star, as beautiful as Harry Belafonte, plus he'd just put his life on the line to show fellow black Americans they didn't have to take abuse from white cops.

The following day Lane orchestrated a press conference for Newton in Jane's apartment. The event was reminiscent of Leonard Bernstein's gathering for his fashionable friends to benefit the Panthers' Legal Defense Fund. The press, mainly Tom Wolfe and Charlotte Curtis of the *New York Times,* had ridiculed the Bernstein party as "radical chic," and they compared it to the goings-on in Jane's elegant home jammed with white supporters shouting "Right on" and "Power to the people" next to gorgeous black women in huge Afros. Newton made a grand entrance from the bedroom and then swept into the room and sat down — he seemed to pounce. He then held forth in his soft, seductive voice about the injustices being perpetrated at the Panther trial in New Haven.

Jane hovered in the background, serving drinks to the noisy crowd of reporters and TV cameramen. She didn't say a word. The following morning, stories about her involvement with the Panthers appeared in various newspapers, and in one there was mention of Jane's address and phone number, so for days she was bothered by threatening phone calls until she got her number changed, and she received dozens of ugly letters. Even so, her penthouse continued to be filled with Panthers in their trademark leather pants and storm-trooper boots. "Jane lent us her place for meetings because we were being harassed by the FBI," said David Hilliard, acting head of the Panthers. "She was very generous."

There were Black Panthers hanging around the set of *Klute* as well. That summer not only did Jane pay a $2,000 phone bill for the Panthers, she posted bail for Zayd Malik Shakur, Panther minister of education, who'd been arraigned in Manhattan criminal court for possessing dangerous weapons. (Shakur's brother and sister were defendants in the Panther 21 bombing conspiracy trial.) She would continue posting bond for a number of Panthers until one skipped town and she was out $50,000.

Usually she stayed home in the evenings with her daughter until the little girl fell asleep, and then Jane would get restless and start phoning people. Once she phoned Fred Gardner, and he dropped by the penthouse and spent all night in the mirrored bedroom talking politics and asking her why she kept giving him credit for her political awakening—why couldn't she take responsibility for what she was doing and saying? She didn't answer, and then dawn broke and a masseuse appeared and Jane declared, "I'd give up everything for the revolution except my massage." Gardner thought she was kidding but she wasn't, and then she gave him her guitar "because I never have time to practice." Gardner loved to play the guitar.

Another time Vadim came to visit, and he and Jane roamed the city in search of some good strong pot. They ended up at the Regency Hotel where Peter was crashing with supermodel Veruschka. Julie Christie and Warren Beatty joined them and they all got stoned.

Around 4:00 A.M. everyone left except Jane, who'd fallen asleep exhausted on a couch. Peter and Veruschka left the living room and returned to the bedroom where they began making love.

During a lull, Peter opened his eyes and realized his sister was leaning against the doorjamb watching them. He and Veruschka lay there quietly for a while and then went back to making love. Jane returned to the couch in the living room and fell asleep again. Today she has no memory of that night but Peter said, "I'll never forget it."

The filming of *Klute* ended one hot afternoon in early September. Gordon Willis remembered shooting a scene with Jane on Tenth Avenue, and then he watched her get into a cab and disappear, and he didn't see her again until he started work on *Comes a Horseman* some years later. B.J. Bjorkman said, "No one except Alan gave the movie another thought. We didn't think it was that special. For most of us it was just another job." And for Jane, too; she was eager to get back to her activism.

As soon as the shoot was over she dropped by the Vietnam Veterans Against the War office, which was based in the Peace Pentagon on Lafayette Street. (VVAW was made up of thousands of Vietnam veterans who planned antiwar actions and rallies.)

Tod Ensign, one of its founders, remembered, "Around seven o'clock one humid night Jane Fonda suddenly appears in our office. She's with Donald Sutherland who I remembered from *M*A*S*H* and that lawyer Mark Lane. She offers to fundraise for us."

VVAW was just beginning to publicize war crimes — "like what had happened with Calley." (In 1968, five hundred Vietnamese had been slaughtered in a tiny town called My Lai; the massacre had been led by Lt. William Calley, who was egged on by an angry army brigade. Details of the massacre had been exposed by Seymour Hersh the following year, sparking media frenzy and bitter protests.)

Ensign went on, "We'd been getting information about other atrocities, and we'd been organizing citizen committees in Portland, Boston, Cincinnati. We started talking to Jane about it. After that first night she'd come in periodically to stuff envelopes and answer phones, that kind of thing. By that time we were into plans for a national investigation where vets would tie the atrocities to actual U.S. military policy. We'd already decided to call the hearing the Winter Soldier Investigation; the name comes from Tom Paine's characterization of soldiers during the Revolutionary War. According to Paine, a sunshine patriot is one who fights only when the weather is good whereas a winter soldier is dedicated to the cause because he is fighting — in this case the Americans were fighting to preserve democracy. Anyhow, we asked Jane to help organize and raise funds and she agreed immediately."

During 1970 the FBI increased its surveillance on Jane. (The bureau spent a million dollars investigating and collecting information on members of the antiwar movement.) The FBI tracked her on Labor Day at a huge rally in Pennsylvania when she and Sutherland and Mark Lane joined a band of ragtag veterans marching between two American revolutionary sites — Morristown, New Jersey, and Valley Forge — and along that route the vets staged "raids," engaged in mock guerrilla warfare, and reenacted some of the techniques used by the U.S. troops against the Vietnamese.

On the banks of the Delaware River, a crowd of about one thousand listened to a variety of antiwar speakers, including Al Hubbard, who denounced racism, and Mark Lane, who spoke of GI revenge. Donald Sutherland read from Dalton Trumbo's antiwar novel *Johnny Got His Gun,* and Jane stood on a pickup truck to denounce the Nixon administration as "a beehive of cold-blooded killers."

One journalist was so impressed with her rhetoric she dubbed Jane "the next Susan B. Anthony." And the description fit. She continued to incite crowds as soon as she went back on the road to raise money for the Winter Soldier Investigation.

The antiwar organizers were exploiting her celebrity with a vengeance and arranging for a grueling six-week tour. That fall she spoke at fifty-four colleges and universities as well as scores of churches and public meeting halls "where there might be up to a couple of thousand people." A few times marquees advertised COME HEAR BARBARELLA SPEAK! "I began to feel like a sideshow and wondered if what I had to say about the war was getting through all the hoopla," Jane wrote. She made $2,000 a lecture. She didn't know until years later that the VVAW bodyguard who sometimes accompanied her when crowds got too rough was actually an L.A. police department plant who fed information to the FBI.

The *Village Voice* reported that the only luggage she carried, as a political activist, was a Vuitton overnight bag filled with credit cards and vitamins.

After a speech Jane would invite vets in the audience to give her their names and numbers if they wanted to be part of the Winter Soldier Investigation. "I'd get on a pay phone to follow up with a VVAW office in Detroit." She said her schedule was so rough — sometimes several appearances in different cities on the same day — she rarely had time to take a bath. "I was moving too fast. I was actively bulimic. I was depressed. I hadn't seen Vanessa and I felt anguish about that. I wasn't reading anymore. I was barely *thinking*. But I kept going. It never occurred to me not to. I was living in crisis mode. U.S. soldiers were willing to testify about the war — at potential personal risk — and I felt a responsibility to do everything I could to make that possible."

By the end of November she was exhausted. It was after midnight when she arrived at Cleveland International Airport from Vancouver, Canada. Clad in blue jeans, T-shirt, and her sweeping *Klute* leather coat, she planned to sleep in a motel and then go to Toledo the following morning for yet another speech.

She did not know that the FBI had arranged to have her stopped at customs. Without an explanation, officials confiscated her notes, personal papers, and bulging leather phone book that contained the numbers of almost every major left-wing activist in the country.

Then inspectors nosed through her Vuitton overnight bag and discovered her cache of Dexedrine and Valium, as well as 105 vials of vitamins marked "B," "L," and "D." With that Jane was charged with "drug smuggling," taken into a room, and held for three hours.

She was not allowed to call her lawyer, and whenever she tried to get up an FBI agent would push her back into her chair and tell her to shut up. "You're in my control. . . . I'm taking orders from Washington!" Finally Jane phoned Mark Lane in Boston; then she kicked a police officer because he refused to let her go to the ladies' room.

Ultimately she was handcuffed and arrested and spent the next ten hours in a cell with several other women, one of whom had been charged with murdering a man and dismembering his body.

The next day she was brought from jail past a phalanx of TV cameras and reporters. Jane wrote in her autobiography, "As my hands are slender and double-jointed, I easily slipped out of one handcuff and threw a 'power to the people' fist in the air, much to the chagrin of the guards."

(By then newspapers all over the country were headlining JANE FONDA CAUGHT SMUGGLING DRUGS — JANE FONDA ARRESTED FOR ASSAULTING A POLICE OFFICER.)

As soon as she was released on $5,000 bail, she held a press conference and cried out in a fury that she was not a smuggler. "I am a health food freak! I was never hassled until I started speaking out against the war — this was a political arrest!"

Ultimately the drug charges were dropped, but the image of Jane as a drug smuggler stayed in the public mind.

After Cleveland, Jane flew directly to New Orleans to lead a demonstration for a group of Panthers holed up in an apartment in a housing development; the police had surrounded the project, saying the Panthers were "illegally occupying the apartment. They didn't constitute a family." Jane felt this remark was racist and unfair.

So when the group needed to make a getaway to Washington, D.C., to attend a Panther conference, Jane rented four cars for them. Moments after they fled the project they were stopped by a police roadblock and arrested. The police chief of New Orleans told a press conference, "Thanks to Jane Fonda we knew exactly when the militants were going to make a break." By then Jane had left the city for more speaking engagements somewhere in Colorado so she was unavailable for comment.

The FBI surveillance of her increased. At every airport there were at least two agents in dark glasses "observing and intimidating me," she said. "Stress and fatigue began to get to me, but I was determined not to be cowed."

During this period her life was frequently threatened. Steve Jaffe, who continued to handle her press, recalled that once when she was on her way to Bakersfield, California, to speak he received a tip that someone had called a radio station and predicted Jane Fonda would be shot on leaving the lecture hall. Jaffe arranged for extra security with the Bakersfield police. Special guards apprehended a man backstage who was brandishing a handgun.

Another time Jaffe went through Jane's "hate mail" in L.A., "a big sack filled with maybe six hundred letters." He read one that warned that Jane Fonda would be assassinated on a street corner in Beverly Hills by sniper fire. It was signed by some self-ordained minister in Arcadia, California.

Jaffe contacted Ramsey Clark, a radical lawyer and former attorney general, and the FBI, but he didn't hear from either of them, and Jane continued to travel mostly by commercial plane or car, usually with Elisabeth Vailland.

Was she ever frightened? She maintained she didn't have time to think about the dangers. She had become so politicized, so passionate about so many worthwhile things she was involved with, that she lived totally in the moment. But "this was a lonely time for me personally," Jane wrote in her autobiography.

By now she had cut herself off from most of her Hollywood friends and from Actors Studio intimates like Collin Wilcox. She'd dumped most of the people who cared for her but that was her way. Andreas commented, "I kept up with Jane's friends and I used to tell them the reason she dropped them was because they reminded her of another Jane Fonda — Jane Fonda the movie star — and she didn't want to think about those Jane Fondas since she was morphing into somebody else."

By mid-January 1971 Jane had moved to Detroit and was sharing a house with Mark Lane along with several Vietnam vets and some members of the VVAW staff. Everyone there was working on the Winter Soldier Investigation, which was to be composed of a hundred veterans who would be giving testimony to an invited audience and the press reporting on the atrocities they'd either witnessed or committed when they were serving in Vietnam. The catalyst had been Seymour Hersh's investigative reportage for the *New York Times* about the My Lai massacre, for which he won a Pulitzer.

"We were out to prove that My Lai was not a one-time occurrence," said Lt. Bill Crandell, a veteran who helped organize the event. "We intended to indict those who were responsible not just for My Lai but for all the other genocide in Vietnam."

Detroit had been chosen as the site of the investigation because so many blue-collar families lived there and had lost fathers and sons in the war. There was also a big Vietnamese community across the Detroit River in Ontario, and the VVAW wanted to start a dialogue with them. And of course a great many draft resisters were living in Ontario, sixty-five thousand of them.

It had been Jane's job to raise money to fund the investigation — some $50,000 that had come mostly from her lecture fees. She was still raising money for the *Winter Soldier* film. (Barbara Koppell was one of the filmmakers — she was only twenty-two and it was her first documentary.*)

Once Jane arrived in Detroit, she began immediately to win endorsements for the investigation from the local auto workers — from the Business Executives for Peace. She helped get housing for the vets from the Methodist Council of Churches. Along the way she struck up a friendship with Ken Cockrel, the handsome young black attorney who was the lawyer for the League of Revolutionary Black Workers.

Jane confided that she was thinking about giving up acting and joining a film commune. Cockrel told her, "There is no one in the movement, no real activist, who's a movie star. Stay with it, we need you. Own your leadership."

Own your leadership. Jane didn't see herself as a leader but as a staunch lieutenant. His comment had a profound effect on her, however, and for the first time she began thinking that maybe her career

---

* *Winter Soldier* became a series of stark, grainy black-and-white 16mm reels of testimonies — rarely seen in thirty-five years. Back in 1971 after it was finished, it was rejected by all three networks; even PBS didn't run it. A 1972 *Variety* article dubbed it "the film no one wants." It was shown only briefly back then — most reviewers found it important but almost unbearable. In 2005, when the story of the torture and prisoner abuse at Abu Ghraib broke, *Winter Soldier* was shown again at various festivals and campus film societies. Koppel said, "When you look at the footage now and hear what those guys were telling us about the atrocities in Vietnam — it's mind-blowing — like Abu Ghraib."

could move beyond her own personal successes or failures, that being successful could make her more powerful. And maybe she could even figure out a way of making movies that had something of value to say.

She filed Cockrel's advice for future reference and went back to work with Steve Jaffe, who had flown in from L.A. to enlist the media.

She was also dealing with a burglary. In Detroit someone broke into the trunk of her car and stole everything relating to the Winter Soldier Investigation, including mailing lists of supporters and contributors as well as literature for the hearings.

The investigation itself was held in a drab Howard Johnson's motel ballroom in downtown Detroit from January 31 to February 1, 1971. The vets shuffled in, many longhaired and in rumpled army fatigues. Their testimonies were shocking, beginning with the following anecdote from one GI: "You have a little lesson and it's called the rabbit lesson, where the staff NCO comes out and he has this rabbit and . . . then in a couple of seconds after just about everyone falls in love with it . . . he cracks it in the neck, skins it, disembowels it . . . and then they throw the guts out into the audience. You can get anything out of that you want, but that's your last lesson you catch in the United States before you leave for Vietnam."

From then on the stories went from boot camp degradation to combat atrocities—it was kill the gooks, kill the gooks for sport. Shove North Vietnamese prisoners out of helicopters alive—cut off their ears for souvenirs—gang-rape the women—set the villages on fire—shoot dogs and cattle for fun.

Anywhere in North Vietnam was a free-fire zone—there were no forbidden targets; if you didn't find a particular target you wanted to hit, you just drop the bombs anywhere.

"All this, the vets repeated, was done in the presence of officers who said nothing, did nothing, to stop it," Jane wrote. "Some of the vets talked about getting hooked on drugs to numb themselves to what they did." Most of the soldiers who spoke weren't more than twenty years old. Haunted—ravaged—numbed—many of them told their stories as tears rolled down their cheeks. They had the courage to confess to war crimes they'd seen and committed—because they felt responsible to themselves and to the country.

The worst story for Jane, and she started crying when she heard it again at a screening for the *Winter Soldier* documentary that was held a month later, was the story a former marine sergeant, Scott Camil, told — how he'd impassively watched a lieutenant rape a badly wounded sniper victim with an entrenching tool while she plaintively begged for water.

Throughout the testimonies Jane remained in the shadows of the ballroom, listening. She'd been told specifically not to speak to the press or anyone else for that matter. She was thought to be too polarizing. She'd watch John Kerry work the room. He was staying as far away from her as possible. She'd raised all the money for *Winter Soldier,* but "Kerry was scared shitless that Jane might say something embarrassing, which was pretty ridiculous considering what was going down in that room," one of the workers said.

Later, Kerry would make sure Jane was not invited to participate in the mass march on Washington that spring that resulted in Kerry's testimony at the Senate Foreign Relations Committee, summarizing the Winter Soldier Investigation. He wanted to get the attention of Congress and he didn't need unnecessary baggage like Jane.

Jane did not know how to deal with this kind of game playing; she spoke her mind — she spoke from her heart. She felt "numb." Her nerves were shot — she couldn't sleep. Picketers were outside her window, brandishing signs saying she was a Communist. Her father wasn't speaking to her because of the newspaper reports that she was a drug smuggler. Then there were her Hollywood friends who were predicting she would never work again.

On the last day of testimony the activist Tom Hayden showed up. Jane's first impression was that he was funny-looking: Wiry. Bulbous nose, acne-scarred cheeks, black eyes. His cold, uningratiating manner reminded her of her father.

A week later Hayden and Jane appeared together at a student rally at the University of Michigan. Hayden remembered Jane as "slender, nervous . . . eyes darting around — her long taut fingers were tugging at the purple shirt that was pushed into her jeans . . . when she spoke to the crowd about the urgency of stopping the war she was very effective."

They had coffee together afterward. Elisabeth Vailland appeared out of nowhere to join them, explaining in faulty English that she was writing about American radicals. Hayden wished he and Jane were alone, although he found her unsettling. "I thought Jane was high strung as any wire and extremely nervous — almost out of her body. I had never encountered anyone like that before."

Jane, for her part, felt in awe and "incredibly intimidated" by Hayden. He had a long record of selfless organizing and was widely regarded as the chief ideologue of the New Left. He'd drafted the Port Huron Statement, he'd helped start Students for a Democratic Society, and as a member of the "Chicago Seven" he'd been sentenced to five years in prison for conspiracy. He was now out on bail. She knew he'd made three unauthorized visits to North Vietnam and had brought back the first American POWs; she'd heard he'd recently changed his position from being antiwar to pro-Hanoi.

During their conversation Jane managed to blurt out that she was thinking of giving up being a movie star and moving into a political collective.

Hayden cautioned against it. He knew from experience how "collectives confuse professionalism with privilege."

He would recall later that "nothing clicked" between them until the following day when they shared a car ride to the Detroit airport. Tom was in the back, Jane in the front; "everybody was talking intensely about war crimes and suddenly I put my Irish cap on Jane's head," Hayden wrote, "and Jane turned around and looked at me and our eyes locked . . . and we started laughing."

They did not see each other again for another year.

24

AFTER DETROIT JANE moved back to L.A. with Vanessa and Dot. She had very little money, so she rented a ramshackle house overlooking the Hollywood Freeway and decorated it with Salvation Army furniture. She continued to wear her "uniform" of jeans and T-shirt and when it was chilly her long *Klute* leather coat. Her brown hair was a bit unkempt, she wore no makeup, and she was very thin. "It's sort of relaxing to be poor," she told friends.

In addition to selling the farm outside Paris, she was selling the furniture she'd lovingly collected over the years — the blond Biedermeier pieces, the Roy Lichtenstein rug — because she needed the cash.

Her lawyer/business manager, Richard Rosenthal, was worried that the money made from the sale of the farm might go directly to one of her causes and insisted that Jane hire someone to live with her, not only to keep track of expenses but to protect her — which is how a tall, rangy woman named Ruby Ellen came to live with Jane and stayed with her until she married Tom Hayden. Not long after Ruby began coordinating her affairs, Jane decided to stop supporting the Panthers.

She knew she'd been too quick about giving them money; Brando had already advised her that it was unwise, and she didn't like the way they exploited her or demeaned her behind her back, calling her "white honky bitch" and spreading rumors that she'd been sleeping with Huey Newton. "Not true," she said. "We were never, ever alone together."

When the Panthers asked her for $10,000 to finance a documentary about their organization, she said no. She was too busy with VVAW and other causes.

Which, of course, she was, as frantic as ever, appearing at rallies and demonstrations, marching with welfare mothers and lettuce workers, attending church benefits for VVAW. She'd speak at colleges, sitting on the floor with students one on one. Friends asked why she didn't ever stop running on such a treadmill. She'd answer, "I have so much to learn — so much to learn."

She did not mention how she felt when it came to mothering. Every morning she'd take Vanessa, then three, to a preschool, and once a week she'd turn into a parent/helper. "But I was still suffering from bulimia, I didn't do a very good job. I was always tired." She felt she "couldn't get it right." She made a mess of a cake she tried to bake for Vanessa and a group of her friends. "The cake slid off the platter and broke into little pieces on the hardwood floor like a brick, which made the kids howl with laughter."

For a while Vanessa took dance classes at UCLA. Often she'd want to do encores in the living room for Jane, but she always refused to dance unless Jane promised to keep her eyes *closed*. Jane would later write, "I loved her and hated the distance that remained between us. I didn't share the physical closeness she had with her father." Vadim had moved back to France. He and Jane both wanted to be involved in caring for Vanessa, so the little girl was shuttled back and forth from Paris to L.A.

Every time Jane said goodbye to her daughter and watched her toddle off by herself onto an airplane, she felt increasingly empty and alone, and even though she and Donald Sutherland were still together they rarely appeared in public and usually kept to themselves. They were both under surveillance by the FBI; they knew that and knew their phones were bugged, so they often talked in code.

One of the few people she did keep in touch with from the old days was Susan Blanchard ("Mom 2"), who'd married the actor Michael Wager and had given birth to a son. "Jane wanted her life to matter; she was so impatient," Susan recalled. "I never questioned what she was doing. She had to follow her own path. I listened in amazement to everything she was struggling to achieve. I just hoped she wouldn't get hurt."

Soon Jane refocused her attention on the political vaudeville show Howard Levy wanted her to do. The year before, he'd suggested she develop a show designed to lampoon the military, the president, and the war, a project along the lines of *Snafu,* a comedic hit produced during the Second World War. It would be called *F.T.A.,* popular GI slang for "Fuck the Army." To the world it would be called *Free the Army.*

Levy envisioned it as an alternative to Bob Hope's more traditional pro-war patriotic shows; he could see *F.T.A.* touring military bases all over the United States, the Pacific. Jane thought the idea was very powerful. Her own political development had been energized by GIs against the war. The Servicemen's Fund would sponsor the production.

By February 1971 she had enlisted the talents of Donald Sutherland, Dick Gregory, Country Joe McDonald, and Peter Boyle (who went on to create some of show business's most memorable eccentrics: the philosophical cabbie in *Taxi Driver,* the monster in *Young Frankenstein,* and the hilariously insensitive dad on *Everybody Loves Raymond*). For a time, Mike Nichols was set to direct *F.T.A.* — but Alan Meyerson, who'd directed the improvisational group the Committee, eventually took over.

Cartoonist Jules Feiffer wrote skits, as did playwrights Barbara Garson and Herb Gardner, but the main source for the show's material was the GIs themselves, their ideas, their hang-ups drawn from stories in the GI newspapers from around the world.

Jane wanted the show not only to raise soldiers' consciousness but to deal with the unfair treatment of women in the military as well.

She told Herb Gardner as much when he handed in some skits. "She was quite bossy about it and she had absolutely no sense of humor. She kept saying, 'We can't have this show all flying tits and ass — we're not doing a chauvinist show here.'" (Later Jane insisted, "None of the men thought I was funny — but the women in the show found me hilarious.")

For months she'd been having intense discussions about men's oppression of women with *F.T.A.* producer Francine Parker, but until she started putting *F.T.A.* together and traveling to army bases to set up the production she hadn't realized how badly women were being treated in the GI movement and in the military.

(She especially liked the Beverly Grant song she and three other women would sing in *F.T.A.* called "Tired of the Fuckers Fucking over Me.")

"Feminism came suddenly to Jane," recalled Parker. "It was an 'aah!' sort of thing." Jane would write later, "My life has been a series of gigantic leaps of faith based almost always on intuition and emotion, not on calculation or ego — or ideology. As British playwright David Hare has said of himself, 'I'm where I want to be before I can be bothered to go through the dreary business of getting there!'"

Jane devoured books and essays like *Sisterhood Is Powerful* and *The Myth of the Vaginal Orgasm*. She reached out to Gloria Steinem, and she watched Bella Abzug in action. Abzug had just gone to Congress, having run on a women's rights/peace platform, and was part of every skirmish and standoff in the struggle for equality.

For a while Jane joined a consciousness-raising group and listened to other women talk about back-alley abortions and being battered by their men and falling in love with other women.

She even spoke once in a session about her long-dead mother and her anger at being abandoned.

But she was mainly focusing on making *F.T.A.* work as "political vaudeville." Incredibly she had dreamed of taking the production to Vietnam, but of course the Pentagon wouldn't allow it — the army found the script "subversive" — and when she and Levy tried to open at Fort Bragg in Fayetteville, home to thirty-five thousand soldiers, that proved impossible, too. The army was never going to allow such a show on any base. *F.T.A.* subsequently opened at the Haymarket Coffee House down the road from Fort Bragg.

The coffeehouse was a beehive of activity — soldiers milling around, some sporting Tom Paine buttons, others applying for CO status; on the bulletin board were flyers demanding war crime inquiries. Rock music pulsed in a corner, and everywhere on the walls there were signs forbidding the use, possession, and dealing of dope.

Journalist Claudia Dreifus was writing about *F.T.A.* for the *Village Voice*. She attended a dress rehearsal on March 10, 1971, and watched Jane sitting in a corner waiting for her cue. "She looked like a waif in the same sweater and dungarees she'd been wearing for days." When a photographer came over to take her picture, she objected vehemently.

But she did allow Peter Basch, an old friend from Actors Studio days, to take pictures of the performance. Basch was struck by her obsession with feminism and anti-elitism. She kept saying, "There are no stars here — only equals." She didn't want to speak to the press by herself. "We're a collective — everyone keeps referring to Fonda and company but it's not Fonda and company!"

"She was trying so hard to be ordinary," Dreifus noted, "and yet she was using her considerable star power to put on a show that was challenging the army's very existence. That to me seemed her most fundamental contradiction."

Once on a break Jane ran out with the rest of the cast past a strip of rip-off souvenir stores and topless live entertainment shows to a Baskin-Robbins, where she gorged on huge scoops of ice cream — chocolate, coffee, strawberry. Then she disappeared. "Oh, yeah, I vomited up all that ice cream," she admitted decades later. "I was binging and purging like mad during the *F.T.A.* and I was still on Dexedrine — one reason I was so irritable and talked so fast. . . ."

Levy remembered her "obsessive-compulsive behavior in meetings." He never doubted her sincerity, but she often had little patience to negotiate or hear out opposing views.

Others felt she was surrounding herself with mediocrities — lost souls, wannabe actresses. "So many men and women so much less talented than she was would glom onto her because of her fame and her gullibility and her insecurity. She didn't seem to trust her peers," Herb Gardner said. "She gravitated to 'yes' people. She was not the best judge of who she should get close to."

But none of this seemed to matter once the show got off the ground. *F.T.A.* played to standing room only for its first three shows. The police used infrared cameras to take pictures of all the soldiers crowding into the coffeehouse. Then there was a bomb threat. "The army really didn't want the show to go on," Peter Boyle said. To the GIs' delight the cast ignored the bomb threat.

The curtain went up on an earsplitting ten-piece rock band, Swamp Dog, playing "God Bless America — for What?" followed by Barbara Dane belting out the song "Insubordination," which brought the house down. Then Dick Gregory bounded onto the stage to tell the GIs they had to vote as a bloc to raise the draft age to seventy-five "so old farts like John Wayne would be called to Vietnam."

There was huge applause for Donald Sutherland's stentorian reading of Daniel Berrigan's *Catonsville Nine,* a play the Jesuit priest wrote about war resisters pouring homemade napalm onto draft cards, for which they were arrested and then put on trial. The show ended with Jane doing a hilarious imitation of Pat Nixon.

Outside the coffeehouse 150 jeeps and trucks ringed the barracks — security was very tight inside during intermission; dozens of FBI agents were busy taking notes.

F.T.A. was a huge success. From the *L.A. Times:* "Jane Fonda's Anti-War show scores a hit playing outside an Army base — the soldiers roared time and time again in their decision to see the end of war."

Throughout April and much of May, *F.T.A.* played in fifteen cities around the United States, performing outside Fort Ord, Fort Lewis, Fort Sam Houston, and the San Diego Naval Station. The show packed soldiers into high school auditoriums and on makeshift stages. It won an Obie award when it played off-Broadway.

Fred Gardner had come back at Jane's insistence to act as advance man because he knew the GI world so well. "The show started out with good intentions and enthusiasm," he recalled. But by mid-April there were reports of trouble and tension in the cast and a number of actors left, including Peter Boyle, who says he was "scared shitless of the FBI." Folk singer Country Joe McDonald had a bitter parting; he later called a press conference to denounce Jane as a political novice. "I don't want to be any part of her ego trip," he said angrily.

But Gardner added that most people *did* want to be involved with Jane. He said, "Everybody wanted something from her — money, a favor, an endorsement, an introduction. At the same time she was attacked for being an elitist, and on top of that people were trying to make her feel guilty for being famous. No matter how hard she tried, the fact remained Jane was a very big movie star and she couldn't erase that image."

Jane was now busy with Donald Sutherland trying to rally all their movie star friends to join them in their newly formed organization Entertainment Industry for Peace & Justice. They hoped to enlist as many big names as possible to help end the war and bring the troops home. Jane hoped this new organization could also fund *F.T.A.*

She and Sutherland used Steve Jaffe's office as a base and went to Hannah Weinstein for advice. Weinstein was a savvy left-wing producer who'd helped organize a similar group during the Second World War. Jane hoped Weinstein would teach her the ropes about activating Hollywood.

In April 1971, Richard Basehart, Barbra Streisand, Sally Field, and Tuesday Weld came along with many other well-known actors, directors, and screenwriters to the first meeting of EIPJ, held in a hotel on the Sunset Strip. "The problem was that neither Donald nor I had ever started an organization before and weren't equipped to give leadership to this uniquely rambunctious group. . . . We got caught up in more divisive and diversionary issues — like whether or not film studios should be nationalized." By June, Jane had teed everybody off in a speech she gave at another meeting at the Musicians Hall in Los Angeles when she declared that what we really needed in Vietnam was a "victory for the Vietcong."

Soon EIPJ became a hornets' nest of political infighting just like *F.T.A.* By June the Servicemen's Fund withdrew its support of *F.T.A.*, so Jane and Sutherland took over and made plans to take it on a tour of the Pacific with monies raised by EIPJ.

Meanwhile Jane never slowed down; "there were all these storms swirling around her, people yelling and arguing, and she never let anybody see what she was going through," recalled a young volunteer from EIPJ. "She'd bring Vanessa to meetings we had in the basement of this Mexican restaurant. I got the feeling the kid didn't enjoy the meetings very much. One day Jane directed a group of us to dress up as dead Vietcong — in whiteface and black leotards. 'You're gonna demonstrate on Bob Hope's front lawn,' she says. 'Little demonstrations are as important as big ones.' Anyhow, the next afternoon she drove us over to Hope's estate in her beat-up Volvo and we lay down on this huge lawn for like twenty seconds because police and guard dogs chased us off the premises almost immediately. Alarms sounded — the whole bit. Jane was parked down the road behind some trees. We jumped in and hightailed it back to West Hollywood. There was never any more talk about 'little demonstrations.'

"But it didn't matter to us kids. We revered Jane Fonda. She was like a modern-day Joan of Arc to us," the young volunteer went on, "and so articulate about what was going on in Vietnam. We heard she'd just raised funds to start a counseling service for vets with post-traumatic stress disorder. We'd never heard about that or about what Agent Orange did — Jane informed us."

Another volunteer, Miska Sorell, remembered how generous Jane was. "She'd lend us her car whenever we needed it. We were all desperately poor; in fact, she lent us her car so much the gearshift got shot; the car sort of bumped along like it was giving up the ghost. . . ."

Eventually, Miska said, she accompanied Jane to a Volvo dealer. "The dealer shook his head when he looked inside the car. It was like a cyclone had hit it — old beer cans, cigarette butts, newspapers on the floor — it smelled. . . . 'Jesus,' he said, 'what the hell happened here?' Jane shrugged. 'I keep lending it to friends.'" The guy repaired the gearshift and swept out the garbage, and Jane paid the bill and went on lending her car to anyone who asked, right up to July when she and Sutherland moved to Berkeley with Peter Boyle to star in the film *Steelyard Blues*. The movie was described in a publicity release as being "a whacky anti-establishment comedy about a band of social misfits who outwit the law in the tradition of *Bonnie and Clyde*."

Sutherland played a demolition derby driver who steals to supply his habit of smashing up cars; Jane was a happy hooker in an Afro wig, Peter Boyle "a jolly schizophrenic." Alan Meyerson was the director. Julia Phillips produced. "Everybody hoped it would turn out to be an eccentric caper comedy. It turned out to be a bomb," Peter Boyle said.

By the time they'd traveled to Santa Rosa, California, for location shooting, Jane was into a more radical feminist phase of her life, so between filming she'd organize "struggle sessions," as she called them, on and off the set. "We guys were under siege," Boyle said. "We were surrounded by feminist revolutionaries who found fault with everything we were supposedly doing to them. Some of the men were reduced to tears in those meetings. Plus the FBI was hanging around. I hated it."

In the midst of this Jane broke up with Sutherland, saying she was moving into such a different phase of her life she could not share it with one man. "The end of this relationship broke Donald's heart," Herb Gardner said. "He was very much in love with Jane but they continued to work together, they stayed friends."

Jane described their new relationship to one of the cast as "serene. He doesn't feel he possesses me and I don't feel as if I possess him. We don't feel the need to be physically faithful because we know that to sleep with another person doesn't diminish how we feel towards one another."

There were soon rumors that Jane was having liaisons with various activists. Said Paul Krassner, editor of the *Realist*, "Everybody in the movement was hot for her."

Steve Jaffe recalled, "Jane liked to have things in order. This involved her personal needs; when she met someone she dug she scheduled it in."

As for Jane, she supposedly confided during a consciousness-raising session, "My biggest regret is I never got to fuck Che Guevara."

Steelyard Blues filmed around San Francisco and Berkeley for much of the summer. Jane brought Vanessa along and Vadim flew in from L.A. to visit. When they were shooting in Geyserville, where there were natural sulfur baths, he played with their little daughter in the pool. A little boy splashing around near her grabbed a toy of hers and she whacked him very hard. There was much crying and screaming and Vadim was heard to murmur, "Why, Vanessa, didn't your mother teach you there is no such thing as personal property?"

When she wasn't filming, Jane hung out with the "Red Family," a radical collective, which had several houses on Bateson Street near the University of California in Berkeley. Jane was curious about what went on inside those brown-shingled houses — the main living room of the one she visited had a shrine to North Korean leader Kim Il-sung and there was a North Korean flag hanging on the wall. There was a lot of talk about Marxism and feminism and everybody revered the Black Panthers.

The Red Family had been started two years before by *Ramparts* editor Bob Scheer and his then-wife, Anne Weills, both active in the antiwar movement; they were now separated but they still lived in the commune. Jane had started to date Scheer. To make matters more complicated, Anne had just broken off with Tom Hayden, who until recently had been very much one of the leaders of the Red Family. He'd been kicked out of the commune for his sexually manipulative behavior.

Jane didn't know what had actually happened. Someone in the commune described how Weills had denounced Hayden in a self-critical session for being a "male chauvinist pig." Jane hadn't forgotten their brief meeting in Michigan. She'd been intrigued. He had been one of the bright lights of the New Left. She wondered when their paths might cross again.

On July 20, 1971, *Klute* opened to superlative reviews for Jane, the best in her entire career. Wrote Richard Schickel in *Life* magazine, "Jane

Fonda has emerged as the finest actress of her generation with a mercurial, subtly shaded, and altogether fascinating performance . . . she is a rock of integrity . . . and one should see *Klute* if only to be present at her moment of triumph." In *The New Yorker* Pauline Kael exulted, "[Fonda] disappears into Bree, the call girl, so totally that her performance is very pure, unadorned by 'acting.' She never stands outside Bree — she gives herself over to the role and yet isn't *lost* in it — she's fully in control and her means are extraordinarily economical, she has somehow gotten onto a plane of acting at which even her closest close-up never reveals a false note."

The impact the movie had on the women of her generation was profound. Susan Brownmiller, the author of *Against Our Will*, recalled, "Jane Fonda was *the* woman of our time up to a point. We all wanted to be like her — the liberated, sexually free woman. Everybody copied her shag hairdo, the miniskirts and boots, but she *wasn't* a feminist; she was still into depending on powerful men to find her identity."

As the decades passed, Jane's performance as the call girl Bree continued to resonate. The meaning of Jane's Bree goes very deep. Her Bree is shrewd and independent, but her unsettled emotions reflect the price of autonomy for women.

Jane ignored the acclaim she received for *Klute*. She was still seriously thinking of giving up acting and joining a film commune. The only reason she flew to Paris to meet with director Jean-Luc Godard and discuss his projected movie *Tout Va Bien* was because it wasn't a mainstream movie. There was no script. Someone had described it as "part Marxist soap opera — part Brechtian agitprop." That appealed to her.

It had an intriguing premise. Jane would be playing a TV reporter, Yves Montand her New Wave director husband. Together they would be trapped all night in a sausage factory outside Paris during a wildcat strike. What they see and hear that night radicalizes them.

Because Montand and Jane were two of the most famous left-wing activists in the world, their star power combined with Godard's reputation as an avant-garde filmmaker convinced Paramount to fund the project.

Jane was pleased by her meeting with Godard, who hadn't made a commercial film since the 1968 Paris riots. Instead he'd formed a

Marxist film collective and produced experimental agitprop films like *Pravda* — abandoning narrative and emotional suspense in the attempt to shape a style. It would be a challenge to work with him.

She flew back to L.A. in time for auditions at her ramshackle little house over the highway to cast new actors for the upcoming *F.T.A.* tour.

At a break in the auditions there was a heated discussion as to whether *F.T.A.* should accept John Lennon and Yoko Ono's offer to join them. The famous couple was promoting peace all over the world; but both Jane and Sutherland were against "star turns," so they turned them down even though Lennon and Ono offered in all seriousness to wear bags over their heads.

Auditions continued, and in November the troupe moved to New York to try out new material at a huge benefit at Philharmonic Hall. After another show at Fort Bragg they embarked on a three-month-long *F.T.A.* Pacific tour with scheduled stops in Hawaii and the Philippines and Okinawa. Occasionally *F.T.A.* would crisscross the routes traveled by Bob Hope's show — his glossy production numbers and Les Brown's band contrasted sharply with *F.T.A.*'s makeshift props and performers in blue jeans.

The show played to an estimated sixty-four thousand soldiers. Jane returned to the United States confident that *F.T.A.* had accomplished something positive. However, she added that during this particular period of her life she had never been so miserable. Her break with Sutherland had been difficult. She never resolved the tensions and turmoil within *F.T.A.* Mostly she was exhausted — physically and psychologically exhausted.

25

O VER NEW YEAR's Jane hid out in Megève, France, with Vadim and Vanessa, hoping to restore herself after so many frantic months. She confided she really didn't want to work with Godard. He hoped with *Tout Va Bien* to make his first revolutionary work for the bourgeoisie. He thought his casting of Yves Montand as a depressed former New Wave director and Jane as his solemn American journalist wife might meld radical politics with mainstream appeal. But there was no script. Jane decided to get out of the deal by saying she now only wanted to work with women.

When Godard heard the news he panicked. He knew that if Jane, at the height of her celebrity, left the production, funding would dry up, so he sent his partner, Jean-Pierre Gorin, to convince her she must remain with the movie.

Gorin appeared at Vadim's rented chalet and proceeded to harangue Jane for the next six hours. Pacing around the kitchen as she attempted to eat a snack, he threatened that if she didn't honor her commitment her career could be ruined. He became so verbally abusive Vadim ordered him to leave the house. He finally did; Jane later said he threatened her physically, but Gorin denied the incident ever happened. "It's all Jane Fonda's lies."

She ended up making the movie and sharing a Left Bank commune in Paris with five other feminists during the filming. Initially she'd been excited about working with Godard; the outlines of the story had appealed to her.

But after the film began shooting, Jane kept to herself. "I just did my work." (*Times* critic Vincent Canby later described her stellar turn as a solemn American political correspondent as "appealing and very funny.")

She didn't socialize with Montand. "Yves was playing around so much and that was killing Simone whom I loved — I could barely look at him." She felt that Godard treated her badly, and when she saw the rough cut she became indignant; she felt Godard had intentionally made her character a parody of Jane Fonda.

Oddly enough Godard's formula for *Tout Va Bien* (a young woman finds herself in the midst of a transforming experience and, in spite of herself, changes) would be an inspiration for Jane when she began producing and starring in her own "message" films.

In the early spring, Jane returned to L.A. She had lost more weight. She was so tired she could barely drag herself around.

She had no home. She was sleeping on various friends' couches. Desperate for a place where Vanessa could live with her, she borrowed $40,000 from her father and bought a little house on Canton Drive overlooking Studio City. She insisted on signing a promissory note and paid him back within the year. But she was touched. "Dad had his own non-intimate ways of letting me know he was there for me."

The house on Canton Drive soon became a nerve center for antiwar and other related activities. Richard Rosenthal remembered that every time he was there the place was abuzz with people running around and phones always ringing.

As the Academy Awards approached, she realized she had to make a decision. She'd been nominated for her performance in *Klute* and she'd already won the Golden Globe, but she'd asked a bemedaled Vietnam vet to accept the award for her — that had totally politicized the evening.

For a while she thought "maybe I shouldn't accept the Academy Award if I win" (some people were telling her not to). Then she decided, "I *should* accept because it comes from people in the business whom I respect — it's a vote of confidence."

But what kind of statement should she make? An artistic statement? A political one? "I decided to ask Dad for his advice — Dad, who didn't believe in the whole awards business at all ('How can you pick between Laurence Olivier and Jack Lemmon? It's apples and oranges!')."

He was standing in the doorway waiting for her. He didn't say hello. They walked in silence down the long hall. She felt unsettled, as she always did when she was with him. He invariably managed to make her feel physically diminished in his presence.

"But he came through," Jane wrote. "His verbal parsimony paid off: 'Tell 'em there's a lot to say, but tonight isn't the time,' was his recommendation — and the moment I heard it I knew he was right."

She promised him she would say just that. And suddenly, the meeting was over. No chitchat, no relaxing in the living room with its view of the pool, no waiting to see his wife, Shirlee, who was out shopping. Jane bolted — heart pounding, mouth dry.

By the morning of the Oscars she was sick with the flu. Richard Rosenthal, who had flown in from New York to be with her, remembered that Jane was sneezing into a Kleenex when he arrived. He couldn't get over how many colds she caught. She never had enough sleep. She had broken her ankle twice that year. She loved to wear platform sandals. But no matter what the ailment, she reacted with "crusty Fonda stoicism." Nothing got in the way of what she wanted to accomplish.

That morning she greeted Rosenthal cheerfully and they settled down in her living room and tried to deal with everything he had to go over with her. They were interrupted frequently by the telephone, which was in another room. Jane would run in to answer it and then would come back shaking her head and murmuring, "If I win the Oscar they want me to use the time to talk about the bombing and to denounce Johnson and the administration." For the next three hours, "between sneezes and more phone calls," he quietly explained what he had been doing on her behalf as her lawyer, and she listened. As always, most of the talk had to do with money. Rosenthal said, "In those days there was never enough money to cover everything she wanted and needed," not for her personal physical comfort but for her many causes.

She had been shelling out thousands of dollars to one peace group after another, making it virtually impossible for Rosenthal to cover all her personal expenses. She'd okayed his calling in of some of the loans, only to discover that most of the people she'd loaned money to thought she was "loaded." That morning Rosenthal insisted she stop giving so much money away and focus on a project that could produce cash. She told him she'd been reading scripts but she didn't like anything she'd been offered.

By the end of the afternoon it was time to get ready for the Oscars. An hour later Ruby, Donald Sutherland, Steve Jaffe, Francine Parker, Jane, and Rosenthal squeezed into the air-conditioned limousine Warner Bros. had sent. They drove through the hazy sunshine to the Dorothy Chandler Pavilion in downtown Los Angeles.

They were heading for the 44th Annual Academy Awards celebration. The highlights included a special tribute to the inimitable Charlie Chaplin, who was making his first return visit to the United States after twenty years of exile. He'd never become an American citizen, and during the 1950s he refused to testify in front of HUAC at the dawn of the McCarthy era. He hadn't wanted to submit to a witch-hunt so he escaped to Switzerland.

Rosenthal glanced over at Jane who was looking radiant in a simple, high-collared black Mao jacket, an elegant foil for "her fine patrician features." She insisted she wasn't nervous, but her slender, beautiful fingers chafed at her palm as if for reassurance.

There was little conversation. Suddenly, in the midst of the silence, Jane asked the driver, a middle-aged black chauffeur named Harry, "Would you like to attend the festivities?" (Comedian Dick Gregory, who had been invited to use one of Jane's tickets, was recovering from a protest fast and didn't feel up to it.) "Oh, Ms. Fonda, how could I thank you, my goodness," Harry said. Jane handed the chauffeur a gold and silver embossed card.

The limo approached the imposing Dorothy Chandler Pavilion bathed in brilliant sunshine. The whole area around the pavilion was deserted. Steve Jaffe looked at his watch, noting it was barely past 5:00 P.M. Nobody wanted to be too early. Someone suggested a place in nearby Little Tokyo where they could have a cup of tea in total anonymity.

A few minutes later everybody was seated at a long, dim bar illuminated by Japanese lanterns. A loud jukebox blared in the distance. "Well!" Jane exclaimed to no one in particular. "Anyone got a bright idea?" Rosenthal said, "We all knew what she meant: her acceptance speech." She waited. There were no suggestions. Rosenthal remembered he felt she deserved better than she was getting: the harassment and hostility of a shabby administration. There had to be a way to seize the moment and to show everyone what she was made of.

All at once he had an idea. "I know what you should say," he told her.

"What?" Jane eyed him expectantly.

"I think you should say, 'There are a lot of things to say . . .' pause '. . . but now is not the time to say them. Thank you very much,' and exit."

Jane cocked her head, "Say that again."

Rosenthal repeated it very slowly, "There are a lot of things to say."

Jane called the group to attention and repeated Rosenthal's little speech. It was short and sweet and right to the point. Everybody agreed. "The Left would respect her for what she said, the Right for what she didn't."

As they trooped outside an hour later, Jane grabbed Rosenthal's arm and whispered: "Now all I have to do is win."

By the time they reached the Chandler Pavilion it was surrounded by noisy crowds, and cars were backed up three deep. Harry maneuvered the limo in and out of a line inching slowly next to the red carpet at the entrance of the pavilion. Jane sat hunched in her seat, fingers flexing furiously.

Suddenly, there were hands on the roof of the car, slapping it, hitting it, pounding it. Then the car was rocked from side to side, with angry faces pressing against the windows. Outside a roar went up from the bleachers. "Down with Fonda!" placards were waving in the air and chants of "Down with Fonda!" could be heard as the car continued to be rocked from side to side. Finally Harry was able to pull the limousine away and onto the curb between protective cordons.

Then everyone jumped quickly onto the sidewalk. Francine Parker and Steve Jaffe walked in front of Jane and Sutherland, who were being acknowledged by the blinding flash of cameras and the screams of "There they are!" And "Hey, Jane!" — "Hi, Donald!"

They hurried across the lobby of the pavilion and into the packed auditorium. Rosenthal remembered, "I saw a sea of famous faces and then there was a cacophony of voices, everybody exclaiming, 'Jane Fonda! Look at Jane Fonda!'"

They were seated in the front row. Soon the show started with Isaac Hayes, "muscles glistening under a thick necklace of steel, and growling out the theme from the black detective movie *Shaft*," Rosenthal recalled.

The French Connection won for Best Picture, Best Director went to Billy Friedkin, Best Actor to Gene Hackman. It was the year of *Fiddler on the Roof, The Last Picture Show, A Clockwork Orange.* Then came the Chaplin tribute and the old clown gracefully accepted his second honorary Academy Award.

Finally the nominees for Best Actress were called, and as they waited for the winner to be announced, Jane leaned close to Rosenthal and whispered, "Say it again."

Finally it was time. "And the winner is . . . Jane Fonda!"

She ran gracefully up onto the stage to thunderous applause. Surveying the room, she held the gold statue high, took a deep breath, and declared, "Thank you. And thank you to those of you who applauded. There's a lot I could say tonight — but this isn't the time or the place. So I'll just say, 'Thank you.'"

The reaction was huge. Most of the room stood and applauded. Jane wrote, "I was stunned by a feeling of love and support that emanated from the audience." She exited into the wings clutching her Oscar and sobbing, "I am still a part of this industry." And then with disbelief, "How can this have happened *to me* when it hasn't happened to my father?"

Moments later she returned to her seat, and her friends hugged her. When she reached Rosenthal, she threw her arms around him and whispered mockingly in his ear: "I'm such a great actress. I blew the line. Sorry, Richard."

After the ceremonies Jane had to pose for pictures with the other winners backstage before Rosenthal and Sutherland met her, and together they moved outside where they stood and waited for the limousine to pick them up.

Fans pressed close. "Hey, Jane, over here!" Cameras flashed. "Can I have your autograph?" "Sorry," Jane answered, "I don't believe in autographs." The fan continued pressuring her. "Oh, please!" Jane shook her head. "No."

Most of the crowd had left. But there were a couple of young boys standing on the sidewalk and one of them spotted the Oscar clutched in her hand. He gestured approvingly: "Hey, that's good!"

Jane grinned at him. "Wanna hold it? Here!"

"Wow!" He grabbed the statuette, stared at it wonderingly, and repeated, "Wow! It's not even heavy!" So saying he passed it over to the friend who was standing next to him, and that friend passed the statuette to another friend. There were more exclamations of surprise and amazement from this trio of grungy kids.

Just then Harry drove up in the limousine. Before everybody climbed in, Jane asked, "Can you open the back, please?" and without so much as a second glance her Academy Award for Best Actress 1972 was tossed into the trunk next to the spare tire. (It would soon end up on the shelf in Santa Monica as a tarnishing bookend.)

Jane and her group did not go on to the Governors Ball where Chaplin and the other luminaries were being toasted. Instead they returned to another restaurant in Little Tokyo and everybody, including Harry, sat shoeless and gorged on sake, tempura, and sushi. "We all competed for who was worst with chopsticks," Rosenthal said.

Around midnight they left the restaurant and piled into the limousine. The first stop was Jane's house. By then she was burning up with fever and she admitted to being very sick. Harry rushed around to escort her to the front door and then thanked her, his voice full of emotion. "It was the most exciting night of my life, Ms. Fonda. I will never forget it."

"Nor would I," Rosenthal said years later. "Nor would I."

26

AFTER A WEEK she recovered from the flu, but she was starting to ask herself, What next? She needed a new role to play, but she couldn't conceive of appearing in a movie. She'd turned down Mike Nichols's offer to star in *Carnal Knowledge*. She passed on the Faye Dunaway part in *Chinatown*, as well as the mother's role in *The Exorcist*. She explained to her agent she couldn't imagine "acting" after the intensity of the past two years.

She wasn't sure she had any future as an activist. Her frantic tour of New Left politics with its endless marches and violent arguments had left her drained. She had to disband *F.T.A.*, and her attempt to rally Hollywood with her organization Entertainment Industry for Peace and Justice had failed. However much she wanted to be a radical, she could not erase her identity as movie star and daughter of Henry Fonda.

She liked to think of herself as a member of the "loyal opposition" — prominent Americans like the priest Daniel Berrigan; the pacifist David Dellinger; Nobel Prize winner George Wald; Cora Weiss, the fiery head of Women Strike for Peace — who had all protested the bombing of North Vietnam. They had also traveled to Hanoi to demonstrate their commitment to end the brutal conflict. Jane wanted to join them; she wanted to be a visible part of their protest. As a matter of fact, while she was in Paris filming with Godard she had met with various members of the North Vietnamese government, and they'd discussed the possibility of a trip in July.

· · ·

In the meantime she decided to give a lecture at the Embassy Theatre in downtown L.A. and show slides of the latest Hanoi bombings. Some of her Vietnamese friends had given her the slides while she was in Paris.

When she came out onstage, she didn't realize that Tom Hayden was sitting in the audience in the front row. He wore baggy pants and rubber sandals, his hair down to his shoulders in braids. Some of the people in the audience recognized him and said hello. He was a hero to many, one of the few famous 1960s New Left leaders who hadn't given up the fight. He was still trying to end the war. Recently, he had been photographed by Richard Avedon for *Vogue*. He was now out on bail as one of the "Chicago Seven" (he'd been one of the defendants of the Chicago Conspiracy Trial) and was living in a seedy apartment in Venice and writing articles, giving talks, and teaching classes at Immaculate Heart College in Hollywood about the culture and people of Vietnam.

He thought Jane's talk was "more political" than his talks but "effective, persuasive." Afterward he went backstage to say hello; they sat in the wings and chatted, and he suggested they collaborate on a joint lecture sometime. He would like to show her his slides, he said, and with that he put his hand on her knee and "an electric charge had gone through me," Jane wrote. "I . . . gave him my number — he gave me his."

She raced home, giddy with excitement, and told Ruby she'd met the man she was going to spend the rest of her life with. "I wanted a man in my life I could love, but it had to be someone who could inspire me, teach me, lead me, not be afraid of me."

Jane still didn't know much about Hayden, except that this once shining light of the New Left was living in virtual exile in Venice. While she was dating *Ramparts* editor Robert Scheer she'd hear many unflattering things about Hayden — that he was "controlling," Machiavellian, "two-faced."

Jane didn't want to hear any criticisms. What really mattered was that he seemed genuinely interested in *her*. He was a hero in the eyes of people from whom she wanted respect.

A week later Tom drove over to Jane's modest house in Studio City to show her the slide show he'd put together in Indochina.

Jane met him at the door. Vanessa was already asleep, so she introduced him to Ruby, then gave him a tour of the place — the swimming pool, the garden with the fruit trees she'd just planted. He was very quiet. Days later, when they were having coffee, he commented, "Quite an operation you have here." She sensed he didn't approve of the swimming pool or of her employee. "I, of course, felt immediate guilt and wished I were still living in the smoggy house on the cul-de-sac. *Then* he would have seen I wasn't an elitist."

That first evening he did see that she had Salvation Army furniture in the living room and a picture of Ho Chi Minh on the wall. They did not talk about the Oscars or about *Klute,* although he'd seen the movie and hadn't expected to be so shaken by it.

"Jane brought tremendous life to the character of Bree Daniels," he wrote in his own memoir. "Her acting touched me sharply especially in those monologues with her therapist where she talks about the comfort of being numb. . . ." He, too, wanted the comfort of being numb. He didn't want intimacy — not after the brutal dismissal from the Red Family, which had been the center of his life for three years.

They sat on the floor of Jane's shabby living room and watched Hayden's slides projected on her wall. "There . . . unfolded a series of stunning images: children riding water buffalo, slender, reedlike women, graceful in their pastel *ao dais,* Buddhist temples with smiling roofs that curled at the corners, and always the rice fields stretching as far as the eye could see, dotted by Vietnamese in conical straw hats, waist-deep in emerald vastness."

Hayden showed her many slides that night, but it was the slides from the Hoa culture that got to her — especially the close-ups of the teenage prostitutes in the brothels and bars; these images made her cry. One slide affected her in particular, a billboard in Saigon promoting plastic surgery so that these young Asian girls could get round eyes like Barbie dolls and big breasts and buttocks like Marilyn Monroe; apparently prostitutes in Vietnam could increase their price if their faces became more "Americanized."

She began to see her own life with new eyes. The women of Vietnam had been victims of a *Playboy* mentality. She had used pills and a near-starvation diet — she had gone against nature to try to achieve an impossible ideal of beauty too.

Suddenly Hayden realized Jane was crying. "I was talking about the superficial sexiness Jane had once promoted and exemplified in *Barbarella*—and now she was trying to shake. I looked at her in a new way. I could fall in love with someone like this, I thought."

At some point during the evening, "Tom asked if I was living with someone, meaning a live-in lover. I answered emphatically, 'Oh no, never! I don't ever want to live with a man again!'" She was cynical about relationships, she said.

That wasn't quite the truth. She longed to have another sustaining relationship with a man, and Hayden sensed this. He was shrewd and supersensitive when it came to women's needs. He responded to Jane's longing and quickly moved into the void.

They became lovers almost immediately and she let her shag grow out. ("Men prefer women with long hair," she'd murmur. While she was with Hayden her hair would ultimately hang past her shoulders.) She sat in on Hayden's lectures, "captivated by his brilliance" about Vietnamese culture. After class she would ply him with questions about politics, morality, economics.

He saw her as "a rich person out of touch with reality—very, very intense—with a devouring curiosity about what I thought." He was also broke, and she had money and was more famous than he was. He'd been out of the spotlight for too long. He wanted back in. "One thing you have to remember about Tom and Jane," said a former colleague, "they are both very, very, very ambitious."

He was aware that she was insecure about most things, especially about her lack of knowledge of American history and how ashamed she was of her privilege. He disliked any show of possessions. When he mentioned he felt uncomfortable whenever she wore her expensive Cartier wristwatch, she replaced it with a cheap Timex.

Within weeks he brought her to Venice where he lived and introduced her to close friends like his roommate, the left-wing lawyer Leonard Weinglass, the pacifist David Dellinger, and Fred Branfman, a looming giant of a man with large feet and an innocent face who dressed in black and was often stoned. Now he worked in Washington, D.C., running the Indochina Resource Center. From 1967 to 1971 he'd traveled around Southeast Asia, usually on his motorcycle. He soon spoke fluent Laotian and ended up in Vientiane, teaching English to schoolchildren.

While he was in Laos, the peasants told him of the terrible secret bombing. It was the CIA's covert war, and the bombing was savage and aimed specifically at helpless civilians — napalm cluster bombs that sliced and diced human beings to shreds or burned thousands alive. Branfman was outraged and despairing. He became obsessed with the immorality of the bombing and the need to tell the world.

Ultimately, Branfman was the catalyst for most of the major exposés of the "secret war." He supplied information to Sey Hersh, Jack Anderson, and the *New York Times*'s Henry Kamm. He translated for Sydney Shainberg and helped Bernie Kalb and *Newsweek*'s Kevin Buckley get their stories straight about the war. Before the CIA shipped Branfman back to the United States, he'd met antiwar protesters like Daniel Berrigan and Noam Chomsky and first befriended Tom Hayden back in Washington, D.C.

"Tom was — and is — one of my personal political heroes for his courage, leadership, and commitment in the 1960s," Branfman said. "I absolutely revered the guy. I projected my idealism onto Tom. I projected what I wanted to believe about America on him. So did Jane."

Tom Hayden, the only son of Irish Catholic parents, was born in 1939 in Royal Oaks, Michigan, a working-class neighborhood of Detroit. His father, John, a dour monosyllabic man and a drinker, held down a job as an accountant for Chrysler until he retired. His mother, Genevieve ("Genny"), was a tiny bird of a woman who smoked two packs of cigarettes a day. She was one of eleven children from a town in Wisconsin called Oconomowoc.

When Tom was three, his parents divorced. Genny Hayden was determined to prove that as a single woman she could support herself and her son. For the next twenty years she worked as a film librarian in the local library system of Royal Oaks; she never missed a day.

She taught Tom that he must learn to use his mind. At an early age he became known as a "brainy advanced kid" who won spelling bees and read Thomas Aquinas to the nuns at the local parish school.

By the time he was a teenager he was an unsettling presence — pockmarked and brooding, driven and competitive. He devoured books like *Catcher in the Rye* and identified with loner rebels like James Dean. Just before he graduated from high school in 1957 a girl wrote in his yearbook, "There is nobody I despise more at times or adore at others than Tom Hayden."

He spent that summer hitchhiking across the United States, "into every corner of America," sleeping in parks or in doorways, embracing the open road like Jack Kerouac, another of his heroes.

He ended up in Berkeley talking with picketers outside of Woolworth's in support of black workers who were striking for better wages. It was his first taste of the civil rights movement.

Back in college Hayden became editor of the *University of Michigan Daily*, and he covered the 1960 Democratic convention where he interviewed Robert Kennedy and Martin Luther King Jr., who made a big impact. He wrote, "Each of us has to be more than neutral and objective. Every one of us has to make a difference." Hayden strongly identified with King and his commitment to nonviolence in an interracial society; he always thought of himself as a radical, not a liberal. His literary heroes were Albert Camus (who saw history reflected in the lives of ordinary people) and C. Wright Mills, a motorcycle-riding Texas socialist who championed self-government and grass-roots democracy and whose book *The Power Elite* provided the intellectual foundations of the New Left. "Mills validated us personally as a generation and as activist organizers," Hayden wrote. He was disappointed when C. Wright Mills died suddenly before they could meet and talk.

In 1961 Hayden and his new wife, Sandra Cason, headed south to work with the Student Nonviolent Coordinating Committee (SNCC). In Fayetteville, Tennessee, they observed demonstrations for better wages and working conditions. They saw evicted sharecroppers living in tents in the snow; they found a group of toughs waiting for them with belts and clubs. Hayden phoned the police, but the police joined the toughs. "We got in our car and raced out of town. They followed us for fifty miles before we lost them."

After that experience Hayden couldn't remain on the sidelines. He was beginning to realize the importance of direct action. "Working with other SNCC people was a key turning point in the evolution of my political identity," Hayden said. He began to see proof in the South that ordinary people could change conditions.

While working for voter registration in Mississippi along with Bob Moses, the gentle, bespectacled field secretary of SNCC, Hayden was beaten and then jailed, spending his twenty-second birthday behind bars in Albany, Georgia. He wrote a personal account of his experiences, which was published as a letter in *New American*. Journalist

Jack Newfield edited it and pronounced Hayden "a fine natural writer." They became friends.

When Hayden returned to school, he and a group of other activists drafted, amid much argument, the visionary Port Huron Statement, a generational call for direct participatory democracy. "The bottom line," said Jack Newfield, "was that society had to change—that conformity and the status quo had to be pushed aside by direct action."

The Port Huron Statement became the bible for the New Left and the burgeoning student movement.

Hayden said he drove to Washington, D.C., in March 1962, directly to the White House, where he personally delivered a copy to Arthur Schlesinger Jr.

After the assassinations of Martin Luther King Jr. and Robert Kennedy, "Tom changed," Jack Newfield said. "He became angrier—hostile towards the liberal ethic. He began calling himself 'a revolutionary.'" He participated in the violent student strike at Columbia University in 1968, and he helped plan the riots during the Democratic convention in Chicago that same summer, which led to his arrest.

A few months later Hayden, Jerry Rubin, Abbie Hoffman, Dave Dellinger, and Bobby Seale were indicted for conspiracy in what became known as the infamous Chicago Seven trial. (Midway through the raucous proceedings Seale—a Black Panther—was bound and gagged after he shouted obscenities at the judge.)

During and after the trial, while he was awaiting the verdict, Hayden became obsessed with "continuing to make history." By then he and his wife, Sandra (nicknamed "Casey"), who was now a leading feminist, had divorced.* According to Anne Weills, Hayden's girlfriend at the time, "Tom wanted to be President someday. He even talked about it."

Hayden was living with Anne then. She was a tall, WASPy blond, beautiful, extremely intelligent, a committed activist. She'd been one of the first Americans to visit Hanoi in 1968 and escort three American pilots back to the United States following negotiations.

She and Tom stayed together for two years in the famous Red Family commune in Berkeley, and they talked "revolution" and even had

---

* In 1965 Casey Hayden had cowritten a memo with Mary King entitled "Sex and Caste." Directed to Students for a Democratic Society (SDS) and SNCC, it challenged activists to be aware of gender inequality in the movement and in the country.

target practice with guns in the hills above the university campus. But they never would go so far as terrorists like the Weathermen (who blew up buildings and actually killed people) or the Black Panthers; the Red Family couldn't and didn't want to go that far. Mostly they ended up in hours of fierce self-criticism sessions based on the Communist Chinese model.

"Tom had this kind of self-confidence that made others aware of their own insecurities," said a member of the Red Family. "Everybody knew he always had this hidden agenda — he was hugely ambitious. Everything was calculated and everyone a pawn in his master plan. He could be friendly and respectful to friends, particularly women, but when they walked out of the room he could cut them into little pieces."

Weills told Craig Unger of *Esquire* she wanted to understand "who this man was. Every time I was becoming more independent he would pull me back and try to reassert himself. I kept trying to find his soul. Tom's ability to love and connect with someone — that was what was missing. His words and behavior were all about possessing me as an object."

Weills was often away from the commune working. Hayden then went off to New Haven with another member of the Red Family, and when he came back he told Weills he had slept with her.

Many members of the collective slept around, but this was more than mere jealousy — as far as Weills was concerned, it was sexual political warfare, an attempt by Hayden to undermine the unity of the women. "No matter how much he said he loved me, he was using everybody," Weills insisted. "I came to dislike him and disrespect him. He is the most manipulative man, the most power conscious man I have ever known."

Weills called the commune together and "we purged him." "They broke his spell," said Bob Scheer. "Tom had cast a spell over these people; he had worked his magic over them and now it was over. But it was not some flighty thing, these were his closest friends."

Not only was he kicked out of the Red Family but he also no longer had a political base in Berkeley. For the next nine months he camped out in Jack Newfield's apartment in Greenwich Village, trying to figure out what he was going to do next.

He moved to Venice, California, grew his hair long, and hung out with Vietnam vets like Ron Kovic; he decided to use an assumed name — Emmet Garity (the name of his Irish grandfather). He taught at Immaculate Heart College in Hollywood, run by an order of five hundred nuns, who were reflecting the 1960s spirit of independence within the context of the Catholic Church.

"And then he met Jane and began to work his magic on her," David Dellinger said. He became her lover/mentor, father figure. He helped her see she didn't have to give up everything to be a radical. She certainly didn't have to stop being an actress, but she had to learn patience — she had to stop making snap judgments.

"Jane was in too much of a hurry — that was her problem," her brother, Peter, said. "Tom, like Fred Gardner, taught her to pull back, to move more slowly. She was so much in love with Tom she did everything he told her."

So when he said she was spreading herself too thin, that she should drop some causes — "like feminism, like the war movement" — she obediently did as she was told. "The movement sucks people dry, then spits them out and wants them to commit suicide," Hayden told her bitterly. It would be better if she focused on a single cause — one issue, like Vietnam; maybe they could talk about Vietnam in joint lectures.

Hayden had begun talking about creating a national network — an educational speaking tour of vast proportions, which he would call the Indochina Peace Campaign (IPC). In Hayden's words, "It was an ambitious plan to barnstorm America about the war."

"It was Tom's most selfless act," Fred Branfman recalled. He helped Hayden organize the tour, and he wrote one of the main pamphlets for it — official documentation of Nixon and Kissinger's having created "Six Million Victims" since taking office. Branfman felt proud to be associated with what he regarded as a noble effort to stop the killing.

As for Jane, the idea of doing something meaningful *together* with Tom Hayden energized her. It gave her a sense of purpose. "Tom saved my life," she would say over and over again.

She had been struggling so long to prove that she was a committed radical, and she'd always felt herself on trial by her left-wing colleagues. She was sure they thought she was a rich dilettante; she had an insatiable need to prove her sincerity.

"She sat at Tom's feet, literally," remembered David Dellinger. "She looked up to Tom like he was some sort of god. . . . She totally subjugated herself to his point of view."

27

THAT SPRING THERE were reports coming from European scientists and diplomats that American planes were dropping bombs on the Red River delta dikes in North Vietnam. Those who witnessed the bombings felt they were deliberate. When Radio Hanoi first broadcast the news, Washington dismissed it as "enemy propaganda." There were reports that if the bombing continued, there would be massive flooding, drowning, and famine for thousands of Vietnamese.

In late May, Jane received an invitation from the Vietnamese Committee for Solidarity with the American People to come to Hanoi. The Vietnamese Cultural Association and the Vietnam Film Artists Association invited her, too.

She jumped at the chance. She could go to Vietnam, photograph the bombed dikes, and publicize the evidence at press conferences. Somehow it did not occur to her that she would be used by the North Vietnamese as propaganda, that her trip would be "planned," that she would have no control over where she went or how much she would be photographed.

The Committee of Liaison (organized by Cora Weiss and David Dellinger) coordinated the travel of Americans to Vietnam; every month groups of three Americans went to Hanoi with letters for the American POWs and returned with mail for their families. Although Jane went alone to Vietnam, she did bring mail back from the POWs.

Hayden used his own connections to set up the trip. He did not choose to accompany her. Years later when Jane tremulously asked why he hadn't gone with her, he replied coolly, "They invited *you*. Besides . . . at the time, we weren't together publicly as a couple."

She told few people of her plan. Her father didn't know about it until he read accounts in the newspapers.

En route she stopped off in New York to see her lawyer, Richard Rosenthal, at his office to get her will updated. Steve Jaffe, who was there, recalled, "I had the feeling she thought she might not be coming back, that she could be killed by bombs."

After the will was updated, he and Rosenthal taught Jane how to use a 35mm camera. She told them she planned to make a film of the effects of the war on the Vietnamese people. Rosenthal was concerned that she was traveling alone, which was very unusual. Most activists who traveled to North Vietnam traveled in groups.

In Paris she caught a plane to Moscow — the plane that would take her to Hanoi. When she reached Orly, she had little time to catch the connecting flight, so she started to run across the airport lobby and slipped, fracturing her left foot ("Bulimics have thin bones"). She did make her flight, but by the time she reached Moscow her foot had swollen terribly. During the four-hour layover she got an x-ray — there was indeed a fracture. She was bandaged, given a pair of crutches, and hobbled back onto the plane.

The trip to North Vietnam took fourteen hours — she tried to sleep but couldn't. She felt numb with fatigue and pain. She arrived in Hanoi on July 12, 1972. The landing was delayed because American Pantheon jets were in the process of bombing the city. Jane wrote that she watched "the planes recede . . . my country's planes — bombing a city where I am about to be received as a welcomed guest." It was bizarre.

She had difficulty getting out of the plane, juggling crutches, a purse, a camera, and a packet of letters from families of POWs. A group of Vietnamese moved toward her carrying a bunch of flowers.

(Later the local newspapers would report on "the great progressive actress Jane Fonda in Hanoi." The story was printed around the world. Many American activists had come to Hanoi, talked on the radio, and toured the bomb sites; the main difference was that the Pentagon ignored them. But with Jane, the CIA watched her every move and reported it back to Secretary of State Henry Kissinger.)

She was immediately whisked away by uniformed officials and driven into Hanoi; in wartime the city appeared almost ghostly. She was staying at the Thong Nhat (the most popular hotel for foreigners, which served delicious French/Vietnamese cuisine). "I [was] given an enormous room on an upper floor, with a ceiling fan and mosquito netting over the bed. . . . I [was] too tired for a bath but grateful for the luxurious accommodations (piles of towels, hot tea, hard candies)." Her interpreter, Quoc, had already given her the schedule for her visit—it included a trip to an antiaircraft installation. Jane tried to make them understand that she didn't want to go to that installation, but the schedule had already been finalized; there was nothing she could do.

She fell into a deep sleep almost immediately but was awakened around midnight by the sound of air-raid sirens—there would be three air raids that first night, and Jane would hide out in a bunker along with other hotel residents, including John Sullivan, director of the American Friends Service Committee, who didn't recognize her at first and then when he did, wondered why she had come.

Around 5:00 A.M. her Vietnamese hosts drove Jane to the Vietnam–U.S.S.R. Friendship Hospital where she had her foot examined. In the midst of the examination there was another air raid, and she was carried immediately to the air-raid shelter where she joined doctors, nurses, and other patients. Nobody seemed to panic. Jane's interpreter told her everybody was very excited about her presence—because "you're an American." She said, "I search[ed] their eyes for some sign of hostility. There was none."

After yet another air raid Jane's foot was x-rayed. The doctors wrapped it in a crude poultice "made from chrysanthemum roots . . . it is . . . full of healing and strengthening elements," she was told. "Because of the war we have to rely on whatever we have, simple things, to meet our medical needs," the doctors said. Within two days the swelling went down and Jane was able to walk with ease.

From then on she traveled all over North Vietnam with an escort and a translator, speaking to people from all walks of life—workers, peasants, students, artists, dancers, soldiers, and politicians. Again and again the distinction was made between the American people and "the imperialist war-making powers of the Nixon administration."

She heard many ingenious stories of resistance; one was about the floating bridges along the Ho Chi Minh Trail. Every day these pontoon bridges were dismantled and hidden in sections up and down the river; imitation painted bridges replaced them and were systemically bombed by American planes, and every night the real pontoon bridges were reassembled in the dark.

Hanoi had gone literally underground. Jane was shown fallout shelters, office buildings, factories, dug deep into the ground, and everything seemed to be camouflaged. Everywhere she went she saw people running, walking, or on bicycles — thousands of bicycles clanging, whirling, flashing in the sunlight. The streets of Hanoi teemed with bicycles and with life. The noise was deafening. The clanging of streetcars — cocks crowing — the chugging of trains — the drone of Migs overhead . . . People in Vietnam went to work at the crack of dawn and on the outskirts of the city, jeeps and military trucks heavily camouflaged moved into the dusty roads.

She couldn't get over the extent of the devastation — farms leveled, dead animals crushed, orchards obliterated — and she couldn't get over the spirit of resistance either: the determination to rebuild, to keep going — to never give up. The beauty of the land was amazing — terraced rice fields, gleaming rivers, the shifting colors of green on the hills that went from soft chartreuse to deep emerald green — and the weather was misty, tranquil, and very warm.

Often swarms of little boys would run after her car waving and shouting, and finally Jane asked her interpreter what they were saying. "Madame Chi [the interpreter] tells me they are asking where I am from — am I Russian? The driver shouts, 'She's an American,' and they actually cheer!" The little boys jumped up and down, yelling even louder. "Maybe it's the first time they've seen an American close up instead of an American plane," Jane remarked, and she smiled at the little boys and waved back.

Meanwhile the U.S. bombing continued unabated, and Jane experienced many air raids. Once she was pulled into a fallout shelter by a young girl. The shelter resembled a manhole dug in the ground with a cover of plain reeds, straw thatch over it, and "no sooner have I climbed in than she wedges herself in with me, quickly covering us with the straw lid. . . . The girl's cheek is pressed against mine. I can feel her eyelashes and her warm breath. This cannot be happening. I am not jammed in a hole with a Vietnamese girl who has helped me escape American bombs. I know I am going to wake up and this will have been a dream. . . . I begin to cry, saying over and over to the girl, 'I'm sorry, oh, I am so sorry, I'm so sorry.' She stops me and begins speaking to me in Vietnamese, not angry, very calm. Quoc [Jane's guide] translates: 'You shouldn't cry for us. We know why we are fighting. The sadness should be for your country, your soldiers. They don't know why they are fighting us.'"

During another air raid in a larger shelter Jane huddled with various Americans, among them Joseph Kraft, who was writing about the war for *The New Yorker*. She told him very fiercely that it was important to speak out against the bombing of the dikes.

A number of American correspondents were trying to get the real story out about the war, reporters like Gloria Emerson, Morley Safer, Peter Arnett, but most American journalists hung out at the Rex Hotel in Saigon. Every afternoon the U.S. military gave cursory briefings at five o'clock, the "Five O'Clock Follies," they called them. Much of the information, like body counts, said a former colonel later, was totally made up.

Two days after she arrived in Hanoi, Jane began filming the massive bomb craters on the dikes. She filmed villagers carrying dirt in big wheelbarrows and then laboriously filling in the huge holes. They were working furiously because the rains were coming and the river was going to rise. It took days to fill one crater. It took only seconds for American bombs to undo all that work.

As she was filming, so was Gérard Guillaume, a respected filmmaker from France. He was making a documentary about North Vietnam and wanted to include Jane's travels in his footage. She agreed. The two struck up a friendship; "he helped me with what I was doing," she said.

After she'd been in Hanoi for less than a week, she had observed so much civilian devastation — ruined hospitals, schools, homes — that she asked her Vietnamese hosts if she could go on radio and make an appeal to the pilots. "I want to try to tell U.S. pilots what I am seeing here on the ground."

Somehow she didn't understand that the North Vietnamese would use her radio spots for propaganda purposes. They would be broadcast night and day in the POW camps like the Hanoi Hilton. "We heard Jane Fonda yakking till we almost went fucking crazy," one POW said years later.

(The CIA would record all her broadcasts. Americans heard only bits and pieces of them back in the United States. These broadcasts would become the rallying points for charges of treason that were later brought against Jane after she returned home.)

Every morning a man would come to her hotel with a Sony tape recorder, and she would sit down in a room with him and talk extemporaneously. "I would say things like 'yesterday I saw children with their hands and feet blown off and this is the kind of weapon that did it . . . perhaps you're not aware of the bombs you're dropping.'"

She would talk about the horrors of the antipersonnel bombs she'd seen in Hanoi's War Crimes Museum — a ghastly site filled with American weapons of mass destruction like the three-thousand-pound "mother bomb," the bearer of little bomblets so devastating to humans because they float down and explode later. Smaller weapons like cluster bombs and the pineapple bomb were displayed in glass cases with photographs of napalm and phosphorus victims, mutilated survivors, and the dead — children with hands and feet blown off, women with more than five hundred holes in their bodies made by "psychological impact weapons," as the Pentagon called them. Jane would talk about what she felt as an American seeing what our government was doing to the Vietnamese people.

She would read excerpts from the Pentagon Papers, a top-secret Department of Defense document detailing the history of the United States' increasing political-military involvement in Vietnam from 1945 to 1967. In 1971 Daniel Ellsberg, a former government employee, had leaked the papers to the *New York Times* because he wanted to end what he perceived to be "a wrongful war." Jane wrote in her autobiography that the Pentagon Papers revealed "we'd been lied to," and she said as much in her radio broadcasts.

She added that she never asked the soldiers to defect. She hoped her broadcasts accomplished "what speaking out always accomplishes: that it instilled new thought in the minds of even a few . . . if there was one pilot who might have second thoughts."

It's possible that pilots and personnel stationed in carriers offshore could have heard Jane, but it seems unlikely "that pilots would have gone out of their way to tune into Radio Hanoi with or without Jane Fonda," Jerry Lembcke wrote. On a more mundane level, the former POW and war historian Mike McGrath suggested, "Sailors had watches to stand, duty stations to work at, and little time to stand on deck to find the Radio Hanoi station. On another note, they wouldn't have been interested enough to listen to Jane and wouldn't have been demoralized if they had."

And why wouldn't they have been? The *Pacific Stars & Stripes*, a civilian newspaper authorized by the Department of Defense and distributed free to military personnel, printed her remarks as soon as she made them. The July 17 paper carried a story headlined U.S. BOMBS DIKES, JANE FONDA SAYS. It was a straight Associated Press news story without comment or criticism, the same kind of report appearing in newspapers throughout the United States that day. The story quoted her address to pilots: "All of you in the cockpits of your aircraft, all of you who load bombs, work on the ships of the Seventh Fleet, think about what you are doing."

Like so much connected to Jane's trip to Hanoi, the significance of her radio speeches can't be separated from the times in which she made them. There are first of all questions about who, if anyone, heard them. Jerry Lembcke wrote, "Curiously few veterans claim to have heard her. Not only that, most historical accounts of the propaganda war in Vietnam note that Radio Hanoi and Liberation Radio and the Voice of the NLF in the South were regularly jammed by the United States and the South Vietnamese government."

What also should be considered is that nothing Jane said in her broadcasts was big news to the GIs in the field. "Military personnel in Southeast Asia got their news from *Pacific Stars & Stripes*." They already knew what Jane had been telling them.

Between radio broadcasts Jane participated in a staged press conference with seven American POWs — downed pilots, some of whom had been imprisoned since 1968, others more recently. The purpose of their meeting with Jane was to demonstrate that they had not been mistreated by their captors.

(Many Americans had met with POWs, and by now there were many POWs in Hanoi who were opposed to the war. Jerry Lembcke wrote that when Jane was in Hanoi in 1972, there were at most "180 prisoners in Hanoi who could have heard her [on the radio] and many of those had declared their own opposition to the war.")

Jane met with the seven American POWs in an abandoned movie theater on the edge of Hanoi. She interviewed them and filmed them,

Jane in close-up in *Circle of Love,* being directed by her first husband, Roger Vadim. Vadim wanted to immortalize Jane. He wanted to create a sexual persona for her onscreen.

Jane with her baby daughter, Vanessa Vadim.

Jane and Vanessa with Henry
Fonda watching proudly; Dot,
the nanny, in the background;
and Vadim looking on in
Malibu, 1969.

Director Sydney Pollack shot the climax of the dance marathon for *They Shoot Horses, Don't They?* over and over, and Jane continued to dance and dance, defying the circumstances, defying the Depression. One critic said her acting was "heroic."

Jane alone on the set of *They Shoot Horses.* She totally inhabited the character of Gloria, the marathon dancer, the girl without hope.

Jane as Bree Daniels, the tough-talking call girl in *Klute*, her most mercurial, subtly shaded performance. Of it Jane says, "It was like a melding of souls between the character Bree and me."

Jane with Donald Sutherland, the night of the Oscars. A photographer caught her expression just as she heard her name announced as the winner of the Academy Award for Best Actress, 1972.

Jane being led off to jail in Cleveland in handcuffs. She had been falsely accused of smuggling drugs from Canada. The charges were dropped. All she had in her purse were a hundred vitamin pills.

Jane brings her antiwar campaign to Newark, New Jersey. The poster reads: "Six million victims: The human cost of the Indochina War Under President Nixon."

Jane, perched on an antiaircraft gun, sings an antiwar song to North Vietnamese soldiers and journalists in July 1972. For this she was later demonized as "Hanoi Jane."

LIFE

BUSY REBEL

Jane Fonda, Pusher of Causes

A Breakthrough Cancer Test

APRIL 23 · 1971 · 50¢

Jane when she was busy raising money for a variety of causes, such as Vietnam Veterans Against the War and the Winter Soldier Investigation.

Jane and Yves Montand were the most famous left-wing activists in the world when they made *Tout Va Bien.* Their star power, combined with Godard's reputation as an avant-garde director, made this movie especially intriguing.

After a press conference in Stockholm, Sweden, Jane addresses the media to protest continuing U.S. military involvement in the Vietnam War.

Jane with her second husband, political radical Tom Hayden, and their son, Troy. Jane said: "I wanted a man in my life I could love, but it had to be someone who could inspire me, teach me, lead me, not be afraid of me."

Tom and Jane spoke out all over the country for his grass-roots organization, the Campaign for Economic Democracy. They were big environmentalists and one of their top priorities was lobbying against the building of more nuclear plants in California.

Jane and Tom kidding around at home on Wadsworth Avenue in Santa Monica, 1976. For the ten years they lived there, they slept on a mattress on the floor. They were very happy.

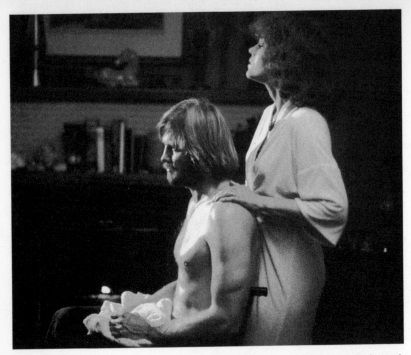

Jon Voight and Jane in *Coming Home*, a drama about Vietnam vets and their wives. Jon and Jane both won Oscars; so did the screenplay.

Jane and Jason Robards in *Julia*. Jane focused on her anger while portraying the difficult, temperamental playwright Lillian Hellman.

The box-office comedy bonanza *Nine to Five,* starring Jane, Lily Tomlin, and Dolly Parton. The movie grossed over $100 million. (1980)

Jane in *The Morning After* playing a drunk has-been movie star. For this performance she was nominated for another Oscar. (1986)

Jane, ecstatic at winning her Oscar for *Coming Home* in 1978.

Jane, Tom, Shirlee Fonda, Troy, and Vanessa watch as Henry Fonda blows out the candles on his birthday cake. He was seventy-seven.

Jane, the Workout queen, with her stepmother Shirlee, who gave her the Workout idea. (1982)

Jane with her third husband, Ted Turner, watching an Atlanta Braves game in 1991. At the time Turner owned the team.

Ted and Jane at the Oscars. Jane is wearing a Versace gown.

Jane, alone again and marching through the streets of Saint-Tropez to Vadim's funeral. (2000)

Jane during the curtain call at the opening-night performance of *33 Variations* on Broadway, March 2009. She was nominated for a Tony.

Jane, back where she started in Hollywood, December 2010.

and later she spoke on the radio about them and stated that she be-lieved they were in good health and good spirits.

They sat in a row in front of her — in striped pajamas. All of them called for an end to the war; they had already given a powerful antiwar letter to a presidential delegation.

A guard was with them at all times. Jane wrote, "It [was] self-con-scious and awkward for all the obvious reasons." She tried to get them to laugh when she asked them point-blank if they'd been brainwashed. They all said no. Later she would say she thought they were all telling the truth but maybe some of them had been lying.

At some point, Jane wrote, "a large impressive man . . . navy captain David Hoffman, proudly raises his arm up and down over his head and says, 'Please, when you go back, let my wife know that my arm has healed.' He tells me that the arm had been broken when he was ejected from his plane. I assure him I will let his wife know (and I do, as soon as I get back)."

Jane did not go on to the infamous "Hanoi Hilton" prison camp where now-senator John McCain was then languishing.

There are erroneous reports that McCain was asked to meet with her and that when he refused he was beaten. Jane said she didn't ask to meet with him. More ugly stories would eventually surface: that Jane met with POWs at the Hanoi Hilton prison who passed her notes for their families back in the United States. According to POW Larry Car-rigan, he had been six years in the Hilton. His wife lived on faith that he would still be alive. He and his group got cleaned up and fed in preparation for Jane's visit. Each man secreted a tiny piece of paper with his Social Security number on it in the palm of his hand. When paraded before Ms. Fonda and a cameraman, each man shook her hand. She took them all and once the cameras had stopped rolling, to the shocked disbelief of the POWs, she turned to the officers in charge and handed them the little papers. Three men died from the subse-quent beatings. Carrigan survived; for a while he was credited with telling this erroneous tale.

One biography of Fonda recounts Carrigan's account not as legend but as truth, as did the *Washington Times* and William Buckley in a syndicated column on November 19, 1999.

However, Mike McGrath, president of NAM-POWs, denounced

these libels online on February 19, 2001. Speaking for specific POWs named in the story, McGrath tried to set the record straight. "Larry Carrigan asked that we get [his] name off that bunch of crap. . . . No torture or beatings to see Fonda. . . . Larry was never near Jane. There were never any POWs killed on account of Jane."

Over her objections to her hosts and her guides, on her last day in Vietnam, Jane visited the air defense installation on the outskirts of Hanoi. She had told her translator to say something to the North Vietnamese government guides, but at the last minute she decided she wouldn't make a fuss. A number of journalists from Russia, Poland, and Japan — no Americans — accompanied her to the site. A Czech reporter named Havranek recounted the incident to Bill Davidson.

"Everybody had lunch with Fonda before lots of toasts of Russian wine and Hungarian slivovitz," Havranek said. "Then they took Fonda to an antiaircraft installation. She had this fixed smile on her face as they moved her towards the aircraft gun. They said this was one of the heroic weapons that was protecting the city from the barbaric American air bombardment.

"Someone put a soldier's helmet on her head and she joked that this was just like a Hollywood publicity opportunity except her hair didn't look right. One of the guides, a woman, then fixed her hair so that it was arranged correctly around the edge of her helmet. They asked her to climb up onto the gun mount, which she did, sitting in the gunner's seat. Everybody laughed, including Miss Fonda. I don't know whether or not she realized a camera crew was filming every moment of the incident."

In retrospect Ron Rosenbaum, a journalist who reported on the incident years later for *Vanity Fair,* said, "The expression on her face looked like another manifestation of Fonda's character; she always said she likes to respond to danger and when she does she makes this manic effort to appear blithe spirited about it.'"

Then the soldiers asked Jane to sing a song called "Day Ma Di" written by the students of South Vietnam who were against the war. Jane as always was prepared. She'd memorized the song back in L.A., and she sang it to the students in Vietnamese while the cameras flashed. As soon as she hopped off the gun, the implications of what had just happened dawned on her. "Oh my God. It's going to look like I was trying to shoot down U.S. planes! I plead with [the translator], 'You have to be sure those photographs are not published. Please, you can't let them be published.'" She was assured the pictures would never be used. She admits today it was possible the Vietnamese had it all planned.

The images of Fonda perched on an antiaircraft gun played a powerful role in her eventual demonizing. American networks immediately picked up the Japanese-shot footage of Jane at the gun site, but only CBS used the film for evening news, and then simply to illustrate Representative Thompson's accusation that Jane was committing treason. Over the years, increasing importance has been attached to that image of Jane on the gun, which lasted only fifty seconds, along with the still photos that were taken at the same time.

"It was my mistake, and I have paid and continue to pay a heavy price for it," she said. "That two-minute lapse of sanity will haunt me until I die. . . . I simply wasn't *thinking* about what I was doing, only about what I was *feeling* — innocent of what the photo implies. Yet the photo exists, delivering its message, regardless of what I was really doing or feeling. . . . I carry this heavy in my heart. I always will."

At the time she wanted to speak to Tom Hayden, but it was virtually impossible to telephone the United States. Back in Washington, D.C., Hayden was locked in a nine-hour talk marathon with Fred Branfman, who remembered, "Tom was worried sick about Jane. He kept wondering if he should have gone with her. He was clearly very much in love with her."

The following day, her translator told Jane portions of her broadcasts from Hanoi had been reprinted in American newspapers. The photograph of her on the antiaircraft gun had not yet appeared.

Jane spent her last hours in Hanoi walking the streets with the foreign minister of North Vietnam. Communication was no problem. Almost everyone Jane met — poets, politicians, schoolteachers — spoke French fluently, as she did. The foreign minister had no bodyguards; he didn't carry a gun.

Jane would later tell friends how civilized people were with each other in Vietnam. So respectful and warm — everyone seemed to be committed to the greater good; she couldn't get over that.

When she boarded the Aeroflot jet for Paris, she carried with her 240 letters from POWs to their families back in the United States. There were reports that as a token of their solidarity her Vietnamese hosts had given her a ring made out of the wreckage of a downed American plane. She also carried with her a part of an antipersonnel weapon made by defense contractor Honeywell that she'd picked up in a bombed-out Vietnamese village.

Former attorney general Ramsey Clark followed Jane to North Vietnam, and in the next weeks he, too, investigated the bombing of the dikes and spoke out about it to the press.

"My trip had called attention to the dikes and so did Ramsey Clark's," Jane said, "and to the fact that Nixon was escalating the war."

"Not long after Clark left Hanoi the U.S. bombing of the dikes slowed down allowing the Vietnamese to repair the damage and avert flooding," Mary Hershberger wrote.

In August 1972 the bombing of the dikes stopped completely. By then they were already largely destroyed.

Jane left Hanoi on July 23. She arrived in Paris on July 25. Roger Pic, a well-known French photographer, hosted an impromptu press conference for her in a screening room off the Champs-Élysées. The place was packed with journalists from around the world as well as Jane's "unique support system," Simone Signoret.

Jane added she wasn't sure whether she or Guillaume had shipped her forty-five-minute film from Hanoi (Guillaume had rough-edited it for her), but when she lifted the reels out of their heavy metal boxes, the soundtrack was missing. She was later told it had been "held up in Paris customs." She had to show the film in silence.

You could have heard a pin drop as the grainy black-and-white images of destroyed villages, schools, and hospitals, the gaunt faces of POWs and little orphaned children, moved across the screen.

Jane stood frail and trembling in front of images of the huge bomb craters on the dikes around Nam Dinh. She pointed out over fifty bomb craters shown in the film, explaining this was unmistakable evidence that Nixon was bombing the dikes that were holding back the Red River.

That same afternoon in Washington, D.C., the State Department announced it would release its own report on the so-called dike system in Vietnam, but after Jane showed her footage the press conference in Washington was abruptly canceled, no reason given. The administration realized that Hanoi also could provide photographs, a reporter wrote. But the administration tried to discredit Jane's evidence by saying she was "escorted by Hanoi to the dikes."

While she was in Paris, Jane phoned Steve Jaffe back in the United States and asked him to set up another press conference in New York so she could show the film to American media. He was in the middle of doing just that when Tom Hayden suddenly appeared in his office. He'd flown in on the redeye and told Jaffe curtly, "From now on I'm handling everything for Jane."

Dozens of reporters were waiting for Jane's plane as it touched down at Kennedy Airport on July 27, 1972. Cries of "Hanoi Jane" and "Pinko slut" came at her, along with a smattering of applause from supporters, as she rushed past the crowd; she was dressed in black Vietnamese pajamas and a coolie hat.

She was kept in customs for a long time while agents pored over her passport and inspected her luggage (on the insistence of Charles Colson, a Nixon aide; the president hoped to prove she'd been "used" by the North Vietnamese). But there were no visas from North Vietnam stamped on the pages. A passport couldn't be confiscated unless it had an "offending" visa stamp, so the customs official had to give Jane back her passport and let her go.

Hayden was waiting for her but he kept to himself, hidden in a corner behind the crowd; he didn't want to be photographed with Jane just yet. Instead, he whisked her off to the Chelsea Hotel, and once in their room they clung together "like refugees." They hadn't been able to communicate at all those past weeks — no phone calls, no letters. "I needed rest, I needed to be held," Jane wrote.

"Tom felt that because he had encouraged me to go [to Vietnam], he was responsible for the trouble I'd gotten into, and he promised to try to make it up to me. Both of us realized that it had been a mistake for me to go alone. But I never felt that he was responsible. I hate buck passers."

• • •

The following day, Jane held another press conference at the Drake
Hotel on Park Avenue. By this time the text of more of her broadcasts from Hanoi had been reprinted in the newspapers, along
with the slow-motion film footage of Jane sitting on the antiaircraft
gun; it was playing on ABC-TV news. The *New York Post* captioned
the image "Hanoi Jane," and that became imprinted in the public's
mind.

(Later critics would say Hanoi Jane's classic film moment was as emblematic as Henry Fonda's last close-up in *The Grapes of Wrath* or Peter Fonda zooming off to his death on the highway as Mister America
in *Easy Rider.*)

The press conference at the Drake was mobbed — and the questions
that followed her little film on the POWs and the bombing of the dikes
weren't especially friendly. One reporter asked, "You've been called a
traitor — how do you respond?"

"What is a traitor? What is a patriot?" was her angry retort. "I cried
every day when I was in Vietnam. I cried for the Vietnamese and I
cried for the Americans too. The bombs are falling on Vietnam but
this is an American tragedy."

Someone else called out, "Were you used as a propaganda tool?"
With that Jane exploded, "Do you think they are blowing up their own
buildings? Bombing their own dikes? Mutilating their women and
children in order to move America?"

David Halberstam attended the press conference, and years later he
was still almost apoplectic about it. "Fonda started lecturing us about
the history of Vietnam. I couldn't believe it. She wasn't that smart. And
she was in way over her head. I've been in Nam. My best friend was
Bernie Fall, who had been killed there. Fonda isn't a politician. She is a
movie star." But as for her role in the 1970 antiwar protests, Halberstam
said: "I'd have to admit she was a — footnote. A one-sentence footnote.
But this woman is not a politician. I repeat: This is a stupid fucking
actress." His colleague Morley Safer from *60 Minutes* also questioned
Jane's importance. But Gloria Emerson, the only women reporter covering Vietnam for the *New York Times,* thought Jane had "terrific impact. She spoke out against the war with great courage and eloquence."

Near the end of the press conference, another reporter asked what
she planned to do with the film once it was properly edited and the

soundtrack was put back in. She said she hoped she could distribute it everywhere.

But that didn't happen. The soundtrack remained in Paris, and after the New York press conference the film mysteriously disappeared. Was it lost? Was it stolen? Jane never found out.

The press, by and large, weren't giving Jane much attention for her trip to Vietnam. By the time she flew back to California, a small story, "Jane Fonda Appeal Reported by Hanoi," appeared on page 9 of the *Times* on July 15, and this was followed by an even smaller story reporting that the State Department had rebuked her for going. *Time* and *Newsweek* ignored the trip until Fonda returned, and then they made little of it. As for her broadcasts — they were never heard in their entirety, but some of her statements were quoted in newspapers, especially her scathing comments about Nixon as a war criminal. This enraged Republicans and supporters of the war; by now hatred of Jane was almost visceral among right-wing members of Congress.

Resolutions to censure her were introduced in the Colorado and Maryland state legislatures. William Manchester, editor of the right-wing *New Hampshire Union Leader,* called for her to be tried for sedition and, if convicted, shot. Another congressman suggested her tongue be cut off.

Throughout this brouhaha Jane declared, "I welcome the Committee members studying the texts of my broadcast from North Vietnam. . . . I have done nothing against the law. . . . Furthermore, Nuremberg rules define Nixon's actions in Vietnam as war crimes and give every American citizen a legal basis and a moral right to resist what is being done in our names." The Justice Department agreed after studying the CIA reports of her radio transcripts; its lawyers could find nothing illegal in her actions. But the White House continued to press the Justice Department to bring treason charges against Jane, causing former Chief Justice Arthur Goldberg to comment, "I'm a great believer in the First Amendment. Miss Fonda hasn't said anything [in Hanoi] that she hasn't said in this country."

Still and all, Representatives Fletcher Thompson and Richard Ichord tried to push through a bill to make it a felony in the future for any American citizen to visit a country at war with the United States.

The measure was unofficially called the "Fonda amendment," and it would be tacked on to the 1950 Internal Security Act, but it didn't pass, probably because the question of whether the United States was really at war with North Vietnam had never been resolved in Congress.

Meanwhile in L.A., Jane's friends rallied, wanting to be there for her, but when they tried to make contact many of them were stopped by Tom Hayden. He screened everybody, including Mark Lane, the hyper-energetic lawyer who had been with Jane constantly ever since she'd become an activist. Lane couldn't believe the sudden cold shoulder treatment he was getting.

At the time he was running what he called a kind of "underground railroad" for cadets from the South Vietnamese air force, who were being trained in Texas to go back and fight the Vietcong. Many of them wanted to desert. Lane had already smuggled thirty of them into Canada.

He'd spent most of his own money to do that, and he was nearly broke when he finally managed to have a few words with Jane and asked her to give $1,000 for airline tickets to three more cadets who were ready to defect. Jane listened quietly and then said, "I appreciate what you're doing but I'm going to pass. From now on all my political contributions and activities will go through Tom."

Lane was sorry she couldn't help out, but he was even more upset by how her trip to Hanoi had "backfired. Jane was a very, very, very important person in the antiwar movement, and she could move many, many, many people. But she'd forfeited that role when the media turned her into 'Hanoi Jane.' It was heartbreaking."

Hayden for his part thought the hostility triggered by her trip was shocking. He had listened to the broadcasts, and her talk of bombed-out villages was the way she talked at home. "If it was anything [the broadcasts] were an expression of naiveté, certainly not treason."

As for Jane, she decided the trip to North Vietnam had changed her life. One night she stood naked in their bedroom and told Hayden she wanted to have a child by him. She was very emotional about it. She said that while she was touring North Vietnam she was introduced to women who had been in labor during the air strikes. As bombs fell they would cry, "Nixon, we fight you with all the joys of a woman in childbirth!" Jane declared she wanted that same kind of dedication and purpose in her life in America. If she and Tom had a child, it would be a way of cementing their love and expressing solidarity with their brothers and sisters in Vietnam. Hayden agreed "with a tearful smile."

A week or so after she returned to L.A., she and Donald Sutherland attended a screening of the movie of *F.T.A.* After they left the theater in Westwood, a group of protesters confronted her with a 1967 popular poster of Jane half-nude on a beach in France. Scrawled across it were the words NAKED CAME THE TRAITOR. Jane ignored the protesters, and she and Sutherland slipped into a waiting car.

F.T.A. was pulled from the theater the day after it opened, no reason given (although reviews had not been very good). *Steelyard Blues* was equally disappointing at the box office — it opened a week later. One critic noted, "After a significant portrayal of a hooker in *Klute* why does Fonda repeat herself in a film that isn't worth watching? *Steelyard Blues* is almost as big a bomb as the recent *F.T.A.* documentary, if that is possible."

Jane moved on, caught up in the excitement and emotion that Tom engendered. "He was fired up to launch the Indochina Peace Campaign," Fred Branfman recalled, "and he got heavyweight people involved." Meanwhile the political smear campaign mounted against Jane by Nixon and Hoover continued. She was surveilled constantly in spite of the fact that the FBI had assessed Jane's and Dr. Spock's files and reached the conclusion to "discontinue surveillance." But it continued, as did the commentary. In one of her rare press conferences First Lady Pat Nixon scolded Jane for going to Hanoi. "She should have told North Vietnam to stop fighting!"

Eventually the smear campaign was taken up by the likes of the American Legion and the Veterans of Foreign Wars. "The attacks on me were not so much from Vietnam vets as they were from veterans of the Korean War or World War II," Jane said.

That summer Jane began to receive assassination threats directly. One letter said in part, "Someday sometime somehow whenever you are in the right place at the right time a shot will ring out ending your life."

In July 1972 she and Hayden campaigned briefly for George McGovern, the Democratic candidate for president. McGovern's people didn't welcome Jane's endorsement, believing that her "traitor" image might damage his chances. Her involvement in American politics occurred during what was probably the most Hollywood-inflected presidential election ever: Nixon versus McGovern. Robert Redford was promoting his personal project, *The Candidate,* with a mock campaign swing, and Warren Beatty pioneered the rock benefit to establish himself as candidate George McGovern's most important fundraiser as well as close adviser. Meanwhile Republicans pulled together a collection of old stars like John Wayne, Frank Sinatra, Charlton Heston, and Bob Hope. The youngest of the Hollywood Nixonites was Clint Eastwood, whom the president had just appointed to the National Council on the Arts.

In August Jane accompanied Tom Hayden to the Republican convention in Miami. Thousands of antiwar activists massed in the streets in downtown Miami. By the afternoon of the first day there were 3,500 demonstrators milling around Flamingo Park. A line of Florida highway patrol cars with four troopers in each car stretched for four city blocks. On the second day 3,000 antiwar activists, including Tom and Jane, circled the convention hall crying out, "Murderers — delegates kill!" to the convention goers.

At the same time 1,300 Vietnam vets led by three disabled vets in wheelchairs conducted a silent march to the Republican headquarters at the Fontainebleau Hotel where Ron Kovic, leader of the march, addressed the delegates assembled outside.

His speech was a scream of rage. He'd started off as an idealistic American kid, he told the throng. He thought he was defending his country when he went to Vietnam. He ended up betrayed, humiliated, neglected, and furious. He was paralyzed from the chest down — his spine had been severed; he was in frequent pain and so he boozed and fought with everyone and was in despair until he stopped being contemptuous of the war protestors and became an activist himself through Vietnam Veterans Against the War.

"You have lied to us too long," he shouted. "You may have taken our bodies but you haven't taken our minds."

Jane was inspired by these words and the image of the angry young man with the ponytail sitting so tall in his wheelchair. She began imagining a film she could make that would not only dramatize the disabled vets' plight but dramatize what was happening to their wives as well.

In the fall, Jane and Hayden went out on the road with their newly formed grass-roots organization, the Indochina Peace Campaign. The idea was to refocus the antiwar movement into energizing local communities around the United States to vote against Nixon.

Jane wrote, "I vividly recall the day Tom sat on the edge of our bed while I cut off his long braid. The event had a ceremonial, rite-of-passage quality: We were leaving behind our counterculture trappings and reentering the mainstream; it wouldn't do if the way we looked turned people off to what we were saying. So I trimmed Tom's hair, bought him a suit and tie, exchanged his rubber sandals for brown leather, and got myself a couple of wrinkle-proof conservative outfits."

The tour began on Labor Day at the Ohio State Fair, emblematic of Hayden's desire to appeal to Middle Americans. They touched down in ninety cities. Jane said, "[It] was the most fulfilling experience of my life up to then. I was living full out, every neuron fired up, every bit of energy being tapped. I wasn't just speaking; I was watching and listening and learning every day, committing every ounce of everything I had to what I believed in, and doing it with someone I loved and admired alongside scores of kindred spirits."

"The trip was another testament to Fonda's extraordinary power to bring her views to the public eye," *L.A. Times* reporter Ron Brownstein wrote. "Armed with Hayden's strategy and Fonda's fame the couple provided a virtual shadow presidential campaign comprised of Fonda, Hayden, Holly Near, and former POW George Smith."

As the tour went on, they picked up other antiwar speakers along the way—*New York Times* reporter Gloria Emerson; Pat Ellsberg (Daniel Ellsberg's wife); Frances FitzGerald, whose book *Fire in the Lake* had just won the Pulitzer Prize. Naturally the FBI created a file on IPC, labeling it a "recently organized Commie infiltration front group."

When the election was over, Nixon had won by a landslide. By then Jane and Hayden were living together in her Laurel Canyon house; it was a hotbed of activity. Friends and coworkers from the Indochina

Peace Campaign came and went as well as members of the "Chicago Seven," who had been found guilty of promoting riots during the Chicago convention in 1968.

In November of 1972 the verdicts were overturned. Hayden had been tireless in pulling together all the evidence needed, and he'd already published a book on the ordeal called *Trial*.

But he wasn't working and she had few movie offers; she was sure it was because she was politically controversial. She had also just found out she was pregnant. So when Joseph Losey asked her to act in *A Doll's House* she agreed immediately.

Losey was a talented blacklisted American director who'd been living in exile in London since the 1950s, collaborating with Harold Pinter on movies like *The Go-Between* and *The Servant*. Jane was initially enthusiastic about working with him, but her enthusiasm evaporated after she became allied with another member of the *Doll's House* cast, the French actress Delphine Seyrig, who was an outspoken feminist. Seyrig had read the Ibsen screenplay (adapted by David Mercer) and found it seriously flawed. She discovered that all the male characters who were somewhat shadowy in the original had been built up in the screenplay and the women had been pared down, except for Nora. Jane agreed, and when she flew to Roros, the beautiful snowy town in Norway, to begin filming, she brought her friend Nancy Dowd along to do rewrites on the screenplay. Also accompanying Jane were Tom Hayden, little Vanessa, and her nanny, Dot.

"Every night we would work together, 'my gaggle of feminists,'" Jane told *Village Voice* critic Molly Haskell. "We were trying to get the most important things back into the script. What I wanted to do was to show from my years in France that women can have an external façade that seems frivolous and superficial but is actually serious. Nora was a vital intelligent woman waiting to explode."

In the mornings before shooting began she would present pages of notes and demands to Losey. Jane added, "The strangest thing happened, I found I had to *become Nora* with Joe Losey. I would bat my eyelashes at him to make it seem to him what we wanted were his ideas. . . ."

Losey told friends that working with Jane was the worst experience of his entire life. "Jane was a fearsome presence — *electric*." Soon a war broke out between the men and women in the cast. Jane refused to socialize with anyone save her inner circle.

Jane said she didn't socialize because she "wanted to be with Tom. The men in the cast were drunk most evenings — they painted us as a conspiracy of dykes — they pitted us against each other. Losey never had the guts to confront me — he wrote me love letters, attacked the women in less powerful positions."

Throughout she insisted, "I was always very professional. I knew my lines; I did my job." Losey admitted Jane's performance as Nora was superb: "Nuanced, vibrant, and impulsive — very, very forceful — but working with her was bloody awful."*

Midway through filming Roger Vadim arrived in Roros, ostensibly to see Vanessa. Jane decided to tell him she was pregnant by Hayden, and Vadim in turn told Jane he planned to marry the blond, beautiful, and very rich Catherine Schneider who'd accompanied him to Roros as well. She was pregnant with his child.

The two couples spent time together in the evenings along with Vanessa and her nanny. One night Losey sought Vadim out and they had a drink together. "You lived with Fonda for over six years," the director marveled, "and you seem in such good shape! How did you manage it?"

As soon as filming ended on *A Doll's House* in late December, Jane and Hayden flew to Oslo to appear at a huge peace rally. At the rally they heard news of the relentless "Christmas bombings" in Hanoi and Haiphong. While speaking to the crowd, Jane was doused with a can of red paint. Undaunted, she wiped the paint from her hair and clothes and continued with her speech. Photographers had a field day snapping pictures of her.

She and Hayden now planned to marry. They'd decided to do so only after Hayden had phoned his mother about the baby and she'd demanded, "Aren't you getting married?" They hadn't even considered it, he said, but Mrs. Hayden pointed out that as a couple they were

---

* When *A Doll's House* was shown at Cannes the following year, critics called Jane's performance remarkable. Molly Haskell wrote, "To this emblematic feminist, Fonda brings her own reverberations, the evolution of an actress-and-woman from Papa's (and Vadim's) little girl to up-front militant."

controversial enough. "Don't add to your problems." They agreed and called a press conference to announce their plans.

Once back in California, Jane and Vadim worked out a joint custody agreement about Vanessa with their lawyer, Richard Rosenthal. They'd rented a suite at the Beverly Wilshire to conduct the meeting; it was dusk. "For some reason nobody bothered to turn on the lights so we ended up speaking in the dark," Rosenthal remembered. "Although everything was cordial there was something terribly sad about it."

Jane flew to the Dominican Republic so she would be able to get her divorce and be free to marry Hayden. There was one more hurdle. Tom refused to sign the prenuptial agreement Jane had Rosenthal draw up. "It offended his sensibilities," a friend said. Jane didn't want to upset him so she dropped the issue. She already seemed intimidated by him. "She was walking on eggshells," another friend said.

28

O N J A N U A R Y 19, 1973, Jane and Tom were married in the living
room of her modest Laurel Canyon home. About forty friends
were present — a mix of antiwar activists, Vietnamese friends,
and show business colleagues. The ceremony was conducted by Reverend Richard York, an Episcopal priest, who concluded by saying,
"Will you, Jane, marry Tom, and will you try in the marriage to grow
together, to be honest, to share responsibility for your children, and to
maintain a sense of humor?"

Jane smiled her dazzling smile; she had written that line herself because she and Hayden had a reputation for being totally humorless.
After the ceremony Vietnamese songs were sung and an Irish jig was
performed in honor of Hayden's forebears (and his tiny chain-smoking
mother). The wedding cake was inscribed with the Vietnamese word
for peace.

Throughout the evening, Jane's devoted press agent, Steve Jaffe,
snapped pictures of the happy couple and their friends.

Hayden had been adamant about keeping the press out; "this is
private and personal," he kept saying. But Steve said the photographs
"would be just for them — it's my present," he insisted. Jane wanted a
record. So Steve kept snapping. "I must have taken close to 500 expo-
sures," he said.

He remembered the "smell of pot very heavy in the air." The guests
lingered for more wine and talk, everybody quite stoned and relaxed.
Vanessa, age four, sat on Grandpa Henry Fonda's lap looking very solemn. Fonda approved of Tom Hayden. Days before they'd gotten together for hamburgers at a local greasy spoon, and the meeting had

gone relatively well. Afterward Fonda had said to Jane, "This fellow is ambitious, energetic, and smart. You'll be a great helpmate to him."

Peter didn't agree. He disliked Tom Hayden. He thought his new brother-in-law was wily and manipulative and totally out for himself. He was worried that Jane would eventually be terribly hurt. Since Jane's return from Vietnam she had received numerous death threats. Just before the ceremony he decided to call on some of his friends from the Hells Angels and had them encircle the Laurel Canyon house on their motorcycles. They remained there until the wedding party was over.

By early the next morning the word was out that Jane Fonda had married Tom Hayden. Steve Jaffe recalled that his phone started ringing at the crack of dawn. Everybody in the world wanted a picture of the wedding. When Steve refused, several wire services threatened to print a picture of Jane wearing the coolie hat she'd bought in Hanoi. Steve kept refusing. He phoned Jane but was unable to get through to her. He was told that "Jane and Tom were in bed and didn't want to be disturbed."

By early evening Steve agreed to release one image of the couple to the wire services. He went to a camera shop he knew and got the negative developed and printed.

The following day he contacted Jane and Tom to explain what had happened. He was surprised by how displeased they were. They accused him of exploiting their celebrity and of making money off them, then they hung up. Steve did not hear from them again until weeks later when he was told, in effect, that his services were no longer needed.

Bit by bit Hayden got rid of all the people who'd been working with Jane for the past three years. He seemed to feel comfortable only with *his* friends.

He'd begun to reconcile with members of the Red Family commune like Bruce Gilbert, who'd run the Red Family nursery and who'd moved from Berkeley to L.A. to help run the newly opened IPC office in Santa Monica along with Carol Kurtz, who later became a lawyer. Carol and her husband, Jack Nichol, also Red Family members, ultimately shared the shabby two-family house Hayden and Jane would eventually buy in Ocean Park.

. . .

On January 23, 1973, a cease-fire agreement was signed in Paris, and the United States agreed to withdraw all its troops from Vietnam and supply Saigon with military and economic aid. But under the terms agreed to by the Nixon administration, North Vietnamese units remained in position in the South.

Days after the accord was signed Hanoi released more than 102 POWs, and soon one could watch them on TV, emerging from transport planes and looking gaunt and frail. They received a hero's welcome. Many of them soon began to recount horror stories of how they'd been tortured in the camps.

The Pentagon had carefully chosen a small group of hard-line officers — the most conservative in the military — to participate in a tightly controlled script called Operation Homecoming, which would create the impression that torture was routine in the camps (the vast number of POWs refused to go along with this story).

For the next couple of weeks an unending stream of press conferences was organized around the country with these hard-line officers — all of whom not only described the terrible conditions of the camps and the brutality they'd been subjected to but also badmouthed the antiwar movement as anti-American.

With the Watergate scandal bubbling to the surface and the Vietnam War slipping into an embarrassing defeat, Nixon needed a boost — Shana Alexander in *Newsweek* commented that the return of the POWs resembled a "carefully prepared TV commercial on behalf of the White House."

Then came the charge that some of the POWs had been tortured and beaten unless they'd agreed to meet with Jane Fonda and Ramsey Clark. Jane immediately denied the charges on TV, stating that the POWs had volunteered to meet with her. She called the POWs who'd told the torture story that implicated her "liars and hypocrites" and said they were being used as "pawns by Nixon to rewrite history." She added that the true heroes of the war were the young men who refused to fight — who resisted the military.

A barrage of criticism erupted from around the country at Jane. Secretary of Defense Elliot Richardson called her remarks "egregious and insulting to all returning prisoners." The *Wall Street Journal* referred to her as outlandish, shrill, and repugnant. But Jane stuck to her guns — and repeated her charges against Nixon's "POW pawns."

To undercut her comments the Pentagon quickly arranged a press conference for David Hoffman, one of the POWs who'd met with Jane in July of 1972. ABC, NBC, and CBS covered the press conference and broadcast his remarks. He maintained he did not want to meet Fonda so the Vietnamese had tortured him by hanging him from a hook in the ceiling by his broken arm. He admitted he had met Fonda, but only because he had been tortured, and then he went on to repudiate everything he had said in his Hanoi news conference against the bombing.

His remarks got huge play in the media and his story was widely circulated. After that he refused to ever talk again about the so-called torture he'd undergone. Jane repeatedly tried to reach him, but he would never answer her calls. She remembered distinctly that when she met him with the other POWs he showed her that his arm had healed. Indeed she'd filmed him and also phoned his family to tell them he was okay when she returned to the United States.

When Nobel Prize–winning biologist Dr. George Wald heard Hoffman's claim of being tortured into meeting with Jane, he felt something wasn't right and came to Jane's defense. He had visited Hanoi in February 1972 and met Hoffman and tape-recorded their conversation. They talked about the condition of his arm. It was healing very nicely, and he said he was being treated well by his captors. Other activists met with Hoffman, too. In September 1972 he met with an American group made up of Reverend William Sloane Coffin Jr., Cora Weiss, and David Dellinger. To all of them his arm looked healthy.

Wald contacted the Pentagon and attempted to get his doubts about Hoffman's allegations to Defense Department officials, but he got no response. He also wrote a piece about it and sent it to *The New Yorker*, but they turned it down. It was obvious that the torture allegations were introduced to discredit Jane. But they also had a bigger political purpose. "They were used to deny reconstruction aid to Vietnam and to create images of the Vietnamese as barbaric," historian Mary Hershberger wrote.

In the *Times* Steve Roberts wrote, "The hard line officers exhibited an almost desperate belief that the Vietnam War had been worth it — and that Nixon had gained peace with honor."

The POW stories were the beginning of a long line of lies, ingredients that fed into the myth of the traitorous "Hanoi Jane." The vilifying of Jane Fonda took shape in the 1970s and in the next thirty years grew to gargantuan size. By 2002, with the advent of the Internet, there were seven thousand Jane Fonda hate sites.

In the meantime, Jane went on. Hayden was launching a national campaign for IPC (they would soon have offices in twenty-five cities) and Jane, despite being a lightning rod, was invaluable as a fundraiser. Together she and Hayden lobbied in Washington with other peace groups to prevail on Congress to cut government funding of the war. Everyone on the Hill came to hear them because of Jane. A veteran politician said, "Everyone came away impressed at how articulate and informed she was."

Still, it was an unsettling time for Jane — usually there was a phalanx of police and voluntary security guards circling her whenever she traveled because Hayden believed his wife's life was in constant danger. "He was quite starry-eyed about her," then-journalist Ken Kelly remembered. "He didn't want to lose her."

In the midst of her pregnancy, Hayden decided they should relocate their home closer to the IPC office in Ocean Park, a section of Santa Monica. "Sell my house? That I'd only had one year? I loved my house!" Jane wrote. "But more than anything I wanted to do what Tom thought was right. Though he never said so outright, I believe Tom felt that how you lived reflected whether you were pure in your politics . . . or just an armchair liberal."

She didn't even see the place before they bought it (for $45,000), and when she did, her heart sank as she moved through the dark little rooms of the shabby two-family house on Wadsworth Avenue. Outside, the narrow street was lined with old cars and battered vans. The other frame houses had enclosed porches and roofs sagging with age. The Pacific Ocean was two blocks away.

The entire place smelled of mildew, but she felt better as soon as she painted the walls rainbow psychedelic colors — red, orange, yellow, and blue. She put plants and flowers everywhere and mixed thrift shop furniture with fine antiques.

She and Hayden lived on Wadsworth for close to ten years. For close to ten years they slept on a mattress on the second floor and ate and worked at a big rough-hewn wooden refectory table covered with a Madras cloth. Jane's Oscar served as a bookend.

To save money they rented the ground-floor apartment to Carol Kurtz and Jack Nichol, who moved in with their little son. "Carol in particular was a pillar of support, stability, and tenderness. . . . [She and Jack were] the only other couple we worked with who had started a family. . . . I actually loved being there. This was community living of a kind I'd never experienced."

"Jane loves her shack," Henry Fonda noted. "It's her new reality." And it was. She enjoyed shopping at the local supermarket, eating pizza barefoot near the beach, and driving her battered Volvo to pick up Vanessa at her school. Right up until a week before she had her baby she was doing her forty-five-minute slide shows about Vietnamese women: how Ho Chi Minh connected the movements of women's liberation and Vietnamese revolutionary nationalism. She'd invariably pass hostile picket lines, the picketers calling out threats. Sometimes she was burned in effigy. Hayden told *Playboy* he was worried "Jane might be martyred like Martin Luther King or the Kennedys." He felt the public couldn't reconcile Barbarella turning into a revolutionary.

After her incendiary remarks about POWs, life was not that easy. Their little house was often under siege. Their record player was stolen. Jane had to put wire over the windows because so many people threw things, especially rotten eggs.

When the pressures got too great, she'd sneak up to the attic and light up a joint. Hayden wouldn't allow smoking in the house so Jane hid her drugs in various places. Once a friend borrowed her Volvo, and the police stopped the car and discovered a bag of weed under the seat. Jane had to go down to the station and pay a $500 fine.

In the midst of all this, she decided to stop binging and purging; she was tired of being so depressed and irritable. She was sure that by now many of her unwise and impulsive decisions, her outbursts, and even the POW remarks had been triggered by the bulimia.

But what finally made her stop was the realization that "my life was important to me — the choice was between being a good wife and mother or a bulimic. I wasn't as good a mother to Vanessa as I wanted to be. How could I be? I was preoccupied with food." For years Jane had rarely eaten a meal, subsisting on dozens of vitamins prescribed by doctors. Like most bulimics, she overused vitamins in the mistaken belief that they replaced the nutrients she kept vomiting up.

She went "cold turkey." "It was tough. I had to learn how to eat all over again." She began a regime of three small meals a day, mostly stir-fried vegetables, fresh fish, or chicken. She had to fight the constant urge to vomit. For a while she suffered cold sweats and insatiable cravings for her favorite foods (roast chicken and Toll House cookies). She kept battling feelings of hopelessness and despair. She went to a psychiatrist. She attended support groups. Week by week the bulimic urges subsided — but she became a chain smoker again.

Hayden was unaware that Jane was struggling to overcome her bulimia. "I never talked about it to him." Vadim hadn't known either. Only Andreas Voutsinas, who'd served as mother/father surrogate, had witnessed her obsession with food and her obsession with keeping thin at all costs.

"I didn't really win the fight until January 1974," Jane said. During her last month of pregnancy she began classes given by Femmy DeLyser, a nurse with special training in obstetrics. Femmy gave lectures to expectant couples in her sun-drenched living room in Santa Monica.

Jane (and often Hayden) attended the classes religiously, and they learned the breathing exercises and how to relax so that when the contractions finally came and Jane went into labor, she felt the pain but none of the panic or the loneliness she'd experienced when she was giving birth to Vanessa.

The natural childbirth was psychologically and spiritually healing. Hayden and Femmy were with her. In spite of the pain, she felt as if she had control over her body.

Troi (né Hayden) was born on July 7, 1973. Incredibly, he was originally named after Nguyen Van Troi, the Vietcong martyr who tried to assassinate Robert McNamara when he was visiting South Vietnam in 1966. Jane and Hayden quickly realized the name Troi would not exactly be an asset, so they changed their son's name to Troy. They also felt he shouldn't be burdened by the last name Hayden or Fonda either, so they gave him his grandmother's maiden name as a surname: Garity.

• • •

Hayden drove Jane and the baby home from the hospital and they went directly to bed. Hayden remembered lying naked beside their baby while Jane lay next to him, "blissful and tired," and he thought, "This house is my cave." He began whispering words of love to Troy, and then he put him on his stomach and realized that he and Jane had created a new life together, and he started to sob. The following day he impulsively sent snapshots of his newborn son to his father in Detroit along with a handwritten note. There was no reply.

Jane was exultant about becoming a mother again. Troy's birth had a profound effect on her. And it was the same for Hayden, too. They both doted on Troy, showering him with love and attention. A friend recalled, "Having Troy meant more to them than just having a baby. Troy was emblematic of all the things they were fighting for: a new order in America, a place where men and women could be respected equally. . . ." If anything, Troy's birth deepened Jane's commitment to the marriage and their causes. She became intensely zeroed in on what exactly it was that motivated her and what she wanted to do.

During the next weeks Vanessa Vadim observed her new brother from the sidelines. She watched her mother tenderly nursing Troy, rocking him back and forth in her arms and calling him her "love child."

Vanessa did not feel a part of the Hayden family. She would always feel apart and detached. She retreated, shuttling back and forth to Paris to be with her father, whom she adored. She began addressing Vadim as *Maman,* and she sent him Mother's Day cards. Jane was hurt. Vadim thought Jane was subconsciously re-creating the atmosphere she'd experienced as a little girl when her mother had rejected her in favor of Peter, but Jane refused to believe she was doing this.

In October of 1973 Hayden was cleared of all contempt charges in the Chicago Seven conspiracy trial. "Free at last!" he cried exuberantly as he carried baby Troy on his shoulders out of the federal court building in Chicago.

Throughout the remainder of that year he and Jane toured ten states for IPC, demanding that Nixon cut off all funding to South Vietnam. They always traveled with Troy; Jane was still breastfeeding. Sometimes she'd nurse Troy as she sat and spoke with students. A junior at

Northwestern remembered, "There was Jane Fonda with her blouse open, her baby sucking at her nipple, telling us about Nixon spying and wiretapping American citizens."

At Wellesley students jammed the auditorium to hear Jane talk about the Watergate Senate hearings, which were documenting more and more official criminality.

Afterward Jane tried to slip out a side door to avoid the press. She and Hayden met in an alley (he'd been rather sullenly baby-sitting Troy backstage). Suddenly a pack of photographers emerged from behind some parked cars with cameras poised.

Hayden told them angrily to "fuck off!" He raised an object over his head and appeared ready to throw it at the paparazzi. "The object turned out to be Troy's empty bassinet," a *Time* reporter noted dryly.

Jane was having an increasingly difficult time with Hayden, although she wouldn't admit it. "He was fucking jealous of how famous she was," the actor Peter Boyle commented. When Barbara Walters asked Tom, "What is the hardest part about living with Jane Fonda?" he'd snapped, "The attention. No one person deserves that much attention."

Jane always tried to melt into the background when they were together, but that was impossible because whenever they were together, all eyes were on her. Still, she usually managed to defuse his black spirits. She'd had plenty of experience coping with her father's moodiness. And at that point she could handle Hayden's drinking. "He was a closet drinker in those days," reporter Jack Newfield said. Soon Jane became Hayden's enabler as she had been Vadim's. She endured her role silently, except once she did confess to a high school friend, "Oh, God, why do I always marry alcoholics?"

That fall Jean-Luc Godard's *Tout Va Bien*, which she'd made with Yves Montand, had opened at the New York Film Festival to mixed reviews. Much of the criticism was focused on the feature that accompanied it: a fifty-five-minute filmed essay Godard and his collaborator, Jean-Pierre Gorin, had added entitled *Letter to Jane*, which excoriated Jane's controversial trip to North Vietnam. Once again the public was reminded of "Hanoi Jane."

The piece is an analysis of a single grainy black-and-white news close-up of Jane listening intently to the words of a Vietnamese peasant. The picture was taken by Guillaume during her trip to Hanoi and published in *L'Express.*

Jean-Pierre Gorin (in a droning voice-over) zeroed in on that one photograph in compelling and compulsive detail, asking all sorts of unanswerable questions, such as what exactly does the expression on Jane Fonda's face *mean*? They're criticizing not Jane but "the function of Jane." They find her behavior in Hanoi wanting, and as for her expression, "It's an expression of an expression and it isn't even her own." (According to the film critic Kent Jones in an eloquent essay, it seems to echo the compassionate look originated by Henry Fonda in *The Grapes of Wrath.*) They ask why the in-focus actress is so ideologically fuzzy while the out-of-focus Vietnamese peasant is so ideologically clear.

More than anything Godard seemed to be saying that Jane had given the American antiwar movement the stamp of celebrity — she heralded the advent of celebrity advocacy, which in turn meant that her motives, her intentions, her sense of strategy, and the ultimate impact of her sitting on the gun or doing radio broadcasts were still open to questioning.

But the lesson Godard kept harping on after staring at Jane's anguished close-up for fifty-five minutes was that it may be better for Americans, especially celebrities, to keep their mouths shut when it comes to politics — don't try to dictate solutions to the world.

The film didn't deal with the cries of "treason" on the part of American congressmen or the harassment of the FBI. Why did Jane arouse such ire? Jane herself had an explanation, which she gave to David Frost. She speculated that the reason so many people disliked her was because she had chosen to break out of her role as sex symbol and think independently. "I stopped being an object. . . . A lot of people — especially men — didn't like that." In another interview Hayden added: "When your fantasy life is threatened and Barbarella becomes a revolutionary, it is very upsetting."

The bottom line, however, was that Jane simply would not go away. "Jane Fonda cannot be dismissed," *Washington Post* reporter Nick von Hoffman said; "the public remains fascinated with her in all her permutations." If Godard found her ridiculous, others found her increasingly impressive.

Milton Viorst, the *New Yorker* columnist, went to Georgetown University to hear this "Hanoi Jane" person speak and see for himself what all the controversy was about. "Some two thousand students had packed the hall. Daniel Ellsberg was on the program but it was Jane Fonda without makeup and in blue jeans they had come to see. She held them captivated. I was a little surprised by her manner — no dramatics, no hip slang, no affectation." Jane's message was that the United States, despite the withdrawal of American troops, was perpetuating a brutal war in Vietnam by its huge subsidies to the unpopular regime of President Thieu. "Most Americans think the Vietnam War is over," she said. "Our problem begins with letting Americans know that thousands of Vietnamese are still being killed every month with American arms and American money. How do you end a war that people don't even know about?"

As far as Jane was concerned, there were equally important issues to deal with, such as Tom Hayden's image. He was seriously considering running for public office. Ever since the 1972 McGovern campaign he had committed to "working within the system." By now he had lobbied Congress enough to know the system, he told Jane.

He had been following Jerry Brown's fight to become governor of California, and he would soon write about the campaign for *Rolling Stone.*

He related to Brown personally and they would soon become close friends; they were both rebels and they were both Irish Catholic. Hayden related to Brown's new-generation theme, and he felt energized by the possibilities of being in the mainstream.

After Brown got elected, he began consulting Hayden and reaching out to him for advice regarding labor and economic strategies. Brown was constantly over at the house. Many thought he was more interested in Jane.

Jane totally supported Tom's political aspirations. After all, he had given her security by supplying her with more confidence and the acceptance of his movement buddies, something she had been starving for ever since her affair with Fred Gardner back in 1970. Hayden was helping her refine *her* political ideology and soften her rhetoric (he would occasionally tell her to shut up). He also convinced her she shouldn't write her autobiography just yet. She'd received a hefty advance from a publisher, which she now returned. It was better that she focus on their political concerns as a team, he said.

So Jane set out to make Tom Hayden visible after a long eclipse. She would make him famous; she believed that as a couple they could "make history."

With the help of Pat Kingsley, and later Stephen Rivers, two of the canniest press agents in Hollywood, Jane orchestrated story after story about Tom Hayden and herself in every major magazine and newspaper in the country. The first one appeared in the *L.A. Times* three weeks after Troy's birth.

Jane would be relentless with the press. Stories about "Tom and Jane" would appear without letup for the next seventeen years. (It was never "Jane and Tom" because Tom insisted on his name coming first.)

Many of the first interviews with reporters took place in their ramshackle house. As Jane spoke of the ins and outs of New Left politics, she might be nursing Troy and then handing him over to Hayden for burping.

Occasionally they were referred to as "Beauty and the Beast" because Jane's radiant persona contrasted so sharply with Hayden's pock-marked dishevelment.

Although the couple never displayed any show of affection — no kisses or hugs — Barbara Harrison noted in *Redbook* magazine, "Jane's eyes turn two shades darker blue when she is with Hayden and she blushes like a girl when she greets him. They never touch but I feel like a voyeur."

Jane liked to chatter on about his "impishness," which nobody else picked up on. In the early days of her marriage she was deliriously happy.

"I was both in love with and in awe of Tom," she wrote. "For me he was friend, mentor, lover, savior, pillar of support, and example of what I hoped I could become. I saw him as a pure person who could not be corrupted."

Others, however, were already calling him a "total user." Gore Vidal said scathingly, "Tom Hayden gives opportunism a bad name."

The fact was Hayden had quickly realized that being married to Jane Fonda gave him a kind of cachet and access he'd never experienced before. "Tom went a little bananas," another friend said.

Vadim, who observed the marriage from the sidelines, thought "the whole thing was like a movie but Jane was living it." The events and the people they associated with were designed to get "ink." There were confabs with politicos (always photographed); intimate dinners with the likes of Governor Brown, Costa-Gavras, and Dan Ellsberg; and the cheering throngs mixed with boos whenever "Tom and Jane" appeared in public. "She was acting the part of Jane Fonda in a big adventure and Tom was the hero of her movie."

Every morning she and Hayden checked their battered Volvo for bombs. The couple did have grandiose fantasies about themselves. Tom wanted to be president; Jane sometimes saw herself as a martyr. "If it had been the 1950s I would have been electrocuted like the Rosenbergs," she declared once.

29

JANE REMAINED CONCERNED about her FBI surveillance. She decided to do something about it after muckraking Washington columnist Jack Anderson sent her one of her FBI files. Anderson had just completed a series on the federal government's surveillance of prominent Americans like Joe Namath and Martin Luther King. During the course of his research he had obtained one of Jane's FBI files from an unnamed source. "It was so thick you could choke a hippopotamus," Anderson said. "It was stuffed to overflowing with memos, discussions of her personal finances, children, travels, all sorts of gossip . . . information that had been obtained illegally."

In October 1973, supported by the American Civil Liberties Union, Jane called reporters to the Los Angeles Press Club to announce that she was suing the president. She said she had filed a million-dollar suit against Richard Nixon, Henry Kissinger, Charles Colson, and what she called "the entire Watergate crew" for conspiring to destroy her credibility and disrupt her life. She described the FBI's plot as "part of an organized systematic attempt by the Nixon administration to discredit me, to make us appear irresponsible, dangerous, and foul-mouthed. I never have and never will raise money or spend money for guns. . . . I don't use foul language and I never said I wanted to kill Nixon. Those are totally fabricated for the purpose of slandering me and making me appear a violent and irresponsible person."

The suit wasn't settled until 1979 when the government agreed to release all the files it had gathered on her and admitted wrongdoing in her case. Jane dropped the financial claim against the government. "We got what we wanted; we were trying to illustrate a principle."

Then there was another reality: Jane was completely supporting the Hayden household. This irked Peter, who would occasionally zoom up to the house on his motorcycle, yelling, "Hayden, get a job!"

Jane ignored her brother's jibes. She worried about their dwindling bank account. Her lawyer, Richard Rosenthal, kept reminding her that she was spending $7,000 a month and still owed back taxes. His advice: start generating some income or cut back on expenses (she was virtually bankrolling IPC and its staff).

Jane started telling people she was being "graylisted" because of her politics and she couldn't find any socially relevant scripts. "The studios were scared of her—no doubt about it," said Paula Weinstein, Jane's onetime agent and closest friend. "And she no longer socialized in Hollywood; she didn't like to play that game."

Paula was the daughter of the left-wing producer Hannah Weinstein. Her godmother was the legendary playwright Lillian Hellman. Defiant and beautiful, Paula was reading scripts for then-agent Mike Medavoy.

Paula had met Jane when she was still a student at Columbia in 1970, right after *Klute* and at the height of the antiwar movement. "Jane was my idol," she said. "Here was this great actress who was also against the war like all my friends. She was so brave and challenging. I've never understood why she isn't taken more seriously. She's always had the guts to live her life in public—to let us see her *becoming* Jane Fonda. She's like Marlon, a true original. She genuinely wants to help people. She pushes and promotes causes. She really can make a difference because of who she is; she really understands how to use her fame."

Starting in 1973, Weinstein began talking to Jane on the phone about various projects and reading scripts, which Jane insisted Hayden should read first "because he notices what's wrong with them."

Paula sent Jane the galleys of Lillian Hellman's memoir *Pentimento*. A few years before, Hellman, angered that she was not listed along with Arthur Miller and Tennessee Williams as one of America's finest living playwrights, engineered her own renaissance by batting out two memoirs in succession. Each was a huge bestseller, and suddenly her turbulent life — as a writer, dramatist, and activist, and as mystery writer Dashiell Hammett's longtime lover — was being acknowledged all over again.

There were four portraits in *Pentimento.* The one that sparked Jane's interest was the story of the playwright's friendship with an elegant aristocrat named Julia, an antifascist. Hellman claimed that Julia had asked her to smuggle $50,000 into Nazi Germany in 1939 to save Jewish refugees from concentration camps.

Paula thought Jane would want to play Julia, but Jane wanted to play Hellman "because I was fascinated by her egotism." "She had this incredible ego, which she *had* to have to make it in a man's world." Hellman, however, wanted Barbra Streisand to play her. Streisand was unconventional, "*and* she's Jewish and I like the way she smokes!" Streisand was talked out of the role by her agent, Sue Mengers, so Hellman reluctantly agreed on Fonda, although she wasn't sure "Jane had the *substance* to play me."

Julia took six years to make, but when it opened it was hailed as "the first female buddy movie." The whole time she worked on it, Jane thought about her deep friendship with Sue Sally Jones; she always kept a small picture of Sue Sally with her whenever she worked.

But what Jane really wanted to do was to make her own films, "films that were stylistically mainstream — films that Americans could relate to," but that would combine her personal interests with Hollywood's demands. In the evenings she, Nancy Dowd, and Bruce Gilbert, another Red Family alum who was running the IPC office, would sit in the house on Wadsworth Avenue and try to think up projects they could develop.

Jane had spent hours listening to the former soldier Ron Kovic, author of *Born on the Fourth of July,* talk about adjusting to life as a paralyzed Vietnam veteran. "Good idea for a movie," Jane thought. "We could wrap it around a sexy love story." In the summer of 1973, she paid her friend Nancy Dowd $4,000 to write a screenplay. Dowd had been an antiwar activist who'd had a romance with a disabled vet. She maintained that the original idea for *Coming Home* came out of that raw experience.

That same summer Jane and Bruce Gilbert joined forces and

formed IPC Films "to make movies which in turn could bankroll our concerns."

Jane also hoped to star in another movie with Peter and her father, set at the time of the American Revolution. She was keeping in close touch with her father now. They saw each other once a week — usually at his home in Bel Air, almost always with his wife, Shirlee, hovering nearby.

Jane was jealous of the fact that her father and Shirlee *talked*. "I never had a real long conversation with my dad in my entire life. . . . Dad wasn't about talking. . . . Then I'd meet somebody at a party and they'd tell me they'd had this great conversation on an airplane with my father. . . . He could be downright garrulous with perfect strangers but with his kids . . . never."

Jane just couldn't stop obsessing about her mythic father — dreaming about him. She simply could not disentangle from the Hydra-like hold he had on her. "Oh, I'd dream about him almost every night." She kept hoping he'd praise her for *something* (he never did). He admitted he didn't always agree with her politically, but he resented it when people wanted him to denounce her: "Hers is not my way of life, but I respect her right to say what she believes."

Jane had just declared her support for the Palestinian state in the wake of the Arab-Israeli War, and she was now being labeled an anti-Semite because she wouldn't back down. She insisted that she would rather leave acting than bow and scrape to various studio heads who were pro-Israel.

Her father winced but said nothing. Nor did he comment when she told him she planned to travel to North Vietnam to make a documentary on the rebirth of that country called *Introduction to the Enemy*; it would be the first film IPC would produce.

The distinguished cinematographer Haskell Wexler joined Jane, Hayden, and baby Troy, then nine months old, on a flight to Hanoi in April 1974. A moody, irascible man of strong opinions, Wexler had won two Oscars (for *Who's Afraid of Virginia Woolf?* and *Bound for Glory*, about Woody Guthrie). He'd met Tom Hayden in Chicago when he was filming his counterculture classic *Medium Cool* about the battles between the antiwar demonstrators and the police during the Democratic convention. He was the perfect person for the Haydens to team up with. "We were all radicals," he would say.

Wexler and Jane bonded immediately, "over our sense of privilege," she said (Wexler's father had made a fortune in electronics, which later became the Radio Shack empire).

Jane recalled that one morning at breakfast, "Haskell suddenly asked me, 'How did you do it? How did you give up everything?' I don't remember what I answered but of course I hadn't given up everything, although I knew what he meant. When you're born into privilege you live with an unending amount of tension and expectation. Are you not giving back enough? Are people suspicious of your motives? Are you suspicious of people's motives? It's a no-win situation. You forget about it and do what you believe in — at least that's what I've done."

The two weeks filming in North Vietnam were intense and emotional for everybody. Jane said, "We were trying to show the Vietnamese not as victims but as people." Near the very end they witnessed a bombing of the Bach Mai Hospital (Wexler actually filmed it), and several doctors they knew personally were killed. Hayden broke down and cried. In a review of *Introduction to the Enemy* in the *New York Times,* Nora Sayre wrote, "This pensive and moving film serves as a chapter of our own education about the Vietnamese past and the rhythm of life in that country now." Molly Haskell in the *Village Voice* called the film a "tiny jewel."

But *Variety* disagreed. Citing the sequences in which a crowd of locals watches Jane and Hayden toss around a Frisbee, the scene wherein Jane argues with a North Vietnamese man who defends the American people, and "the actress's constant use of an incongruously dippy smile to show her fondness for the peasantry," the reviewer invoked *Letter to Jane* as proof of Fonda's tendency for self-dramatization.

After they completed filming in North Vietnam, they flew to Paris to pick up Vanessa, who was staying with her father and his new wife, Catherine. Catherine had recently given birth to Vadim's son Vania. The Vadims had bought a luxurious apartment overlooking the Champ de Mars, the immense garden that extends from the Eiffel Tower to the École Militaire.

While Jane received leftist activists like Regis Debray, one of Che Guevara's intimates, in one opulent living room, the president of France, Valéry Giscard d'Estaing, held forth in another living room, fresh from an official dinner at the Élysée Palace.

Giscard was curious about Jane and made a point of wandering into the other living room to converse with her. While they were talking, Tom Hayden appeared from the kitchen holding a roast chicken leg in his hand. He plopped down on the floor next to Jane and proceeded to bite into it greedily, holding the greasy meat between his fingers.

"He was seated on this incredibly expensive Kenneth Noland rug my wife and I had bought in New York," Vadim wrote. "Catherine was going crazy. She was sure he was going to drop some food onto that carpet, but he didn't."

Around midnight Jane and Hayden went to bed in the guest room. Giscard stayed on for a nightcap. "These young American radicals," he murmured, shaking his head, "so relaxed, so casual . . ." One thought bothered him: "Do you think he will be President of the United States one day?"

Shirlee Fonda had phoned Jane in Paris to tell her that her father's heart had been fibrillating; he'd had a temporary pacemaker put in his chest. Instead of flying to L.A., Jane stopped off in New York and went directly to Lenox Hill Hospital. Peter joined her there.

Fonda was supposedly on the road to recovery, but he looked very frail and his skin was the color of putty. Only weeks before, he'd been starring on Broadway as Clarence Darrow to great acclaim. Jane wondered whether he would act again, or if he would ever be able to take that favorite New York walk of his — from 57th Street to 89th Street, up one side of Madison and down the other, dropping into the Whitney and the Guggenheim and various art galleries.

To cheer him up she and Peter discussed possible films all three of them could star in, including one based on Howard Fast's novel *Conceived in Liberty,* which was set during the Revolutionary War. George Stevens had agreed to direct it.

When she was assured by his cardiologist that her father was on the mend, she and Hayden moved to Washington, D.C., for six weeks to focus all their efforts on lobbying Congress to cut funding to South

Vietnam. But Jane remained worried about her father. She was on the phone to Shirlee a couple of times a day. Since she'd seen him he'd had a permanent pacemaker put in his chest.

"Tom was always very loving towards Jane when it came to Mr. Fonda," Carol Kurtz recalled, "tender, sympathetic—I think the father-daughter bond, the father-son bond, the importance of parents to children—it really got Tom where he lived."

Fonda made a slow recovery. Recuperating at his home in Bel Air, he shuffled about tending his plants and his vegetables as well as his beehives, which he kept behind his fruit trees. For a short while he returned to play Darrow in Los Angeles to sold-out houses.

In August 1974, Richard Nixon, who'd been elected by the largest popular margin in history less than two years earlier, was forced to resign the presidency to avoid impeachment for high crimes and misdemeanors.

Jane and Hayden sat glued to the TV set watching the president march stiffly across the White House lawn to the waiting helicopter. Climbing aboard, he gave his weird little salute before being choppered off to San Clemente.

30

THE EFFECT OF NIXON'S resignation on Jane's career was almost immediate. For years she had been speaking out against the war and Nixon's criminality — she'd been proven right on both counts. Her graylisting was over. Offers began slowly coming in, and Tom urged her to go back to acting full-time.

In January of 1975 she flew to Leningrad to work on *The Blue Bird*, her first bigtime Hollywood movie in five years. George Cukor would be directing, and the cast included Elizabeth Taylor, Ava Gardner, Cecily Tyson, and James Coco. Jane was accompanied by Tom, a male friend of his, baby Troy, and Genny Hayden, who'd come along to baby-sit Troy. They all lived in a suite at the Leningrad Hotel overlooking the frozen Neva River.

Jane enjoyed herself. *They Shoot Horses* had just played in the Soviet Union and was very popular. In Leningrad, crowds followed her wherever she went. But it wasn't politics they were interested in; young women clustered around her demanding to know, "Where did you buy those skintight blue jeans?"

Hayden was restless in Leningrad. Nobody knew or cared who he was. After staying only a couple of days he flew back to Washington, where he conferred with colleagues about America's political future and his own. After Watergate the public was disoriented and restless, and a combination of inflation and recession had the country in deep distress.

One friend, a McGovern aide, John Holum, suggested he run for the Senate seat then held by moderate California Democrat John Tunney. His reason was that California was one of the first states to reflect the country's political and economic disorientation by electing the eccentric young former seminarian Jerry Brown as governor.

Hayden had covered Brown's gubernatorial campaign for *Rolling Stone* and been impressed with him as a candidate. He had strong appeal to the young working-class voter with his promises to overthrow the privileged few in California and bring power directly to the people.

By the time Jane returned to L.A. in April, Tom had pulled together a makeshift staff. He was going to challenge the incumbent Tunney for the Senate nomination, and he would soon embark on a "highly quixotic campaign," given his and his wife's controversial reputations. So began the next phase of Jane Fonda's serial life, this time as the wife of a candidate for the U.S. Senate.

The first organizational meeting was held at an International House of Pancakes, Carey Beauchamp remembered. She was the assistant to campaign manager Bill Zimmerman, a longtime activist. Another who came on board was Sam Hurst, who'd worked for Daniel Ellsberg.

Hayden said he decided that instead of a conventional campaign platform he would draft an update of the Port Huron Statement. Dick and Mickey Flacks helped him shape the draft. They titled it "Make the Future Ours — the Radicalism of the Sixties Has Become the Common Sense of the Seventies."

The paper defined the fundamental choice between government of the corporations and government by the people. "We proposed an economic democracy in which accountability would be expected of the large corporations along with the communities and consumers they impacted," Hayden added.

Hayden gave Fred Branfman the title of Director of Research, which meant it was his job to find out all the dirt about Tunney and his corporate connections like the Gallo brothers.

Branfman moved from Washington, D.C., where he'd been heading the Indochina Resource Center. He'd served as a kind of think tank for Jane and Tom every time they came to the capital. Sometimes they'd talk up to nine hours at a stretch.

For the next year and a half Branfman camped out on the Haydens' back porch with his tiny Vietnamese wife, who became Troy's nanny.

Branfman and his wife were part of the extended family in the little house on Wadsworth Avenue. However, he and Jane never talked much. But they shared an obsession: Tom Hayden.

"The more I think about it, Jane and I were in similar positions," Branfman said. "Before we knew Tom we'd had separate identities, she as an actress, I as a peace activist. We'd lived abroad through most of the sixties. We'd idolized Tom but we didn't know him personally."

Branfman said that during his five years working with Hayden he had met dozens of people "who'd been close to Tom at one time or another and were now extremely critical of him. I couldn't tell if their feelings were legitimate or due to competitiveness. But in those days Jane and I still felt unsure about how to operate in American politics and were extremely grateful to Tom for providing us with a clear and healthy direction. In retrospect, I believe we were also — like most political people — subconsciously looking for 'immortality projects.'"

Even as they committed themselves to ending the war in Vietnam, they dedicated themselves to advancing Tom's political career. Jane was always attracted to powerful cold men, like her distant father, and Branfman was always looking for the strong father he'd never had. Tom filled both their needs.

Branfman and his wife spent a Thanksgiving with Henry Fonda and the rest of the Fondas. "It was some experience crammed into that tiny house. Henry and Shirlee (nice lady); Peter and his wife; Jane and Tom; Vanessa and Troy." Peter was smoking some strong dope. It permeated the place. Jane kept busy roasting the turkey. Henry Fonda just sat there very stiffly, surveying the scene, but not saying a word.

"Troy was about three or four then, an adorable little tyke, cute as a button — he was jumping up and down on the couch like it was a trampoline and Henry didn't like it one iota. Finally he got up with great difficulty and shuffled over to where Troy was bouncing on the couch and he glared at him. His disapproval was so huge it was scary." Branfman had a vision of how Jane must have felt when she was a little girl and Henry had glared at her when she'd done something he didn't like. But Troy ignored him. He just kept jumping up and down and up and down while Peter sucked on his pot. Deathly silence, and then they sat down for an absolutely delicious Thanksgiving dinner.

At first nobody thought Hayden had much of a chance against Tunney, but because Jerry Brown had just succeeded Ronald Reagan as governor and Jimmy Carter would soon be the Democratic nominee for president, anything was possible in America at that point.

Hayden campaigned up and down the state. He had no real constituency to speak of apart from a small cadre of aging hippies and disillusioned out-of-work vets. He had no real financial base, and his one friend in California politics was the newly elected Governor Brown, who had already agreed to be John Tunney's co-campaign chairman.

Hayden soon found support in César Chávez, the charismatic leader of the United Farm Workers, whom Jane had known when she was picketing with the lettuce workers back in 1970.

Chávez bluntly told Hayden he thought his idea of running for the U.S. Senate would be a waste of time and money unless he built a machine — not a political machine like Mayor Daley's in Chicago, but a machine for the people. In essence, Chávez gave Hayden the idea for the Campaign for Economic Democracy, Hayden's multiplatform grass-roots organization.

While Hayden was busy campaigning, Jane had started filming an edgy little comedy called *Fun with Dick and Jane* opposite George Segal. It would be a surprise hit and reestablish her as a major movie star.

The story revolves around a prosperous young couple who are very happy together until Dick loses his job and Jane suddenly realizes that everything they own was bought on credit. Soon even their lawn is repossessed. Dick becomes a basket case — he simply can't cope with all these reversals — and suddenly Jane takes over. She becomes daring and aggressive — their roles are reversed. Together they embark on a life of crime, robbing everything from supermarkets to the phone company in order to survive.

Jane thought the film was entertaining but also had something significant to say "because it's about the evils of consumerism." "Everybody can relate to that," she added.

As with any project she worked on, she was bursting with ideas. "Jane is always turned on when she's escaping into a new role," press agent Steve Rivers recalled.

On the first day of filming she'd noticed the set didn't look "lived in," so she insisted that children's drawings be Scotch taped to the fridge, and "there *has* to be an avocado plant in the living room — every suburban home has an avocado plant."

She even imagined she should wear a certain kind of perfume as

Jane, maybe Charlie by Revlon, and she improvised a scene in the bathroom where she carries on a conversation while perched on the toilet.

"Jane turned in an absolutely hilarious performance," one of her producers, Max Palevsky, recalled. When the movie was released the following year, *New York Times* critic Vincent Canby wrote, "Fonda's comedy has a mixture of intelligence and abandon. There is one sequence when she tries to be a fashion model in a crowded restaurant and it's priceless modern slapstick." All the time Jane was filming she never stopped campaigning for Tom. She'd solicit funds between takes, which often annoyed the politically unsympathetic crew.

Sometimes the producers were barred from a location site because of Jane's political reputation. "A supermarket let us shoot *outside*," producer Peter Bart remembered, "but not *inside* — it was if Jane might contaminate the produce!"

While doing a scene in an auditorium, Jane carried a bag of quarters so she could make fundraising calls between takes. The manager of the auditorium wouldn't let her use the lobby phone (he hated her politics), so she'd run across the street to another pay phone.

At night she'd go on the radio as "the candidate's wife" and talk about middle-class issues — daycare and the price of gas. She was determined to change her image from gung-ho radical to Mrs. Tom Hayden, middle-of-the-road Democrat. The public ultimately bought it. The following year she would be listed as one of the most admired women in a *Redbook* poll.

All the while she was convincing celebrities like Lucille Ball, James Taylor, Linda Ronstadt, Groucho Marx, and Danny Kaye to come out for Hayden. She persuaded her father not only to campaign for him, but to hold a fundraiser in his Bel Air mansion. She also cajoled him into doing some paintings that could be auctioned off. ("I bought them myself," she later confided.)

Hayden kept insisting he didn't want his campaign to be "too Hollywood," but he'd quickly learned what it meant to be Jane Fonda's husband. He had access to everyone in the entertainment industry — including the power group called the "Malibu Mafia," a group that included television producer Norman Lear; Ted Ashley, head of Warner Bros.; Max Palevsky, who'd made millions selling his computer company to Xerox. Sidney Sheinberg, economist and philanthropist, had taken a special shine to Hayden and talked openly about his "presidential qualities."

Hayden knew he had to soften his left-wing stance in order to work within the system. He had to make compromises. Some of his radical friends thought he was betraying them.

Jane wouldn't hear a word of criticism about him. The volatile Palevsky (who was coproducing *Fun with Dick and Jane*) saw Tom "using Jane shamelessly." "I couldn't understand how she could be so stupid. Everyone else saw what he was doing. . . . Hayden was often publicly contemptuous of her."

"Jane — come in here!" he'd bark, and she'd rush in from wherever she was. Her eyes would glaze over when he was talking to her. "His brilliance intimidated me," she said. "I constantly worried I was never political enough."

Carey Beauchamp remembered, "I had to pick her up and drive her to some early-morning meeting in the Valley. I came around eight thirty and found Jane still in her nightgown, crumpled in a chair, sobbing. 'I can't do it. I can't do it,' she sobbed. There were Tom's position papers scattered all over the floor. She'd been trying to memorize them. 'I can't do this — I'm a failure. I can't face his public.'

"I told her, look — the women you are going to see want to meet you, Jane Fonda, movie star. All you have to do is walk in and say, 'I'm Jane Fonda and I'd like you to vote for my husband. He's a great guy,' and they'll believe you. You have credibility as Jane Fonda. Women know you, respect you, even love you.

"She didn't really seem to believe that, but somehow she pulled herself together and got dressed and made up. We left the house and of course at the meeting she charmed everybody, which she always did. She'd pull herself together time and time again. Only the people in the campaign knew how insecure she actually was."

"But Jane, to her credit in my view, couldn't stop being honest with reporters," Fred Branfman said. Near the end of the campaign she accused Tunney of "dating teenagers." Her comments got a huge amount of press.

Branfman said, "I asked Jane, 'Why did you say that?' and she answered, 'Because it's true! I was dating Ted Kennedy and Tunney was dating a teenager the night we all went out.' I admired that about Jane. Yes, she wasn't always 'politically correct.' But she was honest."

She often talked too much. She felt terrible about it but Tom's expectations kept her off balance. It seemed to be part of the dynamic of their relationship.

Often when she was with him, she'd act like a little girl, obedient, self-sacrificing (as she had with Vadim — although inside she might be seething). Away from Hayden she'd turn opinionated, imaginative. "You are a completely different woman when you're away from Tom," Bob Scheer once told her. "You're almost unrecognizable."

She continued to campaign throughout the state, raising thousands of dollars for Hayden's "war chest." Meanwhile, as a sign of dedication to the grass-roots aspect of his politics, Hayden began a thousand-mile walk across California. Three weeks before the primary, it ended on May 17, 1976, with him carrying Troy on his shoulders across the Golden Gate Bridge.

Up to this point Tunney had tried to ignore Hayden, even as he kept rising in the polls. With three weeks to go Tunney finally began a big "counterattack" on radio and TV. He flew in high-powered media consultants like Dave Garth and Jeff Greenfield. Even so, Hayden continued to rise in the polls. "Our message was getting through to them," Jane said, loyally.

In the end, Hayden lost the primary although he got 40 percent of the vote. "1.2 million Californians had cast their votes for a New Left radical, co-founder of SDS, and co-conspirator of Chicago," Jane wrote. "This was unprecedented in recent political history."

That November, California voters elected Tunney's exact opposite, S. I. Hayakawa, president of San Francisco State University, as their junior United States senator.

Hayden kept his promise to Chávez. He immediately began forming his grass-roots organization, which he would call Campaign for Economic Democracy, "to promote progressive causes and candidates from around the state." CED would help launch his Senate bid for 1982.

CED would have an office near the house on Wadsworth Avenue. Jane occasionally could be found manning the phones in the evening.

CED initially focused on economic issues, but the organization soon acquired other causes like solar energy, nuclear disarmament, and women's rights. However, it achieved its biggest success with the battle for rent control laws in Santa Monica.

"Tom was at his best when it came to organizing small local issues," Jack Newfield recalled. "He was a terrific analyst and strategist, and he had a real talent for galvanizing people to work with him. There were a great many families who *rented* in Santa Monica. Tom and Jane literally organized renters into a formidable political force." Eventually they voted a landlord-dominated group out of office and elected a much more liberal City Council. They proceeded to institute one of the strongest rent control laws in the United States. At one point the situation got so heated that right-wingers posted signs that said YOU ARE NOW ENTERING THE PEOPLE'S REPUBLIC OF SANTA MONICA.

To better house CED meetings and conferences, Jane bought (for $700,000) a 120-acre ranch north of Santa Barbara. It was set on rolling hills and dales overlooking the Pacific Ocean. She got a bank loan to do it. The property was called Laurel Springs Ranch.

She and Hayden planned to run a summer arts camp for kids on the property as well. "It's gonna look like a rainbow coalition," Jane told a friend. "Black, Chicano, Puerto Rican — rich kids mixed in with poor." She was very excited about it.

Although she didn't talk about it, Jane was still distressed that she had to keep using her own money to fund Hayden's career. Richard Rosenthal said, "It caused her a lot of angst."

She'd paid for his entire Senate campaign ($500,000). The Tunney people complained that she'd violated federal election laws that limited donations to $1,000, but Rosenthal was able to argue that California community property laws gave Tom Hayden power over Jane's funds. There is no law restricting how much money you personally use.

By the fall of 1976, *Fun with Dick and Jane* had opened. It marked her comeback as a mainstream actress. Its success made it possible for her to tackle offbeat projects like *Coming Home*. Paula Weinstein, who was now her agent, was even able to renegotiate her *Julia* contract and get her more money.

At long last, a tiny bit of security. Jane felt she could finally concentrate on *Julia*, though she was feeling a bit intimidated about portraying Lillian Hellman. Hellman was still very much alive, and her just-published third memoir, *Scoundrel Time,* was a bestseller. In it she described how she'd stood up to the FBI and HUAC all the while she was blacklisted.

Hellman had recently posed for a Blackglama fur ad that had run in many magazines, including a full-page portrait in *Harper's Bazaar.* Swathed in mink, she stared defiantly out at the world underneath the caption "What becomes a legend most?" The phrase seemed to define the exhibitionistic Hellman to the world — this irascible seventy-year-old lady who reveled in self-promotion, money, and fame.

Jane had already immersed herself in Hellman's volatile life, which spanned the Depression, the Cold War, and the Nixon years. She'd read her memoirs but responded even more to her plays. (She read *The Children's Hour* up until the middle of the second act and then, as an acting exercise, "I wrote the rest of the play myself as if Hellman never completed it.")

She thought *The Children's Hour* reflected Hellman's spirit, but her subconscious memories were most apparent in *The Little Foxes,* where she re-created her own eccentric family: her passive, beautiful mother, her voracious, seductive father, her greedy relatives, "all New Orleans Jews."

"Lillian has this uncanny ability to write very vivid characters obsessed with love and hate and money and sex and power," Jane said. "And she inhabited these characters to an amazing degree."

But how could *she* inhabit such a woman, especially because she looked nothing like her? ("Hellman's face resembles that of an old basset hound," Leonard Bernstein once quipped.)

"Okay, so I don't look like her, but I can focus on certain physical qualities," Jane decided. Her lipstick could be a dash of dark red, which would make her mouth appear thinner. Her hair would be a kind of helmet. Clothes could reflect her character, too, she thought as she studied the portrait of Hellman taken by Irving Penn for *Vogue* in 1948. In the photograph, Hellman appeared pensive and immaculate. Her outfits were always elegant and expensive, and she enjoyed wearing hats with veils and very good gloves.

Then, of course, there was her anger. In *Julia* Jane shows what anger can do to a person; it boxes you in, it won't let you relax. In the movie there's a scene in Sardi's, when Jane (as Hellman) strides in after the smash opening of *The Children's Hour* and is twitching with drunken nervousness — reveling in the attention she's getting while stiffly trying to live up to the image of herself as the distinguished playwright. She gets on the pay phone to Dashiell Hammett out in Hollywood and almost spits out, "They liked it, Dash! *I am famous now!*"

Months before in New York, Jane had appeared at a gala held in Hellman's honor — a benefit for the Committee for Public Justice. It was a committee Hellman had formed in 1970 after she'd been alarmed by the FBI's abuse and harassment of dissenters to the Vietnam War.

The evening had been a triumph for Hellman. Jane and Jason Robards had read from the screenplay of *Julia* at Circle in the Square Theatre. Other actors had performed scenes from several of Hellman's plays. Afterward, there was a dinner and reception at Gallagher's Steakhouse.

Many of the biggest names in the theater turned out, including Henry Fonda, Shirley MacLaine, Lauren Bacall, Betty Comden and Adolph Green, Julie Harris, and Hal Prince. The place was packed and everyone talked a mile a minute. "The energy was very high," the actor Patrick O'Neal remembered.

Finally, there were speeches, but nobody seemed that interested when MIT president Jerome Wiesner got up to speak; the room just wouldn't quiet down.

Jane watched as Hellman fumed for several minutes, then, grabbing a microphone, she climbed on top of a table to harangue the crowd. *"Shut up!"* she roared in her hoarse voice. *"Stop talking drivel and listen to something important!"*

Sure enough, the room went deathly silent, after which Hellman could be heard muttering, "Drunken bastards" before climbing down from the table. Wiesner gave his speech.

This was the key to Hellman, Jane decided, and she set about learning to embrace Hellman's volatile personality.

She remembered that tirade when she shot a scene in *Julia* in which actor John Glover teasingly accuses Julia of being a lesbian and by inference Hellman, too. Jane was supposed to slap Glover in response to his comment. During rehearsal she tapped his chin, but when the scene was shot she hauled off and socked him so hard she knocked him out cold.

Jane had previously met Hellman just once, at agent Sue Mengers's home in L.A., but before she left to film the movie, she flew up to Martha's Vineyard to spend a day and a half with her.

She wanted to see Hellman in her own surroundings — in this case a charming house, all windows and decks, in Vineyard Haven overlooking the sea.

Outside a gale-force wind was blowing; a hurricane had been predicted, and Hellman and Jane spent the first couple of hours trying to prepare the house. They cut back flowers in the garden, took mirrors off the walls, battened down storm windows. Jane noted with amusement how nervous Hellman was — she kept running around crossing herself and muttering, "Oy, vey!" at the same time.

The hurricane blew over. Only then did the two women sit down and begin to talk about Alvin Sargent's script — which Jane loved, she said, "because it was full of flashbacks and shifting perspectives. It was mercurial, too, because the suspense comes late, when Hellman has to smuggle the money into Nazi Germany to help the Jews."

Hellman, however, had specific criticisms. She told Jane she hated "the fake butch scenes" where she was constantly smoking (she said this as she chain-smoked compulsively). "I called Dashiell 'Dash' — not 'Hammett'; that's being fake butch, too." Above all, she wanted more tenderness, more love expressed between them. "It was the Kate Hepburn/Spencer Tracy paradigm," Jane said, "two sexy equals who adored each other, except it wasn't true, it was Hellman's fantasy of her relationship with Hammett, the master mystery writer, author of *The Thin Man* and *The Maltese Falcon* — epic drunk and womanizer."

And Hellman added that Julia should be the focus of the story *Julia*, not Lillian Hellman. Near the end of the afternoon, Jane tried to find out more about Julia,* but Hellman evaded her questions and said she couldn't reveal her identity because her family might sue.

Jane spent much of the time observing Hellman move about the living room, stiff-necked and unyielding. Every so often she would sit down, shapely legs slightly apart so Jane could see the hem of her white satin slip. Her dainty feet were shod in expensive pumps.

Later, Jane would tell Dan Rather in a *60 Minutes* interview (March

---

* In mid-1976 psychiatrist Muriel Gardiner published a memoir, *Codename Mary*, in which she accused Hellman of stealing her life story. Hellman denied the charges. A great scandal ensued about Hellman having fabricated her role in Julia's life completely. She and Gardiner made halfhearted attempts to meet, but both died before a meeting could be arranged.

8, 1977) that "Hellman has a way of sitting . . . lounging in chairs, her skirt kind of came up above the knee and you see she was wearing silk and satin underwear . . . she sits with a regal quality, like Queen Nefertiti. . . ."

Hellman said nothing about that interview, but when Jane told *Newsweek,* "Lillian is a homely woman but she moves like Marilyn Monroe," Hellman exploded and fired off a letter to Jane in which she maintained she'd never bought expensive underwear. "The underwear I bought was from a dry goods store in Martha's Vineyard . . . and the night you saw me at Sue Menger's [*sic*] I was sitting in a straight chair because I have a bad back."

Jane replied immediately with a handwritten note saying her remarks had been taken out of context. She went on to explain her *60 Minutes* interview. "I said that one of the most appealing and unexpected things about you is your sensual presence. Your legend, your writing, being an intellectual, does not prepare one for the femininity and accessibility.

"I wish I was more of an actress to have captured the totality of what I experienced with you. My stupidity was in not anticipating how easy it is for a discussion to be twisted out of shape. . . ."

Hellman fired back impatiently that Fonda might be jealous of her, and she told her to "watch it."

She went on to say she had spoken of this to no one because "the falling out of women offends me and always has in my old fashioned woman's personal liberation way. . . ."

They saw each other again when the Academy decided to honor Hellman at the Oscars by asking her to present an award for Best Documentary. Jane, who'd been nominated as Best Actress for *Julia,* accompanied her back across the stage. They were met with thunderous applause.

The *Julia* shoot took four intense months, spread out over multiple locations in Germany and France. Most of the interiors were filmed at Elstree Studios in London.

The Haydens had never been separated for that long. Jane hired a full-time nanny to take care of Troy. "She was a nice, attractive young woman; I thought she was sexy and told Tom so," Jane said.

Once in London, Jane shared an apartment with her makeup girl.

She fasted and "tried to get rid of my extra baggage, cleaning out the last character I'd played — the last character being me." As usual, no matter how tired she was, she went to ballet class every night after filming. She was in almost every scene of the movie.

She didn't get along with her director, Fred Zinnemann, but she was too professional to show it. She complained about him in a letter to Richard Rosenthal. Zinnemann was cold and dictatorial, and he could not be crossed on anything. "He was always right," *Julia*'s producer, Richard Roth, said.

Later, however, Jane would have to admit that she had collaborated with a master; the final *Julia* is classical moviemaking with every detail worked out, every shot perfectly, lustrously composed by cinematographer Douglas Slocombe. The movie glides along, with Zinnemann taking a romantic view of his heroines.

Jane especially enjoyed her scenes with the craggy ex-alcoholic Jason Robards Jr., who played Hammett. His low-key encouragement of Hellman, his stubborn protection of her, as well as his cryptic remarks, are high points in the movie.

Even so, Robards kept complaining genially, "I have nothing the fuck to do." (He won an Oscar for doing "nothing.") He and Jane both noticed the singular talents of twenty-six-year-old Meryl Streep, disguised in a black wig and playing the bitchy socialite who keeps badmouthing Hellman, implying she's a lesbian.

"My part was great but it was ultimately cut," Streep said, years later. Before it was, she and Jane did a lot of improvising together in their scenes. "I was right out of Yale so I *loved* to improvise and so did Jane until the tears rolled down her cheeks."

"Meryl was absolutely amazing," Jane said.

She gave the younger actress advice as to where to stand — "step into the light so they can see you — that kind of thing. . . ." When she got back to California, "Jane told people about me so I got work because of her." (Jane wanted her to play her girlfriend in *Coming Home* but Streep took a part in *The Deer Hunter* instead.)

The actress Rosemary Murphy, who played Dorothy Parker (Hellman's oldest friend), remembered Jane on the set very differently. "Cold, haughty, and almost businesslike." The two had starred in *Any Wednesday* together in 1966. "Back then she'd been giggly and sexy. We were constantly going to massages and she was confiding how Max

Schell wanted to seduce her and she had to stay faithful to Vadim. But while we were filming *Julia* she was like a different person. She just wouldn't loosen up. Max Schell was in the cast, too, playing the down-at-the-heels refugee, the political activist who gets Lillian to go smuggle the money for Julia. I never knew how Jane reacted to him, although their scenes together were quite amazing. There was this intense subtext which I always imagined had a kind of nostalgic undercurrent . . . but even though we had a lot of scenes together, offscreen we barely spoke."

Jane didn't communicate much with Vanessa Redgrave either; they decided that in order to get along they would not talk politics. Jane now called herself a "Progressive Democrat," whereas Redgrave was a Trotskyite. During lunch she would proselytize with the electricians and prop men about joining the Trotsky revolutionary party.

Whenever she was free, Vanessa spoke on behalf of the Palestinian cause. Redgrave had just appeared in *The Palestinian*, a documentary in which she danced wildly and brandished a gun in support of the Palestine Liberation Organization.

In the early seventies Redgrave had been Jane's activist idol, but Jane now found herself telling reporters she had *not* named her daughter after Vanessa Redgrave. (Months later when she returned to California, Redgrave tried to visit the Haydens to get them to support some causes, and Hayden barred the door and wouldn't let her in.)

About a month into the filming, however, Jane forgot about their political differences because she realized how important the movie could be. "It hit me when Vanessa and I did that scene sitting on the hill; we're quite young and she's reciting poetry and then I say, 'I love you, Julia.' The two of them were creating a dreamlike friendship together. You see the gallant adventurous Julia opening up a world of art and mortality and conscience to Lillian who absolutely worships her."

"People will see this movie about two women who think and care for one another!" Jane went on. "It's so wonderful to see women taken seriously. In every other movie I've ever been in women are either falling in and out of love with men or are game playing. There is no game playing in *Julia*."

"Vanessa Redgrave and Jane were an absolutely magical team," Fred Zinnemann said. "They had totally different acting methods. Jane was all about technique. She could cry on cue and she created a splendid portrait of a stubborn driven angry Lillian who gulps down whiskey — puffs on cigarettes as she's trying to finish a play. Finally, in exasperation, she tosses the typewriter out of the window!"

Zinnemann continued, "As for Redgrave, with her majestic walk and ethereal storybook face, she never seemed to be acting."

Jane added, "I recall never being sure where Vanessa was drawing her inspiration from, what choices she was working off of, and this invariably threw me slightly off balance — which worked in the film. The only other time I had experienced this with an actor was with Marlon Brando. . . . Like Vanessa, he always seemed to be in another reality, working off some secret, magnetic, inner rhythm that made me have to adjust to *him* rather than maintaining my own integrity in the scene."

Midway through filming Tom Hayden visited Jane in London for ten days bringing Troy, who was now three. They toured the city together, walking up and down the Thames riverbank. They tiptoed through Canterbury Cathedral. By chance they ran into Afdera Fonda, who had been living in England for the past eight years.

"We embraced like lovers," Afdera recalled. "Jane seemed genuinely glad to see me. I impulsively invited them back to my apartment for pasta and they came."

Afdera had never remarried. Her little flat was like a shrine to Henry Fonda. Mementos of their years together — his paintings, postcards, snapshots — were all decorating a big screen. As she boiled the water for the spaghetti and fried tomatoes and garlic in olive oil, she reminisced. Jane and Hayden listened impassively.

Afdera's impressions: "Jane seemed tense. Hayden was sullen, glum, and *Dio mio!* so unattractive. Bulbous nose, many acne scars. As far as the little boy, Troy, he was a perfect monster and spoiled rotten. He kept butting his head into Jane's stomach and calling her 'dummy' and farting! He farted the entire time and his parents never said a word."

Even so, Afdera thought it had been a "relatively pleasant reunion," but then Jane wrote in her memoir "that Italian woman . . . a phony." Afdera added, "Perhaps Jane was jealous because her father and I had had such passionate love."

Months later Afdera ran into Henry Fonda in London, too, and "he seemed overjoyed to see me. We embraced and then walked about the city for a while and I invited him over for pasta but he resisted. 'I have to get back to Shirlee,' he told me. I never saw him again."

The next time Tom Hayden visited Jane she was filming in Paris and living in a flat in the futuristic Tour Espace. She was spending most evenings with Redgrave, discussing the scenes they would be filming in the following days.

"One night in Paris during his visit, he told me he wanted to talk to me about something," Jane said. "It was about the babysitter, he said. He reminded me that I thought she was sexy, and from the way he then hesitated, I sensed what was coming and told him not to say any more. . . . I assumed he was going to tell me he had slept with her. I was going to have to be by myself for another month once he was gone, and I didn't want to be angry . . . neither one of us ever broached the subject of infidelity again."

Jane added that she never discovered if anything happened between Tom and the babysitter. However, this marked the beginning of a "less harmonious time in the marriage," Jane wrote in her memoir. She left a great deal unsaid, she says, possibly because "Tom vetted all the chapters he was in. I didn't want to hurt Troy, who so adores his father."

31

A S SOON AS Jane finished *Julia*, she flew back to California and plunged into work on *Coming Home*. She had been researching the project since 1973, interviewing disabled Vietnam vets and their wives and listening to how they coped. The first version of the script, called *Buffalo Ghost*, by Nancy Dowd hadn't worked out. (Dowd said, "Jane found the screenplay too dark and unsettling.") When Jane asked her agent, Mike Medavoy, to give her names of other screenwriters, he told her to forget it. "Nobody will want to do a love story about a paralyzed Vietnam vet. It's the least commercial idea I've ever heard of," he said. But Jane wouldn't give up. She went to Waldo Salt, a veteran screenwriter who'd just won the Oscar for *Midnight Cowboy*, and gave him Dowd's version to read. He didn't like it, but he wanted to write a movie about the plight of returning Vietnam vets; he was currently helping Ron Kovic with his memoir, *Born on the Fourth of July*. For a while Salt worked pro bono for Jane, interviewing disabled Vietnam vets and their wives. He developed the lead characters out of these interviews and wrote a treatment. With Jane's blessing he brought in director John Schlesinger and producer Jerome Hellman, with whom he'd made *Midnight Cowboy*. That completed the team for *Coming Home*. Both men agreed to work on spec until they could raise development money from a studio.

Sometime in 1975 Hellman took Salt's treatment to United Artists where he'd made *Midnight Cowboy*, and he convinced UA head Arthur Krim to finance the film. "Arthur gave us five million. It was barebones but we accepted it," Hellman said.

When Jane returned from London after finishing *Julia*, she heard from John Schlesinger that he'd decided he couldn't direct a movie "about vets and piss bags. You don't need a British fag for this one," he joked.

Haskell Wexler, who had already signed on as cinematographer, immediately suggested Hal Ashby, with whom he'd just worked on *Bound for Glory.*

"Hal was as active as I was in opposing the Vietnam War," Wexler said. "I thought he'd be an ideal choice." Ashby was an eccentric pot-smoking hippie type, with long, gray, stringy hair, love beads around his neck. "I don't think Hal liked people very much," Jane said. "That's why he was stoned all the time." Stoned or not, Ashby had previously directed *Shampoo* with Warren Beatty and *The Last Detail* with Jack Nicholson, as well as the cult favorite *Harold and Maude* about a young boy who keeps trying to commit suicide until he falls madly in love with a gray-haired lady old enough to be his grandmother.

Ashby read Waldo Salt's partial draft for *Coming Home,* and he agreed to direct even though he'd have only six weeks to prepare (usually a director has at least six months of preproduction). He was turned on by the ideas in the film — it would be one of the first to deal with a disabled vet and the very first to deal with a disabled vet's sexuality. The movie could affect the perceptions of the public about the war and the antiwar movement, he thought. But he refused to defer his usual fee the way the other principals had. He insisted on $400,000 up front, and he got it. "Hal, the guy who didn't care about money, was now going to be the highest-paid guy on the movie," said Hellman. "So what else is new?"

Over Thanksgiving weekend of 1976, he and Ashby had a tense meeting with Salt. The two men found the screenwriter in very frail shape. He had completed only thirty-six pages of the script, but he assured them that he would be able to finish it soon.

The day after the meeting, Salt was felled by a massive heart attack. "We panicked," Hellman recalled. "We didn't want United Artists to know how sick Waldo was so we played it down." They immediately enlisted the help of Robert C. Jones, an aspiring writer who had worked as Salt's film editor on *Midnight Cowboy.* Jones and Bruce Gilbert helped pull all the rough drafts together into some semblance of order. But everyone was worried. Jones had never written a script before and neither had Gilbert.

There were casting difficulties, too. Jon Voight had originally been set to play Officer Bob, the buttoned-down conventional professional soldier, but Voight was lobbying to play Luke, the paraplegic. The producers wanted either Al Pacino or Jack Nicholson. They both turned the part down.

Voight kept bugging Ashby. He'd take long walks with him and tell him, "Luke is a lover and I'm a lover. This is a love story." He'd read an early draft of the script and felt it was too polemical. Finally the producers agreed to cast him, as Jane and he were friends from the antiwar movement; she felt comfortable with him.

The actor Bruce Dern lived next door to Ashby in the Malibu colony. "One day Hal drops by and says, 'Dernsy, you want to do this?' and hands me the *Coming Home* script. I knew I wasn't the first choice for Bob but as soon as I read it I agreed."

It was a far cry from recent roles Dern had taken on, like the murderous Tom in *The Great Gatsby* or the killer in *The Cowboys*.

Meanwhile, Hellman tried and failed to get government cooperation from the Veterans Administration to film in army camps and army hospitals. The army, the navy, the Marines, and the National Guard turned down Fonda and company.

"We ended up shooting at a hospital for spinal cord injuries in Downey, California," Hellman said. (Only after *Coming Home* opened to great acclaim and praise did the VA approve of the film — unofficially.)

Max Cleland, a triple amputee who'd toured with Jane and Hayden for IPC, was technical adviser and later became a Democratic senator from Georgia. He advised Bruce Dern about the vets' psychological trauma. "I asked him about my character, Bob, who comes back from the war but he's no hero, right? He's survived the war but he is a lost soul, and Max says, 'You're the tragic figure in this one, buddy. You're like thousands of guys who've come back physically intact but psychologically you're lost.'"

Jon Voight had many talks with Cleland, too. He'd already spent five weeks living at a vets' hospital, hanging out with dozens of disabled vets who were playing themselves in the movie. They helped him learn the intricacies of pushing his body in and out of his wheelchair and learning how to drive it, sometimes very fast, down the hospital halls. "The vets were so committed to the film and to helping me, they taught me how to play basketball in a wheelchair," Voight said. "I'll never forget them."

Some of them didn't agree with Jane's politics, and at first the reaction to her was pretty chilly on the set. "Jane made it her business to have conversations with every one of them. She was a strong, admirable lady," Hellman said. "It took guts to do what she did."

Sally Hyde was nothing like Jane, so she felt challenged about playing this docile, unopinionated American housewife who's married to a Marine Corps captain, a gung-ho patriot. When he goes to Vietnam she volunteers at a veterans' hospital and meets Luke, a paraplegic who happens to be a former high school classmate. They fall in love. She starts to change. She loses her inhibitions and reaches out to people. After their lovemaking Sally feels sexually fulfilled for the first time in her life. Luke has given her a beautiful sense of satisfaction, something her husband has never been able to do.

Ashby filmed various rap sessions the men were having with the VA psychiatrist. One such session opens the movie. Everybody is sitting around in their wheelchairs; some of the men have no legs, some no arms — they are all very damaged amputees.

Although it was 1977, the movie was set in 1973, so talk about the war was a very hot topic. One question: "If you could, would any of you go back to Nam?"

Dern said, "I watched this particular session from the sidelines. One guy raises his nub and says simply, 'How could I go back unless I had a purpose? There was no purpose when I went. Is there one now?'"

None of this was scripted — everything was improvised. Voight lay on his gurney and listened, and Ashby zeroed in to a giant close-up of his beautiful baby face. He said nothing. He had lines to say, but he didn't say them. It was better if he just shut up and listened.

"Hal did a lot of that in the film," Bruce said. "Just cutting back and forth to the faces — the torment — the remembering. It was all in the expressions."

"By the fifth week of shooting the guys really got to Jane," Bruce finished. "I saw her sitting on the set one day — all alone — and she was looking at them and weeping. . . ."

•   •   •

As the movie progressed, Hellman marveled at Jane's investment in the project. *Julia* had opened to superlative reviews — it would go on to win three Oscars and Jane won the Golden Globe — "but we didn't talk about that," he said. "Oh, we congratulated her, but she shrugged it off. She was concentrating on this movie. Nothing meant more to her than this movie — except maybe Tom. Jane took her responsibilities as a producer and star to a degree I've never seen before in terms of involvement, promotion, publicity, advertising. Making sure the right people knew about the film and came on set. . . ."

She was worried about the script. It was still unfinished. Salt lay in bed recuperating, unable to contribute anything. Scenes remained incomplete — just sketched out. Hellman recalled, "Sometimes we'd all show up with various revisions of a scene. We'd put them under the door of Hal's trailer, and he'd paste them together and the actors would start improvising. . . ." Eventually the young novelist Rudolph Wurlitzer was called in to do major rewrites.

Wurlitzer told journalist Nick Gagne in 2005 that he didn't want to take any credit because "the main writer was Waldo Salt, whom I revered. I was a friend of Ashby's, so I wrote scenes with Jane in the hospital and the sex scene and I went through the script and tuned it up in various places and added some juice here and there. It was a real rewrite. I was actually writing while they were shooting, too." But he refused to take any name credit.

Near the end of the shoot, Jane and Bruce Dern were still improvising entire scenes. "Like the one when I come at Jon with a bayonet cuz I find out he's been humping my wife," Dern said. "That scene hadn't ever been written so Jane and I improvised it, took notes as we improvised, and then we shot it. But it's our dialogue, Jane's and mine. . . ."

Ashby would shoot up to forty-five takes of a scene, and then at the end of the day he'd disappear into the editing room. "He would take a glance here, a sigh from me there, a slight turn of Jon's head, and would edit them together in a way we hadn't expected — or in some cases hadn't intended," Jane said.

There were disagreements, too, especially about the controversial love scene between Luke and Sally (it would feature what had previously been a taboo subject: sex with a disabled man).

Jane and Voight had talked to several paraplegics and their wives about the adjustment they have to make with respect to sexual dysfunction. Most paraplegics never know when they are going to have an erection. Jane and Ashby had a running argument, as Jane put it, "over the battle of penetration." Jane was opting for the suggestion of oral sex. Ashby wanted to suggest penetration.

"Both of us knew that the scene had to be really hot," Jane said. "Not as arbitrary sex but as the centerpiece of their relationship, emblematic of her transformation and . . . of a masculinity sans erection."

Jane had always felt, she told Peter Biskind, "that an unconventional politicized love story presents the opportunity to talk about what really makes a man. Is he a gung-ho guy who's going over to get the gooks and come back and fuck his brains out? Or is he the guy who is more sensitive and knows how to use other parts of himself like his hands and his mouth?" (Ron Kovic had told Jane that his injuries "really helped my sex life.")

The first day Ashby shot the body doubles for the long shots (the couple are entirely nude in the scene). When Jane came in the next day and watched the rushes, she saw that Ashby had not done what she wanted. "She cannot be riding him that way! She can't. He can't get an erection. I thought we'd agreed," she exploded angrily.

But Ashby was not about to do what Jane wanted, so Jane decided that when she and Voight did the scene, she would move in such a way that Ashby couldn't match her close-ups nor would he be able to intercut the footage.

"Jon and I spent most of the day in bed, naked under the sheets, being filmed from various angles. It's a strange experience doing this kind of scene: There is a sexy, electric charge in the air, and everyone overcompensates by becoming very businesslike. . . . Hal had saved the key shot for last, the one with me/Sally sitting on top of Jon/Luke with the camera framing me from my shoulders up. For me, Sally was experiencing oral sex, and I was moving and reacting accordingly when Jon suddenly whispered, 'Jane, Hal's yelling at us!' From far away behind the hanging sheets, I heard Hal's voice, 'Ride him! Dammit! Ride him! Move your body, goddammit!' But I wouldn't. Finally he gave up and stormed off the set."

Afterward Bruce Dern remembered slipping into Ashby's trailer and finding the director cursing softly to himself as he lit up a joint. Before Dern could find out what had happened, Jane appeared in a robe, barefoot, looking like a little girl and apologizing. "Oh, Hal, please forgive me! I couldn't help it. . . ." Ashby said nothing.

He used both shots. The double didn't match the close-up, but in the end nobody seemed to notice. Everyone had a very strong reaction to the scene.

A couple of weeks later Ashby showed a rough, unedited cut to a small group of people close to the film, including Tom Hayden. When it was over Hayden got up and marched right past Jane, who was sitting with Voight, Gilbert, and Jerome Hellman. "Nice try," he whispered loudly and left the screening room.

"The coldness of his response was devastating for all of us," Jane said. "Tom was not used to seeing rough cuts, and it was true that the film was too long and had problems; but it also had powerful moments, even at that early stage. Yet Tom chose to dismiss all our work outright." He later told her angrily it was the watered-down politics, but Jane was sure what got to him was the emotion and passion in the love scene — "He'd never seen me do a love scene before . . . I guess he was jealous."

For a few days she actually considered getting the scene totally cut. She confided as much to writer Barbara Harrison, who was interviewing her for a *Redbook* cover story. "I couldn't believe what I was hearing," Harrison said. She'd seen the rough cut, too, and had been "very moved by the beauty and tenderness of the love scene and the inherent power of the sex — it was quite revolutionary.* I'd never seen anything like it and yes it was crucial to the movie, but Jane was seriously thinking of cutting it. She didn't tell me why, but one of her associates let it drop that she was extremely upset about Tom's negative reaction. She was scared; she didn't want to do anything to upset him."

She had to contend with her father, too. Henry Fonda had seen the rough cut and had informed his daughter he was "frankly appalled. The love scene has to be cut — it is almost pornographic."

He was so incensed he phoned Jerome Hellman and tried to persuade him to get the scene cut. Hellman held his ground and Fonda

---

* In *Screening Sex*, published in 2008, Linda Williams wrote, "Fonda's sexual performances [in *Klute* and *Coming Home*] were as crucial to the 1970s cinematic knowledge of sex and perhaps as important and influential in their own female sphere as Marlon Brando's animal sexuality was in that of the male. It's not accidental that the quintessential American sexuality of both actors was forged in relation to European and specifically French associated movies."

threatened to "ruin him in the business and whenever I'd run into him at a party after that, he'd turn his back on me." (However, a year later, Fonda changed his mind after he saw the final cut at a screening. He phoned his daughter and brusquely told her, "Good work, I'm proud of ya." He never learned that the last scene in the movie had been totally improvised.)

Hellman said, "We did have an ending which none of us liked, where Bob, after he finds out his wife had been unfaithful, crashes his car on the wrong side of the highway and is killed."

Jane thought he should turn the gun on himself.

"By now we're at the end of the shoot," Dern recalled, "only a couple more days. It's the weekend, Jane is off to make a speech for Tom, she tells Hal and me, just film *something*.

"So on Saturday Hal has me walk down to the beach, strip off my uniform, and disappear into the sea. That's it. He films it every which way — close-ups, long shots, the whole bit — I had the idea of placing my wedding ring on top of my carefully folded uniform, boots, and cap. I leave them on the sand before I wander off into the waves. It felt right to me."

The following Monday Ashby screened all the takes for Jane but she didn't like any of them. She thought it should be more violent, that after what he'd been through he should've turned the gun on Luke and Sally. But Hellman believed that there was enough violence already, that the movie shouldn't end in violence. "At any rate, it was too late to change the ending of Bruce walking into the sea. It stayed."

For the next six months, Ashby cut and edited *Coming Home*. He worked his magic on it, just as he had on *Shampoo* and *Harold and Maude*.

Wexler recalled that he'd come into the editing room and watch him piece the scenes carefully and artfully together. "There's this one scene where Jon Voight is making a speech to high school kids about the horrors of war; it didn't work. Hal had allowed Jon to ramble on, and frankly he made very little sense and it could have been embarrassing if it had ended up in the movie the way I first saw it. 'Jesus,' I say to Hal, and he answers, 'Not to worry. It'll be okay.' And by God he did put it together in such a way the scene was absolutely dynamic. I'm sure it won Jon his Academy Award!"

32

J ANE WASN'T ABLE to watch Ashby edit *Coming Home* because she was in Colorado most of the summer, filming *Comes a Horseman* for Alan Pakula.

Vanessa was in Paris with Vadim, but Troy was on location for a while, playing with his toys in the dirt outside Jane's trailer. Then Tom took him back to L.A. and Jane was left to wail, "Oh, I want to be with my kids more!"

But she had to concentrate on her work. She was playing Ella, a fiercely independent woman rancher from Montana who is fighting to keep greedy investors from grabbing up her land.

Her adored childhood friend Sue Sally was the inspiration for Ella. "Sue Sally had grown up tough and strong," Jane said. "She was running a horse ranch all by herself."

During the shoot Jane learned to ride herd, rope calves, and even brand them, and she kept a picture of Sue Sally looking very jaunty on horseback on her dressing table. But in the movie Jane captures none of Sue Sally's joie de vivre. Instead her expression — especially in the close-ups — is as stubborn and weather-beaten as her father's when he played in the great Western *My Darling Clementine*.

As soon as she finished the picture, she flew back to L.A. and began focusing on projects that she was developing for IPC. Around this time she and Barbra Streisand were also working on a treatment based on the infamous Triangle Shirtwaist Factory fire of 1911.

Herb Gardner had been hired to write the screenplay. "It was a helluva story — 150 young seamstresses trapped on the tenth floor of a factory building in Greenwich Village — their bosses had locked the door to keep union organizers out . . . they left those poor girls to die. . . . Some of them jumped out the windows." Gardner added: "Barbra and Jane and I would meet and talk for hours . . . the combined energy of those two superstars gave me shortness of breath!"

He recalled that after one meeting he took Jane by herself to the building in Greenwich Village where the fire had taken place (it still stands on Greene Street between Washington and Waverly Places with a plaque to commemorate the tragedy).

"We go up to one of the rooms in the building. Jane is looking positively sensational: almost Amazonian with these big boots she liked to wear — lotsa makeup, jangly hoop earrings — all that great Jane Fonda hair tumbling down past her shoulders; and of course that body — amazing — toned — sinewy. Suddenly she strides over to the window and climbs up on the sill. She's teetering there — I'm afraid she's going to jump off . . . 'Jane — *Jane!*' I cry. 'What in hell are you doing?'

"She doesn't answer right off — just keeps teetering on the sill. *The window is open, by the way.* We're ten stories from the street. Then she turns and says defiantly, 'I'm doing this to see how it *feels!* What do you suppose it felt like to have a fire burning your ass? Do you jump or do you let the fire consume you?' She waits for my answer but I can't give it, so she hops down and eyes me. '*Herb?* What would *you* do?' I still don't answer so she continues in that finishing-school accent of hers: 'You are about to be burned alive in a fire. *Do you jump? Or let the fire consume you?*' She glares at me. 'Well? *What would you do?*'

"'It's a no-win situation, Jane,' I say weakly.

"'Well, I'd jump!' Jane insists, her tone impatient. 'I'd jump because I'd just assume there'd be a net to catch me!'"

Gardner finished: "I worked on a script for over two years and in the end the girls passed. Barbra was all caught up with *Yentl*, and Jane was very much into developing a script with Joe Eszterhas (a fictionalized version of the Karen Silkwood story)."*

However, when Jane and Eszterhas presented the Silkwood idea to

---

* Silkwood, a young technician in a nuclear plant, had died in a mysterious car crash on her way to tell the press what she knew about safety violations in her plant. The Haydens had been lobbying all over California, protesting the building of more nuclear plants; this was one of CED's top priorities. In 1983, Mike Nichols directed another movie called *Silkwood*, with a screenplay by Nora Ephron and Alice Arlen.

Columbia Pictures, Columbia passed. The studio was in turmoil. Its president, David Begelman, had been caught embezzling funds. Sherry Lansing had just taken over as head of production, and paradoxically another movie, *The China Syndrome* with a screenplay by Mike Gray, about a near meltdown in a nuclear plant, was her first "go" project. Michael Douglas was producing. It was his first film since he'd won six Oscars for *One Flew over the Cuckoo's Nest*.

He'd already signed Jack Lemmon to play the idealistic engineer who blows the whistle on his corrupt plant bosses. Douglas was going to play the smart-ass cameraman who inadvertently gets the meltdown on film. Richard Dreyfuss had agreed to play the TV reporter on the story, and then *Jaws* opened (he was one of the stars) and his asking price went up. Douglas refused to pay it.

That's when he thought maybe the Dreyfuss role could be transformed into a muckraking girl reporter. Soon after, Roz Heller, another producer at Columbia, sent Jane a script of *The China Syndrome*. Jane liked the script and liked the idea; she met with Michael Douglas to talk further. Within days she'd agreed to costar as well as coproduce for IPC. "But I want real input into the production," she added.

Douglas had worked on *China Syndrome* six years with Michael Gray, who wrote the original screenplay for the movie. Gray had studied to be a nuclear engineer and really knew what could go wrong with technology in a nuclear plant. He'd also directed many documentary films, including the award-winning *Murder of Fred Hampton*. Douglas had promised Gray he could direct *China Syndrome*. But now Douglas realized what it meant to have a star of Jane's magnitude who was also a producer. "I'd have to give in on some things," he said.

A few nights later, after Jane had decided to do the movie, she and Gray and Douglas had dinner at El Coyote, a Mexican restaurant on Melrose Avenue.

Gray recalled, "Jane loved my *China Syndrome* script. She thought it was timely and important but . . ." At the end of the meal she put her hand on his arm and gazed at him "with those steely blue eyes so like Henry Fonda's. And she said, 'Michael, I'm forty years old and hard to light.' It was her way of saying, 'I don't want you to direct,' which was a tremendous disappointment to me since I'd worked on the project and Michael Douglas promised me I would be directing. But I had never directed a feature film. Jane was one of the biggest stars in America and she had her image to protect. She was not about to take a chance on me — an unknown director. She told me she wanted Jim Bridges [who'd directed *The Paper Chase* and would go on to direct *Urban Cowboy* with John Travolta] to rewrite and direct. So I bowed out gracefully — what else could I do?" He and Jane remained friendly and he got co-credit for the screenplay. Michael Douglas, however, later admitted he felt a little "bent out of shape."

Bridges met with Michael Gray a couple of times but Gray said, "He really didn't want me around; I made him nervous. Then Jim proceeded to direct the movie, in documentary fashion, just as I would have."

Gray added that he visited the set only once, on the last day of the shoot, when the cast was on location at a plant. "Jane pulled me into her trailer and shut the door. 'Listen,' she said, 'we don't have an ending for the movie. Could you think one up right now?'" Gray said: "I told her, 'I wouldn't even consider it,' and then we sort of chuckled together and she marched out on the set and adlibbed an entire last monologue — it stayed in the picture and it was terrific."

Much of *China Syndrome* was shot in a remarkably accurate power control plant built at Columbia Studios. The cast got along very well. Jane confided to Lemmon at one point that she'd had a terrible crush on him when she was a kid (she'd met him on the set of *Mister Roberts* — he'd played Ensign Pulver and he'd won an Oscar for his performance). "So why didn't you tell me then?" Lemmon shot back. "I was only eleven, Jack." "So what, I don't give a shit; you shoulda told me. . . ."

As for Douglas, he maintained he'd always had huge admiration for Jane. "She's such an example of how much you can accomplish if you just stick to your goals." Then he would add impishly, "She's got a real good body, solid as a rock; I like to talk dirty to her so I can hear her giggle."

Throughout filming, Jim Bridges was rewriting dialogue — making sure the movie would be packed with details about both the nuclear and broadcasting worlds. He wanted it to crackle at a fever pace reminiscent of the movie *Z*, Costa-Gavras's political thriller: a picture that combined authentic events, star players, and a restless, journalistic way of presenting the action. "He knew how important *China Syndrome* could be," his longtime partner, Jack Larson, said. "Every morning before he drove off to the studio, Jim got down on his knees and asked God to help him do a good job."

Jane told Bridges she was dyeing her hair red in tribute to Brenda Starr, girl reporter. She was also spending hours with Connie Chung and other pioneering women TV reporters, noting how hard they had to work to cover news events instead of trite features.

Nobody was supposed to breathe a word about what the movie's subject matter was. It was then entitled *Power*, but Jane fought to keep the name *China Syndrome*, a term that means meltdown in a plant's cooling system that could theoretically cause the installation to sink all the way to China.

Eventually, although they weren't allowed into nuclear facilities, they did shoot in a couple of actual power plants. "It was at these power plants that we ran into trouble with the hard hats," Jack Lemmon recalled. "They didn't know what we were up to — the script was kept secret — but they correctly assumed the worst. That's when they called Jane a Commie bitch and they called me and Michael Commie fag perverts and worse.

"It was tougher for Jane than it was for us. They brought up the Hanoi shit again, and they threw things at her. One guy let a wrench fall where she was standing. If it had hit her, it would have cracked her skull."

She'd leave location "wound tight as a drum," longtime Fonda press agent John Springer recalled. "Jane was doing one movie after another without a break. Plus *China Syndrome* was the first movie her company was producing, so there was a lot riding on it. She was having all sorts of vivid dreams of waves crashing, her dog drowning, her marriage suddenly in trouble, Tom leaving her."

"There were rumors surfacing about Tom screwing around," a CED staffer said. "His drinking had increased but Jane seemed oblivious to it."

On a day off she took the entire family (Hayden, Vanessa, and Troy) to a Grateful Dead concert that was being given as a benefit for CED's pet cause, Solar Cal. This was CED's attempt to establish a public corporation to manage the California solar energy market, which was facing monopoly from gas and oil companies.

Jane never had time to shop for clothes, so she just threw on a combination of costumes from different movies: a blouse from *Julia*, a skirt from *Coming Home*, the platform sandals from *The China Syndrome*. She didn't put on the blond, tousled Farrah Fawcett wig she sometimes wore when she didn't have time for a shampoo; instead, she let her newly dyed red hair tumble past her shoulders.

Later, she walked regally through the concert crowds — hand in hand with Vanessa and Troy, Hayden slouching behind. Some people stared, others whispered, a few turned away, but the image of this striking, complicated super-celebrity decked out in so many styles — all thoughtlessly thrown together — was a paradox of self-doubt and assurance.

During the last week Jane was shooting *The China Syndrome*, she fractured her foot. "What to do?" she wrote in her autobiography. "I had to get in shape for my next movie, *California Suite*, in which I had to appear in a bikini." Her stepmother Shirlee suggested she go to see Gilda Marx, who taught dance classes in Century City. In 1963, Marx had opened the Body Design by Gilda studio, which featured aerobic exercises and choreographed movement to music. It was an upbeat innovation to exercise, and soon hundreds of women were attending her classes. Everybody wanted tummies flattened and thighs firmed up. By 1977, Marx had opened a chain of extremely successful studios around the country. She also manufactured a best-selling line of exercise clothing in rainbow colors.

Jane attended Marx's classes religiously. The routines were a revelation to her. Unlike in ballet, she was sure she was now using every single part of her body. She loved stretching and bending to pulsing rock music like Kenny Loggins.

As usual, she was worried about money. She would be receiving $1 million for *California Suite*, John Springer said, "but she wasn't keeping any of it." She was on her way to being the biggest female star in the world along with Streisand, but her first financial obligation was to Tom Hayden's Campaign for Economic Democracy. Eventually she would see to it that every one of her movies from *Julia* on served as a benefit for CED, and whenever she came to New York she would fundraise relentlessly.

Gil Shiva, who was married to Jane's college roommate, Susan Stein, recalled "Jane visiting our apartment at the Dakota for brunch. She must have stayed on for close to four hours trying to convince us to give money to CED. She wouldn't let up."

Often she would host little fundraisers at Richard Rosenthal's apartment at the Apthorp, charming the likes of hippie millionaire Stewart Mott, who gave money to a host of causes from Planned Parenthood to Vietnam vets. Mott was a great gardener, and Jane fancied herself one, too; he invited her to see his immense roof garden in the penthouse he kept on East 57th Street so they could compare notes on planting.

Jane would usually stay at the Rosenthals' with four-year-old Troy. Teddy Rosenthal (Richard's ex-wife) remembered "how close we were, sharing confidences and having breakfast together. I used to baby-sit for Troy."

She added that although Richard had other high-powered clients such as Richard Burton and Elizabeth Taylor, he was especially devoted to Jane and caught up in all phases of her multifaceted career. Included in these phases was Laurel Springs Ranch, which was not only serving as a meeting ground for CED members, but also would soon be a children's summer art camp.

Rosenthal had found the property for Jane in early 1977: 157 acres outside Santa Barbara, high in the mountains, featuring breathtaking views of the Pacific Ocean. There were some cabins on the property which Jane was renovating and decorating — she had paid for a windmill generator and solar panels so that the place could function as a research and demonstration project for CED, exploring ideas for alternative energy. "Laurel Springs was our command post — our camp house," she said. She and Tom lived in one of the log cabins.

Every time she was in New York, Jane would urge Rosenthal to pick up stakes and move to L.A. so he could oversee her career from every angle. Even Tom Hayden would gruffly mumble, "What the fuck are you doing with a lawyer who lives on the East Coast?" For a long while Rosenthal resisted — he'd just bought a country place in Quogue — but he and his family finally did move to California in 1977.

In the meantime Jane and he would brainstorm about other ways to get money. For a brief period she considered opening an auto repair shop where people wouldn't be ripped off.

Jane was still attending Gilda Marx's dance classes. When she raved to Shirlee about how wonderful this made her feel and she noticed that other women in the class felt the same way, her stepmother told her, "You could open a studio too, you know." A light went on in Jane's head. She *knew* how important exercise was. This could be the answer for funding CED.

The main instructor at Gilda Marx's, Leni Cazden, was fabulous. Jane hired her to help her master the routines in private.

Part V

Workout Guru / Tycoon Wife: 1988–2000

[Jane's] never going to play anything but Jane Fonda. . . . She's a more important character than any she'll ever play.

— TOM HAYDEN

33

As workout plans slowly took shape in Jane's mind, she grew increasingly concerned about her father's health. He hadn't been well since his heart attack in 1974, and he'd been in and out of hospitals. He'd had a tumor removed; then he got an infection, and he lost forty pounds as well as 40 percent of his hearing in both ears. He looked gaunt and frail and was losing his hair. He recuperated at home with Shirlee hovering nearby. "Shirlee's lasted . . . because I've mellowed," he told *Playboy*. "I'm easier to live with."

He rallied. In December of 1977, he starred in a play called *First Monday in October*, which he loved. It was about a crusading justice of the Supreme Court who gets riled when the president appoints a conservative woman to sit on the court. (Jane Alexander played the judge and Fonda enjoyed working with her, calling her "my other Jane"). The show had brief but sold-out runs in Los Angeles and New York. It later moved to Chicago, where Fonda fell ill again and was forced to return home. For the first time, he seriously contemplated his mortality.

The year before Jane had arranged for Richard Rosenthal to represent him and draw up his will; he also managed his financial affairs and set up a deal for Fonda's lithographs to be sold.

Rosenthal remembered Fonda giving him a tour of his Bel Air home, pointing out the corner of the living room where he painted. Half-finished canvases were scattered about; frail as he was, Fonda always kept busy. He worked part of the day in his vegetable garden and he tended his beehives. Every so often Rosenthal would be given a jar labeled "Fonda Honey."

· · ·

Both Jane and Peter were trying to stay close. On February 28, 1978, they joined their father as he received the American Film Institute's Lifetime Achievement Award at the Beverly Hills Hotel. They hoped for reconciliation although they had no expectations of real intimacy with him. For his part, said Shirlee, he was tired of fighting with "the kids." He told one reporter, "I've never dealt with personal problems at all. Eventually if you just sit there long enough they fall away."

Still, Fonda did not feel close to either Jane or Peter. He thought Jane was away too much. She would phone him and say she was coming over, and then she would call again and say she had to make a speech in San Francisco. He disapproved of his son's restless lifestyle. Peter had spent months sailing around the world on his boat, leaving his wife, Susan, and his children, Bridget and Justin, behind. Then he divorced Susan and married Becky McGuane, and they moved to a three-hundred-acre spread in Livingston, Montana. On one wall of his rustic ranch house was a huge portrait of Henry Fonda as Wyatt Earp. On another wall in a glass case was Peter's jacket from *Easy Rider*.

Fonda had no problems with his grandchildren. They had a relaxed, loving relationship. Often, when Jane was away, Vanessa would stay with Fonda and Shirlee in Bel Air. "Granddad was wonderful to me," she said. "We spent hours weeding, pruning, mulching, and planting in his gardens. He could make anything bloom. I wanted to become a landscape architect because of Granddad."

Her attitude toward her mother was different. Although she loved her terribly and was in awe of her accomplishments, Vanessa was hypercritical of Jane. As Jane became more and more fixated on developing a Workout studio, Vanessa refused to exercise with her. "I would never do that," she'd say, almost contemptuously. "Mom kept promising to be different," she recalled years later, "promising she'd spend more time with me, promising she'd take me to such and such a place on Wednesday, and then Tom would come home and say, 'We have to do something on Wednesday,' and then Mom would say okay without batting an eye." Jane's promises to her daughter were often forgotten.

"I wasn't a good mother," she would admit on *Oprah* years later. "I didn't show up; I wasn't there." She rationalized that since she'd been raised by nannies and nurses, with narcissists for parents, that was all she knew and she behaved accordingly. Vanessa was cared for by a series of babysitters when Jane wasn't around. Tom Hayden wanted their little boy to have a much more "hands-on" approach. He hired a worker from the CED office, twenty-one-year-old Suzanne Tenner, who took care of Troy and became like a member of the family.

The atmosphere at home bothered Vanessa. She always felt "it was Tom and Jane and Troy," and she wasn't part of that family. She was glad to be away half the year in Paris with Vadim, but Jane didn't think being moved back and forth from parent to parent was healthy. "It splits a child in two." Vanessa would tell people, "I was raised by my father. Vadim was my mother. Even he said that."

As it turned out, in 1977 Catherine Schneider divorced Vadim, and he moved to California to be closer to eleven-year-old Vanessa, renting a shabby beach cottage a couple of blocks away from the Haydens on Beverly Street.

Vanessa was ecstatic. She declared more than once she hated Tom Hayden — hated being in the same room with him, hated seeing him demean her mother.

Vadim had a new girlfriend named Ann Biderman, a slender young screenwriter with slanting eyes and a quirky manner. She cared for him, and Vanessa loved her for that. She virtually camped out in the house on Beverly, often sharing their bed until Ann complained to Vadim, "She's too old" and he countered with *"C'est ridicule!"*

Ann met Jane when she dropped by Vadim's place to do some laundry in their laundry room. "Tom wouldn't let Jane have a washing machine or a dishwasher. Are you ready for that? She usually did everything by hand. Anyhow, she dropped by that afternoon lugging this laundry bag."

She announced that she'd just come from exercise class. Ann continued: "I thought she was the most beautiful woman I'd ever seen — she radiated energy — she shimmered. She and Vadim started talking very rapidly in French and that was lovely to listen to. We became friends. We still are."

Soon Jane found opportunities to drop by Vadim's funky little place on Beverly. She was drawn back into the seductive, life-loving atmosphere he always created.

Everybody loved Vadim. "Dogs — children — everybody," Suzanne Tenner said. Everybody loved Vadim except Tom Hayden, who treated him with veiled contempt; Vadim responded with cool indifference. "The door was always open in his little house, everybody was welcome," Ann said. "He was either cooking some delicious stew or out digging in his garden or listening to music. Typical Vadim, he had invited a former actress friend — a big alcoholic — to camp out in the spare bedroom — her name was Barbara Laage. They were drinking buddies."

"Oh, yes, he was an alcoholic," Ann went on; "he was absolutely open about it. Jane was so funny — critical of his drinking whereas she wasn't critical of Tom who was an alcoholic, too. But he was a secret drinker. His drinking went on for years and Jane seemed to be in denial about it."

While he was living in California, Vadim filmed a remake of *And God Created Woman* in Santa Fe as well as a documentary in Africa and some TV shows in Hollywood. At home he'd write songs or compose music; he worked all the time but he was often broke. When he badly needed money he would paint Jane a picture, and she'd hand him $10,000 in cash and run off before he could thank her.

He was probably still in love with her. He never said as much to Ann, but he sometimes called her Jane in his sleep; he said he dreamed about her all the time. Every so often Vadim would show up at Laurel Springs Ranch because it was so beautiful and because Vanessa was there. Once a stranger ran into him at the ranch. Vadim was sitting on the grass smoking a cigarette and gazing dreamily out at the landscape. The stranger asked him if he was driving back to L.A. Vadim obviously had nothing better to do so he said he was, and he chauffeured the stranger halfway there before the man realized this was Roger Vadim, the guy who'd directed Jane Fonda in *Barbarella*.

By mid-1978 Jane had completed Neil Simon's *California Suite,* giving a pitch-perfect performance as a cynical, high-powered *Newsweek* editor, with Alan Alda playing her estranged husband. The drama was a battle for custody of their daughter. They were in only one segment of the film, so work lasted just two weeks. It was a relief. "I'd done four movies back to back," Jane said. "I was exhausted and exhilarated."

She had reason to be. The media was full of references to "Jane Fonda rising like a phoenix from the ashes, reclaiming her career, transforming herself from girl toy to La Passionata of the New Left to Progressive Democrat wife." She won the Golden Globe Best Actress award for *Julia*, and the Women's Press Club gave her its Golden Apple for "cooperating with the press."

The many interviews she gave for the women's magazines and on TV in those months were as much for Hayden's benefit as for her own career. He was planning to run for office again, this time for a seat in the California State Senate. Sometimes he joined Jane with reporters. "Tom and Jane," Craig Unger wrote in *Esquire*, "it was hard to think of one without the other. Theirs is not just a marriage but a partnership to which Jane brings glamour and money and a Hollywood-based constituency and Hayden brings a political agenda and intellectual credibility." Together they seemed much more potent and secure than either would be alone. Their shared sense of purpose was a powerful bond.

By now she had developed her own brand of performance art when she spoke for Tom in public. Usually clad in faded jeans, a T-shirt that complimented her magnificent figure, and long brown hair streaming past her shoulders, she would let loose with a soliloquy that was equal parts populism, morality, standup comedy, and free association, all rendered in her beautifully modulated finishing-school accent. Everybody, young or old, whether they hated her or loved her, wanted to see Barbarella/Hanoi Jane/Mrs. Tom Hayden in the flesh. If she overshadowed her dour, glowering husband, it didn't matter. They were often called "the Mork and Mindy" of left-wing politics, and when Hayden was in a good mood, he'd repeat the joke, "We're Beauty and the Beast."

That said, Hayden's ambitions couldn't be underestimated. His long-range goal was to create a populist movement (CED was the start) that could elect members to Congress and a president — himself — in twenty years. Jane often said Tom would make a very good president; privately, Hayden discussed with advisers his chances of getting on the 1980 ticket as vice president. Both Teddy Kennedy and Jerry Brown were challenging Jimmy Carter for the nomination. Hayden had no chance with Carter, but he speculated whether a Kennedy/Hayden or Brown/Hayden ticket might happen. He seemed convinced that he would be a key figure for social change in his lifetime.

CED lobbied for solar commissions and rent control initiatives;

statewide, it was a powerful grass-roots organization. Its three hundred active members were largely white and college-educated. Some of Hayden's critics felt he was using CED to build on his 1982 senatorial race, that he shouldn't be head of CED as well. "CED wasn't really an independent organization," *Mother Jones* magazine wrote. "Hayden is built into the driver's seat and Fonda buys most of the gas. Through direct contributions, film benefits, concerts, and celebrity events arranged through her connections, Fonda finances the majority of CED's impressive budget."

At home the phone never stopped ringing. Scripts were piling up, telegrams were being delivered. In the spring of 1978, *Coming Home* had played at Cannes, and Jane and Jon Voight had won the Palme d'Or; the entire cast had been there to share in the acclaim. As soon as the movie began screening in L.A., excitement about it increased.

Although *The New Yorker*'s Pauline Kael dismissed the movie as an abstraction and Vincent Canby wrote that it lacked substance, *Time Magazine*'s Frank Rich called it "a devastating vision of this country's recent history. *Coming Home* is one long howl of pain." And *Playboy* said, "*Coming Home* is an emotionally rich romantic film played for the adult market. Jane and Jon produce the kind of chemistry that prompts movie goers to line up around the block."

Interest in the movie peaked the following year when both *Coming Home* and *The Deer Hunter* (the two competing films about Vietnam) were lavished with Oscar nominations.

Behind the scenes, the three writers involved with the screenplay of *Coming Home* had gone into a credit arbitration hearing with the Writers' Guild. Nancy Dowd was demanding sole credit for her story. Up to that point, she hadn't met Salt or Jones, and they were maintaining that they hadn't read her original draft. Jane was furious that Dowd was calling the story her own because Jane believed the screenplay was based on source materials and developed collectively.

After much discussion, the Guild came up with the following credit line for *Coming Home*: "Screenplay by Waldo Salt and Robert C. Jones; Story by Nancy Dowd." Jane made no comment on the Guild's judgment.

"At the ceremony, Jane and Jon both won Oscars and the screenplay won Oscars for Waldo [Salt], Jones, and Nancy Dowd," Bruce Dern recalled. "That was the capper. The three writers hadn't spoken to each other since arbitration. Waldo had just gotten out of the hospital. He comes up on stage with Bob and Nancy. Everybody looks stunned and annoyed and then Jane thanks everybody profusely, especially Tom Hayden, but pointedly neglects Nancy, a former friend. Oh, and Jane did her speech in sign language for the deaf."

The Deer Hunter won the Best Picture and Best Director Oscars for Michael Cimino; Christopher Walken won Best Supporting Actor. Jane was furious that *Coming Home* hadn't won Best Picture. (In some quarters *The Deer Hunter* was viewed as a racist defamation of Vietnamese culture, and Jane picked up on that and lambasted the movie to reporters. When questioned, she had to admit she hadn't seen the film yet.)

But that was Jane — impulsive, speaking before she considered the consequences; her behavior was anything but gracious. When Cimino tried to shake her hand backstage, she abruptly turned away. Around 1:00 A.M. she walked out of the awards dinner to call her father. He was at the Michael Reese Hospital in Chicago undergoing tests on his left hip. He'd watched the Oscar ceremonies on TV and told Jane he was thrilled for her. What he didn't tell her was that he'd been diagnosed with prostate cancer and that the cancer had spread to his hip; nor did he say he was flying back to L.A. to be operated on. She would not learn of Henry Fonda's condition for more than a week.

The day after she won the Oscar she and Bruce Gilbert marched into ABC and made a deal with its president, Brandon Stoddard, to star in *The Dollmaker* (which she would also produce). She'd been dreaming of doing this project for nine years and now she was going to do it.

At the same time, *The China Syndrome* had opened to terrific reviews and big crowds. Film critic Foster Hirsch noted, "In this movie Jane Fonda recycles her off-screen radicalization. Here she plays a TV anchorwoman with bright red hair, knowingly acting the female object role until she gets her breakthrough story about the danger in this nuclear plant." Several critics thought the story presented in the film was far-fetched. George Will in *Newsweek* sniped, "The film falsely suggests that nuclear power companies carelessly risk destroying their million dollar investments."

Then came the Three Mile Island disaster, a nuclear plant malfunction in the Pennsylvania farm country of Middletown. It was eerily like the plot of *The China Syndrome*, about a faulty water pump that causes a nuclear plant meltdown. The movie became a cultural phenomenon, inspiring cover stories in *Time* and *Newsweek*, and of course *The China Syndrome* did landslide business. Jane and Michael Douglas were on the cover of *People* and described as courageous producers with vision and prescience. Columbia later took the movie to the Cannes Film Festival. "Incredible reactions. Standing ovation," wrote director James Bridges in his journal.

Jane was showered with praise; everyone she cared about was getting in touch with her to say bravo. On May 19 there was a CED celebrity fashion show at the Beverly Wilshire. The stars were out for this fundraiser hosted by Jane and Jon Voight. Seven hundred celebrity supporters of CED's antinuke program attended, including Margaret Trudeau, Jack Nicholson, Warren Beatty, and Lily Tomlin. The atmosphere was warm and enthusiastic. Near the end the audience watched as Jane handed over the microphone to Tom, only to be astounded as Hayden turned an afternoon of cheers into a chorus of boos as he declaimed the establishment as "always using fashion as a decadent diversion from the real issues."

"What an ass," Richard Rosenthal said. He was there with his wife, Teddy, and he remembered, "You could feel that thought take over the entire ballroom. How not to win friends and influence people." Jane grabbed the microphone and attempted to smooth the troubled waters. "Tom had set off his self-destruct button but then again that's what he really felt. He couldn't help himself."

It was the same at home. At this point, Tom had started exerting such negative vibes around the house that friends felt uncomfortable when they dropped by. Jane was receiving too much attention. He simply could not take it. Within days he'd curtly ordered a "self-criticism encounter" for Jane (rather like the ones he'd been part of at the Red Family commune). It would be held at Laurel Springs. He asked Bruce Gilbert to attend along with Paula Weinstein, "to clear the air," Hayden said. "We would discuss our shortcomings, hear one another out," Jane said. "Neither Paula, Bruce nor I was entirely sure what the air needed to be cleared of, but these sorts of meetings were not unusual . . . we all assumed it would be constructive."

Everybody arrived at the ranch with some trepidation. As soon as the meeting started, Hayden lit into Jane, accusing her of hogging the limelight and not giving Bruce Gilbert the credit he deserved for *Coming Home*. It quickly became clear that Bruce was just an excuse for Hayden to express his rage at Jane for what he viewed as, she later wrote in *My Life So Far,* "the injustice of a movie star receiving so much attention when the 'real' people — who risk their lives every day and work hard to change the balance of power in the world — never get public credit. They, Tom said, are the unsung heroes, and it's not fair."

She'd lived with fame so long she hardly noticed it, but to Tom it was very disturbing. When she fell in love with him, she thought his sense of self was so secure that her celebrity would never threaten him. She'd been blinded by what she believed was their genuine closeness: what they'd worked for together — the Indochina Peace Campaign, CED. They'd been through so much politically, they'd been committed to so much — she thought he believed in their *love.*

Tom's mean streak toward Jane was often discussed among CED staffers. Nobody could figure out why she put up with it.

Jane has her own theories: "Because Tom's emotional coldness was like my father's. It was familiar, almost comfortable — it was a habit. Tom often made me feel stupid and superficial and my dad had made me feel that way, too."

At the time, she still believed that Tom had saved her life. Tom made her slow down; he helped her focus her huge energies on fewer projects and concentrate on him and their marriage and Troy. She felt fulfilled with Tom; she felt "real." She learned about politics through him, how to articulate ideas and issues. He encouraged her to return to the movies.

But her huge success overshadowed their life. Something terrible was happening between them, but they never talked about it. Jane could find no answers and nothing was resolved that afternoon at Laurel Springs. She would endure his treatment of her — no matter how belittling — for the next eight years, agreeing with him on everything from what kinds of vacations they went on to the political positions they took. "I simply didn't think that my ideas or feelings were as important or credible as his," she said.

• • •

At the same time the public saw Jane Fonda as the biggest female star of the decade and a genuine force in the business as a producer. She lived with a duality: outspoken, creative, independent lady versus victimized, inferior little girl. Such extremes! But she played both roles to a fare-thee-well.

Unable to sort out these contradictions, Jane resorted, as always, to exercise. She was exercising as much as three hours a day. And she had an affair — "It was wonderful, and traumatic," she wrote in *My Life So Far.* "I felt joyously liberated . . . but I knew I had to end it.

"I never spoke of this to Tom, nor did I know that he himself was seeking solace elsewhere. We simply continued in our unusual, seemingly successful partnership. . . . I would say, 'I think we should see a therapist,' and he would say no and I'd fall silent."

She befriended a young woman, an *All About Eve*–type wannabe actress who hung on her every word. Jane occasionally traveled with her, jogged with her. Some people assumed they were sleeping together because Jane often confided she had enjoyed sleeping with women since boarding school.

There was always her core group of close women friends who nurtured her: Paula Weinstein, Mignon McCarthy (earnest, devoted, she would travel with Jane and ghost her Workout books), and Suzanne Tenner, Troy's babysitter.

Suzanne was nineteen, small, dark-haired, waiflike; she had been recruited by Hayden in late 1979 from the CED office. "I'd been working there and he decided I'd be the perfect person to care for Troy . . . who was four years old when I came. . . . One of the reasons we bonded right away was that we both suffered from asthma."

Now a successful still photographer for movies, Suzanne had begun taking pictures before she started baby-sitting for Troy but remembered how Jane encouraged her and gave her an expensive camera. Suzanne said, "Jane often called me her third child. I didn't mind that because I hadn't had a happy childhood. I liked the family situation with Jane and Tom. They opened up worlds for me. I got close to Henry and Shirlee Fonda. Shirlee's my friend to this day. I traveled with Jane and Tom to Sundance, Utah, Africa, and New York — I even went to Santa Fe when Vadim was filming *And God Created Woman.*

"Jane and Tom were very private about whatever they were going through; they never acted out in front of us. I believe for a long time she was happy in that little house. With Tom she came closest to showing who she was deep inside."

Most weekends, Jane would drive out to Laurel Springs Ranch. Nestled among scrub oak and laurels in the hills high above Santa Barbara, the place offered spectacular views of the Pacific Ocean in the distance. It had begun as a CED retreat center, but it was used for all kinds of political and film meetings as well. There were endless discussions about the pros and cons of nuclear energy, to which Governor Jerry Brown often brought singer Linda Ronstadt, whom he was dating at the time. Jane and Bruce Gilbert were there often to talk about future movie projects. The second summer, Jane started a performing arts camp for children, which would run until 1991. Fifty campers from all walks of life attended: children of Black Panthers and Mexican American migrant farmers attended along with those of movie stars, such as Jon Voight's daughter, Angelina Jolie. Troy and Vanessa were there every summer, too.

"We stressed environmental education and the arts," said David Hodges, the young lawyer who ran the camp with his wife, Laurel Lyle, a sweet, fair-skinned actress who organized issue-oriented plays for the kids and would later be Jane's stand-in in several movies.

During those years, Jane built a swimming pool, a gymnasium, and a theater. She had a pond dug so Tom could fish, and she had a baseball diamond laid out on the great lawn so he could play baseball with Troy. It was their favorite sport.

"Every Easter we had a celebration for CED members and their families," Hodges recalled, "with an Easter egg hunt for the kids and Jane dressed up as the Easter Bunny, and we all sang—with Tom, too—'Puff the Magic Dragon.'

"It was a magical time, a transforming time," he finished. "We all believed we were making a difference with these young people and I think we did. We organized adventure trips, hiking into the mountains, river rafting."

"Jane was a real presence whenever she was at the camp," a counselor remembered. "She'd wander around the camp saying hello, stopping to hug some of the smaller kids. She was always in blue jeans and a T-shirt. Her hair was very long, past her shoulders, no makeup, she was so beautiful!"

Jane frequently accomplished something unexpected. David Hilliard, former president of the Black Panthers, was now working as an aide to Tom Hayden for CED in the L.A. ghettos.

"We'd have meetings at the camp which Jane often attended," Hilliard said. "She noticed I had a hard time getting the words out whenever I spoke about what I was doing. So for a while I don't think anyone else knew this. Jane taught me public speaking. She just took me aside and had me recite stuff. She'd record it, film it, we'd play it back on a monitor, I'd watch myself, listen to myself. Eventually I gained self-confidence. It helped me a lot in the next phase of my life when I began teaching black history to kids in Oakland."

And then there was Lulu, a shy girl who became Jane's informally adopted daughter. Lulu was a beautiful eleven-year-old, the child of two Black Panthers, Mary and Randy Williams, whom Jane had met in the early seventies, when she was friendly with Huey Newton.

Lulu had spent her early years in a Panther commune, surrounded by drugs and noise and violence. When she arrived at Laurel Springs, Jane remembered, "she was frightened and angry — she didn't like herself as a person."

Lulu had never been outside of Oakland; she had never been to the country before. She thought the ranch was absolutely gorgeous. "That first summer opened my eyes to so much. I saw white people for the first time in another reality. I started listening to them, had meals with them, realized they were not necessarily 'the enemy.'"

Lulu attended the camp for five years and eventually became a counselor. "Jane singled me out — noticed me, spoke to me. I couldn't get over it. I'd only seen her in *Barefoot in the Park*. She didn't teach classes or go on hikes with the other kids, but she was around a lot because she and Tom had a cabin on the property and their kids were there. Vanessa, Troy, and even Vadim — he was so sweet and funny. Suddenly Jane would just appear among us and ask us questions. She was very natural and really interested in what we were doing. We responded to each other almost instantly. We started talking to each other and we never stopped. I think we must have told each other everything over the years.

"We got very close — sometimes she'd drive me from L.A. to Santa Barbara. I started telling her about my family in Oakland." Lulu had been molested sexually by a man who threatened to kill her and her family if she told anyone. She was suffering from severe post-traumatic stress disorder and getting Ds and Fs in school despite her innate intelligence. She'd come back to the camp because she needed to tell someone. Jane made a deal with her that if she brought her grades up to Bs by the end of the school year, Jane would get her into a school in Santa Monica and she could move in with the Haydens.

Lulu started living with Tom and Jane when she was fourteen. "I didn't know what to expect — I'd grown up with a lot of drugs around, violent sex, no money, arguments, noise, slaps, and kicks. It was the way people communicated. You live like that and you expect nothing out of life and you think you deserve to be treated like shit. But of course Tom and Jane were gentle and loving. It was a huge surprise.

"Vanessa could have been jealous of me but she wasn't. She welcomed me and so did Troy. They have always been wonderful to me — kind, reassuring. Vanessa is a difficult person, outspoken, very smart — she had every reason to resent me because I was so close to her mother and because she and her mother were often at odds. But Vanessa was — is — terrific. I think of her as my sister. I was immediately accepted into the family, and Tom accepted me, too, and Vadim was always so cuddly and funny! I traveled with Jane a lot — to Mexico when she did *Old Gringo,* to Canada when she made *Stanley & Iris.*"

Lulu went on to graduate from college and enrolled in graduate school at Boston University, "with no help from me," Jane said admiringly. After college she started working as a fundraiser in the Atlanta office of the International Rescue Committee, which resettles refugees in the United States. Today Lulu calls herself Mary Lou Williams; she is a forest ranger in Alaska.

34

ARLY IN THE SUMMER of 1978, Jane began organizing her office
for her expected appointment to the California State Arts Council.
The position hadn't been ratified, but Governor Jerry Brown told
her it was a fait accompli. Jane hired a special assistant and flew to
Mexico to meet with the president of Mexico and his wife. She had
plans to develop arts programs between the United States and Mexico.

That same summer, Brown made another appointment. He named
Edison Miller, a former POW in Vietnam, to fill a recent vacancy on
the Orange County Board of Supervisors. Miller had been recommended by Jane, who had met him when she was broadcasting her
radio messages from Hanoi during the war. She had recently served as
matron of honor at Miller's second marriage. Tom Hayden served as
best man.

"Jerry Brown hadn't really wanted to appoint Miller," a colleague
recalled. "But he kind of had to, since Jane had promised to raise two
million dollars for his presidential campaign."

Miller was controversial with state legislators on both sides of the
aisle. Why had Jane and Hayden pushed the appointment? Some
think it was Hayden testing the governor. It was a power play, and it
backfired.

Fred Branfman said, "The California Democratic establishment
was furious at Jerry's choice. Edison didn't have a clue about how to
be a board supervisor. I was supposed to help Miller get acclimated. I
didn't have a clue as to what he was supposed to do either, but I moved
in with him in his house in Orange County. The whole thing turned

out to be a nightmare. Edison was simply not suited to the job in any way."

Since the appointment couldn't be blocked, the California Senate took revenge by rejecting Jane's appointment to the arts council twenty-eight to five, and Republican Robert Nimmo raised the issue of Jane's radio broadcasts in Hanoi, calling them "acts of treason."

Jane heard the news at the hairdresser's. She is said to have burst into angry tears. Brown quickly denounced the Senate as a "group of small-minded politicians." Jane accused them of "McCarthyism," and three hundred celebrities, including Henry Fonda, echoed the charge in a full-page ad in the *L.A. Times.* When the Senate refused to budge, Jane had to withdraw.

At the same time, reports of the North Vietnam bloodbath engulfing Laos and Cambodia hit the front pages, including stories of "boat people" trying to escape the massacre. Singer Joan Baez circulated a protest letter to her friends and colleagues condemning Hanoi and asking for signatures. Jane responded with a blistering attack against Baez; in essence she defended Hanoi.

Meanwhile the state legislature was deluged with letters and telegrams and phone calls praising its vote against Jane. "She was stunned," her lawyer, Richard Rosenthal, remembered, "by the intensity of the hatred being leveled at her."

In reaction to this latest wave of hostility, Rosenthal believed, "Jane became even more obsessed with having money — a lot of money. Money was power — money could protect her — and Tom and her family."

The China Syndrome was a big commercial success. Rosenthal reported to Jane how far she'd come financially since she returned to filming. "Your fee for *Julia* and *Dick and Jane* was $350,000, for *China Syndrome,* $500,000." In the most recent year, 1979, her price had actually doubled to $1 million, enabling her to pay off her debts. Now, he told her, "it has begun to be possible to realistically anticipate your having the required capital to participate in the kind of investment situation that we would both prefer."

But Rosenthal's memo didn't satisfy her. She'd been hanging out with rock stars who'd been salting away money for years — and she felt poor by comparison. Though Rosenthal continued to assure her that she was solvent and that he had been investing in Treasury bills and diligently tucking away extra dollars in a campaign war chest in case Tom ran for office again, she seemed unimpressed. Rosenthal noticed that she had grown cooler toward him since he'd moved to L.A. and they began meeting on a more regular basis.

In fact, there was a great deal of backbiting within the CED circle, and one of Jane's intimates had suggested that maybe Rosenthal was not doing well enough by her. It was the kind of second-guessing she was most vulnerable to. However good her own instincts were about parts and how to play them, she often listened to the wrong people about scripts or business decisions. She didn't trust herself. She had been spreading herself too thin, and on occasion she was impulsive. Only recently she'd been sitting on a plane next to an insurance salesman who struck up a conversation with her. She had all but agreed to sign some policy of his until Rosenthal told her it wasn't wise.

She was dissatisfied with her William Morris agents, too, and would ultimately switch to ICM. Money was on her mind constantly. In the years that followed, Jane would channel her phenomenal energy into making money; she would eventually be worth more than $50 million. Within the next year, she finally established herself in the exercise business. In the spring of 1979 she invested $100,000 in a large, light-filled studio lined with floor-to-ceiling mirrors. It was located in Beverly Hills on Robertson Boulevard. She was offering jazz and ballet; she had lined up good teachers, and she also planned to teach classes herself.

Gilda Marx heard about Jane's plans in a roundabout way. One afternoon a young woman with a heavy British accent came into Marx's studio and started scribbling notes on a pad. Marx said, "Can I help you?" and the woman answered, "Where do you buy your exercise mats and bars?" Marx asked who the woman was and why she was there. The woman answered, "I'm working for Jane Fonda, and I'm getting this information for her." Marx showed her the door.

Before the Workout opened in September 1979, the Haydens set out on a tour around the United States. It was ostensibly to raise money for CED and call attention to "corporate irresponsibility" and the danger of nuclear reactors, but it was really to test the waters for Hayden's Senate bid and Jerry Brown's presidential possibilities. Reporters found this the most fascinating aspect of what they were doing. "Tom and Jane and Jerry were in this flirtatious political dance," Jeffrey Klein wrote in *Mother Jones*. "If the political wind shifted, they could turn away immediately." But for the moment, the three of them were taking full advantage of each other. Jane called their barnstorming a "blitz pilgrimage."

Their kickoff appearance in Battery Park was described by *Time Magazine* as "the biggest anti-nuke rally in U.S. history." To the rollicking tunes of Bonnie Raitt, Pete Seeger, and Jackson Browne, 200,000 blue-jeaned couples — along with Bella Abzug and Ralph Nader — cheered as Tom Hayden cried out, "There will be a nuclear Armageddon unless something is done!" Jane followed with "We have to be like Paul and Pauline Revere going from city to city and town to town warning everybody of the dangers of nuclear pollution and chemical waste dumps!"

In less than a month's time, Jane and Hayden made appearances in seventy-five cities around the country, joined the picketing outside a nuclear waste dump, and protested the building of another nuclear plant in Seabrook, New Hampshire. There were side trips as well to the crippled Three Mile Island plant in Middletown, Pennsylvania (the largest local industry and steady source of jobs), constant interviews, and appearances on *Face the Nation,* where they were grilled by some very skeptical journalists who found them to be ill prepared and naive.

The trip cost $150,000 for travel and expenses, so between appearances they gave extra lectures at colleges for $5,000 a pop. Wherever they went, Jane was the main attraction. Fans crowded around for autographs while enemies such as members of the Catholic War Veterans and the American Legion waved placards saying HANOI JANE GO HOME.

For Hayden the trip was not accomplishing what he'd hoped it would. He'd imagined that together they would boost CED's membership by 5,000 additional people. They attracted only 2,500 new members.

Near the end of the tour, Jill Krementz photographed the couple for *Life* magazine behind the scenes. She caught their worried expressions as they watched themselves on late-night TV in some shabby motel room. In one telling image Jane is slumped stone-faced on a couch. She is suffering from a heavy cold and has broken her big toe. Hayden is sitting nearby, carefully sewing a button onto his jacket.

Just before they returned to California, Jane made a whirlwind solo tour of six cities — New York, Boston, Baltimore, Pittsburgh, Dayton, and Cincinnati — to urge female workers to organize and become a force as women and clerical workers. During every appearance, Jane would announce to her audience that she was about to make a movie about rebellious secretaries. She'd been inspired by her friend Karen Nussbaum, whom she had met when both were protesting the war. Nussbaum was now executive director of Working Women, a national organization devoted to organizing women office workers who were sick of earning low wages and experiencing sexual harassment.

Thanks to Nussbaum, Jane had met with forty secretaries and listened to their ideas about getting even with their male chauvinist bosses. "My movie's gonna be a feminist revenge fantasy," she would joke. She would get a standing ovation.

Jane envisioned *Nine to Five* not only as a message film, but as popular entertainment. She'd hired young screenwriter Patricia Resnick, who had worked for Robert Altman, to go undercover as a secretary in a large insurance company to hear secretaries' stories. Resnick came back with a script that Mike Nichols liked and was set to direct. Then the usual happened. Twentieth Century Fox didn't like the rewrites, so Mike Nichols walked. When Colin Higgins was hired to direct, he wanted to rewrite the script himself and Resnick was out. "At least Jane fired me personally," Pat said. "But I cried and cried." (Thirty years later Resnick would write *Nine to Five* as a Broadway musical with Dolly Parton writing lyrics and music.)

Jane cast Lily Tomlin as the efficient office manager and country and western singer Dolly Parton as the executive secretary to a male chauvinist honcho. Jane would be the newly divorced Judy Bernly, who has gotten her first job in an office and is constantly screwing up. The three women become friends and plot to undermine their male superior.

Originally the part of Judy had been a driven woman patterned after ambitious producer Paula Weinstein, Jane's closest friend, but as rewrites proliferated Judy became a bland nothing character. It didn't seem to matter to Jane that she was being diminished in favor of her two costars. Paula kept asking Jane, "What are you doing? You're one of the stars of the picture *and* the producer *and* you're earning a million dollars." Jane would murmur, "I'll deal with that later."

She did not tell Paula that since the ugly meeting with Tom months before at Laurel Springs Ranch she'd started losing confidence as an actress. What was worse, Jane said, "I was starting to lose interest in the business as well."

When her thirtieth film, *The Electric Horseman* with Robert Redford, became the biggest moneymaker in the fall of 1979, she hardly cared.

The public flocked to the film but critics weren't that enthusiastic. "Will we ever see Jane Fonda and Robert Redford play un-virtuous people?" asked critic Jack Kroll in *Newsweek*.

The filming of *Nine to Five* would begin in January of 1980, but a few days before it did Jane suddenly worried that Dolly Parton, who had never acted in a movie before, might feel self-conscious in front of the cameras. She called Marty Fried (her old friend from Actors Studio days) and asked him to fly out to coach Parton.

Within forty-eight hours Fried, by then a successful Broadway director, found himself sitting in Jane's office at Twentieth Century Fox watching her expertly carve a wooden apple with a knife. She explained that one of her next projects was going to be *The Dollmaker*, about a hillbilly woman who supports her five children by whittling little wooden figures.

"Then she switched subjects to Dolly," Marty recalled, "and how she thought I might be able to help her. She was cold and businesslike. We hadn't seen each other in a decade and a lot had happened to both of us, but Jane had no interest in the shows I was directing in New York — or my kids — she just wanted to talk about Dolly. I took her cue, but I was disappointed."

That same afternoon Fried visited Parton in her trailer. "We yakked about the script. Was she worried about anything? I asked her. 'Hell no!' Parton hooted. 'I'm raring to start filming!'" She was so full of life and jokes and energy, and besides, she'd been concertizing all over the country for years. Marty went back to Jane and told her that Dolly didn't need any coaching. Jane agreed with him and wrote him a generous check, and, Marty said, "I was off. But I felt let down. I'd wanted to schmooze with Jane."

The following morning he had time to kill before catching his plane back to New York. "I was curious about the Workout so I stopped by the place on my way back to the airport." The Workout had opened only three months before and was creating a sensation. Barbara Walters and Merv Griffin had already filmed segments of the class for their shows. Over two thousand women a week were packing into the studio in Beverly Hills to take a roster of classes. There were ballet, jazz disco, kids' disco, prenatal exercise, and postnatal recovery programs. The cost was a moderate $5.50 a class; Jane often taught a class at 5:00 A.M. before she filmed. She was giving interviews to every magazine and newspaper. "What's the connection between the Workout and progressive politics?" a reporter asked. She answered: "There is a direct financial relationship because the Workout is a CED business, and the profits go to CED. That's one aspect of it; the other is a concern for health and self-reliance." Jane credited Tom with coming up with the notion.

When Fried arrived at the Workout at 8:00 A.M., there were hordes of photographers and reporters milling outside the building along with a sizable crowd attempting to get in. A sign on the door announced: BENEFIT FOR E.R.A. BUY A TICKET FOR $100 & BE IN A CLASS TAUGHT BY JANE FONDA.

Marty let himself be swept along by the paparazzi, who were pushing their way into the Workout studio — a sunny room lined with mirrors. The photographers made a beeline for Jane, who was standing in the center of the room in a leotard and leg warmers, directing a group of forty women who were all bending and stretching and groaning to the beat of throbbing rock music. Ali McGraw was in one corner and Tina Louise, voluptuous and bathed in perspiration, was in another.

Jane was whooping it up in cheerleader fashion, barking out instructions. "Does it hurt? Does it burn? Because if it doesn't burn, you aren't doing it right!" Her minions yelled back: *"Yeah!"* As Marty watched sweat darken around Jane's tiny waist and crotch, he had "this epiphany . . . she looked like *Barbarella* in her tights and striped top. Was that intentional?" And then when she rolled around on the floor, he thought of the scenes in that movie when she was simulating orgasms, or in *Coming Home* when she'd gone down on a guy, "and hey, wait — ! In *Klute* she played a prostitute." No wonder she'd been identified as a consummate sex object. Her transformations were dizzying. She was empowering women to be in charge of their bodies — to take control of their bodies — and they were loving it. Yes, in spite of her transformations, she continued to "give orders in that finishing-school accent." Marty decided that at heart, "Jane is still Henry Fonda's privileged little girl."

When class was over, Jane called out, "Thanks for being patient with the press!" Everybody applauded her. Photographers continued snapping pictures. Within minutes, representatives from the National Women's Political Caucus moved front and center and Jane announced, "We thought this would be a fun and easy way of raising several thousand dollars for the ERA." Someone asked, "How much do you think you'll raise?" and Jane laughed. "Forty women signed up for hundred-dollar tickets. You figure it out."

Marty didn't see Jane again, although they spoke on the phone a couple of times during the filming of *Nine to Five* and she confided she'd never laughed so hard, especially with Dolly Parton. *Nine to Five* would go on to be IPC's biggest hit: it grossed over $150 million. One reviewer would call it "a zany slapstick of a romp."

Then came *Rollover*. Alan Pakula was directing. Shooting began in the spring of 1980; it was a lavish production filmed on location in New York. A great deal was riding on it for Jane. It would be her fourth production venture for IPC. Her previous three films had been hits.

The first scene took place in the midst of a glamorous benefit with three hundred extras milling around the Ocean Room of the Museum of Natural History. Behind them electric eels swam unceasingly through the display caves set in the walls. In the forefront, surveying the crowd, Jane stood looking supremely elegant in a shimmering beaded gown.

She could not stop worrying about the script. *Rollover* was ostensibly about corporate greed, and it had gone through endless rewrites and now began with a murder in the first fifteen minutes because Mike Medavoy, head of Orion Pictures and one of the producers, had insisted on it.

In the final version, Jane's character, Lee Winters, a former actress and powerful CEO, becomes romantically involved with a renegade banker named Hub Smith. Together they become enmeshed in an international intrigue involving the transfer of billions of dollars from powerful U.S. banks by Arab investors. Jane wasn't sure about this version, which rested on global financial collapse; she wasn't sure it was very dramatic.

Nor was she sure that her costar, Kris Kristofferson, was right as the renegade banker because Kris looked like a cowboy and preferred jeans to a suit and tie. He had already told her he hadn't wanted to shave off his beard because he used it as a protective mask. He felt naked without it, he complained. The fact was, he told people, he was wrong for the part but wanted to work with Jane.

The best part of the *Rollover* experience was her reconciliation with her stepdaughter, twenty-one-year-old Nathalie Vadim. Slender, blond, and bilingual, Nathalie had been a script supervisor for a couple of years, working for directors like Mike Nichols. When she decided she needed a change, Jane got her a job as third assistant director on *Rollover.*

"We hadn't spoken much in twelve years," Nathalie said, "although I'd seen her off and on. I finally was able to tell her how angry and hurt I'd been when she left my father and went off to protest the war. She insisted she hadn't been aware of how I felt and I believed her because Jane can often be unaware of the most obvious things. Anyhow she said she was sorry."

The two became close again. Jane needed to have people to confide in whom she could trust — especially when, during the filming of *Rollover,* she "flipped out for Kris. She thought he was very hot; she talked about him all the time," Nathalie said.

Hume Cronyn (who played the villain in *Rollover*) added: "Kris knew he was in trouble when it came to women but he just shrugged and went along with it. He was quite something to watch — soft-spoken, unhurried — he projected this genial sexiness. He created an instant intimacy with every woman on the set. Who better than Kris to placate a stubborn, often jittery star like Jane Fonda?"

Soon, Jane and Kris could be seen jogging in Central Park and going to an out-of-the-way gym to exercise together. Then the *National Enquirer* ran stories implying that the couple were having an affair.

They expressed outrage. But it was Nathalie Vadim who insisted she was having a romantic involvement with the shaggy-haired folk singer, not her stepmother. She had no idea whether Jane did. "I didn't ask her."

Besides, during *Rollover,* Jane's concentration was split. She spent every spare minute promoting the Workout on radio, TV, and newspaper interviews. She kept stressing the importance of keeping fit ("It'll change your life"), and thousands of women were starting to listen to her. She was her own best advertisement; at forty-two she was sleek and toned and bursting with energy.

By 1980, the Workout in Beverly Hills was doing phenomenally — women of all ages were continually jamming the place. It was a "must visit" site for tourists from around the world.

"Our accountants were amazed," Jane said. She would soon open two other Workouts in Encino and San Francisco and would consider franchising when the three Workout studios began generating $20,000 a month. (She would also sign with Simon & Schuster for a Workout book and not long after that appear in a video, which would revolutionize the video business.)

In the midst of the Workout's soaring success, Jane fired Richard Rosenthal and replaced him with Barry Hirsch, a high-profile lawyer whose clients included Sydney Pollack and later Julia Roberts and Jennifer Lopez. Unlike Rosenthal, Hirsch was a Hollywood insider who knew every agent and star in the industry. Hirsch and other associates would negotiate and advise Jane as her empire grew. Rosenthal hadn't seen it coming — although for the last three months Jane had been questioning him more and more about their "business management relationship" as well as management fees and percentages. She had never questioned him before. He was also a bit put off when she sent him an abrupt note, criticizing him for not praising the Workout enough.

"I need more sophisticated people with more clout and leverage," Jane told him when they met in his office. "You're okay with little people like my father. You're into other things. You're very creative. This will probably be the best thing that ever happened to you," she added.

"We argued, sulked, laughed, cried, and in the end hugged and kissed," Rosenthal said. "After three hours of back-and-forth, I put my arms around her. She put her head on my shoulder, and I knew it was over."

But it wasn't until he was driving east on Wilshire that reality hit him: "After a dozen years of looking after Jane Fonda, her legal, business, and financial affairs and literally thousands of related subjects — people, personal matters — my dear friend had come to tell me she didn't want me to represent her anymore — she didn't think me sufficiently positioned to give her the kind of investment advice and direction she thought she now required. I was a jumble of conflicting thoughts and emotions as I aimed my Ford wagon up Beverly Glen. How would I break the news to my family? Part of me rejoiced at the lifting of a burden that had of late become intolerable."

Rosenthal went on: "This Jane Fonda was not the same earnest, innocent, high-minded young woman I first met and admired in December 1968. Not the same brave, selfless soul who inspired my unflagging devotion and service in days gone by. Fate and her overwhelming need to satisfy a long, aching lack of self-esteem had propelled her to a larger-than-life stardom on the stage of contemporary human history. It had taken its toll."

A couple of days later, he had a "weird moment in the men's room of a hotel whose name I can't remember. I'm standing at a urinal and suddenly I realize Tom Hayden is standing next to me. We had never been close but suddenly he said to me: 'Just wanted you to know I had nothing to do with Jane's decision to let you go. No hard feelings I hope.' And then he zipped up his pants and was gone."

In 1988 Rosenthal sued Jane for $2 million. "In the process," he said, "I would find out just how iffy it was to challenge a star of Jane's magnitude and the corrupting force of her wealth, power, and personality. I would learn just how good an actress she'd become and, to my eternal sadness, how dangerously far she had traveled along the road of expediency in her quest for identity, acceptance, and, yes, power. My idol turns out to have feet of clay." Movie stars fire agents, lawyers, and managers all the time. But Rosenthal thought he was more than Jane's lawyer; he thought he was her friend. That was his big mistake.

Their oral agreement stipulated that, in return for performing a variety of personal services, he would receive 10 percent of all gross professional income derived from the projects that were initiated during his tenure as her lawyer and business manager from 1972 through 1980, including *On Golden Pond.* They went to trial. The court determined that New York law controlled this dispute rather than California, and that the statute of frauds barred Rosenthal's claim against Fonda for breach of an oral contract. Jane won the suit. Rosenthal charged that falsified documents were produced to discredit his claim.

After his break with Jane, Rosenthal continued to represent Henry and Shirlee Fonda, and their relationship was amicable. In January 1981 Rosenthal drew up Henry Fonda's last will and testament, and he was listed as one of the executors.

Fonda was frailer than ever — quite ill from heart problems. He was observing his daughter's stupendous success with pride. A reporter asked him, What would she do next? "Beats me," he said.

What she did do next was produce a movie for him. "For years I had wanted to do a movie in which all the Fondas — Henry, Peter and I — could act together. . . . Even though there was no role for Peter and mine was very much a supporting one, I believed that in the role of Norman Thayer, Dad would win the Oscar that had eluded him for so long."

35

I T WAS ROSENTHAL who'd sent *On Golden Pond* to Henry Fonda. He passed it on to Jane, who then read the Broadway comedy by Ernest Thompson and surprised her father by not only buying the film rights but saying she wanted to play the part of the daughter.

It was clear it was the perfect vehicle to unite them on the screen. "But it's not a starring role," he'd protest. "I don't care, Dad," she'd cried. "I want to act in a movie with you."

The story: crusty, taciturn, eighty-year-old Norman Thayer, a retired college professor, has come to spend the summer at his vacation home on Golden Pond, New Hampshire. He faces death with fear and loathing; he's alternately sarcastic and loving to his longtime wife, Ethel, and chilly to his daughter, Chelsea, and her dentist fiancé; Chelsea and Norman's relationship has always been tense. Norman has never been able to show love, let alone interest, in his daughter, and Chelsea has been actively rebelling all her life, hoping he'll pay attention to her.

"It's so close to our story," Jane insisted, "an archetypal story of love and loyalty about the difficulty of resolving generational differences." On top of that she was sure "Dad will win an Oscar for his performance." She was determined to help him get it.

She felt that playing the part of Chelsea might finally change the public's perception of them as a dysfunctional family, at the very least shift the perception of her (to use John Houseman's phrase) "from that of an Electra to that of a Cordelia."

For his part Henry Fonda wanted to keep an artistic distance in the movie. He confided to playwright David Rintels that he was "afraid his real-life relationship with Jane might interfere." He could not abide that thought.

Jane asked Mark Rydell to direct. Rydell, with his soft brown eyes and tough-guy manner, had just had a huge success directing Bette Midler in *The Rose*.

Jane agreed with him that Katharine Hepburn would be the perfect Ethel in *On Golden Pond*. Hepburn liked the script and agreed to star in it almost immediately.

They decided to shoot the film in New Hampshire in the summer of 1981. "But we had to move fast," Rydell said. "Hank was very frail, and it gets cold up there in early September. Then the actors struck the Motion Picture Association and nobody was sure we could even go ahead with the movie."

Luckily Bruce Gilbert, Jane's coproducer, got a waiver "so we could begin to film," Rydell finished. "Since our movie was released by a British distributor it didn't fall under MPAA jurisdiction. There were some grumbles from union members who felt Jane's clearance showed favoritism, but the grumbles soon died away."

The entire production was shot on location in Laconia, New Hampshire, an idyllic spot surrounded by four lakes, bordered by rustic lodges and cottages hidden from view by thick groves of trees: oak, birch, poplar, and fir.

Jane rented a virtual compound, which she needed because Hayden would be there along with Troy, Vanessa, and Suzanne, the babysitter, as well as members of the CED steering committee; they were meeting frequently to discuss CED business and Hayden's run for the state Senate.

Henry and Shirlee Fonda had a house ten minutes from Jane's and so did Katharine Hepburn. Everybody else in the production lived in houses scattered about the woods.

The first morning, Rydell remembered, "We all were waiting for La Hepburn to arrive. Hank and Shirlee were perched on stools drinking coffee. The rest of the cast and crew hovered, and then Hepburn appeared, dressed in costume — an old fisherman's sweater and slacks. Her palsy was quite pronounced. She was visibly shaking. She marched over to Fonda holding a battered hat in her hand. 'This was Spencer's favorite hat. Thought you'd like it,' she said in quavery tones. Hank mumbled thanks. I could tell he was moved. It was one of three hats he wore throughout the picture, and when the film ended he made a painting of the three hats so real you could feel the texture. He had lithograph prints of the painting made for the entire cast and crew."

For the first couple of days all Kate talked about was Spencer Tracy this and Spencer Tracy that. Everybody listened politely, but finally Rydell took her aside and said she must stop talking about Spencer; she was working with Henry Fonda now. She stopped immediately. And then she zeroed in on Jane.

"Kate recognized qualities in Jane that she had," Rydell said; the toughness—neither one of them ever fit the mold. They were both so proud and so unconventional, and they both had the same kind of vulnerability that comes from daring to lay themselves on the line. Kate had been very political during the Blacklist, speaking out, telling L. B. Mayer to, "in essence, go fuck himself."

Throughout the filming Kate kept Jane on the defensive. "She'd berate me for not being an active enough producer," Jane said. "She was horrified when she learned that CED workers shared our house. She kept telling me: 'You do too much, you spread yourself too thin . . . you certainly shouldn't have had children.'"

Jane did not tell her how much her family meant to her and how much she'd needed to create a family, to be surrogate mother to Nathalie and Christian and Lulu. "But Hepburn never stopped being hypercritical of the way I was leading my life."

Mark Rydell felt just the opposite. "Jane used her obsessive-compulsive behavior in a wonderfully creative way. Oh, yeah, she suffers from obsessive-compulsive behavior bigtime! But I have never seen anyone who accomplished as much as Jane did in one day."

Once Jane showed Rydell her daily diary. "Every fifteen minutes to half-hour was scheduled with *something*. At the crack of dawn she'd lead a Workout session for cast and crew, then she'd make phone calls. Then she'd work with her assistant, maybe on mail, then if she wasn't filming she'd be writing her Workout book or conferring with Michael Jackson. He came up to location (got very friendly with Kate Hepburn—what a pair). He was giving Jane some of his music to use on her video for free (because all proceeds went to CED). Then there were the meetings with Tom. He'd just launched a very expensive two-year campaign for the California State Assembly, so he had his people come up to confer. And then every weekend the Haydens held a 'salon' in their compound. Jerry Brown came up and Dan Ellsberg; sometimes they'd invite me to join their discussions about the upcoming election . . . Reagan and Bush on the Republican ticket . . . Carter was running again as president . . . Teddy Kennedy backed out. I remember another piece of news. Cathy Wilkerson, a member of the Weather Underground, had surrendered to the police. It was funny. During these discussions at the compound Tom would be talking and Jane would look at him as if waiting for a cue so she could speak. She constantly deferred to him. It didn't seem genuine; as soon as she was away from Tom she seemed more herself."

He recalled: "Once we were in my car having a very intense conversation about some script point. Jane loves to talk; she can get very wound up and talk and talk and so articulately even when she goes off on tangents, she can be brilliant. And she's funny too — ironic. I can't remember what we talked about, but it was so enjoyable that when it was over I leaned over and gave her a peck on the cheek, and with that she kissed me full on the mouth. I went with it and then we both laughed. She was so ripe and blooming and lovely! The kiss was meaningless. Nothing like that ever happened again between us. She had obviously wanted me to know she was still very much a sexual, sensual woman — and I knew that — I'd heard things were not that great between her and Tom. But I knew she could be a very wild creature."

On Golden Pond culminated with the filming of the scene between Jane and her father. "From the first, every time I read the script I would come to that scene and tears would pour down my cheeks. Finally the day of reckoning came. I woke up and ran to the bathroom to vomit, more scared than I had ever been before a scene and knowing it was because I had to say intimate words to my father that I had never been able to say in real life."

First the exchange with her mother: "I can't talk to him, I've never been able to . . ." And her mother counsels her, "Remember Norman is eighty years old and he has heart problems."

Jane had spent her entire life reaching out to Henry Fonda — comparing him to other men, seducing men who reminded her of him. Loving men who resembled him in their coldness and detachment. Oh, how she longed for her father to recognize her! — speak to her — really connect. She raged at him and raged at herself for forever fighting with that part of herself who yearned only to be Daddy's little girl. Sometimes in her dreams the image of Tom Hayden shifted and merged with the image of Henry Fonda.

So on the day they shot the scene Jane couldn't stop crying; her tears flowed — until she had to play her close-up and then she dried up. "*Oh, no,* the actor's worst nightmare: I was bone dry, spent, unable to call up any emotions. What to do?

"There was Hepburn, crouching in the bushes just within my line of vision. Nobody could see her but me. She fixed me intensely with her eyes, and slowly she raised her clenched fists and shook them as if to say 'Do it! Go ahead. You can do this!'"

So Norman and Chelsea rehash old wounds and open new ones. "I want to be your friend." Jane chokes out the words, then touches Henry Fonda's arm, and he draws back with a shudder — he hadn't expected that.

"I saw Dad fighting to keep the tears back and I couldn't keep my tears from flowing," Jane remembered. "It was such a moment — a moment of such intimacy . . . I don't even care how it looks onscreen!"

(Depending on how you feel about the scene, it is over the top or uncomfortably raw. Nathalie Vadim said: "I found *Golden Pond* almost impossible to watch, it is so naked. I knew too much of the backstory." Pauline Kael's comment was brutal: "Chelsea is a terrible role and Jane Fonda plays it so intensely she's like an actress telegraphing her psychiatric miseries.")

That evening Jane asked her father if she could come over to supper because "the scene had been so utterly personal for me, so intimate in a way that he and I had never been. I was raw and felt so close to him, and I needed to acknowledge it and see if he felt the same . . . mostly I wanted to know if he had changed in any way as a result of the intimacy.

"I told him about drying up and asked if such a thing had ever happened to him.

"'Nope.'

"I couldn't believe it. 'Not ever once in your whole career?'

"'Nope.'

"My heart sank. That was it, just 'Nope.' Why did these things happen to me and not to him? What was I doing wrong? Moreover . . .

he was no more open or forthcoming now than he'd been before the scene. I was so sad. I felt like a dope for getting all soft and fuzzy over what to him was obviously just a scene."

However, Shirlee had a different memory. After Jane left, Fonda became agitated and clung to Shirlee. He was almost crying. "He had been very upset about doing the scene and of course he felt something, but he just couldn't admit it to Jane."

When *On Golden Pond* wrapped, Henry Fonda returned to his home in Bel Air. In the mornings when it was warm and sunny, he planted more flowers and fruit trees and he took care of his bees. He loved being in his gardens — especially his organic vegetable garden. That fall he constructed a scarecrow and stuck it in the midst of the corn and the carrots, potato plants, onions. He dressed the scarecrow in his old clothes — a wonderful shirt, battered pants, a tie. He'd painted the face with a rather woebegone expression on it. Ann Biderman said: "That scarecrow was a work of art."

As the months went by, Henry Fonda grew frailer and more grumpy, said George Peppard, who visited him. Usually a full-time nurse accompanied Fonda as he shuffled between the immaculate rooms of his house and outside onto the patio or near the pool; Shirlee was invariably with him, too.

He'd already undergone surgery to remove a benign tumor the size of a grapefruit. Doctors had discovered that his prostate cancer had metastasized — he kept losing weight. But Jane said: "Shirlee hadn't allowed us to admit he wasn't going to get better, so we all went around pretending he'd be up and about in no time. I hated it. It all rang so false but I felt I had to honor her wishes."

She was afraid her father might not live long enough to see *On Golden Pond* so she phoned Mark Rydell and asked him to screen a rough cut of the movie for him.

Fonda shuffled into the theater alone on two canes. Rydell said: "I was too nervous to sit with him so I waited outside. When it was over I came back into the theater to find Hank struggling to get to his feet. He managed to, but then he literally fell into my arms and I held him and felt him shuddering and I thought, 'My God, he's gonna die right here and now!' But after a few minutes he whispered to me, 'Thank you for the most important film of my life. Thank you.'"

He rallied. The picture opened in December of 1981, got good reviews, and did huge business. It received a reverential cover story in *Time* and everyone began talking about Fonda's performance and how he deserved an Academy Award.

He knew how much he owed Jane. "I am not a religious man," he said, "but I thank God every morning I've lived long enough to play this role."

He did, of course, win the Oscar in April 1982, and so did Katharine Hepburn—her fourth. A radiant and tearful Jane, wearing her overblown Farrah Fawcett wig, accepted the award for her father. "This is the happiest night of my life," she told the cheering audience. Then Jane brought the award home and handed it to her father as he sat wrapped in blankets. The entire family surrounded him: Peter, Bridget, Amy, Vanessa, Troy, Shirlee.

For the next months he was in and out of hospitals. Jimmy Stewart, his oldest friend, came to visit three times a week, and they tried to talk but it was difficult; they were both quite deaf and got tired of shouting to each other, so they would sometimes just sit in silence. Fonda had stopped painting but his work was all around him: the meticulously rendered watercolors, the still lifes of fruit and flowers, the rooftops of London. It was all part of his effort to express himself in vivid images in ways he could not and would not express in words.

Jane came to the house almost every day, and she kept trying to talk to him, but he just sat there and never responded. Then one afternoon she blurted out that she loved him and she was sorry for the things she'd done to hurt him. Suddenly he started to cry and she got scared. "I hurt for him, and was scared of this display of his pain and sadness. I stayed for a while in an effort to comfort him but then had to leave because I could sense he hated to be crying in front of me. Shirlee told me that when she got home a little later she found him still in the chair, sobbing."

And he cried again when Peter visited. Peter had come from his ranch in Montana to tell his father about the trips he'd taken on his boat—and the movies he hoped to make and how his children were growing, but mostly how much he loved him. He'd already phoned about six times and kept saying, "I love you very much, Dad."

That afternoon as they were moving very slowly back into the garden, Henry Fonda took Peter by the shoulders. "It was as if he was pushing me away but at the same time he was drawing me close. Tears streamed down his cheeks. 'I love you very much, son. I want you to know that.'"

Peter said, "I hugged him so hard, I could feel the pacemaker in his chest. I told him I loved him very much and I kissed him on the lips."

Throughout the spring and summer Jane campaigned for Tom Hayden, who was running for the California State Assembly in the heavily Democratic 44th District. For six hours a day, six days a week, Jane trudged all over, urging people to vote for her husband. The 44th was an eclectic mix of rich and poor — including Santa Monica, West L.A., and Malibu. Hayden used to kid, "The district has the greatest divergence of incomes in the state — mine and my wife's." But behind the scenes he'd brag about his rich wife; with her millions he believed nothing could stop him. He even confided to a friend once as he surveyed the landscape at Laurel Springs, "I'd always dreamed of having a ranch and being married to a movie star." Now he had both.

Whether Jane ever knew her husband's true thoughts, she was determined he'd win this election. She was in on every political decision he made — even though she downplayed her role: "I'm just around to see that he's happy," she'd say.

When Hayden's opponents began implying he was pro-PLO, Jane helped orchestrate their highly publicized trip to Israel to change that view. In Tel Aviv they were photographed visiting soldiers wounded in the Israel-Lebanon conflict, and they even marched to the front where they were photographed watching impassively as Israeli gunners fired shells into the residential neighborhood of Beirut ("nearby a radio blared the Beatles singing "Eight Days a Week," Chris Andersen, author of *Citizen Jane,* noted). Once back in Santa Monica, Hayden spoke to voters defending Israeli actions. "The PLO's use of terrorism makes Israeli actions inevitable," he said. He wanted everyone to believe he had never in his radical past supported the Palestine Liberation Front.

Back in L.A. Jane helped hire a top-flight media consultant to soften Hayden's left-wing image, and soon a TV spot began playing all the time promoting the image of the Haydens as a happy, middle-of-the-road Democratic family. Only Vanessa rebelled. At a Hayden rally she mugged shamelessly for photographers in clown whiteface makeup, and at a dinner in a restaurant as Jane was slipping a credit card under the table for Tom to pay, Vanessa cried, "Oh, Mom, puh-leeeese!"

Jane kept forging ahead — she felt this campaign could be the start-up for Tom's presidential ambitions. "He should be in the White House someday," she told friends.

On August 12, 1982, Henry Fonda died. Shirlee phoned Jane at home, and she raced to the hospital. She was so frantic she forgot to put her car in park and it had started to roll into the street before a hospital employee jumped in and applied the brakes.

Jane was not allowed to stay with her father; the nurse ordered everyone to leave. Peter had hoped he could wipe "the death's grin off Dad's face," but he couldn't.

The entire family gathered outside the house in Bel Air and spoke briefly to the press, saying that Henry Fonda had "died quietly and is at peace," and then everybody disappeared inside.

Jane had decided she should mourn for her father by staying at his house; she slept in the spare room for the next week. Sometimes Bridget and Justin Fonda, Peter's kids, dropped by, and they joined Jane and Vanessa and watched the endless tributes to Henry Fonda on television. "It was like the departure of a president or a king," Vanessa remembered. Bridget, who would soon become an actress, took her grandfather as her inspiration. "My dad and Jane are very out there, very intense. What drives them is very different from what I saw in Henry. He was cool; he didn't show a lot of things, and that's the way I am."

Throughout the week friends moved in and out of the Fonda home. Jane spoke to Henry's longtime makeup man. "He told me how much Dad talked about me, worried about me. 'You can't imagine how much he talked about you.' Funny, I thought, how Dad talked to others *about* me but never directly *to* me."

Henry Fonda had specified in his will that he wanted to be cremated and his ashes "thrown out with the trash." Jane and Peter hated that idea and so did Shirlee Fonda. So she held on to the ashes and kept them under her bed. Jane and Peter tried to figure out a way of getting the ashes away from her so they could scatter them on the Nebraska plains or bury them somewhere, "so we could visit Dad now and then."

No words were exchanged between them but Shirlee got wind of their plan. She proceeded to hide the ashes somewhere else. Jane and Peter tried in vain to find them but they ultimately gave up.

"It wasn't my decision to make about Dad's ashes, but that's when I decided I wanted to be buried with a gravestone," Jane said.

For much of the week she wandered about the Fonda home, mostly ending up in the garden. She seemed lost and adrift. Her purpose in life, which had been to prove herself to her father and make him love her, had melted away. What would she do now?

Peter meanwhile had holed up in the gatehouse with James Garner. They smoked a lot of pot and played the documentary Peter had filmed of his father. "Jim and I talked. I felt at peace. I felt closure. My dad had told me he loved me. I felt good," Peter said.

One morning he glanced out the window and saw Jane standing next to one of the fruit trees her father had planted not long before he died. She had her arms around the tree and she was hugging it for dear life and crying her eyes out.

Peter wrote later: "I can still see Jane, in the early morning, sitting under one of [Dad's] apple trees . . . and softly crying. It touches my heart in such a sad way. My sister deserves to be a happy person."

A week after he died, Henry Fonda's will was filed for probate. He left nearly all of his considerable estate to Shirlee Fonda and to Amy, his adopted daughter from his marriage to Susan Blanchard. He left nothing to Jane or Peter "because," as he stated brusquely in his will, "in my opinion they are financially independent."

When he heard the news, Peter retorted sadly, "Yeah, sure that's right. We didn't *need* anything. But it would have been nice to have a token — just one measly token from our dad."

As for Jane, "It was a bitter pill to swallow," Susan Blanchard said. "She had tried — oh, God, how she had tried — to connect with her father. She had done everything." Several of Jane's friends called him a son of a bitch.

To which Jane would reply, "Yeah, but he's *my* son of a bitch."

Months after his death she would start to cry if someone mentioned the word *dad*. "My father has come to me in dreams," Jane said, "stepping out from behind a bush, radiantly happy, to tell me not to worry about him."

36

FOUR MONTHS AFTER Henry Fonda's death Tom Hayden won a seat in the California State Assembly. His opponent, Republican Bill Hawkins, had campaigned almost solely on the idea that Hayden's newly crafted "moderate politics" were false, that he was still a "dangerous radical." But that didn't convince voters. Tom Hayden won 164,373 votes to Hawkins's 153,388.

There was a noisy victory celebration at the Santa Monica Hotel with Jane smiling and waving beside Hayden, who was smiling and waving, too. One couldn't have guessed that they had buried his father earlier that day in Detroit (they'd flown there at the crack of dawn to do so).

In fact he eulogized his father in his speech. "My dad wanted to live for this night," he said. "But he had to die . . . a proud supporter . . . Dad may you rest in peace."

Hayden's campaign had been the most expensive state legislature campaign in U.S. history — a huge investment of money ($1.3 million, $615,000 from Jane personally, not to mention the hundreds of thousands of dollars in Workout profits that poured into CED); that and her glamour and her dedication had made the victory possible, more so than Hayden's "Growing Up with America" slogan and his new moderate positions, which seemed to make him more attractive to voters. It was Jane who'd made his election possible. She had appeared at rallies and malls all over the Los Angeles area. "I have never seen anyone give as much to another human being as Jane did with Tom," added Lauren Weissman, Jane's new assistant at IPC and a close friend.

"I'm not just talking about money," Weissman went on. "It was her influence, her celebrity — her connections." Weissman and Jane shared an office at Twentieth Century Fox. "I saw her every day, saw her call in her connections — make long lists — she was relentless. She did everything in her power to make Tom's dream come true."

During the campaign Jane had been hunting for a larger house. She found a nice property on Alta Avenue in Santa Monica and began renovating, filling the place with lots of chintz-covered furniture and the four Andy Warhol portraits of herself. There was a big cluster of family photographs arranged on a center table — images of Henry Fonda at every phase of his career and close-ups of Jane and Fonda looking very happy together. The Haydens moved in right after the election.

In the last five years Jane had accomplished everything she'd wanted. She'd made millions from her four "message" films, she'd ensured her father his Oscar, she'd helped Tom win his Senate seat, and she had many projects in the works. Success for any future IPC project seemed a given.

IPC Films had grossed more than half a billion dollars since its initial production, *Coming Home. On Golden Pond* grossed $119 million, and *Nine to Five* had raked in $103 million. This financial bonanza came to an abrupt stop with *Rollover. Rollover* opened the week after *On Golden Pond* and it was a complete disaster, grossing only $10 million worldwide. The reviews were brutal — Janet Maslin carped in the *Times: "Rollover* isn't dull but it is so bungled it is riveting."

Jane blamed the script — then she privately blamed Bruce Gilbert, who'd insisted on a story line she hadn't agreed to. Gilbert had no movie experience: before Jane met him, he was running a nursery school Vanessa was attending. By 1983, she and Gilbert parted ways.

Jane would not make another movie for three years. She would instead concentrate on her evolving fitness empire. Her three Workout studios (in Beverly Hills, Encino, and San Francisco) were flourishing. In the spring of 1982, the first Jane Fonda Workout book was published, featuring the phrase "Go for the burn!" The book was a huge bestseller and was translated into fifty languages. It was illustrated with photographs of Shirlee Fonda gracefully demonstrating all the routines, muscle stretches, and leg lifts. Using Shirlee as the model in the book had been a way of placating her. Shirlee was miffed because Jane had never credited her publicly with the Workout idea. "It *was* my idea," Shirlee said.

After the book sold 2 million copies in hardcover, Simon & Schuster threw Jane a champagne party in their conference room and presented her with a $1.2 million royalty check. "It was the highest royalty check Simon & Schuster had ever paid out," publicity director Dan Green remembered, "but Jane didn't seem impressed. She was an hour late for the party and then she only stayed five minutes. She didn't thank a soul." Another publicist thought, "Maybe she'd decided this was how a businesswoman behaves. She was hard as nails. But you gotta give this woman credit. She is the greatest self-publicist of all time."

Jane went on to produce another Workout book: *Pregnancy, Birth and Recovery Workout* with her friend Femmy DeLyser. It sold 250,000 copies. Jane had tried to write the text, her editor, Nan Talese, remembered, "but the words were dead on the page." Instead Mignon McCarthy wrote it with Jane. She'd also written the first Workout book. Jane told Nan she was very upset she hadn't been able to write the books herself.*

Then came the Workout tape. Stuart Karl, the father of "how to" videos, had called Jane after his wife read the Workout books and said, "This should be a video." Jane remembered writing the first script on the floor of her living room in pencil: "I wanted to save money so we didn't have a hairdresser or makeup people, no teleprompter—we winged it." She even performed the routines barefoot. "But it didn't matter how we made the video because there was no competition—all that mattered was that people could follow what we were doing." When Jane's first Workout video appeared in stores in 1982, it soared to the top of the charts, remaining there for three years. Until Jane had made her Workout tape, every hit video had been a movie. She virtually invented the video home fitness industry. People bought her tapes rather than renting them. Soon everyone in the business was wondering how to duplicate her act.

"Jane Fonda became the complete American heroine of the '80s,"

---

* Thirty years later, after her memoir, *My Life So Far*, was topping the bestseller charts, she ran into Talese at a party. "I wrote that book, you know," she told her triumphantly. "I *really* wrote *that book!*"

film critic David Thomson declared. "Not just as an actress and producer but as the starring body of her Workout books and tapes." Another critic, Richard Schickel, added, "The exercise guru was perhaps
her most remarkable act of self-recreation. . . . The implications of
the workout woman are rich. Fit, buff women become feminist exem-
plars. In fitness there is freedom. It also plays to her particular brand
of sexuality — we see this beautiful body twisting into erotic-seeming
postures. A lot of look, but don't touch. It was also perfectly timed — a
tamed, earnest, liberationist feminism, without the threatening hyste-
ria of the movement's earlier days. It accomplished a political goal. But
better still, it makes her a bunch of money and redeems her in the eyes
of most Americans, as success stories always do."

The first Workout tape is still the biggest-selling home video of all
time: 17 million copies. All of Jane's unending procession of Workout
tapes, some sixty in all, sold phenomenally well, too. "Like so many of
her films, all of these tapes were ardent, solemn, and modestly erotic,"
Thomson concluded. "She was true to herself."

By the end of 1982 the Workout empire had earned an astonishing
$20 million, and a fitness craze — an obsession with health, youthful-
ness, and sex appeal — was sweeping the country. The generation that
had grown up in the fifties and been involved in civil rights and antiwar activism was now more interested in running clubs than in demonstrations or protests. "This was feminism in the age of narcissism.
Private. Self-centered. Self-consciously apolitical. Jane Fonda was the
great standard-bearer for this new self-empowerment ethic," Judith
Warner wrote.

Letters began pouring in to Jane from all over the world — "by the
basketful" — letters from women "doing Jane," as they called it. "They
were touching, handwritten letters that I have kept to this day," Jane
said. "Some were about my Workout book, some about the videotapes
or the audiotape version. These women poured their hearts out, about
weight they had lost, self-esteem they had gained, how they were finally able to stand up to their boss or recover from a mastectomy. . . .
A Peace Corps volunteer wrote me about how she 'did Jane' using the
audiotape every day in her mud hut in Guatemala."*

---

* The legacy of "doing Jane" has lived on. The artist Mickey Avalon came out with a song in 2006 in
which he directs girls to "do the Jane Fonda." He says: "Work it out, shake it little momma / Lemme

In the next two years Jane would promote the Workout in Europe and Asia—on radio, on TV, and in personal appearances. Soon there would be other Workout spinoffs—calendars, a *Women Coming of Age* book (how to cope with midlife, menopause, etc.), which would earn Jane another $5 million in spite of protests from respected women's health expert Barbara Seaman, who said some of the original material in the book had been lifted from her book. No lawsuits were ever filed because, Seaman said, "I didn't want to sue a feminist."

But lawsuits were filed by three of her instructors in her San Francisco studio, charging Jane with sexism because she paid them less than her male instructors. And some of the dancers on her exercise videos maintained they had not been paid as performers. Jane tried to settle everything amicably, but she decided she would not franchise Workout and go national. Her plans to produce a Workout clothing line proved to be a failure. The clothes were overpriced and they sold poorly.

Meanwhile, exercise queen Gilda Marx, whose classes Jane had initially attended in Century City, had been observing the Workout videos' phenomenal success and accused Jane of "ripping [her] off." She consulted a lawyer, who asked her if her business had been hurt. Marx admitted it hadn't. The lawyer said, "Then don't make yourself miserable. Forget about it and just go on with what you're doing." So Marx took his advice and was as successful as ever. Today she says, "Jane helped me. I began the exercise business. She made it world-famous."

Jane insisted, "None of the exercises were new but we made them our own. We concentrated on each muscle group and gave the exercises a total approach." She and Marx never spoke but they did eventually appear together at a huge fitness event where Marx was introduced as "the Grande Dame of the Exercise Movement" and Jane was described as the woman who popularized it.

By 1984, Jane abandoned her "go for the burn" approach to exercise after it was revealed that nearly half of those engaged in high-impact aerobics suffered such injuries as stress fractures and back problems. She began promoting an easier regime with low-impact aerobics.

---

see you do the Jane Fonda." In his song he fuses sex and exercise, much the way Fonda did with her Workout moves.

Jane also decided to separate the Workout from CED. "I wanted to grow the business but could not because all the income was being paid out in dividends to the organization. By that time, the Workout had brought $17 million into CED, and I felt we had fulfilled our mission of providing it with a solid financial base. As long as I owned the Workout business, I could grow it while continuing to donate money to CED as needed."

Later that summer, Jane flew to France to promote the Workout in Paris, and she appeared on the TV show *Apostrophe;* she was one of the few Americans Bernard Pivot ever interviewed without an interpreter.

In Saint-Tropez Roger Vadim sat on the beach with his old friend Monique Caron and they watched Jane on *Apostrophe* at an outdoor café TV. *"Mon dieu!"* Vadim exclaimed. "Jane Fonda is no longer an artiste — she is now a businesswoman."

Jane worried about that, too. She thought: "Hey, wait a minute! What about me as an actor? What about the causes I'm fighting for? The Workout phenomenon, it seemed, had superseded everything else about me. . . . I didn't want pelvic tilts to define me."

But indeed her body did define her; her body remained central to her iconography — a throughline in her career from her movies with Vadim to her Workout tapes in the 1980s.

New Yorker film critic Pauline Kael went even further. She wondered, "Does Jane Fonda still have the bones of an artist when she devotes so much time to goody-good causes and being an exercise guru? Where is the down-and-dirty Bree of *Klute* or the fierce, unblinking nihilism she showed in *They Shoot Horses, Don't They?* She used to have enough desperation in her voice to nick at your insides."

David Thomson wrote, "Jane Fonda's is an uncoordinated career, torn between the personalities of her father and her husbands."

Many people in the industry were wondering if she'd ever make a film again. Unbeknownst to anybody, she now had a shooting script for *The Dollmaker,* which was based on a novel by Harriette Arnow and written by Hume Cronyn and Susan Cooper for ABC-TV. Against her agent's advice, she'd been working on it for the past two years along with all her other projects.

The Dollmaker was about a rawboned Kentucky farmwoman, Gertie Nevels. Jane loved Gertie's bravery, humility, and capacity for mothering in the face of extreme poverty and loss, including the death of one of her children, who was crushed by a train. To support her family, Gertie carved figures out of wood and sold them.

What had attracted Jane to *The Dollmaker*? "Gertie Nevels is so much like Tom Joad, the character my father played in *Grapes of Wrath.*" Jane was determined to portray a woman as gentle and gallant as Joad — the female equivalent of a Prairie Galahad. She wanted to be like Henry Fonda, whom she saw as a part of the American myth. While filming she would insist she felt "my father's voice coming out of my mouth as I played Gertie!"

Dolly Parton took Jane to Appalachia and introduced her to a couple named Lucy and Waco Johnson. Jane stayed with them for two weeks in a "log cabin covered with clematis." Seventy-four-year-old Lucy was big-boned with thick glasses and new dentures. She became Jane's inspiration. They talked a lot and exchanged stories. "She carved apple dolls (faces carved into apples, which then shriveled into interesting weathered expressions)."

By the time she arrived on the film location in the Smoky Mountains of Tennessee, she'd gained twenty pounds and she'd captured all the Kentucky speech patterns (she'd been coached by the dialect expert Bob Eston as well). It was almost impossible to believe this was the Jane Fonda of Brentwood, Vassar, and Paris.

Jane had always juggled roles and personas and "acted" in order to survive ever since she was a little girl — to survive her mother's suicide, to survive her father's detachment, to survive in Hollywood, to hold on to her family, to run her fitness empire. She was unaware that the deceptiveness, the pretending, the huge need to be liked, were so much a part of her character.

In her memoir she confided, "I think most of us have many personas. . . . The difference with actors is we are paid to *become* all the people inside us." But what happened when betrayals, temptations, and secrets bubbled inside of her, got in her way, and contradicted her work and her marriage? She always worried about accountability — accountability to colleagues, to friends, to Tom. "Tom's the intelligent one; I'm just a chameleon," she'd explain as if that made it all right. Maybe she was a "Zelig," as in the Woody Allen movie — someone who can disappear in and out of situations, adjust, and accommodate. It was all part of her intense quest for an identity. It was about the emptiness of celebrity, too, and the fickleness of the public.

She mobilized a group called the "Brat Pack" (a collection of young, talented stars like Whoopi Goldberg, Ally Sheedy, Demi Moore, Alec Baldwin, and Rob Lowe); together they campaigned for the ERA and traveled with Tom and Jane on a bus around California promoting a bill that was meant to force the state government to list and eliminate all chemicals that caused toxic waste. It was called Proposition 65.

There was a lot of resistance to Proposition 65; the oil companies, the chemical companies, and agribusiness poured millions of dollars into TV commercials to defeat the bill, but Jane rallied all kinds of support. She got on the phone, she made speeches, she spoke eloquently about how important it was to make drinking water safe. "It was due to Jane that the bill was passed," one of Hayden's associates said.

More than any other star, Jane was responsible for the creation of a new political Hollywood where no career could be complete without a cause.

As always, Jane barely had time to catch her breath. Nan Talese remembered dropping by the house to do some edits on a Workout book and Jane dashed in minutes after. "She'd been in Japan doing publicity for *Nine to Five*. She dropped her bag, and her first words were, 'Gimme a double vodka,' and she raced upstairs to see her son."

Talese had the impression that "this was a woman on the fast track who didn't want to stop moving because she had things she didn't want to face."

At another meeting, Jane asked Talese point-blank, "How do you juggle work and marriage and being a mother?" Talese said she told her she had great communication with her husband, Gay. Jane shook her head and then confided that she and Vanessa didn't get along. But she would not admit that her marriage was in trouble. The overwhelming success of the Workout was putting her relationship with Hayden in great jeopardy.

"Tom hated, loathed, despised the Workout," Nathalie Vadim said. "Now Jane was not only a movie star; she was a one-woman conglomerate, a veritable household word—an icon. She had embedded herself in the middle-class consciousness in a way that she could not have with her films. She was a symbol, for God's sake! Tom could not take it.

The Workout overwhelmed his politics, his sense of self, as well as everything in their life together. It was awful. He started drinking more and he continued to play around. Jane closed her eyes to it."

She must have sensed something was up. Her assistant, Lauren Weissman, recalled Jane saying: "'If Tom ever had a lover I would just try to get close to this woman and make her my best friend.' It was weird; I think she must have known he was screwing around with all these women and she didn't want to admit it to herself."

The marriage might have been in trouble but by 1984 Jane was at the height of her career. The *World Almanac* had listed her as the fourth most influential woman in the world, ranked behind Mother Teresa, Margaret Thatcher, and Nancy Reagan. The Gallup Poll stated she was the most admired.

These tributes coincided with the publication of her third book, *Women Coming of Age,* filled with scientific research about nutrition and beauty and menopause. She was especially proud of this book because "I'm talking about what I'm going through now at forty-seven. I'm getting lines and gray hairs, but I want to think of menopause as an adventure." She insisted, "I am looking forward to my first hot flash."

As usual she promoted the book relentlessly all over the country until it was number three on the charts. It remained a bestseller for months. When *People* magazine asked her, "Aren't you spreading yourself too thin?" she snapped, "Nope. I spread myself very carefully." She didn't stop promoting the book even as she filmed *Agnes of God* with Anne Bancroft in the fall of 1984. Between takes on location in a gloomy abbey outside Quebec she would conduct lengthy interviews on a pay phone. She was fighting a terrible head cold.

Agnes of God was her first movie in three years. It had been hard to find a good script. In the early seventies there had been a flurry of quite wonderful feminist-inspired films like *An Unmarried Woman* with Jill Clayburgh, but overall the industry made few concessions to women; Jane had been very lucky with the four very distinctive films she'd produced and starred in. The roles she'd played specifically reflected her political evolution — from the Vietnam veteran's wife in *Coming Home* to the secretary turned rebel in *Nine to Five.* Now she wanted to return to the screen in a project that would make the public forget the disaster of *Rollover*. That picture's failure had been painful for her. She still felt insecure even though she was currently listed along with Streisand and Goldie Hawn as one of three actresses with box office clout.

Norman Jewison, who was directing *Agnes of God*, said, "When Jane agreed to do the picture it was a 'go' project." But she couldn't get that excited about it. She'd agreed to do it because it was based on a successful Broadway play. Her role was that of a cynical, court-appointed psychiatrist named Martha Livingston. In the course of the movie, she tries to solve the case of a young nun (Meg Tilly) who has mysteriously given birth to a baby, then strangles it and stuffs it into a trash bin. Anne Bancroft would be playing the watchful mother superior who defends her young postulant, maintaining she's innocent not because she's innocent but because she's been "touched" by God.

Jane felt challenged by working with Bancroft, of whom she had been in awe ever since their meeting at the Actors Studio back in the sixties. But overall she felt as if she was playing a variation of the women she'd played in *The China Syndrome* and *The Electric Horseman*: crisp, cool, female professionals who when they come home from work always listen to messages from their mothers on their answering services. Director Jewison insists that it was wonderful "to watch Annie and Jane working with each other." But he admitted that Jane was depressed most of the time. "She didn't tell me what was bothering her but something definitely was." She was worried about Tom's reported infidelities. Friends kept describing more women, more trysts. But she didn't confront him.

During filming, it wasn't long before Jane reached out to Sven Nykvist, Ingmar Bergman's legendary cinematographer. He had agreed to work on *Agnes of God* mainly so that he could photograph Jane.

"The two became close," Jewison said. "Sven was a tender, sexy, very intuitive guy. He'd been with Mia Farrow before Jane, and Mia had gotten him through the suicide of his son the year before. So he was hurting a lot, too." Jewison added that he doesn't know whether Jane and Sven had an affair, but other friends say Jane fell in love with Sven and hoped their relationship could work, but he could not make a commitment. A member of the cast recalled Jane and Sven whispering to each other off camera, and then Jane running back to her dressing room in tears.

Over the holidays Tom Hayden arrived in Quebec to spend time with Jane. Mel Brooks came up to see Anne Bancroft. "We had Thanksgiving dinner together," Jewison remembered.

Just before the filming was over, Jane presented Jewison with a small blue velvet pillow. She had embroidered a little saying on it from *Peter Pan*: "The reason birds fly is they have perfect faith, faith to have wings." The pillow remains on Jewison's office couch, and to this day he remains resolutely enthusiastic about Jane. "She was a big star then. Columbia hadn't wanted to make a movie about nuns. I thought the movie was wonderful."

Critics were respectful but not that enthusiastic when the film opened the following year. "*Agnes of God* hasn't been hurt or helped by being transplanted to the big screen," the *Wall Street Journal* noted. "The story hits you over the head with its conundrum of faith vs. reason. . . . Tilly looks beatific. Bancroft is fierce and funny but she has the best part. . . . Ms. Fonda's nerves seemed frayed. . . . Still, she makes us feel the ache inside the brittle psychiatrist."

The picture did not do well at the box office, although Bancroft and Tilly did get Oscar nominations. Jane didn't. That was another disappointment for her. She continued on. She was already researching her next character, Alex, a has-been movie star and lush in a movie called *The Morning After,* which Sidney Lumet would be directing.

Jane had been intrigued by the idea of playing a movie star alcoholic, and she'd read up on some of the most famous and tragic ones like Lana Turner and Ava Gardner. Jane said she modeled her character after Gail Russell, who at thirty-six was found dead in her apartment among empty liquor bottles.

Because Jane was never one to waste a second, she continued her research right after the premiere of *Agnes of God* in Montreal in December of 1985. As soon as the usual round of interviews and press parties ended, she returned to her penthouse suite at the Château Champlain and proceeded to down an entire fifth of vodka to see how it felt — "I wanted to see if you can really black out and then not remember what happened the next morning."

In *The Morning After,* Alex blacks out and wakes up to find a bloodied dead man next to her on the pillows — the rest of the movie is spent with Alex trying to find out how the body got in her bed.

Jane said, "So I drank that fifth of vodka and proceeded to black out and the next day couldn't remember what the hell happened so my research was worthless!"

She'd already attended AA meetings and hung out in seedy late-night bars in West Hollywood as another part of her research on being a drunk. So many lost, lonely, out-of-it women smoking and drinking their lives away. By the time she started filming with costar Jeff Bridges, Jane had a hard, tortured look under her fluffy blond hair and she developed an angry, defensive humor as part of her characterization, which was reminiscent of Bree in *Klute*.

(Later Pauline Kael would write in *The New Yorker*: "After 10 years of dull constricted performances in movies like *Nine to Five* and *On Golden Pond* Fonda shows that her talent may still be intact. In *The Morning After* she's playing a bright woman who's squandered her life and her down-in-the-dirt performance has some of the charge of her Bree in *Klute* and her Gloria in *They Shoot Horses, Don't They?*")

On the set Jane developed a bantering friendship with Jeff Bridges, and between takes he'd snap pictures of her. He was a talented photographer, and there's one shot (in a book he later published) where he captured her outside her dressing room in an old bathrobe, no makeup on, looking haunted and vulnerable, a sad smile on her face as if to say, "Whoops! You caught the real me."

Everything that was going on in her tumultuous private life seemed reflected in her resigned expression. While she was making the movie she was also dealing with Tom's drinking — it had gotten so bad friends had insisted on an intervention. Press agent Steve Rivers had been present, as had Stuart Rosenberg, Paula Weinstein's husband. "Tom was furious. The intervention didn't work," said Jane. She was in despair. Alcohol seemed to have him licked.

He was away more and more — not just in Sacramento (where he had an apartment), but consulting for Michael Dukakis, who was about to run for president. There were rumors Hayden was playing around with Margot Kidder and Morgan Fairchild. But Jane was really worried when she heard he'd been spending a lot of time with Vicky Rideout, a sexy Harvard graduate twenty years younger than Jane, who was Dukakis's head speechwriter.

Somewhere there'd been a terrible disconnect — between Jane's wildly romantic ambitions for "Tom as president" to Hayden's cool sense of what his reality could actually be. "Their marriage had been over for a long time," said Roger Vadim, who observed his former wife with compassion. "It was supposed to be the kind of marriage that leads to social good — for that reason it went on and on."

Paul Zotos, an instructor from the Workout, recalled: "Tom would make a big show of coming for the Christmas party. But otherwise you never saw them together. She'd take us to dinner and he wasn't there. We had a party and she'd come alone. It suddenly dawned on me that she was sort of like one of the Kennedys. Everyone had this image of her but basically she was kind of sad and lonely."

They were about to celebrate their fifteenth wedding anniversary. A reporter came to the house and asked, "What's the secret to a lasting marriage?" Jane stumbled. "Difficult to say . . . I think we are understanding of each other . . . we respect each other's work, we try to take good vacations . . . Tom and I go out to dinner just the two of us . . . I drive around and see these old couples walking along holding hands; I keep thinking we'll be like that when we're old and then I think, Will we?"

Life was moving so fast and in so many directions. She'd accompanied Vanessa to Brown University in Rhode Island and been "all choked up because my daughter was leaving me!" Vanessa had been longing to get away from home and she was uncomfortable at Brown where, as usual, her mother became the center of attention on campus. Vanessa insisted Jane leave before the faculty-parent dinner — so Jane did, feeling very rejected. She'd wanted to experience the college atmosphere again; she remembered how her favorite stepmother, Susan, had been with her at Vassar.

There was always so much to do — expand the exercise business, turn out more fitness tapes — then she had to deal with Vadim's new tell-all memoir, *Bardot, Deneuve, Fonda,* to be published by Simon & Schuster, which recounted, in detail, three-in-a-bed romps. Jane insisted he cut out the "gamier parts," and then she had a long, emotional talk with Vanessa, who was shocked by the revelations. Vanessa knew Vadim had upset many people she cared about with his book, including Jane, and it was hard on her — she loved her father and was quite protective of him.

When Jane could she'd hang out at her development office at Twentieth Century Fox. She was producing the TV series *Nine to Five* (it lasted one season), and she had all sorts of projects in development, including the novel *Hearts* by Hilma Wolitzer and a novel by Carlos Fuentes called *The Old Gringo*. Roger Friedman was working for her (he would go on to become the much-talked-about journalist), and she'd just hired Susan Lyne (who later headed ABC-TV programming). "Everyone was very smart, everyone was very paranoid — jockeying for position — we were supposed to be on the lookout for movies buried in all the great journalism that was being published in magazines like *Rolling Stone*," Friedman said. "Jane was especially close to her main assistant, Lauren Weissman; she listened to her too much." It was Lauren who advised her to turn down the thriller *Jagged Edge*, which had been written by Joe Eszterhas and went on to become a hit starring Glenn Close.

That didn't stop her from phoning Eszterhas one day in 1987 and saying she had a great idea for him. "We met at the Beverly Wilshire," Eszterhas said. "She looked absolutely sensational in a little derby hat — we sat and drank tequilas and talked and talked. Christ, she can be so disarming.

"First off she apologized for not doing *Jagged Edge*. 'Worst mistake I ever made in my life turning down that script,' she said. 'I am so sorry.'" She wanted Eszterhas to write a remake of *All About Eve* set in Hollywood in the eighties. "I didn't want to; I knew too much about Hollywood in the eighties." But then Eszterhas — the son of Hungarian refugees — found himself telling Jane about a story he'd had in his head for years. It was inspired by John Demjanjuk, a Ukrainian who, after years as a Cleveland auto worker, is accused of being Ivan the Terrible of Treblinka during the war — he'd been responsible for the killing of thousands of Jews. His daughter, a lawyer, defends him at a hearing that could cost him his citizenship. At first she's totally in his corner, then, as evidence mounts, she starts losing faith that he's innocent.

Jane loved the idea. "I want to do it!" she said.

As soon as her name was attached to *The Music Box*, it was a "go" project at Columbia Pictures. Eszterhas wrote the script and then Costa-Gavras signed on to direct. He'd just completed *Betrayed* and was famous for the classics *Z* and *Missing*. Jane knew Costa-Gavras from Paris. "It was too good to be true," Eszterhas said. "I handed in the final draft and everybody loved it. We all thought it would be Oscar material for Jane.

"Then the president of Columbia Pictures phoned me and said: 'We have a problem. Costa thinks Jane is too old for the part of the daughter.' And Irwin Winkler, who was producing, agreed. Jane was forty-seven and as gorgeous as ever as far as I was concerned and she'd just been nominated for an Oscar for *The Morning After*.

"Jane got word and asked me point-blank: 'What is going on?' I told her and she said, 'What can I do?' Costa then asked her to audition.

"This amazing, gifted woman — this incomparable actress — did a screen test, and it was terrific but it didn't change Costas's mind. The studio paid her a million dollars to go away; none of this was ever publicized. Jessica Lange ended up doing the part and I think it shook Jane up. If anything, it turned her off from the movie business."

Indeed, although she made no mention of *The Music Box* in her autobiography, she did write: "By the mid-eighties . . . I was in emotional limbo, plowing through life by sheer force of will . . . but willpower can be anathema to creativity. Creativity requires a looseness, a letting go, an openness that allows the psyche to plumb the moist depths where the stuff of dreams and myths percolate.

"I just didn't want to be doing it anymore. I was experiencing creative disintegration, and I didn't understand that my inability to be honest about the disintegration of my long marriage, the shutting down of my body, *and* my feeling totally responsible for it all was slowly draining me of *life*."

She couldn't bear to think of all the things Tom had been doing to upset her; he'd ridiculed her at a big benefit dinner at which he'd been very drunk; she'd heard he hated being called "Mr. Jane Fonda," that he resented it when she sent a private jet to pick him up in Sacramento so he could come home at night to be with Troy.

Early in 1987 she had an eyelift done by Dr. Frank Kramer in Beverly Hills. Hayden said nothing; maybe he didn't notice.

He was immersed in writing his memoir, *Reunion*. As part of his research he traveled all over the South with his ex-wife, Casey Hayden, in an effort to re-create their days together during the civil rights movement. He wrote a glowing account of his marriage to Jane — but he seemed almost embarrassed by the hypocrisy of it. He confided he was afraid that by painting such a "rosy" picture of their life together it might all fall apart. "He was really bugged," Jane said. "He wasn't facing all that was wrong in our marriage. I kept assuring him it would be okay, even though of course it wasn't."

As always work kept her occupied — so she wouldn't have to think about what was going on at home. She was about to star in *The Old Gringo* — it was the first film produced by Jane's new company, Fonda Films. She and Bruce Gilbert had dissolved their partnership, IPC Films, in 1986, and she was now working with Lois Bonfiglio, a chain-smoking, fast-talking New Yorker. They worked together in an office that was sparsely furnished except for a huge exercise bike, which they took turns using.

Jane was smoking more than ever. *The Old Gringo* was the biggest movie she'd ever been involved with and the most complicated. Like all of her projects, it had taken years to get off the ground. She had gone to Mexico in the eighties and "been struck by this common border shared by the richest country in the world and the poorest. I was very moved by the history we shared." When she returned home she found that Hayden had been entertaining the novelist Carlos Fuentes at Laurel Springs. She told him she wanted very much to do a movie about their two countries — he told her he was finishing a novel called *The Old Gringo* about an American spinster schoolteacher who finds herself caught up in the Mexican Revolution. She becomes involved with the celebrated American newspaperman Ambrose Bierce and a young rebel general in Pancho Villa's army. Jane especially liked the father-daughter aspect between the schoolteacher and Bierce, an acerbic old man in his seventies.

Jane optioned it immediately, "but it was complicated and nonlinear," she said, "and we had a hard time getting screenwriters or convincing studios to back it." She hired John Gregory Dunne and Joan Didion to write the screenplay, but she had so many arguments with them that Dunne told her bluntly the only way they would continue to write the script was if they never had to see or talk to her again. She ended up working with Luis Puenzo, who would direct the movie as well as write the screenplay along with Aída Bortnik.

The movie started shooting on location in the wilds of Mexico in December 1988. It was a difficult shoot — weather delays, editing problems. Lulu was there to keep Jane company. Jane had cast Gregory Peck as Bierce and Jimmy Smits (the handsome young star of *L.A. Law*) as the rebel general. Soon the tabloids began spreading rumors that they were having an affair after Jane burbled to a reporter, "I'm blown away. Stardom has a lot to do with sexuality . . . and [Jimmy] is going to be a very big star. He is very, very sexy."

When Tom Hayden read the item he flew down to see Jane unannounced. She was at first furious—then she threatened a nervous breakdown. Peck was extremely sympathetic—"I'd look around at the hundreds of people on the set . . . and then look at Jane. . . . God, this is the reason we're all here. It all rests on her slender shoulders."

Peck didn't seem to mind Jane's perfectionism. She insisted they shoot and reshoot a scene where the two kiss—they performed it over and over until Peck kidded, "It's benevolent fanaticism."

It wasn't just the problems within the movie or Hayden's presence that was making Jane so edgy—after *Gringo* she was to star in another movie, *Stanley & Iris,* with Robert De Niro. Earlier her press agent, Steve Rivers, had flown down to see her bearing the following news: MGM had announced that Waterbury, Connecticut, would be one of the locations for *Stanley & Iris.* War veterans started to protest, in particular Guy Russo, leader of the Waterbury Veterans of Foreign Wars. He threatened to organize a massive protest if Fonda set foot in the town. Soon "I'm Not Fond'a Hanoi Jane" posters popped up all over the place, as did bumper stickers on cars.

Jane kept hoping the protests would die down, but they erupted in other towns around Connecticut and elsewhere. Her controversial reputation as an antiwar activist would not go away.

The year before, a feature film called *The Hanoi Hilton,* directed and written by Lionel Chetwynd, had opened to tepid reviews. It was supposedly a tribute to the heroism of POWs held prisoner in Hanoi. It starred Michael Moriarty, Lawrence Pressman, and an actress named Gloria Carlin playing a Jane Fonda character in a shag wig. In one sequence she lectures the POWs shrilly about their obligation to apologize to the Vietnamese people for bombing civilians. Other POWs tell her the food is lousy in the prison—then the Jane Fonda character betrays the POWs by telling their commanding officer about their complaints.

The movie did not do any business commercially but was shown to veterans groups all over the country—many bought the story. In fact, "the mythical portrait that later became imbedded in Internet web sites of Jane Fonda in Hanoi as a naïve, willfully ignorant woman—a traitor — comes straight out of this film, itself a product of Chetwynd's imagination," the historian Mary Hershberger wrote.

When Jane returned to L.A., Rivers said the protests hadn't stopped, but he'd conducted a public opinion poll in Waterbury and 73 percent of the men and women polled said Jane Fonda should not be prevented from making a movie in their town. Rivers had also gotten a lot of support from pro-Fonda Vietnam vets — from Tip O'Neill and Max Cleland, the disabled vet who was Georgia's secretary of state.

Now they discussed the pros and cons of Jane making a public apology for some of her actions in North Vietnam. She'd done it before as a side issue in many interviews as early as 1981 in the *Ladies' Home Journal.*

Rivers, a "master of spin control" who went on to work with producer Mike Ovitz when he was a Hollywood power broker, said they considered two minutes with Brokaw, then they decided fifteen minutes with Barbara Walters on *20/20.* Jane later told Rosenbaum in *Vanity Fair* that she "had doubts about making an apology. What I had done in Hanoi was not at all negative. After all, about a week after I spoke about the bombing of the dikes the bombing stopped. And maybe I helped shorten the war, but the overriding *fact* was that I owed something to the real guys out there — their wives, their parents — they're the ones I'd been trying to help and they had been led to believe I was anti-GI. I was only anti what our government had put them through."

ABC aired the show the Friday night before filming started in Waterbury in June 1988. However, the taping was done March 31. Jane said she didn't sleep and was almost numb from fatigue.

The taping took place in her living room, decorated with chintz couches and lovely antiques. She wore a tailored shirt and pastel print skirt — not much makeup; she was nervous. She knew the show would open with the famous newsreel of her as Hanoi Jane, sitting on the gun and laughing. In fact, that's the first question Barbara Walters asked her: "Why did you sit on that gun?"

"It was a thoughtless, careless thing to do knowing the power of images," Jane answered. "I take full responsibility for having gotten on the gun. I am a strong woman but I'm naive and make mistakes, but I was a big girl and should have said no."

With regard to the allegation that she told soldiers to disobey orders and referred to officers as war criminals, she said, "I only recall saying the weapons were illegal and had been outlawed by rules of warfare. I wanted to say to them 'let's think about what we're doing.' I was angry that Nixon was using the POWs to make war look noble . . . trying to rewrite history. I'm not a revolutionary woman today. It was preposterous that I said that in 1971. I didn't know what 'revolutionary woman' meant. But I didn't want to be known as some starlet. I used words and rhetoric I didn't understand — I'm not proud of that."

She ended with "I'm proud of most of what I did and sorry for *some* of what I did . . . my intention was to help end the killing and the war."

The Walters interview helped tamp down the resentment against Jane that had been simmering sixteen years after she went to North Vietnam. But the "hate Jane" core was still there and might always be there. However, two-thirds of the Waterbury populace favored Jane in the polls.

The real turning point came when she flew to meet with twenty-six Vietnam vets in Naugatuck (a town near Waterbury). She had asked for the meeting. The press was barred; Reverend John McColley, a Vietnam vet who moderated the session, said it went on for three and a half hours. There was a lot of arguing and explaining, and some of the men even cried. Jane admitted she'd romanticized the war and had been wrong to do so. By the end of the session everybody was emotionally drained. "I think we learned a lot," she said. "It was a very moving experience."

Jane arrived in Waterbury July 25 to begin filming. She looked wan and tired and complained of being overweight ("too many tortillas in Mexico"). She asked director Martin Ritt to find her a gym where she could work out — then she disappeared into the private home that had been rented for her. There were no pickets or posters in sight.

On July 26 filming started — the set was the old Waterbury brass factory on South Main, where Robert De Niro (playing a baker) was supposed to work. That day one thousand people pressed against police barricades in an effort to catch Jane and De Niro acting in their first scene together. Nobody noticed the few hard-core demonstrators, Guy Russo among them, who were struggling to be heard above the din.

Throughout the shoot there were always a few who taunted and called Jane names, and demonstrators chanted "traitor" and held plac-

ards: HANOI JANE: YOUR FATHER WAS ASHAMED OF YOU AND
SO ARE WE.

When she wasn't filming Jane made herself visible in Waterbury;
she ate in local restaurants like No Fish Today, she was gracious and
friendly, she signed autographs.

Then on July 29 she and De Niro appeared at a fundraising event
in nearby Quassy Amusement Park for the benefit of handicapped
children of vets who had been exposed to Agent Orange in Vietnam.
A crowd of twenty-five thousand showed up on a sweltering summer
night, and the two stars posed for endless pictures with fans, some of
whom waited over an hour. By the evening's end $10,000 had been
raised by the group that had organized the event, Veterans Who Care.

The main filming of *Stanley & Iris* was later done in Toronto, Canada.
The story was a preachy one: Jane played a compassionate widow who
works in a cake factory. De Niro works with her; he is illiterate. She
teaches him to read; he teaches her to love and live again. By now, Jane
was at her lowest ebb — physically and emotionally exhausted by all
that was happening in her life. She had never felt so alone.

She wrote in her memoir that she sat in her hotel room in Toronto
and asked herself, "'What will I do with my life? What is there for me?'
I saw only a joyless road ahead."

Although Hayden had been helpful and supportive during the Waterbury protests, they were barely communicating on other levels. But
she couldn't admit "there was no future in the marriage. It was incon-
ceivable to me that my couplehood with Tom was not going to be forever. Leaving would be a sign of defeat, and defeat was not an option.
Besides, without Tom what would I be?"

Months before he had asked her, "Do you love me?" and she'd answered, "Yes," and "he asked me to write him a letter telling him why.
Once I'd finished the part about him being a wonderful father, I got
stuck. Why couldn't I think of reasons for loving him? Why did my
hand want to write only anger?

"My wonderful, loyal, always intelligent body kept sending me signals by repeatedly attracting mishaps the way abandoned bodies do:
Pay attention to me, listen to me. This hadn't happened to me since my
injury-prone days in Greenwich when my parents' marriage was de-
laminating. When I ignored my body signals I was paid back in broken

bones: fingers, ribs, feet. On his desk Tom kept a photo of me that he'd taken when I broke my collarbone. When I broke my nose . . . during *Stanley & Iris* Tom asked for a photo of that as well. Maybe he liked me better broken."

Jane and Tom separated in December 1988 but they kept it a secret for three months. Hayden had been working for Governor Michael Dukakis, and he'd been seen with a number of women, but there were ongoing rumors that he was really involved with Vicky Rideout, Dukakis's main speechwriter.

Jane supposedly hired detectives. She spoke to Hayden, gave him an ultimatum: he had to give up all his girls.

Then on the night she turned fifty-one Tom announced to her he was in love with another woman. He and Jane were in Aspen with Troy, Vanessa, and Lulu, sharing a small rented condo. "I didn't want to spoil everyone's vacation, so I said nothing — stiff upper lip and all that. So as not to let on there was trouble, I'd wait until everyone had gone to bed and then I'd lie on the living room couch alternately sobbing and reading a novel by Amos Oz."

She added, "I don't think Tom expected it to be the end. I think he believed, as did others, that I had known all about his infidelities and didn't really mind." Jane felt such overwhelming shame about the breakup she didn't tell anybody for weeks, although she did tell her friend Paula Weinstein and she even stayed with her for a while.

But she wasn't able to ask Tom to move out until Lulu inadvertently "pushed the button." Lulu said later, "I never knew Tom and Jane's marriage was in trouble. They never acted out in front of us and Jane never said anything to me. But I do remember sometime in late 1988 coming home and there was Tom hurrying up the stairs with a horsey-faced girl with very curly blond hair. He and the girl went up to the bedroom he and Jane shared and shut the door. I didn't think anything of it because Tom always had meetings with people.

"About a week later Jane asked me, 'Did Tom come to the house with another woman?' I said, 'Yes, he did.' Turns out it was the girl Tom had been carrying on with — Vicky Rideout — I hadn't known that. Next thing I knew Tom and Jane had split. After that Tom would never speak to me again," Lulu said. "That hurt but I felt I had to tell the truth." Jane gathered up all of Tom's belongings into large plastic bags and threw them out the window into the garden.

On February 15, Steve Rivers sent out a press announcement. "Jane Fonda and Assemblyman Tom Hayden have decided to separate on a trial basis. Tom and Jane consider this a private matter and will have no public comment." The story made headlines all over the world. It was on page 1 of the *L.A. Times*. And it surprised many of their friends who had recently received a Hayden-Fonda Christmas card, which said, "Enjoy the Holidays and have a kinder, gentler New Year," and there was a photo of Jane, Tom, Troy, Vanessa, and Shirlee laughing it up at Zucky's, a Jewish deli in Santa Monica.

Reporters started phoning from all over the country; a *Newsweek* reporter was finally able to ask, "How do you feel?" Jane answered faintly, "I'm on my exercise bike — I've been on it for five hours pedaling till my butt started bleeding but the physical pain is nothing compared to what I am feeling emotionally. I am breaking apart."

37

During the first weeks without Tom Hayden, Jane could barely speak above a whisper. She was having a hard time swallowing food or even water; she soon lost so much weight she appeared almost skeletal. At the one benefit she did attend in Beverly Hills, photographers caught her hanging on to fifteen-year-old Troy's arm; she seemed totally dazed and out of it.

Sometimes she'd spend all day at the house wandering around in her nightgown, moving slowly around the cavernous living room, stopping to cuddle Spencer, the golden retriever, or Taxi, the black lab. The female mutt Scott was her favorite, but she didn't really respond to any of her animals. There was no air conditioning because she opposed it on environmental grounds, so the house was especially warm in the summer. She didn't notice the temperature; she didn't notice anything because she was contemplating her own death.

She decided to stipulate in her will that Tom would not be able to speak at her funeral. "I was convinced that he would opportunistically try to do so and couldn't imagine that we would ever again be close enough friends to justify it." Earlier she'd spoken to Michael Jackson about death when he visited Laurel Springs Ranch. "We'd walked all over the place, which he loved (he later bought his own ranch, Neverland, nearby), then I showed him the spot where I wanted to be buried and he had a meltdown: he shrieked and bent over and cried out, 'No! No! No!' 'What's the matter?' I asked. 'Don't ever talk about death, don't even think about it,' Michael said. But I thought about it all the time and still do; death is what gives meaning to life."

Peter had taken her to his Montana ranch in the first painful week — they had gone fly-fishing and hiking. "We'd hardly talked at all." She knew he'd never had any use for Tom Hayden — but they didn't speak about that. He'd always felt so protective; he'd always tried to be there for her. Years ago he'd been arrested in a Denver airport for defacing a poster that read FEED JANE FONDA TO THE WHALES. As they dragged him down to the station, he yelled at the police: "She's my sister and in my neck of the woods you don't get away with saying anything bad about your mother, grandmother, or sister." Before he was released he had to pay a large fine but he didn't care.

After the weekend in Montana he and Jane spent a lot of time together talking. They often became quite emotional. Jane taped their conversations and played them over and over. She finally admitted she'd detested him during much of their childhood because he seemed much closer to their mother. She'd felt especially unloved and abandoned when he disappeared with Frances and she didn't know where. He explained they'd gone together to Johns Hopkins when she'd had a hysterectomy and she insisted he be examined for a tapeworm because he was so extremely thin; he'd experienced a painful and unnecessary rectal examination (about which he still suffers nightmares). Jane felt better for knowing. Peter also told her he'd felt guilty for bonding so quickly to Mom 2 (Susan Blanchard) after their mother committed suicide. Bonding with Susan made him stop thinking about their real mother's death.

Jane shot back that he should never feel guilty, because they had both been abandoned, both been emotionally abused. It was their father's fault — Henry Fonda left everything important in their lives unsaid.

Once at Jane's insistence they went to see her therapist together. "She was a nice, middle-aged lady," Peter said. Jane ranted on and on about Tom and their parents. After about fifteen minutes, the therapist interrupted with "What do you have to say about this, Peter?"

He hadn't known how to react, because "Jane was cutting to the chase — leaving out all the details. Yeah, our mother was a victim, yeah, our father was larger than life — and we had survived, we were survivors, almost in spite of ourselves. But Jane didn't get what happened along the way. Anyhow, her version of her life is different from my version. But what the fuck? The end result is the same."

• • •

By April of 1989 Jane and Hayden were meeting to discuss a divorce settlement. Under California's community property laws he stood to walk away with half of Jane's fortune. According to *Forbes* magazine, Jane had made an estimated $20 million.

In 1989, Fonda Films was worth about $40 million. She had many other assets: the Santa Monica house was about $2.5 million. Then there was Laurel Springs Ranch in Santa Barbara, another $8 million, not counting income from a spa operating on the property that charged clients $3,500 a week. Not to mention the fitness empire: the Workout tapes and books were another $35 million. Jane offered Hayden $1 million in cash and $1,000 a month, which he turned down; her lawyers argued she'd poured at least $10 million of her own hard-earned cash into his political campaigns. His lawyers argued it had been a gift between spouses so it didn't figure into the agreement; it was a joint property settlement under California law.

In between lawyers' meetings, Jane held to a busy schedule at her production office. She had to deal with the editing and marketing problems surrounding *The Old Gringo*. It had been shown at Cannes in the spring, receiving boos. At Hollywood screenings critical response had been tepid. Nevertheless, a gala opening was held in October 1989, and Jane flew to New York to attend. She invited Vanessa, who was then a senior at Brown, to come, too. The premiere was noisy and crowded, and Jane was photographed and interviewed so much that as soon as the movie was over she told her daughter she had to get back to the Regency Hotel and go to sleep. She'd already been told that *The Old Gringo* was being panned.

Vanessa went on to the East Village with a boyfriend. They were arrested at eight the following morning near a seedy tenement where drugs were being sold. Headlines screamed: JANE FONDA'S DAUGHTER, VANESSA VADIM, IS JAILED FOR MOUTHING OFF AT A DRUG BUST!

Apparently her boyfriend had been arrested after it was discovered he had two envelopes of heroin in his pocket. Vanessa shouted, "If you're going to arrest him, you're going to have to arrest me too!" She added that they were buying drugs for a school project. She never mentioned that Jane Fonda was her mother. The two young people spent the night in jail.

Lawyers hastened down to the precinct and settled the matter. Vanessa was not arrested on drug charges but faced six months in jail and a fine for obstructing an arrest, loitering, and disorderly conduct.

When Vanessa came back to the Regency Hotel, Jane showed no anger. "Vanessa is a good daughter and a serious student, of whom I am very proud. I stand behind her in all this."

Vanessa telephoned her father in Paris to explain everything. Then he spoke with reporters. "She is really annoyed with herself. She said spending the night in jail was nothing compared to her misgivings about the worry she probably caused us." Vadim added he was confident his daughter had done nothing wrong. "Any problems Vanessa has are connected with her mother's image. Any child would have trouble growing up in the shadow of such a strong image. At college, she joined the drama association but had to give it up. She said, 'I'll never be as good as Mom.' Now she's interested in a career in journalism. She wants to make her own mark."

After graduation Vanessa went on to help build a school in Nicaragua and she began working on documentary films with one of her college friends, Rory Kennedy.

After the little crisis with Vanessa, Jane returned to California and began reviewing a number of projects with Lois Bonfiglio — in particular Neil Sheehan's *A Bright Shining Lie,* about the war in Vietnam, which she planned to produce. She had no movies lined up to star in. She'd started to date a blond hairdresser named Barron Matalon instead of the brash media tycoon billionaire Ted Turner, who had been actively pursuing her ever since he'd heard about her divorce. "She seemed thrilled Ted kept asking her out," her adopted daughter, Lulu, remembered. But she was ambivalent. "She wasn't sure she should see him."

She had no recollection that she had actually met Turner in 1988 when they had breakfast to talk about a film on the Fonda family. She had then been so preoccupied with her crumbling marriage to Hayden that she had paid no attention to Turner's advances. She had heard about his voracious sexual appetite and his inability to sustain personal relationships. She knew he'd had countless affairs with other women, including a Playboy Bunny, the female pilot of his private plane, and a CNN anchor.

There were also his manic depression and wild mood changes;

Turner had a bipolar personality. He had a short attention span and was frequently bored, and it was often difficult to have a two-way conversation with him.

Jane said as much to her brother on the phone when they were discussing whether or not she should date Turner, and Peter practically shouted at her: "You gotta go out with him! The guy is a class act. He not only created CNN, he's a serious environmentalist, he loves movies. C'mon, Sis, be reasonable!"

Jane finally agreed to see him, but when the day came she was so anxious she had her entire family (Vanessa, Troy, Nathalie, Lulu) milling about her living room to back her up emotionally. Peter sat on the sidelines, strumming his guitar.

Jane was still in her bedroom making up when Turner rang the bell. She heard Peter open the door and cry out, "I'm the brother!" and Turner shout back, "Hey, Montana, give me five!" (Peter's ranch in Livingston, Montana, was twenty-five miles from Turner's homestead.) The two men compared notes on their properties, pleased they had that in common.

A few minutes later Jane came downstairs. There was Turner, over six feet tall in cowboy boots and a rumpled business suit. He had a Clark Gable mustache and a cleft in his chin, and he exuded sexuality. They shook hands formally and he hustled her out into the night after shouting goodbye in a loud, rasping drawl to the family. "They seemed subdued," Jane wrote, "as if in the wake of a tornado."

In the limo Turner announced, "I got CNN to do a printout of your archives and I read through it. The stack was about a foot tall. So . . . ahh . . . then I had them do a printout of my files and mine is about three feet tall. Mine's bigger than yours! Pretty cute, huh?" And he smiled a shark's grin, revealing a gap between his front teeth. "All I could do was shake my head and laugh," Jane wrote in her memoir. "He was bowling me over and my whole body was abuzz."

Once in the restaurant Turner wouldn't stop talking; his unnerving, watchful eyes never left her face except when they roved down to stare lustfully at her cleavage. Throughout the meal he kept up a rambling, self-involved monologue, which ranged from anecdotes about his famous acquaintances ("I have friends who are Communists. . . . I've been to the Soviet Union several times because of the Goodwill Games. Gorbachev is my buddy and so is Castro") to a description of his unhappy childhood spent on various plantations in the South. He'd been raised by a hard-drinking, manic father who beat Turner regularly with coat hangers. Robert Edward Turner II would then make his son beat *him*. But Ted always insisted his father really loved him. (The elder Turner shot himself in the head when he was fifty-two.) Later, Turner would tell Jane that they had something in common since her mother had committed suicide, too.

The fact that they were both suicide survivors connected them in an unsettling way. For a long time, whenever Turner was depressed and on lithium, he contemplated killing himself. Until recently he had kept his father's gun in his desk drawer, and his office had windows that he could easily jump out of.

But he didn't mention any of this to Jane; he kept his mood light and flirtatious, although he was very nervous and left the table four times to disappear into the men's room. He would return and continue to talk manically about himself and his media empire.

Jane didn't think she said a word during the entire evening but at the end of it Turner declared, "I'm smitten!" She was exhausted.

A couple of weeks later Jane accompanied Turner on his private plane to a ranch he was thinking of buying in Montana — a place called the Flying D. She was enthralled by the size and beauty of the property — the 125,000 acres of land, stretching as far as the eye could see, close to Yellowstone National Park, and across rolling hills that spread right up to the snowcapped Spanish Peaks, which seemed to rise into the cloud-filled sky. The ranch was near the Great Northern Trail and the rushing Gallatin River.

Sitting on a ridge, they watched the sun going down behind the Rocky Mountains. "It took my breath away," Jane said, "to see light and shadow crisscross over those undulating plains."

That same night they made love in a plain little log cabin on the property (later Turner would point out to guests: "This was where Jane and I first did it"). He often referred to "sex with Jane" and Jane would describe to girlfriends how great sex was with *him*. They were both powerful sexual beings and enjoyed acting on their urges. Turner, of course, was a famous, crude womanizer; Jane liked to keep everybody guessing. Did she or did she not have a longtime affair with Warren Beatty? Had she run off with Mick Jagger for a weekend, played around with Geraldo Rivera after a game at the Garden? Slept with

Sven Nykvist, Ingmar Bergman's great cameraman, after Mia Farrow had left him? Was it true she'd once seduced a leading black activist and been paramour to a Kennedy? (Nobody knew which one and she wasn't telling, although she would later admit she did describe a few of her lovers to Turner: "We were both very curious about each other sexually.")

The rest of the weekend, when they weren't talking their heads off, they were exploring his land. Occasionally Turner would go down on his knees and recite his own poetry in a loud, rasping voice. "'At the feet of Hannibal / Then like a ripe plum Rome once lay. . . .' I wrote that myself, in high school," he declared. "I know his *History of the Peloponnesian War* and everything about Alexander the Great. He was my hero until I switched from war to peace. Martin Luther King and Gandhi are my heroes now."

He continued with another nonstop monologue about his childhood rebellions; he pulled ornaments off Christmas trees and smeared mud on neighbors' sheets as they were hanging in the sun to dry. He said his life changed when his beloved younger sister, Mary Jane, died at fifteen from lupus. He'd prayed so hard for her to recover. Before her death he had once wanted to be a missionary, but when she was gone he lost his faith in God. He decided he would become successful, a super-achiever, because "super-achievers are insecure like me. Being insecure can make you a workaholic."

At Brown University he didn't study, he drank and gambled, and in his junior year he was expelled for sneaking a girl into his room. He enlisted in the Coast Guard and married his first wife, Judy Nye, in June of 1960. They were both twenty-one. They had two children. After his father's death, he decided not to continue in the family business, even though it was one of the most successful billboard companies in the United States. He thought billboard advertising was boring.

Instead, while he was still in his twenties, he moved into broadcasting, buying radio stations and then a UHF television channel in Atlanta. Within a decade, he'd turned his local TV station into a cable channel seen across the country. He worked nonstop. By then, he'd divorced Judy and married Jane Shirley Smith; they had three children but he was very rarely home. He was restless. He had many girlfriends. By the 1980s he was rich; he bought sports teams and film libraries to provide programming for his cable channel; he bet on the company twice, gambling on building the first twenty-four-hour news network, CNN, and then buying the MGM film library to start new cable channels. In between, he captained his boat, *The Courageous,* to victory at the America's Cup, while performing his "Captain Outrageous antics" and continuing his habit of stirring controversy. And all the time he was acquiring properties — plantations in Florida and islands off the South Carolina coast.

He told Jane his empire now consisted of CNN, TNT, TBS, New Line Cinema, and the Atlanta Braves. There were periods when he was almost broke, he confided. He'd always been in fierce competition with men like Rupert Murdoch and Barry Diller, who had bigger fortunes than he had. But he had revolutionized the news industry and now had dreams of saving the planet from pollution. He was an ardent conservationist — had been ever since he was a kid and realized the sea turtles were disappearing off the Savannah coast.

Once again Jane listened to him. She could barely get a word in edgewise and when she did, she was almost sure he hadn't heard her. Because he wasn't all there — he hadn't connected.

By the end of the weekend he was declaring passionately, "I think you're perfect for me." And she was arguing, "We barely know each other." He then countered with "We care about the same issues, we're both over-achievers . . . you need someone who is as successful as you — and I'm *more* successful than you, which is good. There's only one negative as far as I'm concerned . . . your age" (she was fifty-one; he was fifty). Before she could say anything, he penciled in the times they could be together again on his calendar, although Jane kept protesting that it was too fast, that they should get to know each other better. He wasn't listening.

They drove to the airport two hours early, because Turner needed to fly back to Atlanta to keep a date with another girlfriend. They were attending a *Gone with the Wind* celebration (his favorite movie, which he now owned; he now possessed the entire MGM film library). His girlfriend would be costumed as Scarlett O'Hara, he said, and he would be dressing up as Rhett Butler, he added proudly.

Jane felt let down and angry as Turner kissed her goodbye and then walked jauntily off to his private jet. The following day she wrote him a letter saying essentially that they couldn't work as a couple. Then she started scrutinizing her appearance in the mirror. Her body was in good shape but she suddenly didn't think she looked seductive enough.

She decided to have more work done on her face. She went to Dr. Frank Kramer, who'd done some tweaking in 1987; this time she spent $5,000 having her upper and lower eyelids lifted. On an impulse she also went to Dr. Norman Leaf for two small C cup silicone implants. She felt younger and sexier but her children were horrified. And so were many of her friends and colleagues at the Workout. She had been perfectly proportioned; the enlarged breasts were too big for her frame. At the same time she began work with a journalist on her autobiography. The journalist happened to be an ex-lover. They started spending afternoons together taping her reminiscences. At one point he supposedly couldn't resist commenting on her overly curvaceous figure. "Why did you do it?" he asked. With that Jane angrily ripped open her blouse, exposing her big new bosoms. "I think they're great!" she cried. "Okay," he murmured, "but I liked your little breasts better."

In the next weeks she began an affair with Lorenzo Caccialanza, a hunky former hockey player turned actor, sixteen years her junior. "He makes me feel like a young girl again," she told *People* magazine. And Lorenzo countered with "All I want to do is sit at home and have Jane cook me spaghetti." In the midst of their affair Jane flew to Montana and spent time with Peter and took classes at the Orvis fly-fishing school in Bozeman, which was close to Turner's ranch. Turner heard she was there and showed up at the class; he invited her to dinner at his ranch and she went. It was quite uncomfortable because the Scarlett O'Hara girlfriend was with him. Peter was there, too, and he helped lighten the situation. Turner paid no attention to his girlfriend and instead focused all his attention on Jane. That evening, they found themselves alone and he made an urgent comment: "Enough of this stuff with younger men, what about older men's rights?" And in another moment he whispered, "It would be a shame if we were eighty by the time we finally get together." Just before they said goodbye, Turner added, "I'll take Italian lessons [and] I'll get myself stretched to six feet five" (the height of her Italian lover). Jane couldn't help smiling.

Nevertheless she returned to her romantic idyll with Lorenzo, and in the next weeks they flew to Milan to meet his mother. Signora Caccialanza took one look at Jane and said, "No way. You are too old to give Lorenzo babies."

So eventually he stopped seeing her and Jane was upset; her ego was bruised. For a while she dated a doctor and a real estate agent. She kept busy; she took over Hayden's CED, renamed it Campaign California, and began making fundraising appearances around the state. She went on working with Lois Bonfiglio on various projects, including an American version of Pedro Almodóvar's *Women on the Verge of a Nervous Breakdown*. She traveled to Eastern Europe with Mignon McCarthy. All the while Ted Turner kept sending flowers and messages.

He wouldn't give up; he knew she was no longer seeing Lorenzo. One afternoon he appeared outside the Workout studio in Beverly Hills where she was leading a session, and he waited until she was finished so he could speak to her. The idea of Ted Turner waiting for anyone was amazing — he'd never done that before; he was usually too impatient. He was not an easy man to be with. He had no capacity for small talk. His restless energy was draining to be around. But as soon as he did start seeing Jane again on a regular basis, he really tried to be charming and thoughtful — he tried to pull back on his womanizing; he would not let her out of his sight until he could be certain she belonged to him.

It didn't take Jane long to realize she and Ted Turner were closely matched personalities, and so similar in their drives, their ambitions, their self-absorption that they were like twins. She had become an American icon; his life was now assuming legendary proportions as he revolutionized the broadcasting industry and cobbled together a communications empire despite regular brushes with insolvency and fierce competition with better-funded rivals.

There was no question about it — Jane and Ted Turner could make a great team. They were highly keyed, nonstop talkers, insatiably curious about the world, addicted to publicity, and, being celebrities, loved being in the spotlight. Jane's goal was to make a difference in the world; Turner kept a list in his pocket of all the things he wanted to change — end pollution, stop wars, eradicate poverty, curb population growth.

Their courtship was covered relentlessly by the world's press. Turner took Jane everywhere with him: to the CNN Tenth Anniversary Gala, and to all of his plantations and ranches. He brought her to a White House dinner (where Barbara Bush refused to shake her hand), and to the Élysée Palace to meet President Mitterrand. At the Kremlin, Gorbachev paid attention only to her. Every day Turner sent her flowers and presents. She told Suzanne Tenner, "No man has ever loved me the way Ted loves me."

"Ted knows how to treat a lady," a friend of Jane's told the *L.A. Times*. "It's the old-fashioned Southern stuff — gifts and flowers and caring. Tom wasn't good at that. Turner acknowledges Jane in public and she responds to that kind of chivalry. Tom could never acknowledge Jane. I remember she'd be sitting next to him in public and she'd have to place his arm around her shoulder so it would look like they were close, that he cared. It was pathetic."

Late in the summer of 1989 Jane began showing up in Bozeman, near the Flying D Ranch, which Turner had purchased; he told her he was planning to build a house on a golden pond for her, and he did. She stayed at the inn close by the ranch and they took fly-fishing lessons together. In the fall, Tom Hayden agreed to Jane's ultimatum: he would receive an estimated $3 million and an annual allowance of $200,000 for the next several years. They would get joint custody of Troy.

Jane began keeping steady company with Turner again in the summer of 1990; it was at a critical juncture in his career, CNN's coverage of the Gulf War.

In order to do it right, Turner hired Tom Johnson, the highly respected former publisher of the *Los Angeles Times,* to be the president of CNN. They met for the first time in July 1990 at Jane's home. "We had a fifteen-minute interview," Johnson remembered, "and Ted hired me." Jane added, "Ted always goes by his instincts. He thought Tom was perfect for the job." Turner liked the fact that Johnson was from a working-class family in Macon, Georgia. He had a low-key, genial manner and had worked his way through Harvard Business School, had been special assistant to President Johnson, and then was editor, then publisher, of the *Dallas Times Herald* before Otis Chandler brought him to Los Angeles as publisher of his company's flagship paper.

Johnson was to start work at CNN the following day, but that night they all went out to dinner to celebrate. Johnson remembered how "at the restaurant Jane and Ted could not keep their hands off each other. My wife and I felt like we were watching a couple of teenagers."

Johnson's first day on the job at CNN was August 1, 1990. On that day Saddam Hussein's Iraqi army invaded Kuwait. Johnson knew exactly what he had to do. He had a Rolodex bulging with important names and numbers. He posted reporters in Baghdad, Amman, Saudi Arabia, Israel, and the White House as well as the Pentagon and the State Department and had them reporting around the clock. CNN spent $22 million covering the war; the other networks wouldn't make that kind of commitment.

Throughout the fall and early winter Jane remained glued to her TV set whenever she could. Johnson remembered being at Jane's house watching CNN with Ted on the evening of January 16, 1991. "I'll never forget it. Bernie Shaw, Peter Arnett, John Holliman delivering gripping coverage as the bombs began to fall. For the first time in history a war was being televised from behind the lines. We were all euphoric."

Up until that point CNN had drawn maybe a million viewers. During Desert Storm, there were an estimated 60 million people watching CNN. It was almost sexually exciting for Jane to be in love with a man who'd been responsible for scoring the journalistic scoop of the century. *Time Magazine* named him "Man of the Year."

By now, Jane was anxious to get her family's approval of Turner, so he arranged to take everyone to dinner: Troy, Vanessa, Nathalie, and Lulu. "He tried so hard to endear himself to us," Lulu said. "I loved him right away. I think Nathalie did, too. Troy and Vanessa were a harder sell." They were afraid their mother was going to give herself away again to another man and that made them angry.

At first Jane didn't live with Turner. She remained at her home in Santa Monica because Troy was still in high school and Vanessa in her last year of college. Turner would spend weekends with her and then fly back to Atlanta, and they would speak on the phone for hours. He was honest about spending those nights away from her with his other women. She was angry about that but she didn't say anything.

Eventually, he brought her to Atlanta to introduce her to the people closest to him. "The way he introduced me to everyone in Atlanta made me realize that despite his unquestionable importance in the world, Ted was like a kid, so proud to have me on his arm." She met his five children. She met Turner's trusted "surrogate daddy," his chauffeur, Jimmy Brown, who had been with him since he was a boy. He had taught him to sail and fish; he helped him raise his kids. Turner said, "Jimmy knows me better than anybody in the world."

Jane also got to know Dee Woods, his trusted assistant of twenty-five years. Dee told her, "He's a male chauvinist pig and he always will be." She laughed when she said it and Jane chose to think she was being funny. Later she realized Dee was not so subtly trying to tell her something.

After Jane began "going steady" with Turner, she decided she would give up work completely. She would stop acting and producing and she would devote herself totally to the relationship. But she made him promise he would be faithful to her, to give up his other women, and he agreed. And she convinced herself that he would.

She knew he was high maintenance. She knew he was the kind of man who loves the one he's with and then fools around on his wives and his girlfriends when he's away from them. But Jane's marriage to Hayden had suffered because she was away from him so much. She didn't want that to happen again. She imagined she wanted to be taken care of totally by Ted Turner. She'd never in her life been taken care of by a man, unless she counted her father, who had always come through for her when she needed him to. He had given her the money for a house when she needed a place to live. He had let her stay with him in his house in Bel Air when she and Vadim separated, and of course she always had a bedroom in the townhouse in New York. She realized she had never been with a businessman before, not to mention a billionaire businessman. "[Ted] had the heart of a rebel and social values that didn't put money first. Ted understands money, but he's not *about* money," she said.

She did, however, want to hold on to her financial independence. That was essential. The money she made, the fortune she worked so hard to accumulate, made her feel strong. It was funny. She was momentarily enjoying the abundance of everything Ted Turner had, his billions that made life so comfortable and easy and luxurious. His world — his empire — was quite overwhelming. But there was still part of her that wanted to be free. "Part of her didn't want me to pay for stuff," Turner confided once. "She wouldn't even let me buy her a plane ticket," he complained. "Of course, we usually traveled in my private jet."

She continued to oversee the Workout business with Julie LaFond; it flourishes to this day. She made only one more video — the *Lean Routine*. As usual, she created the choreography and promoted the video on Larry King's show. Turner made a surprise appearance with her.

Not long after the King show aired, Jane put her house in Santa Monica on the market — as well as the Santa Barbara ranch — and she moved to Atlanta full-time with Turner. Her stepdaughter, Nathalie, was thrilled: "I have never seen you so happy," she told Jane. Lulu felt the same way and she absolutely adored Ted — he was the surrogate father she'd never had. She began spending time with him and Jane at his various ranches, watching movies with him. He watched his favorite movies over and over again; he'd seen *Citizen Kane* fifty times. "He would cry when he saw *The Wizard of Oz*," Lulu said.

Vanessa was still furious. She didn't like the idea of Jane giving herself away again, of being subsumed by yet another man. Even Troy confided when he was visiting Jane on one of Turner's ranches that he "[didn't] want a mom who doesn't work."

Both of them thought she was wrong to give up her identity as an actress, a businesswoman, a political activist. She would be disappearing into the glitzy world of corporate media — on the arm of a Goldwater Republican. They didn't see how it could work. Once again she'd chosen a powerful, opinionated man to run things — she seemed to need a man like that to anchor her.

Some of Turner's male colleagues were appalled — Southern good ol' boys who drank with him and sailed with him couldn't figure out how this great embodiment of the capitalist system was planning to marry "Hanoi Jane." Turner defended his decision on the Larry King show. "Jane is the love of my life. She holds her own with me — we are good together."

It made sense. Turner was a maverick billionaire — an eccentric, an original, something of a legend, who was giving Jane the farmlands, the horses, that were reminiscent of the bucolic lifestyle of the childhood that Henry Fonda had created for his family. Turner was actually the kind of character that Henry Fonda might have played in a movie. "Oh yes!" Jane exclaimed. "Ted is very much like my father but with none of the bad parts. He sounds like him, even looks like him at times," she insisted. "He loves to fish. My dad was a great fisherman. One big difference, and I can't say it in English, Ted is *bien dans son peau*. Ted feels good in his own skin. He loves women, understands women, feels comfortable with women, and is not threatened by them. My dad was."

Jane was sure she could achieve with Ted "the true, deep soul connection that had eluded me. Ted was not intimidated by me. I loved him! I loved his smell, his skin, his playfulness, his world view, his transparency." She wanted to convince herself that she could finally overcome her fear of intimacy. "Oh, I wanted this so to work!"

Jane stayed up half the night rewriting the wedding vows, cutting out all references to the word *obey*. Before they were married on December 21, 1991, at Turner's 8,100-acre Avalon Plantation outside Tallahassee, Florida, helicopters buzzed overhead, circling over the three tiers of lush gardens and the huge man-made lake. The ear-shattering clatter was such that the entire bridal party left the plantation's small private chapel for the relative quiet of the main house nearby.

Turner dressed in a white linen suit and brown leather cowboy boots, and he appeared very trim; Jane had insisted he exercise and lose twenty pounds. She looked radiant. She had chosen a formal high-waisted, high-necked empire gown she'd resurrected from *Old Gringo*, and she'd pinned yellow and white freesias in her blond-streaked tresses. Vanessa was the maid of honor. Troy was the best man and gave her away. The only other attendant was tall, heavyset Jimmy Brown. Friends and family included Peter Fonda; Lulu; Paula Weinstein; Shirlee Fonda; Dee Woods, Turner's special assistant; and Barbara Pyle, one of Turner's many former girlfriends.

The guests ate fresh quail that Jane had shot, candied yams, collard greens, and plenty of corn bread. The wedding cake was a creamy wonder; it smelled of fresh gardenias. Afterward there were countless champagne toasts. Peter Fonda insisted, "It was a wonderful, joyous moment. We were all crying and laughing."

Turner and Jane honeymooned on the Flying D Ranch in Montana, and after New Year's they attended yet another party in Hollywood with the so-called A-list, including Barbara Walters, Lily Tomlin, Quincy Jones, Meg Ryan, Jon Voight, Barry Diller, Jeff Bridges, and Gregory Peck, most of whom had worked with Jane or Turner. Around midnight, Dolly Parton tipsily raised her glass to "Man of the Year, Woman of the Hour, Couple of the Century." Everyone cheered, but there were a few cynics in the crowd, one of whom murmured that this was different from Jane's other transformations. She was now a trophy wife, with all its severe implications. Roger Vadim, the artist, and Tom Hayden, the driven politician, were pussycats in comparison to Ted Turner. Jane called him "my buccaneer," but there were those at the party that night who believed Jane had made a pact with the devil — that she'd sold out.

A month later Jane discovered Turner was sleeping with another woman.

"The discovery was pure fluke," Jane said. She'd been sitting in their car waiting for Turner. She saw a woman she thought she recognized. She'd seen her earlier that day in the CNN building. Jane called out to her from the car and the woman hid behind a pillar.

"In my gut I knew. I called Ted's office on the car phone, and when his assistant, Dee, answered I put it to her straight. 'He pulled a nooner, didn't he.' (This was Ted's term for lunchtime dalliances.) She stammered and denied it (probably thinking, Hey, Fonda, didn't I warn you?). She told me Ted was on his way down to meet me."

When he slid into the car, Turner's face was ashen and Jane began hitting him over the head and shoulders with the car phone, then she poured her bottle of water over his head. "[I was] crying and shaking. . . . 'I sure hope it was a great fuck because you just blew it with me. I'm outta here!' Hitting someone is not my style. But it also occurred to me I'd never cared enough before to express this kind of balls-out rage. 'Why did you do it? Haven't things been great with us?'"

He stopped at a red light and put his face in his hands. "Yes, I love you madly and our sex is great. I don't know. I guess it's like . . . it's like a tic . . . something I've gotten used to doing. I've always needed a backup in case something happens between us."

"Well, you've succeeded in making sure something would happen and now you'll be stuck with your backup. I hope you're happy."

That same evening Jane flew to L.A., booked herself into the Bel Air, and stayed there for two weeks, telling no one where she was except for Leni Cazden, the woman who'd taught her the Gilda Marx routines for the Workout and who now happened to be Ted's trainer when he was in California. She knew and understood him, and Jane sensed she would be the one she could talk to — "She would come to my room every day, sit by the bed, give me hard Coffee Nips candies (they're comforting), and hold my hand while I cried and kvetched."

After two weeks Jane and Turner reconciled, and Jane gave Turner an ultimatum "that he would never betray me again — would never see that woman again, and would go into counseling with me [with Beverly Kitaen Morse and Jack Rosenberg]." Turner agreed to all three conditions.

They spent the next six hours with Beverly and Jack and continued to see them on and off for the next eight years whenever they were in L.A.

For seven of those years Turner supposedly kept his promise, despite rumors to the contrary. Is Jane sure he was faithful? "I won't answer that question," she said.

38

J ANE INSISTS SHE was happy with Turner — for a while. At first she loved "winging back and forth around his beautiful properties." She liked being privy to so many exciting events; she got a kick out of the extremes of their lifestyles — from muddy jeans to tuxedoes in a twenty-four-hour period thanks to the private jet.

There was even something appealing about surrendering to Turner's fierce demands, giving in and abandoning the fight for independence; it relaxed her momentarily. And there was one amazing thing: she'd stopped having the recurring nightmare she'd been having ever since she was a little girl.

For forty years she'd been plagued with the same terrible dream. "I was in the wrong room and desperately needed to get out, get back to where I was supposed to be. It was dark and cold and I could never find the door. In my sleep I would actually move large pieces of furniture around my bedroom trying to find the way out, and then, because it was futile, I would give up and get back in bed. The next morning the furniture would have to be moved back into place. It was a nightmare that stayed with me . . . until I married Ted Turner when I was fifty-four."

So for the next seven years Jane was the perfect trophy wife — she guarded their privacy, gave no interviews, tried to adjust to Atlanta, where their home was a cramped penthouse at the top of the CNN building. It was difficult; at first she had no friends there. She felt isolated and alone, but she was determined to change that and she did.

Soon she was part of many social circles: the "Ladies Who Lunch"; heavyweights like President Carter and his wife, Rosalynn, and Andrew Young. Everybody wanted to meet Jane Fonda. She was charming and beautiful and a celebrity—that helped, too.

As Mrs. Ted Turner she dutifully accompanied her husband everywhere—to his ranches and plantations, to conferences and meetings and forums all over the United States. In 1994, they embarked on a long CNN-related around-the-world trip. A CNN executive remembers Turner being surprised, but not displeased, when Jane attracted more attention than he did in Hong Kong. Then at a banquet in the Great Hall of the People in Beijing hosted by the Chinese government, a crowd of a thousand approached Turner's table with cameras. He stood up to pose and was stunned when he was told, "No, no, we want Jane." In Tokyo, another crowd of a thousand guests was invited to a hotel reception that Turner was hosting. Jane was still upstairs getting dressed; he came down alone and noticed that hundreds of guests were milling behind a rope waiting to enter the ballroom. He ordered that the guests be let in so he could greet them. "Not a single person would come in without Jane at the door," recalled a CNN executive. For the next twenty minutes, Turner stared at the crowd and they stared back at him. He had a fever and he wanted to go home, but instead he and Jane flew on to India, and then there was an emergency stop at an airport in Canton at 2:00 A.M. The jet's thrust reverser had to be repaired and they had to refuel. Jane remained on the plane and slept, while Turner wandered into a darkened terminal and curled up in a fetal position.

At dawn Turner told an associate that he'd had a terrible nightmare: the Chinese mechanics would say the plane was repaired, and then it would crash in the Himalayas. His associate assured him, "The plane has been repaired and it won't crash." "But I haven't gotten to my nightmare yet," Turner went on. He was still feeling pretty sick, but he couldn't resist a good punch line. "The nightmare is that the headline will be 'Jane Fonda and Others Die in Plane Crash.'" Turner, who claimed he had a fever of 103, arranged to abort the trip and fly home with Jane on a commercial airliner from Hong Kong.

Jane told journalist Ken Auletta that Ted was never jealous of the attention she received. "He doesn't have that kind of an ego," she said when Auletta reported the anecdote to her. "He put me on a pedestal. He loved my successes; he did not love my failures." "Although he is not an introspective or patient man, Turner probably opened up more to Jane than he ever had to anyone else, male or female," Auletta said.

But they were always on the go. "Given everything that happened to Ted when he was a child, the beatings, the psychological manipulations — there is a fear of abandonment that's deeper than with anyone I've ever known," Jane said. They had relatively little time to themselves to reflect. They never seemed to stop. She had to endure endless cocktail hours with slightly loaded corporate executives — mostly right-wing Republicans as well as other business tycoons. They would drone on and on. Sometimes Jane would want to jump in and argue with them about some point or other, take issue with what they were saying, but she didn't. As for Turner, he would ramble on and every so often utter his piercing laugh or exclaim "Ahhhhhh!!!" as a punctuation to his thoughts before he veered off in another direction, which sometimes didn't make sense.

At such times she would remember something a former CNN colleague and friend of Turner's had said: "Ted is a mixture of genius and jackass — he could be president if it weren't for his jackass side." For a while Turner confided to her his dream to be president, but Jane vetoed that dream. She had been married to one politician and would not be married to another one, she told him.

She was now seeing to it that Turner started paying attention to his family, his five children, Beau, Rhett, Ted, Jenny, and Laura. Like him they'd had brutal beginnings and were practically abandoned as kids. Ted's chauffeur had really raised them. In any event, Jane brought them all together. "I know how important it was and I was a good stepmother."

She organized boisterous get-togethers at Thanksgiving and Christmas for the entire family at the Flying D Ranch. She was pleased when she watched two of Ted's sons graduate from college. "I eventually saw all the kids get married and have babies. It was wonderful."

"Jane is a terrific stepmother and an amazing woman. She did wonders for my father and she brought us close. It would not have happened without her," said Laura Seydel, Turner's eldest daughter. Her oldest son, John R., said, "Grandma Jane is a special grandmother. She does things. She doesn't sit around watching TV."

Jane was also working hard to patch up the difficulties with her own daughter, Vanessa, who at that point was a defiant young feminist. (She'd cofounded MayDay Media with her best friend Rory Kennedy. The two had been making documentary films together.)

Vanessa was still finding fault with her mother and with Turner, whom she disliked. "Mom has the worst judgment of anybody I've ever known. She is so smart and yet she makes decisions too fast." It was different with Troy. He never criticized his mother. Jane doted on him. She still seemed to love him more than anybody in the world. When he insisted that *both* his parents celebrate his twenty-first birthday with him, Jane agreed. They had a party at Laurel Springs, which still hadn't been sold, and Hayden arrived with his new wife, Barbara Williams. He and Jane spoke — a bit hesitantly since their bitter divorce.

"I wanted to be friends with Tom again for Troy's sake," Jane said. They began to see each other; every so often they spoke on the phone. Jane cared for Hayden; she never stopped. She would dream about him "when I'm not dreaming about my dad."

In the first years of their marriage Turner acquired four more ranches in Montana within four hours of each other. It wasn't unusual for Jane and Turner to have breakfast at one ranch, fish in the early morning, then have lunch and a late-afternoon fish at another ranch, and then drive to a third and fish in the evening.

Ultimately, Turner's properties ranged from a coastal island off South Carolina to a glass house overlooking the Pacific Ocean at Big Sur. By 1994 he'd bought two more ranches in Montana, another two in Nebraska, two in South Dakota, and three in New Mexico. They comprise 600,000 acres, starting in the Rockies and ending in the Great Plains.

Near the end of the nineties he purchased two more spectacular properties in Patagonia and one in Tierra del Fuego. Jane protested. She'd been decorating most of the ranches — "what a stupendous job." She threatened to leave him if he bought another ranch. But he did anyway, and she didn't leave. She kept saying, "Please don't have so many ranches!"

Their flagship home was still the Flying D in Montana. One afternoon when they were at the D, Turner blindfolded her and drove her into the hills, pointing out a location where "we will build a house." He gestured to a valley with a tiny stream running through it. "Right there I'm gonna create a lake that will reflect the Spanish Peaks. It will be our Golden Pond." And he did, and Jane helped him design the place. "I wanted to have one home that reflected me with a ceiling under which no one before me had made love to Ted."

By 1995 Turner was more restless than ever; he wanted to create a bigger CNN empire. He was worried that his company was too small. He wanted to merge with a network or a studio, so he tried to merge with CBS, but that didn't work out; then he almost bought Paramount Pictures. He had talks with Bill Gates about partnering Microsoft with CNN to create an online news site. Rupert Murdoch, his archenemy, wanted to buy CNN. Turner scoffed at the idea. Ultimately, Murdoch created Fox Cable News to compete with CNN.

Everyone wanted to merge with Turner — no one more than Gerald R. Levin, CEO of Time Warner. He and Turner had many discussions. Meanwhile Levin did all he could to block any other deal from happening. When Turner tried to acquire NBC, Levin used his ties with the network to stop the merger and make way for one with Time Warner instead.

ABC was also making moves. Meanwhile Levin kept advancing. He told colleagues he wasn't going to stop until Time Warner had taken over CNN. Turner became very paranoid about Levin's motives and Jane noticed it. She was afraid he might make a public statement about Levin; she kept him away from reporters whenever they phoned. That spring he had to make a speech at the National Press Club in Washington. Jane told Ken Auletta she was aware of the fragility of the relationship between Levin and Ted. One false move and their possible merger might fall apart. "The night before the speech I didn't sleep. Ted slept like a baby."

The following day at the National Press Club he spoke without notes. He liked to improvise; it made him think faster. Even so the audience was startled when he for no reason mentioned a story CNN had just done on clitoridectomies. Suddenly, he started to compare the mutilation of women to what Gerald Levin was doing to him. He cried out, "Talk about barbaric mutilation. I'm angry. I'm being clitorized by Time Warner.'"

Jane recalled, "I slid under my seat." Levin commented later, "Ted is Ted. He was peeved at the time. He actually called me up and we talked about it. There wasn't a problem."

Even so Levin knew he had to move fast. Time Warner was burdened by a $16 billion debt; its stock kept falling. Meanwhile Turner Broadcasting kept building; Murdoch still wanted to buy CNN. GE was interested, too. Without telling any of his directors at Time Warner, Levin phoned Turner and asked if he could fly to Montana to discuss an important matter. When Levin's plane landed in Bozeman, Jane picked him up at the airport.

"You better not upset my husband," she told Levin, who assured her he was going to make Ted Turner very, very happy. Jane had a great many guests at the ranch that weekend so she disappeared as soon as she deposited Levin with Turner in the living room.

The two men wandered out on the deck to survey the magnificent view of the Spanish Peaks. Levin rapidly explained why he thought the merging of Time Warner and CNN would be a perfect fit. He then jotted down a couple of notes on a piece of paper.

The offer was pretty astounding: $7 billion in Time Warner stock for 100 percent of Turner Broadcasting, twice the market value of TBS. Turner would become Time Warner's largest individual shareholder with an 11 percent equity stake. Levin would be CEO, and Turner would be vice chairman.

Turner appeared to agree to all points. But Levin said, "He said 'Wait a second, I gotta talk to Jane.'"*

He reappeared within minutes, shouting hoarsely. "Okay, we made a deal!" And with that he walked back into the living room, where guests were starting to congregate, among them Tom Brokaw, his wife, Meredith, and their daughter.

"We're gonna merge," Turner announced to the startled Brokaw.

---

* Jane doesn't remember this. "Ted was his own man. I never influenced him in any way about his business. I think Gerry wanted to make Ted look like he couldn't make up his own mind; that he wanted to make him look bad."

Then he added gleefully, "Maybe we will buy CBS or NBC and then you could work for us!"

Meanwhile Jane had been very busy on her own. "Ted was so occupied with his work I could finally start doing things I'd been wanting to do for a long time." In 1994 she'd been asked by the UN to be a goodwill ambassador of the Conference on Population and Development in Cairo, Egypt. The purpose of the conference was to figure out how to stabilize population growth. It was something she and Ted Turner had often discussed. It was one of his obsessions.

She remembers going through the halls, meeting women from all over the world — Buddhist, Christian, Hindu, Muslim; it was the first time in her life she'd been on her own in such an international gathering and she felt exhilarated and intimidated.

Said another woman delegate: "Jane was eager to be involved in something other than her marriage. She'd been out of the loop too long. She was very aggressive about sitting with Bella Abzug and Gerry Ferraro and learning from them." She knew she would have to head a foundation in order to be a major player in the nonprofit and government aid world.

By the end of the conference she'd not just discovered strategies to reduce population growth, she'd started relating it to her own experiences "of vulnerability to pressure from men around *their* sexual pleasure, around acquiescence and needing to be acceptable; [these pressures] were universal issues for women . . . in developed as well as in developing countries."

When she returned to Atlanta, Ted Turner was so busy with new projects that he didn't mind her traveling around the state to "examine the realities of adolescent life at home." Jane felt that many poor girls in Georgia had limited identities apart from their sexuality.

The following year she founded the Georgia Campaign for Adolescent Pregnancy Prevention with the help and support of the Turner Foundation. In the next decade, the teenage pregnancy rate in Georgia dropped significantly, due in part to the organization's outreach programs in churches and schools. Over the years, Jane has raised millions of dollars to support these efforts.

• • •

It was now 1996. Jane had been with Turner for close to eight years. She knew she had made him happy and had played a centering role in his life. When he shared his idea of making a billion-dollar gift directly to the UN, Jane cried and told him, "I'm proud to be married to you." But she still suppressed all the things he did that hurt her, all the things she agreed to do even it if went against her sense of well-being.

She decided to publish a cookbook (Turner published it for her). It was a good cookbook, *Cooking for Healthy Living,* and she wrote about her father's love of organic vegetables and preparing meals for Bardot and Vadim in Paris. She did not mention Tom Hayden, but she did describe all the meals she planned for Ted. The menus and recipes were put together with Ted's chef, Karen Averitt. In the winter of 1996 she promoted the book around the country. She was interviewed for the first time in years; she was nervous and ill at ease, reporters noted. She was also painfully thin.

She was drinking more to numb her feelings as she tried to accommodate Turner's frantic moving about the country. Energetic though she was, she was exhausted from traveling from ranch to ranch. He now owned twenty-two properties.

She was getting tired of having to arrange to meet with her children on Turner's schedule. She was constantly disappointing Troy and Vanessa. They told her she was losing herself and they were right. "[Ted] tried [to understand my needs], but only when my needs didn't interfere with his own," Jane said.

Occasionally they would have an out-and-out fight. Once they came out of a Waldorf Astoria elevator, their voices raised. They kept on yelling at each other as they marched into a ballroom where they were to be guests of honor.

Turner vaulted to the dais and announced, "My wife and I are having a discussion and I want to finish it." Without further ado he pulled Jane out of the ballroom to continue their argument.

Jane was about to turn sixty. It occurred to her it would be her "third act." She wanted to figure out what to do with the rest of her life, and she wanted to answer the question "Who the hell am I?"

She decided to make a short video of her life to discover its different themes. She said she wanted to do it for her children and her stepchildren, but she really wanted to do it for herself. She decided to give a big party to celebrate her sixtieth birthday and invite all her friends and give them copies of the video as a gift. She had already gathered plenty of material. Her father had made home movies when she was a little girl; she'd kept archives of interviews, pictures, and press clippings. And there were her movies and TV interviews. All the raw material was there to help her piece together the puzzle of her identity.

Jane asked Vanessa to help her put the movie together. Her daughter's answer: "Why don't you just get a chameleon and let it crawl across the screen?" Jane winced. It was true, of course. "I had so many personalities in my lifetime it was easy to think, 'Who is she?'" How could such a seemingly strong woman keep on repeating the same mistake — losing herself with another man?

Choosing the images was almost impossible because there were thousands of pictures. Trying to shape and edit the film was unsettling. Who was the real Jane? And what exactly was her story? Hundreds of Janes in black and white and color melting together one after the other. There was a masterful Irving Penn portrait of twenty-one-year-old Jane and her father. Her arm around his neck, her head resting on his shoulder, she appears lost in love. Henry is pleased but implacable. This image could have been juxtaposed with an arch, placating Jane of *Jane* (the documentary), so completely under mentor/lover Andreas's preening control, or the round-cheeked cheerleader in *Tall Story*. The desperate, voracious whore in *Walk on the Wild Side*. The go-getting ingénue in *Barefoot in the Park* and, of course, *Barbarella*. No one had ever seen such a delectable bonbon as this seductive, funny, girly comic book heroine. There were images from the Workout, her mug shot when she was arrested in Cleveland, and the iconic candid of her as "Hanoi Jane."

A few of these images were used, along with her narration, which resulted in a video called *A Work in Progress*. She showed it on her birthday on December 21, 1997, to three hundred of her friends. Her favorite stepmother, Susan, thought it was too personal. There was something upsetting about Jane presenting these raw fragments without much context because she couldn't really explain what the images revealed; they were fragments of a life story that was always in flux. Repeating it was how Jane channeled the flow.

· · ·

Shortly after Jane's birthday Vanessa became pregnant. She had already phoned her father in Paris and he was worried — not that she was having a baby, but that she wouldn't be able to do everything by herself. Vanessa was working on a farm in Florida as an organic gardener. "I didn't know what to say to Mom. She came to visit. We went somewhere to eat and suddenly she's talking about how I mustn't get pregnant until I have my life together. She lists all the reasons why I shouldn't get pregnant. Why she's doing this I don't know. Maybe she has a sixth sense, because I hadn't said anything to her — yet. She keeps on rambling and finally I interrupt with 'Mom, it's too late. I'm going to have a baby.' She really freaks out, lets me have it for twenty minutes or so till I think I'm going crazy. We get back to this place I'm staying in. We bunked together. She is still going on about it. Finally, we fall asleep. The next morning Mom wakes up and her attitude has completely changed. She's all excited. 'I'm going to be a grandmother! I'm going to be a grandmother! I know where I can get you the most adorable crib.' From then on she supports me a hundred percent in what I'm doing."

When Jane told Turner she wanted to be with Vanessa — be there for her as much as possible — he exploded in a rage. "I think he sensed that my energy would be drawn away from him for a while."

From the very beginning, Jane had informed Turner she planned to stay with Vanessa during the ten days surrounding her due date. The home birth would take place at Turner's Crabapple Farm outside of Atlanta; there was a midwife in attendance. Jane kept phoning Turner to come by; he did very briefly.

Right after the baby was born — a boy, Malcolm — Vanessa weakly asked Jane to phone her father in Paris, but she couldn't remember the number and had to hunt around for it. Meanwhile Jane's assistant was filming the whole event. Then the nurse ran in and said, "You're not phoning anybody until we cut the placenta." Vanessa insisted on speaking to her father anyway, and then they rushed her to the hospital where she almost died. She'd lost 60 percent of her blood because they hadn't cut the placenta when they should have.

For the next four days Jane remained at Crabapple Farm with Vanessa and baby Malcolm. She sat in a rocking chair on the porch for hours at a time while her daughter slept, and she held Malcolm to her breast singing the lullabies she'd sung to Vanessa thirty years before.

A May breeze wafted through the air as she gazed out over the freshly blooming dogwood and azalea. "Malcolm had enabled me to discover the combination to the safe where the soft part of my heart had been shut away for so long. Depths of feelings washed over me, cleansing me. . . . Perhaps Ted knew it would be this way and that's why he had gotten so upset at the news I would be a grandmother."

She realized she had to change her relationship with Ted Turner; she could no longer agree, acquiesce, accommodate his every need. She had to think of herself. She had to demand things. It would be hard.

In June when they returned to the Flying D Ranch to fish, she blurted out, "I need us to try to do some things differently in our marriage, because otherwise I'm not sure I can show up for you the way you want me to." She mentioned his infidelities; they had to stop. She could not travel as much, simply could not. She wanted to spend more time with her children. Was any of this too much to ask?

He was glowering when she finished. "Let's go fishing and we'll discuss this later," he told her brusquely. But that evening when they got back into the car, "he freaked out." When they returned to the ranch, Jane watched Turner bang the wall with his fists and his head. She was stunned.

More and more along with the frantic public life they lived together Jane began creating a parallel inner life for herself. She had been talking religion a lot to Nancy McQuirk, who was married to a top Turner executive. The two women had met seven years before at business receptions. While their husbands would go off to talk shop in one corner, Nancy and Jane would talk about Jesus. Ms. McQuirk teaches Bible classes to hundreds of women. "Eventually I began studying the Bible, too," Jane said.

She'd started attending services at Providence Missionary Baptist Church in Atlanta. Turner's chauffeur had taken her there one afternoon when he'd noticed her crying in the back of the limousine. He'd suggested going to a service; it might be helpful. For a while she attended services there until the media got wind of it and Jane Fonda becoming a born-again Christian became a huge news story.

Turner couldn't get over it. "She was not a religious person," he said. "That's a pretty big change for your wife of nine years to tell you. That's a shock. I mean, normally that's the kind of thing your wife or husband would discuss with you before they did it or while they were thinking about it. . . . Obviously we weren't communicating very well at that time."

Jane knew that when she became a Christian he would be very upset. "I chose not to discuss it with him — because he would have talked me out of it. He's a debating champion. He saw it as writing on the wall." It was other things, too. She wanted to visit Troy more; to be with Vanessa and Malcolm, and with Lulu, who was now in Atlanta, too.

For a while they weren't going to get divorced; they were always going to stay married but separate and every so often have these "little sexual interludes." Jane told friends that just before they finally did separate they had the greatest sex ever. She was drinking a lot then and sometimes in public at a benefit or dinner she'd suddenly start telling some perfect stranger an intimate detail about her love life. "Ted was very much around," another friend said. "They'd talk on the phone and he'd fly in to one of the ranches where she was staying."

Then suddenly it was over.

On January 4, 2000, the Turners announced their separation. As soon as this happened Frederique Darragon, a statuesque blond who'd been in and out of Turner's life for thirty years, appeared on his arm. In fact, when Jane left the big ranch in Santa Fe and returned to Atlanta on Turner's jet, Frederique was waiting at the airport hangar to replace her.

Jane had asked Vanessa if she could camp out with her at her shingled house outside Atlanta. "I had gone from twenty-three kingdom-size properties and a private plane that could sleep six to a small guest room with no closet in a modest house in a charming but not quite gentrified section of Atlanta," Jane said.

It was very quiet at Vanessa's. The place was surrounded by old trees and a lovely garden, and Jane and Vanessa spent time outside talking about fathers and husbands and marriages.

There were complications; Vadim was dying in Paris and Vanessa wanted to be with him. When she found out he didn't have much longer to live, she flew to France and Jane stayed with Malcolm. "He was showing me how to love," Jane said. "I would lie in bed with his sleeping body draped across me. . . . Later [when he could speak] Malcolm would take my face in his hands and say, 'I yuv you, grandma.'"

· · ·

Within weeks she joined Vanessa in Paris, because she wanted to say goodbye to Vadim, too. She stood by his bedside along with his mother and sister and friends, and looking down at his pale, emaciated frame, she realized with a pang that he had probably made her happier than any other man in her life.

Vadim died on February 11, 2000. The following day, Jane joined his friends, his women and wives and Vanessa, and together they marched through the cobblestoned streets of Saint-Tropez, his favorite place in the world. He was going to be buried in the little churchyard he had taken Vanessa to see when she was a little girl.

Paris Match covered the funeral march and crowds gathered on the sidewalk to watch. It was quite dramatic. Bardot, dumpy and tearstained, walked arm in arm with an impassive, beautiful Catherine Deneuve; Vanessa cradled baby Malcolm in her arms, and the current Madame Vadim, Marie-Christine Barrault, seemed prostrate with grief; she was bent over and sobbing loudly as she walked.

Jane stood alone, separate and apart from all the other women — hair streaming in the breeze, a fashionable scarf knotted around her neck, she strode to the gravesite in chic Barbarella-style black leather pants and boots.

Vadim had encouraged her to be herself — to believe in herself. In spite of her sadness she suddenly felt strangely triumphant. She was by herself and she was starting to like it. When she returned to Atlanta, she began yet another phase of her incredible serial life.

Epilogue

As soon as Jane returned from Vadim's funeral in Paris, she plunged into her new life as a free and independent woman. For the next ten years, while I wrote about her transformations — from movie star to political actress to exercise guru — she was recycling these various selves. She has survived as many people; they are a genuine part of her and she can inhabit them at will. She markets them brilliantly, in order to remain relevant and visible to the public.

It's not possible to describe the wild variety and scope of everything she tried to do in the last decade. As usual, she never stopped. (Except when she had hip and knee replacement surgery in 2005. Friends insisted that she rest and she did, for a while, at her ranch.)

Some highlights: May 2001, at a tribute at the Lincoln Center Film Society to honor her stellar career, the theater was packed, and the audience applauded as Jane told them, "I'm on a quest. Who knows what's ahead?" She went on to appear at the Rome Film Festival, where she was also honored. In Rome Jane saw her half sister, Pan, for the first time in twenty-five years; they talked about their mother for hours and what she had meant to both of them.

In April 2005, Jane's autobiography, *My Life So Far,* was published with the usual publicity blitz (Jane dedicated the book to her mother). Two segments on *60 Minutes* were to be aired on the publication date, accompanied by book serialization in both *Time* and *People* magazines, "because my autobiography is a news event," she told somebody. She was upset when the Pope died on the publication date, which meant that the *60 Minutes* segments had to be put off. She went on Larry King's show and talked about that.

On the heels of her book, which was a bestseller, she starred in *Monster-in-Law,* her first movie in fifteen years, opposite Jennifer Lopez. Jane told me she adored playing the part of a celebrated TV interviewer à la Barbara Walters who goes nuts after her youth-obsessed network bosses unceremoniously fire her. Jane's portrayal of Viola is a self-obsessed, mocking caricature of the same conflicted persona she reveals in her autobiography. *New York Times* critic Steven Holden wrote, "Fonda informed this disagreeable character with a zany, good-natured verve even when she was behaving atrociously." The movie was a box-office success.

At the time, I was deep into my own book interviewing directors like Sydney Pollack and flying to Greece to speak to Andreas Voutsinas. Jane and I met periodically. Mostly, I e-mailed her, telling her I was working hard. One time she e-mailed back: "I was wondering. The book must be even harder to do cause mine came first. Glad you haven't given up." Then she switched subjects: "I am very happy and falling in love. Who knows where it will lead."

Earlier that year, she had complained on the Larry King show that she was tired of being celibate: "Ted says, if you wait too long, it'll grow over." Not long after that, at a book signing in Grand Central Terminal, she noticed a handsome, rugged man who bore a faint resemblance to Henry Fonda waiting in line for her autograph. She told him he looked like a movie star. He slipped her his card. She lost it. The following week when she was a guest on the David Letterman show, she declared, "Will the man who gave me his card please call my office."

They were together for two years. But it ended finally: "I got bored," Jane said. And she was busy touring all over the world with Eve Ensler in *The Vagina Monologues.* She had also started researching her new book, *Prime Time: Creating a Great Third Act,* about aging in our culture, and she was interviewing men and women around the country, couples in their seventies and eighties who were still vital, still doing things that mattered to them. "Being active keeps you young."

In 2007, Jane's beloved dog Roxie died and she replaced her with a ball of white fluff: a tiny dog named Tulea. She took Tulea everywhere with her. She said, "I can't have a big dog anymore because I no longer have a husband with a private plane."

Speaking of husbands with private planes, Jane continued to travel with Ted Turner to his various ranches — her favorite is in Tierra del Fuego in southern Argentina — and occasionally mediated conflicts among his three mistresses when they called her for advice.

She never stopped promoting her celebrity for a cause at charity auctions and movie premieres, usually for her main foundation, the Georgia Campaign for Adolescent Pregnancy Prevention (G-CAPP). She was often accompanied by her brother, Peter, her daughter, Vanessa, her son, Troy, and her adopted daughter, Lulu.

A friend told me Jane decided to sell her celebrity ten years ago when she was at an AIDS benefit chaired by Elton John. "All sorts of stuff was being auctioned off: a trip to Bermuda, a Jeep. Suddenly Jane says, 'I'm going to auction myself off.' I tried to stop her. But she runs up to the stage, grabs the mike, and calls out, 'Who wants to go out to dinner with Jane Fonda for $5,000?' A guy shouts, 'I do!' I was worried he might be a freak or a weirdo, but he turned out to be a very nice man who owned a business in Atlanta. Jane and he have since become friends."

At another benefit for G-CAPP in Atlanta, writer Claudia Glenn Dowling reported that Jane appeared in Tweety Bird slippers and flirted with Ted Turner who was in the audience, "teasing him with lascivious looks and encouraging him to bid $12,000 for a ski weekend with Jane at her ranch." The "pajama party with Jane" outsold everything else and she didn't stop. She picked up a fishing rod and announced that people could also buy "a weekend with Jane at Ted Turner's Soque River house. She adds, 'The fish are huge, it's Ted's place, and I'll make breakfast.'" The auction was a great success. When it was over, Fonda looked for Turner in the crowd, but he'd left. "Ted?" she called out. "He's got a short attention span," she told the audience.

Once I asked her, "How do you cope with strangers who are paying to be with you for a weekend?" She answered briskly, "I handle it. We have dinner together and then I say good night and I go off to my room and they go off to theirs. It works out and I make money for my foundations."

In the ten years I was writing this book I saw Jane fall apart only once. She had been traveling nonstop for a variety of causes, ending up at an international women's conference at a Hilton hotel in New York, where she gave one of the keynote speeches. Afterward, I went up to her suite to say hello and found her pacing back and forth. When she saw me, she whirled away. I could tell she wished I weren't there. "Are you okay?" I asked. With that, she yanked off the dark glasses she was wearing. One eye was hideously bloodshot. "I am breaking apart," she cried in an angry panic. At that moment, Eve Ensler came into the room and tried to make her eat something but she refused. "I have to have my picture taken tomorrow for my book cover. What am I going to do?" Eve and I assured her she was going to be all right, but she had to relax and take it easy. I stayed with her for a few more minutes and then slipped away. I realized then how much this driven, complicated woman keeps inside herself and at what cost. Months later, when I saw her book cover, she looked absolutely beautiful and serene.

She began practicing yoga and went off to Zen retreats outside of Santa Fe; she learned to meditate and it calmed and centered her.

We had dinner together and I told her I'd never seen her so mellow or laid back. "Try not talking. Try existing in silence," she said. She had been doing just that for eight days and she found it to be very healing.

On March 10, 2009, Jane made her Broadway comeback in Moises Kaufman's *33 Variations*. She told me she chose the play "because it's about life and death and the creative process. I am learning so much as I inhabit the character Katherine Brandt, this musicologist who's dying but determined to find out why Beethoven was so obsessed with composing thirty-three variations on a mediocre little waltz."

The opening night party was a bit surreal, with what seemed like the entire audience jammed into a restaurant on West 16th Street. Guests included Dolly Parton, Tony Kushner, and novelist Joan Didion. They crowded around Jane, who sparkled in sequins. She had arrived flanked by two bodyguards with walkie-talkies.

The play received mixed reviews but was a personal success for Jane. She was nominated for a Tony Award. I went back to see the show over and over, and each time I couldn't help wishing she'd devoted herself solely to her acting. If she'd wanted to, she could have been one of the most interesting and challenging women ever onstage and on film. To me, she is far more compelling as Bree Daniels than she ever was as Hanoi Jane. The motives and needs of an actress are so deeply embedded in the subconscious. Jane's finest performances will never be figured out. They are a mystery.

But maybe she knows that, too. In a recent documentary, *Searching for Debra Winger,* Jane admits how hard it's been to juggle the roles of wife, mother, movie star, and political activist. She becomes most energized when she describes with fervor how, in the midst of terror and tension, she managed to give a great performance on film, and how rare it is and how amazing it feels: "Like a plane taking off." She could've been channeling her father. Henry Fonda was never far from her thoughts while she was acting on Broadway "because Dad loved the theater so much."

During the run of the show, she established her blog. On it she wrote about her father a great deal. She wrote on her blog every day, even during intermissions of her play. And after her play closed, she continued to do so, blogging about her daily life: her work, her concerns, her fitness videos, and her dog, Tulea. She also began selling T-shirts and totes decorated with her police mug shot dating back to her arrest in Cleveland in 1970. All proceeds go to G-CAPP.

Although I saw her periodically, I mostly kept in touch with her via her blog, which she says now has more than fifty thousand visitors.

It was on her blog that I first learned that she was in love again, this time with Richard Perry, a well-known record producer who has fashioned best-selling albums for Barbra Streisand, Carly Simon, and Rod Stewart. Carrie Fisher had introduced them. They soon realized they had met thirty years before when Jane was married to Tom Hayden: "It was in Aspen at a party and we danced together for hours," Jane said. "It was very sexy."

They have been together for a year. He accompanied her to Paris when she made *Et si on vivait tous ensemble,* directed by Stéphane Robelin, and he was also in upstate New York while she was making *Peace, Love, and Misunderstanding* for Bruce Beresford, in which Jane played Catherine Keener's hippie mother. Perry was also in the audience when she played the narrator in the opera version of *The Grapes of Wrath,* which had one performance at Carnegie Hall.

In the fall of 2010 she sold her loft in Atlanta and moved to Hollywood to be with Perry. She went on *Oprah* that November to promote her first exercise video in thirty years, *Jane Fonda Prime Time.* Oprah devoted much of the hour to Jane's life: her children, her marriages. There were even film clips of Ted Turner talking rather uncomfortably about Jane and clips of Jane and Richard Perry slowly dancing a foxtrot in the living room of his home. "We dance every night before we go to sleep," Jane said. "It's relaxing." Then she added, "I'm over seventy but I feel like I'm fifty." The audience cheered and clapped.

Today Jane remains a woman who moves easily through the worlds of politics, feminism, the movies, and philanthropy. She is rich and free and can do exactly what she wants. The difference is that now her family is her first priority. She has become a matriarch: she funds foundations that her children run; she brings them with her on most of her trips; she keeps close to Turner's children, as well as Vadim's other children and grandchildren. She helped plan Troy's wedding and she was thrilled to be at Vanessa's wedding in Saint-Tropez last summer.

When she toured rural Alabama in search of outsider art, she took Vanessa and her three-year-old son, Malcolm, with her. Vanessa hadn't accompanied Jane on many trips when she was a little girl, but now she was with her mother. She ended up making a documentary about the trip called *The Quilts of Gee's Bend,* which was shown at the Whitney Museum and other galleries, alongside African American artwork from the southeastern United States that Jane helped to publicize and sponsor.

She brought Vanessa, Malcolm, and Vanessa's young daughter, Viva, along when she spoke at a big peace march on the National Mall in Washington, D.C., in 2007. More than one hundred thousand people — along with Jesse Jackson, Sean Penn, Susan Sarandon, and Dennis Kucinich — came together to persuade Congress to stop funding President Bush's escalation of the Iraq war.

It was the first time Jane had participated in an antiwar march in thirty-four years and it was touching to hear her explain how she declined to participate in public protests before because she had been afraid her notoriety as Hanoi Jane might hurt rather than help the effort. "Silence is no longer an option," she said.

A final note. Not long after Jane appeared on *Oprah,* we had lunch, and she described her new self-help book, *Prime Time.* "It's about love and creativity and sex. It's about how to keep healthy and fit. It's about everything I've learned in my seventy-three years on earth." The book will be promoted on blogs and to her 140,000 Twitter followers. "I'm a role model," she said.

Hearing that, I thought, Oh, wow, she is redefining herself yet again. This has always been her strategy for survival as she tries to create a final Jane. "I enjoy getting old!" she insists. "I wouldn't want to be young again."

She is also eager to remind the public of her younger, less aware self. This past April I received an invitation from her to attend a benefit for the Women's Media Center, an organization that she started in 2005 with feminist writers Robin Morgan and Gloria Steinem. The goal of the center is to fight sexism and bias against women and to encourage women to tell their stories. At the benefit there was a screening of D. A. Pennybaker's *Jane,* the behind-the-scenes saga of her Broadway flop *The Fun Couple,* which her domineering Greek mentor/lover, Andreas Voutsinas, directed in 1962. Back then she thought the experience had been a disaster. But after watching it again she seems visibly upset. She describes the film as a study in "gender, power, and perception."

The audience observes Jane as she observed herself forty-nine years ago, a raw child/woman hung up on her father and the romance of fame. Throughout the documentary, she plays to the camera beautifully. Even back then she seemed to be pondering her own authenticity.

Acknowledgments

I had originally wanted to title my book *Becoming Jane Fonda;* I still see her story as primarily the evolution of a unique, contradictory, archetypal American woman whose huge appetite for life and love and work remains unparalleled.

I also think the details and significance of her singular career as an actress have often been overshadowed by her equally huge celebrity. That said, I hope I have given equal weight to her contributions in theater and film, and I also hope my book has supplied the historical, critical, and political positioning that Jane sometimes didn't address in her autobiography, *My Life So Far.*

This book took ten years to complete, and so I have a debt to many, many people who helped me bring it to fruition. First and foremost, I want to thank Jane Fonda, who not only generously gave of her thoughts and time, but shared some personal family papers, as well as her FBI files to read, and her contacts with Vietnam War historians like Mary Hershberger.

I am most indebted to all those friends and family members of Jane Fonda who helped me document Jane's life in taped interviews and conversations: Peter Fonda, Vanessa Vadim, Shirlee Fonda, Nathalie Vadim, Afdera Fonda, Mary Lou Williams, Susan Blanchard Widmark, Daniel Selznick, Maria Cooper Janis, Jill Robinson, Paula Weinstein, Robin Morgan, Hildy Brooks, Brooke Hayward, Tanya Everett, Tom Hatcher, Olga Horstig, Monique Caron, Bruce Dern, George Gaynes and Allyn Ann McLerie, Lily Tomlin, Ray Powers, Geoffrey Horne, Collin Wilcox, Michael Thomas, Edna O'Brien, John Springer, Ralph Blum, Sandy Whitelaw, Ted Turner, Laura Seydel, George Furth, Lois Bonfiglio, Tom Johnson, Judith Bruce, Lauren Weissman, David Hodges, Laurel Lyle, Mignon McCarthy, and Pat Mitchell.

I am especially grateful to Marty Fried, Susan Strasberg, Jeanne Fuchs, Tanya Lopert, Richard Rosenthal, Fred Branfman, Andreas Voutsinas, Peter De Rome, Mark Rydell, Suzanne Tenner, Madeleine Sherwood, and Gilda Marx.

I can't forget Jane's colleagues in Hollywood and New York: Peter Basch, Arthur Penn, Sydney Pollack, Sidney Lumet, Norman Jewison, Patricia Resnick, Joe Eszterhas, Haskell Wexler, Richard Roth, Max Palevsky, Jerome Hellman, Gordon Willis, Ann Roth, B.J. Bjorkman, Julia Phillips, Rosemary Murphy, Elliot Gould, Michael Gray, Jack Larson, Mike Medavoy, Gene Saks, Dan Green, Richard Clayton, Nan A. Talese, Buck Henry, John Gregory Dunne, and Dick Cavett.

For helping me define and describe Jane's years as a political activist: Mark Lane, Barbara Koppel, Fred Gardner, David Dellinger, Jack Newfield, Todd Gitlin, Charles Kaiser, Nick von Hoffman, Jack Anderson, Miska Sorel, Tod Ensign, David Hilliard, Ken Kelly, Carey Beauchamp, Peter Davis, Craig Unger, Cathy MacKay, Hamilton Fish, Richard Reeves, Francine Parker, Susan Brownmiller, Gloria Steinem, and Stephen Rivers.

I also must acknowledge my own dear friends for their help and support, including Vivian Nathan, Claudia Dreifus, Kent Jones, Joanna Ney, Jeanine Basinger, Richard Schickel, Peter Boyle, Janet Coleman, Gore Vidal, Susan Dryfoos, Eileen Finletter, Dinitia Smith, Peter Bogdanovich, Tammy Grimes, Arthur Kopit and Leslie Garis, Lily Lodge, David Nasaw, Robert Caro, Rex Reed, Martha Fay, Diana Rico, Bobby Zarem, Michael Anderson, Molly Haskell, Joan Schenkar, Betsy von Furstenberg, Barbara Grizzuti Harrison, Lucy Rosenthal, Diane Sokolow, Linda Healey, Andrew Coppa, and Astrida Valigorsky.

I want to give special thanks to Eve Ensler, Jane Silver, Irene Diamond, and Stanley Cohen.

Deep appreciation must be given to Michael Janeway and András Szántó and the National Arts Journalism Program at Columbia University where I was a senior fellow. I received generous support for a year and so was able to work uninterrupted researching Jane's impact on the media during the Vietnam War and conversely the media's impact on her.

I also spent a summer at Yaddo and a lovely spring at Omi International Arts Center in upstate New York working on the book and reading chapters to fellow writers for feedback.

Thanks as well to the staff of the Theater Collection of New York's Lincoln Center Library and to the staffs of the New York Society Library and the Library of the Academy of Motion Picture Arts and Sciences for their unstinting help.

And to Till Osterland, Emily Feder, Chelsea McGettigan, Brooke Mazurek, Jaime Lubin, Anna Wainwright, Tim Meyers, Joan Martorano, and Sharon Nettles — I could not have done this book without their amazing diligence and commitment to detail and accuracy. To Mark Jacobson, who helped me choose images of Jane from the thousands of pictures in archives and galleries, and to Erika Frankel, who did the dog work of tracking the pictures. Thank you.

Finally, I am most indebted to my agents, Andrew Wylie (whose idea it was that I write about Jane) and Jeff Posternak. Both have always been there for me.

Last, but by no means least, thanks to my editor, George Hodgman, who believed in my book since its inception and in his own inimitable way has shown me what to do and not to do to make my biography of Jane Fonda work on so many levels.

Notes

ABBREVIATIONS:

Susan Blanchard — SB
Patricia Bosworth — PB
Afdera Fonda — AF
Jane Fonda — JF

Peter Fonda — PF
Marty Fried — MF
Andreas Voutsinas — AV

PROLOGUE

page

xi "We are so many selves": Gloria Steinem, *Revolution from Within: A Book of Self-Esteem* (Little, Brown and Company, 1992), p. 323.

1 *"and I was there"*: Eve Ensler, *The Vagina Monologues* (Villard, 1998), p. 105.

2 "I did it!": JF to PB, interview, February 2001.
"The weird thing": JF to PB, interview, March 2003.

3 "I'm going over": Ibid.
"Deep breath": JF to PB, e-mail, January 2003.

4 "It won't be easy": All quotes are from JF to PB, interview, March 3–7, 2003.

CHAPTER ONE

15 "My only major": JF, *Ms. Magazine* (June 1979), p. 46.

18 "I admire your pictures": Jan Herman, *A Talent for Trouble: Hollywood's Most Talked About Director: William Wyler* (Da Capo Press, 1997), p. 181.
"There is a strong": Lillian Ross, *The Player: A Profile of the Art* (Simon & Schuster, 1962), p. 83.

20 "She was always": JF, *My Life So Far* (Random House, 2005), p. 22.

21 "My mother was from old Canadian stock": Frances Fonda, autobiography she started in 1949 at Austen Riggs Psychiatric Hospital, p. 1.

22 "the fastest typist": Henry Fonda, *My Life as Told to Howard Teichmann* (New American Library, 1981), p. 109.

"Don't you think it's about time?": Fred Guiles, *Jane Fonda: The Actress in Her Time* (Doubleday, 1981), p. 4.

23 "Then Mother carried": JF, *My Life So Far*, p. 29.

"Frances was very gay": Jay Watson Webb to Donald Spoto, unpublished interview, circa 1995.

"Arriving in New York": Ibid.

24 "My first memory of Henry": Ibid.

"because it made me feel too different": JF to PB, interview, March 2003.

25 "Oh, he'll be back": Jay Watson Webb to Donald Spoto, unpublished interview, circa 1995.

"She had the most amazing": Ibid.

26 "Dad never said": JF to PB, interview, March 2003.

27 "[He] keeps his own grace and talent": Manny Farber, *Movies* (Hillstone, 1971), p. 177.

28 "There is possibly no more touching": Peter Bogdanovich, *Who the Hell's in It: Conversations with Hollywood's Legendary Actors* (Ballantine, 2004), p. 317.

29 "He would take me into his arms": JF, *My Life So Far*, p. 43.

30 "Hank would wipe us all": Joshua Logan, *Josh: My Up and Down, In and Out Life* (Delacorte Press, 1976), p. 145.

"Acting was a game of make believe": G. Barry Golson, ed., *The Playboy Interview II* (Wideview/Perigee, 1983), p. 445.

"adorable little clown": Fonda, *My Life as Told to Howard Teichmann*, p. 82.

31 a vacation in Chile: Jay Watson Webb to Donald Spoto, unpublished interview, circa 1995.

CHAPTER TWO

32 "I was not happy": JF to PB, interview, March 2003.

33 "Jane told me her mother": AV to PB, interview, January 2002.

"Darling — I am giving you": Ibid.

"Our families were united": Brooke Hayward to PB, interview, October 2003.

34 "Theirs was": Joshua Logan, *Josh: My Up and Down, In and Out Life* (Delacorte Press, 1976), p. 112.

"Maggie was": Ibid.

"cream and sugar on a bed of hot ashes": Peter Collier, *The Fondas: A Hollywood Dynasty* (G. P. Putnam's Sons, 1991), p. 32.

"It's all a blur": Henry Fonda, *My Life as Told to Howard Teichmann* (New American Library, 1981), p. 64.

35 "I'd lean against": Ibid., p. 65.

"A man was": Ibid., p. 66.

"This is a mistake": Ibid., p. 106.

36 "He and Maggie would": Jay Watson Webb to Donald Spoto, unpublished interview, circa 1995.

"Frances' favorite subjects were": Logan, *Josh: My Up and Down, In and Out Life*, p. 112.

"Pan and Jane and I had picnics together": PF to PB, interview, January 2004.

37 "It was quite something": Daniel Selznick to PB, interview, May 2000.

"It had shingles": Lillian Ross, *The Player: A Profile of the Art* (Simon & Schuster, 1962), p. 93.

38 "My best friends were rabbits for a while": JF to PB, interview, March 2003.

"Oh, no, I always wore what my dad wore": Ibid.

"And the richest ice cream you ever tasted": Jill Robinson to PB, interview, March 2002.

39 "Every morning she would": JF, *My Life So Far* (Random House, 2005), p. 57.

"She made me get out of the tub": Ibid.

"We were brought up in an atmosphere": JF to PB, interview, March 2003.

40 "Barbara was the best fuck I ever had": AF to PB, interview, March 2002.

"In private, Fonda was": Ibid.

41 "We had": PF, *Don't Tell Dad: A Memoir* (Hyperion, 1998), p. 15.

"in a large banqueting hall": Thomas Kiernan, *Jane: An Intimate Biography of Jane Fonda* (G. P. Putnam's Sons, 1973), p. 36.

CHAPTER THREE

42 "They were practically on an assembly line": Irene Diamond to PB, interview, December 2000.

"What do fuckin' gunner's mates": Otto Friedrich, *City of Nets* (Harper & Row, Perennial Library, 1987), p. 105.

43 "It was a real publicity gimmick": John Springer to PB, interview, December 1999.

"I never dreamed": G. Barry Golson, ed., *The Playboy Interview II* (Wideview/Perigee, 1983), p. 453.

"I gave her an extra hug": Henry Fonda, *My Life as Told to Howard Teichmann* (New American Library, 1981), p. 138.

44 "Busy, busy, busy": Ralph Blum to PB, interview, December 2000.

"It was a full-time job": Ibid.

45 "I have already lost my looks!": PF to PB, interview, January 2004.

"Lady, if I gain any extra weight": JF to PB, interview, March 2003.

46 "My long, smooth patrician neck!": Jay Watson Webb to Donald Spoto, unpublished interview, circa 1995.

"He was divinely attractive": JF, *My Life So Far* (Random House, 2005), p. 23.

"had taken a fledgling musician": Ibid.

"out of the blue": Ibid.

"I think my mother had an affair with him": PF, *Don't Tell Dad: A Memoir* (Hyperion, 1998), p. 10.

47 "a woman standing beside a fireplace": Fonda, *My Life as Told to Howard Teichmann*, p. 154.

"I am living now on a big ship": Ibid., p. 153.

"Frances really appreciated": Jay Watson Webb to Donald Spoto, unpublished interview, circa 1995.

"We thought the school was terrific": Jill Robinson to PB, interview, March 2002.

48 "Jane is well-adjusted": JF, *My Life So Far*, p. 55.

"she painted the school": JF and Jill Robinson to PB, interview, April 2003.

"Sex was starting to confuse": JF, *My Life So Far*, p. 55.

49 "I would watch her": Fonda, *My Life as Told to Howard Teichmann*, p. 169.

"We had so much fun": JF to PB, interview, April 2003.

"I couldn't believe such a close, loving relationship could exist": Ibid.

50 "The qualities Sue Sally had": Ibid.

CHAPTER FOUR

53 "Dad was most angry": JF to PB, interview, March 2003.

54 "She was very un-Hollywood": Peter Collier, *The Fondas: A Hollywood Dynasty* (G. P. Putnam's Sons, 1991), p. 66.

"She is a good little girl": Frances Fonda in her unpublished autobiography, 1949, p. 2.

55 "This is just like": PF, *Don't Tell Dad: A Memoir* (Hyperion, 1998), p. 28.

"Dad wasn't attracted to Mother anymore": JF, *My Life So Far* (Random House, 2005), p. 59.

"We had to make up": PF, *Don't Tell Dad*, p. 38.

"She meant everything to me": Ibid., p. 54.

56 "His face would get purple": JF to PB, interview, March 2003.

"We were all scared of Henry Fonda": Jill Robinson to PB, interview, March 2002.

"The worse things got": Brooke Hayward to PB, interview, October 2003.

"Dad was playing the part": PF to PB, interview, January 2004.

58 he would never forget Hank's laugh: Joshua Logan, *Josh: My Up and Down, In and Out Life* (Delacorte Press, 1976), p. 145.

"because I [didn't] have to be me": Henry Fonda, *My Life as Told to Howard Teichmann* (New American Library, 1981), p. 14.

CHAPTER FIVE

60 "Peter and I waited": JF, *My Life So Far* (Random House, 2005), p. 61.

61 "He was a perfectionist": Ruth Mitchell to PB, interview, February 2001.

"We felt we'd been kicked out of paradise": PF to PB, interview, January 2004.

"No orange groves, no avocado trees": PF, *Don't Tell Dad: A Memoir* (Hyperion, 1998), p. 36.

62 Jane learned to "take horses": JF, *My Life So Far*, p. 63.

"I was scared when we'd come to a jump": Ibid., p. 64.

"They have cut me in half": Jay Watson Webb to Donald Spoto, unpublished interview, circa 1995.

"We'd stay overnight": PF to PB, interview, January 2004.

"Jane and I really acted up in school": Brooke Hayward to PB, interview, October 2003.

63 her present, "a Mohawk": JF, *My Life So Far*, p. 64.

"It was about that time": Ibid., p. 65.

64 "Susan was absolutely ravishing": Shirley Clurman to PB, interview, April 2002.

"make sure Pan knows": Jay Watson Webb to Donald Spoto, unpublished interview, circa 1995.

65 "If anyone mentions that your father": JF to PB, interview, March 2003.

"The shock of Hank wanting to remarry was almost too much for me": Frances Fonda letter to Jay Watson Webb, quoted in PF, *Don't Tell Dad*, p. 43.

66 "She is definitely suicidal": Dr. Margaret Gibson to PB, interview, July 2002.

67 "He was a cold, self-absorbed person": Ibid.

"She has bounced back": Ibid.

68 "My mother was a hypochondriac": JF to PB, interview, March 2003.

"fragrant with perfume": PF, *Don't Tell Dad*, p. 44.

"At least I can go potty by myself!": Jay Watson Webb to Donald Spoto, unpublished interview, circa 1995.

69 "What did my mother want to tell me?": JF to PB, interview, March 2003.

"Don't enter the bathroom": Jay Watson Webb to Donald Spoto, unpublished interview, circa 1995.

"You've done everything possible": Frances's note to doctor, quoted in Henry Fonda, *My Life as Told to Howard Teichmann* (New American Library, 1981), p. 202.

70 "I don't want you to go out": JF to PB, interview, March 2003.

71 "I'm going to go on": Joshua Logan, *Josh: My Up and Down, In and Out Life* (Delacorte Press, 1976), p. 147.

"Hank walked out on the stage": Eli Wallach to PB, interview, November 2005.

CHAPTER SIX

73 "No one talked about her": PF, *Don't Tell Dad: A Memoir* (Hyperion, 1998), p. 46.
"I thought it was better not to tell them": G. Barry Golson, ed. *The Playboy Interview: Volume II* (Perigee Books, 1983), p. 453.
"Her face was absolutely expressionless": Brooke Hayward to PB, interview, October 2003.

74 "Jane would wake up": Ibid.
"Before my mother's death": JF to PB, interview, March 2003.
"Dad introduced us": JF, *My Life So Far* (Random House, 2005), p. 75.
"They were the saddest brother and sister": SB to PB, interview, May 2000.
"She'd studied": JF, *My Life So Far*, p. 77.

75 "Susan Blanchard became the mother": AV to PB, interview, January 2002.
to this day he does show off the big scar: PF, *Don't Tell Dad*, p. 55.

76 "grand mansion, built by William Randolph Hearst": Ibid., p. 56.
"Dad and Susan would often": JF, *My Life So Far*, p. 79.
Jane had started wearing her hair: AV to PB, interview, January 2002.
"I told him jokes": SB to PB, interview, May 2000.

77 "That note meant a lot to me": Ibid.
"But he was never cruel": Ibid.

78 "I was in awe of Hank": Ibid.
"I'd put his very expensive watch": Ibid.

79 "I loved her deeply for that": JF to PB, interview, March 2003.
"No one had raised the subject": JF, *My Life So Far*, p. 77.
she'd learned about the suicide: Ibid.

80 She became friendly: Kevin Bellows to PB, interview, May 2002.
"I could always make people believe": JF, *My Life So Far*, p. 93.

81 "I was on vacation from Harvard": Ashton Hawkins to PB, interview, June 2002.

CHAPTER SEVEN

82 "Congratulations": JF, *My Life So Far* (Random House, 2005), p. 95.

83 "He was our hero": Jill Robinson to PB, interview, March 2002.
"We started off at an ice cream parlor": Daniel Selznick to PB, interview, January 2001.
"I didn't want anyone to stop me": JF, *My Life So Far*, p. 88.

84 "I was young then": SB to PB, interview, May 2000.

85 "It was the first time": Ibid.

86 "she surprised the hell out of me": Henry Fonda, *My Life as Told to Howard Teichmann* (New American Library, 1981), p. 239.

87 "It was supposed to be a great vacation": SB to PB, interview, May 2000.
"I had tried to make him see a therapist": Ibid.
"Why did it take you so long?": PF to PB, interview, January 2004.

88 "Susan's leaving Dad!": Ibid.
"Oh fuck, Jane! Oh, fuck!": PF, *Don't Tell Dad: A Memoir* (Hyperion, 1998), p. 83.
"But generally": JF, *My Life So Far*, p. 98.
"Mummie's suicide": PF, *Don't Tell Dad*, p. 84.

89 "Whenever I asked questions about my mother's death": Ibid., p. 85.
"I didn't like college": JF to PB, interview, March 2003.
"Jane was hugely popular": Bobby Zarem to PB, interview, June 2003.
"listening breathlessly": Dick Cavett and Christopher Porterfield, *Cavett* (Harcourt, Brace, Jovanovich, 1974), p. 76.
"Jane was beautiful and icy": Michael Thomas to PB, interview, July 2001.

90 "And I bewitched him": AF to PB, interview, April 2002.

"but he was never mean to me": Ibid.

91 "He had the ability": Ruth Mitchell to PB, interview, February 2001.
"He was blond, blue-eyed, and movie star handsome": JF, *My Life So Far*, p. 99.

92 "We waited until fall": JF to PB, interview, March 2003.
"Jane had no lines": Fonda, *My Life as Told to Howard Teichmann*, p. 251.
"This time she really knocked me over": Ibid.
"I'd left the Riviera": AF to PB, interview, April 2002.

93 "He acted like a lovesick schoolboy": Ibid.
"I thought of myself": Ibid.
"I had been trying": JF to PB, interview, March 2003.

94 "He wore me down": AF to PB, interview, April 2002.
"What do you want me to do": PF, *Don't Tell Dad*, p. 95.

95 "[They] both concentrated": Ibid., p. 102.
"I ate": Ibid.
"I drank too much": JF to PB, interview, March 2003.

96 "How could we be so thoughtless": PF, *Don't Tell Dad*, p. 106.
"I was always amazed at Peter": JF, *My Life So Far*, p. 104.

97 "It was like watching": AF to PB, interview, April 2002.
"So was Teddy Kennedy": Ibid.
"It was absolute madness": Ibid.

CHAPTER EIGHT

98 "Everything smelled": Christopher Andersen, *Citizen Jane: The Turbulent Life of Jane Fonda* (Henry Holt and Company, 1990), p. 57.
"I felt clumsy and stupid": Ibid., p. 60.
"It reminded me": JF, *My Life So Far* (Random House, 2005), p. 108.

99 "When she got up to dance": Roger Vadim, *Bardot, Deneuve, Fonda: My Life with the Three Most Beautiful Women in the World* (Simon & Schuster, 1986), p. 210.
"He was a friend of Susan's": JF, *My Life So Far*, p. 109.
"I think": Ibid., p. 110.

100 "I was at a loss": Ibid.
"Are you telling": Arthur Penn to PB, interview, March 2001.

101 "Afdera's lifestyle": JF to PB, interview, March 2003.
"I'd come home": AF to PB, interview, April 2002.
"Jane caused a scandal": Nan Talese to PB, interview, February 2002.
"flung it": AF to PB, interview, April 2002.
"getting along pretty well": Ibid.

102 "young, fresh-faced": Christopher Plummer, *In Spite of Myself: A Memoir* (Knopf, 2008), p. 237.
"And you're": Sandy Whitelaw to PB, interview, June 2003.
"We'd go up to the Cloisters": JF to PB, interview, March 2003.

103 "That's what I really wanted to do": Lillian Ross, *The Player: A Profile of the Art* (Simon & Schuster, 1962), p. 97.
"The subtext was": Michael Thomas to PB, interview, July 2002.

104 "You should study": Susan Strasberg to PB, interview, December 1998.

CHAPTER NINE

105 "I never wanted Jane": AV to PB, interview, January 2002.
107 "The summer of 1958": JF to PB, interview, April 2002.

"We'd walk along": Jill Robinson to PB, interview, March 2002.

108   "I am terribly depressed": JF, *My Life So Far* (Random House, 2005), p. 110.
      "What a pair they were": AF to PB, interview, April 2002.
      "I will never love": Susan Strasberg to PB, interview, January 1999.
      "but she couldn't concentrate": MF to PB, interview, March 2000.

110   "Lee teaches Marilyn": Ibid.

111   "He was fucking scary": Shelley Winters to PB, interview, May 2004.
      "Lee is going to like you": MF to PB, interview, March 2000.
      "So, darling?": JF to PB, interview, March 2003.

112   "Maybe this": Henry Fonda, *My Life as Told to Howard Teichmann* (New American Library, 1981), p. 264.
      "I suppose we": MF to PB, interview, March 2000.

113   "Everybody came": Shelley Winters to PB, interview, May 2004.
      "He was alternately": Susan Strasberg to PB, interview, January 1997.
      "Yes, darling": JF to PB, interview, March 2003.

114   "Paula gives": MF to PB, interview, March 2000.
      "bringing the light": JF, *My Life So Far*, p. 115.

CHAPTER TEN

117   "She behaved like": Thomas Kiernan, *Jane: An Intimate Biography of Jane Fonda* (G. P. Putnam's Sons, 1973), p. 91.

118   "[Lee] made comments": JF, *My Life So Far* (Random House, 2005), p. 124.
      "I closed my eyes": Ibid., p. 120.
      "But she still": MF to PB, interview, March 2000.

119   "I was panting": Al Aronowitz, "America's Answer to Bardot: The Young Jane Fonda," *Saturday Evening Post*, March 23, 1963.
      "I don't know": Ibid.

120   "Wear bohemian clothes": Ray Powers to PB, interview, February 2002.
      "We were thrown together": Suzanne Finstad, *Warren Beatty: A Private Man* (Harmony Books, 2005), p. 184.
      "Kazan called me down": JF, *My Life So Far*, p. 134.
      "Yes, I was ambitious": JF to PB, interview, March 2003.

121   "Jane was so insecure": Kiernan, *Jane*, p. 115.
      "she had doubts": Ray Powers to PB, interview, April 2000.

122   "Jane willed": MF to PB, interview, March 2000.
      "Josh had": JF to PB, interview, March 2003.

124   "I hated the way": JF, *My Life So Far*, p. 124.
      A last suggestion: Ibid.

125   He was a sad, gentle, refined young man: Peter Collier, *The Fondas: A Hollywood Dynasty* (G. P. Putnam's Sons, 1991), p. 124.

126   "It was not": Kiernan, *Jane*, p. 113.
      "Josh gave me no comfort": JF to PB, interview, March 2003.

127   "I'm a girl": AF to PB, interview, April 2002.
      "I just happened": Ibid.
      "She was so neurotic": Sandy Whitelaw to PB, interview, June 2002.
      "There were other": JF to PB, interview, March 2003.

128   "Jane has made more": *Life* magazine, February 1960.
      "He said he would": Ray Powers to PB, interview, February 2002.
      "Jane went from": Collier, *The Fondas*, p. 130.

129   "One night Jane": Kiernan, *Jane*, p. 117.
      "Those two were": MF to PB, interview, March 2000.

129 "Jane liked": Tanya Everett to PB, interview, June 2010.
"Jane was desperate": Ray Powers to PB, interview, February 2002.
"Timmy Everett showed up": Patton Campbell to PB, interview, April 2001.

130 "I don't think you can": Ibid.
"Oh, youth, youth, youth": Christopher Andersen, *Citizen Jane: The Turbulent Life of Jane Fonda* (Henry Holt and Company, 1990), p. 74.
"Why, she's": MF to PB, interview, March 2000.

131 "I've never seen anyone": Kiernan, *Jane*, p. 119.

132 "Jane took one and I took one": Henry Fonda, *My Life as Told to Howard Teichmann* (New American Library, 1981), p. 287.
"I'd created": JF to PB, interview, March 2003.
"Timmy made me": Ibid.

133 "Timmy made Fonda": AF to PB, interview, April 2002.
"He grabbed": MF to PB, interview, March 2000.

134 "He'd pay me": PF to PB, interview, January 2004.

CHAPTER ELEVEN

136 "Vassar girl, strong handshake": AV to PB, interview, January 2002.
"Andreas looked like": Susan Strasberg to PB, interview, January 1997.

137 "I wanted to perform!": AV to PB, interview, January 2002.
"Andreas immediately": MF to PB, interview, March 2000.
"he quickly gained": Linda Marsh to PB, interview, February 2008.

138 "He's treacherous": AV to PB, interview, June 2002.
"He was a homosexual": Jeanne Fuchs to PB, interview, May 2002.

139 "because I was": AV to PB, interview, January 2002.
"he fell in love": Ibid.

140 "We had fun": Geoffrey Horne to PB, interview, March 2001.
"I knew he was getting to her": Ibid.
"She'd be": Tom Hatcher to PB, interview, March 2001.

141 "She was wearing": AV to PB, interview, January 2002.
"Because I was": AF to PB, interview, April 2002.
"I remember": AV to PB, interview, January 2002.

142 "It was a very exciting": AF to PB, interview, April 2002.
"Sleeping Beauty": MF to PB, interview, March 2000.

143 "A mother doesn't": Arthur Laurents to PB, interview, March 2001.
"It was a gentle": Madeleine Sherwood to PB, interview, July 2002.
"Are you afraid": Arthur Laurents to PB, interview, March 2001.

144 "My father said": PF to PB, interview, March 2003.
"And [Bridget] said": Brooke Hayward, *Haywire* (Knopf, 1977), p. 252.
"a certain kind": Ibid.

145 "without anesthetic": Madeleine Sherwood to PB, interview, July 2002.
"Madeleine told": AV to PB, interview, January 2002.
"For Jane and me": Madeleine Sherwood to PB, interview, July 2002.

146 "She was still the same": Thomas Kiernan, *Jane: An Intimate Biography of Jane Fonda* (G. P. Putnam's Sons, 1973), p. 132.
"I needed someone": JF to PB, interview, March 2003.

147 "Once she was finished": MF to PB, interview, March 2001.
"I became": AV to PB, interview, January 2002.
"Three years of depression": JF to PB, interview, March 2003.
"it was so sad": JF, *My Life So Far* (Random House, 2005), p. 129.
"I couldn't help": AV to PB, interview, January 2002.

148 "Jane was unhappy": Madeleine Sherwood to PB, interview, July 2002.
"Up to a point": AV to PB, interview, January 2002.
"because I knew": Ibid.
"Bulimics do": Ibid.
150 "For Jane it was": Ibid.
"Everyone was waiting": MF to PB, interview, March 2001.
"hearing her vomit": Hildy Brooks to PB, interview, April 2001.
"She's gonna heave": MF to PB, interview, March 2001.

CHAPTER TWELVE

152 "I played": AV to PB, interview, January 2002.
153 "Good and bad": Ibid.
154 "It was the hardest": Ibid.
155 "I think that's": Linda March to PB, interview, February 2008.
"We all drank": Jeanne Fuchs to PB, interview, May 2002.
"there was": AV to PB, interview, January 2002.
157 "If she'd been": Collin Wilcox to PB, interview, June 2003.

CHAPTER THIRTEEN

160 "Cukor laughed": JF to PB, interview, March 2003.
161 "I've let you do": *Los Angeles Times,* July 8, 1962.
"She overacts": Ibid.
"I thought he might": JF to PB, interview, March 2003.
162 "I like fame": Collin Wilcox to PB, interview, June 2003.
"Any man": *Saturday Evening Post,* March 23, 1963.
163 "I've just taken": Tom Hatcher to PB, interview, March 2001.
164 "It was a huge": AV to PB, interview, January 2002.
"She was seductive": Peter Basch to PB, interview, February 2003.
"You could actually see": AV to PB, interview, January 2002.
165 "It's ridiculous": Ibid.
169 "We went to": AF to PB, interview, April 2002.
"Henry Fonda conveyed": Marian Seldes to PB, interview, February 2010.
170 "I never knew": JF to PB, interview, March 2003.

CHAPTER FOURTEEN

171 "like an octopus": Collin Wilcox to PB, interview, June 2003.
"That son-of-a-bitch": Henry Fonda, *My Life as Told to Howard Teichmann* (New American Library, 1981), p. 288.
"Oh, yes": JF to PB, interview, March 2003.
"and in front of everybody": MF to PB, interview, March 2001.
172 "I realized that": AV to PB, interview, January 2002.
"Whores, jilted mistresses": Molly Haskell, *From Reverence to Rape: The Treatment of Women in the Movies,* 2nd ed. (University of Chicago Press, 1987), p. 327.
173 "ingénue[s]": Ibid., p. 330.
"Think Marilyn Monroe": Ibid.
she never: Susan Strasberg to PB, interview, January 1999.
174 "Somehow [it] gets": Thomas Kiernan, *Jane: An Intimate Biography of Jane Fonda* (G. P. Putnam's Sons, 1973), p. 42.

"I didn't want": AV to PB, interview, January 2002.

"It wasn't until": JF to PB, interview, March 2003.

175   "Everybody in the": Marios Voutsinas to PB, interview, August 2010.

176   "Jane merely": AV to PB, interview, January 2002.

"It should have": Ibid.

178   "I did": Jay Julien to PB, interview, September 2002.

"You wanna see": JF to PB, interview, March 2003.

"Jane was totally": Lee Pennebaker to PB, interview, August 2005.

179   "Jane told": Collin Wilcox to PB, interview, June 2003.

180   "Andreas was": Geoffrey Horne to PB, interview, February 2000.

181   "If I had a child": Alfred Aronowitz, "Lady Jane," *Saturday Evening Post,* March 23, 1963.

182   "It was a role": JF to PB, interview, March 2003.

"She was a real good sport": John Springer to PB, interview, August 2000.

"For the past two years": AV to PB, interview, June 2002.

184   "I could separate myself": JF to PB, interview, March 2003.

"I want you": AV to PB, interview, June 2002.

185   "You will marry": Betsy von Furstenberg to PB, interview, September 2001.

CHAPTER FIFTEEN

187   "Jane could be ... sweet": Roger Vadim, *Memoirs of the Devil* (Hutchinson and Co., 1975), p. 128.

190   "I was a habit": AV to PB, interview, June 2002.

"I remember watching Simone": JF, *My Life So Far* (Random House, 2005), p. 138.

191   "wall-to-wall teeth": George Haddad-Garcia, *The Films of Jane Fonda* (Citadel Press, 1981), p. 105.

"It was a magical time": JF, *My Life So Far,* p. 140.

192   "but I put it": Dick Clayton to PB, interview, July 2001.

"Kennedy's been shot": JF, *My Life So Far,* p. 141.

193   "Why doesn't": Eileen Finletter to PB, interview, May 2000.

194   "I thought the two of you": Olga Horstig to PB, interview, June 2002.

195   "She would avoid me": Roger Vadim, *Bardot, Deneuve, Fonda: My Life with the Three Most Beautiful Women in the World* (Simon & Schuster, 1986), p. 214.

"Her chest was heaving": Ibid., p. 215.

196   "His lovemaking was": JF, *My Life So Far,* p. 147.

"I was Jane's senior by only ten years": Vadim, *Bardot, Deneuve, Fonda,* p. 220.

197   "I thought": JF to PB, interview, March 2002.

"There's no doubt": JF, *My Life So Far,* p. 147.

198   "Jane never thought Vadim": Dick Clayton to PB, interview, July 2001.

"an independent little boy": Roger Vadim to Aljean Harmetz, interview in the *New York Times,* September 6, 1970.

"My parents loved each other": Vadim, *Memoirs of the Devil,* p. 22.

199   "I grew up fast": Roger Vadim to Aljean Harmetz, interview in the *New York Times,* September 6, 1970.

"The only time": Ibid.

"I was 16 years old": Vadim, *Memoirs of the Devil,* p. 54.

200   "We were kindred spirits": Roger Vadim to Aljean Harmetz, interview in the *New York Times,* September 6, 1970.

"I was going": Vadim, *Bardot, Deneuve, Fonda,* p. 282.

But "dancing": Vadim, *Memoirs of the Devil,* p. 69.

Brigitte "took to lovemaking": Vadim, *Bardot, Deneuve, Fonda,* p. 36.

201 "What struck me": Ibid., p. 80.
202 "Passion is Brigitte's drug": Vadim, *Memoirs of the Devil*, p. 80.
203 "The uproar was based": Vadim, *Bardot, Deneuve, Fonda*, p. 113.
204 "You could be": Ibid., p. 164.
   "If you marry": Ibid., p. 191.
205 "What were you": Ibid., p. 218.
   "I also wanted": Ibid.
206 "There was a huge fireplace": Ibid., p. 220.
   "Vadim had created": JF, *My Life So Far*, p. 153.
   "Jane always thought": Thomas Kiernan, *Jane: An Intimate Biography of Jane Fonda* (G. P. Putnam's Sons, 1973), p. 168.
207 "One of the things": JF to PB, interview, June 2003.
   "His gentleness kills me": Ibid.
   "I was badly hurt in a motorcycle crash": Gordon Miller to PB, interview, March 2002.
208 "I didn't tell Jane": Monique Caron to PB, interview, June 2002.
209 "I'm scared": Ibid.
   "Her voice was": Ibid.
   "Andreas had": Vadim, *Bardot, Deneuve, Fonda*, p. 223.
210 "They were about": Thomas Quinn Curtis to PB, interview, June 2002.
   "I'm not totally": Ibid.
211 he was "able to savor": Vadim, *Bardot, Deneuve, Fonda*, p. 328.
212 "After their first night together": Ibid., p. 222.
   "It was true": Nathalie Vadim to PB, interview, August 2002.
   "the map room": Ibid.
213 "During the years with Vadim": JF, *My Life So Far*, p. 153.
   "At the time": Ibid.
   "It took me": JF to PB, interview, March 2003.
   "by sheer force": Monique Caron to PB, interview, June 2002.
   "I loved Vadim": JF to PB, interview, March 2003.

CHAPTER SIXTEEN

214 "She was all caught up": AV to PB, interview, January 2002.
   "From the top of the dunes": Nathalie Vadim to PB, interview, July 2002.
215 "Christian, Nathalie, and me": JF, *My Life So Far* (Random House, 2005), p. 160.
   "If someone coveted": Thomas Kiernan, *Jane: An Intimate Biography of Jane Fonda* (G. P. Putnam's Sons, 1973), p. 173.
216 "[Vadim] helped me": JF, *My Life So Far*, pp. 156–57.
   "I saw her": Roger Vadim, *Bardot, Deneuve, Fonda: My Life with the Three Most Beautiful Women in the World* (Simon & Schuster, 1986), p. 259.
217 "Vadim and I": JF, *My Life So Far*, p. 193.
218 "I wanted to defend": JF to PB, interview, March 2003.

CHAPTER SEVENTEEN

219 "I wanted to modernize": JF to PB, interview, March 2003.
220 "Jane had a thing": Nathalie Vadim to PB, interview, July 2002.
   "She worked": Ibid.
   "Still, Vadim was": Monique Caron to PB, interview, June 2002.
221 "I was her secret": AV to PB, interview, January 2002.

223 "bare-assed on a bed": John Springer to PB, interview, December 1999.
"The image was crude": JF to PB, interview, March 2003.
"The media went": John Springer to PB, interview, December 1999.
"It remained fresh": Dick Clayton to PB, interview, October 2002.

226 "What's the matter": JF to PB, interview, March 2003.
"BBS quickly became": Peter Biskind, *Easy Riders, Raging Bulls: How the Sex-Drugs-and-Rock 'n' Roll Generation Saved Hollywood* (Touchstone, 1998), p. 76.
"The French film world": Collin Wilcox to PB, interview, July 2002.

227 "an amorphous subculture": Thomas Kiernan, *Jane: An Intimate Biography of Jane Fonda* (G. P. Putnam's Sons, 1973), p. 177.
"how sweet Jane was": Glyn Vincent to PB, interview, June 2010.

228 "Jane loved having a tan": Nathalie Vadim to PB, interview, July 2002.
"Look, . . . can't we": JF to PB, interview, March 2003.
"Oh, yeah": PF to PB, interview, January 2004.

229 "I was in deep denial": JF to PB, interview, March 2003.
"It was a memorable party": Jill Robinson to PB, interview, March 2002.

231 "I didn't believe": JF to PB, interview, March 2003.
"I wasn't perhaps": Roger Vadim, *Bardot, Deneuve, Fonda: My Life with the Three Most Beautiful Women in the World* (Simon & Schuster, 1986), p. 238.
"One thing is certain": Ibid.

232 "Vadim wanted": Monique Caron to PB, interview, June 2002.
"My mother liked Jane": Vadim, *Bardot, Deneuve, Fonda*, p. 239.
"She kept": Dick Clayton to PB, interview, October 2002.
"Boy, if he": JF to PB, interview, March 2003.

233 "It was at Arthur's": Ibid.

234 "Unlike all the others": JF, *My Life So Far*, p. 166.
"But I wouldn't have": JF to PB, interview, March 2003.

235 "I forgot to send you": Roger Vadim, *Memoirs of the Devil* (Hutchinson & Co., 1975), p. 157.

236 "We could see": Brooke Hayward to PB, interview, October 2003.
"feeling like": JF to PB, interview, March 2003.
"I'm married": AV to PB, interview, January 2002.

237 "After stepping up to bat five times": Henry Fonda, *My Life as Told to Howard Teichmann* (New American Library, 1981), p. 291.
"He would phone": Michael Freedland, *Jane Fonda. A Biography* (St. Martin's Press, 1988), p. 94.

238 "And if your wife": Vadim, *Bardot, Deneuve, Fonda*, p. 257.

239 "He validated": JF to PB, interview, March 2003.
"I took my cues": JF, *My Life So Far*, p. 154.

240 "We just laughed": Michael Wager to PB, interview, April 2002.
"It was not exactly": Brooke Hayward to PB, interview, October 2003.
"Later, Jane would react": Vadim, *Bardot, Deneuve, Fonda*, p. 258.
"I was disgusted": Nathalie Vadim to PB, interview, August 2002.

241 "Like Jack's giant beanstalk": Vadim, *Bardot, Deneuve, Fonda*, p. 252.

243 "Jane put Vadim on a pedestal": Nathalie Vadim to PB, interview, July 2002.
"Jane peeked out from behind": Monique Caron to PB, interview, June 2002.

244 The motel they stayed at: JF, *My Life So Far*, p. 171.
"Locals peered": Ibid.
"The atmosphere in the street": Vadim, *Memoirs of the Devil*, p. 160.

245 "As we drove out of town": Ibid.
"Jane had gone all out for the dinner": Sandy Whitelaw to PB, interview, July 2000.
"Vadim calls me": Madeleine Sherwood to PB, interview, July 2000.

CHAPTER EIGHTEEN

248 "some of the most": PF, *Don't Tell Dad: A Memoir* (Hyperion, 1998), p. 221.
"after a fabulous meal": Ibid.
249 "She was a photographer's dream": Peter Basch to PB, interview, February 2003.
250 "She was offered everything": AV to PB, interview, January 2002.
252 "Will I have to": Christopher Andersen, *Citizen Jane: The Turbulent Life of Jane Fonda* (Henry Holt and Company, 1990), p. 158.
"So I became": AV to PB, interview, January 2002.
253 "It was a physical": Nathalie Vadim to PB, interview, July 2002.
"The actual shooting": AV to PB, interview, January 2002.
"It ended": Ibid.
254 "because I'd heard": Buck Henry to PB, interview, August 2001.
"The tensions and insecurities": JF, *My Life So Far* (Random House, 2005), p. 180.
255 "I was also growing more remote": Ibid.
257 "weird stuff": AV to PB, interview, January 2002.
"But nobody took it seriously": Ibid.
259 "about two": PF to PB, interview, January 2004.
"you're both ripped": PF, *Don't Tell Dad*, p. 246.
"In the sixties": Julia Phillips to PB, interview, February 2000.

CHAPTER NINETEEN

260 "A week after": JF, *My Life So Far* (Random House, 2005), p. 182.
"I had to grow up!": JF to PB, interview, June 2003.
"I saw images": JF, *My Life So Far*, p. 192.
261 "It was horrifying to me": JF to PB, interview, June 2003.
"We ate at a fancy": Dick Perrin and Tim McCarthy, *G.I. Resister* (Trafford, 2001), p. 88.
262 "What does it matter?": JF, *My Life So Far*, p. 196.
"betrayed as an American": Ibid.
"You will know": Ibid., p. 200.
263 Jane "equated anything": Roger Vadim, *Bardot, Deneuve, Fonda: My Life with the Three Most Beautiful Women in the World* (Simon & Schuster, 1986), p. 282.
265 "Ten thousand students": JF, *My Life So Far*, p. 200.
"This added to the alienation": Ibid., p. 201.
266 "the doped-up, numbers-running": Ibid.
"I knew Jane": AV to PB, interview, January 2002.
"How can you love me": Ibid.
267 "I woke up": JF, *My Life So Far*, p. 203.
268 "Brigitte sent me a cabbage": Ibid., p. 204.
"If you guys": Peter Collier, *The Fondas: A Hollywood Dynasty* (G. P. Putnam's Sons, 1991), p. 168.
"which meant I had": JF, *My Life So Far*, p. 204.
"I am looking down at the baby": Ibid.
"Nobody knew much": Ibid., p. 206.
269 "I do much more": Jay Cocks to PB, interview, January 2004.

CHAPTER TWENTY

270 "Jane Fonda having sex on wilted feathers": Pauline Kael, *5001 Nights at the Movies* (Holt, Rinehart, and Winston, 1984), p. 40.
271 "*Barbarella* will be": Molly Haskell to PB, interview, June 2001.

272 "They had a mind-boggling": Richard Rosenthal to PB, interview, March 2009.

273 "A house made": Roger Vadim, *Bardot, Deneuve, Fonda: My Life with the Three Most Beautiful Women in the World* (Simon & Schuster, 1986), p. 291.

"When you come home": Thomas Kiernan, *Jane: An Intimate Biography of Jane Fonda* (G. P. Putnam's Sons, 1973), p. 225.

"I had the vision": Vadim, *Bardot, Deneuve, Fonda*, p. 293.

274 "This incident revealed": Ibid., p. 295.

"Actually Larry Peerce": Richard Rosenthal to PB, interview, March 2009.

"I remember sitting with Sydney": JF, *My Life So Far*, p. 207.

275 "Gig came to": Sydney Pollack to PB, interview, May 2001.

It's okay for a daughter": Al Aronowitz, "America's Answer to Bardot: The Young Jane Fonda," *Saturday Evening Post*, March 23, 1963.

"something very black": JF to PB, interview, June 2003.

276 "We shot it": Sydney Pollack to PB, interview, May 2001.

"Jane worked like a demon": Allyn Ann McLerie to PB, interview, May 2001.

277 "I would spend days and nights": JF, *My Life So Far*, p. 211.

"I was having a mini-breakdown": Ibid.

278 "I began to feel": Roger Vadim, *Memoirs of the Devil* (Hutchinson and Co., 1975), p. 171.

"It was obvious": Sydney Pollack to PB, interview, May 2001.

"Jane Fonda's stubborn life-loathing": Manny Farber, *Movies* (Hillstone, 1971), p. 4.

279 "It was like": Christopher Andersen, *Citizen Jane: The Turbulent Life of Jane Fonda* (Henry Holt and Company, 1990), p. 176.

"like Henry Fonda": Rex Reed, "Jane: 'Everybody Expected Me to Fall on My Face,'" *New York Times*, January 25, 1970, p. 87.

"Can't she be saved?": Sydney Pollack to PB, interview, May 2001.

"It changed my career": Ibid.

280 "less in love": Vadim, *Bardot, Deneuve, Fonda*, p. 294.

"She raised money": Julia Phillips to PB, interview, February 2000.

282 "She had this dissatisfied": Yvonne Sewall-Ruskin to PB, interview, February 2002.

"Eric has suggested kidnapping me": Vadim, *Bardot, Deneuve, Fonda*, p. 261.

283 "What's going on in there?": Ibid., pp. 296–97.

"La Fonda": Jill Robinson to PB, interview, March 2002.

284 "I realized": JF to PB, interview, June 2003.

285 "I knew that things": PF, *Don't Tell Dad: A Memoir* (Hyperion, 1998), p. 301.

286 "everybody who was anybody": Peter Biskind, *Easy Riders, Raging Bulls: How the Sex-Drugs-and-Rock 'n' Roll Generation Saved Hollywood* (Touchstone, 1999), p. 79.

287 "I was trying": JF, *My Life So Far*, pp. 213–15.

288 "Something's happened": *Show Magazine*, March 1971.

289 "Peter had written": JF to PB, interview, June 2003.

"It was not": Vadim, *Memoirs of the Devil*, p. 167.

"He talked about": Peter Collier, *The Fondas: A Hollywood Dynasty* (G. P. Putnam's Sons, 1991), p. 184.

290 "Somehow I want": Richard Rosenthal to PB, interview, March 2009.

CHAPTER TWENTY-ONE

292 "She arrived in San Francisco": Peter Collier, *The Fondas: A Hollywood Dynasty* (G. P. Putnam's Sons, 1991), p. 301.

294 "Dad's way of relating": JF, *My Life So Far* (Random House, 2005), p. 218.

"Well, he approves": Thomas Kiernan, *Jane: An Intimate Biography of Jane Fonda* (G. P. Putnam's Sons, 1973), p. 286.

295 "Jane was not": Roger Vadim, *Bardot, Deneuve, Fonda: My Life with the Three Most Beautiful Women in the World* (Simon & Schuster, 1986), p. 302.

"I'd been": Fred Gardner to PB, interview, April 2001.

296 "Jane happened": Ibid.

297 "We wanted": Ibid.

"She gives me": Ibid.

"But only for": JF to PB, interview, June 2003.

"The atmosphere was": JF, *My Life So Far*, p. 224.

298 "to be careful": Fred Gardner to PB, interview, April 2001.

299 "Jane Fonda forgot": *New Yorker*, May 27, 1972.

300 "She had good instincts and a conscience": Fred Gardner to PB, interview, April 2001.

"When Jane came to New York": Kiernan, *Jane*, p. 291.

301 "She felt as if": Ibid., p. 284.

"Do you remember": *The Dick Cavett Show*, March 13, 1970.

302 Jane was often: Mark Lane to PB, interview, April 2001.

"The guy almost": Ibid.

303 "You could tell": Ibid.

"When Jane wants": AV to PB, interview, January 2002.

"Yes and no": JF and Vanessa Redgrave to PB, interview, May 2003.

304 "My world": Nathalie Vadim to PB, interview, July 2002.

CHAPTER TWENTY-TWO

307 "Jane Fonda is important": Tim Findley, "Hanoi Jane Fonda," *Rolling Stone*, May 25, 1972, in *The Rolling Stone Film Reader: The Best Film Writing from Rolling Stone Magazine*, ed. Peter Travers (Pocket Books, 1996), pp. 25–28.

310 "I like your": Roger Vadim, *Bardot, Deneuve, Fonda: My Life with the Three Most Beautiful Women in the World* (Simon & Schuster, 1986), p. 256.

"Did you enjoy": JF, *My Life So Far* (Random House, 2005), p. 232.

311 "She may just ruin": Dick Clayton to PB, interview, July 2001.

312 "because my life": JF, *My Life So Far*, p. 237.

313 "They wanted me": Ibid., p. 242.

314 "She really believed": Elisabeth Vailland, *Voyage dans l'Amérique de gauche* (*Travel in the American Left*) (Librairie Arthème Fayard, 1972), p. 117.

315 "Suddenly I feel": Ibid., p. 118.

"I hadn't heard": JF, *My Life So Far*, p. 242.

316 "Those men may very well": Ibid., p. 244.

317 "There was a tightening": Ibid., p. 239.

318 "we would stop": JF to PB, interview, May 2003.

319 "In those first years": JF, *My Life So Far*, p. 227.

320 "like a pilgrim": Nicholas von Hoffman to PB, interview, July 2002.

CHAPTER TWENTY-THREE

322 "something sheer": Ann Roth to PB, interview, July 2009.

"The more important": JF, *My Life So Far* (Random House, 2005), p. 249.

"Even the pimps": Ibid.

323 "Most of them": JF to PB, interview, May 2003.

"She'd tell us": Roy Scheider to PB, interview, September 2003.

"The first thing you do": Ibid.

"Jane's politics": B.J. Bjorkman to PB, interview, May 2010.
324 "Jane would sometimes": Roy Scheider to PB, interview, September 2003.
"Alan was paranoid": Michael Small to PB, interview, June 2000.
"surely the most indelible": Gordon Willis to PB, interview, May 2010.
325 "Jane found sources": Vivian Nathan to PB, interview, March 2000.
326 "Don't you think": Ibid.
"It gave me": Ibid.
327 "He was madly": Ibid.
328 "This is just one": Jack Anderson to PB, interview, April 2002.
"She was very": Mark Lane to PB, interview, April 2001.
329 "Jane lent us": David Hilliard to PB, interview, May 2001.
330 "I'd give up everything": Fred Gardner to PB, interview, April 2001.
"I'll never": PF, *Don't Tell Dad: A Memoir* (Hyperion, 1998), p. 203.
"No one": B.J. Bjorkman to PB, interview, May 2010.
"Around seven o'clock": Todd Ensign to PB, interview, August 2001.
332 COME HEAR BARBARELLA: JF, *My Life So Far*, p. 263.
"I was moving": Ibid.
333 "You're in my": Ibid., p. 261.
"As my hands": Ibid.
334 "Stress and fatigue": JF, *My Life So Far*, p. 263.
"this was a lonely": Ibid., p. 257.
"I kept up": AV to PB, interview, June 2002.
335 "There is no one": JF, *My Life So Far*, p. 268.
336 "You have a little lesson": Ibid., p. 266.
"All this, the vets": Ibid., p. 265.
337 "slender, nervous": Tom Hayden, *Reunion: A Memoir* (Random House, 1988), p. 440.
338 "everybody was talking": Ibid., p. 441.

CHAPTER TWENTY-FOUR

340 "But I was still": JF, *My Life So Far* (Random House, 2005), p. 270.
"I loved her": Ibid.
"Jane wanted": SB to PB, interview, May 2000.
341 "She was quite bossy": Herb Gardner to PB, interview, September 2000.
"None of the men": JF to PB, interview, June 2003.
"Feminism came": Francine Parker to PB, interview, July 2002.
"My life has": JF, *My Life So Far*, p. 228.
342 "She looked like a waif": Claudia Dreifus to PB, interview, February 2005.
"There are no stars": Peter Basch to PB, interview, February 2003.
343 "She was trying": Claudia Dreifus to PB, interview, February 2005.
"Oh, yeah": JF to PB, interview, June 2003.
"So many men": Herb Gardner to PB, interview, September 2000.
"The army really": Peter Boyle to PB, interview, September 2000.
344 "The show started": Fred Gardner to PB, interview, April 2001.
"I don't want to be": Fred Guiles, *Jane Fonda: The Actress in Her Time* (Doubleday, 1981), p. 191.
"Everybody wanted": Fred Gardner to PB, interview, April 2001.
345 "The problem was": JF, *My Life So Far*, p. 270.
"She'd lend us": Miska Sorell to PB, interview, June 2006.
346 "Everybody hoped": Peter Boyle to PB, interview, September 2000.
"The end of this": Herb Gardner to PB, interview, September 2000.

347 "Why, Vanessa": Julia Phillips, *You'll Never Eat Lunch in This Town Again* (Random House, 1991), p. 102.
348 "Jane Fonda was": Susan Brownmiller to PB, interview, July 2000.

CHAPTER TWENTY-FIVE

350 "I just did my work": JF to PB, interview, November 2003.
351 "Yves was playing": Ibid.
    "Dad had his own": JF, *My Life So Far* (Random House, 2005), p. 279.
    "maybe I shouldn't accept": Richard Rosenthal to PB, interview, March 2009.
    "I decided to ask Dad": JF, *My Life So Far*, p. 279.
352 "But he came through": Ibid.
    "If I win the Oscar": Richard Rosenthal to PB, interview, March 2009.
353 "Would you like": Ibid.
    "Well!": Ibid.
354 "I saw a sea": Ibid.
355 "I was stunned": JF, *My Life So Far*, pp. 279–80.
    "I'm such a great actress": Richard Rosenthal to PB, interview, March 2009.
    "Can I have your": Ibid.
    "Hey, that's good!": Ibid.
356 "Can you open": Ibid.
    "We all competed": Ibid.
    "It was the most": Ibid.

CHAPTER TWENTY-SIX

358 "an electric charge": JF, *My Life So Far* (Random House, 2005), p. 282.
    "I wanted a man": Ibid.
359 "I, of course, felt": Ibid., p. 283.
    "Jane brought tremendous": Tom Hayden, *Reunion: A Memoir* (Random House, 1988), p. 443.
    "There . . . unfolded a series": JF, *My Life So Far*, p. 283.
    "I was talking": Hayden, *Reunion*, p. 446.
360 "Tom asked if I": JF, *My Life So Far*, p. 283.
361 "Tom was — and is": Fred Branfman to PB, interview, November 2008.
362 "Each of us has to be more": Craig Unger, "Tom Hayden's Original Sin," *Esquire*, June 1989, p. 178.
363 "The bottom line": Jack Newfield to PB, interview, December 2004.
    "Tom wanted to be": Unger, "Tom Hayden's Original Sin," p. 184.
364 "Tom had this kind": Ibid.
    "No matter how much": Ibid.
    "They broke his spell": Ibid.
365 "And then he met Jane": David Dellinger to PB, interview, July 2002.
    "Jane was in too much": PF to PB, interview, January 2004.
    "It was Tom's": Fred Branfman to PB, interview, November 2008.
    "She sat at": David Dellinger to PB, interview, July 2002.

CHAPTER TWENTY-SEVEN

366 "They invited *you*": JF, *My Life So Far* (Random House, 2005), p. 291.
367 "Bulimics have thin": Ibid., p. 292.

"the planes recede": Ibid., p. 293.

368 "I [was] given": Ibid., p. 297.
"I search[ed] their eyes": Ibid., p. 298.
"made from chrysanthemum": Ibid., p. 299.

369 "Madame Chi": Ibid.
"no sooner have I": Ibid., p. 311.

370 "I want to try": Ibid., p. 304.

371 "I would say things": Mary Hershberger, *Jane Fonda's War: A Political Biography of an American Antiwar Icon* (The New Press, 2005), p. 89.
"that pilots would": Jerry Lembcke, *Hanoi Jane: War, Sex, and Fantasies of Betrayal* (University of Massachusetts Press, 2010), p. 25.

372 U.S. BOMBS DIKES: Ibid., p. 26.
"Curiously few veterans": Ibid., p. 23.
"Military personnel": Ibid., p. 24.
"180 prisoners in Hanoi": Ibid., p. 28.

373 "It [was] self-conscious": JF, *My Life So Far*, p. 315.
"a large impressive man": Ibid.

374 "Larry Carrigan asked": Mike McGrath, "NAM-POWs Want to Set the Record Straight," e-mail published online February 19, 2001, http://www.military-money-matters.com/nam-pows.html.
"Everybody had lunch": Bill Davidson, *Jane Fonda: An Intimate Biography* (Dutton, 1990), p. 170.

375 "Oh my God": JF, *My Life So Far*, p. 316.
"It was my mistake": Ibid.
"Tom was worried": Fred Branfman to PB, interview, November 2008.

377 "I needed rest": JF, *My Life So Far*, p. 321.

378 "You've been called": Mary Hershberger, ed., "Traitors and Patriots," in *Jane Fonda's Words of Passion and Politics* (The New Press, 2006), p. 34.
"Fonda started lecturing": David Halberstam to PB, interview, June 2002.

379 "I welcome the": Hershberger, *Jane Fonda's War*, p. 115.
"I'm a great believer": Ibid., p. 114.

380 "I appreciate": Mark Lane to PB, interview, April 2001.
"Jane was a very": Ibid.
"If it was": Tom Hayden, *Reunion: A Memoir* (Random House, 1988), p. 450.

381 "with a tearful smile": Ibid., p. 448.
"He was fired up": Fred Branfman to PB, interview, November 2008.
"She should have told": "Mrs. Nixon Asserts Jane Fonda Should Bid Hanoi End War," *New York Times*, August 9, 1972.

382 "You have lied to us": Jerry Lembcke, *The Spitting Image: Myth, Memory, and the Legacy of Vietnam* (New York University Press, 1998), p. 66.

383 "I vividly recall": JF, *My Life So Far*, p. 335.
"[It] was the most fulfilling": Ibid.
"The trip was another": Ronald Brownstein, *The Power and the Glitter: The Hollywood-Washington Connection* (Pantheon, 1990), p. 260.

384 "Every night": Molly Haskell, *Village Voice*, November 7, 1974.

385 "You lived with Fonda": Davidson, *Jane Fonda*, p. 184.

386 "For some reason": Richard Rosenthal to PB, interview, March 2009.

CHAPTER TWENTY-EIGHT

387 "Will you, Jane": Peter Collier, *The Fondas: A Hollywood Dynasty* (G. P. Putnam's Sons, 1991), p. 231.

"I must have taken": Bill Davidson, *Jane Fonda: An Intimate Biography* (Dutton, 1990), p. 184.

388   "Jane and Tom were in bed": Ibid., p. 185.

389   "carefully prepared TV commercial": Shana Alexander, "Prisoners of Peace," *Newsweek*, March 5, 1973, p. 32.

389   "pawns by Nixon": Tom Hayden, *Reunion: A Memoir* (Random House, 1988), p. 455.

390   "They were used": Mary Hershberger, *Jane Fonda's War: A Political Biography of an American Antiwar Icon* (The New Press, 2005), p. 151.
  "The hard line": Steven Roberts, "Two Pilots, Two Wars," *New York Times Magazine*, June 10, 1973, p. 16.

391   "He was quite": Ken Kelly to PB, interview, April 2001.
  "Sell my house?": JF, *My Life So Far* (Random House, 2005), p. 345.

392   "Carol in particular": Ibid., p. 346.
  "Jane loves her shack": Shirlee Fonda to PB, interview, August 2003.
  "my life was important": Leo Janus, "Jane Fonda, Finding Her Golden Pond," *Cosmopolitan*, January 1985, p. 170.

393   "It was tough": Ibid.
  "I never talked": JF to PB, interview, May 2005.
  "I didn't really": Janus, "Jane Fonda, Finding Her Golden Pond," p. 170.

395   "He was fucking": Peter Boyle to PB, interview, September 2000.
  "He was a closet drinker": Jack Newfield to PB, interview, December 2004.

396   "Jane Fonda cannot be dismissed": Nicholas von Hoffman to PB, interview, July 2002.

397   "Some two thousand": Hershberger, *Jane Fonda's War*, p. 126.

398   "Jane's eyes": Barbara Grizzuti Harrison, *Off Center* (The Dial Press, 1980), p. 170.
  "I was both in love": JF, *My Life So Far*, p. 341.
  "Tom Hayden gives": Gore Vidal to PB, interview, February 2003.

399   "the whole thing was": Collier, *The Fondas*, p. 227.

CHAPTER TWENTY-NINE

400   "It was so thick": Jack Anderson to PB, interview, April 2002.
  "part of an organized": JF and Tom Hayden, interview by Ron Ridenour, *Playboy*, April 1974.

401   "The studios were scared": Paula Weinstein to PB, interview, September 2001.
  "Jane was my idol": Ibid.

402   "She had this incredible": JF to PB, interview, June 2003.
  Hellman, however, wanted: Deborah Martinson, *Lillian Hellman: A Life with Foxes and Scoundrels* (Counterpoint, 2005), p. 11.

403   "I never had a real": JF to PB, interview, June 2003.
  "Hers is not": T. Thompson, *McCall's*, September 1973.

404   "over our sense": Haskell Wexler to PB, interview, September 2001.
  "Haskell suddenly": JF to PB, interview, June 2003.

405   "He was seated": Roger Vadim, *Bardot, Deneuve, Fonda: My Life with the Three Most Beautiful Women in the World* (Simon & Schuster, 1986), p. 239.

406   "Tom was always": Carol Kurtz to PB, interview, October 2001.

CHAPTER THIRTY

408   "We proposed": Tom Hayden, *Reunion: A Memoir* (Random House, 1988), p. 469.

409   "The more I think": Fred Branfman to PB, interview, November 2008.
  "It was some experience": Ibid.

410   "Jane is always": Steven Rivers to PB, interview, April 2005.

411 "Jane turned in": Max Palevsky to PB, interview, June 2001.
"I bought them": JF to PB, interview, August 2005.
412 "I couldn't understand": Max Palevsky to PB, interview, June 2001.
"His brilliance": JF to PB, interview, August 2005.
"I had to pick her up": Carey Beauchamp to PB, interview, October 2001.
"But Jane, to her credit": Fred Branfman to PB, interview, November 2008.
413 "You are a completely": JF to PB, interview, August 2005.
"1.2 million Californians": JF, *My Life So Far* (Random House, 2005), p. 368.
414 "Tom was at his best": Jack Newfield to PB, interview, December 2004.
"It caused her": Richard Rosenthal to PB, interview, March 2009.
415 "I wrote the rest": Barbara Grizzuti Harrison, *Off Center* (The Dial Press, 1980), p. 168.
417 "because it was full": JF to PB, interview, August 2005.
418 "Lillian is a homely woman": *Newsweek,* October 10, 1977.
"The underwear I bought": Lillian Hellman letter to JF, October 4, 1977, Harry Ransom Humanities Research Center, Special Collections, Lillian Hellman and Dashiell Hammett Collection, Austin, Texas.
"I wish I was": JF letter to Hellman, undated [1977], Harry Ransom Humanities Research Center, Special Collections, Lillian Hellman and Dashiell Hammett Collection, Austin, Texas.
"watch it": Hellman letter to JF, November 7, 1977, Harry Ransom Humanities Research Center, Special Collections, Lillian Hellman and Dashiell Hammett Collection, Austin, Texas.
"She was a nice": JF, *My Life So Far,* p. 366.
419 "He was always": Richard Roth to PB, interview, April 2009.
"Cold, haughty": Rosemary Murphy to PB, interview, March 2000.
420 "It hit me": *Time Magazine* Research File, JF interview, September 7, 1977, p. 8.
"Vanessa Redgrave and Jane": Fred Zinnemann, *Fred Zinnemann, An Autobiography: A Life in the Movies* (Bloomsbury Publishing, 1992).
421 "I recall never being sure": JF, *My Life So Far,* p. 364.
"We embraced": AF to PB, interview, April 2002.
422 "One night in Paris": JF, *My Life So Far,* p. 366.
"Tom vetted": JF to PB, interview, August 2005.

CHAPTER THIRTY-ONE

423 "Nobody will want": Jerome Hellman to PB, interview, December 2004.
"Arthur gave us": Ibid.
424 "about vets and piss bags": Peter Biskind, "The Vietnam Oscars," *Vanity Fair,* March 2008, p. 268.
"Hal was as active": Haskell Wexler to PB, interview, September 2001.
"I don't think Hal": Biskind, "The Vietnam Oscars," p. 268.
"Hal, the guy who": Jerome Hellman to PB, interview, December 2004.
425 "Luke is a lover": Bruce Dern to PB, interview, November 2006.
"One day Hal": Ibid.
"We ended up": Jerome Hellman to PB, interview, December 2004.
"I asked him": Bruce Dern to PB, interview, November 2006.
"The vets were so committed": Janet Maslin, "For Jon Voight a Coming Home," *New York Times,* February 13, 1978.
426 "Jane made it": Jerome Hellman to PB, interview, December 2004.
"If you could": Bruce Dern to PB, interview, November 2006.
"Hal did a lot": Ibid.
427 "but we didn't talk": Jerome Hellman to PB, interview, December 2004.

"Like the one": Bruce Dern to PB, interview, November 2006.

"He would take a glance": JF, *My Life So Far* (Random House, 2005), p. 374.

428 "Both of us knew": Ibid., p. 371.

"that an unconventional": Biskind, "The Vietnam Oscars."

"Jon and I spent": JF, *My Life So Far,* p. 372.

429 "Oh, Hal, please": Bruce Dern to PB, interview, November 2006.

"The coldness of": JF, *My Life So Far,* p. 374.

"He'd never seen me": JF to PB, interview, August 2005.

"I couldn't believe": Barbara Grizzuti Harrison to PB, interview, June 2000.

"frankly appalled": Jerome Hellman to PB, interview, December 2004.

430 "ruin him in": Ibid.

"By now": Bruce Dern to PB, interview, November 2006.

"At any rate": Jerome Hellman to PB, interview, December 2004.

"There's this one": Haskell Wexler to PB, interview, September 2001.

CHAPTER THIRTY-TWO

431 "It was a helluva story": Herb Gardner to PB, interview, September 2000.

433 "But I want": Michael Gray to PB, interview, September 2008.

"I'd have to give": Ibid.

"Jane loved": Ibid.

434 "He really didn't": Ibid.

"He knew how important": Jack Larson to PB, interview, August 2008.

435 "It was at these power plants": Bill Davidson, *Jane Fonda: An Intimate Biography* (Dutton, 1990), p. 218.

"Jane was doing": John Springer to PB, interview, December 1999.

436 "What to do?": JF, *My Life So Far* (Random House, 2005), p. 387.

"but she wasn't keeping": John Springer to PB, interview, December 1999.

"Jane visiting our": Gil Shiva to PB, interview, May 2000.

437 "how close we were": Teddy Rosenthal to PB, interview, August 2000.

"What the fuck": Richard Rosenthal to PB, interview, March 2009.

438 "You could": Shirlee Fonda to PB, interview, August 2003.

CHAPTER THIRTY-THREE

439 "[Jane's] never going": Peter Collier, *The Fondas: A Hollywood Dynasty* (G. P. Putnam's Sons, 1991), p. 296.

441 "Shirlee's lasted": G. Barry Golson, ed., *The Playboy Interview II* (Worldview/Perigee, 1983), p. 458.

442 "Granddad was": Vanessa Vadim to PB, interview, November 2001.

"I wasn't a good mother": JF, *The Oprah Winfrey Show,* October 27, 2010.

443 "it was Tom and Jane": Vanessa Vadim to PB, interview, November 2001.

"She's too old": Ann Biderman to PB, interview, January 2002.

"Dogs — children": Suzanne Tenner to PB, interview, October 2001.

444 "The door was always open": Ann Biderman to PB, interview, January 2002.

"I'd done": JF to PB, interview, August 2005.

446 "CED wasn't really": Jeffrey Klein, "The Essential Tom and Jane," *Mother Jones,* March 1980.

"At the ceremony": Bruce Dern to PB, interview, November 2006.

447 "In this movie": Foster Hirsch, *Acting Hollywood Style* (Harry N. Abrams, Inc., 1991), p. 257.

448 "always using": Richard Rosenthal to PB, interview, March 2009.
"What an ass": Ibid.
"We would discuss": JF, *My Life So Far* (Random House, 2005), p. 401.
449 "the injustice": Ibid.
"Because Tom's": JF to PB, interview, August 2005.
"I simply didn't think": JF, *My Life So Far*, p. 403.
450 "It was wonderful": Ibid., pp. 405–6.
"I'd been working": Suzanne Tenner to PB, interview, October 2001.
451 "We stressed": David Hodges to PB, interview, April 2002.
452 "We'd have meetings": David Hilliard to PB, interview, April 2002.
"That first summer": Mary Lou Williams to PB, interview, November 2002.
453 "with no help from me": JF, *My Life So Far*, pp. 383–84.

CHAPTER THIRTY-FOUR

454 "The California Democratic": Fred Branfman to PB, interview, November 2008.
455 "She was stunned": Richard Rosenthal to PB, interview, March 2009.
"Your fee for *Julia*": Richard Rosenthal to JF, July 30, 1979. This letter is part of court record CV84-1620RMT, U.S. District Court, Central District, California.
456 "Can I help you?": Gilda Marx to PB, interview, October 2001.
457 "Tom and Jane and Jerry": Jeffrey Klein, "The Essential Tom & Jane," *Mother Jones*, March 1980.
"There will be a nuclear": Ibid.
458 "My movie's gonna": Patricia Resnick to PB, interview, October 2001.
"At least Jane": Ibid.
459 "What are you doing?": Paula Weinstein to PB, interview, October 2001.
"Then she switched": MF to PB, interview, March 2000.
"We yakked": Ibid.
460 "Does it hurt?": Ibid.
462 "We hadn't spoken": Nathalie Vadim to PB, interview, July 2002.
"flipped out for Kris": Ibid.
"Kris knew": Hume Cronyn to PB, interview, February 2001.
463 "I didn't ask her": Nathalie Vadim to PB, interview, July 2002.
"Our accountants": JF to PB, interview, August 2005.
"I need more": Richard Rosenthal to PB, interview, March 2009.
465 "For years I had": JF, *My Life So Far* (Random House, 2005), p. 425.

CHAPTER THIRTY-FIVE

466 "It's so close to our story": JF to PB, interview, June 2003.
467 "But we had to": Mark Rydell to PB, interview, May 2001.
468 "She'd berate": JF to PB, interview, June 2003.
"Jane used her": Mark Rydell to PB, interview, May 2001.
469 "From the first": JF, *My Life So Far* (Random House, 2005), p. 435.
470 "*Oh, no*, the actor's worst nightmare": Ibid.
"I found *Golden Pond*": Nathalie Vadim to PB, interview, July 2002.
"the scene had been": JF, *My Life So Far*, p. 437.
471 "He had been very upset": Shirlee Fonda to PB, interview, August 2003.
"That scarecrow": Ann Biderman to PB, interview, January 2002.
"Shirlee hadn't allowed": JF, *My Life So Far*, p. 442.
"I was too nervous": Mark Rydell to PB, interview, May 2001.

472 "I am not": Henry Fonda, *My Life: As Told to Howard Teichmann* (New American Library, 1981), p. 282.

"I hurt for him": JF, *My Life So Far,* p. 443.

"I love you very much, Dad": PF, *Don't Tell Dad: A Memoir* (Hyperion, 1998), p. 442.

473 "The district has": Christopher Andersen, *Citizen Jane: The Turbulent Life of Jane Fonda* (Henry Holt and Company, 1990), p. 316.

474 "It was like": Vanessa Vadim to PB, interview, November 2001.

"He told me": JF, *My Life So Far,* p. 445.

"thrown out with": PF, *Don't Tell Dad,* p. 152.

475 "It wasn't my decision": JF to PB, interview, June 2003.

"Jim and I": PF to PB, interview, January 2004.

"I can still see Jane": PF, *Don't Tell Dad,* p. 454.

"Yeah, sure": PF to PB, interview, January 2004.

"It was a bitter": SB to PB, interview, May 2000.

"My father has come to me": JF, *My Life So Far,* p. 447.

CHAPTER THIRTY-SIX

476 "My dad wanted": Tom Hayden, *Reunion: A Memoir* (Random House, 1988), p. 481.

"I have never seen": Lauren Weissman to PB, interview, October 2001.

478 "It *was* my idea": Shirlee Fonda to PB, interview, August 2003.

"It was the highest": Dan Green to PB, interview, February 2002.

"but the words were": Nan Talese to PB, interview, February 2002.

"I wanted to save": JF to PB, interview, June 2003.

"Jane Fonda became": David Thomson, *A Biographical Dictionary of Film* (Knopf, 1995), p. 252.

479 "The exercise guru was": Richard Schickel to PB, interview, January 2011.

"This was feminism": Judith Warner, *Perfect Madness: Motherhood in the Age of Anxiety* (Riverhead, 2005), p. 183.

"by the basketful": JF, *My Life So Far* (Random House, 2005), p. 394.

480 "I didn't want": Barbara Seaman to PB, interview, February 2004.

"Then don't make yourself": Gilda Marx to PB, interview, October 2010.

"None of the exercises": Ibid.

481 "I wanted to grow": JF, *My Life So Far,* p. 396.

"Mon dieu!": Monique Caron to PB, interview, June 2002.

"Hey, wait": JF, *My Life So Far,* p. 395.

"Does Jane Fonda": Pauline Kael to PB, interview, January 2001.

"Jane Fonda's": Thomson, *A Biographical Dictionary of Film,* p. 252.

482 "Gertie Nevels": JF to PB, interview, April 2009.

"log cabin": JF, *My Life So Far,* p. 417.

"I think most": Ibid., p. 457.

483 "She'd been in Japan": Nan Talese to PB, interview, February 2002.

"Tom hated, loathed, despised": Nathalie Vadim to PB, interview, July 2002.

484 "If Tom ever": Lauren Weissman to PB, interview, October 2001.

485 "When Jane agreed": Norman Jewison to PB, interview, August 2010.

486 "I wanted to see": Sandra Lee to PB, interview, July 2005.

"So I drank": Ibid.

487 "Tom was furious": JF to PB, interview, June 2003.

"Their marriage had been": Peter Collier, *The Fondas: A Hollywood Dynasty* (G. P. Putnam's Sons, 1991), p. 292.

488 "all choked up": JF to PB, interview, June 2003.

489 "Everyone was very": Roger Friedman to PB, interview, September 2004.

"We met at": Joe Eszterhas to PB, interview, July 2005.

"It was too good": Ibid.

490 "By the mid-eighties": JF, *My Life So Far*, p. 458.

"He was really": JF to PB, interview, June 2003.

492 "I'm blown away": Christopher Andersen, *Citizen Jane: The Turbulent Life of Jane Fonda* (Henry Holt and Company, 1990), p. 331.

"I'd look around": Ibid., p. 330.

"It's benevolent": Ron Rosenbaum, "Dangerous Jane," *Vanity Fair*, November 1988, p. 208.

"the mythical portrait": Mary Hershberger, *Jane Fonda's War: A Political Biography of an American Antiwar Icon* (The New Press, 2005), p. 177.

493 "had doubts": Interview with Barbara Walters on ABC's *20/20*, June 17, 1988.

"Why did you sit": Ibid.

495 "What will I do": JF, *My Life So Far*, p. 458.

"he asked me": Ibid.

496 "I didn't want to": Ibid., p. 462.

"I never knew": Mary Lou Williams to PB, interview, November 2002.

CHAPTER THIRTY-SEVEN

498 "I was convinced": JF, *My Life So Far* (Random House, 2005), p. 463.

"We'd walked": JF to PB, interview, April 2007.

499 "We'd hardly": PF to PB, interview, January 2004.

"She was a nice": Ibid.

500 JANE FONDA'S DAUGHTER: James S. Kunen, Victoria Balfour, and Georgina Oliver, "Jane Fonda's Daughter, Vanessa Vadim, Is Jailed for Mouthing Off at a Drug Bust," *People*, October 23, 1989.

"If you're going": Ibid.

501 "Vanessa is a good": Ibid.

"She is really annoyed": Ibid.

"She seemed thrilled": Mary Lou Williams to PB, interview, November 2002.

502 "They seemed subdued": JF, *My Life So Far*, p. 470.

"I got CNN": Ibid., p. 472.

"I have friends who are Communists": Ibid., p. 470.

504 "We were both": JF to PB, interview, April 2007.

"At the feet": JF, *My Life So Far*, p. 476.

505 "I think you're perfect": Ibid., p. 481.

506 "Enough of this stuff": Ibid., p. 486.

508 "No man has ever": Suzanne Tenner to PB, interview, August 2009.

"We had a fifteen-minute interview": Tom Johnson to PB, interview, April 2009.

509 "at the restaurant": Ibid.

"I'll never forget": Ibid.

"He tried so hard": Mary Lou Williams to PB, interview, November 2002.

"The way he introduced": JF, *My Life So Far*, p. 492.

510 "He's a male": Ibid., p. 493.

"[Ted] had the heart": Ibid., p. 492.

"Part of her": Ted Turner to PB, interview, April 2009.

511 "I have never": Nathalie Vadim to PB, interview, July 2002.

"He would cry": Mary Lou Williams to PB, interview, November 2002.

"[didn't] want a mom": JF, *My Life So Far*, p. 495.

"Ted is very much": Jennet Conant, "Married . . . with Buffalo," *Vanity Fair*, April 1997, p. 230.

512 "the true, deep soul": JF, *My Life So Far*, p. 496.

"It was a wonderful": PF to PB, interview, January 2004.

513 "The discovery was pure fluke": JF, *My Life So Far*, p. 524.

"[I was] crying": Ibid.

514 "She would come": Ibid., p. 525.

"that he would never": Ibid.

"I won't answer": JF to PB, interview, April 2007.

CHAPTER THIRTY-EIGHT

515 "I was in": JF, *My Life So Far* (Random House, 2005), p. 15.

516 "No, no, we want Jane": Ken Auletta, *Media Man: Ted Turner's Improbable Empire* (W. W. Norton and Company, 2004), p. 60.

"Not a single person": Ibid.

"The plane has been repaired": Ibid., p. 61.

"He doesn't have": Ibid.

517 "Given everything that happened": Ted Turner and Bill Burke, *Call Me Ted* (Grand Central Publishing, 2008), p. 329.

"Ted is a mixture": Jennet Conant, "Married . . . with Buffalo," *Vanity Fair*, April 1997, p. 230.

"I know how": JF to PB, interview, May 2009.

"Jane is a terrific": Laura Seydel to PB, interview, April 2009.

518 "Mom has": Vanessa Vadim to PB, interview, November 2001.

"I wanted to be friends": JF to PB, interview, May 2009.

"what a stupendous job": Ibid.

519 "we will build": Ibid.

"The night before": Auletta, *Media Man*, p. 66.

520 "Talk about barbaric": Ibid.

"I slid under": Ibid.

"You better not": Ibid.

"He said": Turner and Burke, *Call Me Ted*, p. 320.

521 "Maybe we will buy": Ibid.

"vulnerability to pressure": JF, *My Life So Far*, p. 515.

522 "I'm proud": Turner and Burke, *Call Me Ted*, p. 346.

"[Ted] tried": JF, *My Life So Far*, p. 529.

524 "I didn't know what": Vanessa Vadim to PB, interview, November 2001.

"I think he sensed": JF, *My Life So Far*, p. 548.

"You're not phoning": Vanessa Vadim to PB, interview, November 2001.

525 "Malcolm had": JF, *My Life So Far*, p. 548.

"I need us to try to": Ibid., p. 549.

"Eventually I began": JF to PB, interview, May 2009.

"She was not": Auletta, *Media Man*, p. 94.

526 "I chose not to discuss it": Ibid.

"I had gone from": JF, *My Life So Far*, p. 554.

"He was showing": Ibid., p. 555.

EPILOGUE

528 "I'm on a quest": Diana Kennedy, "An Unscripted Life Starring Herself," *New York Times*, May 6, 2001.

529 "I was wondering": JF e-mail, January 2, 2007.

"Being active": JF to PB, interview, May 2006.

530 "I can't have": JF to PB, interview, July 2007.

"teasing him with lascivious looks": Claudia Glenn Dowling, "Hear Jane Roar," unpublished article, circa 2002.

531 "Try not talking": JF to PB, interview, January 2009.
    "because it's about": Ibid.
532 "It was in Aspen": JF to PB, interview, September 2009.
533 "No one else": JF to PB, interview, November 2010.

Bibliography

Abramowitz, Rachel. *Is That a Gun in Your Pocket? Women's Experience of Power in Hollywood* (New York: Random House, 2000).

Adams, Cindy. *Lee Strasberg* (Garden City, NY: Doubleday & Co., 1980).

Andersen, Christopher. *Citizen Jane: The Turbulent Life of Jane Fonda* (New York: Henry Holt and Company, 1990).

Atkinson, Brooks. *Broadway* (New York: Macmillan Publishing Co., 1974).

Auletta, Ken. *Media Man: Ted Turner's Improbable Empire* (New York: W. W. Norton & Co., 2004).

Basinger, Jeanine. *The Star Machine* (New York: Knopf, 2007).

Bibb, Porter. *Ted Turner: It Ain't as Easy as It Looks* (Boulder: Johnson Books, 1997).

Biskind, Peter. *Easy Riders, Raging Bulls: How the Sex-Drugs-and-Rock 'n' Roll Generation Saved Hollywood* (New York: Touchstone, 1998).

Brownmiller, Susan. *In Our Time: A Memoir of a Revolution* (New York: Delta, 1999).

Brownstein, Ronald. *The Power and the Glitter: The Hollywood-Washington Connection* (New York: Pantheon, 1990).

Burke, Carol. *Camp All-American, Hanoi Jane, and the High-and-Tight* (Boston: Beacon Press, 2004).

Clinton, James W. *The Loyal Opposition: Americans in Northern Vietnam, 1965–1972* (Boulder: University Press of Colorado, 1995).

Collier, Peter. *The Fondas: A Hollywood Dynasty* (New York: G. P. Putnam's Sons, 1991).

Davidson, Bill. *Jane Fonda: An Intimate Biography* (New York: Dutton, 1990).

Dern, Bruce, with Robert Crane and Christopher Fryer. *Things I've Said but Probably Shouldn't Have* (Hoboken, NJ: Wiley, 2007).

Eliot, Marc. *Jimmy Stewart: A Biography* (New York: Harmony Books, 2006).

Emerson, Gloria. *Winners & Losers: Battles, Retreats, Gains, Losses, and Ruins from the Vietnam War* (New York: Random House, 1975).

Farber, Manny. *Movies* (New York: Hillstone, 1971).

Farber, Stephen, and Marc Green. *Hollywood Dynasties* (New York: Delilah, 1984).

Fonda, Afdera. *Never Before Noon* (New York: Weidenfeld & Nicolson, 1986).

Fonda, Henry. *My Life as Told to Howard Teichmann* (New York: New American Library, 1981).

Fonda, Jane. *Jane Fonda's Workout Book* (New York: Simon & Schuster, 1981).

——. *My Life So Far* (New York: Random House, 2005).

——. *Women Coming of Age* (New York: Simon & Schuster, 1986).

Fonda, Peter. *Don't Tell Dad: A Memoir* (New York: Hyperion, 1998).

Freedland, Michael. *Jane Fonda: A Biography* (New York: St. Martin's Press, 1988).

Friedrich, Otto. *City of Nets: A Portrait of Hollywood in the 1940s* (New York: Harper & Row, 1986).

Gitlin, Todd. *The Sixties: Years of Hope, Days of Rage* (New York: Bantam Books, 1987).

Guiles, Fred Lawrence. *Jane Fonda: The Actress in Her Time* (New York: Doubleday & Co., 1981).

Haddad-Garcia, George. *The Films of Jane Fonda* (Secaucus, NJ: Citadel Press, 1981).

Haskell, Molly. *From Reverence to Rape: The Treatment of Women in the Movies,* 2nd ed. (Chicago: University of Chicago Press, 1987).

Hayden, Tom. *Reunion: A Memoir* (New York: Random House, 1988).

Hayes, Harold, ed. *Smiling Through the Apocalypse: Esquire's History of the Sixties* (New York: McCall Publishing Co., 1960).

Herman, Gary, and David Downing. *Jane Fonda: All American Anti-Heroine* (New York: Quick Fox, 1980).

Herman, Jan. *A Talent for Trouble: Hollywood's Most Talked About Director: William Wyler* (Cambridge, MA: Da Capo Press, 1997).

Hershberger, Mary. *Jane Fonda's War: A Political Biography of an American Antiwar Icon* (New York: The New Press, 2005).

——, ed. *Jane Fonda's Words of Politics and Passion* (New York: The New Press, 2006).

——. *Traveling to Vietnam: American Peace Activists and the War* (Syracuse, NY: Syracuse University Press, 1998).

Hirsch, Foster. *Acting Hollywood Style* (New York: AFI Press, 1991).

Kael, Pauline. *For Keeps: 30 Years at the Movies* (New York: Dutton, 1994).

Kaiser, Charles. *1968 in America: Music, Politics, Chaos, Counterculture, and the Shaping of a Generation* (New York: Grove Press, 1988).

Kanin, Garson. *A Gift of Time* (New York: Random House, 1962).

Kiernan, Thomas. *Jane: An Intimate Biography of Jane Fonda* (New York: G. P. Putnam's Sons, 1973).

Lembcke, Jerry. *Hanoi Jane: War, Sex, and Fantasies of Betrayal* (Boston: University of Massachusetts Press, 2010).

Lewis, Robert. *Method — Or Madness?* (New York: Samuel French, Inc., 1958).

——. *Slings & Arrows: Theater in My Life* (New York: Applause, 1984).

Martinson, Deborah. *Lillian Hellman: A Life with Foxes and Scoundrels* (New York: Counterpoint, 2005).

Mellen, Joan. *Hellman and Hammett* (New York: HarperCollins, 1996).

Monaco, James. *The New Wave: Truffaut, Godard, Chabrol, Rohmer, Rivette* (New York: Oxford University Press, 1976).

Montand, Yves. *You See, I Haven't Forgotten* (New York: Knopf, 1992).

Navarsky, Victor. *Naming Names* (New York: Viking Press, 1980).

Near, Holly. *Fire in the Rain . . . Singer in the Storm* (New York: Quill, 1990).

Newfield, Jack. *Somebody's Gotta Tell It: The Upbeat Memoir of a Working-Class Journalist* (New York: St. Martin's Press, 2002).

O'Hara, John. *BUtterfield 8* (New York: Modern Library, 2003).

Phillips, Julia. *You'll Never Eat Lunch in This Town Again* (New York: Random House, 1991).

Reeves, Richard. *President Nixon* (New York: Simon & Schuster, 2001).

Richards, David. *Played Out: The Jean Seberg Story* (New York: Random House, 1981).

Ross, Lillian. *The Player: A Profile of the Art* (New York: Simon & Schuster, 1962).

Sewall-Ruskin, Yvonne. *High on Rebellion: Inside the Underground at Max's Kansas City* (New York: Thunder's Mouth Press, 1998).

Shorto, Russell. *Jane Fonda: Political Activism* (Brookfield, CT: Millbrook Press, 1991).

Signoret, Simone. *Nostalgia Isn't What It Used to Be* (New York: Harper & Row, 1978).

Spada, James. *Fonda: Her Life in Pictures* (Garden City, NY: Doubleday, 1985).

Springer, John. *The Fondas: The Films and Careers of Henry, Jane and Peter Fonda* (New York: Citadel Press, 1970).

Strasberg, Susan. *Bitter Sweet* (New York: G. P. Putnam's Sons, 1980).

——. *Marilyn and Me: Sisters, Rivals, Friends* (New York: Warner Books, 1992).

Thomson, David. *A Biographical Dictionary of Film* (New York: Knopf, 1995).

Turner, Ted, and Bill Burke. *Call Me Ted* (New York: Grand Central Publishing, 2008).

Vadim, Roger. *Bardot, Deneuve, Fonda: My Life with the Three Most Beautiful Women in the World* (New York: Simon & Schuster, 1986).

——. *Memoirs of the Devil* (London: Hutchinson, 1975).

Vailland, Elisabeth. *Voyage dans l'Amérique de gauche* (Paris: Librairie Arthème Fayard, 1972).

Williams, Linda. *Screening Sex* (Durham: Duke University Press, 2008).

Photo Credits

Jane Fonda, age 23: © Peter Basch, Basch LLC. *Henry Fonda:* © John Swope Trust/mptvimages .com. *Henry and Frances with baby Jane:* Moviestore Collection Ltd./Alamy. *Eating cake:* © John Swope Trust/mptvimages.com. *Peter, Jane, and Frances at Tigertail:* Courtesy of the Academy of Motion Picture Arts and Sciences. *Fonda family picnic:* Photo by Genevieve Naylor. Courtesy Staley-Wise Gallery/Reznikoff Artistic Partnership. *In her first apartment:* Globe Photos, Inc. *With her father backstage:* © John Swope Trust/mptvimages.com. *Fonda family, en route to Rome:* © Bettmann/Corbis. *Hollywood cocktail party:* Photo by Allan Grant/Time Life Pictures/Getty Images. *With Josh Logan:* Photo by Leonard McCombe/Time Life Pictures/Getty Images. *With Basch, Strasberg, and Voutsinas, 1961:* Photo by Bob Gomel/Time Life Pictures/Getty Images. *Actors Studio Theatre, 1963:* AP Photo. *Lee Strasberg:* Photofest. *On the set of* Walk on the Wild Side: © Peter Basch, Basch LLC. *Between takes:* Collection of Patricia Bosworth. *Henry, Jane, and Peter:* MGM/Photofest. *Roger Vadim and Jane, in love:* © Peter Basch, Basch LLC. *Cavorting with Robert Redford:* © Bert Reisfeld/DPA/Zumapress.com. *The infamous nude billboard:* Photofest. *With Vadim in 1966:* Films Marceau/Cocinor/Mega/The Kobal Collection. *In her* Barbarella *costume:* © David Hurn/Magnum Photos. *Close-up,* Circle of Love: Courtesy Everett Collection. *With daughter Vanessa:* © Bruce McBroom/mptvimages .com. *With Henry Fonda watching proudly:* © Bob Willoughby/mptvimages.com. *Continued to dance and dance:* © Cat's Collection/Corbis. *Alone on the set:* © 1978 Bob Willoughby/mptv images.com. *As Bree Daniels:* HPS/Camera Press/Retna Ltd. *With Donald Sutherland:* © JP Laffont/Sygma/Corbis. *In handcuffs:* © Reuters/Corbis. *Brings her antiwar campaign to New Jersey:* AP Photo. *Perched on an antiaircraft gun:* AP Photo/Nihon Denpa News. *Cover of* Life: Photo by Bill Ray/Time Life Pictures/Getty Images. *In* Tout Va Bien: Courtesy Everett Collection. *After a press conference:* AFP/Getty Images. *With Tom Hayden and son, Troy:* © Steve Schapiro. *Speaks out all over the country:* Globe Photos, Inc. *Kidding around at home:* © Steve Schapiro. *In* Coming Home: United Artists/Photofest. *With Jason Robards:* Twentieth Century Fox Film Corp./Photofest. *In* Nine to Five: Twentieth Century Fox Film Corp./Photofest. *In* The Morning After: Lorimar/Photofest. *Ecstatic at winning her Oscar:* Peter C. Borsari. *Henry Fonda blows out the candles:* © Suzanne Tenner 2011. *The Workout queen:* © Steve Schapiro. *With her third husband, Ted Turner:* Focus on Sport/Getty Images. *With Ted at the Oscars:* Photofest. *In Saint-Tropez:* HADJ/SIPA. *Curtain call:* Walter McBride/Retna. *Jane, back where she started:* Photo by Jon Kopaloff/FilmMagic.

Index